Managing Organizations
Readings and Cases

Managing Organizations
Readings and Cases

DAVID A. NADLER

MICHAEL L. TUSHMAN

NINA G. HATVANY

Little, Brown and Company
Boston   *Toronto*

Library of Congress Catalog Card No. 81–82389

ISBN   0–316–596833

9 8 7 6 5 4 3 2

BP

Published simultaneously in Canada
by Little, Brown & Company (Canada) Limited

Printed in the United States of America

Designed and Produced by Ron Newcomer & Associates

Preface

During the last few years we've witnessed the burgeoning of collections of readings related to organizational behavior and management. The plethora of new books reflects the growth of the field of organizational behavior (OB) and the increasing number of OB courses and seminars in different settings. Still, one might rightfully ask, "Why another volume?"

The answer is simple. We've tried to do something a little different with this book. We've tried to present an integrated and consistent selection of readings and cases, organized around a basic diagnostic model of organizations.

Part of the answer also lies in the history of this book. The effort began in 1975 when Nadler and Tushman arrived at the Graduate School of Business at Columbia charged with teaching the basic management/OB course—B6012 (Managerial Behavior in Organizations). They encountered a paradoxical situation which is not uncommon in business schools. The Columbia Business School provided an intellectual environment which was culturally and methodologically supportive to the systematic study of organizations, yet the student body was hostile. The challenge was to build a basic OB/Management course which would reflect developments in the field *and* be regarded as useful by skeptical students.

The two began by building a course organized around a conceptual model of organizations (see Reading 3). They built a course which had the following characteristics:

- It used the model as both an organizing scheme and a basic analytic tool.
- It used other theories or concepts as "sub-models" to aid in more detailed analysis.
- It placed an emphasis on using models as pragmatic management tools to analyze and solve real problems.
- It pushed students to apply these tools by using cases, simulations, and exercises that reflected the problems and settings of modern management.

Needless to say, finding the appropriate text for such a course was difficult, so a collection of readings and cases was begun. When Hatvany joined the group several years later, she collaborated in the continuing development of the course. This book is the culmination of that work and the materials developed as a result.

This volume is designed to provide a set of materials to aid in the teaching and/or learning about organizational behavior and management. It continues in the tradition of our early course development efforts by providing an integrated model, by containing readings on individuals, groups, and organizations which reflect varying but consistent views. It maintains a focus on learning environments by including cases and exercises to use for the application of the various models, concepts, and tools.

The book is primarily intended for use in organizational behavior and management courses in business and professional schools and for use in management development programs. It can stand alone or be used with a basic text. Its structure is designed to be consistent with *Managing Organizational Behavior* (Nadler, Hackman, and Lawler, 1979), but it can also be used independently or with other texts.

So many people have aided us in the development of the course and this book that it would be futile to attempt to name them all. The list would have to include many colleagues, students, and clients. A few, however, have made such significant contributions that we would be remiss should we omit them.

We have been inspired, encouraged, and supported by two of our senior colleagues in the OB field—Edward E. Lawler and J. Richard Hackman. They served as midwives to our model development efforts by publishing the first paper on our diagnostic model in their readings book with Lyman Porter in 1976. They have served as examples for us as well as mentors, and we are deeply grateful.

Major work on the development of our congruence model was supported by Robert Maher, manager of the Organizational Effectiveness Group, American Telephone and Telegraph Company. This support followed in AT&T's long tradition of support of organizational behavior research and experimentation.

We wish to thank E. Kirby Warren, Samuel Bronfman Professor of Management at Columbia University, for providing us with the opportunity to take hold of and shape the B6012 course.

Finally, this book would not exist were it not for the efforts of Joy Glazener, who pulled our scattered attempts at administering this project into a coordinated drive that finally got the book into print. Thank you, Joy.

In summary, we remain firm in our belief that, in the spirit of Kurt Lewin, the best theory is a practical and useful one. We view the fundamental role of the OB field as the development and dissemination of tools to aid in the creation and management of effective and healthy organizations. This book is part of that effort.

David A. Nadler
Michael L. Tushman
Nina G. Hatvany

Contents

Cases   477

The Manager, Models, and Organizational Effectiveness

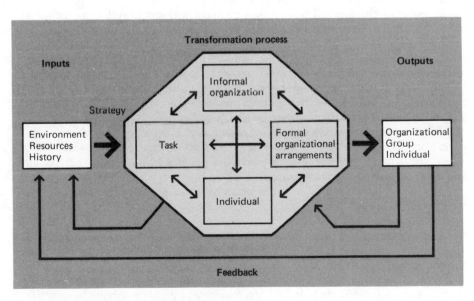

Focus of Section I—Inputs and Outputs

OVERVIEW AND INTRODUCTION

Most of the work of society gets done in organizations. The production of goods and services, the functions of government, and even our spiritual and leisure activities come about as a consequence of the activities of organizations. As a result, the role of management is extremely important to the effective functioning of society. Without people who understand organizations and make them work, we would be in serious trouble.

Over the past few decades the job of management has become more complex, more difficult, and more demanding. Changes in technology, environments, the state of knowledge, and individual attitudes, have made it more difficult to understand and control organizations. Today's typical manager in a multinational corporation may be concerned with coordinating the activities of people who live very far apart, work in different cultures, relate with different types of technologies, and need to coordinate their activities with very different individuals, both inside and outside of the corporation. This manager's job is very different from the job of a typical plant manager in a manufacturing organization at the turn of the century. There is more uncertainty to deal with; there are more factors to keep in mind; there are more relationships to manage.

Just as the nature of organizations has changed over the years, so have the jobs of managers. Rather than administering relatively stable, predictable, and unchanging work systems, the manager is almost constantly involved in collecting data, identifying problems, developing solutions, and implementing changes. The modern manager is less an administrator and more a problem finder, diagnostician, and implementer of change. All these functions occur within the very complex social system we call the organization—a web of different relationships and behaviors among large sets of people.

With the greater complexity of the managerial role and the attending changes in the managerial job have come new managerial tools. The last twenty-five years have brought vast new knowledge about the way organizations function, the way behavior occurs in organizational settings, and the ways managers can understand and influence the patterns of organizational behavior. One of the most basic tools which have been developed are models of organizational behavior. Models are frameworks, organizing schemes, or road maps that help us to understand and predict organizational behavior. Behind any model is the basic assumption that certain factors in an organization are more critical than others and therefore should be considered in greater detail. A model also provides a sense of how the different critical factors are related.

Models of organizational behavior are critical for managers. In any situation, a manager is faced with more information than he or she can possibly collect, process, or act on. Models provide a means for selecting among and interpreting that information. In addition to guiding the manager in collecting and interpreting data, the model helps the manager formulate and implement action to solve problems. Models are therefore important for both problem finding and problem solving in organizations.

Most people already use organizational models, but these models are usually vague and simple, and rarely explicit. By their nature, such models present problems. Simplistic models are inadequate to analyze or deal with the complex situations most managers face. The vague and implicit nature of such models makes them awkward for use in or study of organizations, and it is even more difficult to transmit these models to others. The basic thrust of this book is that people who want to understand and shape organizational behavior would benefit greatly by becoming acquainted with scientifically developed and field tested models of organizational behavior. Properly used, these models can be important managerial tools.

OVERVIEW OF THIS BOOK

The goal of this book is to provide a set of integrated models and perspectives on organizational behavior. To do this, we will present one general model of organizations (see Nadler and Tushman Reading 3, page 35). This is not the only model of organizations, nor is it necessarily the best model available. We chose it because it has been used successfully by a large number of managers and students of organizational behavior during recent years. It has proved useful as a way of understanding the patterns of what happens in organizations.

The model, called the *congruence model of organizational behavior*, is the basic integrative device for the book; we use it as an organizing framework for presenting the material. This model is the general road map by which we will find our way through organizations. In each section, we have selected readings that present concepts or theories relevant to different parts of the congruence model. In a sense, many of the readings present submodels that explain some of the relationships in the larger model. These submodels are also road maps, but in greater detail. If the congruence model is analogous to a map of the United States, the submodels are similar to more detailed maps of particular states, regions, or metropolitan areas. This book attempts, through the general model, to organize many different theories, concepts, and models of organizational behavior into a single, integrated, and thus usable format. Throughout the book we will relate the sets of readings to the different components of this general model.

THE CONGRUENCE MODEL

In Reading 3 we will present and discuss the congruence model in detail. It is useful to give here a brief overview of the model so that we can begin immediately to use it as an integrating device and organizing framework for the book.

There are many different ways of thinking about organizations and the patterns of behavior that occur within them. During the past two decades organizations have come to be seen as complex, open social systems (Katz and Kahn, 1966, 1978). Organizations are seen as mechanisms that take input from the larger environment and transform that input into outputs.

While the systems perspective is useful, systems theory by itself may be too abstract to be a useful managerial tool. For this reason, there have been attempts to develop more specific models based on the general systems paradigm. Building on the input, transformation process, and output perspective, we can describe the system of organizational behavior and effectiveness (Figure I-1). The major inputs to the system of organizational behavior are the environment, which provides constraints, demands, and opportunities; the resources available to the organization; and the history of the organization. A fourth input, and perhaps the most crucial,

Figure I-1. The Systems Model Applied to Organizational Behavior

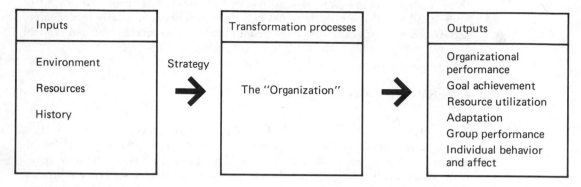

is the organization's strategy. Strategy is the set of key decisions about how to configure the organization's resources in light of the demands, constraints, and opportunities of the environment and the context of history.

The output of the system of organizational behavior is the behavior and performance of the organization: how well it achieves the goals specified by strategy. Specifically, the output includes organizational performance as well as the contributing factors of group behavior and individual behavior and affect.

The organization, then, is the mechanism that takes inputs and transforms them into outputs. The organization has four major components. The first component is the task of the organization, or the work to be done and its critical characteristics. The tasks to be done reflect the strategic decisions of managers about the nature of the organization's core mission and how it will be achieved. A second component is the individuals, organization members basically hired to perform tasks. Given tasks and individuals to perform them, the organization needs a third component, formal organizational arrangements. These include all the various formal structures, processes, systems, relationships, and jobs that motivate individuals and facilitate their performing organizational tasks. Finally, there are the informal organizational arrangements. These emerge over time, are neither written nor formalized, but influence much behavior. These arrangements include patterns of communication, power, and influence; values and norms; and the like.

How do these four components relate to one another? Each component can be thought of as having a relationship with each other component (Figure I-2). Each pair, then, can be thought of as having a relative degree of congruence and consistency, or fit. There are six possible relationships in the model; the basic hypothesis of the model is that *organizations will be most effective when their major components are congruent with each other.* Problems of organizational effectiveness, if they are caused by management or organization-related factors, stem from lack of congruence or fit among the organizational components.

The model is a contingency approach to thinking about organizational effectiveness. There is no one best organization design, style of management, or method of working. The question is whether the organizational design, for example, fits with the nature of the work being done, the individuals, and the informal arrangements. Different patterns of organization and management will be more appropriate in some situations than others.

Figure I-2.   A Congruence Model of Organizational Behavior

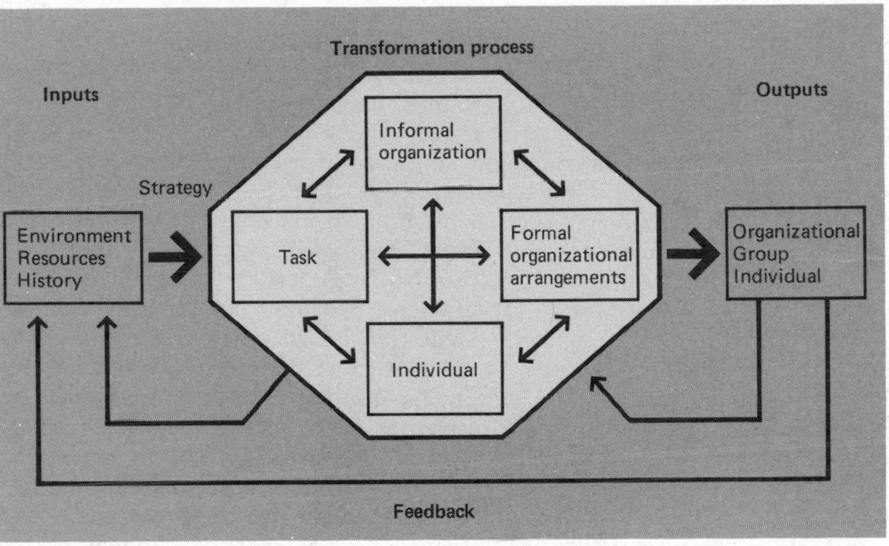

Source: D. A. Nadler and M. L. Tushman, "A Diagnostic Model for Organization Behavior," in *Perspectives on Behavior in Organizations*, ed. J. R. Hackman, E. E. Lawler, and L. W. Porter (New York: McGraw-Hill, 1977), pp. 85–100.

THE ORGANIZATION OF THIS BOOK

The readings are organized into a number of different sections; each relates to a specific part of the congruence model. Section I provides an introduction to the general model and to the role of the manager and organizational behavior. It gives a detailed description of the model and includes readings on the input and output sections of the model (see page 1). Section II focuses on the individuals component and its relationship to other components (see page 73). Section III concerns various aspects of the informal organization, including groups, leadership, and conflict. This section also addresses how the informal organization fits with individuals, tasks, and the formal arrangements (see page 183). Section IV deals with organizational design questions, or how structure, control, and coordination mechanisms can be managed so that they are congruent with the task, the individuals, and the informal organization (see page 287). Finally, Section V concerns how organizations change and can be managed over time. This section presents a different way of looking at all of the components and their relationships. Although dynamic, the components are seen as responsive to management (see page 371).

At the beginning of each of these five sections there is a brief introduction. This introduction gives an overview of the section, links the topic areas to the appropriate portions of the general congruence model, and discusses briefly the role of each reading within the section.

THE READINGS IN SECTION I

Section I sets the stage for a systematic approach to thinking about organizational behavior. In the first half of the section (Part I.A) two readings provide different perspectives on what managers do in organizations and what kinds of tools they use. In his classic article, "Skills of an Effective Administrator," Robert Katz identifies a number of key skills—technical, human, and conceptual—that every manager should have. In Reading 2, Nina Hatvany discusses the role of models in managerial thinking, in particular how models of organization influence the ways in which managers identify, define, and solve organizational problems.

The second half of this section (Part I.B) includes three readings aimed at providing a basic perspective on organizations. Reading 3, by David Nadler and Michael Tushman, "A Congruence Model for the Diagnosis of Organizational Behavior," presents and discusses the congruence model briefly described above. The two remaining readings deal with the input and output side of this model (see page 1). In Reading 4, "When Is an Organization Effective," Richard Steers provides some insight into the output side of the model. He focuses on what is involved in the concept of organizational effectiveness. Ian MacMillan's paper, "Business Strategy Formulation," examines many of the issues related to the input side of the model. He pays particular attention to the questions of how organizational strategy is determined and how organizational tasks are decided upon.

As a whole, then, Section I provides some insight into the general skills, roles, and tools associated with the management of organizations and organizational behavior. In particular, it focuses on one tool, a model of organizational behavior, and provides some general perspectives on the major inputs and outputs of that model. In doing this, the section provides the basis for in-depth examination in the rest of the book of the different components of the organization and the relationships among them.

REFERENCES

Katz, D., and Kahn, R. *The social psychology of organizations.* New York: Wiley, 1966 (1st edition).
——— . *The social psychology of organizations.* New York: Wiley, 1978 (2nd edition).

I.A
What Managers Do, and How

Robert L. Katz

1

Skills of an
effective administrator

Although the selection and training of good administrators is widely recognized as one of American industry's most pressing problems, there is surprisingly little agreement among executives or educators on what makes a good administrator. The executive development programs of some of the nation's leading corporations and colleges reflect a tremendous variation in objectives.

At the root of this difference is industry's search for the traits or attributes which will objectively identify the "ideal executive" who is equipped to cope effectively with any problem in any organization. As one observer of U.S. industry recently noted:

> The assumption that there is an executive type is widely accepted, either openly or implicitly. Yet any executive presumably knows that a company needs all kinds of managers for differ-

ent levels of jobs. The qualities most needed by a shop superintendent are likely to be quite opposed to those needed by a coordinating vice president of manufacturing. The literature of executive development is loaded with efforts to define the qualities needed by executives, and by themselves these sound quite rational. Few, for instance, would dispute the fact that a top manager needs good judgment, the ability to make decisions, the ability to win respect of others, and all the other well-worn phrases any management man could mention. But one has only to look at the successful managers in any company to see how enormously their particular qualities vary from any ideal list of executive virtues.[1]

Yet this quest for the executive stereotype has become so intense that many companies, in concentrating on certain specific traits or qualities, stand in danger of losing sight of their real concern: *what a man can accomplish.*

It is the purpose of this article to suggest what may be a more useful approach to the selection and development of administrators. This approach is based not on what good executives *are* (their innate traits and characteristics), but rather on what they *do* (the kinds of skills which

Source: Reprinted by permission of the Harvard Business Review. "Skills of an Effective Administrator" by Robert L. Katz (September–October 1974). Copyright © 1974 by the President and Fellows of Harvard College; all rights reserved. (Originally published in 1954)

Author's note: This article is based on a study prepared under a grant from the Alfred P. Sloan Foundation.

7

they exhibit in carrying out their jobs effectively). As used here, a *skill* implies an ability which can be developed, not necessarily inborn, and which is manifested in performance, not merely in potential. So the principal criterion of skillfulness must be effective action under varying conditions.

This approach suggests that effective administration rests on *three basic developable skills* which obviate the need for identifying specific traits and which may provide a useful way of looking at and understanding the administrative process. This approach is the outgrowth of firsthand observation of executives at work coupled with study of current field research in administration.

In the sections which follow, an attempt will be made to define and demonstrate what these three skills are; to suggest that the relative importance of the three skills varies with the level of administrative responsibility; to present some of the implications of this variation for selection, training, and promotion of executives; and to propose ways of developing these skills.

THREE-SKILL APPROACH

It is assumed here that an administrator is one who (a) directs the activities of other persons and (b) undertakes the responsibility for achieving certain objectives through these efforts. Within this definition, successful administration appears to rest on three basic skills, which we will call *technical, human,* and *conceptual.* It would be unrealistic to assert that these skills are not interrelated, yet there may be real merit in examining each one separately, and in developing them independently.

Technical Skill

As used here, technical skill implies an understanding of, and proficiency in, a specific kind of activity, particularly one involving methods, processes, procedures, or techniques. It is relatively easy for us to visualize the technical skill of the surgeon, the musician, the accountant, or the engineer when each is performing his own special function. Technical skill involves specialized knowledge, analytical ability within that specialty, and facility in the use of the tools and techniques of the specific discipline.

Of the three skills described in this article, technical skill is perhaps the most familiar because it is the most concrete, and because, in our age of specialization, it is the skill required of the greatest number of people. Most of our vocational and on-the-job training programs are largely concerned with developing this specialized technical skill.

Human Skill

As used here, human skill is the executive's ability to work effectively as a group member and to build cooperative effort within the team he leads. As *technical* skill is primarily concerned with working with "things" (processes or physical objects), so *human* skill is primarily concerned with working with people. This skill is demonstrated in the way the individual perceives (and recognizes the perceptions of) his superiors, equals, and subordinates, and in the way he behaves subsequently.

The person with highly developed human skill is aware of his own attitudes, assumptions, and beliefs about other individuals and groups; he is able to see the usefulness and limitations of these feelings. By accepting the existence of viewpoints, perceptions, and beliefs which are different from his own, he is skilled in understanding what others really mean by their words and behavior. He is equally skillful in communicating to others, in their own contexts, what he means by *his* behavior.

Such a person works to create an atmosphere of approval and security in which subordinates feel free to express themselves without fear of censure or ridicule, by encouraging them to participate in the planning and carrying out of those things which directly affect them. He is sufficiently sensitive to the needs and motivations of others in his organization so that he can judge the possible reactions to, and outcomes of, various courses of action he may undertake. Having this sensitivity, he is able and willing to *act* in a way which takes these perceptions by others into account.

Real skill in working with others must become a natural, continuous activity, since it involves sensitivity not only at times of decision making but also in the day-by-day behavior of the individual. Human skill cannot be a "sometime thing." Techniques cannot be randomly applied, nor can personality traits be put on or removed like an overcoat. Because everything which an executive says and does (or leaves unsaid or undone) has an effect on his associates, his true self will, in time, show through. Thus, to be effective, this skill must be naturally developed and unconsciously, as well as consistently, demonstrated in the individual's every action. It must become an integral part of his whole being.

Because human skill is so vital a part of everything the administrator does, examples of inadequate human skill are easier to describe than are highly skillful performances. Perhaps consideration of an actual situation would serve to clarify what is involved:

When a new conveyor unit was installed in a shoe factory where workers had previously been free to determine their own work rate, the production manager asked the industrial engineer who had designed the conveyor to serve as foreman, even though a qualified foreman was available. The engineer, who reported directly to the production manager, objected, but under pressure he agreed to take the job "until a suitable foreman could be found," even though this was a job of lower status than his present one. Then this conversation took place:

Production Manager: I've had a lot of experience with conveyors. I want you to keep this conveyor going at all times except for rest periods, and I want it going at top speed. Get these people thinking in terms of 2 pairs of shoes a minute, 70 dozen pairs a day, 350 dozen pairs a week. They are all experienced operators on their individual jobs, and it's just a matter of getting them to do their jobs in a little different way. I want you to make that base rate of 250 dozen pairs a week work! [Base rate was established at slightly under 75% of the maximum capacity. This base rate was 50% higher than under the old system.]

Engineer: If I'm going to be foreman of the conveyor unit, I want to do things my way. I've worked on conveyors, and I don't agree with you

on first getting people used to a conveyor going at top speed. These people have never seen a conveyor. You'll scare them. I'd like to run the conveyor at one-third speed for a couple of weeks and then gradually increase the speed.

I think we should discuss setting the base rate [production quota before incentive bonus] on a daily basis instead of a weekly basis. [Workers had previously been paid on a daily straight piecework basis.]

I'd also suggest setting a daily base rate at 45 or even 40 dozen pair. You have to set a base rate low enough for them to make. Once they know they can make the base rate, they will go after the bonus.

Production Manager: You do it your way on the speed; but remember it's the results that count. On the base rate, I'm not discussing it with you; I'm telling you to make the 250 dozen pair a week work. I don't want a daily base rate.[2]

Here is a situation in which the production manager was so preoccupied with getting the physical output that he did not pay attention to the people through whom that output had to be achieved. Notice, first, that he made the engineer who designed the unit serve as foreman, apparently hoping to force the engineer to justify his design by producing the maximum output. However, the production manager was oblivious to (a) the way the engineer perceived this appointment, as a demotion, and (b) the need for the engineer to be able to control the variables if he was to be held responsible for maximum output. Instead the production manager imposed a production standard and refused to make any changes in the work situation.

Moreover, although this was a radically new situation for the operators, the production manager expected them to produce immediately at well above their previous output—even though the operators had an unfamiliar production system to cope with, the operators had never worked together as a team before, the operators and their new foreman had never worked together before, and the foreman was not in agreement with the production goals or standards. By ignoring all these human factors, the production manager not only placed the engineer in an extremely difficult operating situation but also, by refusing to allow the engineer to "run his own show," discouraged the very assumption of responsibility he had hoped for in making the appointment.

Under these circumstances, it is easy to understand how the relationship between these two men rapidly deteriorated, and how production, after two months' operation, was at only 125 dozen pairs per week (just 75% of what the output had been under the old system).

Conceptual Skill

As used here, conceptual skill involves the ability to see the enterprise as a whole; it includes recognizing how the various functions of the organization depend on one another, and how changes in any one part affect all the others; and it extends to visualizing the relationship of the individual business to the industry, the community, and the political, social, and economic forces of the nation as a whole. Recognizing these relationships and perceiving the significant elements in any situation, the administrator should then be able to act in a way which advances the over-all welfare of the total organization.

Hence, the success of any decision depends on the conceptual skill of the people who make the decision and those who put it into action. When, for example, an important change in marketing policy is made, it is critical that the effects on production, control, finance, research, and the people involved be considered. And it remains critical right down to the last executive who must implement the new policy. If each executive recognizes the over-all relationships and significance of the change, he is almost certain to be more effective in administering it. Consequently the chances for succeeding are greatly increased.

Not only does the effective coordination of the various parts of the business depend on the conceptual skill of the administrators involved, but so also does the whole future direction and tone of the organization. The attitudes of a top executive color the whole character of the organization's response and determine the "corporate personality" which distinguishes one company's ways of doing business from another's. These attitudes are a reflection of the administrator's conceptual skill (referred to by some as his "creative ability")—the way he perceives and responds to

the direction in which the business should grow, company objectives and policies, and stockholders' and employees' interests.

Conceptual skill, as defined above, is what Chester I. Barnard, former president of the New Jersey Bell Telephone Company, is implying when he says: ". . . the essential aspect of the [executive] process is the sensing of the organization as a whole and of the total situation relevant to it."[3] Examples of inadequate conceptual skill are all around us. Here is one instance:

In a large manufacturing company which had a long tradition of job-shop type operations, primary responsibility for production control had been left to the foremen and other lower-level supervisors. "Village" type operations with small working groups and informal organizations were the rule. A heavy influx of orders following World War II tripled the normal production requirements and severely taxed the whole manufacturing organization. At this point, a new production manager was brought in from outside the company, and he established a wide range of controls and formalized the entire operating structure.

As long as the boom demand lasted, the employees made every effort to conform with the new procedures and environment. But when demand subsided to prewar levels, serious labor relations problems developed, friction was high among department heads, and the company found itself saddled with a heavy indirect labor cost. Management sought to reinstate its old procedures; it fired the production manager and attempted to give greater authority to the foremen once again. However, during the four years of formalized control, the foremen had grown away from their old practices, many had left the company, and adequate replacements had not been developed. Without strong foreman leadership, the traditional job-shop operations proved costly and inefficient.

In this instance, when the new production controls and formalized organizations were introduced, management did not foresee the consequences of this action in the event of a future contraction of business. Later, when conditions changed and it was necessary to pare down operations, management was again unable to recognize the implications of its action and reverted to the old procedures, which, under the circumstances, were no longer appropriate. This compounded *conceptual* inadequacy left the company at a serious competitive disadvantage.

Because a company's over-all success is dependent on its executives' conceptual skill in establishing and carrying out policy decisions, this skill is the unifying, coordinating ingredient of the administrative process, and of undeniable over-all importance.

RELATIVE IMPORTANCE

We may notice that, in a very real sense, conceptual skill embodies consideration of both the technical and human aspects of the organization. Yet the concept of *skill*, as an ability to translate knowledge into action, should enable one to distinguish between the three skills of performing the technical activities (technical skill), understanding and motivating individuals and groups (human skill), and coordinating and integrating all the activities and interests of the organization toward a common objective (conceptual skill).

This separation of effective administration into three basic skills is useful primarily for purposes of analysis. In practice, these skills are so closely interrelated that it is difficult to determine where one ends and another begins. However, just because the skills are interrelated does not imply that we cannot get some value from looking at them separately, or by varying their emphasis. In playing golf the action of the hands, wrists, hips, shoulders, arms, and head are all interrelated; yet in improving one's swing it is often valuable to work on one of these elements separately. Also, under different playing conditions the relative importance of these elements varies. Similarly, although all three are of importance at every level of administration, the technical, human, and conceptual skills of the administrator vary in relative importance at different levels of responsibility.

At Lower Levels

Technical skill is responsible for many of the great advances of modern industry. It is indispensable to efficient operation. Yet it has greatest impor-

tance at the lower levels of administration. As the administrator moves further and further from the actual physical operation, this need for technical skill becomes less important, provided he has skilled subordinates and can help them solve their own problems. At the top, technical skill may be almost nonexistent, and the executive may still be able to perform effectively if his human and conceptual skills are highly developed. For example:

In one large capital-goods producing company, the controller was called on to replace the manufacturing vice president, who had been stricken suddenly with a severe illness. The controller had no previous production experience, but he had been with the company for more than 20 years and knew many of the key production personnel intimately. By setting up an advisory staff, and by delegating an unusual amount of authority to his department heads, he was able to devote himself to coordination of the various functions. By so doing, he produced a highly efficient team. The results were lower costs, greater productivity, and higher morale than the production division had ever before experienced. Management had gambled that this man's ability to work with people was more important than his lack of a technical production background, and the gamble paid off.

Other examples are evident all around us. We are all familiar with those "professional managers" who are becoming the prototypes of our modern executive world. These men shift with great ease, and with no apparent loss in effectiveness, from one industry to another. Their human and conceptual skills seem to make up for their unfamiliarity with the new job's technical aspects.

At Every Level

Human skill, the ability to work with others, is essential to effective administration at every level. One recent research study has shown that human skill is of paramount importance at the foreman level, pointing out that the chief function of the foreman as an administrator is to attain collaboration of people in the work group.[4] Another study reinforces this finding and extends it to the middle management group, adding, that the administrator should be primarily concerned with facilitating communication in the organization.[5] And still another study, concerned primarily with top management, underscores the need for self-awareness and sensitivity to human relationships by executives at that level.[6] These findings would tend to indicate that human skill is of great importance at every level, but notice the difference in emphasis.

Human skill seems to be most important at lower levels, where the number of direct contacts between administrators and subordinates is greatest. As we go higher and higher in the administrative echelons, the number and frequency of these personal contacts decrease, and the need for human skill becomes proportionately, although probably not absolutely, less. At the same time, conceptual skill becomes increasingly more important with the need for policy decisions and broad-scale action. The human skill of dealing with individuals then becomes subordinate to the conceptual skill of integrating group interests and activities into a whole.

In fact, a recent research study by Professor Chris Argyris of Yale University has given us the example of an extremely effective plant manager who, although possessing little human skill as defined here, was nonetheless very successful:

This manager, the head of a largely autonomous division, made his supervisors, through the effects of his strong personality and the "pressure" he applied, highly dependent on him for most of their "rewards, penalties, authority, perpetuation, communication, and identification."

As a result, the supervisors spent much of their time competing with one another for the manager's favor. They told him only the things they thought he wanted to hear, and spent much time trying to find out his desires. They depended on him to set their objectives and to show them how to reach them. Because the manager was inconsistent and unpredictable in his behavior, the supervisors were insecure and continually engaged in interdepartmental squabbles which they tried to keep hidden from the manager.

Clearly, human skill as defined here was lacking. Yet, by the evaluation of his superiors and by his results in increasing efficiency and raising profits and morale, this manager was exceedingly effective. Professor Argyris suggests that employees in modern industrial organizations tend to have a "built-in" sense of dependence on superiors which capable and alert men can turn to advantage.[7]

In the context of the three-skill approach, it seems that this manager was able to capitalize on this dependence because he recognized the interrelationships of all the activities under his control, identified himself with the organization, and sublimated the individual interests of his subordinates to *his* (the organization's) interest, set his goals realistically, and showed his subordinates how to reach these goals. This would seem to be an excellent example of a situation in which strong conceptual skill more than compensated for a lack of human skill.

At the Top Level

Conceptual skill, as indicated in the preceding sections, becomes increasingly critical in more responsible executive positions where its effects are maximized and most easily observed. In fact, recent research findings lead to the conclusion that at the top level of administration this conceptual skill becomes the most important ability of all. As Herman W. Steinkraus, president of Bridgeport Brass Company, said:

One of the most important lessons which I learned on this job [the presidency] is the importance of coordinating the various departments into an effective team, and, secondly, to recognize the shifting emphasis from time to time of the relative importance of various departments to the business.[8]

It would appear, then, that at lower levels of administrative responsibility, the principal need is for technical and human skills. At higher levels, technical skill becomes relatively less important while the need for conceptual skill increases rapidly. At the top level of an organization, conceptual skill becomes the most important skill of all for successful administration. A chief executive may lack technical or human skills and still be effective if he has subordinates who have strong abilities in these directions. But if his conceptual skill is weak, the success of the whole organization may be jeopardized.

IMPLICATIONS FOR ACTION

This three-skill approach implies that significant benefits may result from redefining the objectives of executive development programs, from reconsidering the placement of executives in organizations, and from revising procedures for testing and selecting prospective executives.

Executive Development

Many executive development programs may be failing to achieve satisfactory results because of their inability to foster the growth of these administrative skills. Programs which concentrate on the mere imparting of information or the cultivation of a specific trait would seem to be largely unproductive in enhancing the administrative skills of candidates.

A strictly informative program was described to me recently by an officer and director of a large corporation who had been responsible for the executive development activities of his company, as follows:

> What we try to do is to get our promising young men together with some of our senior executives in regular meetings each month. Then we give the young fellows a chance to ask questions to let them find out about the company's history and how and why we've done things in the past.

It was not surprising that neither the senior executives nor the young men felt this program was improving their administrative abilities.

The futility of pursuing specific traits becomes apparent when we consider the responses of an administrator in a number of different situations. In coping with these varied conditions, he may appear to demonstrate one trait in one instance— e.g., dominance when dealing with subordinates—and the directly opposite trait under another set of circumstances—e.g., submissiveness when dealing with superiors. Yet in each instance he may be acting appropriately to achieve the best results. Which, then, can we identify as a desirable characteristic? Here is a further example of this dilemma:

A Pacific Coast sales manager had a reputation for decisiveness and positive action. Yet when he was required to name an assistant to understudy his job from among several well-qualified subordinates, he deliberately avoided making a decision. His associates were quick to observe what appeared to be obvious indecisiveness.

But after several months had passed, it became clear that the sales manager had very unobtrusively been giving the various salesmen opportunities to demonstrate their attitudes and feelings. As a result, he was able to identify strong sentiments for one man whose subsequent promotion was enthusiastically accepted by the entire group.

In this instance, the sales manager's skillful performance was improperly interpreted as "indecisiveness." Their concern with irrelevant traits led his associates to overlook the adequacy of his performance. Would it not have been more appropriate to conclude that his human skill in working with others enabled him to adapt effectively to the requirements of a new situation?

Cases such as these would indicate that it is more useful to judge an administrator on the results of his performance than on his apparent traits. Skills are easier to identify than are traits and are less likely to be misinterpreted. Furthermore, skills offer a more directly applicable frame of reference for executive development, since any improvement in an administrator's skills must necessarily result in more effective performance.

Still another danger in many existing executive development programs lies in the unqualified enthusiasm with which some companies and colleges have embraced courses in "human relations." There would seem to be two inherent pitfalls here: (1) Human relations courses might only be imparting information or specific techniques, rather than developing the individual's human skill. (2) Even if individual development does take place, some companies, by placing all of their emphasis on human skill, may be completely overlooking the training requirements for top positions. They may run the risk of producing men with highly developed human skill who lack the conceptual ability to be effective top-level administrators.

It would appear important, then, that the training of a candidate for an administrative position be directed at the development of those skills which are most needed at the level of responsibility for which he is being considered.

Executive Placement

This three-skill concept suggests immediate possibilities for the creating of management teams of individuals with complementary skills. For example, one medium-size midwestern distributing organization has as president a man of unusual conceptual ability but extremely limited human skill. However, he has two vice presidents with exceptional human skill. These three men make up an executive committee which has been outstandingly successful, the skills of each member making up for deficiencies of the others. Perhaps the plan of two-man complementary conference leadership proposed by Robert F. Bales, in which the one leader maintains "task leadership" while the other provides "social leadership," might also be an example in point.[9]

Executive Selection

In trying to predetermine a prospective candidate's abilities on a job, much use is being made these days of various kinds of testing devices. Executives are being tested for everything from "decisiveness" to "conformity." These tests, as a recent article in *Fortune* points out, have achieved some highly questionable results when applied to performance on the job.[10] Would it not be much more productive to be concerned with skills of doing rather than with a number of traits which do not guarantee performance?

This three-skill approach makes trait testing unnecessary and substitutes for it procedures which examine a man's ability to cope with the actual problems and situations he will find on his job. These procedures, which indicate what a man can *do* in specific situations, are the same for selection and for measuring development. They will be described in the section on developing executive skills which follows.

This approach suggests that executives should *not* be chosen on the basis of their apparent possession of a number of behavior characteristics or traits, but on the basis of their possession of the requisite skills for the specific level of responsibility involved.

DEVELOPING THE SKILLS

For years many people have contended that leadership ability is inherent in certain chosen individuals. We talk of "born leaders," "born executives," "born salesmen." It is undoubtedly true that certain people, naturally or innately, possess greater aptitude or ability in certain skills. But research in psychology and physiology would also indicate, first, that those having strong aptitudes and abilities can improve their skill through practice and training, and, secondly, that even those lacking the natural ability can improve their performance and over-all effectiveness.

The *skill* conception of administration suggests that we may hope to improve our administrative effectiveness and to develop better administrators for the future. This skill conception implies *learning by doing*. Different people learn in different ways, but skills are developed through practice and through relating learning to one's own personal experience and background. If well done, training in these basic administrative skills should develop executive abilities more surely and more rapidly than through unorganized experience. What, then, are some of the ways in which this training can be conducted?

Technical Skill

Development of technical skill has received great attention for many years by industry and educational institutions alike, and much progress has been made. Sound grounding in the principles, structures, and processes of the individual specialty, coupled with actual practice and experience during which the individual is watched and helped by a superior, appear to be most effective. In view of the vast amount of work which has been done in training people in the technical skills, it would seem unnecessary in this article to suggest more.

Human Skill

Human skill, however, has been much less understood, and only recently has systematic progress been made in developing it. Many different approaches to the development of human skill are being pursued by various universities and professional men today. These are rooted in such disciplines as psychology, sociology, and anthropology.

Some of these approaches find their application in "applied psychology," "human engineering," and a host of other manifestations requiring technical specialists to help the businessman with his human problems. As a practical matter, however, the executive must develop his own human skill, rather than lean on the advice of others. To be effective, he must develop his own personal point of view toward human activity, so that he will (a) recognize the feelings and sentiments which he brings to a situation; (b) have an attitude about his own experiences which will enable him to re-evaluate and learn from them; (c) develop ability in understanding what others by their actions and words (explicit or implicit) are trying to communicate to him; and (d) develop ability in successfully communicating his ideas and attitudes to others.[11]

This human skill can be developed by some individuals without formalized training. Others can be individually aided by their immediate superiors as an integral part of the "coaching" process to be described later. This aid depends for effectiveness, obviously, on the extent to which the superior possesses the human skill.

For larger groups, the use of case problems coupled with impromptu role playing can be very effective. This training can be established on a formal or informal basis, but it requires a skilled instructor and organized sequence of activities.[12] It affords as good an approximation to reality as can be provided on a continuing classroom basis and offers an opportunity for critical reflection not often found in actual practice. An important part of the procedure is the self-examination of the trainee's own concepts and values, which may enable him to develop more useful attitudes about himself and about others. With the change in attitude, hopefully, there may also come some active skill in dealing with human problems.

Human skill has also been tested in the classroom, within reasonable limits, by a series of analyses of detailed accounts of actual situations involving administrative action, together with a number of role-playing opportunities in which the individual is required to carry out the details of the action he has proposed. In this way an individual's understanding of the total situation and his own personal ability to do something about it can be evaluated.

On the job, there should be frequent opportunities for a superior to observe an individual's ability to work effectively with others. These may appear to be highly subjective evaluations and to depend for validity on the human skill of the rater. But does not every promotion, in the last analysis, depend on someone's subjective judgment? And should this subjectivity be berated, or should we make a greater effort to develop people within our organizations with the human skill to make such judgments effectively?

Conceptual Skill

Conceptual skill, like human skill, has not been very widely understood. A number of methods have been tried to aid in developing this ability, with varying success. Some of the best results have always been achieved through the "coaching" of subordinates by superiors.[13] This is no new idea. It implies that one of the key responsibilities of the executive is to help his subordinates to develop their administrative potentials. One way a superior can help "coach" his subordinate is by assigning a particular responsibility, and then responding with searching questions or opinions, rather than giving answers, whenever the subordinate seeks help. When Benjamin F. Fairless, now chairman of the board of the United States Steel Corporation, was president of the corporation, he described his coaching activities:

> When one of my vice presidents or the head of one of our operating companies comes to me for instructions, I generally counter by asking him questions. First thing I know, he has told me how to solve the problem himself.[14]

Obviously, this is an ideal and wholly natural procedure for administrative training, and applies to the development of technical and human skill, as well as to that of conceptual skill. However, its success must necessarily rest on the abilities and willingness of the superior to help the subordinate.

Another excellent way to develop conceptual skill is through trading jobs, that is, by moving promising young men through different functions of the business but at the same level of responsibility. This gives the man the chance literally to "be in the other fellow's shoes."

Other possibilities include: special assignments, particularly the kind which involve interdepartmental problems; and management boards, such as the McCormick Multiple Management plan, in which junior executives serve as advisers to top management on policy matters.

For larger groups, the kind of case-problems course described above, only using cases involving broad management policy and interdepartmental coordination, may be useful. Courses of this kind, often called "General Management" or "Business Policy," are becoming increasingly prevalent.

In the classroom, conceptual skill has also been evaluated with reasonable effectiveness by presenting a series of detailed descriptions of specific complex situations. In these the individual being tested is asked to set forth a course of action which responds to the underlying forces operating in each situation and which considers the implications of this action on the various functions and parts of the organization and its total environment.

On the job, the alert supervisor should find frequent opportunities to observe the extent to which the individual is able to relate himself and his job to the other functions and operations of the company.

Like human skill, conceptual skill, too, must become a natural part of the executive's makeup. Different methods may be indicated for developing different people, by virtue of their backgrounds, attitudes, and experience. But in every case that method should be chosen which will enable the executive to develop his own personal skill in visualizing the enterprise as a whole and in coordinating and integrating its various parts.

CONCLUSION

The purpose of this article has been to show that effective administration depends on three basic personal skills, which have been called *technical, human,* and *conceptual.* The administrator needs: (a) sufficient technical skill to accomplish the mechanics of the particular job for which he is responsible; (b) sufficient human skill in working with others to be an effective group member and to be able to build cooperative effort within the team he leads; (c) sufficient conceptual skill to recognize the interrelationships of the various factors involved in his situation, which will lead him to take that action which is likely to achieve the maximum good for the total organization.

The relative importance of these three skills seems to vary with the level of administrative responsibility. At lower levels, the major need is for technical and human skills. At higher levels, the administrator's effectiveness depends largely on human and conceptual skills. At the top, conceptual skill becomes the most important of all for successful administration.

This three-skill approach emphasizes that good administrators are not necessarily born; they may be developed. It transcends the need to identify specific traits in an effort to provide a more useful way of looking at the administrative process. By helping to identify the skills most needed at various levels of responsibility, it may prove useful in the selection, training, and promotion of executives.

RETROSPECTIVE COMMENTARY

When this article was first published nearly 20 years ago, there was a great deal of interest in trying to identify a set of ideal personality traits that would readily distinguish potential executive talent. The search for these traits was vigorously pursued in the hope that the selection and training of managers could be conducted with greater reliability.

This article was an attempt to focus attention on demonstrable skills of performance rather than on innate personality characteristics. And, while describing the three kinds of administrative skill (technical, human, and conceptual), it also attempted to highlight the importance of conceptual skill as a uniquely valuable managerial capability, long before the concept of corporate strategy was well defined or popularly understood.

It still appears useful to think of managerial ability in terms of these three basic, observable skills. It also still appears that the relative importance of these skills varies with the administrative level of the manager in the organization. However, my experience over the past 20 years, in working with senior executives in a wide variety of industries, suggests that several specific points require either sharp modification or substantial further refinement.

Human Skill

I now believe that this kind of skill could be usefully subdivided into (a) leadership ability within the manager's own unit and (b) skill in intergroup relationships. In my experience, outstanding capability in one of these roles is frequently accompanied by mediocre performance in the other.

Often, the most internally efficient department managers are those who have committed themselves fully to the unique values and criteria of their specialized functions, without acknowledging that other departments' differing values have any validity at all. For example, a production manager may be most efficient if he puts all his emphasis on obtaining a high degree of reliability in his production schedule. He would then resist any external pressures that place a higher priority on criteria other than delivering the required output on time. Or a sales manager may be most efficient if he puts all his emphasis on maintaining positive relationships with customers. He would then resist all pressures that would emphasize other values, such as ease of production or selling the highest gross margin items. In each case, the manager will probably receive strong support from his subordinates, who share the same values. But he will encounter severe antagonism from other departments with conflicting values.

To the extent that two departments' values conflict with each other, skillful intergroup relationships require some equivocation. But compromise is often perceived by departmental subordinates as a "sellout." Thus the manager is obliged to choose between gaining full support from subordinates or enjoying full collaboration with peers and/or superiors. Having both is rarely possible. Consequently, I would revise my original evaluation of human skill to say now that internal *intragroup* skills are essential in lower and middle management roles and that *intergroup* skills become increasingly important in successively higher levels of management.

Conceptual Skill

In retrospect, I now see that what I called conceptual skill depends entirely on a specific way of thinking about an enterprise. This "general management point of view," as it has come to be known, involves always thinking in terms of the following: relative emphases and priorities among conflicting objectives and criteria; relative tendencies and probabilities (rather than certainties); rough correlations and patterns among elements (rather than clear-cut cause-and-effect relationships).

I am now far less sanguine about the degree to which this way of thinking can be developed on the job. Unless a person has learned to think this way early in life, it is unrealistic to expect a major change on reaching executive status. Job rotation, special interdepartmental assignments, and working with case problems certainly provide opportunities for a person to enhance previously developed conceptual abilities. But I question how easily this way of thinking can be inculcated after a person passes adolescence. In this sense, then, conceptual skill should perhaps be viewed as an *innate* ability.

Technical Skill

In the original article, I suggested that specific technical skills are unimportant at top management levels. I cited as evidence the many professional managers who move easily from one industry to another without apparent loss of effectiveness.

I now believe this mobility is possible only in very large companies, where the chief executive has extensive staff assistance and highly competent, experienced technical operators throughout the organization. An old, established, large company has great operational momentum that enables the new chief executive to concentrate on strategic issues.

In smaller companies, where technical expertise is not as pervasive and seasoned staff assistance is not as available, I believe the chief executive has a much greater need for personal experience in the industry. He not only needs to know the right questions to ask his subordinates; he also needs enough industry background to know how to evaluate the answers.

Role of the Chief Executive

In the original article, I took too simplistic and naïve a view of the chief executive's role. My extensive work with company presidents and my own personal experience as a chief executive have given me much more respect for the difficulties and complexities of that role. I now know that every important executive action must strike a balance among so many conflicting values, objectives, and criteria that it will *always* be suboptimal from any single viewpoint. *Every* decision or choice affecting the whole enterprise has negative consequences for some of the parts.

The chief executive must try to perceive the conflicts and trace accurately their likely impact throughout the organization. Reluctantly, but wittingly, he may have to sacrifice the interests of a single unit or part for the good of the whole. He needs to be willing to accept solutions that are adequate and feasible in the total situation rather than what, from a single point of view, may be elegant or optimum.

Not only must the chief executive be an efficient operator, but he must also be an effective strategist. It is his responsibility to provide the framework and direction for overall company operations. He must continually specify where the company will place its emphasis in terms of products, services, and customers. He must define performance criteria and determine what special competences the company will emphasize. He

also needs to set priorities and timetables. He must establish the standards and controls necessary to monitor progress and to place limits on individual actions. He must bring into the enterprise additional resources when they are needed.

Moreover, he must change his management style and strike different balances among his personal skills as conditions change or as his organization grows in size and complexity. The *remedial* role (saving the organization when it is in great difficulty) calls for drastic human action and emphasizes conceptual and technical skills. The *maintaining* role (sustaining the organization in its present posture) emphasizes human skills and requires only modest technical or strategic changes. But the *innovative* role (developing and expanding the organization) demands high competence in both conceptual and intergroup skills, with the technical contribution provided primarily by subordinates.

In my view, it is impossible for anyone to perform well in these continually changing roles without help. Yet because effective management of the total enterprise involves constant suboptimizing, it is impossible for the chief executive to get unanimous or continuous support from his subordinates. If he is overly friendly or supportive, he may compromise his effectiveness or his objectivity. Yet somewhere in the organization, he needs to have a well-informed, objective, understanding, and supportive sounding board with whom he can freely discuss his doubts, fears, and aspirations. Sometimes this function can be supplied by an outside director, the outside corporate counsel, or the company auditor. But such a confidant requires just as high a degree of conceptual and human skills as the chief executive himself; and to be truly helpful, he must know all about the company's operations, key personnel, and industry. This role has been largely overlooked in discussions of organizational requirements, but in my view, its proper fulfillment is essential to the success of the chief executive and the enterprise.

Conclusion

I now realize more fully that managers at all levels require some competence in each of the three skills. Even managers at the lowest levels must continually use all of them. Dealing with the external demands on a manager's unit requires conceptual skill; the limited physical and financial resources available to him tax his technical skill; and the capabilities and demands of the persons with whom he deals make it essential that he possess human skill. A clear idea of these skills and of ways to measure a manager's competence in each category still appears to me to be a most effective tool for top management, not only in understanding executive behavior, but also in the selection, training, and promotion of managers at all levels.

NOTES

1. Perrin Stryker, "The Growing Pains of Executive Development," *Advanced Management*, August 1954, p. 15.

2. From a mimeographed case in the files of the Harvard Business School; copyrighted by the President and Fellows of Harvard College.

3. *Functions of the Executive* (Cambridge, Harvard University Press, 1948), p. 235.

4. A. Zaleznik, *Foreman Training in a Growing Enterprise* (Boston, Division of Research, Harvard Business School, 1951).

5. Harriet O. Ronken and Paul R. Lawrence, *Administering Changes* (Boston, Division of Research, Harvard Business School, 1952).

6. Edmund P. Learned, David H. Ulrich, and Donald R. Booz, *Executive Action* (Boston, Division of Research, Harvard Business School, 1950).

7. *Executive Leadership* (New York, Harper & Brothers, 1953); see also "Leadership Pattern in the Plant," [*Harvard Business Review*] January–February 1954, p. 63.

8. "What Should a President Do?" *Dun's Review*, August 1951, p. 21.

9. "In Conference," [*Harvard Business Review*] March–April 1954, p. 44.

10. William H. Whyte, Jr., "The Fallacies of 'Personality' Testing," *Fortune*, September 1954, p. 117.

11. For a further discussion of this point, see F. J. Roethlisberger, "Training Supervisors in Human Relations," [*Harvard Business Review*] September 1951, p. 47.

12. See, for example, A. Winn, "Training in Administration and Human Relations," *Personnel*, September 1953, p. 139; see also, Kenneth R. Andrews, "Executive Training by the Case Method," [*Harvard Business Review*] September 1951, p. 58.

13. For a more complete development of the concept of "coaching," see Myles I. Mace, *The Growth and Development of Executives* (Boston, Division of Research, Harvard Business School, 1950).

14. "What Should a President Do?" *Dun's Review*, July 1951, p. 14.

2
Decision making:
Managers and cognitive models

Nina G. Hatvany

The manager's unique access to information and his or her special status and authority place the manager at the central point in the system by which significant or strategic organizational decisions are made. The manager responds to existing and potential problems by initiating changes, restoring equilibrium, allocating resources, and persuading other individuals to cooperate. Mintzberg (1973) calls this set of activities the manager's decisional roles and suggests that they are the most crucial part of the manager's work.

The author recently completed a study of managerial decision making in the retail division of a major commercial bank. The middle managers in this division each have several branch managers as subordinates. Significant decisions made by the managers include formulating strategic plans, distributing resources, launching promotions, and, perhaps most important, allocating their own time. An example of a decision that many managers are making is where to install the new automated teller machines (ATMs), which should reduce the length of lines in the branches.

This [reading] will discuss the key managerial activity of decision making, the choices integral to solving problems. The process of decision making will be outlined and the need for simplifying models of reality will be addressed. The [reading] will focus on the biases and inaccuracies that typically occur in the use of such models. Decision-making problems are not unique to managers; strategies for avoiding or alleviating the deficits inherent in the typical decision-making process will be recommended.

THE PROCESS OF DECISION MAKING

The kinds of decisions that bank managers make vary a great deal, as do the kinds of decisions that

all managers make. Some, such as the best location for an ATM, are made only once. Some, such as whom to promote within the branches, are made twice a year. Some, such as which branches to inspect, are or could be made every day.

The frequency of particular decisions varies, as does the duration of the decision-making process. Managers can make some choices in a microsecond but may spend months making others, such as those choices involved in a business plan that makes predictions and allocates resources for the coming year. Typically, the more significant the manager perceives the decision to be, the more time he or she will spend on it. Allocation of time according to perceived importance is not always the case, however, particularly with decisions that are repeated several times.

In all cases, though, four decision phases ideally occur. First, the problem or opportunity is defined. Second, alternative solutions are generated and examined in terms both of their feasibility and expected consequences. Third, solutions are evaluated and a choice is made. Fourth, the choice is implemented.

In the first, or problem-finding phase (Pounds, 1969), the decision maker notes an event or occurrence, such as an increase in customer complaints. The causes of this symptom, the problem itself, must be identified before a solution can be found.

Classical models of rational choice specify the procedures to be followed in the second and third phases of alternative generation and evaluation. These models require that decision makers have complete knowledge of all the alternative solutions possible as well as of the consequences or outcomes that will follow from each of the alternatives. Each outcome must then be compared against the particular value or combination of values that the decision maker is attempting to maximize.

Extensions of the classical model include discussions of decision making under risk, rather than certainty, when outcomes have a certain probability of occurring. The value of the outcome must then be multiplied by the probability of its occurrence; the best outcome is one that maximizes the expected utility of the outcome. Further extensions discuss decision making under uncertainty, when probabilities are not known and must be estimated by the decision maker. In this extension, subjective expected utility replaces simple utility in a decision maker's calculations (Edwards, 1954).

Once alternatives have been generated and evaluated and the choice made, that choice must be implemented. This step in itself entails a series of decisions about how to implement so that the choice will be effected correctly and successfully.

When generating and examining alternative solutions, decision makers should have as much information as can be gathered in the available time by the available personnel. Implicit in all four phases is the need to search for and be open to new information, which may change the nature of the decision and hence call for a reiteration of the process. Clearly, too, the four phases are not rigidly separated, and there may be extensive interaction among them.

Take the example of a bank manager making a fairly simple decision in the way prescribed. An ATM is to be installed. As many customers as possible should make use of it. The manager identifies the key issue as selecting a machine location that is both attractive and accessible to as many customers as possible. There are three potential sites: branches A, B, and C. The manager inspects the attractiveness of the sites; gathers information about the daily traffic in each branch; and requests a small survey that asks customers whether A, B, or C is the most desirable site for an ATM. He or she gathers data on future market and demographic trends. While gathering this and other inputs, the manager is consistently open to changes in the status of the information already gathered.

Once the manager feels enough information has been obtained, he or she can assess the desirability of the three locations by in some way aggregating the estimates of attractiveness and accessibility. The next step is to combine the assessment of desirability in a multiplicative fashion with his or her own estimate of the likelihood that the sites will remain at their present level of desirability. For example, branch A might be the most desirable at the present time, but an exodus of industry from the area is taking place. This change may make the branch far less desirable as an ATM site. This probability estimate may affect the likelihood of choosing branch A, so that even though branch B is less attractive and accessible, the high probability that the level of these attributes will remain unchanged causes the manager to favor it over A; that is, branch B has higher subjective expected utility. Once the manager chooses B as the site, he or she must begin the process of implementing the decision. This process, in turn, requires that a whole new set of decisions be made.

What is noteworthy about even such a simple choice is that an enormous number of simplifying assumptions and choices are made. To take just a few examples: the key issue in the installation of an ATM is its location (finding the problem); the two major factors to consider when choosing a location are attractiveness and accessibility (choosing what to maximize); ATMs must be located in branches (selecting alternative solutions); customers will use ATMs (assuming a causal relation between accessibility and use); opinion surveys are a guide to customer actions (assuming a causal relation between attitudes of sample population and actions of total population); and an exodus of industry results in fewer customers (assuming a two-step causal relation between number of industries, attractiveness and accessibility, and use). Each of the assumptions of causal relationships could be challenged. The manager could have spent the time making a decision about something other than location; factors other than accessibility and desirability may well be key variables in increasing customer use; an ATM could be located outside a branch; customers may be afraid to use the newfangled ATMs; opinion surveys are often notably poor predictors of the future behaviors of the population represented by the survey; and an exodus of industry might result in an influx of high-income residents.

The point is not, however, to challenge all this hypothetical manager's assumptions, but rather to indicate the fact that they exist. Indeed, without such assumptions it is most unlikely that a decision could ever have been reached. The problem had to be defined. Limits on the information to be gathered were set, both because of the extent of the manager's capacity to process information and because of realistic deadlines for installing the ATM. Not every possible outcome could be evaluated. Not every possible probability or contingency could be estimated. The validity or truth of every causal assumption could not be evaluated. At some juncture, the manager had to choose to ignore novel incoming information. A simplifying model for the decision had to be formulated and adhered to. The next section will discuss the nature of such models or schemas.

MODELS OF REALITY

The limit of a person's capacity for processing information in immediate or short-term memory is about seven "chunks" of information (Miller, 1956). The size of a chunk depends on the person's familiarity with the kind of information, and hence a list of seven words is retained in short-term memory as easily as a list of seven letters such as "qalctsp" because each word forms one chunk. Given this limited capacity, even for familiar information, an individual has great difficulty trying simultaneously to consider all the available alternative solutions to a problem. Each choice has attendant outcomes and probabilities of success. To try to gather all the requisite information and then to juggle the tradeoffs among all the variables at once is simply an impossible task for a human being. The capacity of the human mind for formulating and solving problems is very small compared with the number and complexity of the problems that require solution. Herbert Simon terms this phenomenon bounded rationality (Simon, 1957).

To deal with his own bounded rationality, a human being develops models of reality. A model is an abstraction of reality, a set of causal relationships by which the effects of given conditions can be predicted. Such models are, in essence, simple conceptions of reality gleaned from the information with which the person is constantly bombarded. The information and causal relationships that make up such models can be based on experience or on theoretical knowledge (Pounds,

1969). A model may include any number of relationships within it, each of which may be examined as a model in its own right. A manager's models may include the internal workings of the organization, the behavior of subordinates, the trends in the organization's environment, the habits of associates, and so on.

Although an individual may have every intention of making rational decisions, to do so the individual must construct a simplified model of the real situation in order to deal with it. His or her decisions may be rational in the logical terms of this model; but to understand and predict choices, we must understand the way the manager constructed this simplified model.

Sometimes such models are very powerful and lead to effective decisions; at other times they are crude and lead to gross errors (Mintzberg, 1973). Sometimes these models consist of relationships that are testable and can be proved incorrect; sometimes the relationships are inherently less testable. It is, for example, hard to establish the relationship of saccharin to cancer in humans, since it is unethical to experiment with inducing cancer in human beings.

The most powerful models, those that lead to the most effective decisions, are those that most closely resemble reality yet remain simple enough to be useful. They must encompass the complexity of the phenomenon (requisite variety) without exceeding an individual's bounded rationality. Models that are unconscious or intuitive may be as powerful as explicit or conscious models. Every reader has experienced the "gut feel" that turns out to be correct. However, such "gut" or intuitive models remain closed to testing and hence closed to verification. Use of an intuitive model may achieve effective results, but it will never be clear whether success was due to the power of the model or just to luck. A manager who allows models to remain intuitive and unarticulated not only deprives peers and subordinates of the benefits of the model, if indeed it does reflect reality, but also runs the grave risk of having an incorrect and hence a weak model. This risk lies in the nature of human information processing. The human being, because of bounded rationality and the attendant use of heuristics, is not an accurate information processor. The next section of this reading will discuss the several limitations and biases that occur in the decision-making processes of human beings in general, with a particular focus on managers.

INADEQUACIES IN MODELS

This reading will examine limitations and biases in all four phases of decision making. Several frequently occur in gathering information, evaluating alternatives, estimating probability of outcomes, and selecting the model.

Information Gathering

The quality of available information. Managers tend to rely on orally communicated information rather than written information, as Mintzberg (1973) points out and other researchers (for example, Allen and Cohen, 1969; Tushman, 1977) confirm. This oral information comes not only from subordinates but also from people at the same or higher ranks both within and outside the organization. The manager should be aware of two processes that can distort this oral information. These operate in concert with the more general persuasive techniques that any interested party will adopt when trying to sell a point of view to a manager.

Managers very often do not receive information at first hand. Indeed, because of their preference for oral communication, they often receive their news distilled several times. Each person in the information chain is likely to distort the information in line with his or her own expectations and preconceptions, and those people who are closest to the raw information exercise a great deal of power when they abstract and synthesize the information. The result, as Downs (1967) calculated, is that in a six-level hierarchy, there may be a 98 percent loss of informational content between the lowest and highest level of the organization.

Aside from naturally occurring distortions, distortions occur because subordinates are frequently unwilling to confront a manager with information about the true state of affairs in their part of the organization, especially if they feel

that the information will not conform to the manager's expectations. Subordinates do not want their own inadequacies or failures to be noticed or punished, so they use window dressing and make overoptimistic predictions. By omitting vital facts subordinates paint a rosy picture that may please the manager, but leaves inadequate data for formulating models that reflect reality (Lawler, Porter, and Tannenbaum, 1968; Roberts and O'Reilly, 1979).

Self-imposed limits to information gathering. Even given high-quality information, the manager is limited by his or her bounded rationality, the opportunity-costs of attention given to any one decision arena, and the constraints of deadlines. The result is that the manager often "satisfices" (March and Simon, 1958).

Decision makers do examine alternatives carefully. However, as soon as they find a solution that is satisfactory as measured against some global criterion, they might implement that choice and cease to examine other available alternatives. The global criterion against which the solution is measured might be "will offend no one," "does not cost more than $100,000," or "will show some results quickly." Often the decision maker opts to take a course of action that is "good enough." The greatest liability inherent in this strategy is that alternatives that are, for whatever reason, considered early in the decision process are most likely to be chosen. Such choices may be made at the expense of better, but unexamined, alternatives.

A similar phenomenon often noted among administrators is incrementalism (Lindblom, 1959). This term describes situations in which the decision maker examines only those solutions that are marginally different from policies or situations already in effect. This approach reduces the number of alternatives considered and also drastically simplifies the analysis of each. Rather than thoroughly investigating the ramifications of an alternative, the manager considers only those respects in which the proposed solution and its consequences differ from the status quo. March and Simon (1958), in a similar vein, suggest the existence of a programmed search for solutions in organizations. In this search, routine solutions are found for recurring problems or solutions are selected simply because they happen to be available (Cohen, March, and Olsen, 1972).

Alexander (1979) examined the process of making a strategic choice in three different organizations. In all three cases, the sources for policy options were largely accepted ideas within the organizations. Alexander further reports that the process of decision making did not involve the uninhibited development of alternatives for subsequent formal evaluation, but rather an "intuitive, informal, or semiformalized evaluation process which occurs before formal evaluation even begins" (p. 398). This report is substantiated by data collected in other descriptive studies of decision making, such as that by Mintzberg, Raisinghani, and Theoret (1976).

This limited search naturally reduces the probability of innovative solutions. Various cognitive processes involved in evaluating alternatives and making choices tend also to uphold the status quo.

Evaluating Alternatives

Further distortions due to cognitive limitations may occur in evaluating alternatives. Not only does satisficing take the form of examining only a limited set of alternatives, but also the form of suboptimizing (March and Simon, 1958), a strategy that maximizes the probability of only a few desirable outcomes at the expense of other perhaps equally desirable outcomes. This is really a question of the choice of factors to maximize. In selecting the location of a site for an ATM, the branch manager attempted to maximize attractiveness and accessibility at the expense of even considering, for example, relative installation costs.

Tversky (1972) suggests that we do not consider alternatives separately and sequentially, but rather concurrently in the form of a set of attributes or aspects. At each stage in the choice process, an aspect is selected (with probability proportional to its weight), and all the alternatives that do not include the selected aspect are eliminated. The process continues until all alternatives are eliminated (Tversky, 1972, p. 281). Thus, for example, the manager might examine alternative branches A, B, and C at the same time, focusing first on the size of the branch and

eliminating any branch not large enough, then focusing on the distance of the branch from a shopping area and eliminating any branch too far away, and so on. This model of choice, which has substantial empirical support (for example, Payne, 1976), again has potentially deleterious consequences in that it is highly dependent on the order in which alternatives are selected.

These methods of choice distort the optimal decision-making process. In addition, human beings have difficulty making tradeoffs along different dimensions, such as attractiveness versus accessibility (Steinbruner, 1974; Jervis, 1976). Also, we never know what values we will be attempting to maximize in the future because we do not know what our future desires and needs will be (March, 1976). Such complications make the question of the objective evaluation of alternatives enormously difficult.

In spite of the insuperable difficulties of making a really rational choice, human beings, and in particular members of organizations, tend to enjoy thinking of themselves as rational beings. Decisions, even those made on the spur of the moment, will often later be reexamined and justified.

Bolstering. After a person makes an important decision that has both positive and negative consequences, he or she will often dwell on the positive consequences of the decision. The mechanism underlying this bolstering of behavioral outcomes is often characterized as a self-justification process in which individuals seek to rationalize their previous behavior or psychologically defend themselves against a perceived error in judgment (Festinger, 1957; Aronson, 1968; Janis and Mann, 1977). Such bolstering is particularly likely during a significant decision, such as taking a new job (Lawler, Kuleck, Rhode, and Sorenson, 1975). It usually takes place after a commitment to a choice has been made, but it may take place when the decision is imminent. Thus, a manager about to make the major decision to close a branch in an urban area may spend a great deal of time reading reports about urban blight in the United States and avoiding optimistic reports of the move of industry back into the cities. This tendency to selectively avoid information that contradicts a chosen course of action helps an individual feel satisfied with a choice, but it may lead to an inability to reevaluate earlier decisions in the light of new information or unforeseen consequences.

What is even more pernicious is that evaluations formed and attendant choices of behavior may turn out to be self-fulfilling prophecies. If a person perceives another as hostile, he or she may treat the other in a hostile way and so in fact elicit the perceived behavior. Snyder, Tanke, and Berscheid (1977) led people to believe (falsely) that a partner with whom they were interacting, but whom they could not see, was either highly attractive or unattractive. Not only were those partners perceived as unattractive treated differently than those perceived as attractive; partners also came to adopt either more attractive or unattractive behavior as a result of the expectations held about them.

Perseverance. Another cause of an inability to reevaluate earlier decisions in the light of new information is the phenomenon of perseverance. When information presents itself, the decision maker often tries to explain that information. People usually do not assume events "just happen"; they assume events have a cause. The explanation that the decision maker generates may or may not reflect the true state of affairs. When key information about a person, product, or entity is explained by the decision maker, the explanatory framework and the conclusion based on it are often enduring, even when subsequent contradictory information is presented (Walster, Berscheid, Abrahams, and Aronson, 1967; Ross, Lepper, and Hubbard, 1975). For instance, students' erroneous impressions of their own problem-solving abilities (and their academic choices in a follow-up measure one month later) persevered even after the students learned that good or poor teaching procedures provided a totally sufficient explanation for success or failure (Lau, Lepper, and Ross, 1976). Thus, a decision maker who is given negative information about an employee and who actively seeks to explain that negative information may tend to continue to view the employee in a negative light even after it transpires that the negative information was untrue.

Commitment. Perhaps still more pervasive is the phenomenon of commitment to a choice already made: a solution is still evaluated highly even in the light of evidence that suggests the evaluation should be lowered. Once a decision has been made, it is often difficult to change one's mind about it. If the decision was public, people may fear appearing foolish or weak when they alter it. Also, the sequence of events inherent in the implementation of the decision seems to roll on inexorably. A manager who decides to open a new branch enters into a chain of events, from negotiating leases and parking space to requesting market studies and staff. Not only may the manager fear looking foolish by changing his or her mind suddenly; also, that change might be impossible.

There are real constraints to changing one's mind. More subtly, the bolstering and explanation forming discussed above may give rise to a psychic rather than simply a behavioral commitment to a particular choice. Staw (1976) has shown that individuals who are personally responsible for an unsuccessful investment are more likely to choose to invest more money in the same area than individuals who did not make the earlier decision, although no logic dictates that previous misinvestment should make reinvestment more likely. Fox and Staw (1979) have shown that commitment actually increases with the decision maker's job insecurity and resistance from others to his policies.

When a manager decides to invest money in opening a new branch, he or she is likely to bolster the choice mentally during and after the decision. That manager will summon all the reasons for the decision, thus forming an enduring explanatory framework. This psychological commitment to the decision serves a valuable purpose during the unstable early days of implementation. It serves no good purpose if it causes the manager to ignore warning signals or become more committed to a choice by pouring in additional resources even when customers fail to come and superiors and peers begin to question the decision.

Probability Estimates

The deleterious effects of unwise commitment to choices and evaluations already made may be exacerbated by errors in the probability estimates of the choice. Managers, as mentioned earlier, rely more on orally communicated information than on written reports or figures. The spoken word is quick, easy, and enjoyable. It should be noted, though, that the preference for vivid, immediate information demonstrates a tendency toward ignoring statistical information and using convenient heuristics or such rules of thumb as representativeness, availability and anchoring. Even sophisticated people exhibit this tendency. A few illustrations of each heuristic, drawn largely on Tversky and Kahneman's (1974) work in this area, will be given. Note that these heuristics are usually useful in making decisions. Sometimes, however, they result in serious biases.

Representativeness.   This heuristic is used when judging such problems as the likelihood that a given person is a member of a category or the likelihood that a given outcome can be explained by a given set of antecedent conditions.

Consider the following questions:

> A bank manager has two customers requesting a loan. One is a man who has just opened a bookstore specializing in Eastern philosophy and meditation. The other has just opened a small grocery store. One of these two customers is shy, retiring, and extremely mild-mannered. He often hesitates to venture an opinion, but when he does so he is often amazingly insightful and his comments are tinged with a gentle humor. Which one of the two customers is he? (after Ross, 1977)

If one entertains the option of his being the bookstore owner more seriously than his being the grocery store owner, one is using the representativeness heuristic. The bookstore owner sounds like a person interested in philosophy and meditation. Consider, however, how few such bookstores there are and how many more grocery stores. Such base-rate information of a pallid statistical nature is frequently ignored, although it should have greater utility than the case information. Recent research has begun to investigate the boundary conditions of this tendency to overutilize case example information (Ajzen, 1977; Carroll and Siegler, 1977; Wells and Harvey, 1977; Kassin, 1979).

Similarly, people predicting performance from data known to be correlated with performance make far more accurate use of the data in prediction when the data seem causally related to the performance, or "ecologically" valid (Chapman and Chapman, 1967; McMiller, 1971; Nisbett and Ross, 1980). Thus, if customers' ability to repay a loan is known to be equally highly related to both their income level and to the price of their shoes, income level is more likely to be used as a predictor of their ability to repay the loan because it seems more representative of a typical causal relationship than the price of shoes which does not seem as realistic.

Another statistical concept that is hard to grasp and easily replaced by more colorful explanations of events is regression toward the mean. We may learn about tall fathers having shorter sons in a statistics class, but we really expect the predictor of an outcome (height of fathers) and the outcome itself (height of sons) to be equally extreme. This simply makes "better sense." An example of this inability to grasp regression to the mean was reported in a group of flight instructors. Experienced instructors noted that praise after an exceptionally smooth landing was typically followed by a poor landing, while harsh criticism after a rough landing was usually followed by an improved landing. The flight instructors reached the erroneous and potentially harmful conclusion that punishment is more effective than reward (Tversky and Kahneman, 1974, p. 1127). A bank manager might easily surrender to a similar misconception in dealing with subordinates.

A final common error is overreliance on data generated from a very small sample. The assumption is made that the sample is representative of the population as a whole, yet it may not be unless careful attention has been given to sampling randomly. No survey should be relied upon unless it includes careful examination of the characteristics of the sample selected.

Availability.   Use of the availability heuristic is illustrated by the fact that events, scenarios, or explanations that come or could be brought to mind easily are often deemed more likely or probable than those that do not. Frequency or probability are assumed to be directly given by availability (Schiffman, Cohen, Nowik, and Selinger, 1978).

A simple question illustrates this heuristic: "Are there more English words that begin with the letter *r* than have *r* as the third letter?" If one answers yes, one has used the availability heuristic. It is easier to think of words that begin with *r*, so there appear to be more of them. In fact, there are fewer (after Nisbett and Ross, 1980).

Similarly, sequences of events that have occurred before—the lessons of the past (May, 1973)—are often deemed more likely than sequences of events that have not occurred. They are made more readily available by memory. It is easy to compare the present problem with some similar or representative past state of affairs and to suggest that what happened then is bound to happen now.

The ease with which one can imagine an outcome, another type of availability, often plays a role in estimates of its probability. It is a common experience, when one drives past a gruesome accident on the freeway, to notice that one's estimate of the likelihood of an accident rises for a period of time. Carroll (1978) showed that people asked to imagine Jimmy Carter winning the 1976 presidential election (prior to the election) predicted that he was more likely to win than people asked to imagine Gerald Ford winning. They did so whether or not they were asked to explain what they were instructed to imagine.

Vividness also has a substantial impact, presumably because it mediates how easy it is to imagine the information or the event in question. It has been found, for example, that a stated organizational policy of avoiding layoffs is more likely to be believed if supported by a vivid story of what happened the last time layoffs seemed imminent than if supported by statistical information concerning the frequency with which pay cuts and layoffs had occurred in the past (Wilkins and Martin, 1980).

Consider the following example of a vivid story having more impact than dry statistical information.

Let us suppose that you wish to buy a new car and have decided that on grounds of economy and longevity you want to purchase one of those solid, stalwart, middle class Swedish cars— either a Volvo or a Saab. As a prudent and sensible buyer, you go to *Consumer Reports*, which informs you that the consensus of their experts is that the Volvo is mechanically superior, and the consensus of the readership is that the Volvo has the better repair record. Armed with this information you decide to go and strike a bargain with the Volvo dealer before the week is out. In the interim, however, you go to a cocktail party where you announce this intention to an acquaintance. He reacts with disbelief and alarm! "A Volvo! You've got to be kidding. My brother-in-law had a Volvo. First, that fancy fuel injection computer thing went out. 250 bucks. Next he started having trouble with the rear end. Had to replace it. Then the transmission and the clutch. Finally sold it in three years for junk!" (Nisbett, Borgida, Crandall and Reed, 1976, p. 129.)

Imagine the effect this encounter would have on one's decision. Note also, though, that this isolated experience should carry less weight than the average frequency-of-repair record reported in *Consumer Reports*. Borgida and Nisbett (1977) obtained similar results in further "thought experiments." Slovic and Lichtenstein (1975) have even shown that events presented in the framework of a vivid and easily imagined story are deemed more likely than the same events presented in isolation.

Finally, and perhaps most seriously, it is difficult for people to learn from their past mistakes in estimating probabilities because, after an event occurs, they tend to recall having judged it as more likely to occur than they actually did (Fischoff, 1975; Fischoff and Beyth, 1975). If a new branch turns out to be successful the manager is most likely to say: "I knew it all along."

Anchoring.   A third major heuristic is the anchoring heuristic. When making estimates, one uses a natural starting point as a first approximation or anchor, to the estimate. This anchor is adjusted as one reaches the final estimate, but the adjustment is usually insufficient. Tversky and Kahneman (1974), for example, asked individuals such questions as "What is the percentage of people in the United States today who are age fifty-five or older?" They gave participants randomly chosen starting percentages and asked the individuals to adjust these starting points until they reached their best estimate. Because of insufficient adjustment, those whose starting percentages were too high ended up with higher estimates than those whose starting percentages were too low. Similarly, adjusted estimates of the new branch's profitability may be too low if predicted from the performance of a relatively unsuccessful branch or too high if predicted from the performance of a particularly successful branch.

The probability of a number of events occurring together (conjunctive events) usually is overestimated (Edwards, 1968). Tversky and Kahneman (1974) argue that this too is a result of the anchoring heuristic. People do not adjust their preliminary or partially computed estimates. When deciding whether to open a branch, a manager must estimate the probability of several events. If three events—getting a favorable lease, attracting a certain number of customers, and keeping robberies to a minimum—have probabilities of, respectively, 0.8, 0.7, and 0.6, the probability of all three is 0.3 (not their average, 0.7). However, at first glance the joint likelihood seems high. In addition, the vividness of the scenario of a negotiated lease, an opened branch, and an undisturbed flow of customers makes the conjunctive events available and hence compelling.

A related phenomenon seems to be the overemphasis given to aspects of a choice that are similar to the mode of responding. If, for example, one pays money for an object, its price may influence choice more than any of its other features. Experimental research by Lichtenstein and Slovic (1973) suggests that a used-car buyer may give too much weight to the seller's asking price and too little weight to other factors, such as condition and mileage, when making a counteroffer. Likewise, sums of money granted by juries in personal-injury suits and by bank managers authorizing loans may be overdetermined by the amount of money that the plaintiff or the customer has requested. In such cases, anchoring is operating in tandem with the representativeness heuristic.

In sum, heuristics are most often extremely useful. For example, it is clearly reasonable to use the availability of an event in memory as a rough guide to its frequency of occurrence. However, availability is affected not only by frequency.

When availability is affected by imaginability also, using this convenient heuristic can lead to mistaken conclusions.

The Selection of the Model

Clearly, the biases and heuristics involved in gathering information, evaluating alternatives, and estimating probabilities are all inextricably interlinked. Judgment heuristics are not exclusive to any one cognitive activity. These heuristics occur in all four phases of decision making, not just during the phases of alternative generation and alternative evaluation.

The most negative effects of biases and heuristics may come during the phase of problem finding or model selection. This is the key phase in decision making, since the definition of the problem or opportunity guides and directs the gathering of information and the selection of alternatives for evaluation.

Naturally, problem finding is itself guided by the model that the decision maker has of the causal connections in the environment. A sudden increase in the number of customer complaints is a symptom of some problem. The bank manager's model will play a large role in identifying the problem. The manager might believe that customers' complaints are uniquely mediated by the quality of service they receive. Alternatively, he or she might believe that customers' complaints are uniquely mediated by the ease with which they can obtain loans and mortgages. The model might include some more complex combination of these and other factors. Whatever the model, it will guide the definition of the problem and the search for information about alternative solutions. The model will also delineate what he or she is trying to maximize in evaluating solutions.

The use of a model has a great deal to do with the heuristics of representativeness and availability. If the customer complaints are representative symptoms of a problem that occurred in the past, and if the events that constituted the problem are readily available in memory, then that schema will serve as the model by which to identify the problem (deRivera, 1968; Schank and Abelson, 1977). Let us assume that once in the bank manager's career there was a similar sudden spate of customer complaints. At that time it was found to be due to poorly trained tellers. When the symptoms recur, it is quick and easy simply to assume that the problem is the quality of teller training programs and that the solution is better training of tellers. The solution is reached without searching for information, evaluating solutions, or validating probability estimates. However, this solution is quick and effective only if the problem is identified correctly.

Bearing in mind the impact that limitations, biases, and heuristics have on *all* phases of decision making, we will examine in the next section strategies for reducing that negative impact. The key themes will be awareness and acceptance of the limitations of human information processing capacity.

HELPING HUMAN INFORMATION PROCESSING

Information Gathering

Implicit throughout the foregoing review of the limitations of humans as information processors is the need for as much accurate information as possible. Note that information must be distinguished from data. Information is what the decision maker can extract from the "noise" of the data and profitably use.

Management information systems of all kinds should be used insofar as the organization can afford them. However, simply generating more reports is not usually much help to any manager. The manager needs carefully designed decision support systems (Keen, P.G.W. and Scott Morton, M., 1978).

The decision support system must be based on the manager's own models. If, in the bank example, it is quality of service that mediates customer dissatisfaction, then the manager needs regular, timely, and accurate information on quality of service. In addition, the manager needs regular, timely, and accurate information on those factors, such as the morale of tellers and the physical facilities within the branches, that in his or her view affect quality of service.

Signal levels must be established along with the decision support system. The level of quality of service that signals a problem must be defined, as must the level of teller morale and the state of the physical facilities. If such signal levels are not established, the manager will waste valuable time studying reports that all is well. It is a better use of time to manage "by exception" and react only to signals that all is not well. Exceeding signal levels should constitute an early warning system.

Managers frequently fight management information systems (MIS) because they fear that such systems reduce the role of intuition and hinder free movement (Argyris, 1971), but all an MIS does is provide the potential for accurate information on which to base decisions. However, one difficulty in gathering information and establishing signaling levels is that some data are more easily quantified than other data. There is obviously a general tendency to report and signal what is quantifiable. It is easier, for example, to report profit levels, expenses, and turnover than it is to report the level of morale and commitment to the organization.

Another difficulty is that what is easily quantified is also often easily juggled. For example, at a time of high interest rates, it is light work for a branch manager to make a profit by lending, rather than by generating deposits and thus contributing to the pool of funds used by the bank, if the cost-accounting department has allowed only a 5 percent return on deposits. Similar profits can be realized at a time of very low interest rates by generating deposits and not making loans. Subordinates who wish to look good can usually find ways of doing so. In doing so, however, they may deprive the boss of needed, realistic information.

Since many important indicators can not easily be quantified, and since, in turn, many quantifiable indicators can be manipulated, it behooves the manager to actively seek "soft" information, or information that is difficult to quantify, as well as "hard" information.

Such information often comes to the manager in verbal or observable form, through informal sensing techniques, rather than through formal reporting systems (Lyles and Mitroff, 1980). A comment made during an informal telephone conversation may signal a problem long before the report arrives on the manager's desk. A visit to a branch and the sight of long lines, surly tellers, and a visibly depressed branch manager is a clearer signal of low morale than scores on an attitude or "climate" survey that may be given every six months at most and that take a month to analyze and synthesize.

These observations are not new. The manager should have an open-door policy, make frequent tours of the facilities, and encourage subordinates to express their problems without fear of punishment for doing so. Among our sample of bank managers, almost all favored verbal over written communication. The manager should not rebel against a preference for the timely and efficient vehicle of verbal communication. Accepting this preference is a prerequisite for making the best possible use of a verbal communication network. The manager should strive to make it systematic, comprehensive, and above all, open—as free of error-producing distortion and omissions as possible—and yet remain aware that in a human system some error will always occur. Such communication serves the best interests of the organization and of the humanitarian who is concerned with candor and trust (Argyris, 1973).

Evaluating Alternatives

As has been suggested, decision makers often only consider a few solutions and usually only those that have been used before or happen to be available. In addition, choices are frequently made informally and intuitively before the evaluation phase even begins.

An optimistic approach is based, once again, on awareness and acceptance. Satisficing, suboptimizing, and incrementalism occur. Not only do these processes occur, but also the choice among alternatives examined may be biased by the order in which aspects of the alternatives are examined. Awareness of the crucial role of the order in which alternatives and aspects of those alternatives are examined allows and encourages the manager to amass information about several alternatives. With such awareness, the manager can avoid selecting the first satisfactory one or the one that most closely conforms to the status quo.

Lindblom suggests that we not only accept but also admire our limitations: "The piecemealing, remedial incrementalist or satisficer may not look like an heroic figure. He is nevertheless a shrewd, resourceful problem-solver who is wrestling bravely with a universe that he is wise enough to know is too big for him" (Lindblom, 1968, p. 27).

It is clearly true that an exhaustive information search and an attendant full-blown process of rational choice is not always appropriate. The benefits of more information must always be weighed against the costs of acquiring and considering that information, even though specific techniques for doing such cost benefit analysis are in the developmental stages (Demski, 1972).

It may be that an explicit "mixed-scanning" approach should be adopted. In this approach, fundamental decisions that set directions for the organization are made as rationally as possible, while less significant decisions are made in a more incremental fashion. In this vein, Tversky's (1972) suggestions may be appropriate. He argues that simple choice mechanisms such as elimination by aspects may be most suitable and effective for simple situations. Further research should be considered to assess when this technique is appropriate and when it must be supplemented with computational or other tools.

Available computational techniques for optimizing, such as linear programming, can then assist in evaluating alternative solutions to fundamental problems. Another useful role that computational aids can play is in aggregating utility estimates. Multiattribute utility theory and analysis involves dividing the overall evaluation task into a set of simpler subtasks, each of which is within the judgmental capacities of the decision maker. This subdivision of tasks can facilitate decisions by forcing the decision maker to assign weights to the various factors examined (Huber, 1980). Such explicitness is very helpful in avoiding biased probability estimates.

Probability Estimates

The use of a decision tree forces expression of one's probability estimates and thus opens them to examination and validation. Certainly, this method lessens the chance of such simple mistakes as the overestimation of the joint probabilities of several events.

Awareness and acceptance of the major heuristics makes it more likely that the decision makers will use them only when they are appropriate. There is some evidence that decision makers are helped to avoid heuristics when they are placed in roles, such as jurors in court trials, that by their nature demand rational decisions (Hatvany, 1979; in press). Indeed, it is now illegal in banks for consumer loans to be made by the person who helps the customer complete the application. In this way the maker of the loan is unaware of the ethnic or sexual identification of loan applicants and so avoids the use of representativeness heuristics associated with, as an example, the differential ability of different ethnic groups to repay loans.

Formal training in statistics is also helpful. Confirming this argument is McMiller's (1971) finding that trained statisticians avoided inappropriate use of the representativeness heuristic more successfully than did clinicians, mathematically oriented students, and other students, in that order. It must be stressed here, in accord with Nisbett, that our subjective probabilities or expectations are synonymous with our beliefs about events. It seems obvious that accurate beliefs will result in more successful or effective behaviors.

THE SELECTION OF MODELS

This [reading] proposes not only that managers be aware of their limitations in evaluating alternatives as they are represented within managers' models, but also that they realize that the models they use could probably be replaced or expanded. The only reasonable way to make these judgments is to articulate the model being used and test the model, or at least aspects of it.

By examining the models he or she uses, the decision maker at least becomes more open to the possibility of using alternative models. Obviously, an unarticulated or unconscious model cannot be inspected. Sometimes, however, it is very difficult to accurately articulate what model has been used. People cannot observe their own cognitive processes directly and hence may report inaccurately about them or may simply concoct plausible causal theories or models that they might have used (Nisbett and Wilson, 1977).

In such a case, another approach might be tried: simulating the decision maker's model by examining the information gathered by the decision maker and the choice to which this information led. An example of such a simulation of the decision maker's model, which ultimately argues for replacement of the decision makers, is given in a study (Dawes, 1971) of the decisions to admit graduate students made by the Department of Psychology at the University of Oregon. It was found that the decisions of the admissions committee could be simulated by a linear combination of the criteria it considered (grade point average, GRE scores, and a crude index of the quality of undergraduate institution attended). Fifty-five percent of the applicants the admissions committee considered could have been screened out on this basis without rejecting a single individual whom the admissions committee actually admitted. Furthermore, this simulation, which is independent of the decision maker's mood, fatigue, and other subjective factors, was more valid in predicting future performance than the decision makers were. This "bootstrapping" obviously could save a great deal of administrative time and cost. Bootstrapping has been shown to be more valid than the decision makers themselves in other studies, such as Goldberg's (1970) study of clinical psychologists attempting to differentiate psychotic from neurotic patients.

Bootstrapping frees the decision maker from the boredom of repetitive and routine decisions as well as from vague fears about alertness on a particular day and leaves time to concentrate on key issues, to reflect upon long-term goals, or to reflect on the models that he or she is using. It also leaves more time for play with ideas (March, 1973). It is often in playing, or being a little foolish, that one happens upon different ways of looking at things, novel models, and innovative solutions.

In conclusion, while completely rational decision making may not be possible or even always necessary, an explicit testable model that can be communicated to peers and subordinates will always serve the manager well.

Oxenfelt, Miller, and Dickenson (1978, p. 00) suggest that the following questions be asked to assess the usefulness of a model.

- Can the model be understood and applied without lengthy preparation and practice?
- Can it incorporate many additional variables, if desired?
- Does it permit introduction of dynamic elements—that is, elements that change over time?
- Does it permit easy incorporation of interdependences among some of the variables?
- Does it permit visualization?

A question that they do not ask is whether it is sufficiently complex. A simple model often generates more confidence than a complex one (Dawes, 1976). Naturally, such confidence is misplaced when one operates in the complex open system of an organization.

Once a model has been adopted, its best testing ground is in the implementation phase of the decisions based on the model. Do the solutions work? If not, there may be flaws in the model on which the solutions are based, although it may also be the models of other peoples' reactions or organizational political processes that are at fault. Close observation of implementation allows not only for adjustments in that process but also for information on the adequacy of the model used. However, such feedback is only useful if the decision maker is open to it and is not blindly committed to the choice made. Being aware of and accepting the limitations and conceptual blinders of one's own models is the first step in testing, refining, expanding, or replacing those models.

REFERENCES

Ajzen, I. Intuitive theories of events and the effects of base-rate information on prediction. *Journal of Personality and Social Psychology*, 1977, *35*, 303–314.

Alexander, R. E. The design of alternatives in organizational contexts: A pilot study. *Administrative Science Quarterly*, 1979, *24*, 382–403.

Allen, T. J., and Cohen, S. Information flow in R&D labs. *Administrative Science Quarterly*, 1969, *14*, 12–19.

Argyris, C. Management information systems. The challenge to rationality and emotionality. *Management Science*, 1971, *17*, 6, B275–B292.

———. Some limits of rational man organizational theory. *Public Administration Review*, 1973, *33*, 253–267.

Aronson, E. Dissonance theory: Progress and problems. In R. Abelson, E. Aronson, W. McGuire, T. Newcomb, M. Rosenberg, and P. Tannenbaum (eds.). *Theories of cognitive consistency: A source book*. Chicago: Rand McNally, 1968, 5–27.

Carroll, J. S. The effect of imagining an event on expectations for the event: An interpretation in terms of the availability heuristic. *Journal of Experimental Social Psychology*, 1978, *14*, 88–96.

Carroll, J. S., and Siegler, R. S. Strategies for the use of base-rate information. *Organizational Behavior and Human Performance*, 1977, *19*, 392–402.

Chapman, L., and Chapman, J. The genesis of popular but erroneous psychodiagnostic observations. *Journal of Abnormal Psychology*, 1967, *72*, 193–204.

Cohen, M. D., March, J. G., and Olsen, J. P. A garbage can model of organizational choice. *Administrative Science Quarterly*, 1972, *17*, 1–25.

Dawes, R. M. A case study of graduate admissions: Application of three principles of human decision-making. *American Psychologist*, 1971, *26*, 180–188.

———. Shallow psychology. In J. S. Carroll and J. W. Payne (eds.). *Cognition and social behavior*. Hillsdale, N.J.: Erlbaum, 1976, 3–12.

Demski, J. S. *Information analysis*. Reading, Mass.: Addison-Wesley, 1972.

deRivera, J. *The psychological dimensions of foreign policy*. Columbus, Ohio: Merrill, 1968.

Downs, A. *Inside bureaucracy*. Boston: Little, Brown, 1967.

Edwards, W. The theory of decision making. *Psychological Bulletin*, 1954, *51*, 380–417.

———. Conservatism in human information processing. In B. Kleinmuntz (ed.). *Formal representation of human judgment*. Wiley, 1968.

Festinger, L. *A theory of cognitive dissonance*. Stanford, Calif.: Stanford University Press, 1957.

Fischoff, B. Hindsight ≠ Foresight: The effect of outcome knowledge on judgment under uncertainty. *Journal of Experimental Psychology*: Human Perception and Performance, 1975, *1*, 288–299.

Fischoff, B., and Beyth, R. "I knew it would happen," Remembered probabilities of once-future things. *Organizational behavior and human performance*, 1975, *13*, 1–16.

Fox, F. V., and Staw, B. M. The trapped administrator: Effects of job insecurity and policy resistance upon commitment to a course of action. *Administrative Science Quarterly*, 1979, 24, 449–471.

Goldberg, L. R. Man versus model of man: A rationale, plus some evidence, for a method of improving on clinical inferences. *Psychological Bulletin*, 1970, 73, 422–432.

Hatvany, N. The impact of discredited information: processes and mechanisms underlying perseverance and change. Unpublished Ph.D. thesis, Stanford University, 1979.

Hatvany, N., and Strack, F. The discredited key witness. *Journal of Applied Social Psychology*, in press.

Huber, P. *Managerial decision making*. Glenview, Ill.: Scott, Foresman, 1980.

Janis, I., and Mann, L. *Decision making*. New York: Free Press, 1977.

Jervis, R. *Perception and misperception in international relations*. Princeton, N.J.: Princeton University Press, 1976.

Kassin, S. M. Consensus information, prediction and causal attribution: A review of the literature and issues. *Journal of Personality and Social Psychology*, 1979, 37, 1966–1981.

Keen, P. G. W., and Scott Morton, M. *Decision support systems: An organizational perspective*. Reading, Mass.: Addison-Wesley, 1978.

La Breque, M. On making sounder judgments: Strategies and snares. *Psychology Today*, May 1980, 33–42.

Lau, R. R., Lepper, M. R., and Ross, L. Persistence of inaccurate and discredited personal impressions: A field demonstration of attributional perseverance. Unpublished manuscript, Stanford University, 1976.

Lawler, E. E., Kuleck, W. J., Rhode, J. G., and Sorenson, J. E. Job choice and post decision dissonance. *Organizational Behavior and Human Performance*, 1975, 13, 133–145.

Lawler, E. E., Porter, L., and Tannenbaum, A. Managers' attitudes toward interaction episodes. *Journal of Applied Psychology*, 1968, 52, 432–439.

Lichtenstein, W., and Slovic, P. Response-induced reversals of preference in gambling: An extended replication in Las Vegas. *Journal of Experimental Psychology*, 1973, 101, 16–20.

Lindblom, C. The science of "muddling through." *Public Administration Review*, 1959, 19, 78–88.

——— . *The policy-making process*. Englewood Cliffs, N.J.: Prentice-Hall, 1968.

Lyles, M. A., and Mitroff, M. I. Organizational problem formulation: An empirical study. *Administrative Science Quarterly*, 1980, 25, 102–119.

McMiller, P. Do labels mislead? A multiple cue study within the framework of Brunswick's probabilistic functionalism. *Organizational Behavior and Human Performance*, 1971, 6, 480–500.

March, J. G. Model bias. *Review of educational research*, 1973, 42, 413–429.

——— . Bounded rationality, ambiguity and the engineering of choice. *The Bell Journal of Economics*, 1978, 9, 587–608.

March, J. G., and Simon, H. A. *Organizations*. New York: Wiley, 1958.

May, E. *"Lessons" of the past*. New York: Oxford University Press, 1973.

Miller, G. A. The magical number seven, plus or minus 2. *Psychological Review*, 1956, 63, 81–97.

Mintzberg, H. *The Nature of Managerial Work*. New York: Harper & Row, 1973.

Mintzberg, H., Raisinghani, D., and Theoret, A. The structure of unstructured decisions. *Administrative Science Quarterly*, 1976, 21, 246–275.

Nisbett, R. E., Borgida, E., Crandall, R. and Reed, H. Popular induction: information is not always informative. Carroll, J. S. and Payne, J. N. (eds.). *Cognition and Social Behavior*, 1976, 2, 227–236.

Nisbett, R. E., and Ross, L. D. *Human inference: Strategies and shortcomings of social judgment*. Englewood Cliffs, N.J.: Prentice-Hall, 1980.

Nisbett, R. E., and Wilson, T. D. Telling more than we can know: Verbal reports on mental processes. *Psychological Review*, 1977, 84, 231–259.

Oxenfeldt, A. R., Miller, D. W., and Dickenson, R. A. *A basic approach to executive decision making*. New York: AMACOM, 1978.

Payne, J. W. Task complexity and contingent processing in decision making: An information search and protocol analysis. *Organizational behavior and human performance*, 1976, 16, 366–387.

Pounds, W. F. The process of problem finding. *Industrial Management Review*, 1969, 11, 1–19.

Roberts, K., and O'Reilly, C. Some correlates of communication roles in organization. *Academy of Management Journal*, 1979, 22, 42–57.

Ross, L. D. The intuitive-psychologist and his shortcomings. Distortions in the attribution process. *Advances in Experimental Social Psychology*, 1977, 10, 174–221.

Ross, L. D., Lepper, M. R., and Hubbard, M. Perseverance in self perception and social perception: Biased attributional processes in the debriefing paradigm. *Journal of Personality and Social Psychology*, 1975, 32, 880–892.

Schank, R. C., and Abelson, R. *Scripts, plans, goals and understanding*. Hillsdale, N.J.: Erlbaum, 1977.

Schiffman, A., Cohen, S., Nowik, R., and Selinger,

D. Initial diagnostic hypothesis: Factors which may distort physicians' judgment. *Organizational Behavior and Human Performance*, 1978, *21*, 305–315.

Slovic, P., and Lichtenstein, S. Comparison of bayesian and regression approaches to the study of information processing in judgement. *Organizational Behavior and Human Performance*, 1971, *6*, 649–744.

Snyder, M., Tanke, E. D., and Berscheid, E. Social perception and interpersonal behavior: On the self-fulfilling nature of social stereotypes. *Journal of Personality and Social Psychology*, 1977, *35*, 656–666.

Staw, B. M. Knee-deep in the big muddy: A study of escalating commitment to a chosen course of action. *Organizational Behavior and Human Performance*, 1976, *16*, 27–44.

Steinbruner, J. D. *The cybernetic theory of decision: New dimensions of political analysis*. Princeton, N.J.: Princeton University Press, 1974.

Tushman, M. L. Communication across organizational boundaries: Special boundary roles in the innovation process. *Administrative Science Quarterly*, 1977, *22*, 587–605.

Tversky, A. Elimination by aspects: A theory of choice. *Psychological Review*, 1972, *79*, 281–299.

Tversky, A., and Kahneman, D. Judgment under uncertainty: Heuristics and biases. *Science*, 1974, *185*, 1124–1131.

Walster, E., Berscheid, E., Abrahams, D., and Aronson, E. Effectiveness of debriefing following deception experiments. *Journal of Personality and Social Psychology*, 1967, *6*, 371–380.

Wells, G. L., and Harvey, J. J. Do people use consensus information in making causal attributions? *Journal of Personality and Social Psychology*, 1977, *35*, 279–293.

Wilkins, A., and Martin, J. Organizational legends. Research Paper Series #521. Graduate School of Business, Stanford University, 1980.

Frameworks for Organizational Behavior

3

A model for diagnosing
organizational behavior:
Applying a congruence perspective

David A. Nadler
and Michael L. Tushman

Management's primary job is to make organizations operate effectively. Society's work gets done through organizations and management's function is to get organizations to perform that work. Getting organizations to operate effectively is difficult, however. Understanding one individual's behavior is challenging in and of itself; understanding a group that's made up of different individuals and comprehending the many relationships among those individuals is even more complex. Imagine, then, the mind-boggling complexity of a large organization made up of thousands of individuals and hundreds of groups with myriad relationships among these individuals and groups.

But organizational behavior must be managed in spite of this overwhelming complexity; ultimately the organization's work gets done through people, individually or collectively, on their own

or in collaboration with technology. Therefore, the management of organizational behavior is central to the management task—a task that involves the capacity to *understand* the behavior patterns of individuals, groups, and organizations, to *predict* what behavioral responses will be elicited by various managerial actions, and finally to use this understanding and these predictions to achieve *control*.

How can one achieve understanding and learn how to predict and control organizational behavior? Given its inherent complexity and enigmatic nature, one needs tools to unravel the mysteries, paradoxes, and apparent contradictions that present themselves in the everyday life of organizations. One tool is conceptual framework or model. A model is a theory that indicates which factors (in an organization, for example) are most critical or important. It also shows how these factors are related—that is, which factors or combination of factors cause other factors to change. In a sense then, a model is a roadmap that can be used to make sense of the terrain of organizational behavior.

The models we use are critical because they guide our analysis and action. In any organizational situation, problem solving involves the collection of information about the problem, the interpretation of that information to determine specific problem types and causes, and the development of action plans accordingly. The models that individuals use influence the kind of data they collect and the kind they ignore; models guide people's approach to analyzing or interpreting the data they have; finally, models help people choose their course of action.

Indeed, anyone who has been exposed to an organization already has some sort of implicit model. People develop these roadmaps over time, building on their own experiences. These implicit models (they usually are not explicitly written down or stated) guide behavior; they vary in quality, validity, and sophistication depending on the nature and extent of the experiences of the model builder, his or her perceptiveness, his or her ability to conceptualize and generalize from experiences, and so on.

We are not solely dependent, however, on the implicit and experience-based models that individuals develop. Since there has been extensive research and theory development on the subject of organizational behavior over the last four decades, it is possible to use scientifically developed explicit models for analyzing organizational behavior and solving organizational problems.

We plan to discuss one particular model, a general model of organizations. Instead of describing a specific phenomenon or aspect of organizational life (such as a model of motivation or a model of organizational design), the general model of organization attempts to provide a framework for thinking about the organization as a total system. The model's major premise is that for organizations to be effective, their subparts or components must be consistently structured and managed—they must approach a state of congruence.

In the first section of this article, we will discuss the basic view of organizations that underlies the model—that is, systems theory. In the second section, we will present and discuss the model itself. In the third section, we will present an approach to using the model for organizational problem analysis. Finally, we will discuss some of the model's implications for thinking about organizations.

A BASIC VIEW OF ORGANIZATIONS

There are many different ways of thinking about organizations. When a manager is asked to "draw a picture of an organization," he or she typically draws some version of a pyramidal organizational chart. This is a model that views the stable, formal relationships among the jobs and formal work units as the most critical factors of the organization. Although this clearly is one way to think about organizations, it is a very limited view. It excludes such factors as leadership behavior, the impact of the environment, informal relations, power distribution, and so on. Such a model can capture only a small part of what goes on in organizations. Its perspective is narrow and static.

The past two decades have seen a growing consensus that a viable alternative to the static classic models of organizations is to envision the organization as a social system. This approach stems from the observation that social phenomena display many of the characteristics of natural or mechanical systems. In particular, as Daniel Katz and Robert L. Kahn have argued, organizations can be better understood if they are considered as dynamic and open social systems.

What is a system? Most simply, a system is a set of interrelated elements—that is, a change in one element affects other elements. An *open system* is one that interacts with its environment; it is more than just a set of interrelated elements. Rather, these elements make up a mechanism that takes input from the environment, subjects it to some form of transformation process, and produces output. At the most general level, it should be easy to visualize organizations as systems. Let's consider a manufacturing plant, for example. It is made up of different related components (a number of departments, jobs technologies, and so on). It receives inputs from the environment—that is, labor, raw material, production orders, and so on—and transforms these inputs into products.

As systems, organizations display a number of basic systems characteristics. Some of the most critical are these:

Internal interdependence. Changes in one component or subpart of an organization frequently have repercussions for other parts; the pieces are interconnected. Again, as in the manufacturing plant example, changes made in one element (for example, the skill levels of those hired to do jobs) will affect other elements (the productiveness of equipment used, the speed or quality of production activities, the nature of supervision needed, and so on).

Capacity for feedback—that is, information about the output that can be used to control the system. Organizations can correct errors and even change themselves because of this characteristic. If in our plant example plant management receives information that the quality of its product is declining, it can use this information to identify factors in the system itself that contribute to this problem. However, it is important to note that, unlike mechanized systems, feedback information does not always lead to correction. Organizations have the potential to use feedback to become self-correcting systems, but they do not always realize this potential.

Equilibrium—that is, a state of balance. When an event puts the system out of balance the system reacts and moves to bring itself back into balance. If one work group in our plant example were suddenly to increase its performance dramatically, it would throw the system out of balance. This group would be making increasing demands on the groups that supply it with the information or materials it needs; groups that work with the high-performing group's output would feel the pressure of work-in-process inventory piling up in front of them. If some type of incentive is in effect, other groups might perceive inequity as this one group begins to earn more. We would predict that some actions would be taken to put the system back into balance. Either the rest of the plant would be changed to increase produc-

tion and thus be back in balance with the single group, or (more likely) there would be pressure to get this group to modify its behavior in line with the performance levels of the rest of the system (by removing workers, limiting supplies, and so on). The point is that somehow the system would develop energy to move back toward a state of equilibrium or balance.

Equifinality. This characteristic of open systems means that different system configurations can lead to the same end or to the same type of input-output conversion. Thus there's no universal or "one best way" to organize.

Adaptation. For a system to survive, it must maintain a favorable balance of input or output transactions with the environment or it will run down. If our plant produces a product for which there are fewer applications, it must adapt to new demands and develop new products; otherwise, the plant will ultimately have to close its doors. Any system, therefore, must adapt by changing as environmental conditions change. The consequences of not adapting are evident when once-prosperous organizations decay (for example, the eastern railroads) because they fail to respond to environmental changes.

Thus systems theory provides a way of thinking about the organization in more complex and dynamic terms. But although the theory provides a valuable basic perspective on organizations, it is limited as a problem-solving tool. This is because as a model, systems theory is too abstract for use in day-to-day analysis of organizational behavior problems. Because of the level of abstraction of systems theory, we need to develop a more specific and pragmatic model based on the concepts of the open systems paradigm.

A CONGRUENCE MODEL OF ORGANIZATIONAL BEHAVIOR

Given the level of abstraction of open theory, our job is to develop a model that reflects the basic systems concepts and characteristics, but that is more specific and thus more usable as an analytic tool. We will describe a model that specifies the critical inputs, the major outputs, and the transformation processes that characterize organizational functioning.

The model puts its greatest emphasis on the transformation process and specifically reflects the critical system property of interdependence. It views organizations as made up of components or parts that interact with each other. These components exist in states of relative balance, consistency, or "fit" with each other. The different parts of an organization can fit well together and function effectively, or fit poorly and lead to problems, dysfunctions, or performance below potential. Our *congruence model of organizational behavior* is based on how well components fit together—that is, the congruence among the components; the effectiveness of this model is based on the quality of these "fits" or congruence.

The concept of congruence is not a new one. George Homans in his pioneering work on social processes in organizations emphasized the interaction and consistency among key elements of organizational behavior. Harold Leavitt, for example, identified four major components of organization as being people, tasks, technology, and structure. The model we will present here builds on these views and also draws from fit models developed and used by James Seiler, Paul Lawrence and Jay Lorsch, and Jay Lorsch and Alan Sheldon.

It is important to remember that we are concerned about creating a model for *behavioral* systems of the organization—the system of elements that ultimately produce behavior patterns and, in turn, organizational performance. Put simply, we need to deal with questions of the inputs the system has to work with, the outputs it must produce, the major components of the transformation process, and the ways in which these components interact.

Inputs

Inputs are factors that, at any one point in time, make up the "givens" facing the organization. They're the material that the organization has to work with. There are several different types of inputs, each of which presents a different set of "givens" to the organization (see Figure 1 for an overview of inputs).

The first input is the *environment,* or all factors outside the organization being examined. Every organization exists within the context of a larger environment that includes individuals, groups, other organizations, and even larger social forces— all of which have a potentially powerful impact on how the organization performs. Specifically, the environment includes markets (clients or customers), suppliers, governmental and regulatory bodies, labor unions, competitors, financial institutions, special interest groups, and so on. As research by Jeffrey Pfeffer and Gerald Salancik has suggested, the environment is critical to organizational functioning.

The environment has three critical features that affect organizational analysis. First, the environment makes demands on the organization. For example, it may require certain products or services at certain levels of quality or quantity. Market pressures are particularly important here. Second, the environment may place constraints on organizational action. It may limit the activities in which an organization may engage. These constraints range from limitations imposed by scarce capital to prohibitions set by government regulations. Third, the environment provides opportunities that the organization can explore. When we analyze an organization, we need to consider the factors in the organization's environment and determine how those factors, singly or collectively, create demands, constraints, or opportunities

The second input is the organization's *resources.* Any organization has a range of different assets to which it has access. These include employees, technology, capital, information, and so on. Resources can also include less tangible assets, such as the perception of the organization in the marketplace or a positive organizational climate. A set of resources can be shaped, deployed, or configured in different ways by an organization. For analysis purposes, two features are of primary interest. One concerns the relative quality of those resources or their value in light of the environment. The second concerns the extent to which resources can be reshaped or how fixed or flexible different resources are.

Figure 1. Key Organizational Inputs

Input	Environment	Resources	History	Strategy
Definition	All factors, including institutions, groups, individuals, events, and so on, that are outside the organization being analyzed, but that have a potential impact on that organization.	Various assets to which the organization has access, including human resources, technology, capital, information, and so on, as well as less tangible resources (recognition in the market, and so forth).	The patterns of past behavior, activity, and effectiveness of the organization that may affect current organizational functioning.	The stream of decisions about how organizational resources will be configured to meet the demands, constraints, and opportunities within the context of the organization's history.
Critical features for analysis	1. What demands does the environment make on the organization? 2. How does the environment put constraints on organizational action?	1. What is the relative quality of the different resources to which the organization has access? 2. To what extent are resources fixed rather than flexible in their configuration(s)?	1. What have been the major stages or phases of the organization's development? 2. What is the current impact of such historical factors as strategic decisions, acts of key leaders, crises, and core values and norms?	1. How has the organization defined its core mission, including the markets it serves and the products/services it provides to these markets? 2. On what basis does it compete? 3. What supporting strategies has the organization employed to achieve the core mission? 4. What specific objectives have been set for organizational output?

The third input is the organization's *history.* There's growing evidence that the way organizations function today is greatly influenced by past events. It is particularly important to understand the major stages or phases of an organization's development over a period of time, as well as the current impact of past events—for example, key strategic decisions, the acts or behavior of key leaders, the nature of past crises and the organization's responses to them, and the evolution of core values and norms of the organization.

The final input is somewhat different from the others because in some ways it reflects some of the factors in the organization's environment, resources, and history. The fourth input is *strategy.*

We use this term in its broadest context to describe the whole set of decisions that are made about how the organization will configure its resources against the demands, constraints, and opportunities of the environment within the context of its history. Strategy refers to the issue of matching the organization's resources to its environment, or making the fundamental decision of "What business are we in?" For analysis purposes, several aspects of strategy are important to identify. First, what is the core mission of the organization, or how has the organization defined its basic purpose or function within the larger system or environment? The core mission includes decisions about what markets the organization will serve, what products or services it will provide to those markets, and how it will compete in those markets. Second, strategy includes the specific supporting strategies (or tactics) the organization will employ or is employing to achieve its core mission. Third, it includes the specific performance or output objectives that have been established.

Strategy may be the most important single input for the organization. On one hand, strategic decisions implicitly determine the nature of the work the organization should be doing or the tasks it should perform. On the other hand, strategic decisions, and particularly decisions about objectives determine the system's outputs.

In summary, there are three basic inputs—environment, resources, and history—and a fourth derivative input, strategy, which determines how the organization responds to or deals with the basic inputs. Strategy is critical because it determines the work to be performed by the organization and it defines desired organizational outputs.

Outputs

Outputs are what the organization produces, how it performs, and how effective it is. There has been a lot of discussion about the components of an effective organization. For our purposes, however, it is possible to identify several key indicators of organizational output. First, we need to think about system output at different levels. In addition to the system's basic output—that is, the product—we need to think about other outputs that contribute to organizational performance, such as the functioning of groups or units within the organization or the functioning of individual organization members.

At the organizational level, three factors must be kept in mind when evaluating organizational performance: (1) goal attainment, or how well the organization meets its objectives (usually determined by strategy), (2) resource utilization, or how well the organization makes use of available resources (not just whether the organization meets its goals, but whether it realizes all of its potential performance and whether it achieves its goals by building resources or by "burning them up"), and (3) adaptability, or whether the orga-

nization continues to position itself in a favorable position vis-à-vis its environment—that is, whether it is capable of changing and adapting to environmental changes.

Obviously, the functioning of groups or units (departments, divisions, or other subunits within the organization) contribute to these organizational-level outputs. Organizational output is also influenced by individual behavior, and certain individual-level outputs (affective reactions such as satisfaction, stress, or experienced quality of working life) may be desired outputs in and of themselves.

The Organization as a Transformation Process

So far, we've defined the nature of inputs and outputs of the organizational system. This leads us to the transformation process. Given an environment, a set of resources, and history, "How do I take a strategy and implement it to produce effective performance in the organization, in the group/unit, and among individual employees?"

In our framework, the organization and its major component parts are the fundamental means for transforming energy and information from inputs into outputs. On this basis, we must determine the key components of the organization and the critical dynamic that shows how those components interact to perform the transformation function.

Organizational Components

There are many different ways of thinking about what makes up an organization. At this point in the development of a science of organizations, we probably do not know the one right or best way to describe the different components of an organization. The task is to find useful approaches for describing organizations, for simplifying complex phenomena, and for identifying patterns in what may at first blush seem to be random sets of activity. Our particular approach views organizations as composed of four major components: (1) the task, (2) the individuals, (3) the formal organizational arrangements, and (4) the informal organization. We will discuss each of these individually (see Figure 2 for overviews of these components).

The first component is the organization's *task*—that is, the basic or inherent work to be done by the organization and its subunits or the activity the organization is engaged in, particularly in light of its strategy. The emphasis is on the specific work activities or functions that need to be done and their inherent characteristics (as opposed to characteristics of the work created by how the work is organized or structured in this particular organization at this particular time). Analysis of the task would include a description of the basic work flows and functions with attention to the characteristics of those work flows— for example, the knowledge or skills demanded by the work, the kinds of rewards provided by the work, the degree of uncertainty associated with the work, and the specific constraints inherent in the work (such as critical time demands, cost constraints, and so on). Since it's assumed that a primary (although not the only) reason for the organization's existence is to perform the task consistent with strategy, the task is the starting point for the analysis. As we will see, the assessment of the adequacy of other components depends to a large degree on an understanding of the nature of the tasks to be performed.

A second component of organizations involves the *individuals* who perform organizational tasks. The issue here is identifying the nature and characteristics of the organization's employees (or members). The most critical aspects to consider include the nature of individual knowledge and skills, the different needs or preferences that

Figure 2.   Key Organizational Components

Component	Task	Individual	Formal organizational arrangements	Informal organization
Definition	The basic and inherent work to be done by the organization and its parts.	The characteristics of individuals in the organization.	The various structures, processes, methods, and so on that are formally created to get individuals to perform tasks.	The emerging arrangements, including structures, processes, relationships, and so forth.
Critical features for analysis	1. The types of skill and knowledge demands the work poses. 2. The types of rewards the work can provide. 3. The degree of uncertainty associated with the work, including such factors as interdependence, routineness, and so on. 4. The constraints on performance demands inherent in the work (given a strategy).	1. Knowledge and skills individuals have. 2. Individual needs and preferences. 3. Perceptions and expectancies. 4. Background factors.	1. Organization design, including grouping of functions, structure of subunits, and coordination and control mechanisms. 2. Job design. 3. Work environment. 4. Human resource management systems.	1. Leader behavior. 2. Intragroup relations. 3. Intergroup relations. 4. Informal working arrangements. 5. Communication and influence patterns.

individuals have, the perceptions or expectancies that they develop, and other background factors (such as demographics) that may potentially influence individual behavior.

The third component is the *formal organizational arrangements*. These include the range of structures, processes, methods, procedures, and so forth that are explicitly and formally developed to get individuals to perform tasks consistent with organizational strategy. The broad term, organizational arrangements, encompasses a number of different factors. One factor is organization design—that is, the way jobs are grouped together into units, the internal structure of those units, and the coordination and control mechanisms used to link those units together. A second factor is the way jobs are designed within the context of organizational designs. A third factor is the work environment, which includes a number of factors that characterize the immediate environment in which work is done, such as the physical working environment, the available work resources, and so on. A final factor includes the organization's formal systems for attracting, placing, developing, and evaluating human resources.

Together, these factors create the set of formal organizational arrangements—that is, they are explicitly designed and specified, usually in writing.

The final component is the *informal organization*. Despite the set of formal organizational arrangements that exists in any organization, another set of arrangements tends to develop or emerge over a period of time. These arrangements are usually implicit and unwritten, but they influence a good deal of behavior. For lack of a better term, such arrangements are frequently referred to as the informal organization and they include the different structures, processes, and arrangements that emerge while the organization is operating. These arrangements sometimes complement formal organizational arrangements by providing structures to aid work where none exist. In other situations they may arise in reaction to the formal structure, to protect individuals from it. They may therefore either aid or hinder the organization's performance.

Because a number of aspects of the informal organization have a particularly critical effect on behavior, they need to be considered. The behavior of leaders (as opposed to the formal crea-

tion of leader positions) is an important feature of the informal organization, as are the patterns of relationships that develop both within and between groups. In addition, different types of informal working arrangements (including rules, procedures, methods, and so on) develop. Finally, there are the various communication and influence patterns that combine to create the informal organization design.

Organizations can therefore be thought of as a set of components—the task, the individuals, the organizational arrangements, and the informal organization. In any system, however, the critical question is not what the components are, but what the nature of their interaction is. This model raises the question: What are the dynamics of the relationships among the components? To deal with this issue, we must return to the concept of congruence or fit.

The Concept of Congruence

A relative degree of congruence, consistency, or "fit" exists between each pair of organizational inputs. The congruence between two components is defined as "the degree to which the needs, demands, goals, objectives, and/or structures of one component are consistent with the needs, demands, goals, objectives, and/or structures of another component."

Congruence, therefore, is a measure of how well pairs of components fit together. Consider, for example, two components—the task and the individual. At the simplest level, the task presents some demands on individuals who would perform it (that is, skill/knowledge demands). At the same time, the set of individuals available to do the tasks have certain characteristics (their levels of skill and knowledge). Obviously, if the individual's knowledge and skill match the knowledge and skill demanded by the task, performance will be more effective.

Obviously, too, the individual-task congruence relationship encompasses more factors than just knowledge and skill. Similarly, each congruence relationship in the model has its own specific characteristics. Research and theory can guide the assessment of fit in each relationship. For an overview of the critical elements of each congruence relationship, see Figure 3.

Figure 3. Definitions of Fits

Fit	Issues
Individual/Organization	How are individual needs met by the organizational arrangements? Do individuals hold clear or distorted perceptions of organizational structures? Is there a convergence of individual and organizational goals?
Individual/Task	How are individual needs met by the tasks? Do individuals have skills and abilities to meet task demands?
Individual/Informal organization	How are individual needs met by the informal organization? How does the informal organization make use of individual resources consistent with informal goals?
Task/Organization	Are organizational arrangements adequate to meet the demands of the task? Do organizational arrangements motivate behavior that's consistent with task demands?
Task/Informal organization	Does the informal organization structure facilitate task performance or not? Does it hinder or help meet the demands of the task?
Organization/Informal organization	Are the goals, rewards, and structures of the informal organization consistent with those of the formal organization?

The Congruence Hypothesis

The aggregate model, or whole organization, displays a relatively high or low degree of system congruence in the same way that each pair of components has a high or low degree of congruence. The basic hypothesis of the model, which builds on this total state of congruence, is as follows: "Other things being equal, the greater the total degree of congruence or fit between the various components, the more effective will be the organization—effectiveness being defined as the degree to which actual organization outputs at individual, group, and organizational levels are similar to expected outputs, as specified by strategy."

The basic dynamic of congruence sees the organization as most effective when its pieces fit together. If we also consider strategy, this view expands to include the fit between the organization and its larger environment—that is, an organization is most effective when its strategy is consistent with its environment (in light of organizational resources and history) and when the organizational components are congruent with the tasks necessary to implement that strategy.

One important implication of the congruence hypothesis is that organizational problem analysis

(or diagnosis) involves description of the system, identification of problems, and analysis of fits to determine the causes of problems. The model also implies that different configurations of the key components can be used to gain outputs (consistent with the systems characteristic of equifinality). Therefore the question is not how to find the "one best way" of managing, but how to find effective combinations of components that will lead to congruent fits among them.

The process of diagnosing fits and identifying combinations of components to produce congruence is not necessarily intuitive. A number of situations that lead to congruence have been defined in the research literature. Thus in many cases fit is something that can be defined, measured, and even quantified; there is, in other words, an empirical and theoretical basis for assessing fit. The theory provides considerable guidance about what leads to congruent relationships (although in some areas the research is more definitive and helpful than others). The implication is that the manager who wants to diagnose behavior must become familiar with critical aspects of relevant organizational behavior models or theories so that he or she can evaluate the nature of fits in a particular system.

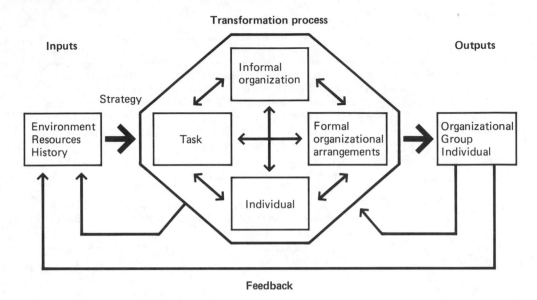

Figure 4.   A Congruence Model for Organization Analysis

The congruence model provides a general organizing framework. The organizational analyst will need other, more specific "submodels" to define high and low congruence. Examples of such submodels that might be used in the context of this general diagnostic model include the following: (1) the job characteristics model to assess and explain the fit between individuals and tasks as well as the fit between individuals and organizational arrangements (job design), (2) expectancy theory models of motivation to explain the fit between individuals and the other three components, (3) the information processing model of organizational design to explain the task-formal organization and task-informal organization fits, or (4) an organizational climate model to explain the fit between the informal organization and the other components. These models and theories are listed as illustrations of how more specific models can be used in the context of the general model. Obviously, those mentioned above are just a sampling of possible tools that could be used.

In summary, then, we have described a general model for the analysis of organizations (see Figure 4). The organization is seen as a system or trans-

formation process that takes inputs and transforms them into outputs—a process that is composed of four basic components. The critical dynamic is the fit or congruence among the components. We now turn our attention to the pragmatic question of how to use this model for analyzing organizational problems.

A PROCESS FOR ORGANIZATIONAL PROBLEM ANALYSIS

The conditions that face organizations frequently change; consequently, managers are required to continually engage in problem-identification and problem-solving activities. Therefore, managers must gather data on organizational performance, compare the data with desired performance levels, identify the causes of problems, develop and choose action plans and, finally, implement and evaluate these action plans. These phases can be viewed as a generic problem-solving process. For long-term organizational viability, some type of

Figure 5. Basic Problem Analysis Steps Using the Congruence Model

Step	Explanation
1. Identify symptoms.	List data indicating possible existence of problems.
2. Specify inputs.	Identify the system. Determine nature of environment, resources, and history. Identify critical aspects of strategy.
3. Identify outputs.	Identify data that define the nature of outputs at various levels (individual, group/unit, organizational). This should include desired outputs (from strategy), and actual outputs being obtained.
4. Identify problems.	Identify areas where there are significant and meaningful differences between desired and actual outputs. To the extent possible, identify penalties; that is, specific costs (actual and opportunity costs) associated with each problem.
5. Describe components of the organization.	Describe basic nature of each of the four components with emphasis on their critical features.
6. Assess congruence (fits).	Conduct analysis to determine relative congruence among components (draw on submodels as needed).
7. Generate and identify causes.	Analyze to associate fit with specific problems.
8. Identify action steps.	Indicate the possible actions to deal with problem causes.

problem-solving process must operate—and operate continuously.

Experience with using the congruence model for problem analysis in actual organizational settings has led to an approach to using the model that's based on these generic problem-solving processes (see Figure 5). In this section, we will "walk through" this process, describing each step in the process and discussing how the model can be used at each stage. Here are the steps in the problem-analysis process:

1. Identify symptoms. In any situation initial information (symptomatic data) may indicate that there are problems, but not what the problems are or what the causes are. Symptomatic data are important because the symptoms of problems may indicate where to look for more complete data.

2. Specify inputs. Once the symptoms are identified, the starting point for analysis is to identify the system and the environment in which it functions. This means collecting data

about the nature of environment, the type of resources the organization has, and the critical aspects of its history. Input analysis also involves identifying the overall strategy of the organization—that is, its core mission, supporting strategies, and objectives.

3. Identify outputs. The third step is an analysis of the organization's outputs at the individual, group, and organizational levels. Output analysis actually involves two elements: (1) defining the desired or planned output through an analysis of strategy that explicitly or implicitly defines what the organization wants to achieve in terms of output or performance indicators, and (2) collecting data that indicate the type of output the organization is actually achieving.

4. Identify problems. Symptoms may indicate problems—in this case, significant difference between desired or planned output and actual output. Such problems might be descrepancies (actual vs. expected) in organizational performance, group functioning, individual behavior, or affective reactions. These data tell us what problems exist, but they still don't tell us the causes. (Note: Where data are available, it's frequently also useful to identify the costs associated with the problems or the *penalties* the organization incurs by not fixing the problem. Penalties might be actual costs—increased expenses, and so on—or opportunity costs, such as revenue lost because of the problem.)

5. *Describe organizational components.* At this step the analysis to determine the causes of problems begins. Data are collected about the nature of each of the four major organizational components, including information about the component and its critical features in this organization.

6. *Assess congruence (fits).* Using the data collected in step 5 as well as applicable submodels or theories, an assessment is made of the positive or negative fit between each pair of components.

7. *Generate hypotheses about problem causes.* Once the components are described and their congruence assessed, the next step is to link together the congruence analysis with the problem identification (step 4). After analyzing to determine which are the poor fits that seem to be associated with, or account for, the output problems that have been identified, the patterns of congruence and incongruence that appear to cause the patterns of problems are determined.

8. *Identify action steps.* The final step in problem analysis is to identify possible action steps. These steps might range from specific changes to deal with relatively obvious problem causes to a more extensive data collection designed to test hypotheses about relatively more complex problems and causes.

In addition to these eight steps, some further steps need to be kept in mind. After possible actions are identified, problem solving involves predicting the consequence of various actions, choosing the course of action, and implementing and evaluating the impact of the chosen course of action. It is, of course, important to have a general diagnostic framework to monitor the effects of various courses of action.

The congruence model and this problem-

analysis process outline are tools for structuring and dealing with the complex reality of organizations. Given the indeterminate nature of social systems, there is no one best way of handling a particular situation. The model and the process could, however, help the manager in making a number of decisions and in evaluating the consequences of those decisions. If these tools have merit, it is up to the manager to use them along with his or her intuitive sense (based on experience) to make the appropriate set of diagnostic, evaluative, and action decisions.

FUTURE DIRECTIONS

The model we've presented here reflects a particular way of thinking about organizations. If that perspective is significant, the model might be used as a tool for handling more complex problems or for structuring more complex situations. Some directions for further thought, research, and theory development could include these:

1. *Organizational change.* The issue of organizational change has received a good deal of attention from both managers and academics. The question is how to effectively implement organizational change. The problem seems to center on the lack of a general model of organizational change. It is hard to think about a general model of organizational change without a general model of organizations. The congruence perspective outlined here may provide some guidance and direction toward the development of a more integrated perspective on the processes of organizational change. Initial work in applying the congruence model to the change issue is encouraging.

2. *Organizational development over time.* There has been a growing realization that organizations grow and develop over time, and that they face different types of crises, evolve through different stages, and develop along some predictable lines. A model of organizations such as the one presented here might be a tool for developing a typology of growth patterns by indicating the different configurations of tasks, individuals, organiza-

tional arrangements, and informal organizations that might be most appropriate for organizations in different environments and at different stages of development.

3. Organizational pathology. Organizational problem solving ultimately requires some sense of the types of problems that may be encountered and the kinds of patterns of causes one might expect. It is reasonable to assume that most problems encountered by organizations are not wholly unique, but are predictable. The often expressed view that "our problems are unique" reflects in part the lack of a framework of organizational pathology. The question is: Are there basic "illnesses" that organizations suffer? Can a framework of organizational pathology, similar to the physician's framework of medical pathology, be developed? The lack of a pathology framework, in turn, reflects the lack of a basic functional model of organizations. Again, development of a congruence perspective might provide a common language to use for the identification of general pathological patterns of organizational functioning.

4. Organizational solution types. Closely linked to the problem of pathology is the problem of treatment, intervention, or solutions to organizational problems. Again, there's a lack of a general framework in which to consider the nature of organizational interventions. In this case, too, the congruence model might be a means for conceptualizing and ultimately describing the different intervention options available in response to problems.

SUMMARY

This article has presented a general approach for thinking about organizational functioning and a process for using a model to analyze organizational problems. This particular model is only one way of thinking about organizations; it's clearly not the only model, nor can we claim it's definitively the best model. It is one tool, however, that may be useful for structuring the complexity of organizational life and helping managers create, maintain, and develop effective organizations.

SELECTED BIBLIOGRAPHY

For a comprehensive review and synthesis of research in organizational behavior, see Marvin Dunnette's *Handbook of Industrial and Organizational Psychology* (Rand-McNally, 1976). Daniel Katz and Robert Kahn's seminal work on organizations as systems, *The Social Psychology of Organizations* (John Wiley & Sons, 1966), has been revised, updated, and extended in their 1978 edition. See their new book for an extensive discussion of organizations as open systems and for a unique synthesis of the literature in terms of systems ideas.

For a broad analysis of organizational behavior, see David Nadler, J. Richard Hackman, and Edward E. Lawler's *Managing Organizational Behavior* (Little, Brown, 1979) and see Charles Hofer and Daniel Schendel's *Strategy Formulation: Analytical Concepts* (West, 1978) for a discussion of strategy.

For an extensive discussion of output and effectiveness, see Paul Goodman and Johannes Pennings's *New Perspectives on Organizational Effectiveness* (Jossey-Bass, 1977) and Andrew Van de Ven and Diane Ferry's *Organizational Assessment* (Wiley Interscience, 1980).

For more detail on organizational arragements, see Jay R. Galbraith's *Designing Complex Organizations* (Addison-Wesley, 1973); on job design and motivation, see J. Richard Hackman and Greg Oldham's *Work Redesign* (Addison-Wesley, 1979); and on informal organizations, see Michael Tushman's "A Political Approach to Organizations: A Review and Rationale" (*Academy of Management Review*, April 1977) and Jeffrey Pfeffer's new book, *Power and Politics in Organizations* (Pitman Publisher, 1980).

Submodels corresponding to the various components of our congruence model would include: J. Richard Hackman and Greg Oldham's job design model; Victor Vroom and Edward Lawler's work on expectancy theory of motivation and decision making—see Vroom's *Work and Motivation* (Wiley, 1964) and Lawler's *Motivation in Work*

Organizations (Wadsworth Publishing Co., 1973); Jay R. Galbraith, Michael Tushman, and David Nadler's work on information processing models of organizational design; and George Litwin and Robert Stringer's work on organization climate— see Litwin and Stringer's *Motivation and Organizational Climate* (Harvard University Graduate School of Business Administration, 1968).

David Nadler's "An Integrative Theory of Organizational Change," to appear in the *Journal of Applied Behavioral Science* in 1981, uses the congruence model to think about the general problems of organizational change and dynamics. Several distinct levers for change are developed and discussed. Other pertinent books of interest include: Jay R. Galbraith's *Organization Design* (Addison-Wesley, 1979), Jay R. Galbraith and Daniel A. Nathanson's *Strategy Implementation: The Role of Structure and Process* (West, 1978), George C. Homans's *The Human Group* (Harcourt Brace Jovanovich, Inc., 1950), Paul R.

Lawrence and Jay W. Lorsch's *Developing Organizations: Diagnosis and Action* (Addison-Wesley, 1969), Harold J. Leavitt's "Applied Organization Change in Industry" in J. G. March's (ed.) *Handbook of Organizations* (Rand-McNally, 1965), Harry Levinson's *Organizational Diagnosis* (Harvard University Press, 1972), Harry Levinson's *Psychological Man* (Levinson Institute, 1976), Jay W. Lorsch and Alan Sheldon's "The Individual in the Organization: A Systems View" in J. W. Lorsch and P. R. Lawrence's (eds.) *Managing Group and Intergroup Relations* (Irwin-Dorsey, 1972), David A. Nadler and Noel M. Tichy's "The Limitations of Traditional Intervention Technology in Health Care Organizations" in N. Margulies and J. A. Adams's (eds.) *Organization Development in Health Care Organizations* (Addison-Wesley, 1980), Edgar H. Schein's *Organizational Psychology* (Prentice-Hall, 1970), and James A. Seiler's *Systems Analysis in Organizational Behavior* (Irwin-Dorsey, 1967).

4
When is an organization effective?
A process approach to understanding effectiveness   Richard M. Steers

While most organizational analysts agree that the pursuit of effectiveness is a basic managerial responsibility, there is a notable lack of consensus

Source: Reprinted by permission of the publisher, from *Organizational Dynamics*, Autumn, 1976, © 1976 by AMACOM, a division of American Management Associations. All rights reserved.

Author's note: An earlier version of this article was presented at the 1976 annual meeting of the American Psychological Association. The author wishes to express his appreciation to the Office of Naval Research for support of the initial study.

on what the concept itself means. The economist or financial analyst usually equates organizational effectiveness with high profits or return on investment. For a line manager, however, effectiveness is often measured by the amount and quality of goods or services generated. The R&D scientist may define effectiveness in terms of the number of patents, new inventions, or new products developed by an organization. And last, many labor union leaders conceive of effectiveness in terms of job security, wage levels, job satisfaction, and the quality of working life. In short, while there is general agreement that effectiveness is something all organizations should strive for, the criteria for assessment remain unclear.

In view of the many different ways in which managers and researchers conceptualize organizational effectiveness, it comes as no surprise that there is equal disagreement over the best strategy for attaining effectiveness. A principal reason for this lack of agreement stems from the parochial views that many people harbor about the effectiveness construct. As mentioned, many define effectiveness in terms of a single evaluation criterion (profit or productivity, for example). But it is difficult to conceive of an organization that would survive for long if it pursued profits to the exclusion of its employees' needs and goals or those of society at large. Organizations typically pursue multiple (and often conflicting) goals—and these goals tend to differ from organization to organization according to the nature of the enterprise and its environment.

Another explanation for the general absence of agreement on the nature of effectiveness arises from the ambiguity of the concept itself. Organizational analysts often assume, incorrectly, that it's relatively easy to identify the various criteria for evaluating effectiveness. In point of fact, such criteria tend to be somewhat intangible; indeed, they depend largely on who is doing the evaluating and within what specific frame of reference.

A number of organizational analysts have tried to identify relevant facets of effectiveness that could serve as useful evaluating criteria. I recently reviewed 17 different approaches to assessing organizational effectiveness and found a general absence of agreement among them. Figure 1 summarizes the criteria used in the 17 models and notes the frequency with which each is mentioned. As this table reveals, only one criterion (adaptability-flexibility) was mentioned in more than half of the models. This criterion was followed rather distantly by productivity, job satisfaction, profitability, and acquisition of scarce and valued resources. Thus there is little agreement among analysts concerning what criteria should be used to assess current levels of effectiveness.

PROBLEMS IN ASSESSMENT

This absence of convergence among competing assessment techniques poses a serious problem for

Figure 1. Frequency of Occurrence of Evaluation Criteria in 17 Models of Organizational Effectiveness

Evaluation criteria	No. of times mentioned (N = 17)	Percent of total
Adaptability-flexibility	10	59
Productivity	6	35
Job satisfaction	5	29
Profitability	3	18
Acquisition of scarce and valued resources	3	18
Absence of organizational strain	2	12
Control over external environment	2	12
Employee development	2	12
Efficiency	2	12
Employee retention	2	12
Growth	2	12
Integration of individual goals with organizational goals	2	12
Open communication	2	12
Survival	2	12
All other criteria	1	6

Source: Reprinted from "Problems in the Measurement of Organizational Effectiveness," by Richard M. Steers. Published in *Administrative Science Quarterly,* 20, #4 (December 1975) by permission of *The Administrative Science Quarterly.* Copyright 1975 by Cornell University.

both managers and organizational analysts. If appropriate assessment criteria cannot be agreed upon, it would be manifestly impossible to agree completely on an evaluation of an organization's success or failure. This inability to identify meaningful criteria to be used across organizations results in part from ignoring several questions (or problems) that must be resolved if we are to derive more meaningful approaches to assessing organizational effectiveness. Eight such issues are:

1. *Is there any such thing as organizational effectiveness?* It is only logical to ask whether there is indeed empirical justification for any such construct. In the absence of any tangible evidence, it may be that organizational effectiveness exists only on an abstract level, with little applicability to the workplace and its problems. But if effectiveness is indeed a viable concept from a managerial standpoint, its definition and characteristics must be made more explicit.

2. *How stable—consistently valid—are the assessment criteria?* A second problem encountered in attempts to assess effectiveness is that many of the assessment criteria change over time. In a growth economy, for example, the effectiveness of a business firm may be related to level of capital investment; during a recession or depression, however, capital liquidity may emerge as a more useful criterion, and high fixed investment may shift from being an asset to being a liability. Clearly, such criteria do not represent permanent indicators of organizational success. In fact, it is probably this transitory nature of many effectiveness criteria that has led some investigators to suggest that adaptability or flexibility represents the key variable in any model of effectiveness.

3. *Which time perspective is most appropriate in assessment?* Contributing to the problem of criterion instability is the question of which time perspective to take in assessing effectiveness. For example, if current production (a short-run criterion) consumes so much of an organization's resources that little is left over for investment in R&D, the organization may ultimately find itself with its products outmoded and its very survival (a long-term criterion) threatened. Thus the problem for the manager is how best to allocate available resources between short- and long-term considerations so that both receive sufficient support for their respective purposes.

4. *Are the assessment criteria related positively to each other?* Most approaches to assessing effectiveness rely on a series of relatively discrete criteria (for example, productivity, job satisfaction, profitability). The use of such multiple measures, however, often leads to situations in which these criteria are in conflict. Consider, for instance, an organization that uses productivity and job satisfaction as two of its criteria. Productivity can often be increased (at least in the short run) by pressuring employees to exert greater energy and turn out more goods in the same period of time. Such managerial efforts are likely, however, to result in reduced job satisfaction. On the other hand, it's possible to increase job satisfaction by yielding to employee demands for increased leisure time and reduced production pressures—but at the price of lower productivity. Thus, while the use of multiple evaluation criteria adds breadth to any assessment attempt, it simultaneously opens the door to conflicting demands that management may not be able to satisfy.

5. *How accurate are the assessment criteria?* A further problem in assessing organizational effectiveness is how to secure accurate measures for assessment purposes. How does an organization accurately measure managerial performance or job satisfaction, if these are to be used as effectiveness criteria? And how consistent are such measures over time? In point of fact, we tend to measure the performance of the individual manager loosely in terms of an overall rating by his superior and to measure job satisfaction frequently in terms of turnover and absenteeism rates. Such operational definitions have their obvious limitations. Performance ratings, for example, may be skewed by personality factors, and a low turnover rate may indicate low performance standards born of a complacent or indifferent management.

6. *How widely can the criteria be applied?* A major problem with many of the criteria suggested for assessing effectiveness is the belief that they apply equally in a variety of organizations. Such is often not the case. While profitability and mar-

ket share may be relevant criteria for most business firms, they have little applicability for organizations like a library or a police department. Thus, when considering appropriate criteria for purposes of assessment, we should take care to ensure that the criteria are consistent with the goals and purposes of a particular organization.

7. How do such criteria help us understand organizational dynamics? The organizational analyst of necessity is concerned with the utility of the effectiveness construct. What purposes are served by the existence of evaluation criteria for assessing effectiveness? Do they provide insight into the dynamics of ongoing organizations? Do they help us make predictions concerning the future actions of organizations? Unless such models facilitate a better understanding of organizational structures, processes, or behavior, they are of little value from an analytical or operational standpoint.

8. At which level should effectiveness be assessed? Finally, managers face the problem of the level at which to assess effectiveness. Logic suggests evaluating organizational effectiveness on an organizationwide basis. Such an approach, however, ignores the dynamic relationships between an organization and its various parts. We must bear in mind that the individual employee ultimately determines the degree of organizational success. If we are to increase our understanding of organizational processes, we must develop models of effectiveness that enable us, to the greatest extent possible, to identify the nature of the relationships between individual processes and organizational behavior. Moreover, a comparison of the relative effectiveness of various departments or divisions is also useful. It is highly likely that certain of these subunits (for example, sales) may be more successful than others within the same organization. The existence of such differences complicates even further any attempts to draw firm conclusions concerning the effectiveness of a given organization.

Even a cursory examination of these problems reveals the magnitude and complexity of the subject. If managers are to reduce their dependence on simplistic criteria for evaluating effectiveness,

we must provide them with a framework for analysis that surmounts these problems.

One solution that at least minimizes many of the obstacles to assessing effectiveness is to view effectiveness in terms of a process instead of an end state. Most of the earlier models of effectiveness place a heavy emphasis on identifying the criteria themselves (that is, the end state). Although such criteria may be useful, they tell us little about the ingredients that facilitate effectiveness. Nor do they help the manager better understand how effectiveness results. Hence it appears that we need to re-examine our notions about the concept of organizational effectiveness and about the kinds of analytical models managers require to help them make their own organizations effective.

EFFECTIVE AND INEFFECTIVE ORGANIZATIONS

Perhaps one of the best ways to understand the notion of organizational effectiveness is to examine several instances of *ineffectiveness*. Consider the following three examples:

1. Farm tractors. There are many examples of organizations that correctly identify the nature of the problem and set relevant goals but then select a less than optimal strategy for attaining those goals.

One such example can be seen in the activities of the first Henry Ford as he tried to maintain the profitability of Ford Motor Company during the depression of the 1930s—when, of course, the demand for new cars had declined. Alfred Chandler reports in his book *Strategy and Structure* that Ford decided to enter the farm tractor market in order to employ some of his unused plant capacity. Within a relatively short period of time, his engineers had designed and built a versatile yet inexpensive tractor. Unfortunately, however, Ford selected an inappropriate marketing and distribution strategy for the new product. He tried to market the tractors through his existing automobile distribution system, which was largely concentrated in major cities and was not attuned to the needs of farms. Hence his product (however good it may have been) never really reached its intended market. The venture failed commercially until Ford realized his mistake and created a supplementary distribution system that reflected market realities and communicated with the farming audience in its own terms.

2. Slide rules.   Whereas Example 1 represents an attempt to apply the wrong strategy to the right goal, Example 2 we may describe as an attempt to apply the right strategy to the wrong goal—a goal that became wrong because of a technological advance that created a shift in market demand.

This example involves a company that manufactures slide rules. For many years, the organization had a reputation for producing and selling high-quality slide rules for a variety of applications. With the advent of relatively inexpensive electronic pocket calculators, however, sophisticated computations could be completed quickly and accurately. Almost overnight, demand shifted from slide rules to calculators. Within two years, sales dropped by 75 percent. The company either failed to predict environmental changes accurately or was unable to adapt to them in order to achieve its profit goal.

3. Regulatory agencies.   A third type of problem exists when an organization chooses an inappropriate strategy to achieve a suboptimal goal. Typically, we find examples of this type of situation in public bureaucracies (perhaps because of a lack of competitive pressure).

Consider the example of the Interstate Commerce Commission, an agency of the U.S. Government charged with facilitating and regulating commerce between the states. Purportedly, its primary goal is to achieve an effective level of operation in such commerce. In actual practice, however, many complain that its operative (or real) goals are just the opposite. For example, in order to ensure "equity" between the various trucking lines, the ICC for many years required certain firms to drive from point *A* to point *B* not directly, but through some out-of-the-way point *C*. The rationale for such a policy was based in part on the belief that smaller firms, which often had less efficient routes, needed to be protected from the larger firms, which had more resources

at their disposal. As a result, costs increased for both the trucking firms and the customers, and delivery times lengthened for all concerned.

In each of these cases, we have a clear example of ineffectiveness. The nature of the problem in each case, however, is quite different. Moreover, the strategies chosen by the organizations to achieve their stated objectives are also quite different. It is this lack of convergence in most approaches to organizational effectiveness that has led to so much confusion—not only over how organizations achieve effectiveness, but indeed over what we mean by the notion of effectiveness itself.

What Is Organizational Effectiveness?

The term *organizational effectiveness* has been used (and misused) in a variety of contexts. As noted above, some equate the term with profit or productivity, while others view it in terms of job satisfaction. While many analysts view these criteria as definitions of organizational effectiveness, a few investigators suggest that such variables actually constitute intervening variables that enhance the likelihood that effectiveness will result.

If we accept the notion that organizations are unique and pursue divergent goals (as the three examples suggest), then such definitions are too situation-specific and value-laden to be of much use. Instead, it appears more useful initially to follow the lead to Talcott Parsons and Amitai Etzioni and define organizational effectiveness in terms of an organization's ability to acquire and efficiently use available resources to achieve their goals. Viewed from this perspective, all three examples cited previously represent a case of goal failure.

Such a definition requires elaboration. First, we are focusing on operative goals as opposed to official goals. It seems more appropriate to assess the relative level of effectiveness against the real intended objectives of an organization rather than a static list of objectives meant principally for public consumption. For example, we often see public advertisements by corporations claiming that "progress is our most important product" or "the things we do improve the way we live." Such statements (or official goals) often give the impression that the company's primary objective is progress, while in fact other goals (for example, profit, growth, or an acceptable rate of return on investment) probably represent more accurate statements of intent (that is, operative goals). Thus whatever objectives the organization truly intends pursuing, it is against these criteria that effectiveness is best judged. Such an approach has the added advantage of minimizing the influence of the analyst's value judgments in the assessment process. While many would argue, for example, that job satisfaction is a desirable end, it remains for the organization, not an outside analyst, to set such a goal.

Inherent in such a definition, moreover, is the notion that effectiveness is best judged against an organization's ability to compete in a turbulent environment and successfully acquire and use its resources. This suggests that managers must deal effectively with their external environments to secure needed resources. Finally, this approach recognizes the concept of efficiency as a necessary yet insufficient ingredient (or facilitator) of effectiveness.

A Note on Efficiency

People often discuss efficiency and effectiveness as being interchangeable. Our approach is to clearly separate the two notions yet to recognize the importance of and interrelation between them. While we define effectiveness as the extent to which operative goals can be attained, we define efficiency as the cost/benefit ratio involved in the pursuit of those goals. An example should clarify this distinction. Shortly after World War II, a ranking German officer observed that the Allies had not "beaten" Germany but had instead "smothered" her. In other words, the officer was suggesting that while the Allies had been effective in the pursuit of their objectives, they had not been particularly efficient.

At some point, however, we would expect that increased inefficiency would have a detrimental effect on subsequent effectiveness. When this notion is applied to a business environment, it appears that the more costly goal effort becomes, the less likely the business is to be effective. As an example of this efficiency-effectiveness rela-

tionship, consider some of the current experiments in job redesign, such as the Volvo and Saab-Scania experiments in Sweden. Several prominent investigators have noted recently that, while job enrichment may have desirable social consequences, the costs associated with such efforts may be so high that they increase the price of the product beyond what customers are willing to pay. Hence the notion of efficiency emerges as an important element of organizational effectiveness.

A PROCESS MODEL FOR ANALYZING EFFECTIVENESS

From a static viewpoint, it may be enough to define effectiveness in terms of attaining operative goals. However, if we are to understand more fully the processes involved in bringing about an effective level of operations, it is necessary to take a more dynamic approach to the topic. The approach suggested here is essentially a "process model" of effectiveness. Its aim is to provide managers with a framework for analysis of the major *processes* involved in effectiveness. This approach contrasts sharply with earlier models that merely listed the requisite criteria for assessing organizational success.

The process model that is proposed here consists of three related components: (1) the notion of goal optimization; (2) a systems perspective; and (3) an emphasis on human behavior in organizational settings. I believe that these three components, taken together, provide a useful vehicle for the analysis of effectiveness-related processes in organizations. This multidimensional approach has several advantages over earlier models—in particular, the advantage of increasing the comprehensiveness of analysis aimed at a better understanding of a highly complex topic.

Goal Optimization

If we examine the various approaches currently used to assess organizational effectiveness, it becomes apparent that most ultimately rest on the notion of goal attainment. A primary advantage of using the operative goal concept for assessing levels of effectiveness is that organizational success is evaluated in the light of an organization's behavioral intentions. In view of the fact that different organizations pursue widely divergent goals, it is only logical to recognize this uniqueness in any assessment technique.

While many variations on the goal approach to evaluating effectiveness exist, the most fruitful approach is to view effectiveness in terms of goal *optimization*. Instead of evaluating success in terms of the extent to which "desired" goals have been maximized, we recognize a series of identifiable and irreducible constraints (for example, money, technology, personnel, other goals, and so on) that serve to inhibit goal maximization. Managers are seen as setting and pursuing "optimized" goals (that is, desired goals within the constraints dictated by the resources available). A company may, for example, feel that a 10 percent return on investment is a realistic goal in view of resource availability, the existing market environment, and so forth. We would argue that it is against this *feasible* goal set, not against an ultimate goal set, that effectiveness be judged. (Note: Goal optimization should not be confused with suboptimization, where less than optimal goals are intentionally pursued. Under suboptimized conditions, a company may intentionally set a 5 percent return-on-investment goal even though 10 percent may be feasible, given the situation.)

The goal optimization approach has several advantages over conventional approaches: First, it suggests that goal maximization is probably not possible and that, even if it were, it might be detrimental to an organization's well-being and survival. In most situations, for example, there appears to be little chance for a company to maximize productivity and job satisfaction at the same time. Instead, compromises must be made—compromises that provide for an optimal level of attainment of both objectives. We can observe such compromises in the ICC case mentioned previously; ideally, such a regulatory agency would try to meet the conflicting needs and demands of the trucking firms, the customers, the public at large, and so forth. Thus the use of a goal optimization approach permits the explicit recognition of multiple and often conflicting goals.

Second, goal optimization models recognize the existence of differential weights that managers place on the various goals in the feasible set. For instance, a company may place on the pursuit of its profit goal five times the weight, and resources, that it puts on its affirmative-action employment goal or its job satisfaction goal. While real-life examples would obviously be far more complex, this simple example emphasizes the differential weighting aspect inherent in any assessment of organizational effectiveness.

Third, the model also recognizes the existence of a series of constraints that can impede progress toward goal attainment. Many of these constraints (for example, limited finances, people, technology, and so on) may be impossible to alleviate, at least in the short run. Consider the case of the slide rule manufacturer. The production of slide rules requires a radically different technology than that required by the production of electronic calculators. Thus this firm, which had a competitive advantage using one technology, lost its edge when market demand shifted. Of course, if this company had anticipated environmental changes, accurately and far enough in advance, it might have developed new applications for existing technology—assuming the infeasibility of changing it. The firm might, for instance, have devoted its energies to developing new precision-measurement instruments not based on electronics. Thus it is important to recognize such constraints—and how a company reacts to them—in any final assessment of success or failure.

Fourth, this approach has the added advantage of allowing for increased flexibility of evaluation criteria. As the goals pursued by an organization change, or as the constraints associated with them change, a new optimal solution will emerge that could represent new evaluation criteria. Hence the means of assessment would remain current and would reflect the changing needs and goals of the organization.

Last, from the standpoint of long-range planning, weighted goals and their relevant contraints could be modeled by using computer simulations to derive optimal solutions for purposes of allocating future resources and effort.

The use of computer-simulation models in long-range planning has become commonplace among larger organizations. The same technique could be applied to examining organizational effectiveness. Major organizational and environmental variables could be systematically manipulated to analyze the impact of such changes on resulting facets of effectiveness (for example, profits, market share, adaptation, and productivity). From such manipulations, optimal solutions could be derived that would help managers direct the future of the enterprise.

Systems Perspective

The second important aspect of a process model of organizational effectiveness is the employment of an open-systems perspective for purposes of analysis. Such a perspective emphasizes interrelationships between the various parts of an organization and its environment as they jointly influence effectiveness.

If we take a systems perspective, we can identify the four major categories of influences on effectiveness (see Figure 2): (1) organizational characteristics, such as structure and technology; (2) environmental characteristics, such as economic and market conditions; (3) employee characteristics, such as level of job performance and job attachment; and (4) managerial policies and practices. While the precise manner in which these variables influence effectiveness goes beyond the scope of this article, it is suggested that these four sets of variables must be relatively con-

sonant if effectiveness is to be achieved. The negative outcomes that result when these characteristics do not fit we saw in the example of the Ford tractor. While the product itself was good, the failure to recognize environmental variations and to adapt the marketing structure accordingly led to ineffectiveness.

Thus managers have a responsibility to understand the nature of their environment and to set realistic goals that accommodate and/or exploit that environment. Given these goals, the more effective organizations will tend to be those that successfully adapt structure, technology, work effort, policies, and so on to facilitate goal attainment.

Behavioral Emphasis

A final aspect of the process approach to understanding and analyzing effectiveness is the emphasis on the role of individual behavior as it affects organizational success or failure. The position taken here is in opposition to the stand taken by many that effectiveness is best examined exclusively on a "macro" (or organizationwide) basis. Instead, it appears that greater insight can result if analyses include consideration of how the behavior of individual employees impacts upon organizational goal attainment. If an organization's employees largely agree with the objectives of their employer, we would expect them to exert a relatively high level of effort toward achieving

Figure 2.   Major Influences on Organizational Effectiveness

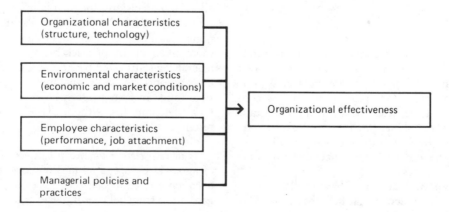

those goals. If, on the other hand, organizational goals largely conflict with employees' personal goals, there is little reason to believe that employees would exert their maximum effort.

As an interesting example of the importance of individuals in goal attainment, consider the controversy over automobile seat belts. In an effort to improve traffic safety, the federal government initially passed a law that required auto manufacturers to install seat belts in all new cars. When this action failed to have the desired consequences (many people simply did not use them), additional laws were passed requiring manufacturers to install warning lights, buzzers, and so forth to remind drivers to use seat belts. Finally, when these measures also proved ineffective, laws were passed requiring manufacturers to install devices that made it mandatory to use seat belts before the ignition could be activated—although even these devices could be circumvented with a degree of ingenuity. While the initial goal was laudatory, the processes (means) used to achieve this goal were largely ineffective because they ignored the predispositions and behavior patterns of most drivers. Perhaps a more effective strategy (certainly in terms of time and cost) would have been simply to pass a law nullifying accident insurance claims for drivers injured while not wearing seat belts.

Hence when we examine organizational effectiveness, it is important to recognize and account for the people who ultimately determine the quality and quantity of an organization's response to environmental demands.

CONCLUSION

Most contemporary organizations exist in turbulent environments in which threats to survival and growth are relatively commonplace. Within such environments, managers must try to secure and properly utilize resources in an effort to attain the operative goals set forth by the organization. The process by which they do so—or fail to do so—is at the heart of the concept of organizational effectiveness.

In the above discussion, I have tried to review the various approaches that have been taken to evaluate organizational effectiveness. Little homogeneity exists between the various approaches. This lack of consensus, in turn, results from the existence of at least eight problems inherent in the existing models. In an effort to overcome many of these problems, I have proposed a process model of organizational effectiveness.

The model described differs from the earlier models. Instead of specifying the criteria for effectiveness (for example, when is an organization effective?), this model focuses on the process of becoming effective (for example, what conditions are most conducive to effectiveness?). It is argued that the actual criteria for evaluation vary depending on the particular operative goals of the organization. Because of this, it appears appropriate to place greater emphasis on understanding the dynamics associated with effectiveness-oriented behavior.

It is further recommended that one way to conceptualize organizational effectiveness *as a process* is to examine three related factors. First, optimized goals (that is, what an organization is capable of attaining) can provide realistic parameters for the assessment process. Given an organization's operative goals, we can ask intelligent questions about the appropriateness of managerial resource-allocation decisions. In other words, is there a better way for managers to expend their limited resources?

Important questions to consider in connection with this first factor include the following:

To what extent are we applying our limited resources toward the attainment of our various goals? In point of fact, organizations often make resource-allocation decisions independent of goal decisions, resulting in "unfunded" goals and "funded" nongoals. This behavior is perhaps most clearly exemplified in the practice by various state and federal legislatures of passing authorization bills and appropriation bills separately. Thus it is possible (and, in fact, it often happens) that a bill (goal) becomes law without the appropriation of resources to implement it.

Is there a clear relationship between the amount of resources we spend on the various goals and the importance of each goal? If, for example, an organization truly believes it places equal weight on making a profit and on improving quality of working life, are such beliefs reflected in the allocation of resources? This does not suggest that equivalent amounts of resources must be spent on each goal. Instead, it implies that sufficient resources be spent to bring about the attainment of both goals.

What kind of return on investment, per goal, are we getting on our resources? If organizations pursue multiple goals, it would seem logical to examine the efficiency of effort invested in each goal. It may be that an organization is highly efficient in realizing its less important goals and relatively inefficient in realizing its more important goals. Where such inefficiencies are noted, decisions must be made concerning the desirability of continuing the pursuit of a goal. Where a goal is viewed as worthwhile (for example, hiring the hard-core unemployed), companies may pursue the goal despite a low return on investment.

Is the entire organization working together for goal attainment? As shown in the Ford tractor example, there are instances in which an organization's existing marketing channels are not suited to newer products—a "bad fit" that leads to suboptimal results. Moreover, a fairly common complaint against research and development departments is that scientists stress basic research projects at the expense of applied projects that generally have more immediate and more certain payoffs.

Is the "fit" between the organization and its environment changing? Organizations should continually raise questions concerning their place in the external environment. We saw in the example of the slide rule manufacturer how a company can lose a major share of its market by failing to adjust to changes in market demand. Under such circumstances, and without the necessary technology to compete with manufacturers of electronic calculators, this firm may find it desirable to establish its niche in the market by specializing in drafting equipment or other instruments not based on electronics. A relatively successful example of such organization-environment fit can be seen in American Motors Corporation (AMC),

which for many years has specialized in small cars and jeeps while the "Big Three" stressed medium- and large-sized cars. As the other auto makers shift their focus toward smaller cars, however, AMC (with fewer resources) may find it necessary to adjust its efforts toward newer markets. Hence flexibility in the face of environmental change remains an important area of concern for effective organizations.

Second, it has been stressed throughout our discussion that the use of a systems perspective allows for the explicit recognition of the ways in which various organizational factors blend together to facilitate or inhibit effectiveness-related activities. This approach forces managers to employ more comprehensive analytical models when they ask questions about why the organization achieved or failed to achieve a particular goal. It facilitates a broader perspective both on the nature of the problem and on its possible solutions.

Third, it is highly desirable to recognize the important link between individual behavior and organizationwide performance. That is, any consideration of how organizations become effective (or more effective) must account for the primary determinant of ultimate organizational performance: the employees of the organization. Recent efforts to institute management-by-objectives programs in organizations represent one such attempt to coordinate the efforts of various employees toward specific organizational objectives. Taken together, these three related factors should help managers and organizational analysts understand the various ways in which organizations move toward or away from goal attainment and organizational effectiveness.

Two general conclusions (with important implications for managers) emerge from our analysis of organizational effectiveness. First, the concept of organizational effectiveness is best understood in terms of a continuous process rather than an end state. Marshaling resources for goal-directed effort is an unceasing task for most managers. In view of the changing nature of the goals pursued in most organizations, managers have a continuing responsibility to recognize environmental changes, to restructure available resources, to modify technologies, to develop employees, and so forth in order to use the talents at their disposal to attain goals that are themselves in perpetual flux.

Second, our analysis also has emphasized the central role of contingencies in any discussion of effectiveness. Thus it is incumbent upon managers to recognize the unique qualities that define their own organization—its goals, structures, technologies, people, environments, and so on—and to respond in a manner consistent with this uniqueness. Our conclusion cautions against the arbitrary use of "rules" or "principles" for achieving success. Such rules and principles are of little use viewed against the background of organizational diversity. Instead, responsibility must fall to the organization and its management to develop employees so that they can better recognize and understand the nature of a particular situation and respond appropriately. When viewed in this manner, organizational effectiveness becomes largely a function of the extent to which managers and employees can pool their efforts and overcome the obstacles that inhibit goal attainment.

SELECTED BIBLIOGRAPHY

Several interesting pieces exist on the subject of organizational effectiveness. For a review of some early formulations of effectiveness that have greatly influenced our current thinking, the reader is referred to Basil S. Georgopoulos and Arnold S. Tannenbaum's "A Study of Organizational Effectiveness," *American Sociological Review*, Vol. 22, pp. 534–540, 1957; Ephraim Yuchtman and Stanley E. Seashore's "A System Resource Approach to Organizational Effectiveness," *American Sociological Review*, Vol. 32, pp. 891–903, 1967; and Thomas A. Mahoney and Peter J. Frost's "The Role of Technology in Models of Organizational Effectiveness," *Organizational Behavior and Human Performance*, Vol. 11, pp. 127–138, 1974. Also of importance is James Price's *Organizational Effectiveness: An Inventory of Propositions* (Irwin, 1968).

A systematic review and analysis of the major problems encountered in attempts to assess effectiveness can be found in a recent article by the author, "Problems in the Measurement of Organizational Effectiveness," *Administrative Science Quarterly*, Vol. 20, pp. 546–558, 1975. A more complete description of the process model of organizational effectiveness, along with a review of the major determinants of effectiveness, is presented in a . . . book by the author entitled *Organizational Effectiveness: A Behavioral View* (Goodyear, 1979).

Several excellent books on organizations are available that are consistent with the process view of effectiveness. In particular, Alfred D. Chandler's *Strategy and Structure* (Anchor, 1964) reviews in detail the growth and adaptation of several major corporations. Chandler's basic hypothesis is that successful organizations structure themselves in accordance with their chosen strategy (goals) for responding to the environment. Paul R. Lawrence and Jay Lorsch's book, *Organization and Environment* (Harvard Business School, 1967), takes a similar stand.

For a somewhat more theoretical treatment of a process model, the reader is referred to Daniel Katz and Robert L. Kahn's *The Social Psychology of Organizations* (Wiley, 1966) and Richard Hall's *Organizations: Structure and Process* (Prentice-Hall, 1972).

BUSINESS STRATEGY FORMULATION

This [reading] will provide a highly condensed overview of a business strategy formulation procedure and will outline and discuss the key steps undertaken in formulating business strategy.

For the purposes of this [reading], focus will be maintained on the area of *business*, as opposed to corporate, strategy formulation.

By corporate strategy is meant the strategy for securing and maintaining a successful portfolio of businesses.

In corporate strategy, major decisions must be made regarding the deployment of resources between different businesses in the corporate portfolio.

By business strategy is meant the strategy for securing and maintaining a position of competitive success in a product/market area.

In business strategy, major decisions must be made regarding the deployment of resources in a specific product/market area, to secure the area from competitive attack, but within the constraints of a broader *corporate* strategy.

There are many ways of viewing strategy formulation, ranging from the evolutionary process described by Mintzberg et al. (1976) and Wrapp (1967), who argue that strategic decisions usually evolve as organization experience evolves, and that in reality a formal, step by step process of strategy formulation is unusual, to a contingency theory approach suggested by Hofer (1975) and Miller (1975), among others, who suggest that specific characteristics of the organization and its environment give rise to a need for strategy formulation processes which are tailored to the specific conditions which the organization faces.

Between these viewpoints are a broad body of authors who argue that strategy formulation needs to be formalized and lay out general ways of approaching strategy formulation, (Ansoff (1965), Newman & Logan (1971), Andrews

(1971), Katz (1970), Hofer & Schendel (1978)). There is still some debate as to the effectiveness of strategy formulation. Among others, Ansoff et al. (1971), Thune & House (1970), Herold (1972), support the hypothesis that strategy "pays," Grinyer & Norburn (1975), Kudla (1979) reject it, and Rue & Fulmer (1973), achieved mixed results.

This [reading] will take the position that the concept of formal strategic planning has survived the market test—studies by Steiner (1972), and Kudla (1979) have indicated a willingness on the part of most of the U.S. Fortune 500 companies to invest time, funds and effort in the process.

The focus will be on strategy *formulation*, as opposed to such implementation problems as organization design, and planning and control systems, to support the strategy. These are discussed elsewhere in the text.

The [reading] will briefly review the following steps, recommended by various authors:

- *Environmental Analysis*—for the purpose of identifying the key threats and opportunities in the future of the business, and the critical factors for success in the industry.

- *Business Analysis*—for the purpose of identifying the critical key strengths and weaknesses.

- *Strategy Formulation*—by which the organization decides on the desired relation between itself and its future environment and develops strategies to determine these.

- *Strategic Anticipation* of opponents' responses.

- *Strategic Planning* by which the key resource allocations to support the strategy, are decided.

ENVIRONMENTAL ANALYSIS

Environmental analysis consists of two major parts: structural analysis and trend analysis:

Structural analysis is done to determine the key relationships of the firm to its environment. This is carried out by: *environmental mapping* which identifies the key organizations which have a vested interest in the strategy of the business; *industry chain analysis* which analyses the entire chain of industries that link the business from its raw material suppliers through to the final customer; and finally *industry attractiveness assessment* which assesses the attractive and unattractive features of the industry in which the firm participates.

Trend analysis is done to determine the key trends which may impact on the business. This consists of analyzing: *macroeconomic trends* which take place in the society as a whole; *industry chain trends* in which the impact of macroeconomic trends on the critical links in the industry chain are estimated, together with trends which are taking place in the industry chain itself.

Structural Analysis: Environmental Mapping

There are a number of organizations surrounding the business who have a vested interest in the decisions that the business makes.

Typical of such interest groups are competitors, suppliers, financial organizations, stockholders, government regulatory bodies, political interest groups, unions, local community groups and others, depending on the organization.

Recent experience, of even the largest corporations, with the ability of such interest groups to influence corporate direction, suggests that strategic decisions cannot be made unilaterally, that realistic strategies may have to take the vested interests of surrounding organizations into account.

Thus an essential ingredient of structural analysis is "environmental mapping," a specific analysis of the interest groups which currently, or may in the future, take an active interest in the business strategy.

In carrying out such an analysis, it may prove useful to do the following: (MacMillan (1978), Kennedy (1965)): First, identify the *key* interest groups that have a vested interest in decisions made by the business. Then identify the key issues which they will raise with the business and the positions which they will take on these issues. Next try to estimate the power of each interest group and the basis of that power. Finally, try to identify any issues over which different groups will be in conflict (such as dividend payments versus wage rates, or profits versus regulatory compliance). Of particular importance are issues where powerful groups are likely to make conflicting demands.

Such an analysis should provide: an estimate of the future points of conflict between organization and its key interest groups, the scope of such conflict, and the basis of this conflict; an indication of what major constraints could be placed on the strategic decisions to be made; where support and opposition can be expected from these interest groups.

With this as background, the next structural analysis that may be worth pursuing is an analysis of the industry chain.

Structural Analysis: Industry Chain Analysis

Few businesses are not part of an industry chain. A typical chain might be depicted by Figure 1.

Analysis of the chain is important, for iden-

Figure 1. Typical Industry Chain

Prime suppliers	1st stage manufacturers	2nd stage manufacturers		
		1st stage distributors	2nd stage distributors	
				Final Customer

tifying the competitive conditions not only in the industry, but also in the rest of the chain.

Chain analysis is concerned with trying to identify the *critical* links in the chain, and the way in which the business is dependent on them.

Factors to look for in such a chain analysis include: recent *shifts in demand* at any link; the *degree of concentration* of competitors, since the more concentration in a particular link, the greater the impact of any disruption in that link; *major social and regulatory pressures* on that link; recent *price level shifts* at that link, since any decrease in real prices at a link in the chain may be transmitted to industries behind it, and any price increase at a link in the chain may be transmitted to industries ahead of it; and finally, *critical resource dependencies* (raw materials, labor, equipment, etc.) at any link increase the probability that disruption might occur at that link, these disruptions may progress up or down the chain.

Chain analysis should be confined to the most important links and may provide warning signals of major cost, price, supply and demand pressures which could impact the business in the strategic planning period.

The preceding analyses provide a contextual background for the next stage of the analysis—assessment of industry attractiveness.

Structural Analysis: Assessment of Industry Attractiveness

The results of environmental mapping and industry chain analysis provides the basis for deciding the attractive and unattractive features of the industry in which the business is operating.

In listing the factors to consider in assessing the attractiveness of the industry, the inputs of the Strategic Planning Institute, Rothschild (1976), Hofer & Schendel (1978), Salter and Weinhold (1979) have been used to generate Table 1.

The systematic analysis of these factors provide guidelines for deciding what the critical factors for success are in the industry.

Table 1. Factors Which Could Enhance Industry Attractiveness

Market factors	Industry factors	Cost factors	Investment factors	Interest group factors
Large market size	High degree of pricing control	Low capital intensity	Short payback on investment	High social acceptability
High market growth rate	Weaker dispersed competition	Low labor intensity	Low potential for excess capacity	Low degree of unionization
High market segmentability	High industry profitability	Low marketing cost/sales	High ease of entry and exit	Low regulatory vulnerability
High customer profitability	Low cyclical vulnerability	Low manufacturing cost/sales	Low degree of vertical integration	
Low concentration of customers	Low inflation vulnerability	Low inventory/sales		
	Low energy dependence	Low R&D/sales		
	High technological stability			
	Low supply vulnerability			
	Low environmental impact vulnerability			

In order to be successful, a company operating in a small, high growth market with many small competitors, high industry profits, high inflation rates, cyclical vulnerability and rapid technological change, needs to do things differently from a company in a large, slow growing market with low industry profits, and a few larger competitors all of which are highly unionized and highly energy dependent.

Success factors for the first company could include: ability to lead in product technology, ability to maintain or gain market share in the expanding market via a strong marketing force, ability to negotiate prices which allow the company to keep up with inflation, ability to identify ways of smoothing the disruptive effects of cyclical sales without increasing costs (such as long term contracts). Success factors for the second company could include: ability to reduce manufacturing and energy costs, ability to negotiate satisfactory contracts with unions with minimum disruption of production; control or near control of the major distribution systems; and ability to efficiently identify, design, develop and manufacture custom products.

Thus the industry attractiveness study highlights key factors which will determine the ability of the business to succeed in that industry.

This concludes the structural component of environmental analysis. The problem is that the environment changes, so now attention needs to be given to trend analysis.

Trend Analysis: Macroeconomic Trends

The origins of change in the industry chain usually stem from trends in the society as a whole. Thus the first level of trend analysis is concerned with trends in the society and economy in which the firm is embedded.

At the national level, the firm should identify trends in the nation as a whole. First, there are broad demographic trends: shifts in the age distribution of the population, the geographical distribution, the distribution of racial groups, the proportions of racial groups, the size of families, the income of families, trends in education and occupations and so on would be identified and projected into the future. Second, there are broad economic trends: projections would be made of the trends in gross domestic product, consumer spending-power, government expenditure, government fiscal and monetary policy, national productivity and general business activity. Third, there are broad sociopolitical trends: trends in cultural values and attitudes would be identified; the policies of the important political parties, particularly those of the incumbent party, would be analysed and the effects of the implementation of these policies would be projected; trends in international politics and their effect on the nation would be projected. Fourth, there are ecological trends: trends in the physical environment of the nation would be projected and the effect of these trends on the nation would be projected.

A detailed analysis of every aspect is not necessary. What the firm requires is some idea of the direction in which the nation is moving. Many of these analyses are done either by government departments or by private consultants specialising in this type of work.

The basic purpose of this analysis is to then identify the possible impacts of these trends on the business, either directly or along links in the industry chain.

For instance, shifts in social demographics may lead to restructuring in the retailing industry, which could cause a reevaluation of a manufacturer's plant locations and distribution channels. (The impact on retailing of the growth and regional concentration trends in the senior citizens population could eventually work back down the chain and affect packaging, branding, pricing and delivery systems.)

Out of the macroeconomic and sociopolitical analyses should emerge some judgments of the major impacts on the industry in which the business operates. Some of these trends may have negative impacts, in which case they are regarded as threats, and some may have positive impacts, in which case they are regarded as opportunities.

The next level of trend analysis involves trends in the industry chain.

Trend Analysis: Industry Chain Trends

Clearly major trends taking place in the industry chain have the potential for impacting the business itself.

In analysing the industry chain trends, it is

important to focus on those *critical* links which were identified in the structural analysis of the chain.

For each *critical* link in the industry chain, it may be necessary to do analyses of the following types: First, consumer spending-patterns and market growth should be projected on the basis of the national analysis, to get an idea of the expected trends in competitive activity at that link. The likelihood of new competitors, and expansion of existing competitors' activity should be identified and their effects on the market estimated. Second would be an analysis of labor. Trends in union activity and attitude, trends towards unionization, trends in wage levels, labor supply, labor efficiency would be identified and their effect projected. Third would be an analysis of raw material supplies. A fourth analysis could concern technology. Current technological development and its effects would be projected. A fifth analysis could concern trends in the money market. Subsequent analyses could analyse trends at regional (state and local) levels.

The object here is to identify whether any of the factors identified in the industry attractiveness assessment are changing in a way that will cause the attractiveness to substantially change.

Major trends which *reduce* industry attractiveness, or the ability of the firm to compete, are identified as *threats*.

Major trends which may *increase* industry attractiveness, or the firm's ability to compete, are identified as *opportunities*.

In the light of these trends, the critical success factors need also to be reviewed to assess what factors will determine success in the *future* as opposed to the present.

The analysis of industry chain trends completes the environmental analysis. The strategist should have the following results:

1. Key future interest groups and the major issues on which conflict/support can be expected on these future issues.
2. Critical factors for future success in the industry.
3. Threats and opportunities facing the industry.

The next step for the strategist is to focus on the business itself, which leads to business analysis.

BUSINESS ANALYSIS

The purpose of business analysis is to identify the strengths and weaknesses of the business in relation to its competitors. Business analysis comprises the following major steps: *Analysis of key strategic variables* such as product policy, market policy to determine where the firm is performing well and poorly, and whether support functions such as manufacturing, and R&D are focussing their efforts *consistently* with the areas of good performance; *competitive analysis*, in which the firm's position compared to competitors identifies areas *where* it is strong and weak. Explanation of the differences determines what the actual strengths and weaknesses of the firm are; and finally a comparison with *future environmental trends* identifies which strengths and weaknesses are likely to persist in the future.

These three major steps will be discussed in turn.

Business Analysis: Key Strategic Variables

Katz (1970) discusses the importance of a clear identification of what he calls the key strategic variables of the firm. These strategic variables represent the policy commitments the firm has made to reflect the desired relationship between the firm and its environment.

Product policy.   Analysis of sales volume and contribution to profits by product category often reveals that a large proportion of sales volume and contribution to profits is generated by a relatively small proportion of the products. It is where these concentrations of sales and profits take place that provides the clues as to what the business' real strengths are.

For instance, in Figure 2, product A is a high contributor to total sales as well as to total profits. This product is one of the major products of the business. Product C may be even more important, since it generates high profits from moderate sales. However it is probably a prime target for competitive attack. Product B could be receiving more attention than it deserves, by virtue of the fact that it is a high sales volume generator but only contributes moderately to profits. Product D

Figure 2. Sales and Profit Contribution Analysis

		Contribution to total profits		
		High	Medium	Low
Contribution to total sales	High	A	B	D
	Medium	C		
	Low			E

needs to be seriously considered: unless there is a very real strategic reason for the low profits (such as share gain) price should be increased which will reduce sales but generate better profits. Product E is a prime candidate for deletion unless there are really compelling reasons why it should be kept.

Thus the key product policy question is: "In what product categories are sales and profits concentrated?" This often requires creative determination of what the key "dimensions" for categorizing products are, since products can be categorized in many ways; by price range, size, color, quality, configuration, materials. Many of these dimensions may be irrelevant, but for each business some are critical. One of the creative challenges of business analysis is the determination of those dimensions which *are* critical.

Market policy.   A similar analysis of sales and profits by markets or customer types will provide clues as to where the real market strengths of the firm lie.

As in the case of product policy, there are many "dimensions" by which they can be categorized; markets can be analyzed by customer type (a host of sociodemographic or socioeconomic dimensions), by geographic region, by end-usage patterns, by reason for puchase (new, replacement), to name but a few dimensions. The strategic challenge is to identify the important dimensions which will answer the key question: "In what market categories are sales and profits concentrated?"

Distribution policy.   Analysis of sales and profits by distribution channel provide the clues for discovering the firm's distribution strengths. As above, the key dimensions need to be identified

to determine which distribution channels provide the bulk of sales and profits.

The above three analyses identify the strong and weak performing products, markets and distribution channels. The next question is whether the firm is deploying its resources appropriately to the strong performers. In line with this, the firm needs to consider other key policy variables. The search here is for *consistency* between the firm's posture in the product/market/distribution arena and *other* major policy decisions for the business.

Katz (1970) and Rothschild (1976, 1979) give indications of what these variables may be.

Promotion policy.   What fundamental ways are being employed to attract the attention of final consumer and intermediate purchasers? Are these appropriate in the light of actual sales and profit concentrations? Desired sales and profits concentrations?

Price policy.   Is the pricing of the products in various markets and channels appropriate? For instance in Figure 2 some concern was expressed with products B and D's low margins. Unless there is some compelling strategic reason not to, their prices could be moved up.

Innovation policy.   Where are the funds expended on R&D? Is this appropriate in the light of product and market concentrations? What research funds are spent on product innovation? On process innovation?

Manufacturing policy.   Are manufacturing, scheduling, inventory, delivery and quality consistent with key products/markets/channels served?

Key personnel policy. Where are the best people being deployed? How are they being promoted and rewarded? Is this consistent with the product/market/channel posture of the firm?

Investment and discretionary spending policy. Are funds of the organization being deployed appropriately? To what product/market/channels do the last few dollars in the various divisional budgets get allocated? An analysis of these discretionary expenditures can indicate differences between the attention which is being focussed in various product/market/channel activities and the degree of success in each area.

Finally, a review of the firm's position in regard to its key interest groups may indicate that certain other key policy commitments are necessary. For instance:

Regulation policy. What will the policy be regarding regulation: Compliance, reluctant compliance, or outright resistance to regulation?

Labor policy. What are the policies toward labor unions? To other forms of organized labor? What is the firm's approach going to be? Fight? Avoid? Compromise?

It is important to recognize that the major analytical challenge is to identify, for the specific industry, what its specific strategic variables are. Each industry and firm has a set of *unique* policy variables that are major determinants of future success. For instance, the mining industry requires key commitments to exploration policy and options policy (options to mine certain explored areas). In the publishing industry, editorial and options policies are important. Hence the list above is merely a specification by Katz of commonly occuring strategic variables. The challenge to the strategist is to identify key strategic variables for the specific business under analysis.

The business analysis highlights inconsistencies between the firm's current posture in the market and its major policy commitments to these markets. Such inconsistencies must be explained or corrected. They could also highlight inconsistencies between the firm's current policy commitments and the critical factors for success in the future.

Finally, the identified areas of product/market/

channel concentrations also highlight *where* the firm is doing well and poorly. The question now is *why* this is happening. To answer this question it is necessary to do comparisons with competitors.

Business Analysis: Competitive Analysis

To the extent that information is available, similar policy analyses need to be carried out for the competitors, as was carried out in the business analysis of the firm itself.

The object here is to identify where the firm is doing *better* than competitors—then the *explanation* of these differences leads to identification of the key strengths. Thus it is important to identify *why* the firm is outperforming competitors rather than merely *where* this is happening. This is what explains the strength of the firm. (For instance, selling more than competitors in Texas is not a strength—the *reason* for selling more in Texas is a strength.)

It is also important to identify *why* the firm is doing worse than competitors. Since this may be the result of a strategic choice not to compete heavily in a certain product, market or channel, it is important to identify whether this relatively poor performance is by *choice* or because of a fundamental weakness. A review of the critical factors for success from the environmental analysis may give valuable clues to explain such weaknesses.

Competitive analysis should therefore yield: *Key strengths of the business*—where the firm outperforms competitors and why; *key weaknesses* of the business—where the firm underperforms and why; and the *key policy variables* which determine the posture of the firm in relation to its environment.

However, these results relate to the *current* environment—what has yet to be considered is whether this is appropriate to the future.

Business Analysis: Comparison with Future Environment

Review of the trend analyses leads to questions as to whether the current strengths of the firm are appropriate to the future.

In this process, the product/market/channel strengths of both the firm and its major competitors are reviewed in the light of expected trends in the environment, and an estimate is made of which current strengths will persist or become obsolete and which current weaknesses will persist or disappear.

This completes the business analysis. The stage is now set for strategy formulation.

STRATEGY FORMULATION

The strategy formulation process consists of: *Mission development* in which the basic purpose of the business is specified; *specification of objectives and constraints* by which objectives are set and the major constraints imposed by corporate strategy or external interest groups are identified: *strategy formulation* in which offensive and defensive strategies are formulated and key policy commitments to support these strategies are formulated; and finally *strategic anticipation* in which competitive counter responses are anticipated.

It should be stressed that though the following discussion of strategy formulation appears to be [a] straight forward step by step process, this may well not be the case. Several iterations may be required, as the strategist revises mission, objectives and strategy in the light of expected competitive and interest group responses.

Strategy Formulation:
Statement of Mission

The determination of the firm's current and future strengths and weaknesses, and the industry's major threats, opportunities and critical success factors finally places the strategist in the position of being able to ask what the mission of the business should be.

The mission statement answers the question: "What business are we in?" It addresses the fundamental raison d'être, or "reason to be" of the business in its environment. In other words, a mission statement specifies the functional role that the business is going to play in the larger economy.

Hofer & Schendel (1978) argue that effective management of a business stems from a clear understanding of this mission on the part of senior management.

In formulating mission, the strategist must make the tradeoff between a broad mission that spreads management and resources thin, and a narrow mission that focusses resources but limits flexibility.

Thus a typewriter manufacturer may have a mission statement as broad as: "We are in the business of providing electro mechanical copy worldwide" or as narrow as "We are in the business of providing portable mechanical typewriters to the Northeastern United States".

The first statement could take the company as far afield as electronic transmission networks, the second is very specific and focussed but leaves little room for flexibility.

Scope of mission can only be decided in the light of major environmental threats and opportunities, which may indicate the need for a broadening or narrowing of the current mission.

The output should be a statement that specifies what part of society the business will participate in and what the functional role of the business will be.

The next step is to specify the objectives which will be sought, and the constraints that will be imposed on the business, in pursuing the mission.

Strategy Formulation: Specification of Objectives and Constraints

Hofer & Schendel (1978) and Katz (1970) list a variety of objectives that the business strategist may consider.

These include growth, profits, resource utilization, efficiency, contributions to various stakeholders such as suppliers, customers, employees, stockholders and society at large, risk/reward tradeoffs and survival.

However, objectives are not unilaterally decided. The key interest group analysis will give indications of what objectives are going to be *demanded* by interest groups surrounding the firm. To the extent that such demands are going to be irrefutable, the strategist should include them as part of the objective set.

At minimum, three major sets of objectives should be included though conscious tradeoffs between them will have to be made. These are growth, profitability and competitive performance (such as market share). In other words, the strategist needs to decide how fast the business should grow, how profitably this growth will take place and how well the business should do in relation to competitors. The extent to which the strategist will be allowed to tradeoff between these objectives is a function of the constraints which will be imposed. These are discussed next.

Constraints are imposed from two sources: *First*, the firm may be subject to corporate constraints emanating from the objectives and key policy decisions of the corporate strategy; *second*, the key interest group analysis will indicate the constraints which may be imposed by powerful suppliers, customers, labor representatives, banks, regulatory bodies and so on.

To the extent that these constraints are non-negotiable, they must be accepted as valid constraints on strategic direction. Having identified the major constraints on strategy and decided on appropriate or acceptable objectives, the next need is the formulation of a strategy to achieve these objectives.

The first stage in strategy formulation is to recognize the option of dividing strategy into two components (MacMillan (1978)): An *offensive strategy*, which seeks to use strengths to take advantage of opportunities; a *defensive strategy*, which seeks to bolster weaknesses that may be reinforced by threats.

Strategy Formulation: Offensive Strategy

In developing the offensive strategy, *the strategic options* available to the firm and its competitors are reviewed.

Rothschild (1979), Hofer & Schendel (1978) identify a number of major offensive strategic options. These are identified in Table 2.

Depending on the specific opportunities in the industry, identified in the environmental analysis, and the status of the competition, identified in the competitive analysis, several of the options in Table 2 may be viable options for selection by *one or more* competitors in the industry.

Success of a strategy often depends largely on what choice of options are made by competitors. If several competitors select the same option as the basis on which they will compete in the future, the result is a "war of attrition" in which all competitors pour resources into matching the latest moves of the others.

So an attempt is made to determine the likelihood that one or more competitors will follow the viable options identified from the industry opportunities.

In trying to assess the likelihood of the competitors' moves, it is important to recognize that few competitors can select *all* options—after all they are subject to their own resource limitations. The problem is to determine whether they will select the same option as the firm and precipitate a war of attrition. The concepts of strategic anticipation discussed below can be of help in trying to determine whether the competitor will commit substantial resources in pursuit of the option.

Of the limited options that are least likely to attract serious competitive followers, those opportunities are sought where maximum usage of the firm's strengths may be deployed.

So the ideal is to find the *limited* number of opportunities where the firm can make maximum use of its various strengths where aggressive competitive response is unlikely, rather than spread its resources across a wide array of options where strong competitive reaction is probable.

Where this ideal situation is not found, the strategist may have to focus on a limited number of opportunities where maximum use is made of strengths, and aggressive competitive response can be contained.

To be avoided is the selection of too many options (Katz (1970)). This tends to dilute effectiveness and lead to mediocre performance across a broad front.

Thus the final offensive strategy selects a number of opportunities on which the firm's efforts and resources can be *focussed* where the probability of success is the greatest.

Unfortunately, it may not be possible for all resources and effort to be deployed to the offensive strategy—since defensive measures may be called for as well. This is addressed in the defensive component of strategy formulation.

Table 2.   Strategic Options: Offensive Strategies

Market segmentation	Whereby the competitor identifies and focusses on specific segments of the market
Product innovation	Whereby the competitor introduces new products as the major thrust of competitive direction
Service competition	Whereby the competitor enhances service as a major competitive weapon
Distribution competition	Whereby the securing of major distribution channels and superior delivery is sought
Promotion competition	Whereby the major emphasis is on promoting of product
Process innovation	Whereby the competitor reduces costs by introduction of the latest process technology
Logistics innovation	Reduction of costs of manufacturing, distribution, inventory
Price competition	Whereby pricing is used as the major competitive weapon
Market diversification	New Markets are sought, either geographically or market segments which were not previously served
Related & unrelated product diversification	New Products are sought for existing markets
Credit competition	Terms of payment, and assistance in funding of purchases by the customer, are used as a means of securing sales
Supply control competition	Securing control of critical supplies or controlling costs of supplies
Forward integration	Moving into activities down the chain
Back integration	Moving into activities up the chain
Conglomerate diversification	New products are brought to new managers

Strategy Formulation: Defensive Strategy

In formulating a *defensive* strategy, threats are reviewed with the object of identifying whether these threats are reinforced by a weakness of the firm. Where threats and weaknesses of the firm coincide, vulnerability of the firm is at its highest. Resources may have to be deployed to reduce this vulnerability.

In particular, if it can be anticipated that competitors will attack the business at these points of high vulnerability, resources may have to be deployed to contain such attacks and bolster these weaknesses.

Katz (1970) argues that resources deployed to defensive purposes such as these should be held to a minimum. Thus the strategist must trade off the limited resources of the business between offensive and defensive strategies.

In making the trade offs between the perhaps substantial resources required to implement of-

fensive and defensive strategies, it should be recognized that, to the extent that the firm "invests" in defensive strategies, it is largely reacting to moves by the environment. To the extent that it can afford to invest in offensive strategies that avoid direct confrontation, it is focussing resources in a way that gives it more control over its own destiny.

To the extent that it cannot find offensive strategic direction, particularly if the industry is highly unattractive, it may have to resort to purely *defensive* options.

Hofer & Schendel (1978) suggest several such options; listed in Table 3.

Once the appropriate offensive and defensive strategies have been decided, the reformulation of strategic variables becomes necessary.

These strategic variables should be reviewed in the light of the strategy selected to ensure consistency, in much the same way as for the original business analysis. In other words, a consistent set

Table 3.   Strategic Options: Defensive Strategies

Scope reduction	Divestiture of assets and reduction of costs to a level where small select segments can be served from an appropriately small asset and cost base
Merger	With some other competitor to pool market share and thus achieve economies of scale
Sale	To a company outside the industry wanting access to the market
Liquidation	Liquidating of the business altogether

of policies to guide product, market, channel, price, promotion, etc., decisions should be made to reinforce the direction to be taken for the future. Finally the entire strategy should be reviewed in light of the statement of mission, the impact on objectives and anticipated competitive responses.

If objectives cannot be met, reformulation of mission, objective or strategy may be necessary.

As far as competition is concerned, the strategic anticipation process may reveal responses which could also cause the business to reformulate strategy.

We turn now to the problem of anticipating competitive responses.

STRATEGIC ANTICIPATION

The guidelines for strategic anticipation will draw heavily on the work of two authors, Allison (1971) and Thompson (1967), who in turn have used many other authors' contributions in the development of their arguments. The topic is discussed more extensively in MacMillan (1978).

Allison (1971) discusses the ways in which complex strategic decisions are made from the perspective of three distinct but not mutually exclusive perspectives: rational actor, organizational process and bureaucratic politics.

Competitor as a Rational Actor

One way of anticipating strategic responses is to consider the competitor as a rational actor. We think of the way in which "Competitor A" would respond, as if the competitor were a single, purposive person with specific goals in mind.

The essence of using the rational actor perspective is to put ourselves in the position of the competitor facing our strategic move and to try to determine what the most rational counterresponses would be.

In order to be able to do this, we need to have as clear an idea as possible of the following:

What are the competitor's objectives? What goals are they emphasizing? What are the major policy commitments that the competitor has made as to products, markets, distribution channels, promotion methods, and pricing? Where is discretionary income being directed? How are key personnel rewarded?

So with some knowledge of the competitor's objectives, strategy, and resource deployments, it is possible to "put ourselves in the shoes" of the competitor and try to decide what responses the competitor could make when faced with a strategic move on our part.

In the next two approaches we try to determine what factors would influence the decisions it *would* choose.

Competitor as an Organization

The problems of coordinating a complex organization are substantial. This coordination problem results in the development of a large number of "bureaucratic" rules, procedures and policies under which the various managers must act.

The opponent must also *control* the activities of its managers to ensure that they carry out these tasks which they have been assigned. In order to cope with this problem, the competitor develops control systems that monitor and then reward managers according to how well the tasks have been performed.

The organizational process model recognizes

that the possible response of a competitor is influenced by these bureaucratic processes in many ways:

If the strategic move we make is something that the manager has never encountered before, it may not *have* a set of rules, policies, or procedures to counter this move. In many cases it may respond to the move by continuing as it has always done, or perhaps by countering the move in the nearest way it can find that "fits the rules."

Policies that act as the guidelines for decision making in the organization may be cumbersome to change, so there is a tendency for the organizations to persist in these policies.

In planning the activities of its divisions, the competitor must commit its resources. It is therefore disruptive if a particular manager makes sudden demands for new resources.

The specific perspective of one division may make them rather unsympathetic to problems encountered in another division and this can give rise to parochial conflicts and conflicts of jurisdiction as *each* division tries to "solve" the problem in terms of its perspective.

Therefore it is important to analyse the following:

What types of *major rules, procedures, policies and programs* are used by the competitor? These may influence the visibility of our move, increase the time it takes to recognize the move, and limit the responses they can generate. What *major control systems* does the competitor employ? How are departments evaluated? How often are they measured? At what level in the organization are decisions relevant to our move made? How is the competitor *organized?* What major departments does it have? Will the strategic move directly affect more than one department? Will it affect them in different ways? Are there likely to be conflicts between departments?

The better our knowledge of these factors, the better we can assess the competitor's likely responses to them.

Competitor as a Political Entity

The last model views the competitor as a political system in which powerful and influential interest groups, surrounding the organization or within it,

place demands on the organization for the purpose of achieving their own purposes.

Key interest groups perceive any response to the firm's strategy in terms of their interests. This has an influence on how the organization *can* react. Certain responses which look "rational" may not be tolerated by an interest group which sees its interests being harmed by that response. This applies at the level of specific decision makers as well. People within the organization will assess their responses to our move in terms of how they will be rewarded for the outcome and the risks associated with that outcome.

With this as a background, it is suggested that the competitor be analysed in a political context, much in the same way as the environmental mapping of the strategist's own organization.

Questions to be asked are: What major *interest groups* have a vested interest in the competitor's response? What issues are they raising? What positions are they taking? How powerful are these interest groups? This analysis should provide a sense of what constraints are imposed on the organization and also what responses will be prescribed unless the organization can convince the relevant interest groups to relax the constraints. What is the *discretion structure* in the organization? Who is responsible for the response decision? What discretion do they have? How does the organization "treat" unsuccessful use of discretion? A knowledge of these factors provides a sense of the riskiness of various responses to the competitors, and the likelihood that some responses will not be considered because the proposal may be too risky for the opposing organization in general or the opposing decision maker in particular.

The results of a political model perspective therefore give an indication of which responses are likely to be *acceptable* to the competitor and its interest groups. From this one is in a position to estimate the competitor's likely counter strategies. The insight provided by applying these three models allows us to develop some estimates of the expected counter responses. These are taken into account in refining the offensive and defensive strategies developed above.

At this stage the strategist should finally have: An *offensive strategy* geared to applying strengths to take advantage of opportunities: a *defensive strategy* to bolster weaknesses that are reinforced by threats; a *set of policy commitments* for the key strategic variables of that business, which are consistent with the strategy and the trends in the environment; an estimate of the *competitive counterresponses;* an assessment of the *key interest groups* who will have a vested interest in the results of our strategy, the issues that will arise and their positions on these issues.

This provides the input to the second major component of strategy—the strategic plan.

STRATEGIC PLAN

Since the development of strategic plans is beyond the scope of this [reading], comments are confined to a few key points:

Rothschild (1976), Katz (1970), Hofer & Schendel (1978) all point out the importance of ensuring that the strategy be adequately supported by appropriate resource deployments, cor-

rectly timed. Key decisions are necessary to determine action steps required for implementation, that the resources (staff, funds, equipment, etc.) to support these action steps are available, and that clear delegation of responsibility for the execution of these action steps has taken place.

MacMillan (1978) points out that it is often possible to get other interest groups to commit resources to assist the firm. Allies can be sought and secured. To the extent that such allies can support the defensive strategy, it preserves the firm's own resources for the offensive.

There is no question that the strategy will turn out differently from anticipated. Particularly where critical assumptions were made regarding environmental trends and competitive responses, it may be important to formulate contingency plans. The number of such contingency plans should be limited, and as Warren (1966) points out, clear trigger points for *when* the contingency plan needs to be launched should be identified.

As the strategic planning period unfolds it is necessary to monitor performance against plan

Figure 3. Cycle of Business Strategy Actions

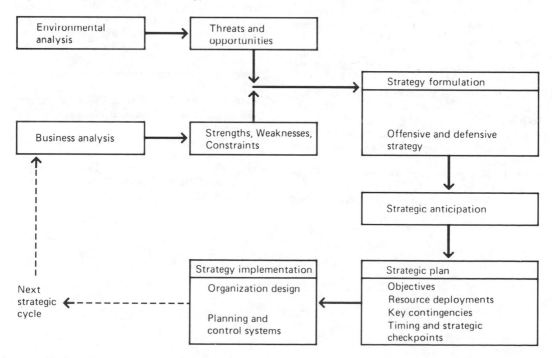

and feed the results back into the strategy formulation process for modification.

A more detailed discussion of organization design and planning and control systems to support the strategic plan are found elsewhere in the text. Without the appropriate strategic plan, organization design, and planning and control systems, the business strategy formulation effort is a paper exercise. The relationship between strategy formulation processes and strategy implementation processes are summarized in Figure 3.

BIBLIOGRAPHY

Allison, G. T. *Essence of Decision.* Boston: Little, Brown, 1971.

Andrews, K. *The Concept of Corporate Strategy.* Homewood, Ill.: Dow-Jones-Irwin, 1971.

Ansoff, H. I. *Corporate Strategy, An Analytic Approach to Business Policy for Growth and Expansion.* New York: McGraw-Hill, 1965.

Ansoff, H. I., R. C. Brandenburg, F. E. Portner, and R. Radosevich. *Acquisition Behavior of U.S. Manufacturing Firms: 1946–65.* Nashville: Vanderbilt University Press, 1971.

Grinyer, P. H., and D. Norburn. "Planning for Existing Markets: Perception of Executives and Financial Performance," *Journal of the Royal Statistical Society Series A,* 138: Part 1: 70–97, 1975.

Herold, D. M. "Long-Range Planning and Organizational Performance," *Academy of Management Journal,* 15:91–102. March 1972.

Hofer, C. W. "Towards a Contingency Theory of Business Strategy," *Academy of Management Journal,* December 1975.

Hofer, C. W., and D. E. Schendel. *Strategy Formulation: Analytical Concepts.* St. Paul, Minn.: West Publishing, 1978.

Katz, R. L. *Management of the Total Enterprise.* Englewood Cliffs: Prentice-Hall, 1970.

Kennedy, J. S. "Practice and Theory in Negotiations." In Webster, R. E.; "New Directions in Marketing" *Proceedings of the 48th National Conference: American Marketing Association.* Chicago: American Marketing Association, 1965.

Kudla, R. J. "The Effects of Strategic Planning on Common Stock Returns," *Academy of Management Journal:* Vol. 12, No. 1: March 1980.

MacMillan, I. C. *Strategy Formulation: Political Concepts.* St. Paul, Minn.: West Publishing, 1978.

Miller, D. "Toward a Contingency Theory of Business Strategy Formulation." *Proceedings of the National Meeting of the Academy of Management.* New Orleans: Academy of Management, August 1975.

Mintzberg, H., D. Raisinghani and A. Theoret. "The Structure of Unstructured Decision Processes." *Administrative Science Quarterly.* Vol. 21, No. 2, June 1976.

Newman, W. H. and J. P. Logan. *Strategy, Policy and Central Management.* Cincinnati: South Western Publishing, 1971.

Rothschild, W. E. *Putting It All Together.* New York: AMACOM, 1976.

Rothschild, W. E. *Strategic Alternatives.* New York: AMACOM, 1979.

Rue, L. W. and R. M. Fulmer. "Is Long Range Planning Profitable?" *Proceedings of the Business Policy and Planning Division of the Academy of Management,* Paper No. 8. Boston: Academy of Management, August 1973.

Salter, M. E., ed., W. A. Weinhold. *Diversification Through Acquisition.* New York: Free Press, 1979.

Steiner, George A. *"Pitfalls in Comprehensive Long Range Planning."* Oxford, Ohio: The Planning Executive Institute, 1972.

Thompson, J. D. *Organizations in Action.* New York: McGraw-Hill, 1967.

Thune, S. S. and R. J. House. "Where Long Range Planning Pays Off." *Business Horizons:* 13:81–87, August 1970.

Warren, E. K. *Long Range Planning.* Englewood Cliffs: Prentice-Hall, 1966.

Wrapp, H. E. "Good Managers Don't Make Policy Decisions." *Harvard Business Review.* Vol. 45, No. 5, Sept.–Oct. 1967.

Individual Behavior in Organizations

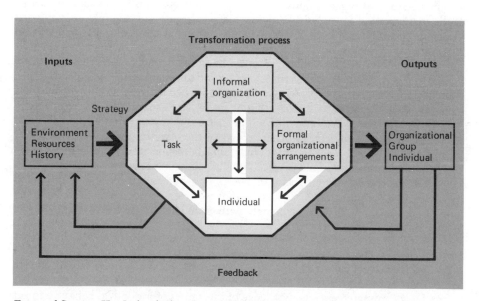

Focus of Section II—Individuals

INTRODUCTION

We have begun our work by thinking about the organization as a system. We started by looking at what managers do and the kinds of skills managers need to have to perform effectively in the different parts of their jobs. We then looked at one of the major tools—conceptual models—that managers use to diagnose problems and determine action steps. We looked at one specific model, a congruence model of organizational behavior, as an approach to thinking about organizations. Our initial focus in Section I was on the input and output sides of the model. In particular we considered issues of strategy (a critical input) and organizational effectiveness (the output). We now turn our attention to the core of the model, the transformation process. We will begin to look at the organization, the mechanism that takes inputs and transforms them into outputs. Using the congruence model, we will look at the basic elements of task, individuals, organizational arrangements, and informal organization in order to identify useful concepts, tools, and theories to help us understand the nature of the fits or congruence that might exist among those different elements.

We could start at one of many places in the models. We might begin by looking at organization design and its links to the components of strategy and task. Another approach, the one we will use here, is to begin with the simplest level of analysis. We will begin our discussion by focusing on the individual's component of the model. Later we will build on concepts of individual behavior to examine concepts of group functioning and total system design.

Why start with the individual? There are several reasons why it makes sense to begin the study of organizations from the perspective of the individual. First, this is the simplest level of analysis. When we move to groups, for example, we will need concepts of individual behavior along with additional concepts to explain group phenomena. A beginning focus on the individual allows us to start with the smallest set of needed concepts and tools. Second, the individual level is the least abstract. Virtually every person reading this book has at some point in their lives been a member of an organization. The questions of why people work as they do and how an individual responds to his or her job, peers, and supervisors are questions to which we can relate. We have all been in that position and experienced what it is like. Third, as we move on to other aspects of the organization, we will continue to come back to some key concepts of individual behavior. It is important to prepare a sound foundation of learning, since we will build upon it later.

What are the important issues or questions when we think about individual behavior in organizations? Our view is that we need to consider a few very key questions if we are to deal adequately with individual behavior patterns. These questions are:

1. Why do individuals in organizations behave as they do?
2. What factors influence individual behavior? Which of these factors can be used by managers?
3. How can managers use knowledge of the causes of individual behavior to get people to behave in a manner consistent with organizational effectiveness?

These questions are the basic concerns that will be addressed in this section. This introduction and the readings we have selected all address these three basic questions in one way or another.

INDIVIDUAL BEHAVIOR IN THE CONGRUENCE MODEL

The individual component is one of the four major organizational components identified in the congruence model (see page **73).** The model gives us a clue as to some of the factors that we have to consider if we are to answer the questions posed above. First, we need to identify in individuals those characteristics that are important for analysis. In particular we need to know what it is that makes one individual different from another and which of these differences are relevant to the purposes of organizational behavior. This step is necessary before we can look at the fit between the individual component and the other elements of the model.

The second concern is the task-individual fit. The question here is how to assess the fit between individuals and the inherent nature of the work to be done. We need to consider what demands the work makes (for skills, abilities, information, expertise, and so on) as well as what rewards the work inherently provides. We also need to consider both the knowledge and skill of individuals as well as the different things that individuals look for in their work. The question is one of congruence or fit between the demands and rewards of the work on the one hand, and the skills and desires of the individuals on the other.

The third concern is the individual–organizational arrangement fit. The question here is how to assess the fit between individuals and the various types of organizational arrangements designed to structure the work situation. Again we need to consider individual desires and capacities as well as demands of and rewards from the organization. We also need to consider whether the organizational arrangements create perceptions that are in line with organizational goals. In this case, the question is one of congruence between individual characteristics and the nature of the formal organizational design.

The final concern is the individual–informal organization fit. The question here is whether the informal organization, the unwritten set of arrangements that emerge over time, indeed meets individual needs as well as the issue of how the informal organization influences patterns of individual behavior.

CAUSES OF INDIVIDUAL BEHAVIOR—AN OVERVIEW

The congruence model, and in particular the place of the individual component in the model, suggests a general approach to thinking about the causes of individual behavior. We will discuss this approach here and then use it as a device for organizing the readings that follow this introduction.

A fundamental view of individual behavior is $B = f(P,E)$, or behavior is a function of factors in the individual and factors in the environment (Lewin, 1947). As Figure II-1 shows, to understand any individual's behavior, particularly in organizations, we need to consider both aspects of the individual as well as aspects of the environment in which the individual functions. If we looked just at the environment, we would not account for the fact that there are significant differences among individuals. Different people have different desires, different capacities, and may tend to view the same events or situations in different ways because of their past

Figure II-1.   Major Influences on Individual Behavior
in Organizations

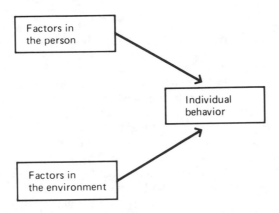

experiences. Yet if we were to think just about individual factors, then we would not account for the reality that individual behavior is influenced by factors in the world around them. When we move an individual from one environment to another, we frequently see significant shifts in behavior. We need to evaluate two factors—the person and the environment—and how they interact if we are to understand and explain individual behavior.

Using the simple formula just presented and working from the congruence model, let us examine in more detail the factors that cause behavior. What specific factors in the individual and in the environment should we keep in mind?

Figure II-2 provides a graphic representation of the key factors that influence individual behavior. Three factors in the individual seem particularly important. The first factor relates to the needs and preferences of individuals when they enter organizations. Each individual may have different desires as a result of his or her background, experiences, and development. Thus different people look for different things at work and are therefore likely to be motivated by different things at different times. A second factor concerns the perceptions that people develop about the environment (the organization around them), and in particular, their expectations about the consequences of a good or bad performance. An important influence on behavior is people's perceptions of the world and the rewards and punishments they associate with different kinds of behavior. Finally, behavior is influenced by the relation of a person's knowledge and skills to the job he or she holds. These three factors in the individual are therefore all important determinants of behavior.

Three determinants of behavior are associated with the environment. (Note that these three correspond roughly to the three other components of the congruence model.) The first factor is the inherent nature of the work to be done. The work may meet different needs and preferences, may be perceived in different ways, and may demand the use of different knowledge and skills. In any case, it is an influence on performance.

A second factor is the nature of the formal organization. An organization elicits certain behaviors through the design of jobs, the reward systems, the methods of managing, the goals set, and so forth. The organization can also influence behavior by providing training, technical assistance, and the like, thus increasing knowledge and skills in individuals.

Figure II-2. Key Factors Influencing Individual Behavior

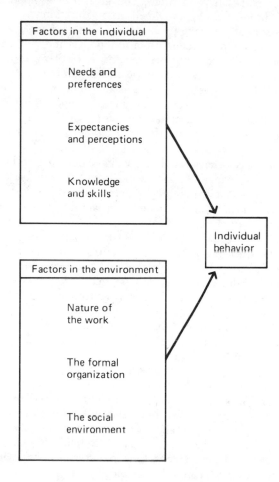

The third factor is the social environment in which the individual functions (largely a manifestation of the nature of the informal organization). The social environment provides for peoples' needs, creates perceptions, and also makes demands on and contributes to an individual's knowledge and skills.

Thus all three factors in the environment—the nature of the work, the formal organization, and the social environment—are potential influences on the patterns of behavior that individuals exhibit in organizations.

THE READINGS IN SECTION II

The readings in this section have been arranged to approximate the sequence of the different factors as they are outlined in Figure II-2. We begin by considering ways to think about individual needs and preferences and how they affect patterns of behavior. Reading 6, by Lawler, makes up all of Part II.A. He discusses different approaches to thinking about needs. He describes the different types of needs researchers and theorists have identified and gives a basic approach to thinking about differences in behavior by individuals in organizations.

The next three readings make up Part II.B. These readings deal with different aspects of perceptions and expectancies of individuals and how these perceptions directly affect patterns of behavior. In Reading 7, Nadler and Lawler describe a theory of motivation and behavior based on the notion that perceptions of performance-reward relationships lead to patterns of behavior. This approach, called expectancy theory, is presented in detail and the implications of the model for management are discussed. Lawler's Reading 8 is on satisfaction and behavior. Lawler continues the expectancy framework and discusses the concept of job satisfaction and how it relates to patterns of behavior. Lawler believes that satisfaction is primarily a consequence of behavior and its associated outcomes rather than a primary cause of behavior. In Reading 9, Staw works from the same basic perspective but puts more emphasis on the importance of perception and how it is the world that people perceive rather than any real or objective world that frequently explains how people behave in organizations.

The third set of readings, Part II.C, deals with matching people, and their knowledge and skills, to appropriate jobs. In Reading 10, Schein discusses different organizational needs for selecting, placing, and developing people as well as the needs of individuals at different stages of their careers. He suggests that organizations need to put into effect some processes that effectively match those individual and organizational needs, or, in terms of the congruence model, to assure a good fit between the individual and the organization. In Reading 11 Van Maanen deals with the issue of how individuals are brought into organizations and prepared to function effectively as organization members.

The Schein and Van Maanen readings deal with questions of individual knowledge and skills, but they also lead into a focus on the environment as a factor influencing individual behavior. The environment is considered explicitly in the final set of readings, Part II.D. In their reading on work design, Hackman and Oldham present a way of thinking about the fit between individuals and tasks. They discuss how the nature of the work influences individual behavior and also how changes in organizational arrangements (and in particular changes in how individual and group jobs are designed) can influence motivation and behavior. Another critical aspect of organizational arrangements is the nature of rewards provided for performance. Hamner devotes Reading 13 to some key issues in developing rewards.

The final issue, the influencing role of the social environment, constitutes a new major area of discussion. A separate section (Section III) is devoted to that topic area.

In summary, the section focuses on the behavior of individuals by looking at the various factors in the individual and in the environment that influence patterns of behavior in organizations. Together, the readings provide a set of models or tools to assess the fit between individuals and the other elements in the organizational system.

REFERENCE

Lewin, K. Frontiers in group dynamics. *Human Relations*, 1947, *1*, 5–41.

II.A
Individual Needs and Behavior

6
Drives,
needs, and outcomes

Edward E. Lawler III

For centuries, psychologists and philosophers have tried to explain why some objects or outcomes seem to be desired by people while others are not. The concepts of instinct, drive, intrinsic motives, functional autonomy, derived motives, and many others have been used to explain this phenomenon. This [reading] will review many of these concepts and present an integrated view of present knowledge about why certain outcomes are desirable or attractive to people.

An adequate explanation of why certain outcomes are desirable must deal with three separate but interrelated questions.

1. What is it about the nature of individuals that causes outcomes to become desirable to them?
2. What general classes or groups of outcomes do people find desirable or undesirable?
3. What factors influence the desirability of outcomes; that is, how does the desirability

Source: From *Motivation in Work Organizations* by E. E. Lawler, III. Chapter 2, pp. 11–40. Copyright © 1973 by Wadsworth Publishing Company, Inc. Reprinted by permission of Brooks/Cole Publishing Company, Monterey, Cal. 93940.

of outcomes change over time and why do individuals differ in the importance they attach to various outcomes?

Unless the second and third questions are answered, it is impossible to predict the kind of behavior choices a person will make. Although the answer to the first question is not needed in order to predict behavior, most theorists have found that answering it is a prerequisite to answering questions two and three. That is, these theorists have found it necessary to make assumptions about what causes outcomes to be important in the first place in order to make statements about the kinds of outcomes people value and the things that are likely to influence the attractiveness of outcomes.

Our first question has typically been answered by a set of assumptions about man's internal state. For example, some theorists have assumed that man has homeostatic drives, others have talked of instincts, while still others have talked of learned drives. The second question has been answered by the development of a number of need or outcome classification systems. Some of these systems assume only two classes of needs while others assume more than 20. The third question has been answered in many different ways. Maslow (1943), for example, has theorized that needs are arrayed in a hierarchy such that the lower-level needs have to be satisfied before the higher-level needs come into play. Other psychologists have stressed that learned associations can cause changes in the attractiveness of outcomes.

Not every theory that has dealt with the attractiveness of outcomes has attempted to answer all of these questions. In fact, some theories have dealt essentially with only one of the questions. For example, in his discussion of the competence motive, White (1959) is concerned with establishing the existence of that motive. He does not present a general classification of motives, nor does he make statements about what influences the importance of other motives. As we discuss the various theories dealing with the attractiveness of outcomes, it is important to note which of the three questions are answered and which are ignored.

Let us now turn to a consideration of some of the more prominent theories.

HISTORICAL APPROACHES

Prior to the 1940s three theoretical approaches to explaining why outcomes are valued dominated the thinking in psychology. The first two, instinct theory and hedonism, do not make scientifically testable predictions of what outcomes people will seek. The third, drive theory, represents an attempt to develop a theory that does make testable predictions.

Instinct Theory

Charles Darwin was the first to call the attention of the scientific world to the possibility that much of human and animal behavior may be determined by instincts. He thought that many "intelligent" actions were inherited, and he provided a number of examples from his research on animals to support this view. William James, Sigmund Freud, and William McDougall developed the instinct doctrine as an important concept in their psychological theories. Some theorists thought of instincts as mechanical and automatic rather than as conscious motivators of behavior, but McDougall, who developed the most exhaustive taxonomy of instincts, thought of them as purposive, inherited, goal-seeking tendencies.

McDougall (1908) wrote that "we may then define an instinct as an inherited or innate psycho-physical disposition that determines the possessor to perceive and pay attention to objects of a certain class, to experience an emotional excitement of a particular quality on perceiving such an object, and to act in regard to it in a particular manner, or at least to experience an impulse to such action" (p. 39). Thus, the "pugnacity instinct" was an instinct that manifested itself in fighting when the organism was exposed to appropriate stimuli. At first McDougall thought he could account for all behavior in terms of about a dozen instincts. However, as time progressed he added more and more instincts to his list so that by 1932 his list included 19 instincts. Other psychologists added more, so that by the 1920s the list of instincts totaled nearly 6000, including the "instinct to avoid eating apples in one's own orchard" (Murray, 1964, p. 6).

In a sense, instinct theory died of its own weight. As more and more instincts were stated, psychologists began to question the explanatory usefulness of the approach. To say that an animal fights because of the instinct of pugnacity or that an individual takes a job because he has an instinct to work is merely to give a redundant description of the observed behavior that adds nothing to our understanding of why the behavior took place. The tendency of some psychologists to add a new instinct to explain each new behavior that was observed also weakened the theory. As instinct theory developed, it seemed to provide unsatisfactory answers to all of our questions. It said that heredity determined which goals or outcomes organisms would seek (which was incomplete and misleading) and that people's goals consisted of the objects they sought (a circular definition). Thus, instinct theory did not allow for the prediction of which outcomes would be sought; it allowed only for the *post hoc* explanation of why certain goals were sought. Instinct theory also failed to provide a useful classification of the type of outcomes people sought. The original list of instincts was too short and the later ones were so long that they proved useless.

Hedonism

The origins of most contemporary conceptions of motivation can be traced to the principle of hedonism (Atkinson, 1964). In turn, hedonism can be traced to the original writings of the English utilitarians. The central assumption is that behavior is directed toward outcomes that provide pleasure and away from those that produce pain. In every situation people strive to obtain those goals or outcomes that provide the most pleasure. Despite its simplicity and popularity, the principle of hedonism fails to answer any of our three questions adequately. Nothing is said about why certain things give pleasure while others don't. There is no specification of the types of outcomes that are pleasurable or painful or even how these outcomes can be determined in advance for a particular individual. Any kind of behavior can be explained after the fact by postulating that particular outcomes were sources of either pain or pleasure. Finally, nothing is said about how the attractiveness of outcomes may be modified by experience or environmental circumstances. In short, the hedonistic assumption has no real empirical content leading to predictions of behavior and, thus, it is untestable.

Despite the fact that hedonism can be described as circular and lacking in content, its influence on psychology has been extensive. As one psychologist stated, "the study of motivation by psychologists has largely been directed toward filling in the missing empirical content in hedonism" (Vroom, 1964, p. 10). It is certainly true that almost all modern theories assume that people direct their behavior toward outcomes that they find pleasurable and away from those that they find unattractive. However, most modern theories do attempt to overcome the circularity of hedonism. They specify in advance how attractive specific outcomes will be to particular individuals and they develop models that predict when the attractiveness of outcomes will change.

Drive Theory

Drive theory developed partially as a reaction to instinct theory and hedonism. It is in the tradition of hedonism, but it is more closely tied to empirical events and therefore more testable. In 1918, R. S. Woodworth published a little book entitled *Dynamic Psychology* in which he advanced the view that psychologists should study what induces people to behave in particular ways. He referred to this inducement as drive, and the concept of drive soon replaced the concept of instinct in the psychologist's glossary of important terms. Later, the term "drive" took on a very precise meaning in the writings of C. L. Hull (1943). He assumed that all behavior is motivated by either primary or secondary drives. According to Hull, the primary drives were biologically based; they represented states of homeostatic imbalance. Hull's position was that:

> The major primary needs or drives are so ubiquitous that they require little more than to be mentioned. They include the need for foods of various sorts (hunger), the need for water (thirst), the need for air, the need to avoid tissue injury (pain), the need to maintain an optimal temperature, the need to defecate, the need to micturate, the need for rest (after protracted exertion), the need for sleep (after protracted wakefulness), and the need for activity (after protracted inaction). The drives concerned with the maintenance of the species are those which lead to sexual intercourse and the need represented by nest building and care of the young [pp. 59–60].

In Hull's theory, outcomes become rewards when they are able to reduce primary drives and thereby reduce homeostatic imbalance and the tension that occurs when organisms are in a state of ecological deprivation. Thus, food is a reward to a hungry person and water is a reward to a thirsty person. Hull also stressed that drive strength can be increased by deprivation and reduced as needs become satisfied. Thus, the hungrier a person gets, the more he desires food; but as he eats food, he becomes less hungry and his desire diminishes. Although Hull assumed that all rewards and drives are ultimately based on the reduction of primary drives, he recognized that certain secondary drives and rewards could develop—or be "learned"—if in the past they were associated with food or other primary rewards. Thus, money is a secondary reward because it is often associated with food and other primary rewards. Social approval becomes a reward for children who are praised for eating well, or dressing themselves, and so on. According to Hull's view, most of the rewards used by work organizations would be considered secondary rewards.

Hull's theory represents a significant advance over the previous theories of motivation. It gives a clear-cut answer to the question of what objects or outcomes have value—that is, objects or outcomes that either reduce primary, biologically based drives or have been related to outcomes that do. It also provides a classification of drives that is still commonly used (it divides them into primary and secondary drives, and it specifies what the primary drives are). Finally, it says that deprivation increases drive strength, whereas obtaining the desired outcomes reduces drive strength. Thus, Hull's theory has answers to all three of our questions. But the real significance of Hull's theory rests in the fact that it is empirically testable. Since it specifies in detail the relationship between such measurable things as deprivation, drive, and learning, the theory can be tested, and it has spawned a large number of research studies.

At this point it is safe to say that these studies have found Hull's theory to be inadequate in a number of important respects. The most important shortcomings have to do with the ability of the theory to explain motivation that is not based on primary drives. Hull's basic point about organisms' possessing certain primary drives that become stronger with deprivation and weaker with satisfaction still seems valid. What does not seem valid is his argument that all secondary motives are learned on the basis of primary physiological or homeostatic drives.

There is no solid evidence that drives can be learned on the basis of their association with positive drives such as hunger and thirst (Cravens and Renner, 1970). There is evidence that organisms will work for rewards that have been associated with the reduction of a primary drive if the primary drive is present. However, when the primary drive is not present, there seems to be no

"acquired" drive to obtain the reward. For example, in the classic experiments of Wolfe (1936) and Cowles (1937), chimpanzees learned to associate tokens with the acquisition of food. Initially, the chimps learned to operate an apparatus that required lifting a weight to obtain grapes. They continued to operate it when the only visible reward was a token that had been associated with the grapes. However, they didn't seem to develop an acquired need for tokens, since they were willing to work to obtain the tokens only as long as they were hungry and the tokens led to something they desired—that is, food. Hence, it is difficult to see how Hull's explanation can help us understand why workers continue to work for more money even when their basic needs are satisfied.

More damaging to Hull's view than the evidence on the failure of animals to acquire learned drives is the great amount of evidence indicating that people and animals are attracted to many outcomes that do not seem to be directly related to primary needs. Rats will learn mazes in order to explore novel environments, monkeys will solve puzzles even though they receive no extrinsic rewards, and people will work simply in order to develop their skills and abilities and to increase their competence. These and many other phenomena cannot be explained easily by drive theory.

CONTEMPORARY APPROACHES

Recently, many psychologists have rejected the emphasis of drive theory on primary drives and have argued that people have many needs. This argument has come particularly from those psychologists who are interested in studying human behavior. As we shall see, they have proposed a number of needs that do not seem to be directly related to homeostatic imbalance, organism survival, or species survival. This recent work on motivation has produced two somewhat different approaches.

Researchers in one group have focused on establishing the existence of one or two human motives that they consider to be particularly important. Thus, McClelland has focused on the achievement motive and White has focused on the competence motive. They have not tried to develop complex need, or motive, classification systems. In other words, they have not tried to answer our second question. They have contented themselves with trying to understand why one set or type of outcomes is attractive to people. Other researchers have tried to develop need, or motive, classification systems in an attempt to predict which kinds of outcomes will be attractive to people. Murray's (1938) list of needs and Maslow's (1943) statement of a need hierarchy are examples of this approach. But before we consider these classification systems, we need to look at some of the needs that have been proposed as necessary additions to the primary drives observed by Hull.

The Affiliation Motive

A number of researchers have presented evidence to show that an affiliation motive exists. They have shown that social interaction is attractive to people and that it is particularly likely to occur under certain conditions. For example, Schachter (1959) has shown that people seek the companionship of others when they are anxious and confused about their motives. In Schachter's work, college students faced with the prospect of being shocked were given the opportunity to be with another person. The subjects under such anxiety were more likely to accept invitations to be with others than were subjects who were not under such anxiety. This result occurred even when the subjects were not permitted to talk to the person they were to be with. Other research suggests that people are likely to seek social interaction at times when they are doubting their self-esteem.

Harlow (1958) has presented some interesting evidence suggesting that the social motive may be innate. As part of his work with monkeys he raised some infant monkeys, providing them with two surrogate mothers in place of their natural mothers. One surrogate mother consisted of a cylinder of wire mesh with an opening in the center of the "breast" for a bottle. The other was similarly shaped but was covered with cotton terry cloth. In the experiment, baby monkeys were placed in cages containing the two "mothers." Half were fed from the cloth mother, the other half from the wire mother. According to drive theory, the monkeys who were fed by the wire mother should have become attached to the wire mother because it provided the drive reduction—that is, the milk. However, it did not work out that way. The monkeys who were fed on the wire mother spent most of their time clinging to the cloth mother. Thus, it appears that monkeys develop their attachment to their mothers based on contact comfort rather than on primary-drive reduction.

However, the important point for us about the research on the need for social contact is not whether this need is innate or acquired but that it exists in most adult human beings. It clearly is an important motivation—one that has a significant impact on behavior in organizations. Many organizations have discovered—to their sorrow—that jobs that do not provide opportunities for social contact have higher turnover and absenteeism rates because employees simply cannot stand the isolation. Frequently, unnecessary social isolation results from mechanical and architectural designs that do not consider employees' needs for social relationships.

Need for Equity

People want to be treated fairly. They observe what happens to other people and if they receive either "too much" or "too little" in comparison to other people it makes them uncomfortable. For example, one study showed that dissatisfaction with promotion was highest in Army units where promotion rates were high. Why? Because the individuals who weren't promoted in these units felt unfairly treated. Adams (1963, 1965) has developed a theory that makes a number of interesting predictions about the effects of wage inequity on work output, work quality, and attitudes toward work. Although this theory is a general theory of social inequity, it has been tested largely with respect to the effects of wage inequity, and it has some interesting things to say about how equity may affect the attractiveness of rewards. Its predictions seem to be particularly relevant to understanding the effects of offering various sizes of pay increases and the effects of paying different wage rate.

Adams (1965) defines inequity as follows:

> Inequity exists for Person when he perceives that the ratio of his outcomes to inputs and the ratio of Other's outcomes to Other's inputs are unequal. This may happen either (a) when he and Other are in a direct exchange relationship or (b) when both are in an exchange relationship with a third party, and Person compares himself to Other [p. 280].

Outcomes in the job situation include pay, fringe benefits, status, the intrinsic interest of the job, and so on. Inputs include how hard the person works, his education level, his general qualifications for the job, and so on. It must be remembered that what determines the equity of a particular input-outcome balance is the individual's perception of what he is giving and receiving; this cognition may or may not correspond to an observer's perception or to reality.

Equity theory states that the presence of inequity will motivate an individual to reduce inequity and that the strength of the motivation to reduce inequity varies directly with the perceived magnitude of the imbalance experienced between inputs and outcomes. Feelings of inequity can be produced in a variety of ways and in a variety of situations. Adams has studied inequity produced by overpayment. His research suggests that overpayment is less attractive to employees than equitable payment is. There is evidence, for example, that when a person is paid on a piece rate and feels overpaid, he will reduce his productivity in order to reduce the amount of pay he receives. The important thing for this discussion about the research on equity theory is that people tend to seek equity in their work activities, which can affect their job behavior.

Activity and Exploration

Too little stimulation is very uncomfortable for humans. In one study, college students were employed at $20 a day to stay in a low stimulation environment (Bexton, Heron, & Scott, 1954). They were asked to remain for as many days as they could, lying on a cot in a lighted, partially sound-deadened room. They wore translucent goggles, gloves, and cardboard cuffs that minimized tactile stimulation. An air conditioner provided a noise that blocked out other sounds, and the students rested their heads on a U-shaped pillow. After a certain period—usually filled with sleeping—the subjects found this situation impossible to tolerate and asked to leave the experiment. Rarely did a subject endure it for as long as 2 days despite the fact that the pay was relatively high. Other studies have reported similar results, stressing that under these conditions people seem to develop a hunger for stimulation and action leading to such responses as touching the fingers together and twitching the muscles.

Research by Scott (1969) has shown that the results are very similar when people are given repetitive tasks to perform. They develop a negative attitude toward the task, and, as time goes on, they take more breaks and try in many ways to vary their behavior. As we shall see, this finding has direct implications for the design of jobs in organizations.

Other studies have shown that both people and animals seek out opportunities to experience novel situations. Butler (1953) has shown that monkeys will learn to push open a window for no reward other than being able to see what is going on in a room, and they will keep doing it. Butler has also shown that the strength of the drive for novel stimulation can be increased by deprivation. An experiment by Smock and Holt (1962) has shown that if children are given a chance to control what they see on a television screen, they will look at objects that offer complex stimuli rather than unconflicting, simple stimuli.

Many studies of rats have shown that they will learn certain behaviors in order to experience novel stimuli. In one experiment, rats preferred a goal box that contained objects to an empty goal box. Miles (1958) found that kittens would learn things when the reward was simply the opportunity to explore a room. There is much evidence that humans and animals will try to solve puzzles simply because of the stimulation provided by working on them. Harlow (1953) has shown that monkeys will persist in solving puzzles for many days. One monkey, who was presented with a square peg and a round hole, persisted for months in trying to get the two to fit together. (The monkey finally died of perforated ulcers.)

Several theorists have suggested that the results of both the stimulus-deprivation studies and the studies of novel-stimulus environments can be explained by considering how novelty affects stimulus attractiveness (Berlyne, 1967). According to activation theory, people become used to a certain level and pattern of stimulation from the environment. For some people this adaptation level may be a relatively low level of stimulation; for others it may be a rather high level. Regardless of where a person's level of adaptation is, however, psychologists hypothesize that deviation from it will have a strong impact on the person. Slight deviations will be experienced as pleasurable and rewarding while large deviations will be experienced as noxious and dissatisfying. Figure 1 illustrates this point graphically. According to this approach, the subjects in the stimulus-deprivation experiment were uncomfortable because the situation fell too far below the adaptation level. The animals who wanted to explore new things were attracted to them because these new things represented stimulus situations that were somewhat above their adaptation levels. Presumably if the stimulus situations had been too far above their adaptation levels, the animals would have avoided them, and indeed there is evidence that both animals and people fear situations that are very unfamiliar to them.

One of the problems with activation theory is that it can be very difficult to measure in advance what a person's adaptation level is. Still, the theory and its related research provide some interesting evidence to support the point that not all drives or needs are either primary or learned on the basis of primary drives. It is hard to see how people's reactions to different levels of stimulation can be explained by reference to a drive that has been learned on the basis of a primary drive.

Achievement

The achievement motive has been extensively studied by D. C. McClelland. It is defined by McClelland (1951, 1961) as a desire to perform in terms of a standard of excellence or as a desire to be successful in competitive situations. McClelland stresses that achievement motivation is present in most people but that the amount people have depends on a number of things, including how they were treated during childhood. One study has shown that high-need-achievement people tend to come from families where high demands were made for independence and performance at an early age. Their mothers evaluated their accomplishments favorably and rewarded them liberally.

McClelland meaures the strength of people's achievement motive by scoring their responses to a series of pictures. The pictures are shown to individuals who are asked to write a five-minute story about what is going on in the picture. The stories are scored on the basis of how frequently achievement-oriented themes are mentioned (for example, "He will try his best to succeed"). The following is an example of a story showing a strong achievement theme. It was written in response to a picture showing a young boy in the foreground and a hazy representation of an operation in the background.

> A boy is dreaming of being a doctor. He can see himself in the future. He is hoping that he can make the grade. It is more or less a fantasy. The boy has seen many pictures of doctors in books, and it has inspired him. *He will try his best* and hopes to become the best doctor in the country. He can see himself as a very important doctor. He is performing a very dangerous operation. He can see himself victorious and is proud of it. He gets world renown for it. He will become the *best doctor in the U.S.* He will be an

Figure 1. The Butterfly Curve

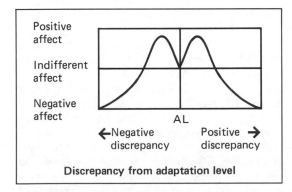

From Haber, R. N. Discrepancy from adaptation level as a source of affect. *Journal of Experimental Psychology*, 1958, **56**, 370–375. Copyright 1958 by the American Psychological Association. Reprinted by permission.

honest man, too. His name will go down in medical history as one of the *greatest men* [Atkinson, 1958, p. 193].

McClelland's research has shown that under certain conditions achievement motivation can be an important motivator of good performance in work organizations. When achievement motivation is operating, good job performance becomes very attractive to people; as a result, the motivation to perform well is higher. Achievement motivation typically does not operate when people are performing routine or boring tasks where no competition is involved. However, when challenge and competition are involved, achievement motivation can stimulate good performance. A study by French (1955) clearly illustrates this point. In French's study, Officer Candidate School cadets performed a simple task under three different sets of instructions. Under the "relaxed" instructions the subjects were told that the experimenter was merely interested in determining what kinds of scores people make on the test. The "task-motivated" instructions said that the task was a measure of people's ability to deal rapidly with new materials. The "extrinsically motivated" instructions said that the best performers could leave while the others had to continue performing. Performance was highest under the "task-motivated" instructions and lowest under the "relaxed" instructions. Subjects with high need for achievement performed better on the "task-motivated" instructions but not under the two other kinds of instructions.

Other studies also support the view that people can be motivated simply by a drive to achieve. For example, Alper (1946) gave two groups of subjects a list of nonsense syllables to learn. Only one group was told it was an intelligence test. A test given 24 hours later showed that the "intelligence test" group remembered more of what they had learned. McClelland (1961) showed that successful people in competitive occupations tend to be universally high in achievement motivation. For example, he showed that successful managers from countries such as the United States, Italy, and India tend to be high in achievement motivation.

Overall, the research on achievement motivation suggests that such motivation is most likely to be present when moderately challenging tasks have to be performed (where about a 50–50 chance of success exists), in competitive situations, in situations where performance is perceived to depend upon some important or valued skill, and in situations where performance feedback is given. The research also suggests that people with a high need for achievement tend to seek out situations in which they can achieve, and they tend to find successful performance attractive once they are in these situations. These points have important implications for the design of jobs in organizations and for the kinds of people that are attracted to jobs in different types of work situations.

Judging from the research cited earlier on the effects of child rearing on the strength of need for achievement, it seems certain that achievement motivation is a partly learned drive. McClelland in fact argues that it is differentially present in certain cultures precisely because child-rearing practices differ. However, even though achievement motivation is a learned drive, it is hard to see how it could develop because of the primary drives. There may be some relationship here, since success often helps people to obtain primary rewards, such as food; but it is hard to see how the primary drive approach can explain the fact that early independence training leads to a strong need for achievement. Thus, even though achievement is a learned drive, it seems that it is only partially learned on the basis of primary drives.

Competence

Robert W. White (1959) has argued for the existence of a competence motive. He uses competence to refer to an organism's capacity to interact effectively with its environment. In organisms capable of little learning, competence is considered to be innate; however, competence in man—that is, his fitness to interact with the environment—is slowly attained through prolonged feats of learning. The human learning that is needed to gain competence is characterized by high persistence and a strong goal orientation. Because of this dedication to learning, White argues that it is necessary to treat competence as having a motivation aspect that is separate from motivation derived from primary drives or instincts. He presents considerable evidence of organisms trying to cope with their environment seemingly for no other reason than that they want to master it. As White notes, there are repeated references in psychological literature

> . . . to the familiar series of learned skills which starts with sucking, grasping, and visual exploration and continues with crawling and walking, acts of focal attention and perception, memory, language and thinking, anticipation, the exploring of novel places and objects, effecting stimulus changes in the environment, manipulating and exploiting the surroundings, and achieving higher levels of motor and mental coordination. . . . Collectively they are sometimes referred to as mechanisms . . . but on the whole we are not accustomed to cast a single name over the diverse feats whereby we learn to deal with the environment. . . . I now propose that we gather the various kinds of behavior just mentioned, all of which had to do with effective interaction with the environment, under the general heading of competence . . . it is necessary to make competence a motivational concept; there is a competence motivation [1959, pp. 317–318].

White argues that competence motivation is aroused when people are faced with somewhat new situations and wanes when a situation has been explored and mastered to the point at which it no longer presents a challenge.

There is an obvious similarity between White's view of when competence motivation is aroused and the activation theorists' view of how stimulus novelty affects motivation. Both argue for high motivation when somewhat novel situations are encountered. White's theory is also very closely related to the theory of achievement motivation, since both talk of man's need to perform adequately. In fact, White says that achievement may be one outcome of competence motivation. White's theory has some interesting implications for the design of jobs in organizations. It suggests that if presented with the right task people can be motivated to perform effectively without the use of extrinsic rewards such as pay and promotion. However, once the task is mastered, competence motivation will disappear. It is also

interesting to note that White, like other recent theorists, argues that the competence motive is not based on any primary drive. Although he does not say exactly where it comes from, he does imply that man's desire to be competent is innate.

Self-Actualization

In the last thirty years a number of psychologists have introduced concepts into their theories that have to do with people's need to grow and develop. Table 1 lists some of these theorists and their concepts. The work of Maslow has had by far the greatest impact on the thinking concerned with motivation in organizations. Maslow uses the term "self-actualization" to describe the need people have to grow and develop. According to him, it is the "desire for self-fulfillment, namely . . . the tendency [for a person] to become actualized in what he is potentially . . . the desire to become more and more of what one is, to become everything that one is capable of becoming . . ." (1954, pp. 91–92). Maslow stresses that not all people function on the self-actualization level. He then goes on to describe the characteristics of people who are motivated by self-actualization. According to him, much of the self-actualizing person's behavior is motivated solely by the sheer enjoyment he obtains from using and developing his capacities. He does not necessarily behave in accordance with extrinsic goals or rewards. For him, the goal is simply to behave in a certain way or experience a certain feeling. Maslow makes the point like this:

> . . . we must construct a profoundly different psychology of motivation for self-actualizing people, e.g., expression motivation or growth motivation, rather than deficiency motivation. Perhaps it will be useful to make a distinction between living and *preparing* to live. Perhaps the concept of motivation should apply *only* to non-self-actualizers. Our subjects no longer strive in the ordinary sense, but rather develop. They attempt to grow to perfection and to develop more and more fully in their own style. The motivation of ordinary men is a striving for the basic need gratifications that they lack. But self-actualizing people in fact lack none of these gratifications; and yet they have impulses. They

Table 1.   List of Theorists Classified as Emphasizing Self-actualization, and the Term Each Uses

---

Kurt Goldstein (1939): Self-actualization

Erich Fromm (1941): The productive orientation

Prescott Lecky (1945): The unified personality; self-consistency

Donald Snygg and Arthur Combs (1949): The preservation and enhancement of the phenomenal self

Karen Horney (1950): The real self and its realization

David Riesman (1950): The autonomous person

Carl Rogers (1951): Actualization, maintenance, and enhancement of the experiencing organism

Rollo May (1953): Existential being

Abraham Maslow (1954): Self-actualization

Gordon W. Allport (1955): Creative becoming

Adapted from C. N. Cofer and M. H. Appley, *Motivation: Theory and Research.* Copyright © 1964 by John Wiley & Sons, Inc. Reprinted by permission.

work, they try, and they are ambitious, even though in an unusual sense. For them motivation is just character growth, character expression, maturation, and development; in a word self-actualization [p. 211].[1]

Thus, like White and others, Maslow is careful to say that all motivation is not tied to the primary drives. Maslow also stresses that people will work to obtain outcomes that are intrinsic, such as feelings of growth. He completely rejects the view that valued outcomes have to be related to such extrinsic rewards as food and water. Maslow probably goes further than any of the other theorists we have reviewed in stressing the differences between motivation based on primary drives and motivation that is independent of primary drives. He says that, unlike motivation based on primary drives, motivation based on growth needs does not decrease as the needs become satisfied. Quite to the contrary, Maslow argues that as people experience growth and self-actualization they simply want more. In his view, obtaining growth creates a desire for more growth, whereas obtaining food decreases one's desire for food.

Maslow argues that the concept of self-actualization can explain a significant amount of the motivation in organizations. He states that, particularly at the managerial level, many people are motivated by a desire to self-actualize. There is

a considerable amount of evidence to support this point. In one study, managers rated the need for self-actualization as their most important need (Porter, 1964). In addition, most large organizations abound with training and development programs designed to help people develop their skills and abilities. Sometimes people do enter these programs in the hope of obtaining a raise or promotion, but on other occasions they do it only because it contributes to their self-development. There is also evidence of people seeking more challenging jobs for no other reason than to develop themselves.

An interesting contrast to Maslow's work on self-actualization is provided by the work of existential psychologists such as Allport (1955) and Rogers (1961). They too talk of people being motivated by desires that are not related to obtaining rewards such as money and status. However, they give less emphasis to the development of skills and abilities and the achievement of goals than does Maslow, and they give more emphasis to the new experiences as a way of learning about one's self. Rogers, for example, talks of people being motivated "to be that self which one truly is." He emphasizes self-discovery and the importance of being open to experience. Perhaps because they don't emphasize skill development and accomplishments as much as Maslow, the existential psychologists have not had much impact on the research of psychologists interested in work organizations. This is unfortunate, and it is important to remember that at times people may be motivated by nothing more than self-discovery and a desire to experience.

Need-Classification Theories

Numerous lists and classifications of needs have been presented by psychologists. One of the most important is Henry A. Murray's (1938) list of "psychogenic" or "social" needs. This list, which contains more than 20 motives, was arrived at on the basis of the study of a number of "normal" people. Although Murray's list has been very influential in the field of psychology, it has not been applied very much to the study of motivation in organizations, probably because its length greatly reduces its usefulness. Like the early lists of instincts, it is so long that there is almost a separate need for each behavior people demonstrate. A look at Table 2, which lists some of Murray's needs, may help the reader gain an impression of the nature of the problem. The issue is not whether Murray has identified separate kinds of behavior (he has) but whether these behaviors might not be better dealt with by a more parsimonious list of needs.

Maslow's hierarchical classification of needs has been by far the most widely used classification system in the study of motivation in organizations. Maslow differs from Murray in two important ways: first, his list is shorter; second, he argues that needs are arranged in a hierarchy.

Maslow's (1943, 1954, 1970) hierarchical model is composed of a five-level classification of human needs and a set of hypotheses about how the satisfaction of these needs affects their importance.

The five need categories are as follows:

1. *Physiological needs,* including the need for food, water, air, and so on.
2. *Safety needs,* or the need for security, stability, and the absence from pain, threat, or illness.
3. *Belongingness and love needs,* which include a need for affection, belongingness, love, and so on.

4. *Esteem needs,* including both a need for personal feelings of achievement or self-esteem and also a need for recognition or respect from others.
5. *The need for self-actualization,* a feeling of self-fulfillment or the realization of one's potential.

More important than the definition of these five need groups, however, is the *process* by which each class of needs becomes important or active. According to Maslow, the five need categories exist in a hierarchy of prepotency such that the lower or more basic needs are inherently more important (prepotent) than the higher or less basic needs. This means that before any of the higher-level needs will become important, a person's physiological needs must be satisfied. Once the physiological needs have been satisfied, however, their strength or importance decreases, and the next higher-level need becomes the strongest motivator of behavior. This process of "increased satisfaction/decreased importance/increased importance of the next higher need" repeats itself until the highest level of the hierarchy is reached. Maslow has proposed in later revisions of his theory (1968, 1970) that at the highest level of the hierarchy a reversal occurs in the satisfaction-importance relationship. He states that for self-actualization, increased satisfaction leads to *increased* need strength. "Gratification breeds increased rather than decreased motivation, heightened rather than lessened excitement" (1968, p. 30).

In short, individual behavior is motivated by an attempt to satisfy the need that is *most important* at that point in time. Further, the strength of any need is determined by its position in the hierarchy and by the degree to which it and all lower needs have been satisfied. Maslow's theory predicts a dynamic, step-by-step, causal process of human motivation in which behavior is governed by a continuously changing (though predictable) set of "important" needs. An increase (change) in the satisfaction of the needs in one category *causes* the strength of these needs to decrease, which results in an increase in the importance of the needs at the next-higher level. Maslow does say that the hierarchy of needs is not a rigidly fixed order that is the same for all individuals. Especially in the case of needs in the

Table 2.   Some Items from Murrray's List of Needs

Social motive	Brief definition
Abasement	To submit passively to external force. To accept injury, blame, criticism, punishment. To surrender. To become resigned to fate. To admit inferiority, error, wrongdoing, or defeat. To confess and atone. To blame, belittle, or mutilate the self. To seek and enjoy pain, punishment, illness, and misfortune.
Achievement	To accomplish something difficult. To master, manipulate, or organize physical objects, human beings, or ideas. To do this as rapidly and as independently as possible. To overcome obstacles and attain a high standard. To excel oneself. To rival and surpass others. To increase self-regard by the successful exercise of talent.
Affiliation	To draw near and enjoyably co-operate or reciprocate with an allied other (an other who resembles the subject or who likes the subject). To please and win affection of a cathected object. To adhere and remain loyal to a friend.
Aggression	To overcome opposition forcefully. To fight. To revenge an injury. To attack, injure, or kill another. To oppose forcefully or punish another.
Autonomy	To get free, shake off restraint, break out of confinement. To resist coercion and restriction. To avoid or quit activities prescribed by domineering authorities. To be independent and free to act according to impulse. To be unattached, irresponsible. To defy convention.
Counteraction	To master or make up for a failure by restriving. To obliterate a humiliation by resumed action. To overcome weaknesses, to repress fear. To efface a dishonor by action. To search for obstacles and difficulties to overcome. To maintain self-respect and pride on a high level.
Defendance	To defend the self against assault, criticism, and blame. To conceal or justify a misdeed, failure, or humiliation. To vindicate the ego.
Deference	To admire and support a superior. To praise, honor, or eulogize. To yield eagerly to the influence of an allied other. To emulate an exemplar. To conform to custom.
Dominance	To control one's human environment. To influence or direct the behavior of others by suggestion, seduction, persuasion, or command. To dissuade, restrain, or prohibit.
Exhibition	To make an impression. To be seen and heard. To excite, amaze, fascinate, entertain, shock, intrigue, amuse, or entice others.
Harmavoidance	To avoid pain, physical injury, illness, and death. To escape from a dangerous situation. To take precautionary measures.
Infavoidance	To avoid humiliation. To quit embarrassing situations or to avoid conditions which may lead to belittlement, the scorn, derision, or indifference of others. To refrain from action because of the fear of failure.
Nurturance	To give sympathy and gratify the needs of a helpless object: an infant or any object that is weak, disabled, tired, inexperienced, infirm, defeated, humiliated, lonely, dejected, sick, mentally confused. To assist an object in danger. To feed, help, support, console, protect, comfort, nurse, heal.

Table 2.   *(Continued)*

Social motive	Brief definition
Order	To put things in order. To achieve cleanliness, arrangement, organization, balance, neatness, tidiness, and precision.
Play	To act for "fun" without further purpose. To like to laugh and make jokes. To seek enjoyable relaxation from stress. To participate in games, sports, dancing, drinking parties, cards.
Rejection	To separate oneself from a negatively cathected object. To exclude, abandon, expel, or remain indifferent to an inferior object. To snub or jilt an object.
Sentience	To seek and enjoy sensuous impressions.
Sex	To form and further an erotic relationship. To have sexual intercourse.
Succorance	To have one's needs gratified by the sympathetic aid of an allied object. To be nursed, supported, sustained, surrounded, protected, loved, advised, guided, indulged, forgiven, consoled. To remain close to a devoted protector. To always have a supporter.
Understanding	To ask or answer general questions. To be interested in theory. To speculate, formulate, analyze, and generalize.

Source: From C. S. Hall and G. Lindzey, *Theories of Personality.* Copyright © 1957 by John Wiley & Sons, Inc. Reprinted by permission.

middle of the hierarchy, the order varies somewhat from person to person. However, this view clearly states that physiological needs are the most prepotent and that self-actualization needs are usually the least.

Two other need-hierarchy theories have been stated. One is by Langer (1937)—predating Maslow's—and another by Alderfer (1969). Alderfer's (1972) theory is the best developed of these two theories. Alderfer argues for three levels of needs: existence, relatedness, and growth. Like Maslow, he argues that the satisfaction of a need influences its importance and the importance of higher-level needs. He agrees with Maslow's hypothesis that the satisfaction of growth needs makes them more important rather than less important to people; however, he also hypothesizes that the lack of satisfaction of higher-order needs can lead to lower-order needs becoming more important to people. He then argues that the importance of any need is influenced by the satisfaction/frustration of the needs above and below it in the hierarchy. He also assumes that all needs can be simultaneously active; thus, prepotency does not play as major a role in his theory as it does in Maslow's.

From the point of view of the three questions we asked at the beginning of the [reading], the hierarchical theories of Maslow and Alderfer provide rather complete answers to the last two questions. These theories make specific statements about what outcomes people will value (outcomes that satisfy whatever need or needs are active). They also make specific predictions about what will influence the attractiveness of various outcomes—for example, satisfaction of relevant needs including those lower on the hierarchy. They provide less complete answers to our first question, since they are not clear on why needs originate. They do, however, imply that the lower-order needs are innate and that the higher-order needs are present in most people and will appear if not blocked from appearing.

The hierarchical concept has received a great deal of attention among those interested in organizations. This interest is undoubtedly because the concept, if valid, provides a powerful tool for predicting how the importance of various outcomes will change in response to certain actions by organizations. It also can provide some important clues concerning what is likely to be important to employees. It suggests, for example, that as people get promoted in organizations and their lower-level needs become satisfied, they will become concerned with self-actualization and growth. It also suggests that if a person's job security is threatened, he will abandon all else in order to protect it. Finally, it suggests that an organization can give an employee enough of the lower-level rewards, such as security, but that it cannot give him enough growth and development. Thus, as employees receive more valued outcomes from organizations, they will *want* more; although the nature of what they want may change from things that satisfy their lower-order needs to things that satisfy their higher-order needs. As more than one manager has noted, "we have given our employees good working conditions, high pay, and a secure future. Now they want more interesting jobs and a chance to make more decisions. Won't they ever be satisfied?" Need hierarchy suggests that they won't!

AN APPROACH TO OUTCOME ATTRACTIVENESS

The approaches of Maslow, McClelland, and others are useful in thinking about motivation in organizations. They clearly indicate a number of important points that need to be included in any approach that tries to deal with the issue of why certain outcomes are attractive to people. However, there are still many questions. The rest of this [reading] will be concerned with answering these questions and with developing an approach to explaining outcome attractiveness.

Drives, Needs, Motives, or Just Outcomes?

All of the theorists discussed so far have assumed that outcomes are attractive to a person because of some drive, motive, or need the person has. On the other hand, Vroom (1964) has taken a different approach. He does not use the terms drive, need, or motive in his theory. He simply says that outcomes have value if they lead to other valued outcomes. Nothing is said about what causes people to value those other outcomes nor about what other outcomes are likely to be

valued. Although it does solve the problem of trying to understand why individual outcomes are attractive, a theory that deals with the problem as Vroom's does sacrifices predictive power, in contrast to a theory of needs that states in advance what outcomes are likely to be valued and what affects their value.

A theory of needs can make some predictions—such as when outcomes will be important and what will be the effects of certain events—that Vroom's theory cannot make. For example, if it is known that pay is important to an individual because it leads to prestige, Vroom's theory can only predict that, as prestige outcomes become less important, so will pay. On the other hand, a need theory such as Maslow's can make further predictions. It can predict what conditions will affect the importance of prestige outcomes—that is, satisfaction of esteem needs or lower-level needs—and can then predict what the effect of a number of factors, such as a promotion, will be on the importance of pay.

The issue of whether needs are innate or learned is an important one; but since we are dealing with adults whose need structures are already developed, it is not crucial for us. This issue is important for us only in the sense that it might provide information about how common it is for people to have a need. Innate needs should be present in a greater proportion of the society than learned needs. Of course, at this point no one seriously argues that any needs other than the basic ones are either purely learned or purely innate. Still, it does seem that the needs that are lower on Maslow's hierarchy are more innate and, therefore, more universally present than are those that are at the top of the hierarchy.

For our purposes a theory of needs does not have to specify why people have needs, since it can say something about the needs people have and the conditions under which certain needs operate without doing this. All it has to say is that certain outcomes can be grouped together because when one is sought the others are sought and when one is obtained the others are no longer sought. People often have several groups of such outcomes. The groups can be called "needs," and, if the same ones are sought by most people, then it is reasonable to speak of a "human need" for the group of outcomes. Perhaps it should be added that before a group of outcomes is called a need the outcomes should be sought as ends in themselves rather than as instruments for obtaining other outcomes. For example, food outcomes are sought as an end in themselves, and thus we speak of a *need* for food; a big office is not an end in itself, and thus cannot be called a need. Once it is decided that people have needs, the question is "how many needs?".

How Many Needs?

Interestingly, theorists defining different categories of human needs usually don't disagree over which specific outcomes are likely to be goals for people, but they do disagree on what kinds of needs lead to outcomes taking on goal characteristics. Psychologists have argued that people have from three to several hundred needs. Part of the reason for this variance rests in the way needs are defined. Originally, the criterion was simple; needs or drives were only said to exist when it could be established that a physiological basis could be found for the attractiveness of the outcomes sought by a person.

The recent research on higher-level needs has clearly shown this approach to be too restrictive. A suggested alternative is to use the term "need" to refer to clusters of outcomes that people seek as ends in themselves. This definition, however, does not solve the problem of how to determine what constitutes a valid cluster. Different foods provide a simple example of the problem. Various food objects can be grouped together in the sense that when a person wants one he often wants the others and when he gets enough of one he may lose interest in the others. Thus, we can say that people have a need for meat rather than saying that people have a need for roast beef or steak. By thinking in terms of outcome clusters such as the one just described, we move to a more general level and begin to group outcomes more parsimoniously. The question that arises now, however, is where to stop. That is, at what level of abstraction or generality should we stop grouping outcomes. Should we, for example, stop at the level of meat or put all food outcomes together and speak of a need for food, since food objects are somewhat similar in attractiveness as shown in Figure 2. The former is a tighter cluster in the sense that the attractiveness of different kinds of meat is probably more closely related than is the attractiveness of meat to the attractiveness of fruit. However, there are still tighter clusters (different kinds of steak), and thus there is no final answer to the question of how tight a cluster should be.

It is also possible to go to a higher level of abstraction and combine food outcomes with water and oxygen and call this combination an existence need (see Figure 3). This existence need includes all the outcomes that people need to sustain life. The criterion for grouping at this

Figure 2.   An Outcome Cluster

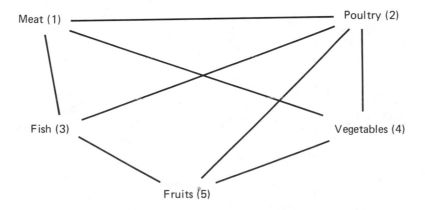

level is different from the criterion stated earlier (when one outcome is sought the other will be sought, and when one is obtained the attractiveness of the other is affected). The grouping in Figure 3 is based on the fact that all the outcomes have a common property: they are necessary for existence. Unlike the cluster shown in Figure 2, the attractiveness of one is not necessarily related to the other. Using this system, we would say that people desire food objects because of a basic need to exist; whereas, if we operated at a lower level, we would say people desire food objects because of a need for nourishment. A somewhat similar grouping problem occurs with achievement, self-actualization, and competence. Although it is possible to say that these concepts each represent separate needs, they also overlap in many respects. They all focus on the attractiveness to people of dealing effectively with challenging problems. Thus, they can be grouped and labeled as "a need for competence and growth" or they can be treated separately.

Ultimately, the best approach to categorizing needs is that which allows the greatest prediction of behavior in organizations. Unfortunately, at the moment there is not enough research evidence to allow us to state conclusively which listing of needs leads to the greatest predictability. Because of this lack of evidence, the best approach would seem to be grouping only those outcomes that have a strong empirical relationship

to each other. By this condition we mean those outcomes that can be observed to have common degrees of attractiveness to people. Using this criterion and thinking in terms of organizations, the following needs can be identified:

1. A number of existence needs—primarily sex, hunger, thirst, and oxygen.
2. A security need.
3. A social need.
4. A need for esteem and reputation.
5. An autonomy or freedom need.
6. A need for competence and self-actualization.

Is There a Need Hierarchy?

Now that we have identified a specific set of human needs, we must consider whether these needs should be arranged in a hierarchy. What does the evidence show about the existence of a need hierarchy?

There is strong evidence to support the view that unless existence needs are satisfied, none of the higher-order needs will come into play. There is also evidence that unless security needs are satisfied, people will not be concerned with higher-order needs. One report shows that subjects kept in a state of hunger think of little else than food (Keys, Brozek, Henschel, Mickelsen, & Taylor,

Figure 3.   An Existence-Need Cluster

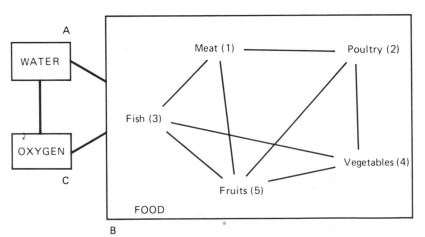

1950). Similar data is available in the literature on brainwashing and concentration camps (Lawler & Suttle, 1972).

There is, however, very little evidence to support the view that a hierarchy exists above the security level. Thus, it probably is not safe to assume more than a two-step hierarchy with existence and security needs at the lowest level and all the higher-order needs at the next level. This line of thinking leads to the prediction that unless these lower-order needs are satisfied, the others will not come into play. However, which higher-order needs come into play after the lower ones are satisfied and in what order they will come into play cannot be predicted. If anything, it seems that most people are simultaneously motivated by several of the same-level needs. On the other hand, people do not seem to be simultaneously motivated by needs from the two different levels. One person might, for example, be motivated by social and autonomy needs, while another might be motivated by hunger and thirst. Once a need appears, it does seem to persist until it is satisfied or the satisfaction of the lower-order needs is threatened. The one exception to this rule is the need for self-actualization and competence. Unlike the other needs, evidence shows that this need does not appear to be satiable and, thus, is not likely to cease to be important unless the satisfaction of one of the lower-level needs is threatened.

Can Outcomes Satisfy More Than One Need?

There is a considerable amount of research evidence indicating that some outcomes are relevant to the satisfaction of more than one need. That is, when these outcomes are obtained they affect the attractiveness of more than one cluster of outcomes. A classic example is pay (Lawler, 1971). Pay appears to have the ability to satisfy not only existence needs but also security and esteem needs. For example, Lawler and Porter (1963) report that the more a manager is paid, the higher is his security- and esteem-need satisfaction. This statement means that when a person is trying to satisfy either security or esteem needs, pay will be important. It is not difficult to see why pay has

the ability to satisfy a number of needs. Pay can be used to buy articles, such as food, that satisfy existence needs, and high pay also earns a certain amount of esteem and respect in our society.

How Important Are Different Needs?

Literally hundreds of studies have tried to measure the importance of different needs and outcomes to employees. Some idea of the importance of different needs can be obtained by looking at the data collected by Porter (1964), which appears in Figure 4. These data show that for over 1900 managers sampled the higher-order needs are clearly the most important. Other data from the study show that the managers are most satisfied with the lower-order needs. Thus, it follows that these lower-order needs should be the least important. Whether this same concern with higher-order need satisfaction exists at the lower levels in organizations is not clear. The data presented in Figure 4 show that higher-order needs do seem to be somewhat less important to lower-level managers than to higher-level managers. Other data suggest that pay and certain lower-level needs are rated as more important by workers than by managers (Porter & Lawler, 1965). Dubin (1956), for example, argues that the work place is not a central part of the life of most industrial workers and that it is unwise to expect the workers to be concerned with fulfilling their higher-order needs within the context of their jobs.

Figure 5 shows the average ratings of the importance of job factors in a large number of studies (16 studies and 11,000 employees). Most of these studies were done on nonmanagerial employees. It shows job security and intrinsic job interest to be the most important factors to the employees. Lawler (1971) reviewed 43 studies in which pay was rated and found that its average rating was third. This is an interesting finding, but, like other findings that are based on employee ratings of how important various needs and job characteristics are, it must be interpreted very cautiously. These ratings are difficult for people to make and are strongly influenced by how the questions are worded. Thus, it is impossible to reach any strong conclusions about which job factors are the most important. Perhaps the most significant

Figure 4.   Importance Attached to Five Needs by Managers from Three Organization Levels

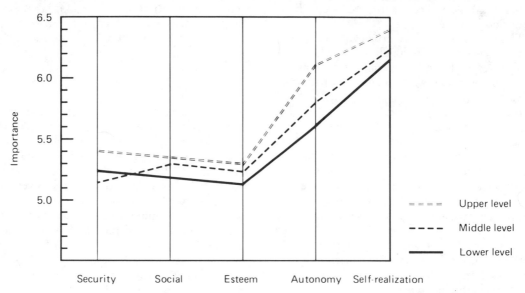

thing to remember from these studies is that employees rate a number of factors as very important. Some of these factors seem to be most strongly related to lower-order needs, while others are related to higher-order needs.

Individual Differences in Need Strength

Large differences clearly exist in the goals and needs people have, and these differences must be considered when viewing individual motivation in organizations. For example, Lawler reports that in about 1/4 of the cases he analyzed, pay was rated as first in importance, while in many other cases it was rated sixth or lower in importance. Because of these differences a pay system that will motivate one person is often seen as irrelevant by others. Porter's (1963) data show that managers at different organization levels differ in the degree to which they are motivated by higher-order needs. Other data show that managers are motivated by different needs; some managers are motivated by self-actualization, while others are motivated by autonomy. There is also evidence that some people seem to be fixated on such lower-order needs as security.

Many individual differences in need strength are understandable if we relate them to personal characteristics and situations. Hulin and Blood (1968), for example, point out that urban workers have different values from those of rural workers. Urban workers seem to be more alienated from work and apparently are less concerned with fulfilling higher-order needs on the job. For an interesting example of the type of individual profile that can be drawn from the research on need strength, consider the profile of a person to whom money is likely to be very important (Lawler, 1971).

> The employee is a male, young (probably in his twenties); his personality is characterized by low self-assurance and high neuroticism; he comes from a small town or farm background; he belongs to a few clubs and social groups, and he owns his own home and probably is a Republican and a Protestant [p. 51].

In summary then, there are significant individual differences among employees in the importance of different needs and outcomes. These differences are not surprising; in fact, many are predictable from what has been said about how the importance of needs is affected by the satis-

Figure 5. Average Importance of Factors in Employee Attitudes (Compiled from 16 Studies, Including over 11,000 Employees)

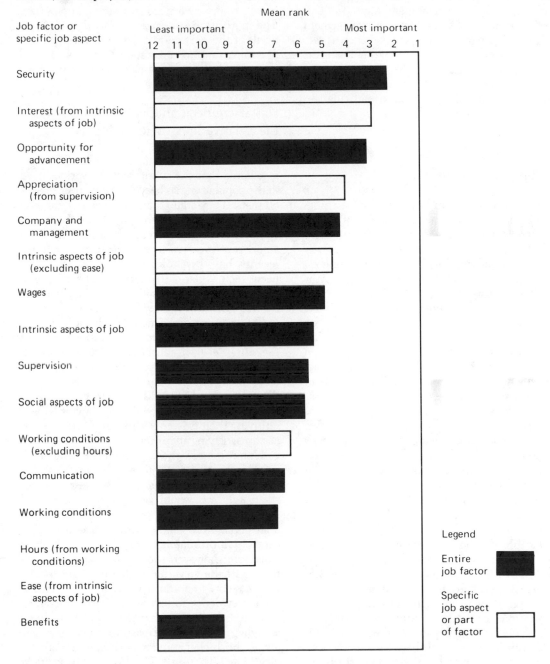

From Herzberg, et al., *Job Attitudes: Review of Research and Opinion* (Psychological Service of Pittsburgh, 1957). Reprinted by permission of Psychological Service of Pittsburgh.

faction of needs and by child-rearing experience. There is also evidence that these individual differences are related in meaningful ways to a number of organizational factors, such as management level, and to personal characteristics, such as age, sex, and education level. This point has some interesting implications for the management of organizations, since it means that it is possible to identify those people for whom a particular reward is likely to be important.

How Changeable Is the Importance of Needs?

There is evidence to indicate that some things can and do influence the importance of needs. Still, the evidence suggests that organizations have relatively little influence over how important various outcomes will be to their members. The importance of needs is determined partly by hereditary factors and partly by childhood experiences—things over which organizations have no control. Organizations can influence only two of the factors that determine need importance: need satisfaction and need arousal. Satisfaction influences importance, and organizational practices strongly influence satisfaction. Achievement motivation can be aroused by certain tasks and situations, as can competence motivation. Since organizations do have partial control over the situation in which their employees work, they can create conditions that will arouse certain needs. However, these needs must be present in the individual in order to be aroused, and whether the needs are present is a function of many things beyond the control of the organization.

Probably the best opportunity organizations have to influence the needs of their employees is provided by the selection process. Since need importance is relatively fixed and it is possible to identify people who are high on particular needs, organizations can select people who have the kinds of need-strength patterns they want. This would seem to be a much better approach than trying to change people's needs once they join the organization. This point also has some interesting implications for managers who have to motivate employees. It suggests that rather than

trying to change the needs of their subordinates, managers should concentrate on placing people in jobs where their need structure is appropriate. The motivation system that is used must fit the needs of the person or it will not work. If pay is not important to an employee, he or she will never be motivated by a pay-incentive system.

Has There Been an Overall Change in the Relative Importance of Needs?

Many writers (for example, Roszak, 1969) have speculated that the strength of the various needs in the population has been changing over the past 60 years. They argue that only recently has a significant proportion of the population been concerned with needs such as self-actualization and autonomy. (And it is interesting to note that only recently have psychologists been concerned with needs such as self-actualization.) The concept of man as a self-actualizing organism is essentially a development of the 1960s.

Two reasons are generally advanced for the emergence of higher-order needs. First, there is the rising level of education in our society; approximately 40 percent of the high school graduates in the United States go to college. Second, the standard of living has constantly increased so that fewer and fewer people are concerned with satisfying their existence needs and, thus, can focus on satisfying their higher-order needs.

Unfortunately, there is very little evidence to either support or disprove the view that the strength of needs is changing. To test this view adequately we would have to compare need-strength data collected 60 years ago from a random population sample with data collected recently. Unfortunately, such data do not exist. There are, however, some data that can be said to support the view that higher-order needs have become more important. We've already seen that there is evidence to support a two-step hierarchy. If we accept the fact that the standard of living is higher, then, on the basis of a two-step hierarchy, this higher standard of living supports the view that higher-order needs probably are more important. In addition, Porter's (1962) data show that younger managers place greater importance on self-actualization than older managers do.

This could, of course, be simply a function of age, but it could also be due to the higher education level of these younger managers and the fact that they never experienced a depression.

There is also some direct evidence that higher-educated people are more concerned with self-actualization. Finally, there is the fact that the idea of self-actualization has gained fairly wide attention in our society. It now seems "in" to talk about self-actualization; and, as we pointed out, the concept of "self-actualization" is now prominent in psychology. Although this evidence is only indirect, it does support the view that concern with self-actualization has increased recently. In summary, although there is little direct data to support the view, it probably is true that, in general, people are somewhat more concerned with satisfying higher-order needs than they used to be.

SUMMARY AND CONCLUSIONS

The following statements summarize the major points that have been made . . . about human needs.

1. Needs can be thought of as groups of outcomes that people seek.
2. Man's needs are arranged in a two-level hierarchy. At the lowest level are existence and security needs; at the other level are social, esteem, autonomy, and self-actualization needs.
3. The higher-level needs will appear only when the lower-level ones are satisfied.
4. All needs except self-actualization are satiable, and as needs become satisfied they decrease in importance.
5. A person can be motivated by more than one need at a given point in time and will continue to be motivated by a need until either it is satisfied or satisfaction of the lower-order needs is threatened.

Thus, we have answered two of the three questions asked at the beginning of the [reading]. A classification system for needs has been developed, and statements have been made about what in-fluences the importance of needs. No conclusions have been reached about why people develop needs or about whether needs are innate or learned because these questions don't seem to be answerable at this time.

NOTE

1. From A. H. Maslow, *Motivation and Personality,* Second Edition (Harper & Row Publishers, Inc., 1970). Reprinted by permission.

REFERENCES

Adams, J. S., Toward an understanding of inequity. *Journal of Abnormal Psychology,* 1963, 67, 422–436.

Adams, J. S., Injustice in social exchange. In L. Berkowitz (Ed.), *Advances in experimental social psychology.* Vol. 2. New York: Academic Press, 1965.

Alderfer, C. P., An empirical test of a new theory of human needs. *Organizational Behavior and Human Performance,* 1969, 4, 142–175.

Alderfer, C. P., *Existence, relatedness, and growth: Human needs in organizational settings.* New York: The Free Press, 1972.

Alper, T. G., Task-orientation vs. ego-orientation in learning and retention. *American Journal of Psychology,* 1946, 38, 224–238.

Allport, G. W., *Becoming: Basic considerations for a psychology of personality.* New Haven: Yale University Press, 1955.

Atkinson, J. W., Towards experimental and anlaysis of human motivation in terms of motives, expectancies, and incentives. In J. W. Atkinson (Ed.), *Motives in fantasy, action, and society.* Princeton, N. J.: Van Nostrand Reinhold, 1958.

Atkinson, J. W., *An introduction to motivation.* Princeton, N.J.: Van Nostrand Reinhold, 1964.

Berlyne, D. E., Arousal and reinforcement. In D. Levine (Ed.), *Nebraska symposium on motivation.* Lincoln: University of Nebraska Press, 1967.

Bexton, W. H., Heron, W., & Scott, T. H., Effects of decreased variation in the sensory environment. *Canadian Journal of Psychology,* 1954, 8, 70–76.

Butler, R. A., Discrimination learning by rhesus monkeys to visual exploration motivation. *Journal of Comparative and Physiological Psychology,* 1953, 46, 95–98.

Cowles, J. T., Food tokens as incentives for learning by chimpanzees. *Comparative Psychology Monograph*, 1937, 14 (No. 71).

Cravens, R. W., & Renner, K. E., Conditioned appetitive drive states: Empirical evidence and theoretical status. *Psychological Bulletin*, 1970, 73, 212–220.

Dubin, R., Industrial workers' worlds: A study of the "central life interests" of industrial workers. *Social Problems*, 1956, 3, 131–142.

French, E. G., Some characteristics of achievement motivation. *Journal of Experimental Psychology*, 1955, 50, 232–236.

Harlow, H. F., Mice, monkeys, men & motives. *Psychological Review*, 1953, 60, 23–32.

Harlow, H. F., The nature of love. *American Psychologist*, 1958, 13, 673–685.

Hulin, C. L., & Blood, M. R., Job enlargement, individual differences, and worker responses. *Psychological Bulletin*, 1968, 69, 41–55.

Hull, C. L., *Principles of behavior*, New York: Appleton-Century-Crofts, 1943.

Keys, A., Brozck, J., Henscheul, A., Mickelsen, O., & Taylor, H., *The biology of human starvation*. Minneapolis: University of Minnesota Press, 1950, 2 vols.

Langer, W. C., *Psychology and human living*. New York: Appleton-Century-Crofts, 1937.

Lawler, E. E., *Pay and organizational effectiveness: A psychological view*. New York: McGraw-Hill, 1971.

Lawler, E. E., & Porter, L. W., Perceptions regarding management compensation. *Industrial Relations*, 1963, 3, 41–49.

Lawler, E. E., & Suttle, J. L., A causal correlational test of the need hierarchy concept. *Organization Behavior and Human Performance*, 1972, 7, 265–287.

Maslow, A. H., A theory of human motivation. *Psychological Review*, 1943, 50, 370–396.

Maslow, A. H., *Motivation and personality*. New York: Harper & Row, 1954.

Maslow, A. H., *Motivation and personality*, (2nd ed.), New York: Harper & Row, 1970.

Maslow, A. H., *Toward a psychology of being*. (2nd ed.), Princeton, N. J.: Van Nostrand Reinhold, 1968.

McClelland, D. C., Measuring motivation in phantasy: The achievement motive. In H. Guetzkow (Ed.), *Groups, leadership, and men*. Pittsburgh: Carnegie Press, 1951.

McClelland, D. C., *The achieving society*. Princeton: Van Nostrand Reinhold, 1961.

McDougall, W., *An introduction to social psychology*. London: Methuen & Co., 1908.

Miles, R. C., Learning in kittens with manipulatory, exploratory, and food incentives. *Journal of Comparative and Physiological Psychology*, 1958, 51, 39–42.

Murray, H. A., *Explorations in personality*. New York: Oxford University Press, 1938.

Murray, E. J., *Motivation and emotion*. Englewood Cliffs, N. J.: Prentice-Hall, 1964.

Porter, L. W., Job attitudes in management: I. Perceived deficiencies in need fulfillment as a function of job level. *Journal of Applied Psychology*, 1962, 46, 375–384.

Porter, L. W., Job attitudes in management: II. Perceived importance of needs as a function of job level. *Journal of Applied Psychology*, 1963, 47, 141–148.

Porter, L. W., *Organizational patterns of management job attitudes*. New York: American Foundation for Management Research, 1964.

Porter, L. W., & Lawler, E. E., Properties of organization structure in relation to job attitudes and job behavior. *Psychology Bulletin*, 1965, 64, 23–51.

Rogers, C. R., *On becoming a person*. Boston: Houghton Mifflin, 1961.

Roszak, T., *The making of a counter culture*. Garden City, New York: Doubleday, 1969.

Schachter, S., *The psychology of affiliation*. Stanford, Calif.: Stanford University Press, 1959.

Scott, W. E., The behavioral consequences of repetitive task design: Research and theory. In L. L. Cummings & W. E. Scott (Eds.), *Readings in organizational behavior and human performance*. Homewood, Ill.: Richard D. Irwin, 1969.

Smock, C. D., & Holt, B. G., Children's reactions to novelty: An experimental study of "curiosity motivation." *Child Development*, 1962, 33, 631–642.

Vroom, V. H., *Work and Motivation*, New York: John Wiley & Sons, 1964.

White, R. W., Motivation reconsidered: The concept of competence. *Psychological Review*, 1959, 66, 297–333.

Wolfe, J. B., Effectiveness of token-rewards for chimpanzees. *Comparative Psychology Monograph*, 1936, 12, 15.

Motivation and Performance

David A. Nadler and Edward E. Lawler III

- What makes some people work hard while others do as little as possible?
- How can I, as a manager, influence the performance of people who work for me?
- Why do people turn over, show up late to work, and miss work entirely?

These important questions about employees' behavior can only be answered by managers who have a grasp of what motivates people. Specifically, a good understanding of motivation can serve as a valuable tool for *understanding* the causes of behavior in organizations, for *predicting* the effects of any managerial action, and for *directing* behavior so that organizational and individual goals can be achieved.

EXISTING APPROACHES

During the past twenty years, managers have been bombarded with a number of different approaches

Source: J. R. Hackman and E. E. Lawler, *Perspectives on behavior in organizations.* New York: McGraw-Hill, 1977.

to motivation. The terms associated with these approaches are well known—"human relations," "scientific management," "job enrichment," "need hierarchy," "self-actualization," etc. Each of these approaches has something to offer. On the other hand, each of these different approaches also has its problems in both theory and practice. Running through almost all of the approaches with which managers are familiar are a series of implicit but clearly erroneous assumptions.

Assumption 1: All employees are alike. Different theories present different ways of looking at people, but each of them assumes that all employees are basically similar in their makeup: Employees all want economic gains, or all want a pleasant climate, or all aspire to be self-actualizing, etc.

Assumption 2: All situations are alike. Most theories assume that all managerial situations are alike, and that the managerial course of action for motivation (for example, participation, job enlargement, etc.) is applicable in all situations.

Assumption 3: One best way. Out of the other two assumptions there emerges a basic principle that there is "one best way" to motivate employees.

When these "one best way" approaches are tried in the "correct" situation they will work. However, all of them are bound to fail in some situations. They are therefore not adequate managerial tools.

A NEW APPROACH

During the past ten years, a great deal of research has been done on a new approach to looking at motivation. This approach, frequently called "expectancy theory," still needs further testing, refining, and extending. However, enough is known that many behavioral scientists have concluded that it represents the most comprehensive, valid, and useful approach to understanding motivation. Further, it is apparent that it is a very useful tool for understanding motivation in organizations.

The theory is based on a number of specific assumptions about the causes of behavior in organizations.

Assumption 1: Behavior is determined by a combination of forces in the individual and forces in the environment.   Neither the individual nor the environment alone determines behavior. Individuals come into organizations with certain "psychological baggage." They have past experiences and a developmental history which has given them unique sets of needs, ways of looking at the world, and expectations about how organizations will treat them. These all influence how individuals respond to their work environment. The work environment provides structures (such as a pay system or a supervisor) which influence the behavior of people. Different environments tend to produce different behavior in similar people just as dissimilar people tend to behave differently in similar environments.

Assumption 2: People make decisions about their own behavior in organizations.   While there are many constraints on the behavior of individuals in organizations, most of the behavior that is observed is the result of individuals' conscious decisions. These decisions usually fall into two categories. First, individuals make decisions about *membership behavior*—coming to work, staying at work, and in other ways being a member of the organization. Second, individuals make decisions about the amount of *effort* they will direct *towards performing their jobs.* This includes decisions about how hard to work, how much to produce, at what quality, etc.

Assumption 3: Different people have different types of needs, desires, and goals.   Individuals differ on what kinds of outcomes (or rewards) they desire. These differences are not random; they can be examined systematically by an understanding of the differences in the strength of individuals' needs.

Assumption 4: People make decisions among alternative plans of behavior based on their perceptions (expectancies) of the degree to which a given behavior will lead to desired outcomes.   In simple terms, people tend to do those things which they see as leading to outcomes (which can also be called "rewards") they desire and avoid doing those things they see as leading to outcomes that are not desired.

In general, the approach used here views people as having their own needs and mental maps of what the world is like. They use these maps to make decisions about how they will behave, behaving in those ways which their mental maps indicate will lead to outcomes that will satisfy their needs. Therefore, they are inherently neither motivated nor unmotivated; motivation depends on the situation they are in, and how it fits their needs.

THE THEORY

Based on these general assumptions, expectancy theory states a number of propositions about the process by which people make decisions about their own behavior in organizational settings. While the theory is complex at first view, it is in fact made of a series of fairly straightforward observations about behavior. (The theory is presented in more technical terms in Appendix A.) Three concepts serve as the key building blocks of the theory:

Performance-outcome expectancy. Every behavior has associated with it, in an individual's mind, certain outcomes (rewards or punishments). In other words, the individual believes or expects that if he or she behaves in a certain way, he or she will get certain things.

Examples of expectancies can easily be described. An individual may have an expectancy that if he produces ten units he will receive his normal hourly rate while if he produces fifteen units he will receive his hourly pay rate plus a bonus. Similarly an individual may believe that certain levels of performance will lead to approval or disapproval from members of her work group or from her supervisor. Each performance can be seen as leading to a number of different kinds of outcomes and outcomes can differ in their types.

Valence. Each outcome has a "valence" (value, worth, attractiveness) to a specific individual. Outcomes have different valences for different individuals. This comes about because valences result from individual needs and perceptions, which differ because they in turn reflect other factors in the individual's life.

For example, some individuals may value an opportunity for promotion or advancement because of their needs for achievement or power, while others may not want to be promoted and leave their current work group because of needs for affiliation with others. Similarly, a fringe benefit such as a pension plan may have great valence for an older worker but little valence for a young employee on his first job.

Effort-performance expectancy. Each behavior also has associated with it in the individual's mind a certain expectancy or probability of success. This expectancy represents the individual's perception of how hard it will be to achieve such behavior and the probability of his or her successful achievement of that behavior.

For example, you may have a strong expectancy that if you put forth the effort, you can produce ten units an hour, but that you have only a fifty-fifty chance of producing fifteen units an hour if you try.

Putting these concepts together, it is possible to make a basic statement about motivation. In general, the motivation to attempt to behave in a certain way is greatest when:

a The individual believes that the behavior will lead to outcomes (performance-outcome expectancy)

b The individual believes that these outcomes have positive value for him or her (valence)

c The individual believes that he or she is able to perform at the desired level (effort-performance expectancy)

Given a number of alternative levels of behavior (ten, fifteen, and twenty units of production per hour, for example) the individual will choose that level of performance which has the greatest motivational force associated with it, as indicated by the expectancies, outcomes, and valences.

In other words, when faced with choices about behavior, the individual goes through a process of considering questions such as, "Can I perform at that level if I try?" "If I perform at that level, what will happen?" "How do I feel about those things that will happen?" The individual then decides to behave in that way which seems to have the best chance of producing positive, desired outcomes.

A General Model

On the basis of these concepts, it is possible to construct a general model of behavior in organizational settings (see Figure 1). Working from left to right in the model, motivation is seen as the force on the individual to expend effort. Motivation leads to an observed level of effort by the individual. Effort, alone, however, is not enough. Performance results from a combination of the effort that an individual puts forth *and* the level of ability which he or she has (reflecting skills, training, information, etc.). Effort thus combines with ability to produce a given level of performance. As a result of performance, the individual attains certain outcomes. The model indicates this relationship in a dotted line, reflecting the fact that sometimes people perform but do not get desired outcomes. As this process of perfor-

Figure 1.   The Basic Motivation-Behavior Sequence

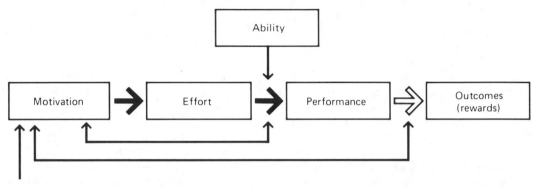

A person's motivation is a function of:

a.   Effort-to-performance expectancies
b.   Performance-to-outcome expectancies
c.   Perceived valence of outcomes

mance-reward occurs, time after time, the actual events serve to provide information which influences the individual's perceptions (particularly expectancies) and thus influences motivation in the future.

Outcomes, or rewards, fall into two major categories. First, the individual obtains outcomes from the environment. When an individual performs at a given level he or she can receive positive or negative outcomes from supervisors, coworkers, the organization's rewards systems, or other sources. These environmental rewards are thus one source of outcomes for the individual. A second source of outcomes is the individual. These include outcomes which occur purely from the performance of the task itself (feelings of accomplishment, personal worth, achievement, etc.). In a sense, the individual gives these rewards to himself or herself. The environment cannot give them or take them away directly; it can only make them possible.

Supporting Evidence

Over fifty studies have been done to test the validity of the expectancy-theory approach to predicting employee behavior.[1] Almost without exception, the studies have confirmed the predictions of the theory. As the theory predicts, the best performers in organizations tend to see a strong relationship between performing their jobs well and receiving rewards they value. In addition they have clear performance goals and feel they can perform well. Similarly, studies using the expectancy theory to predict how people choose jobs also show that individuals tend to interview for and actually take those jobs which they feel will provide the rewards they value. One study, for example, was able to correctly predict for 80 percent of the people studied which of several jobs they would take.[2] Finally, the theory correctly predicts that beliefs about the outcomes associated with performance (expectancies) will be better predictors of performance than will feelings of job satisfaction since expectancies are the critical causes of performance and satisfaction is not.

Questions about the Model

Although the results so far have been encouraging, they also indicate some problems with the model. These problems do not critically affect the managerial implications of the model, but they should be noted. The model is based on the assumption that individuals make very rational decisions after a thorough exploration of all the available alternatives and on weighing the possible outcomes of all these alternatives. When we talk to or observe individuals, however, we find that their decision processes are frequently less thorough. People often stop considering alternative behavior plans when they find one that is at least moderately satisfying, even though more rewarding plans remain to be examined.

People are also limited in the amount of information they can handle at one time, and therefore the model may indicate a process that is much more complex than the one that actually takes place. On the other hand, the model does provide enough information and is consistent enough with reality to present some clear implications for managers who are concerned with the question of how to motivate the people who work for them.

Implications for Managers

The first set of implications is directed toward the individual manager who has a group of people working for him or her and is concerned with how to motivate good performance. Since behavior is a result of forces both in the person and in the environment, you as manager need to look at and diagnose both the person and the environment. Specifically, you need to do the following:

Figure out what outcomes each employee values. As a first step, it is important to determine what kinds of outcomes or rewards have valence for your employees. For each employee you need to determine "what turns him or her on." There are various ways of finding this out, including (a) finding out employees' desires through some structured method of data collection, such as a questionnaire, (b) observing the employees' reactions to different situations or rewards, or (c) the fairly simple act of asking them what kinds of rewards they want, what kind of career goals they have, or "what's in it for them." It is important to stress here that it is very difficult to change what people want, but fairly easy to find out what they want. Thus, the skillful manager emphasizes diagnosis of needs, not changing the individuals themselves.

Determine what kinds of behavior you desire. Managers frequently talk about "good performance" without really defining what good performance is. An important step in motivating is for you yourself to figure out what kinds of performances are required and what are adequate measures or indicators of performance (quantity, quality, etc.). There is also a need to be able to define those performances in fairly specific terms so that observable and measurable behavior can be defined and subordinates can understand what is desired of them (e.g., produce ten products of a certain quality standard—rather than only produce at a high rate).

Make sure desired levels of performance are reachable. The model states that motivation is determined not only by the performance-to-outcome expectancy, but also by the effort-to-performance expectancy. The implication of this is that the levels of performance which are set as the points at which individuals receive desired outcomes must be reachable or attainable by these individuals. If the employees feel that the level of performance required to get a reward is higher than they can reasonably achieve, then their motivation to perform well will be relatively low.

Link desired outcomes to desired performances. The next step is to directly, clearly, and explicitly link those outcomes desired by employees to the specific performances desired by you. If your employee values external rewards, then the emphasis should be on the rewards systems concerned with promotion, pay, and approval. While the linking of these rewards can be initiated through your making statements to your employees, it is extremely important that employees see a clear example of the reward process working in a fairly short period of time if the motivating "expectancies" are to be created in the employees' minds. The linking must be done by some concrete public acts, in addition to statements of intent.

If your employee values internal rewards (e.g., achievement), then you should concentrate on changing the nature of the person's job, for he or she is likely to respond well to such things as increased autonomy, feedback, and challenge, because these things will lead to a situation where good job performance is inherently rewarding. The best way to check on the adequacy of the internal and external reward system is to ask people what their perceptions of the situation are. Remember it is the perceptions of people that determine their motivation, not reality. It doesn't matter for example whether you feel a subordinate's pay is related to his or her motivation. Motivation will be present only if the subordinate sees the relationship. Many managers are misled about the behavior of their subordinates because they rely on their own perceptions of the situation and forget to find out what their subordinates feel. There is only one way to do this: ask. Questionnaires can be used here, as can personal interviews. (See Appendix B for a short version of a motivation questionnaire.)

Analyze the total situation for conflicting expectancies.   Having set up positive expectancies for employees, you then need to look at the entire situation to see if other factors (informal work groups, other managers, the organization's reward systems) have set up conflicting expectancies in the minds of the employees. Motivation will only be high when people see a number of rewards associated with good performance and few negative outcomes. Again, you can often gather this kind of information by asking your subordinates. If there are major conflicts, you need to make adjustments, either in your own performance and reward structure, or in the other sources of rewards or punishments in the environment.

Make sure changes in outcomes are large enough.   In examining the motivational system, it is important to make sure that changes in outcomes or rewards are large enough to motivate significant behavior. Trivial rewards will result in trivial amounts of effort and thus trivial improvements in performance. Rewards must be large enough to motivate individuals to put forth the effort required to bring about significant changes in performance.

Check the system for its equity.   The model is based on the idea that individuals are different and therefore different rewards will need to be used to motivate different individuals. On the other hand, for a motivational system to work it must be a fair one—one that has equity (not equality). Good performers should see that they get more desired rewards than do poor performers, and others in the system should see that also.

Equity should not be confused with a system of equality where all are rewarded equally, with no regard to their performance. A system of equality is guaranteed to produce low motivation.

Implications for Organizations

Expectancy theory has some clear messages for those who run large organizations. It suggests how organizational structures can be designed so that they increase rather than decrease levels of motivation of organization members. While there are many different implications, a few of the major ones are as follows:

Implication 1: The design of pay and reward systems.   Organizations usually get what they reward, not what they want. This can be seen in many situations, and pay systems are a good example.[3] Frequently, organizations reward people for membership (through pay tied to seniority, for example) rather than for performance. Little wonder that what the organization gets is behavior oriented towards "safe," secure employment rather than effort directed at performing well. In addition, even where organizations do pay for performance as a motivational device, they frequently negate the motivational value of the system by keeping pay secret, therefore preventing people from observing the pay-to-performance relationship that would serve to create positive, clear, and strong performance-to-reward expectancies. The implication is that organizations should put more effort into rewarding people (through pay, promotion, better job opportunities, etc.) for the performances which are desired, and that to keep these rewards secret is clearly self-defeating. In addition, it underscores the importance of the frequently ignored performance evaluation or appraisal process and the need to evaluate people based on how they perform clearly defined specific behaviors, rather than on how they score on ratings of general traits such as "honesty," "cleanliness," and other, similar terms which frequently appear as part of the performance appraisal form.

Implication 2: The design of tasks, jobs, and roles.   One source of desired outcomes is the work itself. The expectancy-theory model supports much of the job enrichment literature, in saying that by designing jobs which enable people to get their needs fulfilled, organizations can bring about higher levels of motivation.[4] The major difference between the traditional approaches to job enlargement or enrichment and the expectancy-theory approach is the recognition by expectancy theory that different people have different needs and, therefore, some people may not want enlarged or enriched jobs. Thus, while the design of tasks that have more autonomy, variety, feedback, meaningfulness, etc., will lead to higher motivation in some, the organization needs to build in the opportunity for individuals to make choices about the kind of work they will do so that not everyone is forced to experience job enrichment.

Implication 3: The importance of group structures. Groups, both formal and informal, are powerful and potent sources of desired outcomes for individuals. Groups can provide or withhold acceptance, approval, affection, skill training, needed information, assistance, etc. They are a powerful force in the total motivational environment of individuals. Several implications emerge from the importance of groups. First, organizations should consider the structuring of at least a portion of rewards around group performance rather than individual performance. This is particularly important where group members have to cooperate with each other to produce a group product or service, and where the individual's contribution is often hard to determine. Second, the organization needs to train managers to be aware of how groups can influence individual behavior and to be sensitive to the kinds of expectancies which informal groups set up and their conflict or consistency with the expectancies that the organization attempts to create.

Implication 4: The supervisor's role. The immediate supervisor has an important role in creating, monitoring, and maintaining the expectancies and reward structures which will lead to good performance. The supervisor's role in the motivation process becomes one of defining clear goals, setting clear reward expectancies, and providing the right rewards for different peo-

ple (which could include both organizational rewards and personal rewards such as recognition, approval, or support from the supervisor). Thus, organizations need to provide supervisors with an awareness of the nature of motivation as well as the tools (control over organizational rewards, skill in administering those rewards) to create positive motivation.

Implication 5: Measuring motivation. If things like expectancies, the nature of the job, supervisor-controlled outcomes, satisfaction, etc., are important in understanding how well people are being motivated, then organizations need to monitor employee perceptions along these lines. One relatively cheap and reliable method of doing this is through standardized employee questionnaires. A number of organizations already use such techniques, surveying employees' perceptions and attitudes at regular intervals (ranging from once a month to once every year-and-a-half) using either standardized surveys or surveys developed specifically for the organization. Such information is useful both to the individual manager and to top management in assessing the state of human resources and the effectiveness of the organization's motivational systems.[5] (Again, see Appendix B for excerpts from a standardized survey.)

Implication 6: Individualizing organizations. Expectancy theory leads to a final general implication about a possible future direction for the design of organizations. Because different people have different needs and therefore have different valences, effective motivation must come through the recognition that not all employees are alike and that organizations need to be flexible in order to accommodate individual differences. This implies the "building in" of choice for employees in many areas, such as reward systems, fringe benefits, job assignments, etc., where employees previously have had little say. A successful example of the building in of such choice can be seen in the experiments at TRW and the Educational Testing Service with "cafeteria fringe-benefits plans" which allow employees to choose the fringe benefits they want, rather than taking the expensive and often unwanted benefits which the company frequently provides to everyone.[6]

SUMMARY

Expectancy theory provides a more complex model of man for managers to work with. At the same time, it is a model which holds promise for the more effective motivation of individuals and the more effective design of organizational systems. It implies, however, the need for more exacting and thorough diagnosis by the manager to determine (a) the relevant forces in the individual, and (b) the relevant forces in the environment, both of which combine to motivate different kinds of behavior. Following diagnosis, the model implies a need to act—to develop a system of pay, promotion, job assignments, group structures, supervision, etc.—to bring about effective motivation by providing different outcomes for different individuals.

Performance of individuals is a critical issue in making organizations work effectively. If a manager is to influence work behavior and performance, he or she must have an understanding of motivation and the factors which influence an individual's motivation to come to work, to work hard, and to work well. While simple models offer easy answers, it is the more complex models which seem to offer more promise. Managers can use models (like expectancy theory) to understand the nature of behavior and build more effective organizations.

APPENDIX A: THE EXPECTANCY THEORY MODEL IN MORE TECHNICAL TERMS

A person's motivation to exert effort towards a specific level of performance is based on his or her perceptions of associations between actions and outcomes. The critical perceptions which contribute to motivation are graphically presented in Figure 2. These perceptions can be defined as follows:

a The effort-to-performance expectancy $(E \rightarrow P)$: This refers to the person's subjective probability about the likelihood that he or she can perform at a given level, or that effort on his or her part will lead to successful performance. This term can be thought of as varying from 0 to 1. In general, the less likely a person feels that

Figure 2.   Major Terms in Expectancy Theory

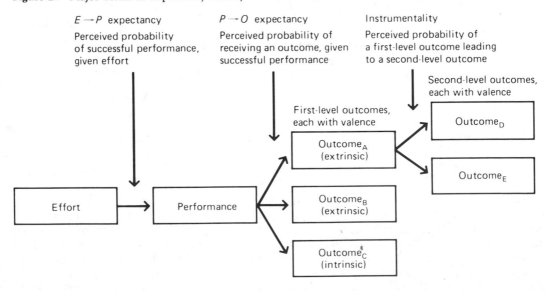

Motivation is expressed as follows: $M \cdot [E \rightarrow P] \times \Sigma [(P \rightarrow O)(V)]$

he or she can perform at a given level, the less likely he or she will be to try to perform at that level. A person's $E{\to}P$ probabilities are also strongly influenced by each situation and by previous experience in that and similar situations.

b The performance-to-outcomes expectancy $(P{\to}O)$ and valence (V): This refers to a combination of a number of beliefs about what the outcomes of successful performance will be and the value or attractiveness of these outcomes to the individual. Valence is considered to vary from $+1$ (very desirable) to -1 (very undesirable) and the performance-to-outcomes probabilities vary from $+1$ (performance sure to lead to outcome) to 0 (performance not related to outcome). In general, the more likely a person feels that performance will lead to valent outcomes, the more likely he or she will be to try to perform at the required level.

c Instrumentality: As Figure 2 indicates, a single level of performance can be associated with a number of different outcomes, each having a certain degree of valence. Some outcomes are valent because they have direct value or attractiveness. Some outcomes, however, have valence because they are seen as leading to (or being "instrumental" for) the attainment of other "second level" outcomes which have direct value or attractiveness.

d Intrinsic and extrinsic outcomes: Some outcomes are seen as occurring directly as a result of performing the task itself and are outcomes which the individual thus gives to himself (i.e., feelings of accomplishment, creativity, etc.). These are called "intrinsic" outcomes. Other outcomes that are associated with performance are provided or mediated by external factors (the organization, the supervisor, the work group, etc.). These outcomes are called "extrinsic" outcomes.

Along with the graphic representation of these terms presented in Figure 2, there is a simplified formula for combining these perceptions to arrive at a term expressing the relative level of motivation to exert effort towards performance at a given level. The formula expresses these relationships:

a The person's motivation to perform is determined by the $P{\to}O$ expectancy multiplied by the valence (V) of the outcome. The valence of the first order outcome subsumes the instrumentalities and valences of second order outcomes. The relationship is multiplicative since there is no motivation to perform if either of the terms is zero.

b Since a level of performance has multiple outcomes associated with it, the products of all probability-times-valence combinations are added together for all the outcomes that are seen as related to the specific performance.

c This term (the summed $P{\to}O$ expectancies times valences) is then multiplied by the $E{\to}P$ expectancy. Again the multiplicative relationship indicates that if either term is zero, motivation is zero.

d In summary, the strength of a person's motivation to perform effectively is influenced by (1) the person's belief that effort can be converted into performance, and (2) the net attractiveness of the events that are perceived to stem from good performance.

So far, all the terms have referred to the individual's perceptions which result in motivation and thus an intention to behave in a certain way. Figure 3 is a simplified representation of the total model, showing how these intentions get translated into actual behavior.[7] The model envisions the following sequence of events:

a First, the strength of a person's motivation to perform correctly is most directly reflected in his or her effort—how hard he or she works. This effort expenditure may or may not result in good performance, since at least two factors must be right if effort is to be converted into performance. First, the person must possess the necessary abilities in order to perform the job well. Unless both ability and effort are high, there cannot be good performance. A second factor is the person's perception of how his or her effort can best be converted into performance. It is assumed that this perception is learned by the individual on the basis of previous experience in similar situations. This "how to do it" perception can obviously vary widely in accuracy, and—where erroneous perceptions exist—performance is low even though effort or motivation may be high.

b Second, when performance occurs, certain amounts of outcomes are obtained by the

Figure 3.   Simplified Expectancy-Theory Model of Behavior

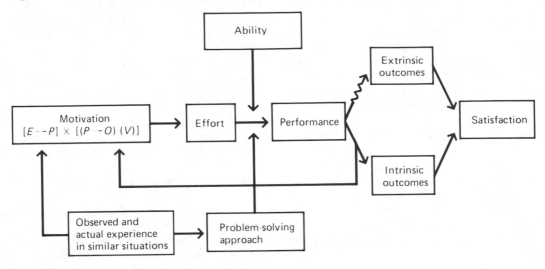

individual. Intrinsic outcomes, not being mediated by outside forces, tend to occur regularly as a result of performance, while extrinsic outcomes may or may not accrue to the individual (indicated by the wavy line in the model).

c Third, as a result of the obtaining of outcomes and the perceptions of the relative value of the outcomes obtained, the individual has a positive or negative affective response (a level of satisfaction or dissatisfaction).

d Fourth, the model indicates that events which occur influence future behavior by altering the $E \rightarrow P$, $P \rightarrow O$, and V perceptions. This process is represented by the feedback loops running from actual behavior back to motivation.

APPENDIX B: MEASURING MOTIVATION USING EXPECTANCY THEORY

Expectancy theory suggests that it is useful to measure the attitudes individuals have in order to diagnose motivational problems. Such measurement helps the manager to understand why employees are motivated or not, what the strength of motivation is in different parts of the organization, and how effective different rewards are for motivating performance. A short version of a questionnaire used to measure motivation in organizations is included here.[8] Basically, three different questions need to be asked (see Tables 1, 2, and 3).

Using the Questionnaire Results

The results from this questionnaire can be used to calculate a *work-motivation score*. A score can be calculated for each individual and scores can be combined for groups of individuals. The procedure for obtaining a work-motivation score is as follows:

a For each of the possible positive outcomes listed in questions 1 and 2, multiply the score for the outcome on question 1 ($P \rightarrow O$ expectancies) by the corresponding score on question 2 (valences of outcomes). Thus, score 1a would be multiplied by score 2a, score 1b by score 2b, etc.

b All of the 1 times 2 products should be added together to get a total of all expectancies times valences ———.

c The total should be divided by the number of pairs (in this case, eleven) to get an average expectancy-times-valence score ———.

d The scores from question 3 ($E \rightarrow P$ expectancies) should be added together and then di-

Table 1. Question 1: Here are some things that could happen to people if they do their jobs *especially well.* How likely is it that each of these things would happen if you performed your job *especially well?*

		Not at all likely		Somewhat likely		Quite likely		Extremely likely
a	You will get a bonus or pay increase	(1)	(2)	(3)	(4)	(5)	(6)	(7)
b	You will feel better about yourself as a person ...	(1)	(2)	(3)	(4)	(5)	(6)	(7)
c	You will have an opportunity to develop your skills and abilities	(1)	(2)	(3)	(4)	(5)	(6)	(7)
d	You will have better job security	(1)	(2)	(3)	(4)	(5)	(6)	(7)
e	You will be given chances to learn new things ..	(1)	(2)	(3)	(4)	(5)	(6)	(7)
f	You will be promoted or get a better job	(1)	(2)	(3)	(4)	(5)	(6)	(7)
g	You will get a feeling that you've accomplished something worthwhile	(1)	(2)	(3)	(4)	(5)	(6)	(7)
h	You will have more freedom on your job	(1)	(2)	(3)	(4)	(5)	(6)	(7)
i	You will be respected by the people you work with	(1)	(2)	(3)	(4)	(5)	(6)	(7)
j	Your supervisor will praise you	(1)	(2)	(3)	(4)	(5)	(6)	(7)
k	The people you work with will be friendly with you	(1)	(2)	(3)	(4)	(5)	(6)	(7)

vided by three to get an average effort-to-performance expectancy score ————.

e Multiply the score obtained in step c (the average expectancy times valence) by the score obtained in step d (the average $E{\rightarrow}P$ expectancy score) to obtain a total work-motivation score ————.

Additional Comments on the Work-Motivation Score

A number of important points should be kept in mind when using the questionnaire to get a work-motivation score. First, the questions presented here are just a short version of a larger and more comprehensive questionnaire. For more detail, the articles and publications referred to here and in the text should be consulted. Second, this is a general questionnaire. Since it is hard to anticipate in a general questionnaire what may be valent outcomes in each situation, the individual manager may want to add additional outcomes to questions 1 and 2. Third, it is important to remember that questionnaire results can be influ-

enced by the feelings people have when they fill out the questionnaire. The use of the questionnaire as outlined above assumes a certain level of trust between manager and subordinates. People filling out questionnaires need to know what is going to be done with their answers and usually need to be assured of the confidentiality of their responses. Finally, the research indicates that, in many cases, the score obtained by simply averaging all the responses to question 1 (the $P{\rightarrow}O$ expectancies) will be as useful as the fully calculated work-motivation score. In each situation, the manager should experiment and find out whether the additional information in questions 2 and 3 aid in motivational diagnosis.

NOTES

1. For reviews of the expectancy theory research see Mitchell, T. R. Expectancy models of job satisfaction, occupational preference and effort: A theoretical methodological, and empirical appraisal. *Psychological Bulletin*, 1974, 81, 1053–1077. For a more general discussion of expectancy theory and other approaches to

Table 2. Question 2: Different people want different things from their work. Here is a list of things a person could have on his or her job. How *important* is each of the following to you?

	Moderately important or less		Quite important			Extremely important	
How Important Is . . . ?							
a The amount of pay you get	(1)	(2)	(3)	(4)	(5)	(6)	(7)
b The chances you have to do something that makes you feel good about yourself as a person	(1)	(2)	(3)	(4)	(5)	(6)	(7)
c The opportunity to develop your skills and abilities	(1)	(2)	(3)	(4)	(5)	(6)	(7)
d The amount of job security you have	(1)	(2)	(3)	(4)	(5)	(6)	(7)
How Important Is . . . ?							
e The chances you have to learn new things	(1)	(2)	(3)	(4)	(5)	(6)	(7)
f Your chances for getting a promotion or getting a better job	(1)	(2)	(3)	(4)	(5)	(6)	(7)
g The chances you have to accomplish something worthwhile	(1)	(2)	(3)	(4)	(5)	(6)	(7)
h The amount of freedom you have on your job	(1)	(2)	(3)	(4)	(5)	(6)	(7)
How Important Is . . . ?							
i The respect you receive from the people you work with	(1)	(2)	(3)	(4)	(5)	(6)	(7)
j The praise you get from your supervisor	(1)	(2)	(3)	(4)	(5)	(6)	(7)
k The friendliness of the people you work with	(1)	(2)	(3)	(4)	(5)	(6)	(7)

Table 3. Question 3: Below you will see a number of pairs of factors that look like this:

Warm weather→sweating   (1)   (2)   (3)   (4)   (5)   (6)   (7)

You are to indicate by checking the appropriate number to the right of each pair how often it is true for *you* personally that the first factor leads to the second on *your job.* Remember, for each pair, indicate how often it is true by checking the box under the response which seems most accurate.

	Never		Sometimes		Often		Almost always
a Working hard→high productivity	(1)	(2)	(3)	(4)	(5)	(6)	(7)
b Working hard→doing my job well	(1)	(2)	(3)	(4)	(5)	(6)	(7)
c Working hard→good job performance	(1)	(2)	(3)	(4)	(5)	(6)	(7)

motivation see Lawler, E. E. *Motivation in work organizations,* Belmont Calif.: Brooks/Cole, 1973.

2. Lawler, E. E., Kuleck, W. J., Rhode, J. G., & Sorenson, J. F. Job choice and post-decision disso-

nance. *Organizational Behavior and Human Performance,* 1975, 13, 133–145.

3. For a detailed discussion of the implications of expectancy theory for pay and reward systems, see Law-

ler, E. E. *Pay and organizational effectiveness: A psychological view.* New York: McGraw-Hill, 1971.

4. A good discussion of job design with an expectancy theory perspective is in Hackman, J. R., Oldham, G. R., Janson, R., & Purdy, K. A new strategy for job enrichment. *California Management Review,* Summer, 1975, p. 57.

5. The use of questionnaires for understanding and changing organizational behavior is discussed in Nadler, D. A. *Feedback and organizational development: Using data-based methods.* Reading, Mass.: Addison-Wesley, 1977.

6. The whole issue of individualizing organizations is examined in Lawler, E. E. The individualized organization: Problems and promise. *California Management Review,* 1974, 17(2), 31–39.

7. For a more detailed statement of the model see Lawler, E. E. Job attitudes and employee motivation: Theory, research and practice. *Personnel Psychology,* 1970, 23, 223–237.

8. For a complete version of the questionnaire and supporting documentation see Nadler, D. A., Cammann, C., Jenkins, G. D., & Lawler, E. E. (Eds.) *The Michigan organizational assessment package* (Progress Report II). Ann Arbor: Survey Research Center, 1975.

8

Satisfaction
and behavior

Edward E. Lawler III

[Compared to what is known about motivation, relatively little is known about the determinants and consequences of satisfaction. Although thousands of studies have been done on job satisfaction during the last thirty years, those studies have not usually been theoretically oriented. Instead, researchers simply have looked at the relationship between job satisfaction and factors such as age, education, job level, absenteeism rate, productivity, and so on.

Originally, much of the research seemed to be stimulated by a desire to show that job satisfaction is important because it influences productivity. Underlying the earlier articles on job satisfaction was a strong conviction that happy workers are productive workers. Recently, however, this theme has been disappearing, and many organizational psychologists

seem to be studying job satisfaction simply because they are interested in finding its causes.

As it turns out, satisfaction is related to absenteeism and turnover, both of which are very costly to organizations. Thus, there is a very practical economic reason for organizations to be concerned with job satisfaction, since it can influence organizational effectiveness. However, before any practical use can be made of the findings, that job dissatisfaction causes absenteeism and turnover, we must understand what factors cause and influence job satisfaction.]—Eds.

A MODEL OF FACET SATISFACTION

Figure 1 presents a model of the determinants of facet satisfaction. The model is intended to be applicable to understanding what determines a

Figure 1. Model of the Determinants of Satisfaction

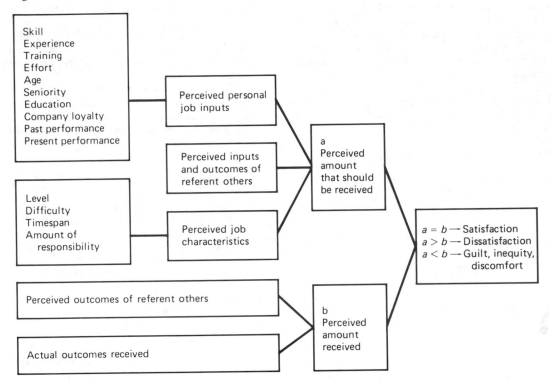

person's satisfaction with any facet of the job. The model assumes that the same psychological processes operate to determine satisfaction with job factors ranging from pay to supervision and satisfaction with the work itself. The model in Figure 1 is a discrepancy model in the sense that it shows satisfaction as the difference between *a*, what a person feels he should receive, and *b*, what he perceives that he actually receives. The model indicates that when the person's perception of what his outcome level is and his perception of what his outcome level should be are in agreement, the person will be satisfied. When a person perceives his outcome level as falling below what he feels it should be, he will be dissatisfied. However, when a person's perceived outcome level exceeds what he feels it should be, he will have feelings of guilt and inequity and perhaps some discomfort (Adams, 1965). Thus, for any job factor, the assumption is that satisfaction with the factor will be determined by the difference

between how much of the factor there is and how much of the factor the person feels there should be.

Present outcome level is shown to be the key influence on a person's perception of what rewards he receives, but his perception is also shown to be influenced by his perception of what his "referent others" receive. The higher the outcome levels of his referent others, the lower his outcome level will appear. Thus, a person's psychological view of how much of a factor he receives is said to be influenced by more than just the objective amount of the factor. Because of this psychological influence, the same amount of reward often can be seen quite differently by two people; to one person it can be a large amount, while to another person it can be a small amount.

The model in Figure 1 also shows that a person's perception of what his reward level should be is influenced by a number of factors. Perhaps the most important influence is perceived job inputs. These inputs include all of the skills, abilities, and training a person brings to the job as well as the behavior he exhibits on the job. The greater he perceives his inputs to be, the higher will be his perception of what his outcomes should be. Because of this relationship, people with high job inputs must receive more rewards than people with low job inputs or they will be dissatisfied. The model also shows that a person's perception of what his outcomes should be is influenced by his perception of the job demands. The greater the demands made by the job, the more he will perceive he should receive. Job demands include such things as job difficulty, responsibilities, and organization level. If outcomes do not rise along with these factors, the clear prediction of the model is that the people who perceive they have the more difficult, higher-level jobs will be the most dissatisfied.

The model shows that a person's perception of what his outcomes should be is influenced by what the person perceives his comparison-other's inputs and outcomes to be. This aspect of the model is taken directly from equity theory and is included to stress the fact that people look at the inputs and outcomes of others in order to determine what their own outcome level should be. If a person's comparison-other's inputs are the same as the person's inputs but the other's outcomes are much higher, the person will feel that he should be receiving more outcomes and will be dissatisfied as a result.

The model allows for the possibility that people will feel that their outcomes exceed what they should be. The feelings produced by this condition are quite different from those produced by under-reward. Because of this difference, it does not make sense to refer to a person who feels overrewarded as being dissatisfied. There is considerable evidence that very few people feel overrewarded, and this fact can be explained by the model. Even when people are highly rewarded, the social-comparison aspect of satisfaction means that people can avoid feeling overrewarded by looking around and finding someone to compare with who is doing equally well. Also, a person tends to value his own inputs much higher than they are valued by others (Lawler, 1967). Because of this discrepancy, a person's perception of what his outcomes should be is often not shared

by those administering his rewards, and is often above what he actually receives. Finally, the person can easily increase his perception of his inputs and thereby justify a high reward level.

As a way of summarizing some of the implications of the model, let us briefly make some statements about who should be dissatisfied if the model is correct. Other things being equal:

1. People with high perceived inputs will be more dissatisfied with a given facet than people with low perceived inputs.
2. People who perceive their jobs to be demanding will be more dissatisfied with a given facet than people who perceive their jobs as undemanding.
3. People who perceive similar others as having a more favorable input-outcome balance will be more dissatisfied with a given facet than people who perceive their own balance as similar to or better than that of others.
4. People who receive a low outcome level will be more dissatisfied than those who receive a high outcome level.
5. The more outcomes a person perceives his comparison-other receives, the more dissatisfied he will be with his own outcomes. This should be particularly true when the comparison-other is seen to hold a job that demands the same or fewer inputs.

Most theories of job satisfaction argue that overall job satisfaction is determined by some combination of all facet-satisfaction feelings. This could be expressed in terms of the facet-satisfaction model in Figure 1 as a simple sum of, or average of, all *a–b* discrepancies. Thus, overall job satisfaction is determined by the difference between all the things a person feels he should receive from his job and all the things he actually does receive. . . .

CONSEQUENCES OF DISSATISFACTION

Originally, much of the interest in job satisfaction stemmed from the belief that job satisfaction influenced job performance. Specifically, psychologists thought that high job satisfaction led to high job performance. This view has now been discredited, and most psychologists feel that satisfaction influences absenteeism and turnover but not job performance. However, before looking at the relationship among satisfaction, absenteeism, and turnover, let's review the work on satisfaction and performance.

JOB PERFORMANCE

In the 1950s, two major literature reviews showed that in most studies only a slight relationship had been found between satisfaction and performance. A later review by Vroom (1964) also showed that studies had not found a strong relationship between satisfaction and performance; in fact, most studies had found a very low positive relationship between the two. In other words, better performers did seem to be slightly more satisfied than poor performers. A considerable amount of recent work suggests that the slight existing relationship is probably due to better performance indirectly causing satisfaction rather than the reverse. Lawler and Porter (1967) explained this "performance causes satisfaction" viewpoint as follows:

> If we assume that rewards cause satisfaction, and that in some cases performance produces rewards, then it is possible that the relationship found between satisfaction and performance

comes about through the action of a third variable—rewards. Briefly stated, good performance may lead to rewards, which in turn lead to satisfaction; this formulation then would say that satisfaction rather than causing performance, as was previously assumed, is caused by it.

[Figure 2] shows that performance leads to rewards, and it distinguishes between two kinds of rewards and their connection to performance. A wavy line between performance and extrinsic rewards indicates that such rewards are likely to be imperfectly related to performance. By extrinsic rewards is meant such organizationally controlled rewards as pay, promotion, status, and security—rewards that are often referred to as satisfying mainly lower-level needs. The connection is relatively weak because of the difficulty of tying extrinsic rewards directly to performance. Even though an organization may have a policy of rewarding merit, performance is difficult to measure, and in dispensing rewards like pay, many other factors are frequently taken into consideration.

Quite the opposite is likely to be true for intrinsic rewards, however, since they are given to the individual by himself for good performance. Intrinsic or internally mediated rewards are subject to fewer disturbing influences and thus are likely to be more directly related to good performance. This connection is indicated in the model by a semiwavy line. Probably the best example of an intrinsic reward is the feeling of having accomplished something worthwhile. For that matter any of the rewards that satisfy self-actualization needs or higher-order growth needs are good examples of intrinsic rewards [pp. 23–24].[1]

Figure 2. Model of Relationship of Performance to Satisfaction

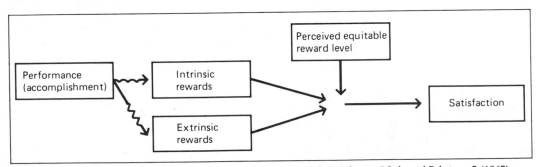

From E. E. Lawler and L. W. Porter, "The Effect of Performance on Job Satisfaction," *Industrial Relations*, 7 (1967), pp. 20–28. Reprinted by permission.

Figure 2 shows that intrinsic and extrinsic rewards are not directly related to job satisfaction, since the relationship is moderated by perceived equitable rewards (what people think they should receive). The model in Figure 2 is similar to the model in Figure 1, since both models show that satisfaction is a function of the amount of rewards a person receives and the amount of rewards he feels he should receive.

Because of the imperfect relationship between performance and rewards and the important effect of perceived equitable rewards, a low but positive relationship should exist between job satisfaction and job performance in most situations. However, in certain situations, a strong positive relationship may exist; while in other situations, a negative relationship may exist. A negative relationship would be expected where rewards are unrelated to performance or negatively related to performance.

To have the same level of satisfaction for good performers and poor performers, the good performers must receive more rewards than the poor performers. The reason for this, as stressed earlier, is that performance level influences the amount of rewards a person feels he should receive. Thus, when rewards are not based on performance— when poor performers receive equal rewards or a larger amount of rewards than good performers— the best performers will be the least satisfied, and a negative satisfaction-performance relationship will exist. If, on the other hand, the better performers are given significantly more rewards, a positive satisfaction-performance relationship should exist. If it is assumed that most organizations are partially successful in relating rewards to performance, it follows that most studies should find a low but positive relationship between satisfaction and performance. Lawler and Porter's (1967) study was among those that found this relationship; their study also found that, as predicted, intrinsic-need satisfaction was more closely related to performance than was extrinsic-need satisfaction.

In retrospect, it is hard to understand why the belief that high satisfaction causes high performance was so widely accepted. There is nothing in the literature on motivation that suggests this causal relationship. In fact, such a relationship is opposite to the concepts developed by both drive theory and expectancy theory. If anything, these two theories would seem to predict that high satisfaction might reduce motivation because of a consequent reduction in the importance of various rewards that may have provided motivational force. Clearly, a more logical view is that performance is determined by people's efforts to obtain the goals and outcomes they desire, and satisfaction is determined by the outcomes people actually obtain. Yet, for some reason, many people believed—and some people still do believe—that the "satisfaction causes performance" view is best.

TURNOVER

The relationship between satisfaction and turnover has been studied often. In most studies, researchers have measured the job satisfaction among a number of employees and then waited to see which of the employees studied left during an ensuing time period (typically, a year). The satisfaction scores of the employees who left have then been compared with the remaining employees' scores. Although relationships between satisfaction scores and turnover have not always been very strong, the studies in this area have consistently shown that dissatisfied workers are more likely than satisfied workers to terminate employment; thus, satisfaction scores can predict turnover.

A study by Ross and Zander (1957) is a good example of the kind of research that has been done. Ross and Zander measured the job satisfaction of 2,680 female workers in a large company. Four months later, these researchers found that 169 of these employees had resigned; those who left were significantly more dissatisfied with the amount of recognition they received on their jobs, with the amount of achievement they experienced, and with the amount of autonomy they had.

Probably the major reason that turnover and satisfaction are not more strongly related is that turnover is very much influenced by the availability of other positions. Even if a person is very dissatisfied with his job, he is not likely to leave unless more attractive alternatives are available.

This observation would suggest that in times of economic prosperity, turnover should be high, and a strong relationship should exist between turnover and satisfaction; but in times of economic hardship, turnover should be low, and little relationship should exist between turnover and satisfaction. There is research evidence to support the argument that voluntary turnover is much lower in periods of economic hardship. However, no study has compared the relationship between satisfaction and turnover under different economic conditions to see if it is stronger under full employment.

ABSENTEEISM

Like turnover, absenteeism has been found to be related to job satisfaction. If anything, the relationship between satisfaction and absenteeism seems to be stronger than the relationship between satisfaction and turnover. However, even in the case of absenteeism, the relationship is far from being isomorphic. Absenteeism is caused by a number of factors other than a person's voluntarily deciding not to come to work; illness, accidents, and so on can prevent someone who wants to come to work from actually coming to work. We would expect satisfaction to affect only voluntary absences; thus, satisfaction can never be strongly related to a measure of overall absence rate. Those studies that have separated voluntary absences from overall absences have, in fact, found that voluntary absence rates are much more closely related to satisfaction than are overall absence rates (Vroom, 1964). Of course, this outcome would be expected if satisfaction does influence people's willingness to come to work.

ORGANIZATION EFFECTIVENESS

The research evidence clearly shows that employees' decisions about whether they will go to work on any given day and whether they will quit are affected by their feelings of job satisfaction.

All the literature reviews on the subject have reached this conclusion. The fact that present satisfaction influences future absenteeism and turnover clearly indicates that the causal direction is from satisfaction to behavior. This conclusion is in marked contrast to our conclusion with respect to performance—that is, behavior causes satisfaction.

The research evidence on the determinants of satisfaction suggests that satisfaction is very much influenced by the actual rewards a person receives; of course, the organization has a considerable amount of control over these rewards. The research also shows that, although not all people will react to the same reward level in the same manner, reactions are predictable if something is known about how people perceive their inputs. The implication is that organizations can influence employees' satisfaction levels. Since it is possible to know how employees will react to different outcome levels, organizations can allocate outcomes in ways that will either cause job satisfaction or job dissatisfaction.

Absenteeism and turnover have a very direct influence on organizational effectiveness. Absenteeism is very costly because it interrupts scheduling, creates a need for overstaffing, increases fringe-benefit costs, and so on. Turnover is expensive because of the many costs incurred in recruiting and training replacement employees. For lower-level jobs, the cost of turnover is estimated at $2,000 a person; at the managerial level, the cost is at least five to ten times the monthly salary of the job involved. Because satisfaction is manageable and influences absenteeism and turnover, organizations can control absenteeism and turnover. Generally, by keeping satisfaction high and, specifically, by seeing that the best employees are the most satisfied, organizations can retain those employees they need the most. In effect, organizations can manage turnover so that, if it occurs, it will occur among employees the organization can most afford to lose. However, keeping the better performers more satisfied is not easy, since they must be rewarded very well. Although identifying and rewarding the better performers is not always easy, the effort may have significant payoffs in terms of increased organizational effectiveness.

NOTE

1. E. E. Lawler and L. W. Porter, "The Effect of Performance on Job Satisfaction," *Industrial Relations* 7 (1967), pp. 20–28. Reprinted by permission.

REFERENCES

Adams, J. S. "Injustice in Social Exchange." In L. Berkowitz (ed.), *Advances in Experimental Social Psychology*, vol. 2. New York: Academic Press, 1965.

Lawler, E. E. "The Multitrait-Multirater Approach to Measuring Managerial Job Performance." *Journal of Applied Psychology* 51 (1967), 369–81.

Lawler, E. E., and Porter, L. W. "The Effect of Performance on Job Satisfaction." *Industrial Relations* 7 (1967), 20–28.

Ross, I. E., and Zander, A. F. "Need Satisfaction and Employee Turnover." *Personnel Psychology* 10 (1957), 327–38.

Vroom, V. H. *Work and Motivation*. New York: John Wiley and Sons, 1964.

9

Motivation
from the bottom up

Barry M. Staw

It can be said that there is nothing so central to an organization's functioning as the motivation of its members. It can also be said that there has been more research on individual motivation than on any other topic within organizational behavior. Yet, somehow, most of the research in this area has either added little to what we already know from early experimental psychology (see, e.g., Thorndike, 1911; Tolman, 1932; Lewin, 1938), or has provided us with few insights which go beyond prevailing common sense.

Source: "Motivation in Organizations: Toward Synthesis and Redirection," by Barry M. Staw in Barry M. Staw and Gerald R. Salancik, *New Directions in Organizational Behavior*, pp. 55–95. Copyright © 1977 by John Wiley & Sons, Inc. Reprinted by permission of John Wiley & Sons, Inc.

In the past decade, a great deal of research has, for example, gone into the question of whether a multiplicative modle (*expectancy* × *valence*) is appropriate to specify motivational force (see Heneman and Schwab, 1972; Behling and Starke, 1973; House, Shapiro, and Wahba, 1974; and Mitchell, 1974, for reviews). This issue has been fraught with methodological and empirical difficulties (Schmidt, 1973; Connolly, 1977) and shows little prospect of being resolved. One might contend, therefore, that research on expectancy theory would be more fruitful if some of its basic questions were rephrased. Instead of testing the statistical significance of an expectancy model or comparing multiplicative versus additive models of motivation, one should ask under what conditions would individual motivation be expected to approximate a subjective expected utility (SEU) model, and when would it be less rational?

It may be true, for example, that many individuals and subgroups do not engage in detailed cognitive arithmetic to decide which organization to join and at what level to perform. Many individuals may merely model the behavior of salient others or follow the path that appears appropriate for a person from a particular family background or socioeconomic group. Individuals may join an organization or perform at a certain level because it "seems the right thing to do," rather than its being the product of subjective expected utility. As Salancik has shown in a series of original studies (Salancik, 1974; Salancik and Conway, 1975), individuals may analyze their behavior in rationalistic terms only when faced with such a task presented to them by an outside researcher.

Although many studies testing expectancy models are subject to the bias that rationality has been retrospectively called (cf. Staw, 1976) rather than concurrently tapped by the researcher, these studies are still unimpressive in their support for the theory. The magnitude of unexplained variance should lead us to look for moderating variables. One such variable might be the fit between occupational status of the job and socioeconomic background of the role occupant. When the individual is upwardly mobile in status, his behavior may be better predicted by an expectancy-value model than when he is satisfied with his social station. Alternatively, if the individual's job occupies a small aspect of his "central life interest" (Dubin, Champoux, and Porter, 1975), the individual should be expected to do little cognitive work in deciding to join a particular organization or perform within it. Expectancy-value formulations may be appropriate only for the most important decisions an individual must make. For those uninvolved in work, day-to-day performance questions or the choice of one of many perceived-to-be similar organizations (e.g., an auto worker's choice of Ford, GM, or Chrysler) may closely resemble impulse purchase decisions of consumers. Many workers may reserve their cognitive prowess for decisions about the allocation of leisure time and durable goods.

Finally, we should not expect individuals to engage *continually* in a cognitive motivational process. Individuals are most attentive to behavior-outcome contingencies in learning a new task or when confronted with a large discrepancy between present reward levels and a salient alternative (e.g., when a new pay plan is introduced). In other situations, the individual's behavior has probably become routinized and this patterning could be represented either in terms of an operant conditioning model (Skinner, 1953, 1974) or as a decision subroutine (March and Simon, 1958).

A DIVERGENT APPROACH

Mapping the cognitive antecedents of behavior is important and research should no doubt continue on it. But at the same time we should begin to examine alternative formulations of individual behavior. One strategy which is helpful in developing new theoretical propositions is to alter the point of view or perspective from which current theorizing addresses behavior.

Many existing theories of individual behavior can be viewed as formulations of individual adaptation to the environment. Certainly Skinner's theory of reinforcement and operant conditioning represents the view that man is extensively shaped by the reward/punishment contingencies around him. However, other motivational models can also be viewed, as White (1959) pointed out, as manifestations of an individual's motivation to be "competent" or positively adapted to his particular social and physical surroundings. For example, Festinger's (1957) theory of cognitive dissonance as well as the attribution models of Kelley (1967), Bem (1967, 1972), and Jones and Davis (1965) are theories about how individuals make sense of their physical and social worlds. Even the maximizing notions of expectancy theory and Simon's (1957) alternative of satisficing can be viewed in this way.

At the organizational level of analysis there has been a concomitant degree of theory development on how organizations can best be adapted to their environments. Work on centralization-decentralization (e.g., Blau and Schoenherr, 1971; Hage and Aiken, 1969; Mackenzie, 1975), integration and differentiation (e.g., Lawrence and Lorsch, 1967; Child, 1974, 1975; Khand-walla, 1974), and matrix organizational designs (Shull, 1965; Galbraith, 1973), are examples of this perspective. The central research question in this line of research has been how the particular structure of an organization interacts with characteristics of the organization's environment (such as uncertainty and technological change) to produce a given level of effectiveness.

Figure 1 represents the above two theoretical perspectives as the directed lines A and B. In Figure 1, the organization is fitted within its environment, while top levels of the organization are shown to constitute the environment of lower participants. From a top-management perspective, societal institutions (including other organizations and the market economy) comprise the external context in which behavior must be en-acted. This environment determines many of the behavior-outcome contingencies which will shape and alter the organization's behavior. From the perspective of lower levels within the organization, the environment primarily consists of the actions and policies set by higher-level management. These policies frequently describe the behavior-outcome contingencies the lower-level participant faces on his job.

As illustrated in Figure 1, each level in the organizational system tends to determine the behavior-outcome contingencies under which the lower level must operate. This is obviously an oversimplification, but it tends to fit a large body of theory and empirical research in organizational behavior. At the micro level, for example, organizational research is often concerned with the

Figure 1. Flow of Influence in Intra- and Extraorganizational Environments

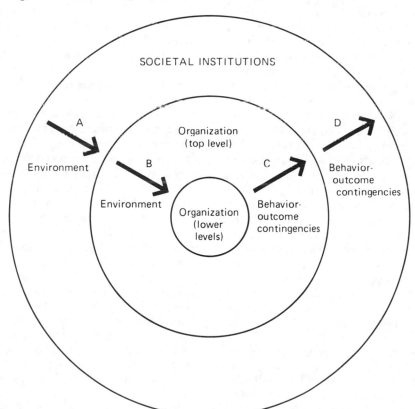

individual's response to incentive schemes, leadership practices, and control mechanisms exerted from higher levels in the organization. Individual behavior is studied largely to show why individuals respond positively to some actions and policies of management but negatively to others. In essence, much of the micro-level research has implicitly taken the perspective of higher management who attempt to control behavior-outcome contingencies and endeavor to increase worker response to them. From this perspective, the individual is viewed as an adaptive organism who responds to the reward contingencies facing him. Thus, if there is little positive response from the individual to a new program (e.g., job enlargement), the problem is conceptualized as due to the fact that the proper valences were not tapped (e.g., individuals may have low growth needs) or the contingencies between behavior and accomplishment or between accomplishment and reward were not clearly specified (e.g., task goals were not clearly set).

I would advocate that we enlarge our perspective of individuals in organizations, and that we attempt to creatively reverse our point of view. As shown in Figure 1, there is an influence process that flows upward in the organization (cf. Mechanic, 1962) and also from the organization to its environment (cf. Thompson, 1967). By reversing our perspective, we not only recognize this upward influence but can build specific hypotheses which are not evident without it. This practice has already occurred to a large extent in the macro literature on organizations. Following Thompson's (1967) seminal work, the organization is viewed as an entity which attempts to shape its environment, reduce potential sources of uncertainty, and enlarge its bases of resources. The organization does not merely adapt to behavior-outcome contingencies facing it from the environment, but it alters these contingencies by *acting on* the environment. A number of empirical studies have tested this basic hypothesis (see, e.g., Selznick, 1949; Zald, 1967; Pfeffer, 1972, 1973).

Micro-level theory could profit by testing the same kinds of hypotheses that are now centered in the sociological literature. The individual should not be viewed as a passive acceptor of behavior-outcome contingencies or merely as an adapter to them, but also an entity which strives

to alter its environment. The individual, like the organization, strives to reduce sources of uncertainty in his day-to-day relations with superiors. One particular source of uncertainty the individual strives to reduce is uncertainty over the allocation of resources. From the individual's perspective, improvement may come in the form of increased control over reinforcement contingencies so that the individual is assured of a given level of reward for a specific behavior. In this regard it should be noted that unionization of the workplace brings increased power to workers and that this power is usually manifested in control over behavior-outcome contingencies. Union demands for weekly wages, rather than piece-rate incentives, and for the implementation of strict work rules can be interpreted as evidence for a demand for control over reinforcement contingencies.

A second method by which the individual may actively improve his situation in the organization is by ingratiation (Wortman and Linsenmeier, 1976). If the individual can manipulate his supervisor's attitudes and opinions of him, he can improve his share of resources allocated by the supervisor. Through ingratiation, the individual may receive more than he deserves for a given level of work or at least assure himself of a positive evaluation of his task output.

In developing a theory of individual action within the organizational environment, one caveat should be kept in mind: Individuals may indeed strive to reduce sources of uncertainty but they do not strive for high probabilities of receiving low rewards. This oversight in the macro-organizational literature has led to an overemphasis on environmental conditions leading to uncertainty and a virtual neglect of the scarcity-munificence of environments. As noted by Staw and Szwajkowski (1975), organizations strive to improve their quantities of resources in addition to reducing uncertainty in resource procurement. Thus, at the individual level of analysis, we must develop hypotheses which include both the magnitude of reinforcement received and the contingency between behavior and outcomes. A sample set of general hypotheses from which specific testable propositions can be derived is stated below:

Hypothesis 1: Individuals strive to increase the probability of receiving positive outcomes and to reduce the probability of receiving negative outcomes within the organization.

Hypothesis 2: Individuals attempt to control the reinforcement contingencies leading to both desirable and undesirable outcomes.

Hypothesis 3: If direct control of the reinforcement contingencies is impossible, individuals attempt to personally influence the allocator of resources so as to improve personal outcomes.

Hypothesis 4: If direct control of the reinforcement contingencies or indirect control through personal influence is impossible, individuals attempt to make the contingencies more predictable.

Hypothesis 5: Individuals strive to reduce the possibility of negative outcomes before attempting to control or make predictable positive outcomes from the organization.

From these hypotheses and others similar to them, it is possible to build a testable theory of upward influence in the organization. The individual, like the organization, may attempt to carve a niche for himself which is both highly munificent and low in uncertainty. The individual can attempt to do this in a one-to-one role relationship with his supervisor, and relations with subordinates and peers. Graen (1976), for example, has suggested that roles are negotiated between the superior and subordinate, and that the role-making process is determined by both interpersonal attraction and bargaining. We would contend that individuals generally follow a strategy of improving interpersonal attraction or ingratiation in one-to-one relationships with supervisors. Outright bargaining with supervisors runs the risk of future sanctions or negative outcomes, except when the individual's expertise is especially high or the individual is nearly irreplaceable. High-skill personnel, and especially those with ready opportunities in alternative organizations are, however, more likely to utilize either overt or implied bargaining in shaping their organizational roles. Low-skill personnel and those with fewer outside opportunities are more likely to use bargaining agents such as unions to help control behavior-outcome contingencies on the job.

A relevant question which follows from the above analysis is, "What are the consequences of behavior-outcome contingencies which are un-

predictable or uncontrollable by the individual?" As implied by the above hypotheses, lack of individual control or predictive ability may be aversive to organizational participants. Several separate areas of research provide data which bear on this question.

Prediction of Behavior-Outcome Contingencies

The most familiar body of research data which is relevant to this issue is that of role conflict and ambiguity (Kahn et al., 1964). When the individual's task is inadequately defined or there is substantial disparity in demands placed upon the individual from his supervisor, peers, or subordinates, the individual may find the situation to be aversive. Under these conditions, the individual has been found to possess low job satisfaction, low trust in supervisors, and poor mental health (Kahn et al., 1964).

In a theoretical sense, both role conflict and ambiguity can be interpreted as factors which reduce the individual's ability to predict behavior-outcome contingencies. When an individual does not know what is expected of him due to the absence of information (i.e., role ambiguity) or conflicting information (i.e., role conflict), his predictive power is reduced. House and his associates' recent work on leadership (House, 1971; House and Dessler, 1974; Szilgyi and Sims, 1974) suggests that increased clarification and supervision (i.e., initiating structure) will improve individual attitudes and behavior on ambiguous tasks. However, when a task is already highly structured and routine, initiating structure has been found to be negatively related to task satisfaction. Presumably, once behavior-outcome contingencies are relatively clear, increased supervision and work directives add little of positive value and may be viewed by many workers as threatening.

If individuals do indeed strive to make the behavior-outcome contingencies they face more predictable, how can this fact be reconciled with the research and theory on achievement motivation that shows high achievers tend to seek out risk-taking situations (Atkinson and Raynor, 1974)? Fortunately, this paradox is more apparent than real. Individuals high in achievement motivation should not be viewed as deriving pleasure from uncertainty itself but from the *process of reducing it.* Behavior-outcome sequences which are either hopelessly impossible or trivially easy do not appeal to high achievers. They view 50-50 situations (termed "calculated risks" by McClelland) as most motivating because of the negative relationship between valence and expectancy (i.e., the most difficult tasks being the most rewarding) and the positive relationship between expectancy and goal attainment. Therefore, the primary contribution of achievement theory is to revise our expectancy-valence models so that the two factors of valence and expectancy are not independent. Achievement theory does not refute the notion that individuals strive to reduce uncertainty.

Control of Behavior-Outcome Contingencies

In recent years there have been a number of experimental studies designed to compare individuals' reactions to controllable and uncontrollable aversive outcomes (see Averill, 1973 and Glass and Singer, 1972, for reviews). Subjects in these studies are typically subjected to aversive stimuli and then either provided or not provided with information on how to terminate the stimulation (e.g., Corah and Boffa, 1970; Glass et al., 1971; Sherrod and Downs, 1974). In most of the studies in this area, subjects who can control aversive outcomes experience less stress than subjects without such control (see Wortman and Brehm, 1976).

Desire to control aversive outcomes makes sense intuitively and can be explained by any number of psychological theories. What is more compelling, in terms of testing an individual need or desire for control per se, is to examine the consequences of receiving positive outcomes under high and low choice. Tests of Brehm's (1966, 1972) theory of psychological reactance provide the most relevant data on individuals' striving for control.

Reactance

Brehm posited that when behavioral freedom is threatened, the individual will become motiva-

tionally aroused or experience reactance. The predicted consequences of psychological reactance are efforts to restore freedom and an increased desire for any lost options. Among empirical studies designed to test reactance theory, it has been shown, for example, that subjects will devalue positive outcomes if they are "forced" to receive them. If the individual expects to choose his outcomes, he will react negatively if they are selected for him—even if they are the very outcomes he had previously preferred (see Hammock and Brehm, 1966). The implications of psychological reactance for applications of reinforcement theory in organizations are quite profound. Will the individual react negatively to the allocation of positive and negative outcomes by supervisors or will he react more positively if he can reduce his dependence on higher authorities?

An answer to this question is likely to be found by examining the parameters posited by Brehm as underlying psychological reactance. According to Brehm (1966, 1972), reactance should only result when there is an initial expectation of freedom, when this freedom is of importance to the individual, and when there is a significant threat of elimination of the freedom. In the experiment described above (Hammock and Brehm, 1966), for example, simply giving the preferred alternative to subjects with no expectation of control led to an increase in its evaluation. Thus, it would seem reasonable to conclude that in organizations with a tradition of hierarchical relations there should be no reactance aroused in employees who have come to expect a topdown approach. Reactance would be more of a problem in organizations with a history of participative management that attempt to institute hierarchical controls. Participation and freedom, following Brehm, are thus easier to expand than to contract.

Learned Helplessness

Recently, a large number of studies have been conducted on a related phenomenon labeled, "learned helpessness" (see Wortman and Brehm, 1976, for a review). In a series of studies using laboratory animals, Seligman (1975) and his associates have found that exposure to uncontrollable, inescapable electric shock leads to a reduction in the ability to respond adaptively to future learning situations. This general finding has also been replicated in a number of task settings using human subjects (Hiroto and Seligman, 1975).

The practical implications of "learned helplessness" seem to conflict directly with those of reactance theory. One model posits that individuals react negatively to reductions in freedom and actively attempt to restore control, while the other posits that exposure to uncontrollable outcomes results in passive acceptance of any negative consequences. However, as noted by Wortman and Brehm (1976), it is possible to integrate learned helplessness and reactance into a single theoretical statement. Their model is presented in Figure 2. If a person expects to be able to control or influence outcomes that are of importance to him (i.e., at point *a* in the figure), exposure to uncontrollable events should arouse psychological reactance and the individual should be motivated to re-exert control. But, if the individual comes to learn through extended helplessness training that he cannot control his environment, he will stop trying. When a person has no expec-

tation of control (i.e., at point *b* in the figure) then reactance will *not* precede helplessness and the individual is predicted to quickly become a passive receiver of future outcomes. Wortman and Brehm report some tentative support for this model from animal research (e.g., Seligman and Maier, 1967; Sidman, Heinstein, and Conrad, 1957) and research using human subjects (e.g., Shaban and Welling, 1972; Glass and Singer, 1972; Krantz, Glass, and Snyder, 1974; Roth and Kuban, in press; Roth and Bootzin, 1974.

The Wortman and Brehm model of individuals' reaction to uncontrollable outcomes has some direct implications for everyday behavior, but these implications appear to turn on the critical variable of "expectation of control." Unfortunately, it is this same variable which is the most difficult to extrapolate across situations and individuals. Thus, following from the model, we must have some knowledge of both the history of upward and downward influence in the organization and the individual's personal reinforcement history in order to make accurate predictions. This is not a shortcoming of Wortman and Brehm's theory, but an empirical reality with which we must deal in applied research.

One factor which *is* a shortcoming of the Wortman and Brehm model is its lack of specificity of the notion of control. Much of the empirical work on reactance theory has dealt with the reduction of control over the distribution of outcomes, while the work on learned helplessness has been concerned with exposure to outcomes (primarily aversive) which are not contingent on the individual's actions. Thus, we can see that the crucial dimension of "exposure to uncontrollable outcomes" in Figure 2 can be interpreted as either inability to influence the allocation of resources or merely as inability to predict the linkage between one's behavior and subsequent allocations by others. The reason that this vagary is so important is that the Wortman and Brehm model, as it stands, can be used to support either increased *or* decreased control by lower-order participants in an organizational setting. If one uses the argument that predictive ability is the most important factor (citing the learned helplessness research as evidence), it is possible to conclude that the organization needs tighter top-down controls and increased power of supervisors to reward

Figure 2. The Integrative Model

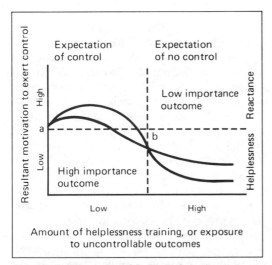

From C. B. Wortman and J. W. Brehm, "Responses to uncontrollable outcomes: An integration of reactance theory and the learned helplessness model," in I. Berkowitz (ed.), *Advances in Experimental Social Psychology* (Academic Press, 1976). Reprinted by permission.

and punish contingently.[1] If, however, one uses the argument that control over resource allocation is the crucial factor (as per reactance theory), then one would be hesitant to institute any top-down controls which inhibit freedom and tend to avoid behavior modification schemes (Luthans and Kreitner, 1975). Recall that reactance theory predicts that even positive outcomes may be devalued if they are not freely chosen by the individual.

It is my opinion that individuals do strive for control over their social environment and that one important source of control is that over behavior-outcome contingencies. If no control is possible, then the ability to predict will be preferred by individuals over random or noncontingent outcomes. Thus, it is possible that individuals *will* prefer top-down controls and contingent reinforcement schemes over situations in which there is no apparent link between behavior and reward. However, this is not to deny that *control over the allocation of outcomes* is probably more preferred than a highly predictable supervisor who controls the rewards.

An alternative model to that of Wortman and Brehm is presented in Figure 3. It shows that individuals follow a decision-making sequence in which they seek first to control and then, if control is not possible, to at least predict behavior-outcome sequences. If neither control nor prediction is perceived to be possible, the individual will either leave the field or become a passive acceptor of externally imposed outcomes. In Figure 3, expectations of control are shown as a moderating variable which determines where individuals begin this decision-making process. With no prior expectations of control, individuals are shown to strive primarily for prediction or clarity in behavior-outcome sequences. Clarity would be sought both in the specification of tasks to be completed and also in the rewards which would result from various levels of task performance. Individual differences in need for autonomy are also shown to affect the entry point in this decision process. With a low need for autonomy the individual may not be as interested in actual control over the allocation of resources as in predicting their distribution by supervisors. In addition, individual differences are relevant for one's personal history of control. Some individ-

uals have had very little exposure to situations in which they were able to influence the allocation of external rewards, while others (e.g., children raised on a communal farm) may have had little experience with highly authoritarian relationships. Finally, as touched upon earlier, the organization's own history of participative versus autocratic style of management will influence initial expectations of control.

As shown in the revised model of Figure 3, if attempts at both control and prediction fail, the individual becomes resigned to his fate or decides to leave the field. This latter option is added to make the model applicable to real-world settings in which turnover is a definite option for the individual faced with uncontrollable outcomes. In laboratory research on learned helplessness, the subject either has no option to leave the field (especially in the studies using animal subjects) or this option is extremely restricted. In organizations, factors such as external labor market conditions, the educational or skill level of the individual, and his visibility to other organizations may determine ease of turnover.

CONCLUSIONS

The theory of motivation presented here is one in which the individual is an active constructor of his social reality. The individual is viewed not merely as an information processor confronting a number of possible behavioral paths—each with their attendant rewards and costs—but as an actor who can attempt to change the parameters or "givens" of traditional motivation models. The individual can bargain, cajole, and ingratiate in order to change the contingencies between behavior and outcomes. In addition, the individual may be able to change the valences attached to the particular outcomes he faces. (For example, an individual may consciously give up security and achievement to concentrate on social gratification.[2]) What we are facing therefore in describing a theory of individual motivation in organizations is a highly complex system in which individuals have constructed a social and physical niche for themselves within the larger environ-

Figure 3. Flow Diagram of Upward Control

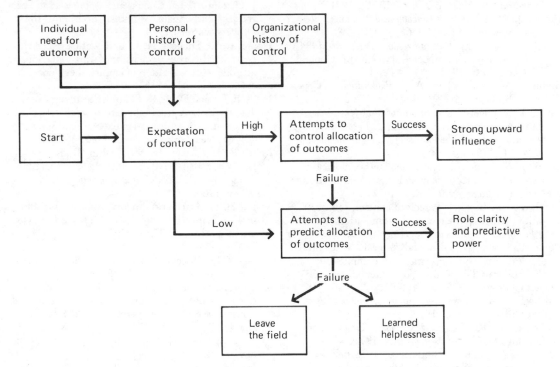

ment. This niche is built upon relationships developed over time with supervisors, subordinates, and peers in the organization and rests, in part, upon a role negotiation process (Graen, 1976). This niche is also built upon the individual's idiosyncratic construction of his social reality (Berger and Luckman, 1967; Weick, 1969). The processes of self-perception, dissonance arousal and reduction, and psychological reactance are but a few of the ways by which individuals come to grips with their social world. We need to know more about how individuals psychologically cope with the demands placed upon them by an organization and how these demands are in turn changed, redefined, or met by subordinates.

NOTES

1. William E. Scott, for example, has previously used the learned helplessness literature as evidence for greater use of contingent reward systems.

2. This point was also raised by William Simons in a graduate organization behavior seminar at Northwestern University, 1976.

REFERENCES

Atkinson, J. W., and Raynor, J. O. *Motivation and Achievement.* New York: Wiley, 1974.

Averill, J. Personal control over aversive stimuli and its relationship to stress. *Psychological Bulletin,* 1973, 80, 286–303.

Behling, O., and Starke, F. The postulates of expectancy theory. *Academy of Management Journal,* 1973, 16, 373–88.

Bem, D. J. Self-perception: The dependent variable of human performance. *Organizational Behavior and Human Performance,* 1967, 2, 105–21.

———. Self-perception theory. In L. Berkowitz (ed.), *Advances in Experimental Social Psychology* (vol. 6), Academic Press, 1972.

Berger, P. L., and Luckman, T. *The Social Construction of Reality.* New York: Anchor, 1967.

Blau, P. M., and Schoenherr, R. A. *The Structure of Organizations.* New York: Basic Books, 1971.

Brehm, J. W. *A Theory of Psychological Reactance.* New York: Academic Press, 1966.

———. *Responses to Loss of Freedom: A Theory of Psychological Reactance.* Morristown, N.J.: General Learning Press, 1972.

Brehm, J. W., and Cohen, A. R. *Explorations in Cognitive Dissonance.* New York: Wiley, 1962.

Child, J. Managerial and organizational factors associated with company performance, Part I: A contingency analysis. *The Journal of Management Studies,* 1974, 11, 175–89.

Connolly, T. Some conceptual and methodological issues in expectancy-type models of work motivation. *Academic Management Review,* 1977.

Corah, N. L., Boffa, J. Perceived control, self-observation, and response to aversive stimulation. *Journal of Personality and Social Psychology,* 1970.

Dubin, R. Champoux, J. E. and Porter, L. W. Central life interests and organizational commitment of blue-collar and clerical workers. *Administrative Science Quarterly,* 1975, 20, 411–21.

Festinger, L. A. *Theory of Cognitive Dissonance.* Stanford University Press, 1957.

Galbraith, J. R. *Designing Complex Organizations.* Reading, Mass.: Addison-Wesley, 1973.

Glass, D. C., Reim, B., and Singer, J. E. Behavioral consequences of adaptation to controllable and uncontrollable noise. *Journal of Experimental Social Psychology,* 1971, 7, 244–57.

Glass, D. C., and Singer, J. E. *Urban Stress.* New York: Academic Press, 1972.

Graen, G. Role making processes within complex organizations. In M. Dunnette (ed.) *Handbook of Industrial and Organizational Psychology.* Chicago: Rand McNally, 1976.

Hage, J., and Aiken, M. Routine technology, social structure and organization goals. *Administrative Science Quarterly,* 1969, 14, 366–76.

Hammock, T., and Brehm, J. W. The attractiveness of choice alternatives when freedom is eliminated by a social agent. *Journal of Personality,* 1966, 34, 546–54.

Heneman, H. G., and Schwab, D. P. Evaluation of research on expectancy theory predictions of employee performance. *Psychological Bulletin,* 1972, 78, 1–9.

Hiroto, D. S., and Seligmen, M. E. P. Generality of learned helplessness in man. *Journal of Personality and Social Psychology,* 1975, 31, 311–27.

House, R. J. A path-goal theory of leader effectiveness. *Administrative Science Quarterly,* 1971, 16, 321–35.

House, R. J., and Dessler, G. The path-goal theory of leadership: Some post hoc and a priori tests. In J. G. Hunt (ed.), *Contingency Approaches to Leadership.* Carbondale, Illinois: Southern Illinois University Press, 1974.

House, R. J., Shapiro, H. J., and Wahba, M. A. Expectancy theory as a predictor of work behavior and attitude: A reevaluation of empirical evidence. *Decision Sciences,* 1974, 5, 481–506.

Jones, E. E., and Davis, K. E. From acts to dispositions: The attribution process in person perception. In L. Berkowitz (ed.) *Advances in Experimental Social Psychology.* New York: Academic Press, 1965.

Kahn, R. L., Wolfe, D. M., Quinn, R. R., Snoek, J. D., and Rosenthal, R. N. *Organizational Stress: Studies in Role Conflict and Ambiguity.* New York: Wiley, 1964.

Kelley, H. H. Attribution theory in social psychology. In D. Levine (ed.) *Nebraska Symposium on Motivation* (vol. 15), University of Nebraska Press, 1967.

———. The process of causal attribution. *American Psychologist,* 1974, 28, 107–28.

Khandwalla, P. N. Mass output orientation of operations technology and organization structure. *Administrative Science Quarterly,* 1974, 19, 74–97.

Krantz, D. S., Glass, D. C., and Snyder, M. L. Helplessness, stress level, and the coronary-prone behavior pattern. *Journal of Experimental Social Psychology,* 1974, 10, 284–300.

Lawrence, P. R., and Lorsch, J. W. *Organization and Environment.* Boston: Harvard University, Graduate School of Business Administration, Division of Research.

Lewin, K. *The Conceptual Representation and the Measurement of Psychological Forces.* Durham: Duke University Press, 1938.

Luthans, F., and Kreitner, R. *Organizational Behavior Modification.* Glenview, Ill.: Scott, Foresman and Co., 1975.

Mackenzie, K. D. *A Theory of Group Structures.* Monograph, Lawrence, Kansas: University of Kansas, 1975.

March, J. G., and Simon, H. A. *Organizations.* New York: John Wiley, 1958.

McClelland, D. *The Achieving Society.* Princeton, N.J.: Van Nostrand, 1961.

Mechanic, D. Sources of power of lower participants in complex organizations. *Administrative Science Quarterly,* 1962, 7, 249–364.

Mitchell, T. R. Expectancy models of job satisfaction, occupational preference and effort: A theoretical, methodological, and empirical appraisal. *Psychological Bulletin,* 1974, 81, 1053–77.

Pfeffer, J. Merger as a response to organizational interdependence. *Administrative Science Quarterly*, 1972, 17, 382–94.

——. Size, composition, and function of hospital boards of directors: A study of organization-environment linkage. *Administrative Science Quarterly*, 1973, 18, 349–64.

Roth, S., and Bootzin, R. The effects of experimentally induced expectancies of external control: An investigation of learned helplessness. *Journal of Personality of Social Psychology*, 1974, 29, 253–64.

Roth, S., and Kubal, L. The effects of non-contingent reinforcement of tasks of differing importance: Facilitation and learned helplessness. *Journal of Personality and Social Psychology*, 1975, Vol. 32, No. 4, 680–691.

Salancik, G. R. Inference of one's attitude from behavior recalled under linguistically manipulated cognitive sets. *Journal of Experimental Social Psychology*, 1974, 10, 415–27.

Salancik, G. R., and Conway, M. Attitude inferences from salient and relevant cognitive content about behavior. *Journal of Personality and Social Psychology*, 1975, 32, 829–40.

Schmidt, F. L. Implications of a measurement problem for expectancy theory research. *Organizational Behavior and Human Performance*, 1973, 10, 243–51.

Seligman, M. E. P. *Helplessness*. San Francisco: W. H. Freeman, 1975.

Seligman, M. E. P., and Maier, S. F. Failure to escape traumatic shock. *Journal of Experimental Psychology*, 1967, 74, 1–9.

Selznick, P. *TVA and the Grass Roots*. Berkeley: University of California Press, 1949.

Shaban, J., and Welling, G. The effects of two kinds of bureaucratic harassment. In D. C. Glass and J. Singer (eds.) *Urban Stress*. New York: Academic Press, 1972.

Sherrod, D. R., and Downs, R. Environmental determinants of altruism: The effects of stimulus overload and perceived control on helping. *Journal of Experimental Social Psychology*, 1974, 10, 468–79.

Shull, F. A. Matrix structure and project authority for optimizing organizational capacity. *Business Monograph*, no. 1, Business Research Bureau, Southern Illinois University, 1965.

Sidman, M., Herrnstein, R. J., and Conrad, D. G. Maintenance of avoidance behavior by unavoidable shocks. *Journal of Comparative and Physiological Psychology*, 1957, 50, 553–57.

Simon, H. A. *Administrative Behavior*. New York: Macmillan, 1957.

Skinner, B. F. *Science and Human Behavior*. New York: Macmillan, 1953.

——. *About Behaviorism*. New York: Alfred A. Knopf, 1974.

Staw, B. M. *Intrinsic and Extrinsic Motivation*. Morristown, N.J.: General Learning Press, 1976.

Staw, B. M., and Szwajkowski, E. The scarcity-munificence component of organizational environments and the commission of illegal acts. *Administrative Science Quarterly*, 1975, 20, 345–54.

Szilagyi, S., and Sims, H. An exploration of the path-goal theory of leadership in a health care environment. *Academy of Management Journal*, 1974, 17, 622–34.

Thompson, J. D. *Organizations in Action*. New York: McGraw-Hill, 1967.

Thorndike, E. L. *Animal Intelligence*. New York: Macmillan, 1911.

Tolman, E. C. *Purposive Behavior in Animals and Men*. New York: Appleton-Century Crofts, 1932.

Weick, K. *The Social Psychology of Organizing*. Reading, Mass.: Addison-Wesley, 1969.

White, R. W. Motivation reconsidered: The concept of competence. *Psychological Review*, 1959, 66, 297–333.

Wortman, C. B., and Brehm, J. W. Responses to uncontrollable outcomes: An integration of reactance theory and the learned helplessness model. In L. Berkowitz (ed.) *Advances in Experimental Social Psychology*, New York: Academic Press, 1976.

Wortman, C. B., and Linsenmeier, J. A. W. Interpersonal attraction and techniques of ingratiation in organizational settings. In B. Staw and G. Salancik (eds.) *New Directions in Organizational Behavior*. Chicago: St. Clair Press, 1977.

Zald, M. N. Urban differentiation, characteristics of boards of directors and organizational effectiveness. *American Journal of Sociology*, 1967, 73, 261–72.

II.C
Staffing Organizations

10

Increasing organizational effectiveness through better human resource planning and development

Edgar H. Schein

INTRODUCTION

In this article I would like to address two basic *questions. First,* why is human resource planning and development becoming increasingly important as a determinant of organizational effectiveness? *Second,* what are the major *components* of a human resource planning and career development system, and how should these components be *linked* for maximum organizational effectiveness?

Source: Reprinted from "Increasing Organizational Effectiveness through Better Human Resource Planning and Development," by Edgar H. Schein, *Sloan Management Review,* Vol. 19, No. 1, pp. 1–20, by permission of the publisher. Copyright © 1977 by the Sloan Management Review Association. All rights reserved.

Author's note: Much of the research on which this paper is based was done under the sponsorship of the Group Psychology branch of the Office of Naval Research. Their generous support has made continuing work in this area possible. I would also like to thank my colleagues Lotte Bailyn and John Van Maanen for many of the ideas expressed in this paper.

The field of personnel management has for some time addressed issues such as these and much of the technology of planning for and managing human resources has been worked out to a considerable degree [10] [24]. Nevertheless there continues to be in organizations a failure, particularly on the part of line managers and functional managers in areas other than personnel, to recognize the true importance of planning for and managing human resources. This paper is not intended to be a review of what is known but rather a kind of position paper for line managers to bring to their attention some important and all too often neglected issues. These issues are important for organizational *effectiveness,* quite apart from their relevance to the issue of humanizing work or improving the quality of working life [13] [21].

The observations and analyses made below are based on several kinds of information:

- Formal research on management development, career development, and human development through the adult life cycle conducted in the Sloan School and at other places for the past several decades [4] [6] [18] [20] [24] [29] [36];

- Analysis of consulting relationships, field observations, and other involvements over the past several decades with all kinds of organizations dealing with the planning for and implementation of human resource development programs and organization development projects [1] [5] [6] [12] [19] [28].

WHY IS HUMAN RESOURCE PLANNING AND DEVELOPMENT (HRPD) INCREASINGLY IMPORTANT?

The Changing Managerial Job

The first answer to the question is simple, though paradoxical. Organizations are becoming more dependent upon people because they are increasingly involved in more complex technologies and are attempting to function in more complex economic, political, and sociocultural environments. The more different technical skills there are involved in the design, manufacture, marketing, and sales of a product, the more vulnerable the organization will be to critical shortages of the right kinds of human resources. The more complex the process, the higher the interdependence among the various specialists. The higher the interdependence, the greater the need for effective integration of all the specialities because the entire process is only as strong as its weakest link.

In simpler technologies, managers could often compensate for the technical or communication failures of their subordinates. General managers today are much more dependent upon their technically trained subordinates because they usually do not understand the details of the engineering, marketing, financial, and other decisions which their subordinates are making. Even the general manager who grew up in finance may find that since his day the field of finance has outrun him and his subordinates are using models and methods which he cannot entirely understand.

What all this means for the general manager is that he cannot any longer safely make decisions by himself; he cannot get enough information digested within his own head to be the integrator and decision maker. Instead, he finds himself increasingly having to manage the *process* of decision making, bringing the right people together around the right questions or problems, stimulating open discussion, insuring that all relevant information surfaces and is critically assessed, managing the emotional ups and downs of his prima donnas, and insuring that out of all this human and interpersonal process, a good decision will result.

As I have watched processes like these in management groups, I am struck by the fact that *the decision emerges out of the interplay*. It is hard to pin down who had the idea and who made the decision. The general manager in this setting is *accountable* for the decision, but rarely would I describe the process as one where he or she actually makes the decision, except in the sense of recognizing when the right answer has been achieved, ratifying that answer, announcing it, and following up on its implementation.

If the managerial *job* is increasingly moving in the direction I have indicated, managers of the future will have to be much more skilled in how to:

1. Select and train their subordinates,
2. Design and run meetings and groups of all sorts,
3. Deal with all kinds of conflict between strong individuals and groups,
4. Influence and negotiate from a low power base, and
5. Integrate the efforts of very diverse technical specialists.

If the above image of what is happening to organizations has any generality, it will force the field of human resource management increasingly to center stage. The more complex organizations become, the more they will be vulnerable to human error. They will not necessarily employ more people, but they will employ more sophisticated highly trained people both in managerial and in individual contributor, staff roles. The price of low motivation, turnover, poor productivity, sabotage, and intraorganizational conflict will be higher in such an organization. Therefore it will become a matter of *economic necessity* to improve human resource planning and development systems.

Changing Social Values

A second reason why human resource planning and development will become more central and important is that changing social values regarding the role of work will make it *more complicated to manage people.* There are several kinds of research findings and observations which illustrate this point.

First, my own longitudinal research of a panel of Sloan School graduates of the 1960s strongly suggests that we have put much too much emphasis on the traditional success syndrome of "climbing the corporate ladder [31]." Some alumni indeed want to rise to high-level general manager positions, but many others want to exercise their particular technical or functional competence and only rise to levels of functional management or senior staff roles with minimal managerial responsibility. Some want security, others are seeking nonorganizational careers as teachers or consultants, while a few are becoming entrepreneurs. I have called these patterns of motivation, talent, and values "career anchors" and believe that they serve to stabilize and constrain the career in predictable ways. The implication is obvious—organizations must develop multiple ladders and multiple reward systems to deal with different types of people [32].

Second, studies of young people entering organizations in the last several decades suggest that work and career are not as central a life preoccupation as was once the case. Perhaps because of a prolonged period of economic affluence, people see more options for themselves and are increasingly exercising those options. In particular, one sees more concern with a balanced life in which work, family, and self-development play a more equal role [4] [22] [25] [38].

Third, closely linked to the above trend is the increase in the number of women in organizations, which will have its major impact through the increase of dual career families. As opportunities for women open up, we will see more new life-styles in young couples which will affect the organization's options as to moving people geographically, joint employment, joint career management, family support, etc. [2] [3] [17] [39].

Fourth, research evidence is beginning to accumulate that personal growth and development is a life-long process and that predictable issues and crises come up in every decade of our lives. Organizations will have to be much more aware of what these issues are, how work and family interact, and how to manage people at different ages. The current "hot button" is *mid-career crisis,* but the more research we do the more we find developmental crises at *all* ages and stages [16] [23] [33] [35].

An excellent summary of what is happening in the world of values, technology, and management is provided in a recent text by Elmer Burack:

> The leading edge of change in the future will include the new technologies of information, production, and management, interlaced with considerable social dislocation and shifts in manpower inputs. These developments are without precedent in our industrial history.
>
> Technological and social changes have created a need for more education, training, and skill at all managerial and support levels. The lowering of barriers to employment based on sex and race introduces new kinds of manpower problems for management officials. Seniority is coming to mean relatively less in relation to the comprehension of problems, processes, and approaches. The newer manpower elements and work technologies have shifted institutional arrangements: the locus of decision making is altered, role relationships among workers and supervisors are changed (often becoming more collegial), and the need to respond to changing routines has become commonplace. . . .
>
> These shifts have been supported by more demanding customer requirements, increasing government surveillance (from product quality to anti-pollution measures), and more widespread use of computers shifting power bases to the holders of specialized knowledge skills [10, pp. 402–403].

In order for HRPD systems to become more responsive and capable of handling such growing complexity they must contain all the necessary components, must be based on correct assumptions, and must be adequately integrated.

COMPONENTS OF A HUMAN RESOURCE PLANNING AND DEVELOPMENT SYSTEM

The major problem with existing HRPD systems is that they are fragmented, incomplete, and sometimes built on faulty assumptions about human or organizational growth.

Human growth takes place through successive encounters with one's environment. As the person encounters a new situation, he or she is forced to try new responses to deal with that situation. Learning takes place as a function of how those responses work out and the results they achieve. If they are successful in coping with the situation, the person enlarges his repertory of responses; if they are not successful the person must try alternate responses until the situation has been dealt with. If none of the active coping responses work, the person sometimes falls back on retreating from the new situation, or denying that there is a problem to be solved. These responses are defensive and growth limiting.

The implication is that for growth to occur, people basically need two things: *new challenges* that are within the range of their coping responses, and *knowledge of results*, information on how their responses to the challenge have worked out. If the tasks and challenges are too easy or too hard, the person will be demotivated and cease to grow. If the information is not available on how well the person's responses are working, the person cannot grow in a systematic, valid direction but is forced into guessing or trying to infer information from ambiguous signals.

Organizational growth similarly takes place through successful coping with the internal and external environment [29]. But since the organization is a complex system of human, material, financial, and informational resources, one must consider how each of those areas can be properly managed toward organizational effec-

tiveness. In this article I will only deal with the human resources.

In order for the organization to have the capacity to perform effectively over a period of time it must be able to plan for, recruit, manage, develop, measure, dispose of, and replace human resources as warranted by the tasks to be done. The most important of these functions is the *planning* function, since task requirements are likely to change as the complexity and turbulence of the organization's environment increase. In other words, a key assumption underlying organizational growth is that the nature of jobs will change over time, which means that such changes must be continuously monitored in order to insure that the right kinds of human resources can be recruited or developed to do those jobs. Many of the activities such as recruitment, selection, performance appraisal, and so on presume that some planning process has occurred which makes it possible to assess whether or not those activities are meeting *organizational needs*, quite apart from whether they are facilitating the individual's growth.

In an ideal HRPD system one would seek to match the organization's needs for human resources with the individual's needs for personal career growth and development. One can then depict the basic system as involving both individual and organizational planning, and a series of matching activities which are designed to facilitate mutual need satisfaction. If we further assume that both individual and organizational needs change over time, we can depict this process as a developmental one as in Figure 1.

In the right-hand column we show the basic stages of the individual career through the life cycle. While not everyone will go through these stages in the manner depicted, there is growing evidence that for organizational careers in particular, these stages reasonably depict the movement of people through their adult lives [11] [14] [32] [34].

Given those developmental assumptions, the left-hand side of the diagram shows the organizational planning activities which must occur if human resources are to be managed in an optimal way, and if changing job requirements are to be properly assessed and continuously monitored.

Figure 1.   A Developmental Model of Human Resource Planning and Development

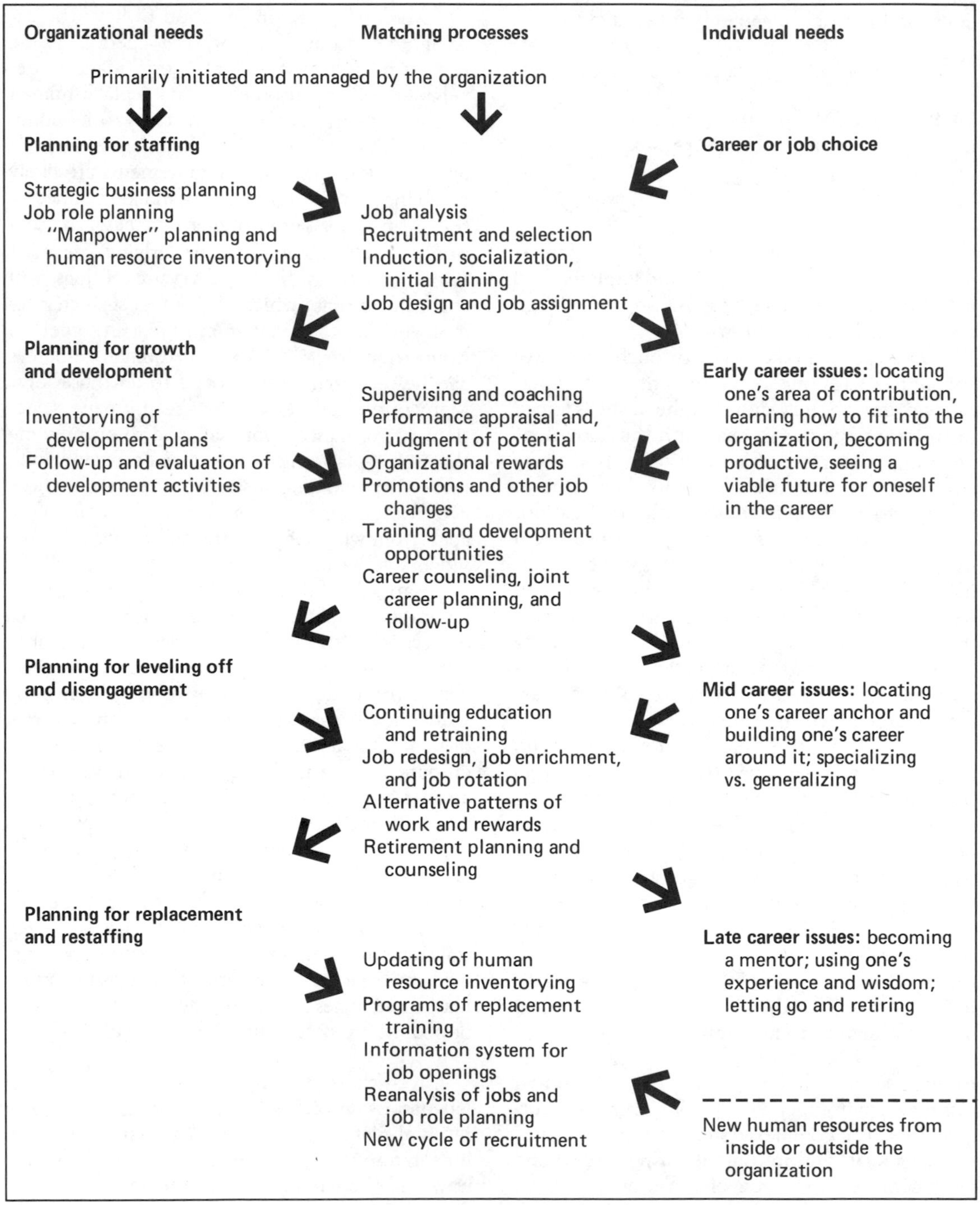

Organizational needs	Matching processes	Individual needs
	Primarily initiated and managed by the organization	

Planning for staffing

Strategic business planning
Job role planning
   "Manpower" planning and
   human resource inventorying

Job analysis
Recruitment and selection
Induction, socialization,
   initial training
Job design and job assignment

Career or job choice

**Planning for growth
and development**

Inventorying of
   development plans
Follow-up and evaluation of
   development activities

Supervising and coaching
Performance appraisal and,
   judgment of potential
Organizational rewards
Promotions and other job
   changes
Training and development
   opportunities
Career counseling, joint
   career planning, and
   follow-up

Early career issues: locating
   one's area of contribution,
   learning how to fit into the
   organization, becoming
   productive, seeing a
   viable future for oneself
   in the career

**Planning for leveling off
and disengagement**

Continuing education
   and retraining
Job redesign, job enrichment,
   and job rotation
Alternative patterns of
   work and rewards
Retirement planning and
   counseling

Mid career issues: locating
   one's career anchor and
   building one's career
   around it; specializing
   vs. generalizing

**Planning for replacement
and restaffing**

Updating of human
   resource inventorying
Programs of replacement
   training
Information system for
   job openings
Reanalysis of jobs and
   job role planning
New cycle of recruitment

Late career issues: becoming
   a mentor; using one's
   experience and wisdom;
   letting go and retiring

New human resources from
   inside or outside the
   organization

The middle column shows the various matching activities which have to occur at various career stages.

The components of an effective HRPD system now can be derived from the diagram. *First,* there have to be in the organization the overall planning components shown on the left-hand side of Figure 1. *Second,* there have to be components which insure an adequate process of staffing the organization. *Third,* there have to be components which plan for and monitor growth and development. *Fourth,* there have to be components which facilitate the actual process of the growth and development of the people who are brought into the organization; this growth and development must be organized to meet *both* the needs of the organization and the needs of the individuals within it. *Fifth,* there have to be components which deal with decreasing effectiveness, leveling off, obsolescence of skills, turnover, retirement, and other phenomena which reflect the need for either a new growth direction or a process of disengagement of the person from his or her job. *Finally,* there have to be components which insure that as some people move out of jobs, others are available to fill those jobs, and as new jobs arise that people are available with the requisite skills to fill them.

In the remainder of this article I would like to comment on each of these six sets of components and indicate where and how they should be linked to each other.

Overall Planning Components

The function of these components is to insure that the organization has an adequate basis for selecting its human resources and developing them toward the fulfillment of organizational goals.

Strategic business planning. These activities are designed to determine the organization's goals, priorities, future directions, products, markets growth rate, geographical location, and organization structure or design. This process should lead logically into the next two planning activities but is often disconnected from them

because it is located in a different part of the organization or is staffed by people with different orientations and backgrounds.

Job/role planning. These activities are designed to determine what actually needs to be done at every level of the organization (up through top management) to fulfill the organization's goals and tasks. This activity can be thought of as a dynamic kind of job analysis where a continual review is made of the skills, knowledge, values, etc. which are presently needed in the organization *and will be needed in the future.* The focus is on the predictable consequences of the strategic planning for managerial roles, specialist roles, and skill mixes which may be needed to get the mission accomplished. If the organization already has a satisfactory system of job descriptions, this activity would concern itself with how those jobs will evolve and change, and what new jobs or roles will evolve in the future [32].

This component is often missing completely in organizations or is carried out only for lower level jobs. From a planning point of view it is probably most important for the highest level jobs—how the nature of general and functional management will change as the organization faces new technologies, new social values, and new environmental conditions.

"Manpower planning" and human resource inventorying. These activities draw on the job/role descriptions generated in job/role planning and assess the capabilities of the present human resources against those plans or requirements. These activities may be focused on the numbers of people in given categories and are often designed to insure that under given assumptions of growth there will be an adequate supply of people in those categories. Or the process may focus more on how to insure that certain scarce skills which will be needed will in fact be available, leading to more sophisticated programs of recruitment or human resource development. For example, the inventorying process at high levels may reveal the need for a new type of general manager with broad integrative capacities which may further reveal the need to start a development program that will insure that such managers will be available five to ten years down the road.

These first three component activities are all geared to identifying the *organization's* needs in the human resource area. They are difficult to do and tools are only now beginning to be developed for job/role planning [32]. In most organizations I have dealt with, the three areas, if they exist at all, are not linked to each other organizationally. Strategic planning is likely to exist in the Office of the President. Job/role planning is likely to be an offshoot of some management development activities in Personnel. And human resource inventorying is likely to be a specialized subsection within Personnel. Typically, no one is accountable for bringing these activities together even on an ad hoc basis.

This situation reflects an erroneous assumption about growth and development which I want to mention at this time. The assumption is that if the organization develops its *present* human resources, it will be able to fill whatever job demands may arise in the future. Thus we do find in organizations elaborate human resource planning systems, but they plan for the present people in the organization, not for the organization per se. If there are no major changes in job requirements as the organization grows and develops, this system will work. But if jobs themselves change, it is no longer safe to assume that today's human resources, with development plans based on *today's* job requirements, will produce the people needed in some future situation. Therefore, I am asserting that more job/role planning must be done, independent of the present people in the organization.

The subsequent components to be discussed which focus on the matching of individual and organizational needs all assume that some sort of basic planning activities such as those described have been carried out. They may not be very formal, or they may be highly decentralized (e.g. every supervisor who has an open slot might make his own decision of what sort of person to hire based on his private assumptions about strategic business planning and job/role planning). Obviously, the more turbulent the environment, the greater the vulnerability of the organization if it does not centralize and coordinate its various planning activities, and generate its HRPD system from those plans.

Staffing Processes

The function of these processes is to insure that the organization acquires the human resources necessary to fulfill its goals.

Job analysis. If the organizational planning has been done adequately, the next component of the HRPD system is to actually specify what jobs need to be filled and what skills, etc. are needed to do those jobs. Some organizations go through this process very formally, others do it in an informal unprogrammed manner, but in some form it must occur in order to specify what kind of recruitment to do and how to select people from among the recruits.

Recruitment and selection. This activity involves the actual process of going out to find people to fulfill jobs and developing systems for deciding which of those people to hire. These components may be very formal including testing, assessment, and other aids to the selection process. If this component is seen as part of a total HRPD system, it will alert management to the fact that the recruitment selection system communicates to future employees something about the nature of the organization and its approach to people. All too often this component sends incorrect messages or turns off future employees or builds incorrect stereotypes which make subsequent supervision more difficult [26] [32].

Induction, socialization, and initial training. Once the employee has been hired, there ensues a period during which he or she learns the ropes, learns how to get along in the organization, how to work, how to fit in, how to master the particulars of the job, and so on. Once again, it is important that the activities which make up this component are seen as part of a total process with long-range consequences for the attitudes of the employee [27] [36]. The goal of these processes should be to facilitate the employees becoming productive and useful members of the organization both in the short run and in terms of long-range potential.

Job design and job assignment.   One of the most crucial components of staffing is the actual design of the job which is given to the new employee and the manner in which the assignment is actually made. The issue is how to provide *optimal challenge,* a set of activities which will be neither too hard nor too easy for the new employee, and which will be neither too meaningless nor too risky from the point of view of the organization. If the job is too easy or too meaningless, the employee may become demotivated; if the job is too hard and/or involves too much responsibility and risk from the point of view of the organization, the employee will become too anxious, frustrated, or angry to perform at an optimal level. Some organizations have set up training programs for supervisors to help them to design optimally challenging work assignments [26].

These four components are geared to insuring that the work of the organization will be performed. They tend to be processes that have to be performed by line managers and personnel staff specialists together. Line managers have the basic information about jobs and skill requirements; personnel specialists have the interviewing, recruiting, and assessment skills to aid in the selection process. In an optimal system these functions will be closely coordinated, particularly to insure that the recruiting process provides to the employee accurate information about the nature of the organization and the actual work that he or she will be doing in it. Recruiters also need good information on the long-range human resource plans so that these can be taken into account in the selection of new employees.

Development Planning

It is not enough to get good human resources in the door. Some planning activities have to concern themselves with how employees who may be spending thirty to forty years of their total life in a given organization will make a contribution for all of that time, will remain motivated and productive, and will maintain a reasonable level of job satisfaction.

Inventorying of development plans.   Whether or not the process is highly formalized, there is in most organizations some effort to plan for the growth and development of all employees. The planning component that is often missing is some kind of pulling together of this information into a centralized inventory that permits coordination and evaluation of the development activities. Individual supervisors may have clear ideas of what they will do with and for their subordinates, but this information may never be collected, making it impossible to determine whether the individual plans of supervisors are connected in any way. Whether it is done by department, division, or total company, some effort to collect such information and to think through its implications would be of great value to furthering the total development of employees at all levels.

Follow-up and evaluation of development activities.   I have observed two symptoms of insufficient planning in this area—one, development plans are made for individual employees, are written down, but are never implemented, and two, if they are implemented they are never evaluated either in relation to the individual's own needs for growth or in relation to the organization's needs for new skills. Some system should exist to insure that plans are implemented and that activities are evaluated against both individual and organizational goals.

Career Development Processes

This label is deliberately broad to cover all of the major processes of managing human resources during their period of growth and peak productivity, a period which may be several decades in length. These processes must match the organization's needs for work with the individual's needs for a productive and satisfying work career. The system must provide for some kind of forward movement for the employee through some succession of jobs, whether these involve promotion, lateral movement to new functions, or simply new assignments within a given area [30] [32]. The system must be based both on the organization's need to fill jobs as they open up and on employees' needs to have some sense of progress in their working lives.

Supervision and coaching. By far the most important component in this area is the actual process of supervising, guiding, coaching, and monitoring. It is in this context that the work assignment and feedback processes which make learning possible occur, and it is the boss who plays the key role in molding the employee to the organization. There is considerable evidence that the first boss is especially crucial in giving new employees a good start in their careers [8] [9] [14] [26], and that training of supervisors in how to handle new employees is a valuable organizational investment.

Performance appraisal and judgment of potential. This component is part of the general process of supervision but stands out as such an important part of that process that it must be treated separately. In most organizations there is some effort to standardize and formalize a process of appraisal above and beyond the normal performance feedback which is expected on a day-to-day basis. Such systems serve a number of functions—to justify salary increases, promotions, and other formal organizational actions with respect to the employee; to provide information for human resource inventories or at least written records of past accomplishments for the employee's personnel folder; and to provide a basis for annual or semiannual formal reviews between boss and subordinate to supplement day-to-day feedback and to facilitate information exchange for career planning and counseling. In some organizations so little day-to-day feedback occurs that the *formal* system bears the burden of providing the employees with knowledge of how they are doing and what they can look forward to. Since knowledge of results, of how one is doing, is a crucial component of any developmental process, it is important for organizations to monitor how well and how frequently feedback is actually given.

One of the major dilemmas in this area is whether to have a single system which provides both feedback for the growth and development of the employee and information for the organization's planning systems. The dilemma arises because the information which the planning system requires (e.g. "how much potential does this employee have to rise in the organization?") may be the kind of information which neither the boss nor the planner wants to share with the employee. The more potent and more accurate the information, the less likely it is to be fed back to the employee in anything other than very vague terms.

On the other hand, the detailed work-oriented, day-to-day feedback which the employee needs for growth and development may be too cumbersome to record as part of a selection-oriented appraisal system. If hundreds of employees are to be compared, there is strong pressure in the system toward more general kinds of judgments, traits, rankings, numerical estimates of ultimate potential, and the like. One way of resolving this dilemma which some companies have found successful is to develop two separate systems—one oriented toward performance improvement and the growth of the employee, and the other one oriented toward a more global assessment of the employee for future planning purposes involving judgments which may not be shared with the employee except in general terms.

A second dilemma arises around the identification of the employee's "development needs" and how that information is linked to other development activities. If the development needs are stated in relation to the planning system, the employee may never get the feedback of what his needs may have been perceived to be, and, worse, no one may implement any program to deal with those needs if the planning system is not well linked with line management.

Two further problems arise from this potential lack of linkage. One, if the individual does not get good feedback around developmental needs, he or she remains uninvolved in their own development and potentially becomes complacent. We pay lip service to the statement that only the individual can develop himself or herself, but then deprive the individual of the very information that would make sensible self-development possible. Two, the development needs as stated for the various employees in the organization may have nothing to do with the organization's needs for certain kinds of human resources in the future. All too often there is complete lack of linkage between the strategic or business planning function and the human resource development function resulting in potentially willy-nilly individual development based on today's needs and individual managers' stereotypes of what will be needed in the future.

Organizational rewards—pay, benefits, perquisites, promotion, and recognition. Entire books have been written about all the problems and subtleties of how to link organizational rewards to the other components of a HRPD system to insure both short-run and long-run human effectiveness. For purposes of this short paper I wish to point out only one major issue—how to insure that organizational rewards are linked *both* to the needs of the individual and to the needs of the organization for effective performance and development of potential. All too often the reward system is neither responsive to the individual employee nor to the organization, being driven more by criteria of elegance, consistency, and what other organizations are doing. If the linkage is to be established, line managers must actively work with compensation experts to develop a joint philosophy and set of goals based on an understanding of both what the organization is trying to reward and what employee needs actually are. As organizational careers become more varied and as social values surrounding work change, reward systems will probably have to become much more flexible both in time (people at different career stages may need different things) and by type of career (functional specialists may need different things than general mangers).

Promotions and other job changes. There is ample evidence that what keeps human growth and effectiveness going is continuing optimal challenge [11] [18]. Such challenge can be provided for some members of the organization through promotion to higher levels where more responsible jobs are available. For most members of the organization the promotion opportunities are limited, however, because the pyramid narrows at the top. An effective HRPD system will, therefore, concentrate on developing career paths, systems of job rotation, changing assignments, temporary assignments, and other lateral job moves which insure continuing growth of all human resources.

One of the key characteristics of an optimally challenging job is that it both draws on the person's abilities and skills and that it has opportunities for "closure." The employee must be in the job long enough to get involved and to see the results of his or her efforts. Systems of rotation which move the person too rapidly either prevent initial involvement (as in the rotational training program), or prevent closure by transferring the person to a new job before the effects of his or her decisions can be assessed. I have heard many "fast track" executives complain that their self-confidence was low because they never really could see the results of their efforts. Too often we move people too fast in order to "fill slots" and thereby undermine their developmnt.

Organizational planning systems which generate "slots" to be filled must be coordinated with development planning systems which concern themselves with the optimal growth of the human resources. Sometimes it is better for the organization in the long run not to fill an empty slot in order to keep a manager in another job where he or she is just beginning to develop. One way of insuring such linkage is to monitor these processes by means of a "development committee" which is composed of both line managers and personnel specialists. In such a group the needs of the organization and the needs of the people can be balanced against each other in the context of the long-range goals of the organization.

Training and development opportunities. Most organizations recognize that periods of formal training, sabbaticals, executive development programs outside of the company, and other educational activities are necessary in the total process of human growth and development. The important point about these activities is that they should be carefully linked both to the needs of the individual and to the needs of the organization. The individual should want to go to the program because he or she can see how the educational activity fits into the total career. The organization should send the person because the training fits into some concept of future career development. It should not be undertaken simply as a generalized "good thing," or because other companies are doing it. As much as possible the training and educational activities should be tied to job/role planning. For example, many companies began to use university executive development programs because of an explicit recognition that future managers would require a broader perspective on various problems and that such "broadening" could best be achieved in the university programs.

Career counseling, joint career planning, follow-up, and evaluation. Inasmuch as the growth and development which may be desired can only come from within the individual himself or herself, it is important that the organization provide some means for individual employees at all levels to become more proactive about their careers and some mechanisms for joint dialogue, counseling, and career planning [15]. This process should ideally be linked to performance appraisal, because it is in that context that the boss can review with the subordinate the future potential, development needs, strengths, weaknesses, career options, etc. The boss is often not trained in counseling but does possess some of the key information which the employee needs to initiate any kind of career planning. More formal counseling could then be supplied by the personnel development staff or outside the organization altogether.

The important point to recognize is that employees cannot manage their own growth development without information on how their own needs, talents, values, and plans mesh with the opportunity structure of the organization. Even though the organization may only have imperfect, uncertain information about the future, the individual is better off to know that than to make erroneous assumptions about the future based on no information at all. It is true that the organization cannot make commitments, nor should it unless required to by legislation or contract. But the sharing of information if properly done is not the same as making commitments or setting up false expectations.

If the organization can open up the communication channel between employees, their bosses, and whoever is managing the human resource system, the groundwork is laid for realistic individual development planning. Whatever is decided about training, next steps, special assignments, rotation, etc. should be jointly decided by the individual and the appropriate

organizational resource (probably the supervisor and someone from personnel specializing in career development). Each step must fit into the employee's life plan and must be tied into *organizational needs.* The organization should be neither a humanistic charity nor an indoctrination center. Instead, it should be a vehicle for meeting both the needs of society and of individuals.

Whatever is decided should not merely be written down but executed. If there are implementation problems, the development plan should be renegotiated. Whatever developmental actions are taken, it is essential that they be followed up and evaluated both by the person and by the organization to determine what, if anything, was achieved. It is shocking to discover how many companies invest in major activities such as university executive development programs and never determine for themselves what was accomplished. In some instances, they make no plans to talk to the individual before or after the program so that it is not even possible to determine what the activity meant to the participant, or what might be an appropriate next assignment for him or her following the program.

I can summarize the above analysis best by emphasizing the two places where I feel there is the most fragmentation and violation of growth assumptions. First, too many of the activities occur without the involvement of the person who is "being developed" and therefore may well end up being self-defeating. This is particularly true of job assignments and performance appraisal where too little involvement and feedback occur. Second, too much of the human resource system functions as a personnel *selection* system unconnected to either the needs of the organization or the needs of the individual. All too often it is only a system for short-run replacement of people in standard type jobs. The key planning functions are not linked in solidly and hence do not influence the system to the degree they should.

Planning for and Managing Disengagement

The planning and management processes which will be briefly reviewed here are counterparts of ones that have already been discussed but are focused on a different problem—the problem of the late career, loss of motivation, obsolescence, and ultimately retirement. Organizations must recognize that there are various options available to deal with this range of problems beyond the obvious ones of either terminating the employee or engaging in elaborate measures to "remotivate" people who may have lost work involvement [2].

Continuing education and retraining.   These activites have their greatest potential if the employee is motivated and if there is some clear connection between what is to be learned and what the employee's current or future job assignments require in the way of skills. More and more organizations are finding out that it is better to provide challenging work first and only then the training to perform that work once the employee sees the need for it. Obviously for this linkage to work well continuous dialogue is needed between employees and their managers. For those employees who have leveled off, have lost work involvement, but are still doing high quality work, other solutions such as those described below are more applicable.

Job redesign, job enrichment, and job rotation.   This section is an extension of the arguments made earlier on job changes in general applied to the particular problems of leveled off employees. In some recent research, it has been suggested that job enrichment and other efforts to redesign work to increase motivation and performance may only work during the first few years on the job [18]. Beyond that the employee becomes "unresponsive" to the job characteristics themselves and pays more attention to surrounding factors such as the nature of supervision, relationships with co-workers, pay, and other extrinsic characteristics. In other words, before organizations attempt to "cure" leveled off employees by remotivating them through job redesign or rotation, they should examine whether those employees are still in a responsive mode or not. On the other hand, one can argue that there is nothing wrong with less motivated, less involved employees so long as the quality of what they are doing meets the organizational standards [2].

Alternative patterns of work and rewards.   Because of the changing needs and values of employees in recent decades, more and more organizations have begun to experiment with alternative work patterns such as flexible working hours, part-time work, sabbaticals or other longer periods of time off, several people filling one job, dual employment of spouses with more extensive childcare programs, etc. Along with these experiments have come others on flexible reward systems in which employees can choose between a raise, some time off, special retirement, medical, or insurance benefits, and other efforts to make multiple career ladders a viable reality. These programs apply to employees at all career stages but are especially relevant to people in mid and late career stages where their own perception of their career and life goals may be undergoing important changes.

None of those innovations should be attempted without first clearly establishing a HRPD system which takes care of the organization's needs as well as the needs of employees and links them to each other. There can be little growth and development for employees at any level in an *organization* which is sick and stagnant. It is in the best interests of both the individual and the organization to have a healthy organization which can provide opportunities for growth.

Retirement planning and counseling.   As part of any effective HRPD system, there must be a clear planning function which forecasts who will retire, and which feeds this information into both the replacement staffing system and the counseling functions so that the employees who will be retiring can be prepared for this often traumatic career stage. Employees need counseling not only with the mechanical and financial aspects of retirement, but also to prepare them psychologically for the time when they will no longer have a clear organizational base or job as part of their identity. For some people it may make sense to spread the period of retirement over a number of years by using part-time work or special assignments to help both the individual and the organization to get benefits from this period.

The counseling function here as in other parts of the career probably involves special skills and must be provided by specialists. However, the line manager continues to play a key role as a provider of job challenge, feedback, and information about what is ahead for any given employee.

Seminars for line managers on how to handle the special problems of pre-retirement employees would probably be of great value as part of their managerial training.

Planning for and Managing Replacement and Restaffing

With this step the HRPD cycle closes back upon itself. This function must be concerned with such issues as:

1. Updating the human resource inventory as retirements or terminations occur;
2. Instituting special programs of orientation or training for new incumbents to specific jobs as those jobs open up;
3. Managing the information system on what jobs are available and determining how to match this information to the human resources available in order to determine whether to replace from within the organization or to go outside with a new recruiting program;
4. Continuously reanalyzing jobs to insure that the new incumbent is properly prepared for what the job *now* requires and *will* require in the future.

How these processes are managed links to the other parts of the system through the implicit messages that are sent to employees. For example, a company which decides to publicly post all of its unfilled jobs is clearly sending a message that it expects internal recruitment and supports self-development activities. A company which manages restaffing in a very secret manner may well get across a message that employees might as well be complacent and passive about their careers because they cannot influence them anyway.

SUMMARY AND CONCLUSIONS

I have tried to argue in this article that human resource planning and development is becoming an increasingly important function in organiza-

tions, that this function consists of multiple components, and that these components must be managed *both* by line managers and staff specialists. I have tried to show that the various planning activities are closely linked to the actual processes of supervision, job assignment, training, etc. and that those processes must be designed to match the needs of the organization with the needs of the employees throughout their evolving careers, whether or not those careers involve hierarchical promotions. I have also argued that the various components are linked to each other and must be seen as a total system if it is to be effective. The total system must be managed as a system to insure coordination between the planning functions and the implementation functions.

I hope it is clear from what has been said above that an effective human resource planning and development system is integral to the functioning of the organization and must, therefore, be a central concern of line management. Many of the activities require specialist help, but the accountabilities must rest squarely with line supervisors and top management. It is they who control the opportunities and the rewards. It is the job assignment system and the feedback which employees get that is the ultimate raw material for growth and development. Whoever designs and manages the system, it will not help the organization to become more effective unless that system is *owned* by line management.

REFERENCES

[1] Alfred, T. "Checkers or Choice in Manpower Management." *Harvard Business Review*, January-February 1967, pp. 157–169.
[2] Bailyn, L. "Involvement and Accommodation in Technical Careers." In *Organizational Careers: Some New Perspectives*, edited by J. Van Maanen. New York: John Wiley & Sons, 1977.
[3] Bailyn, L. "Career and Family Orientations of Husbands and Wives in Relation to Marital Happiness." *Human Relations* (1970): 97–113.
[4] Bailyn, L., and Schein, E. H. "Life/Career Considerations as Indicators of Quality of Employment." In *Measuring Work Quality for Social Reporting*, edited by A. D. Biderman and T. F. Drury. New York: Sage Publications, 1976.

[5] Beckhard, R. D. *Organization Development: Strategies and Models.* Reading, MA: Addison-Wesley, 1969.

[6] Bennis, W. G. *Changing Organizations.* New York: McGraw-Hill, 1966.

[7] Bennis, W. G. *Organization Development: Its Nature, Origins, and Prospects.* Reading, MA: Addison-Wesley, 1969.

[8] Berlew, D., and Hall, D. T. "The Socialization of Managers." *Administrative Science Quarterly* 11 (1966): 207–223.

[9] Bray, D. W.; Campbell, R. J.; and Grant, D. E. *Formative Years in Business.* New York: John Wiley & Sons, 1974.

[10] Burack, E. *Organization Analysis.* Hinsdale, IL: Dryden, 1975.

[11] Dalton, G. W., and Thompson, P. H. "Are R&D Organizations Obsolete?" *Harvard Business Review,* November–December 1976, pp. 105–116.

[12] Galbraith, J. *Designing Complex Organizations.* Reading, MA: Addison-Wesley, 1973.

[13] Hackman, J. R., and Suttle, J. L. *Improving Life at Work.* Los Angeles: Goodyear, 1977.

[14] Hall, D. T. *Careers in Organizations.* Los Angeles: Goodyear, 1976.

[15] Heidke, R. *Career Pro-Activity of Middle Managers.* Master's Thesis, Massachusetts Institute of Technology, 1977.

[16] Kalish, R. A. *Late Adulthood: Perspectives on Aging.* Monterey, CA: Brooks-Cole, 1975.

[17] Kanter, R. M. *Work and Family in the United States.* New York: Russel Sage, 1977.

[18] Katz, R. "Job Enrichment: Some Career Considerations." In *Organizational Careers: Some New Perspectives.* edited by J. Van Maanen. New York: John Wiley & Sons, 1977.

[19] Lesieur, F. G. *The Scanlon Plan.* New York: John Wiley & Sons, 1958.

[20] McGregor, D. *The Human Side of Enterprise.* New York: McGraw-Hill, 1960.

[21] Meltzer, H., and Wickert, F. R. *Humanizing Organizational Behavior.* Springfield, IL: Charles C. Thomas, 1976.

[22] Myers, C. A. "Management and the Employee." In *Social Responsibility and the Business Predicament,* edited by J. W. McKie, Washington, D.C.: Brookings, 1974.

[23] Pearse, R. F., and Pelzer, B. P. *Self-directed Change for the Mid-Career Manager.* New York: AMACOM, 1975.

[24] Pigors, P., and Myers, C. A. *Personnel Administration.* 8th ed. New York: McGraw-Hill, 1977.

[25] Roeber, R. J. C. *The Organization in a Changing Environment.* Reading, MA: Addison-Wesley, 1973.

[26] Schein, E. H. "How to Break in the College Graduate." *Harvard Business Review,* 1964, pp. 68–76.

[27] Schein, E. H. Organizational Socialization and the Profession of Management, *Industrial Management Review,* Winter 1968, pp. 1–16.

[28] Schein, E. H. *Process Consultation: Its Role in Organization Development.* Reading, MA: Addison-Wesley, 1969.

[29] Schein, E. H. *Organizational Psychology.* Englewood Cliffs, NJ: Prentice-Hall, 1970.

[30] Schein, E. H. The Individual, the Organization, and the Career: A Conceptual Scheme. *Journal of Applied Behavioral Science* 7 (1971): 401–426.

[31] Schein, E. H. How "Career Anchors" Hold Executives to Their Career Paths. *Personnel* 52, no. 3 (1975): 11–24.

[32] Schein, E. H. *The Individual, the Organization and the Career: Toward Greater Human Effectiveness.* Reading, MA: Addison-Wesley, forthcoming.

[33] Sheehy, G. "Catch 30 and Other Predictable Crises of Growing Up Adult." *New York Magazine.* February 1974, pp. 30–44.

[34] Super, D. E., and Bohn, M. J. *Occupational Psychology,* Belmont, CA: Wadsworth, 1970.

[35] Troll, L. E. *Early and Middle Adulthood.* Monterey, CA: Brooks-Cole, 1975.

[36] Van Maanen, J. "Breaking In: Socialization to Work." In *Handbook of Work, Organization, and Society,* edited by R. Dubin. Chicago: Rand McNally, 1976.

[37] Van Maanen, J., ed. *Organizational Careers: Some New Perspectives.* New York: John Wiley & Sons, 1977.

[38] Van Maanen, J.; Bailyn, L.; and Schein, E. H. "The Shape of Things to Come: A New Look at Organizational Careers," In *Perspectives on Behavior in Organizations,* edited by J. R. Hackman, E. E. Lawler, and L. W. Porter. New York: McGraw-Hill, 1977.

[39] Van Maanen, J., and Schein, E. H. "Improving the Quality of Work Life: Career Development." In *Improving Life at Work,* edited by J. R. Hackman and J. L. Suttle. Los Angeles: Goodyear, 1977.

11

People processing:
Strategies of organizational socialization

John Van Maanen

Socialization shapes the person—a defensible hyperbole. Organizational socialization or "people processing" refers to the manner in which the experiences of people learning the ropes of a new organizational position, status, or role are structured for them by others within the organization. In short, I will argue here that people acquire the social knowledge and skills necessary to assume a particular job in an organization differently not only because people are different, but, more critically, because the techniques or strategies of people processing differ. And, like the variations of a sculptor's mold, certain forms of organizational socialization produce remarkably different results.

Socialization strategies are perhaps most obvious when a person first joins an organization or when an individual is promoted or demoted. They are probably least obvious when an experienced member of the organization undergoes a simple change of assignment, shift, or job location. Nevertheless, certain people-processing devices can be shown to characterize every transition an individual makes across organizational boundaries. Moreover, management may choose such devices explicitly or consciously. For example, management might require all recruits or newcomers to a particular position to attend a training or orientation program of some kind. Or management may select people-processing devices implicitly or unconsciously. These strategies may simply represent taken-for-granted precedents established in the dim past of an organization's history. The precedent could perhaps be the proverbial trial-and-error method of socialization by which a person learns how to perform a new task on his own, without direct guidance.

Source: Reprinted, by permission of the publisher, from *Organizational Dynamics,* Summer 1978, © 1978 by AMA-COM, a division of American Management Associations. All rights reserved.

Regardless of the method of choice, however, any given socialization device represents an identifiable set of events that will make certain behavioral and attitudinal consequences more likely than others. It is possible, therefore, to identify the various people-processing methods and evaluate them in terms of their social consequences.

BACKGROUND

Three primary assumptions underlie this analysis. First, and perhaps of most importance, is the notion that people in a state of transition are more or less in an anxiety-producing situation. They are motivated to reduce this anxiety by learning the functional and social requirements of their new role as quickly as possible.

Second, the learning that takes place does not occur in a social vacuum strictly on the basis of the official and available versions of the job requirements. Any person crossing organizational boundaries is looking for clues on how to proceed. Thus colleagues, superiors, subordinates, clients, and other work associates can and most often do support, guide, hinder, confuse, or push the individual who is learning a new role. Indeed, they can help him interpret (or misinterpret) the events he experiences so that he can take appropriate (or inappropriate) action in his altered situation. Ultimately, they will provide him with a sense of accomplishment and competence or failure and incompetence.

Third, the stability and productivity of any organization depend in large measure on the way newcomers to various organizational positions come to carry out their tasks. When positions pass from generation to generation of incumbents smoothly, the continuity of the organization's mission is maintained, the predictability of the organization's performance is left intact, and, in the short run at least, the survival of the organization is assured.

A concern for the ways in which individuals adjust to novel circumstances directs attention not only to the cognitive learning that accompanies any transition but also to the manner in which the person copes emotionally with the new situation. As sociologist Erving Goffman rightly suggests, new situations require individuals to reassess and perhaps alter both their instrumental goals (the goals they wish to achieve through their involvement in the organization) and their expressive style (the symbolic appearances they maintain before others in the organization).

In some cases, a shift into a new work situation may result in a dramatically altered organizational identity for the person. This often happens, for example, when a factory worker becomes a foreman or a staff analyst becomes a line manager. Other times, the shift may cause only minor and insignificant changes in a person's organizational identity; for instance, when an administrator is shifted to a new location or a craftsman is rotated to a new department. Yet any of these shifts is likely to result in what might be called a "reality shock" for the person being shifted. When people undergo a transition, regardless of the information they already possess about their new role, their *a priori* understandings of that role are bound to change in either a subtle or a dramatic fashion. Becoming a member of an organization will upset the everyday order of even the most well-informed newcomer. Matters concerning such aspects of life as friendships, time, purpose, demeanor, competence, and the expectations the person holds of the immediate and distant future are suddenly made problematic. The newcomer's most pressing task is to build a set of guidelines and interpretations to explain and make meaningful the myriad of activities observed as going on in the organization.

To come to know an organizational situation and act within it implies that a person has developed some beliefs, principles, and understandings, or, in shorthand notation, a *perspective* for interpreting the experiences he or she has had as a participant in a given sphere of the work world. This perspective provides the rules by which to manage the unique and recurring strains of organizational life. It provides the person with an ordered view of the organization that runs ahead and directs experience, orders and shapes personal relationships in the work setting, and provides the ground rules to manage the ordinary day-to-day affairs.

STRATEGIES OF PEOPLE PROCESSING

Certain situational variables associated with any organization transition can be made visible and shown to be tied directly to the perspective constructed by individuals in transit. The focus here is not on perspectives *per se*, however, but rather on the properties peculiar to any given people-processing situation. These properties are essentially process variables akin to, but more specific than, such generic processes as education, training, apprenticeship, and indoctrination. Furthermore, these properties can be viewed as organizational strategies that distinctly pattern the learning experiences of a newcomer to a particular organizational role.

The people-processing strategies examined below are associated to some degree with all situations that involve a person moving from one organizational position to another. Although much of the evidence comes from studies concerned with the way someone first becomes a member of an organization, the techniques used to manage this passage are at least potentially available for use during any transition a person undergoes during the course of a career. Thus the term "strategy" is used to describe each examined aspect of a transition process because the degree to which a particular people-processing technique is used by an organization is not in any sense a natural condition or prerequisite for socialization. Indeed, by definition, some socialization will always take place when a person moves into and remains with a new organizational role. However, the form that it takes is a matter of organizational choice. And, whether this choice of strategies is made by design or by accident, it is at least theoretically subject to rapid and complete change at the direction of the management.

This is an important point. It suggests that we can be far more self-conscious about employing certain people-processing techniques than we have been. In fact, a major purpose of this article is to heighten and cultivate a broader awareness of what it is we do to people under the guise of "breaking them in." Presumably, if we have a greater appreciation for the sometimes unintended consequences of a particular strategy, we can alter the strategy to benefit both the individual and the organization.

Seven dimensions on which the major strategies of people processing can be located will be discussed. Each strategy will be presented alongside its counterpart or opposing strategy. In other words, each strategy as applied can be thought of as existing somewhere between the two poles of a single dimension. Critically, across dimensions, the strategies are not mutually exclusive. In practice, they are typically combined in sundry and often inventive ways. Thus, although each tactic is discussed in relative isolation, the reader should be aware that the effects of the various socialization strategies upon individuals are cumulative—but not necessarily compatible (in terms of outcome) with one another.

I do not claim that these strategies are exhaustive or that they are presented in any order of relevance to a particular organization or occupation. These are essentially empirical questions that can only be answered by further research. I do claim and attempt to show that these strategies are recognizable, powerful, in widespread use, and of enormous consequence to the people throughout an organization. And, since organizations can accomplish little more than what the people within them accomplish, these people-processing strategies are of undeniable importance when it comes to examining such matters as organizational performance, structure, and, ultimately, survival.

Formal (Informal) Socialization Strategies

The formality of a socialization process refers to the degree to which the setting in which it takes place is segregated from the ongoing work context and to the degree to which an individual's newcomer role is emphasized and made explicit. The more formal the process, the more the recruit's role is both segregated and specified. The recruit is differentiated strictly from other organizational members. In an informal atmosphere, there is no sharp differentiation and much of the recruit's learning necessarily takes place within the social and task-related networks that surround his or her position. Thus informal socialization procedures are analytically similar to the familiar trial-and-error techniques by which one learns, it is said, through experience.

Generally, the more formal the process, the more stress there is influencing the newcomer's attitudes and value. The more concerned the organization is with the recruit's absorption of the appropriate demeanor and stance, the more the recruit is likely to begin to think and feel like a U.S. Marine, an IBM executive, or a Catholic priest. In other words, formal processes work on preparing a person to occupy a particular *status* in the organization. Informal processes, on the other hand, prepare a person to perform a specific *role* in an organization. And, in general, the more the recruit is separated from the day-to-day reality of the organization, the less he or she will be able to carry over, generalize, and apply any abilities or skills learned in one socialization setting to the new position.

From this standpoint, formal socialization processes are often only the "first round" of socialization. The informal second round occurs when the newcomer is placed in his designated organizational slot and must learn informally the actual practices in his department. Whereas the first wave stresses general skills and attitudes, the second wave emphasizes specified actions, situational applications of the rules, and the idiosyncratic nuances necessary to perform the role in the work setting. However, when the gap separating the two kinds of learning is large, disillusionment with the first wave may set in, causing the individual to disregard virtually everything he has learned in the formal round of socialization.

Even when formal socialization is deliberately set up to provide what are thought to be practical and particular skills, it may be still experienced as problematic by those who pass through the process. In effect, the choice of a formal strategy forces all newcomers to endure, absorb, and perhaps become proficient with *all* the skills and materials presented to them, since they cannot know what is or is not relevant to the job for which they are being prepared. For example, in police training academies, recruits are taught fingerprinting, ballistics, and crime-scene investigation, skills that are, at best, of peripheral interest and of no use to a street patrolman. One result is that when recruits graduate and move to the mean streets of the city, a general disenchantment with the relevance of all their training typically sets in.

Even in the prestigious professional schools of medicine and law the relevance of much training comes to be doubted by practitioners and students alike. Such disenchantment is apparently so pervasive that some observers have suggested that the formal processes that typify professional schools produce graduates who have already internalized standards for their everyday work performances that are "self-validating" and are apparently lodged well beyond the influence of others both within and outside the professional and intellectual community that surrounds the occupation.

Formal strategies appear also to produce stress for people in the form of a period of personal stigmatization. This stigmatization can be brought about by identifying garb (such as the peculiar uniform worn by police recruits); a special and usually somewhat demeaning title (such as "rookie," "trainee," or "junior"); or an insular position (such as an assignment to a classroom instead of an office or job). A person undergoing formal socialization is likely to feel isolated, cut off, and prohibited from assuming everyday social relationships with his more experienced "betters."

Informal socialization processes, wherein a recruit must negotiate for himself within a far less structured situation, can also induce personal anxiety. Indeed, the person may have trouble discovering clues as to the exact dimensions of his or her assigned organizational role. Under most circumstances, laissez-faire socialization increases the influence of the immediate work group on the new employee. There is no guarantee, though, that the direction provided by the informal approach will push the recruit in the right direction so far as those in authority are concerned. Classical examples are the socalled goldbricking and quota-restriction tactics invented by employ-

ees in production situations to thwart managerial directives. Such practices are passed on informally but quite effectively to newcomers against the desires of management.

Left to his own devices, a recruit will select his socialization agents. The success of the socialization process is then determined largely on the basis of whatever mutual regard is developed between the agent and the newcomer, the relevant knowledge possessed by an agent, and, of course, the agent's ability to transfer such knowledge. In most Ph.D. programs, for example, students must pick their own advisors from among the faculty. The advisors then act as philosophers, friends, and guides for the students. And among professors—as among organization executives—it is felt that the student who pushes the hardest by demanding more time, asking more questions, and so forth, learns the most. Consequently, the recruit's freedom of choice in the more informal setting has a price. He or she must force others to teach him.

Individual (Collective)
Socialization Strategies

The degree to which individuals are socialized singly or collectively is perhaps the most critical of the process variables. The difference is analogous to the batch versus unit modes of production. In the batch or mass production case, recruits are bunched together at the outset and processed through an identical set of experiences, with relatively similar outcomes.

When a group goes through a socialization program together, it almost always develops an "in-the-same-boat" collective consciousness. Individual changes in perspective are built on an understanding of the problems faced by all members of the group. Apparently as the group shares problems, various members experiment with possible solutions and report back. In the course of discussions that follow, the members arrive at a collective and more or less consensual definition of their situation.

At the same time, the consensual character of the solutions worked out by the group allows the members to deviate more from the standards set by the agents than the individual mode of socialization does. Therefore, collective processes provide a potential base for recruit resistance. In such cases, the congruence between managerial objectives and those adopted by the group is always problematic—the recruit group is more likely than the individual to redefine or ignore agent demands.

Classic illustrations of the dilemma raised by the use of the collective strategy can be found in both educational and work environments. In educational settings, the faculty may beseech a student to study hard while the student's peers exhort him to relax and have a good time. In many work settings, supervisors attempt to ensure that each employee works up to his level of competence while the worker's peers try to impress on him that he must not do too much. To the degree that the newcomer is backed into the corner and cannot satisfy both demands at the same time, he will follow the dicta of those with whom he spends most of his time and who are most important to him.

The strength of group understandings depends, of course, on the degree to which all members actually share the same fate. In highly competitive settings, group members know that their own success is increased through the failure of others. Hence, the social support networks necessary to maintain cohesion in the group may break down. Consensual understandings will develop, but they will buttress individual modes of adjustment. Junior faculty members in publication-minded universities, for instance, follow group standards, although such standards nearly always stress individual scholarship.

Critically, collective socialization processes can also promote and intensify agent demands. Army recruits socialize each other in ways the army itself could never do; nor, for that matter, would it be allowed to do. Graduate students are often said to learn more from one another than from the faculty. And, while agents may have the power to define the nature of the collective problem, recruits often have more resources available to them to define the solution—time, experience, motivation, expertise, and patience (or the lack thereof).

Individual strategies also induce personal changes. But the views adopted by people processed individually are likely to be far less homogeneous than the views of those processed collectively.

Nor are the views adopted by the isolated newcomer necessarily those that are the most beneficial to him in his transitional position, since he has access only to the perspectives of his socialization agents, and they may not fully apprehend or appreciate his immediate problems.

Certainly, the newcomer may choose not to accept the advice of his agents, although to reject it explicitly may well lose him his job. Furthermore, the rich, contextual perspectives that are available when individuals interact with their peers will not develop under individual strategies. In psychoanalysis, for example, the vocabulary of motives a recruit-patient develops to interpret his situation is quite personal and specific compared with the vocabulary that develops in group therapy. Of course, individual analyses can result in deep changes but they are lonely changes and depend solely on the mutual regard and warmth that exist between agent and recruit.

Apprenticeship modes of work socialization bear some similarity to therapist-patient relationships. If the responsibility for transforming an individual to a given status within the organization is delegated to one person, an intense, value-oriented process is likely to follow. This practice is common whenever a role incumbent is viewed by others in the organization as being the only member capable of shaping the recruit. It is quite common in upper levels of both public and private organizations. Because one organizational member has the sole responsibility, he or she often becomes a role model. The recruit emulates that person's thoughts and actions.

Succession to the chief executive officer level in many firms is marked by the extensive use of the individual socialization strategy. Outcomes in these one-on-one efforts depend on the affective relationships that may or may not develop between the apprentice and his master. In cases of high affect, the process works well and the new member internalizes the values of the particular role he is eventually to play quickly and fully. However, when there are few affective bonds, the socialization process may break down and the transition may not take place.

Overall, individual socialization is expensive in terms of both time and money. Failures are not recycled or rescued easily. Nor are individual strategies particularly suitable for the demands of large organizations, which process many people every year. Hence, with growing bureaucratic structures, the use of mass socialization techniques has increased. Indeed, collective tactics, because of their ease, efficiency, and predictability, have tended to replace the traditional socialization mode of apprenticeship.

Sequential (Nonsequential) Socialization Strategies

Sequential socialization refers to transitional processes marked by a series of discrete and identifiable stages through which an individual must pass in order to achieve a defined role and status within the organization. Many banks groom a person for a particular managerial position by first rotating him or her across the various jobs that will comprise the range of managerial responsibility. Similarly, police recruits in most departments must pass successively through such stages as academy classroom instruction, physical conditioning, firearm training, and on-the-street pupilage.

Nonsequential processes are accomplished in one transitional stage. A factory worker may become a shop supervisor without benefit of an intermediary training program. A department head in a municipal government may become a city manager without serving first as an assistant city manager. Presumably, any organizational position may be analyzed to discover whether intermediate stages of preparation may be required of people taking over that position.

When examining sequential strategies, it is crucial to note the degree to which each stage builds on the preceding stage. For example, the courses in most technical training programs are arranged in what is thought to be a progression from simple to complex material. On the other hand, some sequential processes seem to follow no internal logic. Management training is often disjointed, with the curriculum jumping from topic to topic with little or no integration across stages. In such cases, a person tends to learn the material he likes best in the sequence. If, on the other hand, the flow of topics or courses is harmonious and connected functionally in some fashion, the various minor mental alterations a

person must make at each sequential stage will act cumulatively so that at the end, the person may find himself considerably different from the way he was when he started.

Relatedly, if several agents handle different portions of the socialization process, the degree to which the aims of the agents are common is very important to the eventual outcome. For example, in some officers' training schools of peacetime military organizations, the agents responsible for physical and weapons training have very different attitudes toward their jobs and toward the recruits from the agents in charge of classroom instruction. Officer trainees quickly spot such conflicts when they exist and sometimes exploit them, playing agents off against one another. Such conflicts often lead to a more relaxed atmosphere for the recruits, one in which they enjoy watching their instructors pay more attention to each other than they do to the training program. An almost identical situation can be found in many police training programs.

In the sequential arrangement, agents may not know each other, may be separated spatially, and may have thoroughly different images of their respective tasks. University-trained scientists, for example, apparently have considerable difficulty moving from an academic to an industrial setting to practice their trade. The pattern disconcerts many scientists as they discover that their scholarly training emphasized a far different set of skills and interests from those required in the corporate environment. It is often claimed that to become a "good" industrial scientist, you must learn the painful lesson that being able to sell an idea is as important as having it in the first place.

Consider, too, the range of views about a particular job an organizational newcomer may receive from the personnel department, the training division, and colleagues on the job, all of whom have a hand (and a stake) in the recruit's transition. From this standpoint, empathy must certainly be extended to the so-called juvenile delinquent who receives "guidance" from the police, probation officers, judges, social workers, psychiatrists, and correction officers. Such a sequence may actually teach a person to be whatever his immediate situation demands.

Besides the confusion that comes from the contradictory demands that are sometimes made on people, there is also likely to be misinformation passed along by each agent in a sequential process as to how simple the next stage will be. Thus, the recruit may be told that if he just buckles down and applies himself in stage A, stages B, C, D, and E will be easy. Agents usually mask, wittingly or unwittingly, the true nature of the stage to follow. Their reasoning is that if a person feels his future is bright, rewarding, and assured, he will be most cooperative at the stage he is in, not wishing to jeopardize the future he thinks awaits him.

When attempts are consistently made to make each subsequent step appear simple, the individual's best source of information on the sequential process is another person who has gone through it. If the recruit can find organizational members who have been through the process he can use them to help him obtain a more reality-oriented perspective. But some organizations go out of their way to isolate recruits from veteran members. Certain profit-making trade schools go to great lengths to be sure their paying clientele do not learn of the limited job opportunities in the "glamorous and high-paying" worlds of radio and TV broadcasting, commercial art, or heavy equipment operation. Door-to-door sales trainees are continually assured that their success is guaranteed; the handy-dandy, one-of-a-kind product they are preparing to merchandise will "sell itself." When recruits are officially allowed the privilege of interacting with more experienced organizational members, those controlling the process invariably select a veteran member who will present a sanitized or laundered image of the future.

The degree to which an individual is required to keep to a schedule as he goes through the entire sequence is another important aspect of the sequential socialization strategy. A recruit may feel that he is being pressured or pushed into certain positions or stages before he is ready. This position is similar to that of the business executive who does not want a promotion but feels that if he turns it down, he will be damaging his career. A professor may feel that he cannot turn down the chairmanship of his department without rupturing the respectful relationships with his faculty members that he now enjoys.

On the other hand, if the person does not slip, falter, fail, or seriously discredit himself in any fashion, sequential socialization over his full career may provide him with what has been called a "permanent sense of the unobtained." Thus the executive who, at thirty, aims toward being the head of his department by the time he is forty, will then be attempting to make division head by fifty, and so on. The consumer sequence that stresses accumulation of material goods has much the same character as the artistic sequence that stresses the achievement of the perfect work. Sequential socialization of this sort has a rather disquieting Sisyphus-like nature as the person seeks perpetually to reach the unreachable.

Fixed (Variable) Socialization Strategies

Organizational socialization processes differ in terms of the information and certainty an individual has regarding his transition timetable. Fixed socialization processes provide a recruit with a precise knowledge of the time it will take him to complete a given step. The time of transition is standardized. Consider the probationary systems used on most civil service jobs. The employees know in advance just how long they will be on probation. Educational systems provide another good illustration of fixed processes. Schools begin and end at the same time for all pupils. Students move through the system roughly one step at a time. Fixed processes provide rigid conceptions of "normal" progress; those who are not on schedule are considered "deviant."

Variable socialization processes do not give those being processed any advance notice of their transition timetable. What may be true for one is not true for another. The recruit has to search out clues to his future. Prisoners who serve indeterminate sentences such as the legendary and properly infamous "one to ten," must dope out timetable norms from the scarce materials available to them. Apprenticeship programs often specify only the minimum number of years a person must remain an apprentice and leave open the precise time a person can expect to be advanced to journeyman.

Since the rate of passage across any organizational boundary is a matter of concern to most participants, transition timetables may be developed on the basis of the most fragmentary and flimsiest information. Rumors and innuendos about who is going where and when characterize the variable strategy of socialization. However, if a recruit has direct access to others who are presently in or have been through a similar situation, a sort of "sentimental order" will probably emerge as to when certain passages can or should be expected to take place. And whether or not these expectations are accurate, the individual will measure his progress against them.

The vertically oriented business career is a good example of both variable socialization and the "sentimental order" that seems to characterize such processes. Take the promotional systems in most large organizations. These systems are usually designed to reward individual initiative and performance on current assignments and are therefore considered, at least by upper management, to be highly variable processes. But, for those deeply concerned with their own (and others') progress in the organization, the variable process is almost inevitably corrupted, because would-be executives push very hard to uncover the signs of a coming promotion (or demotion). These people listen closely to stories concerning the time it takes to advance in the organization, observe as closely as possible the experiences of others, and develop an age consciousness delineating the range of appropriate ages for given positions. The process is judgmental and requires a good deal of time and effort. However, in some very stable organizations, such as government agencies, the expected rate of advancement can be evaluated quite precisely and correctly. Thus, the process becomes, for all practical purposes, a fixed one.

In some cases, what is designed as a fixed socialization process more closely approximates a variable process for the individual described by the cliché, "always a bridesmaid, never a bride." The transition timetable is clear enough but, for various reasons, the person cannot or does not wish to complete the journey. Colleges and universities have their "professional students" who never seem to graduate. Training programs have trainees who continually miss the boat and remain trainees indefinitely. Fixed processes differ, therefore, with regard to both the frequency and the rate of the so-called role failure—the number of recruits who for one reason or another are not able to complete the process.

Some organizations even go so far as to provide a special membership category for certain types of role failures. Some police agencies, for example, give recruits unable to meet agent demands long-term assignments as city jailers or traffic controllers. Such assignments serve as a signal to the recruit and to others in the organization that the individual has left the normal career path.

To the extent that these organizational "Siberias" exist and can be identified by those in the fixed setting, chronic sidetracking from which there is rarely a return is a distinct possibility. On the other hand, sidetracking is quite subtle and problematic to the recruit operating in a variable socialization track. Many people who work in the upper and lower levels of management in large organizations are unable to judge where they are going and when they might get there because a further rise in the organization depends in part on such uncertain factors as the state of the economy and the turnover rates above them. Consequently, variable processes can create anxiety and frustration for people who are unable to construct reasonably valid timetables to judge the appropriateness of their movement or lack of movement in the organization.

It is clear that to those in authority within the organization time is an important resource that can be used to control others. Variable socialization processes give an administrator a powerful tool for influencing individual behavior. But the administration also risks creating an organizational situation marked by confusion and uncertainty among those concerned with their movement in the system. Fixed processes provide temporal reference points that allow people both to observe passages ceremonially and to hold together relationships forged during the socialization experiences. Variable processes, by contrast, tend to divide and drive apart people who might show much loyalty and cohesion if the process were fixed.

Tournament (Contest) Socialization Strategies

The practice of separating selected clusters of recruits into different socialization programs or tracks on the basis of presumed differences in ability, ambition, or background represents the essence of tournament socialization processes. Such tracking is often done at the earliest possible date in a person's organizational career. Furthermore, the shifting of people between tracks in a tournament process occurs mainly in one direction: downward. These people are then eliminated from further consideration within the track they have left. The rule for the tournament socialization strategy, according to Yale University sociologist James Rosenbaum, is simple: "When you win, you win only the right to go on to the next round; when you lose, you lose forever."

Contest socialization processes, on the other hand, avoid a sharp distinction between superiors and inferiors of the same rank. The channels of movement through the various socialization programs are kept open and depend on the observed abilities and stated interests of all. In perhaps 75 percent of American public high schools, school administrators and teachers have made student tracking decisions by the ninth grade (and even before). Thus only students on a college-bound track are allowed to take certain courses. But some schools practice a contest mode. They give their students great freedom to choose their classes and allow for considerable mobility in all directions within the system.

Although little empirical research has been done along these lines, there are strong reasons to believe that some version of the tournament process exists in virtually all large organizations. Often someone who is passed over for a management job once is forever disqualified from that position. And accounts from the women's movement strongly suggest that women in most organizations are on very different tracks from men and have been eliminated from the tournament even before they began. A similar situation can be said to exist for most minority-group members.

Even the so-called "high-potential employee" has something to worry about in the tournament process. Often the training for the "high potentials" is not the same as that for the other employees. The "high potential" track will differ considerably from the track afforded the average or typical recruit. But tournament strategy dictates that even among the "high potentials" once you are dropped from the fast track you can't get back on it.

As you move through higher and higher levels in the organization, the tournament strategy be-

comes even more pervasive. Perhaps this is inevitable. The point here is simply that the tournament socialization process (particularly if an extreme version is used across all levels in an organization) has widespread consequences.

One consequence is that when tournament processes are used, the accomplishments of an employee are more likely to be explained by the tracking system of that organization than by the particular characteristics of the person. Thus the person who fails in organization X might well have succeeded in organization Y. Also, those who fall out of the tournament at any stage can expect only custodial socialization in the future. They are expected to behave only in ways appropriate to their plateaued position, are treated coolly, and are discouraged from making further efforts. The organization, in other words, has completed its work on them. As can be seen, tournament socialization, more than the contest mode, can shape and guide ambition in a powerful way.

Consider, too, that in tournament processes, where a single failure has permanent consequences, those passing through tend to adopt the safest strategies of passage. Low risk taking, short cycles of effort, and ever-changing spheres of interest based primarily on what those above them deem most desirable at any given time are the norm. It follows that those who remain in the tournament for any length of time are socialized to be insecure, obsequious to authority, and differentiated, both socially and psychologically, from one another. On the other hand, those who do not remain in the tournament tend to move in the other direction, becoming fatalistic, homogeneous, and, to varying degrees, alienated from the organization.

The attractiveness and prevalence of tournament socialization strategies in work organizations appear to rest on two major arguments. One is that such processes promote the most efficient allocation of resources. Organizational resources, its proponents say, should be allocated only to those most likely to profit from them. The other, closely related argument, is based primarily on the faith that an accurate and reliable judgment of an individual's potential can be made early in one's career. They believe that the principles of selection and personnel psychology (which are uncertain at best) can be used to separate the deserving from the undeserving members of the organization. Various tracks are then legitimized by testing and classifying people so that each test and the resulting classification represent another level in the tournament process. The American Telephone & Telegraph Co. is perhaps the foremost proponent and user of this socialization process. Each transition from one hierarchical level to another is accompanied by the rigorous evaluation of the ever-declining cadre still in the tournament.

Contest socialization, on the other hand, implies that preset norms of transition do not exist in any other form than that of demonstrated performance. Regardless of age, sex, race, or other background factors, each person starts out equal to all other participants. As in educational systems, this appears to be the stated policy of most American corporations. However, those who have looked closely at these organizations conclude that this Horatio Alger ideal is rarely even approximated in practice.

There is some evidence (primarily from studies conducted in public schools) that contest socialization processes, where they do exist, encourage the development of such characteristics as enterprise, perseverance, initiative, and a craftlike dedication to a job well done. We also have the occasionally impressive results of the workplace experiments that are designed to create autonomous work groups, open and competitive bidding for organizational jobs, and the phasing out of the predictive types of psychological tests used to locate people in the "proper" career track (sometimes in secrecy). Instead of tests, a few organizations have moved toward simply providing people with more reliable career information and voluntary career counseling so that people can make more knowledgeable choices about where to go in the organization.

In summary, tournament socialization seems far more likely than contest socialization to drive a wedge between the people being processed. In tournament situations, each person is out for himself and rarely will a group come together to act in unison either for or against the organization. Contest strategies, as the label implies, appear to produce a more cooperative and participative spirit among people in an organiza-

tion. Perhaps because one setback does not entail a permanent loss, people can afford to help one another over various hurdles and a more fraternal atmosphere can be maintained.

Serial (Disjunctive) Socialization Strategies

The serial socialization process, whereby experienced members groom newcomers about to assume similar roles in the organization, is perhaps the best guarantee that an organization will not change over long periods of time. In the police world, the serial feature of recruit socialization is virtually a taken-for-granted device and accounts in large measure for the remarkable stability of patrolman behavior patterns from generation to generation of patrolmen. Innovation in serial modes is unlikely, but continuity and a sense of history will be maintained—even in the face of a turbulent and changing environment.

If a newcomer does not have predecessors available in whose footsteps he can follow, the socialization pattern may be labeled disjunctive. Whereas the serial process risks stagnation and contamination, the disjunctive process risks complication and confusion. The recruit who is left to his own devices may rely on definitions for his task that are gleaned from inappropriate others.

But the disjunctive pattern also gives a recruit the chance to be inventive and original. Without an old guard about to hamper the development of a fresh perspective, the conformity and lock-step pressures created by the serial mode are absent. Most entrepreneurs and those people who fill newly created positions in an organization automatically fall into a disjunctive process of socialization. In both cases, few, if any, people with similar experiences are around to coach the newcomer on the basis of the lessons they have learned.

Similarly, what may be a serial process to most people may be disjunctive to others. Consider a black lawyer entering a previously all-white firm or the navy's recent attempts to train women to become jet pilots. These "deviant" newcomers do not have access to people who have shared their set of unique problems. Such situations make passage considerably more difficult, especially if the person is going it alone, as is most often the case.

Sometimes what appears to be serial is actually disjunctive. Newcomers may be prepared inadequately for spots in one department by agents from another department. This is often true when the personnel department handles all aspects of training. Only later, after the newcomers have access to others who have been through the same process, do they discover the worthlessness and banality of their training. Agent familiarity with the target position is a very crucial factor in the serial strategy.

Occasionally, what could be called "gapping" presents a serious problem in serial strategies. Gapping refers to the historical or social distance between recruit and agent. For example, a newcomer to an organization has the greatest opportunity to learn about his future from those with whom he works. But the experiences passed on to him—no doubt with the best of intentions—by those with whom he works may be quite removed from his own circumstance.

Typically, recruits in the first class will set the tone for the classes to follow. This is not to say that those following will be carbon copies, but simply that it is easier to learn from people who have been through similar experiences than it is to devise solutions from scratch. So long as there are people available in the socialization setting the recruits consider to be "like them," these people will be pressed into service as guides, passing on the consensual solutions to the typical problems faced by the newcomer. Mental patients, for example, often report that they were only able to survive and gain their release because other, more experienced, patients "set them wise" as to what the psychiatric staff deemed appropriate behavior indicating improvement.

From this perspective, serial modes of socialization provide newcomers with built-in guidelines to organize and make sense of their organizational situation. Just as children in stable societies are able to gain a sure sense of the future by seeing in their parents and grandparents an image of themselves grown older, employees in organizations can gain a sense of the future by seeing in their more experienced elders an image of themselves further along. The danger exists, of course, that the recruit won't like that image, and will leave the organization rather than face what seems to be an agonizing future. In industrial settings, where worker morale is low and turnover is high, the serial pattern of initiating newcomers into the organization maintains and perhaps amplifies an already poor situation.

The analytic distinction between serial and disjunctive socialization processes is sometimes brought into sharp focus when an organization cleans house, sweeping old members out and bringing new members to replace them. In extreme cases, an entire organization can be thrown into a disjunctive mode of socialization, causing the organization to lose all resemblance to its former self. For example, in colleges with a large turnover of faculty, long-term students exert a lot of control. Organizations such as prisons and mental hospitals, where inmates stay longer than the staff, are often literally run by the inmates.

Investiture (Divestiture) Socialization Strategies

The last major strategy to be discussed concerns the degree to which a socialization process is set up either to confirm or to dismantle the incoming identity of a newcomer. Investiture processes ratify and establish the viability and usefulness of the characteristics the person already possesses. Presumably, recruits to most high-level managerial jobs are selected on the basis of what they bring to the job. The organization does not wish to change these recruits. Rather, it wants to take advantage of their abilities.

Divestiture processes, on the other hand, deny and strip away certain entering characteristics of a recruit. Many occupational and organizational communities almost require a recruit to sever old friendships, undergo extensive harassment from experienced members, and engage for long periods of time in what can only be called "dirty work" (that is, low-status, low-pay, low-skill, and low-interest tasks). During such periods, the recruit gradually acquires the formal and informal credentials of full and accepted membership.

Ordained ministers, professional athletes, master craftsmen, college professors, and career military personnel must often suffer considerable mortification and humiliation to pay the dues necessary before they are considered equal and respected participants in their particular professions. As a result, closeness develops among the people in that occupation and a distinct sense of solidarity and mutual concern can be found. Pervasive and somewhat closed social worlds are formed by such diverse groups as policemen, airline employees, railroad workers, nurses, symphony musicians, and funeral directors.

Investiture processes say to a newcomer, "We like you as you are; don't change." Entrance is made as smooth and troublefree as possible. Members of the organization go to great lengths to ensure that the recruit's needs are met. Demands on the person are balanced to avoid being unreasonable. There is almost an explicit "honeymoon" period. At times, even positions on the bottom rung of the organizational ladder are filled with a flurry of concern for employee desires. Orientation programs, career counseling, relocation assistance, even a visit to the president's office with the perfunctory handshake and good wishes, systematically suggest to newcomers that they are as valuable as they are.

Ordinarily, the degree to which a setting represents an ordeal to a recruit indicates the degree to which divestiture processes are operative. Rehabilitation institutions, such as mental hospitals and prisons, are commonly thought to be prototypical in this regard. But even in these institutions, initiation processes will have different meanings to different newcomers. Some "rehabilitation" settings, for example, offer a new inmate a readymade home away from home that more or less complements his entering self-image. Thus, for some people, becoming a member of, say, the thief subculture in a prison acts more as an investiture than a divestiture socialization process. In such cases, one's preinstitutional identity is sustained with apparent ease. Prison is simply an annoying interval in the person's otherwise orderly career. The analyst must examine socialization settings closely before assuming powerful divestiture processes to be acting homogeneously on all who enter.

Yet the fact remains that many organizations consciously promote initiation ordeals designed primarily to make the recruit whatever the organization deems appropriate. In the more extreme cases, recruits are isolated from former associates, must abstain from certain types of behavior, must publicly degrade themselves and others through various kinds of mutual criticism, and must follow a rigid set of sanctionable rules and regulations.

This process, when voluntarily undergone, serves, of course, to commit and bind people to the organization. In such cases, the sacrifice and surrender on the part of the newcomers is usually premised upon a sort of institutional awe the recruits bring with them into the organization. Such awe serves to sustain their motivation throughout the divestiture process. Within this society, there are many familiar illustrations: the Marine Corps, fraternal groups, religious cults, elite law schools, self-realization groups, drug rehabilitation programs, professional athletic teams, and so on. All these organizations require a recruit to pass through a series of robust tests in order to gain privileged access to the organization.

In general, the endurance of the divestiture process itself promotes a strong fellowship among those who have followed the same path to membership. For example, college teaching, professional crime, dentistry, and the priesthood all require a person to travel a somewhat painful and lengthy road. The trip provides the newcomer with a set of colleagues who have been down the same path and symbolizes to others on the scene that the newcomer is committed fully to the organization. For those who complete the ordeal, the gap separating recruits from members narrows appreciably while the gap separating members from nonmembers grows.

Clearly, divestiture rather than investiture strategies are more likely to produce similar results among recruits. And, it should be kept in mind, the ordeal aspects of a divestiture process represent an identity-bestowing, as well as an identity-destroying, process. Coercion is not necessarily an assault on the person. It can also be a device for stimulating personal changes that are evaluated positively by the individual. What has always been problematic with coercion is the possibility for perversion in its use.

SUMMARY AND CONCLUSIONS

I have attempted to provide a partial framework for analyzing some of the more pervasive strategies used by organizations to control and direct the behavior of their members. For instance, the tightness or looseness of day-to-day supervision could also be depicted as a socialization strategy. So, too, could the degree of demographic and attitudinal homogeneity or heterogeneity displayed by the incoming recruits, since it could affect the probability that a single perspective will come to dominate the group of newcomers. What I have tried to do here, however, is describe those processes that are most often both ignored by organizational researchers and taken for granted by organizational decision makers.

It is true that someone undergoing a transition is not *tabula rasa,* waiting patiently for the organization to do its work. Many people play very active roles in their own socialization. Each strategy discussed here contains only the possibility, and not the actuality, of effect. For example, those undergoing collective socialization may withdraw from the situation, abstaining from the group life that surrounds other recruits. Or a person may undergo a brutal divestiture process with a calculated indifference and stoic nonchalance. A few exceptions are probably the rule in even the most tyrannical of settings.

However, the preponderance of evidence suggests that the seven strategies discussed here play a very powerful role in influencing any individual's conception of his work role. By teasing out the situational processes variables that, by and large, define an organization passage, it becomes apparent that for most people a given set of experiences in an organization will lead to fairly predictable ends.

If we are interested in strategies that promote a relatively high degree of similarity in the thought and actions of recruits and their agents, a combination of the formal, serial, and divestiture strategies would probably be most effective. If dissimilarity is desired, informal, disjunctive, and investiture strategies would be preferable. To produce a relatively passive group of hard-working but undifferentiated recruits, the combination of formal, collective, sequential, tournament, and divestiture strategies should be used. Other combinations could be used to manufacture other sorts of recruits with, I suspect, few exceptions.

At any rate, the single point I wish to emphasize is that much of the control over individual behavior in organizations is a direct result of the manner in which people are processed. By directing focused and detailed attention to the break-

points or transitions in a person's work career, much can be gained in terms of understanding how organizations shape the performances and ambitions of their members. And, most critically, the strategies by which these transitions are managed are clearly subject to both empirical study and practical change.

Increased awareness and interest in the strategies of people processing may be a matter of some urgency. The trend in modern organizations is apparently to decrease control through such traditional means as direct supervision and the immediate application of rewards and punishments and increase control by such indirect means as recruitment, selection, professionalization, increased training, and career path manipulation. To these more or less remote control mechanisms, we might well add the seven strategies described in this paper.

Certain features of organizations promote behavioral styles among subordinates, peers, and superiors. Since many of the strategies for breaking in employees are taken for granted (particularly for employees beyond the raw recruit level), they are rarely discussed or considered to be matters of choice in the circles in which managerial decisions are reached. Furthermore, those strategies that are discussed are often kept as they are simply because their effects are not widely understood.

People-processing strategies are also frequently justified by the traditional illogic of "that's the way I had to do it, so that's the way my successors will have to do it." Yet, as I have attempted to show, socialization processes are not products of some fixed, evolutionary pattern. They are products of both decisions and nondecisions—and they can be changed. Unfortunately, many of the strategies discussed here seem to be institutionalized out of inertia rather than thoughtful action. This is hardly the most rational practice to be followed by managers with a professed concern for the effective utilization of resources—both material and human.

SELECTED BIBLIOGRAPHY

For a much fuller consideration of just how these socialization strategies are linked to one another and how they can be used to help predict the behavioral responses of people in organizational settings, see John Van Maanen and Edgar H. Schein's "Toward a Theory of Organizational Socialization," in Barry Staw's (ed.) *Research in Organizational Behavior* (JAI Press, 1978). Some of the ideas developed in this paper are also to be found in John Van Maanen's "Breaking-In: Socialization to Work," a chapter in Robert Dubin's *Handbook of Work, Organization, and Society* (Rand-McNally, 1976). An examination of the contrast between the content variables of organizational socialization and the process variables treated here can be found in several of the selections in the recent book edited by Van Maanen, *Organizational Careers: Some New Perspectives* (John Wiley, 1977).

The view of the individual presented in this paper places greater emphasis on the social situations and institutions in which a person resides than it does upon the inner personality. This view suggests that man is social to the core not just to the skin and it is presented best by Erving Goffman in his classic works, *The Presentation of Self in Everyday Life* (Doubleday, 1959) and *Asylums* (Anchor, 1961). Goffman has recently published a difficult but ultimately rewarding book, *Frame Analysis* (Harvard University Press, 1974), that summarizes and ties together much of his sometimes obscure earlier writings.

Some of the better treatments of the sociology of human behavior in organizational settings of direct relevance to managers include Everett C. Hughes's *Men and Their Work* (Free Press, 1958), Melville Dalton's *Men Who Manage* (John Wiley, 1959), and, most recently Rosabeth Kanter's *Men and Women of the Corporation* (Basic Books, 1977). A somewhat broader but nonetheless still pertinent examination of the issues addressed in this paper can be found in Orville Brim and Stanton Wheeler's *Socialization After Childhood* (John Wiley, 1964) and Blanch Greer's (ed.) *Learning to Work* (Sage, 1972). And for a most practical effort at weaving many of these sociological ideas into the psychological fabric that presently informs much of our thinking about behavior in organizations, see Edgar H. Schein's suggestive treatment of *Career Dynamics* (Addison-Wesley, 1978).

II.D
Motivating Work Behavior

12
Motivation through
the design of work

J. Richard Hackman and Gregory R. Oldham

How can work be structured so that it is performed effectively and, at the same time, jobholders find the work personally rewarding and satisfying? In this [reading], one approach to answering that question is developed. We begin by examining the basic conditions that promote high performance motivation and satisfaction at work, and then work backwards to determine how those conditions can be created.[1]

When people are well matched with their jobs, it rarely is necessary to force, coerce, bribe, or trick them into working hard and trying to perform the job well. Instead, they try to do well because it is rewarding and satisfying to do so. Consider the following diagnostic question: "What happens when you try to work especially hard and productively on your job?" When there is a good fit between the person and the job, responses to that question will be mostly positive: "I get a nice sense of accomplishment," or "I feel good about myself and what I'm producing."

The term we use to describe this state of affairs is "internal motivation." When someone has high internal work motivation, feelings are closely tied to how well he or she performs on the job. Good performance is an occasion for self-reward, which serves as an incentive for continuing to do well. And because poor performance prompts unhappy feelings, the person may elect to try harder in the future so as to avoid those unpleasant outcomes and regain the internal rewards that good performance can bring. The result is a self-perpetuating cycle of positive work motivation powered by self-generated (rather than external) rewards for good work.[2]

A number of other personal and work outcomes (such as improved work effectiveness and increased job satisfaction) tend also to appear when conditions for internal work motivation are created. For ease of presentation, we will deal solely with internal motivation in the pages to follow, and fold in these additional outcomes toward the end of the [reading].

Source: Hackman/Oldham, *Work Redesign*, © 1980, Addison-Wesley Publishing Company, Inc., Chapter 4, pages 71–94, "Motivation Through the Design of Work." Reprinted with permission.

CREATING CONDITIONS FOR INTERNAL MOTIVATION

When will internal motivation occur on the job? As shown in Figure 1, our theory suggests that there are three key conditions. First, the person must have *knowledge of the results* of his or her work. If things are arranged so that the person who does the work never finds out whether it is being performed well or poorly, then that person has no basis for feeling good about having done well or unhappy about doing poorly.

Secondly, the person must *experience responsibility* for the results of the work, believing that he or she is personally accountable for the work outcomes. If one views the quality of work done as depending more on external factors (such as a procedure manual, the boss, or people in another work section) than on one's own initiatives or efforts, then there is no reason to feel personally proud when one does well or sad when one doesn't.

And finally, the person must *experience the work as meaningful,* as something that "counts" in one's own system of values. If the work being done is seen as trivial (as might be the case for a job putting paper clips in boxes, for example), then internal work motivation is unlikely to develop—even when the person has sole responsibility for

Figure 1. The Three Psychological States That Affect Internal Work Motivation

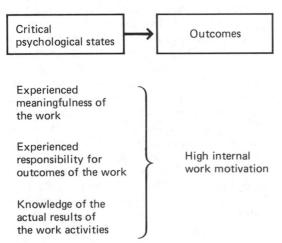

the work and receives ample information about how well he or she is performing.

It appears necessary for *all three* of these factors, labeled "critical psychological states" in Figure 1, to be present for strong internal work motivation to develop and persist. One of your authors, like many college teachers, finds that his day is made or broken by how well the morning lecture goes. The task is meaningful to him (he finds lecturing challenging and believes it to be important); he feels that the quality of the lecture is *his* responsibility (he's never quite learned how to attribute responsibility for a bad class to the students); and his knowledge of results is direct and unambiguous (undergraduates are expert in using subtle cues—and some not so subtle, such as newspaper reading—to signal how much they feel they are learning from the day's class). So all three of the psychological states are present in the lecturing task, and internal motivation to do well is very high indeed.

If any one of the three psychological states were to be removed, your author's internal motivation would drop. If, for example, he did not experience the task as meaningful—perhaps because he did not believe in the lecture as a teaching device, or because he was so good at it (or so poor) that it was not a challenge—then the results would not matter so much. The same would be true if he were merely reading lecture notes prepared by someone else (his personal responsibility for the outcome would be minimal), or if he were insulated from knowledge about how his lecture was being received by the students.

It is ironic that the three psychological states often characterize games played for pleasure better than they do work in organizations. Consider, for example, the game of golf. Knowledge of results is direct and immediate: the player hits the ball and sees at once where it goes. Moreover, tallies of scores for each hole played are kept, providing cumulative and comparative data about performance effectiveness. Experienced personal responsiblity for the outcomes also is clear and high, despite the tendency of golfers sometimes to claim that the slice was due to someone whispering behind the tee, or perhaps to a little puff of wind that came up 100 yards down the fairway just after the ball had been hit. Experienced meaningfulness also is high, despite the fact that the task itself is mostly devoid of cosmic significance.

Why is experienced meaningfulness high for the game of golf? The reason is that golf provides continuous opportunities for players to express and test their personal skills and abilities—specifically their judgment and motor coordination. As will be seen in the next section of this [reading], people tend to experience as meaningful almost *any* task that provides chances to use and test personal skills and abilities, regardless of whether the task is inherently significant (such as performing surgery) or trivial (such as hitting white balls around green pastures). Moreover, the meaningfulness that grows from the challenge to players' skills is often reinforced by golfing partners, who provide social validation of the importance of the activity and may even attach monetary outcomes to the day's play.

So, in golf, the three psychological states are present, and internal motivation among regular golfers is usually quite high. Indeed, golfers exhibit an intensity of behavior that is rarely seen in the workplace: getting up before dawn to be first on the tee, feeling jubilation or despair all day depending on how well the morning round was played, sometimes even destroying the tools and equipment of the game—not out of boredom or frustration with the work (as is sometimes seen in industrial settings) but rather from anger at oneself for not playing better.

Now consider another kind of task, such as assembling aircraft brakes, which clearly is of great human significance. For this task, good versus poor performance can literally mean the difference between life and death for someone aboard an aircraft that must stop before the runway does. An aircraft brake assembler is likely to experience the work as highly meaningful, which provides a good basis for creating conditions of high internal work motivation. The irony is that in many such significant jobs, precisely *because* the task is so important, management designs and supervises the work to ensure error-free performance and destroys employee motivation for high quality work in the process.

For example, managers in one organization were very concerned that an assembly task (not assembling brakes, but similar in many respects)

be performed at the highest possible level of quality, with virtually no errors. A detailed manual was prepared specifying how the assembly should be carried out, with step-by-step instructions about the order of assembly, the use of different tools, and so on. Supervisors were instructed to monitor closely the performance of the assemblers, to ensure that they performed the task exactly "by the book," and to demonstrate the correct use of tools and procedures when they deviated from standard procedure in any way. Moreover, an independent inspection section was created and located in a distant wing of the plant. Also in that wing was a small repair section where any assemblies that failed to pass inspection were to be repaired. Each supervisor received an end-of-week report giving the number of faulty assemblies produced by his group and documenting the nature of the problems discovered by the inspectors. Supervisors were expected to take any corrective action needed to eliminate recurring problems.

The work system described above, which is typical for jobs deemed especially critical by management, seems at first glance appropriate and rational. How did the assemblers respond to the system? The experienced meaningfulness of the work was high: almost to a person the employees agreed that the work itself was significant and important. But they experienced very little *personal* responsibility for the outcomes of the work and felt well insulated from knowledge of the results of their work activities.

The reasons for these perceptions and feelings are not hard to fathom. Because the job required the assemblers to follow the procedure manual to the letter, and because supervisors enforced that requirement, the assemblers viewed themselves as relatively small cogs in a carefully engineered machine. Many employees assumed that if an error were made, or if the assembly materials or tools were out of specification, an inspector would catch it·—that was, after all, their job. Moreover, no assembler learned about the results of his or her work: all testing was done by the inspectors, and the information received by the supervisor at the end of each week was about the group (not the individual). This led many assemblers to conclude that reported problems probably were the fault of *other* members of the work group, not themselves.

In sum, two of the three psychological states were low for most of the assemblers (that is, experienced responsibility and knowledge of results), resulting in a low level of internal work motivation to perform well, despite the inherent significance of the task. And work quality was such a problem that management expressed dismay at the shoddy work being done by the "shoddy people" in the assembly section. Given how the work was designed, with little real chance for assemblers to feel responsibility for what they produced or to learn about the quality of their production, it was almost inevitable that there would be motivational problems among them. But as is often the case, management viewed the problem solely in terms of the apparent impact of the people on the work and failed to consider the effects of the work on the people.

In fact, most people exhibit "motivational problems" at work when their tasks are designed so that they have little meaning, when they experience little responsibility for the work outcomes, or when they are protected from data about how well they are performing. If, on the other hand, a task is arranged so that the people who perform it richly experience the three psychological states, then even individuals who view themselves as chronically lazy may find themselves putting out a little extra effort to do the work well. It appears, then, that *motivation at work may actually have more to do with how tasks are designed and managed than with the personal dispositions of the people who do them.* But what are the task characteristics that create conditions for internal work motivation? We turn to this question next.

THE PROPERTIES OF MOTIVATING JOBS

The three psychological states discussed above are, by definition, internal to persons and therefore not directly manipulable in designing or managing work. What is needed are reasonably objective, measureable, changeable properties of the work itself that foster these psychological states, and through them, enhance internal work motivation. Research suggests that the five job characteristics shown in Figure 2 may be useful in this regard (Hackman and Lawler, 1971; Hackman and Oldham, 1976; Turner and Lawrence, 1965). Three of these five job characteristics are shown in the figure as contributing to the experienced meaningfulness of the work, one contributes to experienced responsibility, and one contributes to knowledge of results.

Figure 2. Job Characteristics That Foster the Three Psychological States

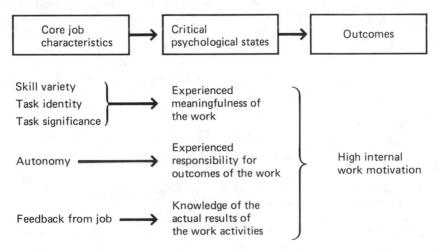

Toward Experienced Meaningfulness

There are a number of different ways that work can take on personal meaning for the person who performs it. Three characteristics of jobs that seem especially powerful in influencing the experienced meaningfulness of work are (1) *skill variety*, (2) *task identity*, and (3) *task significance*.

> **Skill variety:** The degree to which a job requires a variety of different activities in carrying out the work, involving the use of a number of different skills and talents of the person.

As noted earlier, when a task requires workers to engage in activities that challenge or stretch their skills or abilities, they almost invariably experience that task as meaningful, and the more skills involved, the more meaningful the work is likely to be. The link between skill variety and experienced meaningfulness is probably "wired in" for human organisms. Numerous researchers have shown that people, from newborn infants to mature adults, seek out occasions to explore and manipulate their environments and to gain a sense of efficacy by testing and using their skills (Kagan, 1972; White, 1959). The substantive content of the materials being dealt with is not critical in establishing experienced meaningfulness; even work that is not very significant or important in an absolute sense can still be meaningful to a person if doing that work taps and stretches the performer's skills and talents.

> **Task identity:** The degree to which a job requires completion of a "whole" and identifiable piece of work, that is, doing a job from beginning to end with a visible outcome.

People care about their work more when they are doing a whole job. When workers have an intact task, such as providing a complete unit of service or putting together an entire product, they tend to see that task as more meaningful than is the case when they are responsible for only a small part of the job. A social worker in a public welfare department who is responsible for dealing with *all* the needs and problems of his or her clients will find the work more meaningful than a colleague who deals only with issues relating to income maintenance or homemaker as-

sistance. By the same token, it is more meaningful to assemble a complete toaster than to solder electrical connections on toaster after toaster— even if the skill levels required for the two jobs are about the same.

> **Task significance:** The degree to which the job has a substantial impact on the lives of other people, whether those people are in the immediate organization or in the world at large.

Experienced meaningfulness of the work usually is enhanced when workers understand that the work being done will have a substantial impact on the physical or psychological well-being of other people. Employees who tighten nuts on aircraft engines are likely to experience their work as more meaningful than workers who tighten nuts on decorative mirrors, simply because lives are at stake in the first task and are not in the second. When we know that what we do at work will affect someone else's happiness, health, or safety, we care about that work more than if the work is largely irrelevant to the lives and well-being of other people.

Each of the three job characteristics described above contributes to the overall experienced meaningfulness of the work. If a given job is high on all three of the characteristics, an employee is very likely to experience the work as meaningful: putting together a complex heart pacemaker is an example of such a task. Yet because three different task characteristics contribute to experienced meaningfulness, a person can experience the work as meaningful even if one or two of these task characteristics are quite low. Even our assembler of decorative mirrors, whose task is surely below average in significance, could find meaning in the work if it were sufficiently high in skill variety and/or task identity.

Toward Increased Responsibility

The characteristic of jobs that fosters increased feelings of personal responsibility for the work outcomes is *autonomy*.

> **Autonomy:** The degree to which the job provides substantial freedom, independence, and discretion to the individual in scheduling the

work and in determining the procedures to be used in carrying it out.

When the job provides substantial autonomy to the persons performing it, work outcomes will be viewed by those individuals as depending substantially on their *own* efforts, initiatives, and decisions, rather than on, say, the adequacy of instructions from the boss or on a manual of job procedures. As autonomy increases, individuals tend to feel more personal responsibility for successes and failures that occur on the job and are more willing to accept personal accountability for the outcomes of their work.[3]

Toward Knowledge of Results

Knowledge of the results of one's work is affected directly by the amount of *feedback* one receives from doing the work.

> **Job feedback:** The degree to which carrying out the work activities required by the job provides the individual with direct and clear information about the effectiveness of his or her performance.

Note that the focus here is on feedback obtained *directly from the job,* as when a television repairman turns on the set and finds that it works (or doesn't work) after being repaired, when a sales representative closes the deal and receives a check from the customer, or when a physician treats a patient and sees the patient get well. In each case, the knowledge of results derives from the work activities themselves, rather from some other person (such as a co-worker or a supervisor) who collects data or makes a judgment about how well the work is being done. While this second type of feedback (which will be termed "feedback from agents") can also contribute to the overall knowledge an employee has of the results of his or her work, the focus here is on feedback mechanisms that are designed into the work itself.

The Overall Motivating Potential of a Job

Because a given job can be very high on one or more of the five characteristics described above and simultaneously quite low on others, it always is useful to consider the standing of a job on each of the job characteristics. Nevertheless, it also can be informative to combine the five characteristics into a single index that reflects the *overall* potential of a job to foster internal work motivation on the part of job incumbents.

Following the model diagrammed in Figure 2, a job high in motivating potential must be high on at least one (and hopefully more) of the three characteristics that prompt experienced meaningfulness, *and* high on both autonomy and feedback as well, thereby creating conditions that foster all three of the critical psychological states. When numerical scores are available, they are combined as follows:

Motivating potential score (MPS) =

$$\frac{\text{Skill variety} + \text{Task identity} + \text{Task significance}}{3}$$

$$\times \text{ Autonomy} \times \text{ Job feedback}$$

As can be seen from the formula, a very low score on *either* autonomy or feedback will reduce the overall MPS of the job very substantially. This is as it should be, because the model requires that both experienced responsibility and knowledge of results be present if internal work motivation is to be high, and autonomy and feedback, respectively, are the job characteristics that prompt these two psychological states.

On the other hand, a low score on one of the three job characteristics that contribute to experienced meaningfulness cannot, by itself, seriously compromise the overall motivating potential of a job. The other characteristics that prompt experienced meaningfulness can, to some extent, compensate for low scores on one or even two of these three characteristics.

. . . A diagnostic instrument is described there that yields scores for each job characteristic, ranging from a low of 1 to a high of 7. Following the above formula, this means that the lowest possible MPS for a job is 1 and the highest possible is 343 (7 cubed). In practice, the lowest MPS we have ever observed was 7 (an *overflow* typing pool, in which a number of employees sat by their typewriters for hours on end waiting for occasions when one of the regular typing pools was overloaded, at which time they would be given some pages to type until the workload in the regular pools once again became normal). The highest we have observed was over 300, for an autonomous organization development consultant working in a moderate-sized corporation. An average MPS score for jobs in U.S. organizations is about 128.

It should be emphasized that the objective "motivating potential" of a job does not *cause* employees who work on that job to be internally motivated, to perform well, or to experience job satisfaction. Instead, a job that is high in motivating potential merely creates conditions such that *if* the jobholder performs well he or she is likely to experience a reinforcing state of affairs as a consequence. Job characteristics, then, serve only to set the stage for internal motivation. The *behavior* of people who work on a job determines the action that unfolds on the stage. And, as will be seen below, some people are much better positioned to take advantage of the opportunities offered by "enriched" jobs than are others.

THE ROLE OF DIFFERENCES AMONG PEOPLE

Some employees "take off" on jobs that are high in motivating potential; others are more likely to "turn off." There are many attributes of people that affect how they respond to their work, and we cannot review all of them here. We have, however, selected for discussion three characteristics of people that seem especially important in understanding who will (and who will not) respond positively to high MPS jobs. These three factors, which we believe should be taken into account in planning for possible changes in jobs, are identified as "moderators" in Figure 3 and are examined separately below.

Knowledge and Skill

Recall once again the essential property of internal work motivation: positive feelings follow from,

Figure 3. Moderators of the Relationship Between the Job Characteristics and Internal Motivation

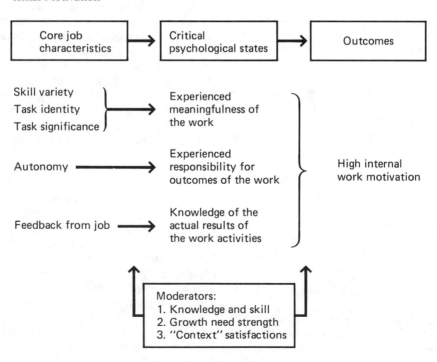

good performance, and negative feelings follow from poor performance. If a job is low in motivating potential, then internal motivation will be low, and one's feelings will not be affected much by how well one does. But if a job is *high* in MPS, then good performance will be highly reinforcing, and poor performance will lead to very unhappy feelings. The consequence of this state of affairs for the work motivation and satisfaction of job incumbents is shown in Figure 4.

For jobs high in motivating potential, then, people who have sufficient knowledge and skill to perform well will experience substantially positive feelings as a result of their work activities. But people who are *not* competent enough to perform well will experience a good deal of unhappiness and frustration at work, precisely because the job "counts" for them and they do poorly at it.

To return to our example of golf, a high MPS task, we find talented golfers frustrated at times with occasional poor performance, but always motivated, returning for more practice, and netting a good deal of self-satisfaction with themselves and the game. However, those of us who

are not blessed with good hand-eye coordination may show equally high motivation early in our experience with the game, but eventually we tend to give it up. Spending a weekend morning trying hard and being miserable at failing, time after time, eventually leads all but the most masochistic to abandon the game in favor of an activity that brings more pleasure than frustration.

A similar phenomenon can occur in organizations when people are given highly motivating tasks that they are unable to perform successfully: rather than continually accept the pain of failing at something that is experienced as important, such individuals frequently opt to withdraw from the job—either behaviorally, by changing jobs, or psychologically, by convincing themselves that in fact they do *not* care about the work. Either outcome is an undesirable state of affairs both for the individual and for the organization.

Growth Need Strength

Jobs high in motivating potential create opportunities for considerable self-direction, learning, and personal accomplishment at work. Not all individuals appreciate such opportunities, even among employees who would be able to perform the work very competently. What determines who will respond positively to a complex, challenging job, and who will not? . . . Some researchers (e.g., Turner and Lawrence, 1965; Blood and Hulin, 1967) have suggested that the critical factor may be subcultural: people from rural settings may more strongly endorse middle-class work norms than people from urban settings, and therefore respond more positively to jobs high in motivating potential. An alternative view, and the one we endorse, is that the *psychological needs* of people are critical in determining how vigorously an individual will respond to a job high in motivating potential (Hackman and Lawler, 1971; Hackman and Oldham, 1976).

Some people have strong needs for personal accomplishment, for learning, and for developing themselves beyond where they are now. These people are said to have strong "growth needs" and are predicted to develop high internal motivation when working on a complex, challenging job. Others have less strong needs for growth and will

Figure 4. The Outcomes of Work on High and Low MPS Jobs as a Function of Employee Knowledge and Skill

| | Motivating potential of the job | |
	Low	High
High	Low internal work motivation, with personal satisfaction not	High internal work motivation, and much satisfaction obtained from doing well.
Low	much affected by how well one performs,	High internal work motivation, and great dissatisfaction obtained from doing poorly.

(Job-relevant knowledge and skill of the employee)

be less eager to exploit the opportunities for personal accomplishment provided by a job high in motivating potential.

Growth need strength may affect how people react to their jobs at two different points in the model shown in Figure 3: first at the link between the objective job characteristics and the psychological states, and again between the psychological states and internal motivation. The first link specifies that people with high growth need strength will *experience* the psychological states more strongly when their objective job is high in MPS than will their low growth need strength counterparts. And the second link means that individuals with high growth need strength will *respond more positively* to the psychological states, when they are present, than will low growth need individuals.

For both of these reasons, individuals with strong needs for growth should respond eagerly and positively to the opportunities provided by enriched work. Individuals with low needs for growth, on the other hand, may not recognize the existence of such opportunities, or may not value them, or may even find them threatening and balk at being "pushed" or stretched too far by their work.

Satisfaction with the Work Context

Up to this point our discussion has focused on the motivating properties of the work itself and on characteristics of people (specifically their job-relevant knowledge and skill, and their growth need strength) that affect how people respond to jobs that are high or low in motivating potential. However, it is also the case that how satisfied people are with aspects of the work *context* may affect their willingness or ability to take advantage of the opportunities for personal accomplishment provided by enriched work.

Consider, for example, an employee who is very upset about her work context. She feels exploitively underpaid for the work she does; she is worried that she is about to be fired, partly because her supervisor seems to go out of the way to make life at work miserable for her; and she doesn't get on at all well with her co-workers, to the point that she believes her co-workers are ridiculing her behind her back.

Now imagine that this woman is asked if she would like to have her (currently rather routine) job made more complex and challenging. Even if she is presently more than qualified to do the work that would be required on the enriched job, would she respond with enthusiasm to the opportunity being offered? It is not very likely. She is *so* dissatisfied with the contextual aspects of life at work that most of her energy is absorbed merely in coping with those issues from day to day. Only if these problems were resolved (or if the employee found a way to adapt psychologically to them) would she become able to experience, appreciate, and respond with high internal motivation to enriched work.

We expect, therefore, that individuals who are relatively satisfied with pay, job security, co-workers, and supervisors will respond more positively to enriched and challenging jobs than individuals who are dissatisfied with these aspects of the work context. And if individuals who are satisfied with the work context also have relatively strong growth need strength, then a *very* high level of internal work motivation would be expected.

What of employees who are both dissatisfied with the work context and low on personal need for growth? For these individuals, work motivation may be only minimally affected by the motivational characteristics of the jobs they do; they are likely to be distracted from whatever richness exists in the work itself (because of their dissatisfaction with contextual factors) and at the same time oriented toward satisfactions *other* than those that can come from effective performance on enriched jobs (because of their low need for personal growth at work).

Research tests of these ideas provide some support for the proposition that the impact of a job on a person is moderated both by the person's needs and by his or her context satisfaction (Oldham, 1976a; Oldham, Hackman, and Pearce, 1976). The findings of the Oldham, Hackman, and Pearce study are summarized in Figure 5. Overall, we found that the higher the motivating potential of a job, the stronger the work motivation and on-the-job performance of the employee. This was not unexpected: task characteristics usually turn out to predict outcomes such as satisfaction and performance in this kind of research.

Yet it also was found in this study that the

Figure 5. Relationship Between the Motivating Potential of a Job and the Motivation and Performance of Job Incumbents

| | Growth need strength | |
	Low	High
Satisfaction with the work context — High	Moderate positive relationship	**Strong positive relationship:** The higher the MPS of the job, the higher the motivation and performance of the job incumbent.
Satisfaction with the work context — Low	**No relationship (or small negative relationship):** Motivation and performance are unrelated (or slightly negatively related) to the MPS of the job.	Moderate positive relationship

strongest relationships between MPS and the outcomes were obtained for those employees who were highly desirous of growth satisfaction and simultaneously satisfied with the work context (that is, those employees in the upper right-hand cell of Figure 5. And when both growth need strength and context satisfaction were at low levels (the lower left-hand cell), some *negative* relationships were obtained between MPS and the outcomes—a quite unusual finding. Apparently those individuals who were both low in growth need strength *and* dissatisfied with the work context found a complex and challenging job so far out of line with their needs that they were unable to perform well on it. When, on the other hand, these individuals worked on a simple and routine job (one low in MPS), they reacted positively to it, probably for two related reasons. First, the job may have fit better with their personal needs (which were for other than growth satisfactions); secondly, because the job was not very challenging, these individuals probably could carry out the work satisfactorily and still have energy left over to use in attempting to deal with the dissatisfying work context.

Summary

In the preceding pages, we have reviewed three factors which qualify the general proposition that increases in the motivating potential of a job foster greater internal work motivation on the part of the people who perform it. These factors are a person's job-relevant knowledge and skill; growth need strength; and level of satisfaction with aspects of the work context, particularly satisfaction with job security, compensation, co-workers, and supervision.

While each of these factors may, in its own right, affect the responses of a person to a job, they become especially significant when they occur in combination. The "worst possible" circumstance for a job that is high in motivating potential, for example, would be when the job incumbent is only marginally competent to perform the work *and* has low needs for personal growth at work *and* is highly dissatisfied with one or more aspects of the work context. The job clearly would be too much for that individual, and negative personal and work outcomes would be predicted. It would be better, for the person as well as for the organization, for the individual to perform relatively more simple and routine work.

On the other hand, if an individual is fully competent to carry out the work required by a complex, challenging task *and* has strong needs for personal growth *and* is well satisfied with the work context, then we would expect both high personal satisfaction and high work motivation and performance. The work, in this case, would fit well both with the talents and the needs of the individual, and the outcomes should be beneficial both to the individual and to the organization.

OUTCOMES OF ENRICHED WORK

Thus far, we have focused on internal work motivation as one key outcome of enriched work. We now broaden our view and examine a number of other personal and organizational outcomes that often are associated with motivating jobs, outcomes that may be affected when the motivational structure of work is changed. The expanded set of outcomes is shown in Figure 6,

Figure 6. The Complete Job Characteristics Model

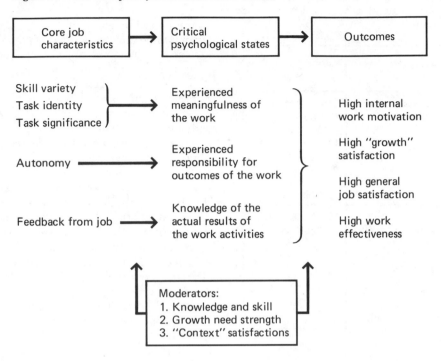

which provides a complete overview of the job characteristics model of work motivation that has been developed in the preceding pages.

Personal Outcomes

The personal outcomes associated with the motivating potential of jobs are, in addition to internal motivation, *growth satisfaction* and *general satisfaction*. When a job is high in MPS, jobholders have enriched opportunities for personal learning and growth at work, and they tend to report that they find those opportunities personally satisfying. Employees on enriched jobs also express relatively high general satisfaction, as measured by questions such as "Generally speaking, how satisfied are you with your job?" and "How frequently do you think of quitting this job?" (reverse scored).

Not included among the outcomes in Figure 6 is satisfaction with various aspects of the work context. What is changed when work is rede-

signed is the relationship between the person and the work itself. While improvements in that relationship should affect the overall satisfaction of individuals with their jobs, there is no reason to expect that it should also lead to specific improvements in satisfaction with job security, pay, supervision, or co-worker relationships. Indeed, . . . job enrichment sometimes leads to decreases in satisfaction with pay and supervision, particularly when compensation arrangements and supervision are not altered to mesh with the new responsibilities and increased autonomy of the persons whose jobs are redesigned.

Work Effectiveness

The model in Figure 6 specifies that employee work effectiveness is expected to be high when jobs are high in motivating potential. As we choose to use the term, work effectiveness includes both the quality and the quantity of the goods or services produced. These two components of overall effectiveness relate to the motivational structure of jobs somewhat differently.

The reasoning regarding work *quality* is straightforward: When a job is high in motivating potential, people who work on that job tend to experience positive affect when they perform *well*. And performing well, for most people, means producing high-quality work of which one can be proud. Thus, on enriched jobs, we find error-free products being manufactured, or especially considerate and helpful service being given to clients, or an extra-careful piece of library research being done.

On the other hand, merely producing a great *quantity* of work—such as making many calls, turning out lots of products, or handling hordes of customers—may not be viewed as a very good reason for patting one's self on the back. Such self-rewards are especially unlikely when, as is sometimes the case, it has been necessary to cut some corners in quality to rack up great quantities of work.

But if the motivational payoff of enriched work has more to do with producing excellent products or services than with producing lots of them, then why are improvements in work quantity obtained in many work redesign projects (Katzell, Beinstock, and Faerstein, 1977)? There are, we believe, three reasons. First, work redesign may remove the "demotivating" effects of a traditionally designed job. . . . If work is extremely routine and repetitive, employees often engage in behaviors that minimize the amount of work they actually have to do. This may involve diversion of attention from the work (daydreaming or sleeping), finding ways to leave the job (taking unnecessary breaks or feigning the need for help from the supervisor), or even engaging in directly counterproductive behaviors (causing machine malfunctions or deliberately restricting output). So even if employees do not become motivated to produce especially great quantities of output when their work is enriched, productivity increases may still be obtained, simply because dysfunctional behaviors such as those noted above are no longer exhibited.

Second, hidden inefficiencies in the use of time and support staff may be eliminated when traditional jobs are redesigned. While in traditional designs each subpart of the work to be done is engineered for maximum efficiency, it often is necessary to add extra coordinating, supervising, and quality control staff for the work system as a whole to function smoothly. Moreover, when work must be passed from person to person repeatedly to complete an entire task, employees necessarily spend nonproductive time receiving the work, getting started on it, and passing it on to the co-worker who is to perform the next operation. In some (not all) work systems, these inefficiencies of time and staff can be reduced substantially when the numerous small parts of the total task are recombined into a meaningful whole.

Finally, it often is possible to refine and simplify the overall work system when jobs within that system are redesigned. Whenever jobs are changed substantially, it usually is necessary to rethink the way related jobs are structured and how work flows from person to person and from job to job. Often such scrutiny of the workflow (which previously may have been taken as "given") unearths some simple systemic inefficiencies—such as redundant work activities, work being done that does not contribute to the final product or service (reports written for files that are never used, for instance), or time-wasting work rules and procedures. Once these inefficiencies are brought to light they are likely to be corrected, resulting in higher system productivity.

In sum, improvements in work effectiveness generally are to be expected when the motivational makeup of jobs is improved through work redesign. The quality of performance should improve as a direct function of the increased motivating potential of the work. The quantity of work produced also may increase, but this is a more complicated and less predictable matter. In our view, the likelihood of quantity improvements depends on the state of the work system *prior* to work redesign, specifically whether (1) employees were exhibiting low productivity because they were "turned off" by exceedingly routine or repetitive work, (2) there were hidden inefficiencies in the use of time or support staff in getting the work done, or (3) there were redundancies or time-wasting procedures built into the work system itself. If one or more of these problems preexisted in the work unit, then increases in the quantity of work performed are likely to appear after the work is redesigned. If these problems were not present, then we would not expect work redesign to yield increases in production quantity.[4] Indeed, decreases in quantity may even be noted as people work especially hard to produce high *quality* work.[5]

Attendance at Work

Why is reduced absenteeism not in the outcome list in Figure 6? One would expect that when jobs are motivationally improved, employees would find the workplace more attractive and would want to come to work more regularly. The fact that general satisfaction (which is typically associated with absenteeism) usually improves when jobs are enriched would further strengthen the expectation that attendance should improve when the design of work is improved. Yet research results on the question are far from conclusive: Some studies report improvements in attendance when jobs are enriched, some report no change, and some have even reported worse absence problems than before (e.g., Hackman, Pearce, and Wolfe, 1978).

Our view is that whether attendance improves or deteriorates as a consequence of work redesign depends heavily on the *competence* of the employees whose jobs are changed. We argued earlier in this [reading] that while jobs high in motivating potential lead to increased occasions for self-reinforcement among people who are competent in the work, they also provide more frequent occasions for self-generated *negative* affect for those who are not. If this is true, then changes in jobs that increase internal motivation might simultaneously prompt decreased absenteeism for more competent employees and increased absenteeism for their less competent co-workers. Any overall indicator of absenteeism for the work group as a whole would be misleading because of the different effects of the change on the absence rate of the two subgroups.

This notion awaits systematic research testing. If it should be borne out, it would have some interesting implications for the management of employee attendance—and, perhaps, even for issues of work-force retention. Specifically, it appears that designing enriched jobs might be one way to foster the retention of the best workers and to ensure their regular attendance, while at the same time creating conditions such that their less competent colleagues would find it advantageous to stay away from work. For some managers, this would be a pleasant reversal of present difficulties in getting competent workers to stay with the organization and in getting incompetents to stay away.

Summary

When the motivational properties of work are improved, one can usually count on increases in internal work motivation, general satisfaction, and growth satisfaction. Employee satisfaction with aspects of the work context, such as job security, pay, supervision, and co-workers are not likely to increase and may even show a decline.

Work effectiveness should improve when jobs are enriched, especially the quality of the work done. Production quantity may also increase, but this is likely only when there were relatively severe motivational problems or built-in inefficiencies in the work system prior to redesign. Although additional research is required before confident predictions can be made regarding the effects of work redesign on absenteeism and voluntary turnover, it may be that enriched work leads to greater behavioral commitment to the work and the organization for more talented employees and to less commitment among employees who are less capable.

Work redesign assuredly is *not* a panacea for all organizational problems. It is a viable and useful change strategy for some personal and work outcomes but not for others. . . . Even to obtain those outcomes listed in Figure 6 requires careful and competent planning to ensure that the changes made are appropriate for the kind of work being done, for the people who do the work, and for the broader organizational context. . . .

NOTES

1. The theoretical position presented in this [reading] is developed in more detail by Hackman and Oldham (1976).

2. Concepts that are related to internal motivation as we use the term here include Deci's (1975) more general notion of "intrinsic motivation" and Csikszentmihalyi's (1975) more focused idea of the "flow experience." Perhaps closest in meaning to internal motivation is Blood's concept of "self-rewarding." Self-administered rewards, according to Blood, are both immediate and contingent on behavior; in colloquial terms, extreme positive self-rewarding can be characterized as pride, and extreme negative self-rewarding as shame (Blood, 1978, p.94).

3. There has been a good deal of research in social and clinical psychology documenting the negative consequences for people of constrained autonomy to make decisions about their life and work (see Wortman and Brehm, 1975 for a review.) Moreover, there are some intriguing findings that suggest that increased control can have beneficial effects on learning (Perlmuter and Monty, 1977), on responses to stressful situations such as crowding (Baron and Rodin, 1978), and on happiness and health (Rodin and Langer, 1977). There are, however, few studies in which control has been increased by direct alteration of task structure, or which provide direct tests of the link proposed here between objective increases in autonomy and enhanced feelings of personal *responsibility* for work outcomes (Sogin and Pallak, 1976; Wortman, 1976).

4. This suggests that findings from laboratory studies of the effects of work redesign on productivity should be interpreted with caution. It is doubtful, in such studies, that control conditions will contain the kinds of systemic inefficiencies that often build up over time in real organizations, or that control subjects in the laboratory will exhibit the kinds of antiproductive behaviors that sometimes appear when employees have extended experience on poorly designed jobs. Thus, a laboratory finding that work redesign has no impact on productivity may not generalize to problem-ridden real organizations.

5. In such circumstances, devices such as goal setting and contingent financial rewards may be helpful in maintaining a balance between the quantity and quality of work produced (cf. Umstot, Bell, and Mitchell, 1976).

REFERENCES

Baron, R. M., and J. Rodin. Personal control as a mediator of crowding. In A. Baum, S. Valins, and J. Singer (eds.), *Advances in environmental psychology.* Hillsdale, N.J.: Erlbaum, 1978.

Blood, M. R. Organizational control of performance through selfrewarding. In B. King, S. Streufert, and F. E. Fiedler (eds.), *Managerial control and organizational democracy.* Washington, D.C.: Winston & Sons, 1978.

Blood, M. R., and C. L. Hulin. Alienation, environmental characteristics, and worker responses. *Journal of Applied Psychology,* 1967, 51, 284–290.

Csikszentmihalyi, M. *Beyond boredom and anxiety.* San Francisco: Jossey-Bass, 1975.

Deci, E. L. *Intrinsic motivation.* New York: Plenum, 1975.

Hackman, J. R. and E. E. Lawler III. Employee reactions to job characteristics. *Journal of Applied Psychology Monograph,* 1971, 55, 259–286.

Hackman, J. R., and G. R. Oldham. Motivation through the design of work: Test of a theory. *Organizational Behavior and Human Performance,* 1976, 16, 250–279.

Hackman, J. R., J. L. Pearce, and J. C. Wolfe. Effects of changes in job characteristics on work attitudes and behaviors: A naturally occurring quasi-experiment. *Organizational Behavior and Human Performance,* 1978, 21, 289–304.

Kagan, J. Motives and development. *Journal of Personality and Social Psychology,* 1972, 22, 51–66.

Katzell, R. A., P. Bienstock, and P. H. Faerstein. *A guide to worker productivity experiments in the United States 1971–1975.* New York: New York University Press, 1977.

Oldham, G. R. Job characteristics and internal motivation: The moderating effect of interpersonal and individual variables. *Human Relations,* 1976, 29, 559–569. (a)

Oldham, G. R., J. R. Hackman, and J. L. Pearce. Conditions under which employees respond positively to enriched work. *Journal of Applied Psychology,* 1976, 61, 395–403.

Perlmuter, L. C., and R. A. Monty. The importance of perceived control: Fact or fantasy? *American Scientist,* 1977, 65, 759–765.

Rodin, J. and E. J. Langer. Long term effects of a control-relevant intervention with the institutionalized aged. *Journal of Personality and Social Psychology,* 1977, 35, 897–902.

Sogin, S. R., and M. S. Pallak. Bad decisions, responsibility, and attitude change: Effects of volition, foreseeability, and locus of causality of negative consequences. *Journal of Personality and Social Psychology,* 1976, 33, 300–306.

Turner, A. N., and P. R. Lawrence. *Industrial jobs and the worker.* Boston: Harvard Graduate School of Business Administration, 1965.

Umstot, D. D., C. H. Bell, and T. R. Mitchell. Effects of job enrichment and task goals on satisfaction and productivity. *Journal of Applied Psychology,* 1976, 61, 379–394.

White, R. W. Motivation reconsidered: The concept of competence. *Psychological Review*, 1959, 66, 297–333.

Wortman, C. B. Causal attributions and personal control. In J. Harvey, W. Ickes, and R. Kidd (eds.), *New directions in attribution research.* Hillsdale, N.J.: Erlbaum, 1976.

Wortman, C. B., and J. W. Brehm. Responses to uncontrollable outcomes. In L. Berkowitz (ed.), *Advances in experimental social psychology* (Vol. 8). New York: Academic Press, 1975.

13
How to ruin
motivation with pay

W. Clay Hamner

MERIT PAY—
SHOULD IT BE USED?

Most behavioral scientists believe in the "law of effect," which states simply that behavior which appears to lead to a positive consequence tends to be repeated. This principle is also followed by most large organizations which have a merit pay system for their management team. Merit pay or "pay for performance" is so widely accepted by compensation managers and academic researchers that criticizing it seems foolhardy.

Despite the soundness of the principle of the law of effect on which merit pay is based, academic researchers have criticized the merit system as being detrimental to motivation rather than enhancing motivation as designed. These criticisms generally fall into one of two categories.

The first group of researchers criticize the failure of the merit plan to increase the motivation of the work force because of mismanagement or lack of understanding of the merit program by managers. The second group of researchers criticize the use of merit pay because it utilizes externally mediated rewards rather than focusing on a system where individuals can be motivated by the job itself. This second criticism centers on the proposition that employees who enjoy their job (i.e., are intrinsically motivated) will lose interest in the job when a merit pay plan is introduced because they soon believe they are doing the job for the money and not because they enjoy their job. Therefore, for the first group of researchers, the recommendation is that compensation managers need to examine ways to improve the introduction of merit plans, while the second group of researchers, albeit fewer in number, would recommend that compensation managers need to deemphasize the merit pay plan system and concentrate on improving other aspects of the job.

The purpose of this presentation will be to examine the research behind both of these positions and then present recommendations which, it is hoped, will enable the compensation manager to utilize a "pay performance" plan as a method of improving the quality and quantity of job performance. Let's begin the discussion by examining possible reasons why merit pay systems fail.

REASONS WHY MERIT PAY SYSTEMS FAIL

As noted earlier, one group of researchers has concluded that the failure of merit pay plans is due not to a weakness in the law of effect, but to a weakness in its implementation by compensation managers and the line managers involved in the merit increase recommendations. For example, after reviewing pay research from General Electric and other companies, H. H. Meyer (1975) concluded that despite the apparent soundness of the simple principle on which merit pay is based, experience tells us that it does not work with such elegant simplicity. Instead, managers typically seemed to be inclined to make relatively small discriminations in salary treatment among individuals in the same job regardless of perceived differences in performance. As a matter of fact, Meyer notes, when discriminations are made, they are likely to be based on factors other than performance—such as length of service, future potential, or perceived need for "catch up," where one employee's pay seems low in relation to others in the group.

Michael Beer (see Beer & Gery, 1972), Director of Organizational Development at Corning Glass, explains why the implementation of the merit system has lost its effectiveness when he states that pay systems evolve over time and administrative considerations and tradition often override the more important considerations of behavioral outcomes in determining the shape of the system and its administration. Therefore, both of these researchers seem to say that it is not the merit pay theory that is defective. Rather, the history of the actual implementation of the theory is at fault. Let us look at the shortcomings— noted in the literature—that may cause low motivation to result from a merit pay program.

Pay is Not Perceived As Being Related to Job Performance

Edward E. Lawler, III, a leading researcher on pay and performance, has noted that one of the major reasons managers are unhappy with their wage system is that they do not perceive the relationship between how hard they work (productivity) and how much they earn. Lawler (1966), in a survey of 600 middle and lower level managers, found virtually no relationship between their pay and their rated performance. Of the managers studied, those who were most highly motivated to perform their jobs effectively were characterized by two attitudes: (1) they said that their pay was important to them and (2) they felt that good job performance would lead to higher pay for them.

There are several reasons why managers do not perceive their pay as being related to performance even when the company claims to have a merit pay plan. First, many rewards (e.g., stock options) are *deferred payments*, and the time horizon is so long that the employee loses sight of its relationship to performance. Second, the *goals* of the organization on which performance appraisals are based are either unclear, unrealistic, or unrelated to pay. W. H. Mobley (1974) found only 36 percent of the managers surveyed from a company using an MBO program saw goal attainment as having considerable bearing on their merit increase, while 83 percent of their bosses claim that they used the goal attainments to determine their pay increase recommendations. Third, the *secrecy* of the annual merit increases may lead managers to conclude that their recommended pay increase has no bearing on their past year's performance. R. L. Opsahl and M. D. Dunnette (1966) claimed that secrecy is due in part to a fear by salary administrators that they would have a difficult time mustering convincing arguments in favor of many of their practices. E. E. Lawler (1971) summarized his extensive research on secrecy of pay by stating that managers did not have an accurate picture of what other managers were earning. There was a general tendency for the managers to overstate the pay of managers at their own level (thereby reducing their own pay, relatively speaking), and at one level below them (again reducing their own pay, relatively speaking), while they tended to under-estimate the pay of managers one level above them (thus reducing the value of future promotions).

Performance Ratings Are Seen As Biased

While many managers working under a merit program believe that the program is a good one, they are dissatisfied with the evaluation of their performance given them by their immediate superior. A merit plan is based on the assumption that managers can make objective (valid) distinctions between good and poor performance. Unfortunately, most evaluations of performance are subjective in nature, and consist of a "summary score" from a general (and sometimes dated) performance evaluation form. As H. H. Meyer (1975) notes, the supervisor's key role in determining pay creates a problem in that it reminds the employee very clearly that he or she is dependent on the supervisor for rewards. Therefore, the merit plan should, whenever possible, be based on objective measures (e.g., group sales, cost reduction per unit, goal attainment, etc.) rather than subjective measures (e.g., cooperation, attitude, future potential, etc.).

As an aside, it should be noted that in the area of fair employment of minorities, both the courts (e.g., see *Rowe v. General Motors Corporation,* 1972) and the new EEOC (1974) guidelines recognize the potential of bias in subjective performance appraisals, and organizations must begin examining the validity of their performance ratings to see if they are, in fact, job related. My recent research has shown that, even when objective measures of job performance are clearly spelled out, supervisors have a tendency to rate blacks differently than whites and females differently than males even though their performance levels are identical (e.g., see Scott & Hamner, 1975; Hamner, Kim, Baird, & Bigoness, 1974). E. E. Lawler, III, feels that the complaints of managers and employees about the subjective nature of their performance evaluations may be a sign of a system of poor leadership. Lawler (1971) notes that many plans seem to fail not because they are mechanically defective, but because they are ineffectively introduced, there is a lack of trust between superiors and subordinates, or the

quality of the supervisor is too low. He adds that no plan can succeed in the face of low trust and poor supervision, no matter how well-constructed it may be. L. W. Gruenfeld and P. Weissenberg (1966) reported support for this theory of poor leadership espoused by Lawler when they found that good managers are much more amenable than poor managers to the idea of basing pay on performance.

Rewards Are Not Viewed As Rewards

A third problem in administering a merit increase deals with management's inability to communicate accurately to the employee the information that they are trying to communicate through the pay raise. There is no doubt that the pay raise is more than money; it tells the employee "You're loved a lot," "You're only average," "You're not appreciated around here," "You'd better get busy," etc. Often management believes it is communicating a positive message to the employee, but the message being received by the employee is negative. This may have a detrimental effect on his or her future potential. Opsahl and Dunnette (1966) warn us that the relation between performing certain desired behaviors and attainment of the pay-incentive must be explicitly specified.

The reasons that the reward message may not be seen as a reward include the following: (1) Conflicting reward schedules may be operating. (2) A problem of inequity among employees is perceived to exist. (3) The merit increase is threatening to the self-esteem of the employee. All three of these problems center on the fact that the pay increases are generally kept secret—thus causing the employees to draw erroneous conclusions—or on the fact that there is little or no communication in the form of coaching and counselling coming from the supervisor during the year, or following the performance appraisal. Instead, the employee is "expected to know" what the supervisor thinks about his or her performance. As Beer and Gery (1972) stated, the more frequent the formal and informal reviews of performance and the more the individual is told about reasons for an increase, the greater his preference for a merit increase and the lower his preference for a seniority system.

Conflicting reward schedules. Such schedules come about because of a defect in the merit plan itself. For example, individual rewards (e.g., the best manager will get a free trip to Hawaii) are set up in such a way that cooperation with other managers is discouraged, or perhaps a cost-reduction program is introduced at the expense of production, and one department (sales) suffers while another department (manufacturing) benefits in the short run. As Kenneth F. Foster, Manager of Composition at Xerox, has noted (see *Harvard Business Review,* July-August 1974), pay plans must be constantly changing because of general business conditions, shifts in management philosophy, competitive pressures, participant feedback, and modification in the structure and objectives of the organization. Nevertheless, these changes should be designed in such a way that the negative side effect of reduced cooperation does not result. For this reason, many companies are using a company-wide merit plan (e.g., the Scanlon Plan; see Frost, Wakeley, & Ruh, 1974) where there is a financial incentive to everyone in the organization based on the performance of the total organization.

Inequity. Inequity in pay can come about for one of two reasons. First, the employee perceives the merit increase to be unfair relative to his own past year's performance. That is, he is dissatisfied with the performance evaluation, or else feels the performance evaluation is fair, but believes his supervisor failed to reward him in a manner consistent with his rating. A much more common problem is that while the employee may agree with the dollar amount of his pay, he perceives that others who are performing at levels below him are receiving as large an increase as he, or else those who are performing at his same level are receiving higher raises. For example, an employee who was rated as above average receives an 8 percent pay increase. He perceives this to be low since he believes that the average increase was 9 percent, when in fact it was 6½ percent. In order to avoid the feeling of inequity, which will contribute to dissatisfaction with pay and possible lower job performance, Lawler (1973) recommends that managers tell their employees how the salary raises were derived (e.g., 50 percent based on cost of living and 50 percent on merit)

and tell them the range and mean of raises given in the organization for people at their job level. Lawler advocated the abandonment of secrecy policies: "There is no reason why organizations cannot make salaries public information" (1965, p. 8).

Threat to self-esteem. H. H. Meyer, in an excellent paper, argues that the problem with merit pay plans may be more than a problem of equity. Drawing on his previous research (Meyer, Kay, & French, 1965), he concluded that 90 percent of the managers at General Electric rated themselves as above average. Bassett and Meyer (1968) and Beer and Gery (1972) found similar results. Meyer concludes that the inconsistency in the information of the merit raise with the employee's evaluation of his or her performance will be a threat to the manager's *self-esteem,* and the manager may cope with this threat by either denying the importance of hard work or disparaging the source. Meyer concludes:

> The fact that almost everyone thinks he is an above average performer probably causes most of our problems with merit pay plans. Since the salary increases most people get do not reflect superior performance (as determined by interpersonal comparisons, or as defined in the guide book for the pay plan), the effects of the actual pay increases on motivation are likely to be more negative than positive. The majority of the people feel discriminated against because, obviously, management does not recognize their true worth (1975, p. 13).

Managers of Merit Increases Are More Concerned with Satisfaction with Pay than Job Performance

Most studies which survey managers' satisfaction with their pay have shown high levels of dissatisfaction. Porter (1961) found that 80 percent of the managers surveyed from companies throughout the United States reported dissatisfaction with their pay. These same findings have been reported in surveys at General Electric (Penner, 1967) and a cross-section of managers from many companies (Lawler, 1965). Beer (Beer & Gery, 1972) points out that too often dissatisfaction with pay is assumed to mean dissatisfaction with amount. However, his research suggests that a change to a merit system with no increase in amount paid out by the company will increase satisfaction if the reasons for the increases are explained.

Opsahl and Dunnette (1966) noted that while there is a great deal of research on satisfaction with pay, there is less solid research in the area of the relationship between pay and job performance than any other field. Because of this failure to deal with the role of pay, Lawler (1966) notes that many managers have come to the erroneous conclusion that the experts in "human relations" have shown that pay is a relatively unimportant incentive.

In fact, Cherrington, Reitz, and Scott (1971) found that the magnitude of the relationship between satisfaction and performance depends primarily upon the performance-reinforcer contingencies that have been arranged (i.e., people who were appropriately reinforced were satisfied with their pay, while those people who were dissatisfied with their pay were those who were inappropriately rewarded). Likewise, Hamner and Foster (1974) found that the best performers working under a contingent (piece rate) pay plan were more satisfied than the poorer performers, but that there was no relationship between satisfaction and performance for those paid under a noncontingent (across the board) pay plan.

Managers need to be concerned with two questions. First, *is the merit raise being based on performance?* Numerous studies (e.g., see Lee, 1969; Belcher, 1974) show that pay is not closely related to performance in many organizations that claim to have merit ranges. Typically, these studies show that pay is much more closely related to job level and seniority than performance. In fact, Belcher (1974) reports that low, zero, and even negative correlations between pay and supervisory ratings of performance occur even among managers where the correlation would be expected to be high.

Second, *who is doing the complaining?* Donald Finn, Compensation Manager at J. C. Penney, says we are often "hung up" as managers about the satisfaction of employees with our pay recommendations. He says:

So who is complaining and why? If low producers are low earners, the pay plan is working—but there will be complaints. If a company wants an incentive plan in which rewards are commensurate with risk, it must be willing to accept a relatively broad range of earnings and corresponding degrees of manager satisfaction. (*Harvard Business Review*, July-August, 1974, p. 8.)

Beer agrees with Finn when he says:

A merit system can probably be utilized effectively by management in motivating employees. This concept has been in disfavor lately, but our findings indicate that more might be done with money in motivating people, particularly those who are work and achievement oriented in the first place.

While a merit system would seem to be less need satisfying to the security-oriented individual and, therefore, potentially less motivating, there is probably a net gain in installing a merit system. Those who are high in achievement-oriented needs will be stimulated by such a system to greater heights of performance, while those high in security-oriented needs will become more dissatisfied and it is hoped, will leave. (Beer & Gery, 1972, p. 330.)

Trust and Openness about Merit Increases Is Low

A merit system will not be accepted and may not have the intended motivational effects if managers do not actively administer a performance appraisal system, practice good human relations, explain the reasons for the increases and ensure that employees are not forgotten when eligibility dates come and go. The organization must provide an open climate with respect to pay, and an environment where work and effort are valued (Beer & Gery, 1972).

The Xerox Corporation has recognized the problem of trust and openness and states a philosophy that "If pay and satisfaction is to be high, pay rates must vary according to job demands in such a way that each perceived increment in a job demand factor will lead to increased pay" (*Xerox Compensation Planning Model*, June 1972). This same document at Xerox notes that organizations expect extremely high levels of trust on the part of their employees, in that:

(a) Only 72% of 184 employing organizations had a written statement of the firm's basic compensation policy covering such matters as paying competitive salaries, timing of wage and salary increases, and how raises are determined.

(b) Only 51% of these same organizations communicate their general compensation policies directly to all employees, while 21% communicate the policy only to managers.

(c) Contrarily, 69% of the firms do not provide their employees with wage and salary schedules or progression plans that apply to their own categories, thus indicating a low trust level toward employees.

(d) Over 50% of the firms do not tell their employees where this information is available.

(e) In only 48% of the firms do managers have access to salary schedules applying to their own level in the organization, and in only 18% of the companies do managers have knowledge of the salaries of other managers at their own level or higher levels. (*Xerox Compensation Planning Model*, June, 1972, pp. 68–69.)

Some Organizations View Money As the Primary Motivator, Ignoring the Importance of the Job Itself

The first five shortcomings deal with the criticism of researchers that the failure of the merit plan is due to poor implementation, and not due to a weakness in the theory of the "law of effect." However, the sixth shortcoming under discussion now centers on the second criticism that employees who have intrinsically interesting jobs will lose interest in the job when a merit pay plan is introduced. An intrinsically motivating job can be defined as one that is interesting and creative enough that certain pleasures or rewards are derived from completing the task itself. Until recently, most theories dealing with worker motivation (e.g., Porter & Lawler, 1968) have assumed that the effects of intrinsic and extrinsic reinforcement (e.g., merit pay) are additive; i.e., a worker will be more motivated to complete a task which combined both kinds of rewards than a task where only one kind of reward is present.

Deci (1971, 1972a, b), among others (Likert, 1967; Vroom & Deci, 1970), criticizes behavioral scientists who advocate a system of employee motivation that utilizes externally mediated rewards, i.e., rewards such as money administered by someone other than the employee. In so doing, according to Deci, management is attempting to control the employee's behavior so he or she will do as told. The limitations of this method of worker motivation, for Deci, is that it only satisfies a person's "lower order" needs (Maslow, 1943) and does not take into account "higher order" needs for self-esteem and self-actualization.

Deci recommends that we should move away from a method of external control, and toward a system where individuals can be motivated by the job itself. He says that this approach will allow managers to focus on higher-order needs where the rewards are mediated by the recipient (intrinsically motivated). To motivate employees intrinsically, tasks should be designed which are interesting, creative, and resourceful, and workers should have some say in decisions which concern them "so they will feel like causal agents in the activities which they engage in" (Deci, 1972a, p. 219).

Deci has introduced evidence which reportedly shows that a person's intrinsic motivation to perform an activity decreases when he or she receives contingent monetary payment for performing an interesting task. Deci concludes from these findings that:

> Interpreting these results in relation to theories of work motivation, it seems clear that the effects of intrinsic motivation and extrinsic motivation are not additive. While extrinsic rewards such as money can certainly motivate behavior, they appear to be doing so at the expense of intrinsic motivation; as a result, contingent payment systems do not appear to be compatible with participative management systems. (1972b, pp. 224–225.)

Deci brings out an important point: Managers should not use pay to offset a boring or negative task. However, like Herzberg before him, his results don't appear to completely support his conclusion about the effect of money as a motivator. Research by both Hamner and Foster (1974) and Calder and Staw (1975) has shown that the effect of intrinsic and extrinsic monetary rewards is additive and that even Deci's results themselves, on close examination, support this more traditional argument. In addition, I am not sure that merit pay plans are incompatible with a participative management system. The noted psychologist B. F. Skinner offers advice to managers on both of these last two arguments.

Skinner recommends that the organization should design feedback and incentive systems in such a way that the dual objective of getting things done and making work enjoyable are met. He says:

> It is important to remember that an incentive system isn't the only factor to take into account. How pleasant work conditions are, how easy or awkward a job is, how good or bad tools are— many things of that sort make an enormous difference in what a worker will do for what he receives. One problem of the production-line worker is that he seldom sees any of the ultimate consequences of his work. He puts on left front wheels day in and day out and he may never see the finished car. . . . (1973, p. 39.)

Skinner also suggested that people be involved in the design of the contingencies of reinforcements (in this case, merit pay plans) under which they live. This way the rewards come from the behavior of the worker in the environment, and not the supervisor. Both Kenneth F. Foster at Xerox and Joe W. Rogers, Chairman of the Board of Waffle House, agree. Foster, commenting on the McDonald pay plan, said, "McDonald's management is to be commended for recognizing a number of important incentive reward axioms. Foremost, the reward system must be meaningful to the recipient. They must also see it as equitable and its financial outcomes and rewards as within their power to control." (*Harvard Business Review*, July-August 1974, p. 5.) Rogers agreed, saying, "In the restaurant industry, a bonus system must be self-monitoring and deal only with the facts. All areas of judgment by a friendly or unfriendly superior should be absent in a bonus system. . . . let people participate in the design of the new pay. Credibility with the participants is much more critical." (Ibid., p. 6.)

Deci's recommendation that jobs be designed so that they are interesting, creative, and resourceful should be wholeheartedly supported by proponents of a merit pay plan. Skinner warns managers that too much dependency on force and a poorly designed monetary reward system may actually reduce performance, while designing the task so that it is automatically reinforcing can have positive effects on performance. He says:

> The behavior of an employee is important to the employer, who gains when the employee works industriously and carefully. How is he to be induced to do so? The standard answer was once physical force: men worked to avoid punishment or death. The by-products were troublesome however, and economics is perhaps the first field in which an explicit change was made to positive reinforcement. Most men now work, as we say, "for money."
>
> Money is not a natural reinforcer; it must be conditioned as such. Delayed reinforcement, as in a weekly wage, raises a special problem. No one works on Monday morning because he is reinforced by a paycheck on Friday afternoon. The employee who is paid by the week works during the week to avoid losing the standard of living which depends on a weekly system. Rate of work is determined by the supervisor and special aversive contingencies maintain quality. The pattern is therefore still aversive. It has often been pointed out that the attitude of the production-line worker toward his work differs conspicuously from that of the craftsman, who is envied by workers and industrial managers alike. One explanation is that the craftsman is reinforced by more than monetary consequences, but another important difference is that when a craftsman spends a week completing a given set object, each of the parts produced during the week is likely to be automatically reinforcing because of its place in the completed object. (From B. F. Skinner, *Contingencies of Reinforcement: A Theoretical Analysis*, © 1969, p. 18. Reprinted by permission of Prentice-Hall, Inc., Englewood Cliffs, N.J.)

RECOMMENDATIONS FOR OVERCOMING FAILURES IN MERIT PAY SYSTEM

In the discussion of the shortcomings of merit pay plans, my suggestions for overcoming these deficiencies have been implied or suggested. Let us briefly review and outline several of these suggestions as a point of departure for our discussion.

1. *Openness and trust should be stressed by the compensation manager.* As a minimum, employees should know the formula for devising the merit increases and should be told the range and mean of the pay increases for people at their job level. This alone should reduce some of the feeling of low self-esteem and inequity present in many organizations today.

2. *Supervisors should be trained in rating and feedback techniques.* Compensation managers should help personnel design and carry out training programs which emphasize the necessity of having consistency between performance ratings, other forms of feedback, and pay increases. In addition, managers should be trained to emphasize objective rather than subjective areas of job performance. Skinner sees one of the greatest weaknesses in the motivation of workers through reinforcement principles as due to poor training of managers. He says that what must be accomplished, and what he believes is currently lacking, is an effective training program for managers. "In the not too distant future, a new breed of industrial managers may be able to apply the principles of operant conditioning effectively." (*Organizational Dynamics*, 1973, p. 40.)

3. *Components of the annual pay increase should be clearly and openly specified.* Compensation managers need to allocate a certain percentage for a cost-of-living increase (not to cover the total cost of living, however) and a percentage for merit. The percentage for merit should be an average and not a maximum, and the manager should be able to distribute this percentage in any way he or she deems appropriate. In other words, it should not be an either-or situation where the worker either gets the full amount of the merit increase or none at all. Any pay increase due to an adjustment for past inequities and pay increases due to promotions should come out of the payroll increase first, but should not be included in the stated average pay increase. Frequently, if the organization can afford a 10 percent increase in wages and benefits, it might take 2 percent of wages and benefits to use for the adjustments mentioned above, and then allocate an 8 percent average increase to cost of living (e.g., 4 percent) and merit (e.g., 4 percent). Therefore, the range of pay increases would be from 4 percent to 12 percent—not including adjustments—where the

average for the department would be 8 percent. Along these same lines, I feel it is important to give the increases in percentages and not dollar amounts since managers have a tendency to "cheat" long-term good performers (i.e., high pay managers) when a dollar amount is used.

4. *Each organization should tailor its pay plan to the needs of the organization and individuals therein— with participation a key factor in the merit pay plan design.* One of the reasons the Scanlon plan has been so successful is that it combines participation with the company's ability to afford a merit increase. Workers understand how they get the increase they do and why it is the amount it is. In addition each company using a Scanlon approach has a unique pay plan designed especially for that organization by the members of the organization.

5. *Don't overlook other rewards.* Compensation managers should work with other staff people in the organization to improve the climate of the organization, the task design, and other forms of feedback to ensure that an employee has as much chance of success as possible.

ETHICAL IMPLICATIONS: EXCHANGE, NOT CONTROL

No discussion of effective uses of merit pay plans would be complete without a discussion of the compensation manager's ethical responsibilities in using pay as a motivator. There is no doubt that poorly designed reward structures can interfere with the development of spontaneity and creativity. Reinforcement systems which are deceptive and manipulative are an insult to everyone's integrity. The employee should be a willing party to an attempt to influence, with both parties benefiting from the relationship.

Nord (1974), referring to a well designed incentive plan, says:

> I would add that to the degree that such approaches increase the effectiveness of man's exchanges with his environment, the potential for expanding freedom seems undeniable. To me these outcomes seem highly humanistic, although, for some reason this approach is labeled

anti-humanistic and approaches which appear to have less potential and human advancement are labeled humanistic.

I concur with Nord, and think the ethical responsibility of compensation managers is clear. The first step in the ethical use of monetary control in organizations is the understanding by managers of the determination of behavior (see Hamner, 1974). Since reinforcement is the single most important concept in the learning process, managers must learn how to design effective reinforcement programs that will encourage productive and creative employees. This presentation has attempted to outline the knowledge and research available for this endeavor.

REFERENCES

Bassett, G. L., & Meyer, H. H. Performance appraised based on self review. *Personnel Psychology*, 1968, **21**, 421–430.

Belcher, D. W. *Compensation Administration*. Prentice-Hall, Englewood Cliffs, N.J., 1974.

Beer, M., & Gery, G. J. Individual and organizational correlates of pay system preferences. In H. L. Tosi, R. House, & M. D. Dunnette (Eds.), *Managerial Motivation and Compensation*. East Lansing, Michigan: Michigan State University Press, 1972.

Blood, M. R. Applied behavioral analysis from an organizational perspective. Paper presented at the 82nd Annual Convention of the American Psychological Association, New Orleans, August 1974.

Calder, B. J. & Staw, B. M. The interaction of intrinsic and extrinsic motivation: Some methodological notes. *Journal of Personality and Social Psychology*, 1975, **31**, 599–605.

Case of Big Mac's pay plans. *Harvard Business Review*, July–August 1974, 1–8.

Cherrington, D. L., Reitz, H. J., & Scott, W. E. Effects of reward and contingent reinforcement on satisfaction and task performance. *Journal of Applied Psychology*, 1971, **55**, 531–536.

Deci, E. L. Effects of externally mediated rewards on intrinsic motivation. *Journal of Personality and Social Psychology*, 1971, **18**, 105–115.

Deci, E. L. Work: Who does not like it and why? *Psychology Today*, August 1972(a), **92**, 57–58.

Deci, E. L. The effects of contingent and noncontingent rewards and controls on intrinsic motivation. *Organizational Behavior and Human Performance*, 1972(b), **8**, 217–229.

Drucker, P. F. Beyond the stick and carrot: Hysteria over the work ethic. *Psychology Today*, November 1973, **87**, 89–93.

Employee survey finds most like their work. *Equinews*, March **18**, 1974 (Vol. III, No. 6).

Equal Employment Opportunity Commission Guidelines (Rev. ed.). Washington, D.C.: U.S. Government Printing Office, 1974.

Frost, C. F., Wakeley, J. H., & Ruh, R. A. *The Scanlon Plan for Organization Development: Identity, Participation and Equity*. East Lansing: Michigan State University Press, 1974.

Gruenfeld, L. W., & Weissenberg, P. Supervisory characteristics and attitudes toward performance appraisals. *Personnel Psychology*, 1966, 143–152.

Hamner, W. Clay. Reinforcement theory and contingency management in organizational settings. In H. L. Tosi & W. C. Hamner (Eds.), *Management and Organizational Behavior: A Contingency Approach*. St. Clair Press, 1974.

Hamner, W. Clay, Kim, J., Baird, L., & Bigoness, W. Race and sex as determinants of ratings by "potential" employees in a simulated work sampling task. *Journal of Applied Psychology*, 1974, **59**, 705–711.

Hamner, W. Clay, & Foster, L. W. Are intrinsic and extrinsic rewards additive? A test of Deci's cognitive evaluation theory. Paper presented at the National Academy of Management, Seattle, 1974.

Lawler, E. E. Managers' perceptions of their subordinates' pay and of their superiors' pay. *Personnel Psychology*, 1965, **18**, 413–422.

Lawler, E. E. The mythology of management compensation. *California Management Review*, 1966, **9**, 11–22.

Lawler, E. E. *Pay and Organizational Effectiveness*. New York: McGraw-Hill, 1971.

Lawler, E. E. *Motivation in Work Organization*. Monterey, Calif.: Brooks/Cole, 1973.

Lee, S. M. Salary equity: Its determination, analysis and correlates. Unpublished doctoral dissertation, University of Georgia, 1969.

Likert, R. *New Patterns of Management* (2nd ed.). New York: McGraw-Hill, 1967.

Maslow, A. H. A theory of human motivation. *Psychological Review*, 1943, **50**, 370–396.

Meyer, H. H. The pay for performance dilemma. *Organizational Dynamics*, 1975, 3(3), 39–50.

Meyer, H. H., Kay, E., & French, J. R. P. Split roles in performance appraisals. *Harvard Business Review*, January–February 1965.

Mobley, W. H. The link between MBO and merit compensation. *Personnel Journal*, June 1974, 423–427.

Nord, W. R. Some issues in the application of operant conditioning to the management of organizations. Paper presented at the National Academy of Management, Seattle, 1974.

Opsahl, R. L., & Dunnette, M. D. The role of financial compensation in industrial motivations. *Psychological Bulletin*, 1966, **66,** 94–118.

Penner, D. D. A study of the causes and consequences of salary satisfaction. General Electric Company, *Behavioral Research Service Report*, 1967.

Porter, L. W. A study of perceived need satisfactions in bottom and middle management jobs. *Journal of Applied Psychology*, 1961, **45,** 1–10.

Porter, L. W., & Lawler, E. E. *Managerial attitudes and Performance*. Homewood, Ill.: Irwin-Dorsey, 1968.

Rowe vs. General Motors Corporation, 457 F 2d. 348 (5th Cir. 1972).

Scott, W. E., & Hamner, W. Clay. The influence of variations in performance profiles on the performance evaluation process: An examination of the validity of the criteria. *Organizational Behavior and Human Performance*, 1975, **14,** 360–370.

Skinner, B. F. *Contingencies of Reinforcement*. New York: Appleton-Century-Crofts, 1969.

Skinner, B. F. Conversations with B. F. Skinner. *Organizational Dynamics*, Winter 1973, 31–40.

Vroom, V. H., & Deci, E. L. An overview of work motivation. In V. H. Vroom & E. L. Deci (Eds.), *Management and Motivation*. Baltimore: Penguin Press, 1970.

Xerox Compensation Planning Model. Rochester, N.Y.: Xerox Corporation, June 1972.

Social Processes in Organizations— Groups and Leadership

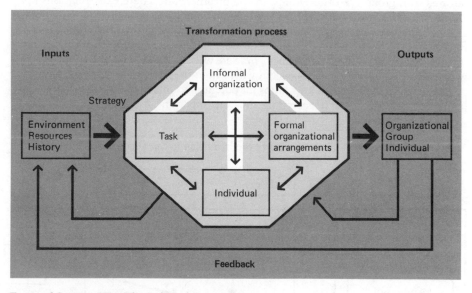

Focus of Section III—The Informal Organization

INTRODUCTION

When we think about the behavior of an individual in an organization, we get an image of one person sitting at a desk, standing at a machine, working at a bench, doing his or her job. Up to this point, we have looked at a number of the factors that influence the behavior of that individual. These have included the needs of the person and some characteristics of the environment, including the design of work and the nature of rewards, goals, and appraisals.

There is another type of environment surrounding the individual. Rarely do people work completely alone in organizations. Most of the time their working lives involve some form of contact with other people. The individual exists within an environment made up of people and relationships. We will call this new environment the social environment, and, as we will see, it is as powerful an influence on behavior as are the other more tangible environments in which the individual exists.

What are the major characteristics of the social environment of the individual in organizations? Figure III-1 provides some sense of the basic relationships that exist. If we look at the box marked "individual," we see a number of lines emanating from that box. Each line indicates a type of relationship that might exist.

Most individuals exist within a group, a set of two or more individuals who interact with each other, are aware of one another, and have a sense of identity as a unit (Schein, 1970). The individual has relationships with other group members, or peers. There is usually some type of formal leader—a supervisor, manager, boss, coordinator, team leader—with whom the individual has a relationship, but frequently that relationship is different from the one with peers. Beyond the boundaries of one's own group are other groups in the organization. There exist relationships among the different groups (the dotted line in Figure III-1), but the individual may also have unique relationships with other groups or individuals within those groups. Finally, the individual may have relationships with other people who do not fall into his or her group or other groups. These are clients, customers, and other people who are not organization members but with whom the individual interacts anyway.

The patterns of these relationships all potentially influence how the individual behaves. The social environment is thus an important influence on individual

Figure III-1.   The Social Environment of the Individual in the Organization

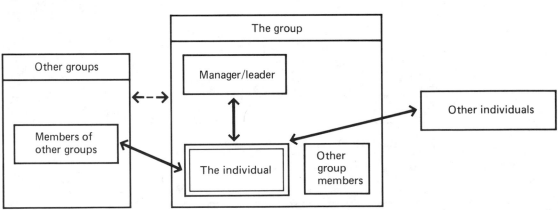

behavior. The significance of the social environment goes beyond this however. The nature of relationships and the patterns of behavior that emerge over time in groups—both among group members and between group members and leaders— have an effect on the work performance of the group. Thus these relationships affect group and organizational performance (or outcomes in the model). Similarly, interaction between different groups also affects both individual behavior as well as the effectiveness of the organization in producing outputs at unit and organization levels. Since these social processes have a great impact on the output of an orga- nization, they are an important aspect of organizational life and need to be examined carefully so that the dynamics of the social environment can be understood and eventually managed.

SOCIAL PROCESSES IN THE CONGRUENCE MODEL

The social processes that we have mentioned—group processes, leadership, and intergroup relations—are all important elements of what we call the informal orga- nization in the congruence model. Remember that the informal organization is the set of organizational arrangements (groupings, relationships, communication pat- terns, working arrangements, and the like) that emerge over time and are basically informal in that they are not written down or formerly prescribed. The informal organization is fundamentally responsive to individual needs and organizational needs unaddressed by the formal organizational arrangements.

The informal organization can work either for or against total organizational goals (the effective transformation of strategies into outputs). In many cases, the organization could not function without informal relationships and working arrange- ments. The formal organizational arrangements simply cannot anticipate all situ- ations or account for situations where judgment, bargaining, or common sense may need to be applied to new problems. In other cases, the informal organization serves to undermine organizational performance. Informal rules that limit, through peer pressure, how much a factory worker is permitted to produce are a well-known illustration of how the informal organization may be at odds with the formal orga- nization. Given that the informal organization has the potential to help or hinder, the manager should strive to understand the informal organization and to develop approaches to shape, influence, and modify that organization to make it congruent with the other organizational components.

It is important to point out that the informal organization goes beyond just the patterns of behavior within groups, between group leaders and group members, and among groups. If we look at the whole informal organization, we need to consider the nature of power relations and political factors, formation of and behavior in coalitions, values and norms in the organization, and so on. We will consider these factors in detail later on in this book, when we focus on the organization as an entire system and on the patterns of organizational behavior over time. For the moment, however, we will limit ourselves to questions of groups, leadership, and intergroup relations.

Obviously, the critical question concerning the informal organization is fit with other components of the organizational model (see page 183). There are three major types of fits to consider. First is the informal organization–individual fit, or congruence of the informal organization with the needs of different individuals. Part of the question is the extent to which the informal organization influences the patterns of behavior in individuals by shaping expectancies, augmenting ability, or even arousing individual needs. Second is the informal organization–task fit. The fundamental question here is whether the informal organization is consistent with the demands of the task. Especially relevant are questions of group effectiveness, or how the relationship among groups influences the performance of the task.

The third fit is the informal organization–formal organizational arrangements fit. The fundamental question here is whether the formal and informal organizations conflict with or complement each other. Do the combined informal and formal arrangements meet the demands of both the task and the individuals in the organization? Again, a key to understanding is taking a large view of the relationships among the different elements of the organization rather than thinking about each element in isolation.

SOCIAL PROCESSES AND ORGANIZATION EFFECTIVENESS: AN OVERVIEW

Building on our definition of the social processes that make up the informal organization and on the role of the informal organization in the congruence model, we can construct a very general approach to thinking about how those factors influence organizational effectiveness (the nature of the outputs of the system).

Figure III-2 reflects a general approach to these social processes. The three factors, group processes and behavior, small group leadership, and intergroup relations, directly influence organizational effectiveness. The relationship, however, is not simple. It is not possible to say that one particular group process will always lead to group and organizational effectiveness. It is more accurate to say that an interaction

Figure III-2.   Factors in the Informal Organization that Influence Organizational Effectiveness

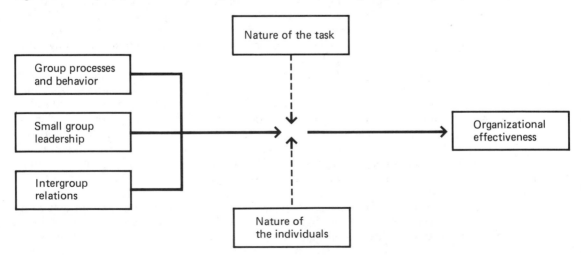

of that group process, leadership, and intergroup relations will result in effectiveness only when two other factors—the nature of the work to be done (the task) and the type of people involved (the individuals)—are congruent. Different work and different individuals will require different patterns of leadership, group functioning, and intergroup relationship.

THE READINGS IN SECTION III

The readings in Section III are organized into three parts (III.A, III.B, III.C). Each part relates to one of the previously named elements of the informal organization. Part III.A deals with group behavior in organizations. In the Reading 14, Leavitt discusses the general role of groups in organizations and presents a case for paying more attention to groups and how they influence individual and organizational behavior. Herold, in the Reading 15, proposes a general model for group effectiveness. He emphasizes the need for different group structures and processes for different types of tasks. The final reading in III.A is by Hatvany and Gladstein. They discuss the role of groups in facilitating decision making in organizations. They emphasize the problems of using groups for decision making and identify methods for improving how groups make decisions and perform work.

Part III.B deals with the question of the leader in relation to the group and its members. In his paper (Reading 17) on the supervisor as a motivator, Locke focuses on the relation between the supervisor/leader/manager and the individual group members. Burke's paper (Reading 18) on leadership summarizes much of the voluminous research on leadership and identifies some consistent patterns that suggest a relationship between certain types of leader behavior and the performance of subordinates. In Reading 19, Vroom and Jago look at the question of how leaders and groups make decisions. In particular they present an approach to help the leader determine which of several decision-making processes is appropriate in a given situation. They give a guide to which kinds of management styles are most effective for certain tasks and in certain situations. Berlew's reading closes III.B. He discusses the emotional roles that a leader can play—how the leader can generate energy within the organization and within group members through patterns of leader behavior.

Reading 20 is the whole of Part III.C, which includes a thorough discussion of conflict between individuals and groups in organizations. In his paper on organizational conflict, Thomas discusses how conflict evolves, how it is experienced, and how managers can develop different strategies for effectively managing conflict.

Together the readings provide a set of concepts, tools, and models for thinking about how the informal organization influences individual behavior and how well it matches the demands of the work. Later in the book, we will revisit the informal organization after we have discussed relevant issues of organizational design and structure. We will then look at the informal organization at the systems, rather than small group, level and see how it emerges over time and how it affects the capacity of an organization to change and adapt.

REFERENCE

Schein, E. H. Organizational Psychology. (2nd ed.). Englewood Cliffs, N.J.: Prentice-Hall, 1970.

III.A
Group Behavior in Organizations

14
Suppose we
took groups seriously . . .

Harold J. Leavitt

INTRODUCTION

This [reading] is mostly a fantasy, but not a utopian fantasy. As the title suggests, it tries to spin out some of the things that might happen if we really took small groups seriously; if, that is, we really used groups, rather than individuals, as the basic building blocks for an organization.

This seems an appropriate forum for such a fantasy. It was fifty years ago, at Hawthorne, that the informal face-to-face work group was discovered. Since then groups have been studied inside and out; they have been experimented with, observed, built, and taken apart. Small groups have become the major tool of the applied behavioral scientist. Organizational development methods are group methods. Almost all of what is called participative management is essentially based on group techniques.

From Harold G. Leavitt, "Suppose we took work groups seriously?" in E. G. Cass and F. G. Zimmer (eds.), *Man and Work in Society* (New York: Van Nostrand, 1975), pp. 67–77. Reprinted by permission of the publisher.

So the idea of using groups as organizational mechanisms is by no means new or fantastic. The fantasy comes in proposing to start with groups, not add them in; to design organizations from scratch around small groups, rather than around individuals.

But right from the start, talk like that appears to violate a deep and important value, individualism. But this fantasy will not really turn out to be anti-individualistic in the end.

The rest of this [reading] will briefly address the following questions: (1) Is it fair to say that groups have not been taken very seriously in organizational design? (2) Why are groups even worth thinking about as organizational building materials? What are the characteristics of groups that might make them interesting enough to be worth serious attention? (3) What would it mean "to take groups seriously?" Just what kinds of things would have to be done differently? (4) What compensatory changes would probably be needed in other aspects of the organization, to have groups as the basic unit? And finally, (5), is the idea of designing the organization around small face-to-face groups a very radical idea, or is it just an extension of a direction in which we are already going?

Haven't Groups Been Taken Seriously Enough Already?

The argument that groups have not been taken "seriously" doesn't seem a hard one to make. The contemporary ideas about groups didn't really come along until the 30's and 40's. By that time a logical, rationalistic tradition for the construction of organizations already existed. That tradition was very heavily based on the notion that the individual was the construction unit. The logic moved from the projected task backward. Determine the task, the goal, then find an appropriate structure and technology, and last of all fit individual human beings into predefined man-sized pieces of the action. That was, for instance, what industrial psychology was all about during its development between the two world wars. It was concerned almost entirely with individual differences and worked in the service of structuralism, fitting square human pegs to predesigned square holes. The role of the psychologist was thus ancillary to the role of the designers of the whole organization. It was a back up, supportive role that followed more than it led design.

It was not just the logic of classical organizational theory that concentrated on the individual. The whole entrepreneurial tradition of American society supported it. Individuals, at least male individuals, were taught achievement motivation. They were taught to seek individual evaluation, to compete, to see the world, organizational or otherwise, as a place in which to strive for individual accomplishment and satisfaction.

In those respects the classic design of organizations was consonant with the then existent cultural landscape. Individualized organizational structures blended with the environment of individualism. All the accessories fell into place: individual incentive schemes for hourly workers, individual merit rating and assessment schemes, tests for selection of individuals.

The unique characteristic of the organization was that it was not simply a race track within which individuals could compete, but a system in which somehow the competitive behavior of individuals could be coordinated, harnessed and controlled in the interest of the common tasks. Of course one residual of all that was a continuing tension between individual and organization, with the organization seeking to control and coordinate the individual's activities at the same time that it tried to motivate him; while the competitive individual insisted on reaching well beyond the constraints imposed upon him by the organization. One product of this tension became the informal organization discovered here at Western [Electric]; typically an informal coalition designed to fight the system.

Then it was discovered that groups could be exploited for what management saw as positive purposes, *toward* productivity instead of away from it. There followed the era of experimentation with small face-to-face groups. We learned to patch them on to existing organizations as bandaids to relieve tensions between individual and organization. We promoted coordination through group methods. We learned that groups were useful to discipline and control recalcitrant individuals.

Groups were fitted onto organizations. The group skills of individual members improved so that they could coordinate their efforts more effectively, control deviants more effectively and gain more commitment from subordinate individuals. But groups were seen primarily as tools to be tacked on and utilized in the pre-existing individualized organizational system. With a few notable exceptions, like Rensis Likert (1961), most did not design organizations around groups. On the contrary, as some of the ideas about small groups began to be tacked onto existing organizational models, they generated new tensions and conflicts of their own. Managers complained not only that groups were slow, but that they diffused responsibility, vitiated the power of the hierarchy because they were too "democratic and created small in-group empires which were very hard for others to penetrate." There was the period, for example, of the great gap between T-group training (which had to be conducted on "cultural islands") and the organization back home. The T-groupers therefore talked a lot about the "reentry problem," which meant in part the problem of movement from a new culture (the T-group culture) designed around groups back into the organizational culture designed around individuals.

But of course groups didn't die despite their difficulties. How could they die? They had always been there, though not always in the service of the organization. They turned out to be useful, indeed necessary, though often unrecognized tools. For organizations were growing, and professionalizing, and the need for better coordination grew even as the humanistic expectations of individuals also grew. So "acknowledged" groups (as distinct from "natural," informal groups) became fairly firmly attached even to conservative organizations, but largely as compensating addenda very often reluctantly backed into by organizational managers.

Groups have never been given a chance. It is as though someone had insisted that automobiles be designed to fit the existing terrain rather than build roads to adapt to automobiles.

Are Groups Worth Considering As Fundamental Building Blocks?

Why would groups be more interesting than individuals as basic design units around which to build organizations? What are the prominent characteristics of small groups? Why are they interesting? Here are several answers:

First, small groups seem to be good for people. They can satisfy important membership needs. They can provide a moderately wide range of activities for individual members. They can provide support in times of stress and crisis. They are settings in which people can learn not only cognitively but empirically to be reasonably trusting and helpful to one another. Second, groups seem to be good problem finding tools. They seem to be useful in promoting innovation and creativity. Third, in a wide variety of decision situations, they make better decisions than individuals do. Fourth, they are great tools for implementation. They gain commitment from their members so that group decisions are likely to be willingly carried out. Fifth, they can control and discipline individual members in ways that are often ex-

tremely difficult through more impersonal quasi-legal disciplinary systems. Sixth, as organizations grow large, small groups appear to be useful mechanisms for fending off many of the negative effects of large size. They help to prevent communication lines from growing too long, the hierarchy from growing too steep, and the individual from getting lost in the crowd.

There is a seventh, but altogether different kind of argument for taking groups seriously. Thus far the designer of organizations seemed to have a choice. He could build an individualized or a groupy organization. A groupy organization will, de facto, have to deal with individuals; but what was learned here so long ago is that individualized organizations, must de facto, deal with groups. Groups are natural phenomena, and facts of organizational life. They can be created but their spontaneous development cannot be prevented. The problem is not shall groups exist or not, but shall groups be planned or not? If not, the individualized organizational garden will sprout groupy weeds all over the place. By defining them as weeds instead of flowers, they shall continue, as in earlier days, to be treated as pests, forever fouling up the beauty of rationally designed individualized organizations, forever forming informally (and irrationally) to harass and outgame the planners.

It is likely that the reverse could also be true, that if groups are defined as the flowers and individuals as the weeds, new problems will crop up. Surely they will, but that discussion can be delayed for at least a little while.

Who Uses Groups Best?

So groups look like interesting organizational building blocks. But before going on to consider the implications of designing organizations around groups, one useful heuristic might be to look around the existing world at those places in which groups seem to have been treated somewhat more seriously.

One place groups have become big is in Japanese organizations (Johnson & Ouchi, 1974). The Japanese seem to be very groupy, and much less concerned than Americans about issues like individual accountability. Japanese organizations, of course, are thus consonant with Japanese culture, where notions of individual aggressiveness and competitiveness are de-emphasized in favor of self-effacement and group loyalty. But Japanese organizations seem to get a lot done, despite the relative suppression of the individual in favor of the group. It also appears that the advantages of the groupy Japanese style have really come to the fore in large technologically complex organizations.

Another place to look is at American conglomerates. They go to the opposite extreme, dealing with very large units. They buy large organizational units and sell units. They evaluate units. In effect they promote units by offering them extra resources as rewards for good performance. In that sense conglomerates, one might argue, are designed around groups, but the groups in question are often themselves large organizational chunks.

Groups in an Individualistic Culture

An architect can design a beautiful building which either blends smoothly with its environment or contrasts starkly with it. But organization designers may not have the same choice. If we design an organization which is structurally dissonant with its environment, it is conceivable that the environment will change to adjust to the organization. It seems much more likely, however, that the environment will reject the organization. If designing organizations around groups represents a sharp counterpoint to environmental trends maybe we should abort the idea.

Our environment, one can argue, is certainly highly individualized. But one can also make a less solid argument in the other direction; an argument that American society is going groupy rather than individual this year. Or at least that it is going groupy as well as individual. The evidence is sloppy at best. One can reinterpret the student revolution and the growth of anti-establishment feelings at least in part as a reaction to the decline of those institutions that most satis-

fied social membership needs. One can argue that the decline of the Church, of the village and of the extended family is leaving behind a vacuum of unsatisfied membership and belongingness motives. Certainly popular critics of American society have laid a great deal of emphasis on the loneliness and anomie that seem to have resulted not only from materialism but from the emphasis on individualism. It seems possible to argue that, insofar as there has been any significant change in the work ethic in America, the change has been toward a desire for work which is socially as well as egoistically fulfilling, and which satisfies human needs for belongingness and affiliation as well as needs for achievement.

In effect, the usual interpretation of Abraham Maslow's need hierarchy may be wrong. Usually the esteem and self-actualization levels of motivation are emphasized. Perhaps the level that is becoming operant most rapidly is neither of those, but the social-love-membership level.

The rising role of women in American society also has implications for the groupiness of organizations. There is a moderate amount of evidence that American women have been socialized more strongly into affiliative and relational sorts of attitudes than men. They probably can, in general, more comfortably work in direct achievement roles in group settings, where there are strong relational bonds among members, than in competitive, individualistic settings. Moreover, it is reasonable to assume that as women take a more important place in American society, some of their values and attitudes will spill over to the male side.

Although the notion of designing organizations around groups in America in 1974 may be a little premature, it is consonant with cultural trends that may make the idea much more appropriate ten years from now.

But groups are becoming more relevant for organizational as well as cultural reasons. Groups seem to be particularly useful as coordinating and integrating mechanisms for dealing with complex tasks that require the inputs of many kinds of specialized knowledge. In fact the development of matrix-type organizations in high technology industry is perhaps one effort to modify individually designed organizations toward a more groupy direction; not for humanistic reasons but as a consequence of tremendous increases in the informational complexity of the jobs that need to be done.

What Might a Seriously Groupy Organization Look Like?

Just what does it mean to design organizations around groups? Operationally how is that different from designing organizations around individuals? One approach to an answer is simply to take the things organizations do with individuals and try them out with groups. The idea is to raise the level from the atom to the molecule, and *select* groups rather than individuals, *train* groups rather than individuals, *pay* groups rather than individuals, *promote* groups rather than individuals, *design jobs* for groups rather than for individuals, *fire* groups rather than individuals, and so on down the list of activities which organizations have traditionally carried on in order to use human beings in their organizations.

Some of the items on that list seem easy to handle at the group level. For example, it doesn't seem terribly hard to design jobs for groups. In effect that is what top management already does for itself to a great extent. It gives specific jobs to committees, and often runs itself as a group. The problem seems to be a manageable one: designing job sets which are both big enough to require a small number of persons and also small enough to require only a small number of persons. Big enough in this context means not only jobs that would occupy the hands of group members but that would provide opportunities for learning and expansion.

Ideas like evaluating, promoting, and paying groups raise many more difficult but interesting problems. Maybe the best that can be said for such ideas is that they provide opportunities for thinking creatively about pay and evaluation. Suppose, for example, that as a reward for good work the group gets a larger salary budget than it got last year. Suppose the allocation for increases within the group is left to the group members. Certainly one can think up all sorts of difficulties that might arise. But are the potential problems necessarily any more difficult than those now generated by individual merit raises? Is there any

company in America that is satisfied with its existing individual performance appraisal and salary allocation schemes? At least the issues of distributive justice within small groups would presumably be open to internal discussion and debate. One might even permit the group to allocate payments to individuals differentially at different times, in accordance with some criteria of current contribution that they might establish.

As far as performance evaluation is concerned, it is probably easier for people up the hierarchy to assess the performance of total groups than it is to assess the performance of individual members well down the hierarchy. Top managers of decentralized organizations do it all the time, except that they usually reward the formal leader of the decentralized unit rather than the whole unit.

The notion of promoting groups raises another variety of difficulties. One thinks of physically transferring a whole group, for example, and of the costs associated with training a whole group to do a new job, especially if there are no bridging individuals. But there may be large advantages too. If a group moves, its members already know how to work with one another. Families may be less disrupted by movement if several move at the same time.

There is the problem of selection. Does it make sense to select groups? Initially, why not? Can't means be found for selecting not only for appropriate knowledge and skill but also for potential ability to work together? There is plenty of groundwork in the literature already.

After the initial phase, there will of course be problems of adding or subtracting individuals from existing groups. We already know a good deal about how to help new members get integrated into old groups. Incidentally, I was told recently by a plant manager in the midwest about an oddity he had encountered: the phenomenon of groups applying for work. Groups of three or four people have been coming to his plant seeking employment together. They wanted to work together and stay together.

Costs and Danger Points

To play this game of designing organizations around groups, what might be some important danger points? In general, a group-type organization is somewhat more like a free market than present organizations. More decisions would have to be worked out ad hoc, in a continually changing way. So one would need to schedule more negotiation time both within and between groups.

One would encounter more issues of justice, for the individual vis-a-vis the group and for groups vis-a-vis one another. More and better arbitration mechanisms would probably be needed along with highly flexible and rapidly adaptive record keeping. But modern record keeping technology is, potentially, both highly flexible and rapidly adaptive.

Another specific issue is the provision of escape hatches for individuals. Groups have been known to be cruel and unjust to their deviant members. One existing escape route for the individual would of course continue to exist: departure from the organization. Another might be easy means of transfer to another group.

Another related danger of a strong group emphasis might be a tendency to drive away highly individualistic, nongroup people. But the tight organizational constraints now imposed do the same thing. Indeed might not groups protect their individualists better than the impersonal rules of present day large organizations?

Another obvious problem: If groups are emphasized by rewarding them, paying them, promoting them, and so on, groups may begin to perceive themselves as power centers, in competitive conflict with other groups. Intergroup hostilities are likely to be exacerbated unless we can design some new coping mechanisms into the organization. Likert's proposal for solving that sort of problem (and others) is the linking pin concept. The notion is that individuals serve as members of more than one group, both up and down the hierarchy and horizontally. But Likert's scheme seems to me to assume fundamentally individualized organizations in the sense that it is still individuals who get paid, promoted and so on. In a more groupy organization, the linking pin concept has to be modified so that an individual might be a part-time member of more than one group, but still a real member. That is, for example, a portion of an individual's pay might come from each group in accordance with that group's perception of his contribution.

Certainly much more talk, both within and between groups, would be a necessary accompaniment of group emphasis; though we might argue about whether more talk should be classified as a cost or a benefit. In any case careful design of escape hatches for individuals and connections among groups would be as important in this kind of organization as would stairways between floors in the design of a private home.

There is also a danger of over-designing groups. All groups in the organization need not look alike. Quite to the contrary. Task and technology should have significant effects on the shapes and sizes of different subgroups within the large organization. Just as individuals end up adjusting the edges of their jobs to themselves and themselves to their jobs, we should expect flexibility within groups, allowing them to adapt and modify themselves to whatever the task and technology demand.

Another initially scary problem associated with groups is the potential loss of clear formal individual leadership. Without formal leaders how will we motivate people? Without leaders how will we control and discipline people? Without leaders how will we pinpoint responsibility? Even as I write those questions I cannot help but feel that they are archaic. They are questions which are themselves a product of the basic individual building block design of old organizations. The problem is not leaders so much as the performance of leadership functions. Surely groups will find leaders, but they will emerge from the bottom up. Given a fairly clear job description, some groups, in some settings, will set up more or less permanent leadership roles. Others may let leadership vary as the situation demands, or as a function of the power that individuals within any group may possess relative to the group's needs at that time. A reasonable amount of process time can be built in to enable groups to work on the leadership problem, but the problem will have to be resolved within each group. On the advantage side of the ledger, this may even get rid of a few hierarchical levels. There should be far less need for individuals who are chiefly supervisors of other individuals' work. Groups can serve as hierarchical leaders of other groups.

Two other potential costs: With an organization of groups, there may be a great deal of in-fighting, and power and conflict issues will come even more to the fore than they do now. Organizations of groups may become highly political, with coalitions lining up against one another on various issues. If so, the rest of the organizational system will have to take those political problems into account, both by setting up sensible systems of intercommunications among groups, and by allocating larger amounts of time and expertise to problems of conflict resolution.

But this is not a new problem unique to groupy organizations. Conflict among groups is prevalent in large organizations which are political systems now. But because these issues have not often been foreseen and planned for, the mechanisms for dealing with them are largely ad hoc. As a result, conflict is often dealt with in extremely irrational ways.

But there is another kind of intergroup power problem that may become extremely important and difficult in groupy organizations. There is a real danger that relatively autonomous and cohesive groups may be closed, not only to other groups but more importantly to staff advice or to new technological inputs.

These problems exist at present, of course, but they may be exacerbated by group structure. I cannot see any perfect way to handle those problems. One possibility may be to make individual members of staff groups part time members of line groups. Another is to work harder to educate line groups to potential staff contributions. Of course the reward system, the old market system, will probably be the strongest force for keeping more groups from staying old-fashioned in a world of new technologies and ideas.

But the nature and degree of many of the second order spinoff effects are not fully knowable at the design stage. We need to build more complete working models and pilot plants. In any case it does not seem obvious that slowdowns, either at the work face or in decision-making processes, would necessarily accompany group based organizational designs.

Some Possible Advantages to the Organization

Finally, from an organizational perspective, what are the potential advantages to be gained from a group based organization? The first might be a sharp reduction in the number of units that need to be controlled. Control would not have to be carried all the way down to the individual level. If the average group size is five, the number of blocks that management has to worry about is cut to 20% of what it was. Such a design would also probably cut the number of operational levels in the organization. In effect, levels which are now primarily supervisory would be incorporated into the groups that they supervise.

By this means many of the advantages of the small individualized organization could be brought back. These advantages would occur within groups simply because there would be a small number of blocks, albeit larger blocks, with which to build and rebuild the organization.

But most of all, and this is still uncertain, despite the extent to which we behavioral scientists have been enamoured of groups, there would be increased human advantages of cohesiveness, motivation, and commitment, and via that route, both increased productivity, stronger social glue within the organization, and a wider interaction between organization and environment.

SUMMARY

Far and away the most powerful and beloved tool of applied behavioral scientists is the small face-to-face group. Since the Western Electric researches, behavioral scientists have been learning to understand, exploit and love groups. Groups attracted interest initially as devices for improving the implementation of decisions and to increase human commitment and motivation. They are now loved because they are also creative and innovative, they often make better quality decisions than individuals, and because they make organizational life more livable for people. One can't hire an applied behavioral scientist into an organization who within ten minutes will not want to call a group meeting and talk things over. The group meeting is his primary technology, his primary tool.

But groups in organizations are not an invention of behavioral types. They are a natural phenomenon of organizations. Organizations develop informal groups, like it or not. It is both possible and sensible to describe most large organizations as collections of groups in interaction with one another; bargaining with one another, forming coalitions with one another, cooperating and competing with one another. It is possible and sensible too to treat the decisions that emerge from large organizations as a resultant of the interplay of forces among groups within the organization, and not just the resultant of rational analysis.

On the down side, small face-to-face groups are great tools for disciplining and controlling their members. Contemporary China, for example, has just a fraction of the number of lawyers in the United States. Partially this is a result of the lesser complexity of Chinese society and lower levels of education. But a large part of it, surprisingly enough, seems to derive from the fact that modern China is designed around small groups. Since small groups take responsibility for the discipline and control of their members many deviant acts which would be considered illegal in the United States never enter the formal legal system in China. The law controls individual deviation less, the group controls it more (Li, 1971).

Control of individual behavior is also a major problem of large complex western organizations. This problem has driven many organizations into elaborate bureaucratic quasi-legal sets of rules, ranging from job evaluation schemes to performance evaluations to incentive systems; all individually based, all terribly complex, all creating problems of distributive justice. Any organizational design that might eliminate much of that legalistic superstructure therefore begins to look highly desirable.

Management should consider building organizations using a material now understood very well and with properties that look very promising, the small group. Until recently, at least, the human group has primarily been used for patching and mending organizations that were originally built of other materials.

The major unanswered questions in my mind are not in the understanding of groups, nor in the potential utility of the group as a building block. The more difficult answered question is whether or not the approaching era is one in which Americans would willingly work in such apparently contra-individualistic units. I think we are.

REFERENCES

Johnson, Richard T. and William G. Ouchi. Made in America (under Japanese management). *Harvard Business Review*, September-October 1974.

Li, Victor. The Development of the Chinese Legal System, in John Lindbeck (ed.), *China: The Management of a Revolutionary Society*. Seattle: University of Washington Press, 1971.

Likert, Rensis. *New Patterns of Management*. New York: McGraw-Hill, 1961.

15
The effectiveness
of work groups

David M. Herold

The success of organizations depends to a large extent upon the performance of various work groups within them. Given the individual's limited capacity to process and store information, the increasing complexity of organizational tasks, environments, and technologies, and the increasing diversity of skills and knowledge required for the performance of organizational tasks, it seems certain that the role of groups in organizations will continue to increase.

Though we all seem to accept the inevitability of groups in organizations, our feelings toward them are often reflective of a love-hate relationship which seems to characterize our experiences in group settings. We think that "two heads are better than one"; yet "too many cooks spoil the broth." "A camel is a horse assembled by a committee," yet we let many important decisions which affect our lives be made by committees. We place great value on democratic process, yet we note with admiration that Mussolini made the trains run on time. These conflicting beliefs are not simply demonstrations of mankind's irrationality, but rather reflect the successes and failures that all of us have known in our experiences with groups.

It is obvious that the group often possesses resources which exceed those of any one of its members and thus, for many tasks, has greater potential for effective performance. Yet we have not been very successful in charting the path which will take us from the mere availability of these resources to the reality of effective performance. In this [reading] we will take a modest stab at charting one such course. This course is but one of many possible, and as such will not be all-inclusive, nor will it reflect or explain every

Source: Reprinted with permission from *Organizational Behavior,* edited by Steven Kerr. Grid Publishing, Inc., Columbus, Ohio, 1979.

Author's note: This paper was written while the author was on leave as a Research Fellow with the National Institute on Alcohol Abuse and Alcoholism.

aspect of the phenomenon. Rather, it represents an attempt to focus on a manageable subset of issues which seem to have the potential to explain a significant portion of what goes on in work groups in organizations.

Some Basic Definitions

What is a group? There are probably as many definitions of groups as there are writers in the field. For our present purpose of understanding the task effectiveness of groups in organizational settings, we may say that a *group* consists of two more people *interacting* (i.e., responding to or having the capacity to influence each other's behavior) for the purpose of accomplishing some goal.

Task groups. We shall further restrict our focus by saying that we are interested in task or work groups. Groups exist for a variety of reasons (goals). Groups like social clubs exist solely to satisfy social needs and the only output of interest is the need satisfaction experienced by the members. Other groups such as Alcoholics Anonymous exist for the purpose of modifying the behavior or characteristics of some members and the output of interest is whether such changes take place. Work groups, on the other hand, come together or are brought together for the purpose of transforming some inputs (raw materials, ideas, concepts, or objects) into an identifiable group product (an object, a decision, a report, or some detectable environmental change).

Group effectiveness. Our primary interest in task groups is the nature, i.e., quality and quantity, of their output. *Effectiveness* can then be narrowly defined in terms of how well a group carries out the task which it has been assigned or which it assigned to itself, recognizing that criteria for quality and quantity of group output may vary widely in clarity or ease of operationalization. Hackman (1976) used a much broader definition of effectiveness. He considered a group effective if:

a. the group meets or exceeds acceptable levels of quantity and quality;
b. the group experience satisfies rather than frustrates the personal needs of members; and
c. the group experience maintains or enhances members' ability to work together on subsequent tasks.

We need not limit ourselves to one or the other of these definitions; either may be useful under certain circumstances. For ongoing organizational groups we need to be aware of the *feedback loop* in which one outcome of any group performance episode (e.g., the personal outcomes experienced by group members) has the potential to influence the group's subsequent performance. It is possible to observe high quality and quantity output, but simultaneously be aware that the group is destroying itself. For example, the New York Yankees won the 1977 World Series, certainly demonstrating effective performance, but even as the champagne was flowing in the winner's dressing room, mention was being made of players wanting to be traded to other clubs. Certainly in this case of an ongoing group, one might want to use the broader definition of effectiveness such that one would be looking at some optimum combination of group performance and member experience which would contribute to future performance effectiveness. However, even in this example one could make a case for applying the narrow definition of maximum, short term performance (and many disappointed Los Angeles Dodger fans were said to be doing just that).

A TASK TYPOLOGY

A great deal of the research on group performance can be analyzed in terms of an input-output model. An *input* is any variable or condition present or "given" at the onset of the group's performance episode. Input variables can typically be divided into three categories:

a. environmental level,
b. group level, and
c. individual level.

Environmental variables are those characteristics of the group's environment which are likely to influence group outcomes, e.g., the authority and reward structures of the organization within which the group operates. Group variables refer to characteristics of the group, such as its size, which can be expected to influence group outcomes. Individual variables reflect the characteristics of individual group members, such as member personalities and intelligence.

Output means any result or consequence of the group's performance episode. Output variables can generally be categorized as task performance variables (such as quantity or quality of performance), personal variables (e.g., participants' satisfaction), or social interaction variables (group cohesiveness, who talks to whom, etc.; Davis, 1969).

Typically, research in the field has used input variables as independent variables . . . to be manipulated for the purpose of noting variations in the output or dependent variables. Several writers have noted that this strategy has failed to produce a coherent body of knowledge concerning the determinants of group performance. These writers go on to note that a partial explanation for this failure is the lack of attention paid to the *process* by which groups become productive. The group's interaction process transforms inputs into outputs, and we need to better understand the nature of that transformation.

Adding this focus on group process to the input-output model, we arrive at the following conceptual model of the determinants of group outcomes [see Figure 1, page 198].

A major problem with the above model is the almost endless list which can be developed of inputs thought to affect outputs through their effects on process. For example, it is not unreasonable to expect temperature, humidity, lighting conditions, state of the economy, spatial arrangement of the work place and the mental and emotional states of group members all to affect performance. As Katzell et al. (1970) noted, "Since the number of inputs having important effects on group outputs is enormous and our abil-

Figure 1. Input-Output Relationships Mediated by Group's Interaction Process

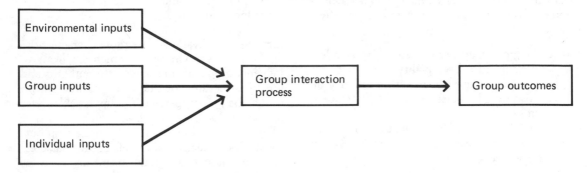

ity to manage more than a few at a time—either conceptually or experimentally—is limited, a strategy for coping with this manifold is essential" (p. 157).

It seems obvious that unless we develop strategies for selectively and systematically studying elements of this totality, the understanding of group phenomena will continue to elude us. This is not to suggest that any one strategy will ultimately lead to a general or comprehensive theory of group functioning. Rather, as noted by Hackman and Morris (1975), we may need to develop different strategies for different purposes, or "mini-theories" which deal with specific aspects of group functioning or are aimed at understanding particular aspects of the phenomenon under specified conditions.

The strategy selected for this [reading] is to focus on one major input variable of interest, the group's task, and to develop a framework within which the effects of the task in determining or influencing group process, and subsequently performance, can be analyzed.

There are several reasons for making the group's task our primary focus. First, the lack of attention paid to experimental tasks and their potential impact on experimental results may be a major reason for the inconsistency which characterizes much of the research on group performance. Selection of tasks for group performance experiments has been anything but systematic. In fact, it has often been noted that tasks are usually selected as an afterthought, as "something for the group to do," while the variables of interest are studied. For example, if one wanted to study the relationship between group size and group performance, one would have to provide something for the group to do which would yield a performance measure. One researcher might ask the group to perform some mechanical assembly, another might have the group solve an intellectual puzzle, another might ask groups to debate an issue, while still another might ask members to estimate the number of marbles in a jar.

As Zajonc (1965) noted, this idiosyncratic choice of tasks has created nearly as many group tasks as there are small group experiments. Furthermore, several writers have cautioned that lack of knowledge concerning the specific impact of the tasks on results obtained makes it difficult, if not impossible, to generalize about situations where groups are performing different tasks. This lack of generalizability has been further demonstrated by writers who have shown that seemingly contradictory findings of different studies investigating the same variables or relationships could be reconciled if one accounted for the different tasks used in these studies (e.g., Herold, 1978; Shaw, 1954).

Second, task characteristics may be considered a major input variable in the input-process-output sequence. It seems obvious that groups' interactions are largely determined by what they are trying to accomplish. Division of labor, interaction patterns, content of communications, emotional states, etc. can all be strongly influenced by the group's task. Studies have shown that what the group is asked to do can be a major factor in determining group process, group structure, and of course the final group product.

The final consideration for our focus on tasks is more practical. The group's task represents a logical, unambiguous starting point for an analysis of how members go about achieving task performance and, more importantly, how performance might be improved. A task-centered analysis requires both knowledge of the task and a framework for relating task characteristics to issues of group process and performance (such a framework being an aim of this [reading]). These requirements are independent of other input factors such as member characteristics, group cohesiveness and leader behavior. While the latter are of legitimate concern and, as will be shown later, can add valuable explanatory power to the task-based analysis, they are more difficult to assess, require more intimate knowledge or experience with the group, are typically less amenable to change by group members themselves or by an outsider, are generally more ambiguous in their operationalization, and their impact is less well understood.

The first step in creating a task-based approach to understanding group performance is to develop a means for classifying tasks according to some dimensions or criteria which will reduce the wide assortment of tasks into a few manageable categories. Herold (1975; 1978) has proposed the task typology presented here. The performance of any task requires that certain activities be carried out by the group, that certain behavioral requirements imposed by the task be satisfied. A useful means of classifying tasks is to do so according to whether the dominant activities required of the group are *social* and/or *technical* in nature. Furthermore, required behaviors along the social and technical dimensions can be classified as being either *simple* or *complex*, that is, as being easily satisfied or difficult to satisfy.

All tasks may demand some socially and some technically oriented behaviors on the part of group members; the real difference between tasks is the degree to which one category is more critical, or more difficult to satisfy, than the other. It is important to differentiate between tasks which are only nominally social (e.g., a tug-of-war, a routine mechanical assembly) and those which require the group to overcome major interpersonal difficulties (such as deciding on a university admissions policy for minorities). Similarly, tasks which are nominally technical (such

as solving a simple mathematical problem) will require very different behaviors from tasks which are technically quite complex (e.g., developing a strategy for large capital investment programs).

Let us now specifically consider what we mean by technical and social complexity of tasks.

Complexity of Technical Demands

This dimension refers to the availability, distribution, and programmability of raw materials, data, resources, and procedures necessary to create an adequate response to the task's demands. The following task attributes may be used to determine the complexity of technical demands which the task imposes on the group.

1. *Programmability*—Tasks can be routine or can confront the group with stimuli such that the group is unsure of the best approach, procedure, or program likely to lead to successful performance. Programmability may be assessed by one or more of the following criteria:
   a. *Solution multiplicity* reflects "the number of acceptable solutions, the number of alternatives for task completion, and the degree to which acceptable solutions can be verified, i.e., can be demonstrated to be correct" (Shaw, 1971, p. 311).
   b. *Population familiarity*, also identified by Shaw (1973), reflects the degree to which the task has been previously encountered by those who are charged with its performance.
   c. *Variability* asks whether task requirements remain constant over time or whether unpredictable changes occur from one performance episode to another or even during a given performance episode.
2. *Difficulty*—Tasks can be easy or difficult, with difficulty reflecting sheer effort requirements, the number of different operations necessary, and the level of skills required.
3. *Information or skill diffusion*—For some tasks (e.g., many mathematical problems), we

may expect that one group member will possess a major portion of whatever skill or knowledge is required, or will represent the group's best chance at task success. For other tasks, such as deciding whether to market a new product, requisite skills or information can be expected to be widely distributed among group members.

In summary, we have identified three task attributes which can be used to classify tasks as being technically either simple or complex. It should be obvious that tasks which are difficult, hard to program, and characterized by diffuse requisite information or skills should be classified as technically the most complex. However, we shall classify as technically complex any task which would be so classified on one or more of these attributes. Figure 2 lists the attributes and corresponding characteristics of technically simple and complex tasks.

Complexity of Social Demands

This dimension refers to the quality of social interaction necessary for the group to perform effectively. Tasks low on this dimension require little or no interaction among members for effective task completion. A tug of war is an example of such a task. Alternatively, tasks low on this dimension may require considerable interaction, but of a kind which is unlikely to create interpersonal difficulties. Tasks high in complexity of social demands require extensive and potentially problematic social interaction, with the group's product shaped and determined by the nature of that interaction process. For example, complex social demands would be placed on a group dealing with an emotionally charged issue for which different group members hold very different positions, or on a jury reaching a verdict likely to engender wide philosophical disagreements.

The following task attributes may be used to diagnose the complexity of social demands which the task imposes on the group.

1. *Ego involvement*—This attribute refers to members' personal investment in the group's task and its outcomes. Tasks which engage deeply rooted values or beliefs (for example, deciding whether to support legalized abortions), which affect important aspects of participants' lives (such as setting budgets for participants' respective departments), or which engage highly valued

Figure 2. Task Attributes Making for Technically Simple and Complex Tasks, and Some Characteristics of Such Tasks

Task attributes	Characteristics of simple tasks	Characteristics of complex tasks
Programmability:	Single acceptable solution, achieved via a single path and easily verified as correct.	Many alternative solutions and means to solution; any given solution not easily verified.
	People who must perform the task have experience with the task.	People who must perform the task do not have experience with the task.
	Task requirements remain constant.	Task requirements vary.
Difficulty:	Little effort is required.	Great deal of effort required.
	Few operations are required.	Many operations are required.
	Involves low-level skills.	Involves complex skills.
Information diffusion:	Requisite knowledge is centralized.	Knowledge and skills are widely distributed.
	Involves few skills or areas of knowledge.	Several skills or areas of knowledge are necessary.

skills such that performance reflects individuals' self-concepts, can all be considered high on the ego involvement dimension.

2. *Agreement on means*—This dimension refers to the extent group members agree on how the group should go about performing its task. For some tasks there may be high agreement on the best approach to the task and on who should do what. For other tasks, different approaches will be favored by different group members. Some subtasks will be more attractive than others such that who performs them becomes an important issue and whether and how the task is divided will be subject to disagreement.

3. *Agreement on ends*—This attribute reflects group members' agreement on what they are trying to accomplish and what criteria will be used to define success. For some tasks it is very clear what the group is trying to achieve and one may expect wide agreement on the part of group members. For example, a fund raising group can often agree that they should raise as much money as possible. For other tasks, the group may have considerable difficulty agreeing on what constitutes a satisfactory outcome. For example, a group of department heads will often disagree about which of them will receive a particular office when offices differ in desirability.

Classifying tasks as socially simple or complex requires that the above three task attributes be considered jointly rather than any one being sufficient for classification purposes, as was the case with the technical attributes. Tasks having high agreement on means and ends and high ego involvement will not create social difficulties for the group. If agreement over means and ends is high but ego involvement is low, one would still expect few social difficulties.

Tasks having low ego involvement which generate disagreement over means or ends will most likely remain socially simple, since no great commitment to positions will be evident if ego involvement is lacking. Such tasks could conceivably become moderately socially complex as the extent of disagreement grows.

Which tasks will create socially complex demands for the group? Tasks which are ego involv-

ing *and* produce disagreement over means and/or ends. In other words, one has to first predict that task content is such that group members will care and be involved and furthermore that there will be unresolved issues concerning goals or procedures.

Illustrating the Task Space

Having said what we mean by the complexity of technical and social demands which tasks create for groups, we can now envision a two-dimensional task space as in Figure 3, in which tasks are categorized by whether they are simple or complex in a social sense and in a technical sense. As an aid, let us select tasks which illustrate each of our categories.

In the lower left-hand corner of Figure 3 (simple technical–simple social) are placed tasks which are highly routine, repetitive or programmed, and which require little social interaction. What social interaction is required consists of routine exchanges concerning routine matters. Such tasks do not present social or technical difficulties which might stand in the way of effective task performance. Routine record keeping functions such as payroll, accounts receivable and

Figure 3. A Cross-Classification of Tasks Based on the Nature of Task Demands and Illustrative Tasks

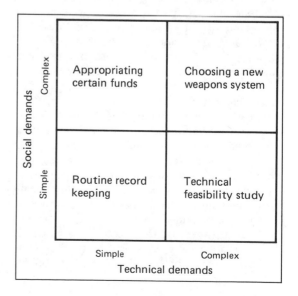

payable, and routine maintenance functions are examples of group tasks in this category.

In the lower right-hand corner (complex technical–simple social) we have tasks which are technically complex in terms of the search required for an optimum solution. These tasks may require technical skills, use of intricate or complex methods or procedures, thorough knowledge of various environmental contingencies, and so on. However, once a response has been arrived at it is evaluated on its technical merits or soundness of approach with social process playing a minor role. As an example, consider a group charged with gathering information on whether a conversion from one source of energy to another is financially advisable. This task requires a technical search which addresses technically complex issues in the areas of finance, taxation, maintenance, construction, environmental regulations, economic projections, and other aspects. On the basis of such a search, a technically optimum recommendation will be made.

Moving to the upper right-hand corner of our space (complex technical–complex social), we find tasks with technical as well as social difficulties which have to be solved. These tasks, like the ones in the lower right-hand corner, are technically complex and require specialized skills, specialized knowledge, and a thorough search of alternatives and their potential impact. However, unlike technically complex-socially simple tasks, selection of the one best alternative may not be obvious, and may involve major disagreements as to desirability of various alternatives, disagreements over group short- and long-term goals, and issues of beliefs, attitudes, or traditions which may stand in the way of a final group product.

As an example of such a task, consider a group of Air Force personnel charged with the selection of a new prototype fighter plane to be the major weapons system for the next decade. Not only is this task technically complex—involving issues of combat effectiveness, cost, serviceability and interchangeability—it may also introduce a host of issues for which group members differ widely in their subjective evaluations. Should the emphasis be on manned aircraft or missiles? Should a design by a foreign manufacturer be chosen if it is technologically superior? Should the financial rescue of one of the bidders be a factor in the

decision? Should past cost overruns by bidders be considered in evaluating costs? Should political considerations, such as geographical areas most likely to benefit from the contract, enter into the decision? Such issues will have to be dealt with as part of the group's deliberations even after technical aspects of the task have been performed.

In the upper left-hand corner (simple technical–complex social) we have tasks which are technically or procedurally simple, but whose response form is based primarily on the outcome of the group's social process. Thus the setting and reviewing of departmental budgets may be the result of strong and often contradictory notions on the part of group members about which functions are more important, which ones have performed best in the past, and which ones are likely to need funds in the future. While technically the allocation of available funds to a unit is simply a ledger entry which represents no difficulties, from a social standpoint the midnight oil might have to burn before task performance (in this case, a budget proposal) takes place.

GROUP PROCESS: A TASK-CENTERED VIEW

In this section we shall temporarily continue our strategy of viewing the group's task as the major input variable of interest, and shall develop our analysis as if the group's task is the only major piece of information we possess.

If, as we have argued, tasks confronting groups place both social and technical demands on group members, then group effectiveness becomes a question of how well the group manages to meet these demands. Thus the group's interaction process may be viewed as assessing task demands (social and technical) and then meeting these demands by task-appropriate planning, utilization, and coordination of group resources during the performance phase.

The location of a task in our task space can help to predict what category of processes (social or technical) is likely to prove troublesome and might hold the key to improved effectiveness. Tasks high on the social complexity dimension can be expected to give rise to social process difficulties, and tasks high on the technical complexity dimension can be expected to create technical process difficulties. In addition to locating the group's task in the task space, one must also consider whether the group understands the dominant demands of the task, whether it is attempting to address these, and whether it is likely to succeed. Finally, having categorized the task, one can make a decision concerning the type of assistance the group will benefit from most. Attempts to help groups manage their technical and social process can be expected to differ in their success, depending upon whether they address demands created by the task.

Changing Group Process

An important aim of understanding group performance must be the development of strategies for improving group effectiveness. Many writers have sought to classify various approaches to group and organizational change. . . . A few of these classifications are particularly convenient for our present purpose. For example, Hackman and Morris (1975) classified intervention techniques as being either interpersonal or procedure-oriented. The former are aimed at improving the quality of relationships among group members, while the latter provide group members with specific strategies for improving their effectiveness.

Leavitt (1965) used a three category scheme based upon technological, people-oriented, and structural approaches to change. *Technological changes* involve direct changes in the tasks, technology, or programs available for the group's work. . . . *People-oriented* approaches focus on changing the behavior of group members. Leavitt's technological and people-oriented categories seem similar to Hackman and Morris' procedural and interpersonal categories, respectively. Leavitt's structural category includes changes in the organization of the group or in organizational systems in which the group is embedded. *Structural changes* do not constitute direct interventions into group process, but rather change the group's environment.

Having distinguished between social and technical demands of tasks and social and technical aspects of the group's interaction process aimed

at satisfying these demands, it makes sense to refer to group intervention strategies as being technical or social in nature depending upon the interaction process they aim to promote. Thus our use of "social" seems equivalent to Hackman and Morris' interpersonal and Leavitt's people categories, while "technical" is similar to Hackman and Morris' procedural and Leavitt's technical categories.

Matching Interventions to Tasks

Since the classification of intervention strategies as either social or technical parallels our classification of tasks, we now have a rough guide to what type of intervention is likely to enhance the effectiveness of groups performing different tasks. Specifically, social skill training and social process interventions are appropriate for tasks low in complexity of technical demands and high in complexity of social demands. Technical process interventions are appropriate for tasks low in complexity of social demands and high in complexity of technical demands. Tasks in our high technical–high social complexity category would benefit from an intervention strategy with both social and technical components.

For tasks low in both social and technical complexity, the prediction of appropriate intervention strategies is more complex. If one assumes that group members possess the minimal skills (both social and technical) and motivation to perform such routine tasks, then any intervention may serve only to distract members from the task and direct their energies toward non-productive behaviors. For example, a social intervention when no complex social task demands are confronting the group may get members involved in the novelty or excitement of the new social process possibilities, but this involvement may be counter-productive in terms of the group's output. Similarly, technical interventions or procedural changes may be dysfunctional when the task is technically so simple that group members perform it correctly more or less automatically.[1] On the other hand, if minimal skills and effort necessary to perform such routine tasks are not represented in the group, some kind of intervention may be in order. The specific strategy will, however, depend on the diagnosis of the problem. In fact, process interventions (of either type) may not be very effective for improving the performance of such groups. Perhaps structural changes would be more effective.

That intervention strategies need to be congruent with task type has been tested in two ways. First, an examination was made of experimental studies which tested the performance consequences of various intervention strategies (Herold, 1978). The group tasks used in these studies were analyzed using our task typology. The intervention strategy suggested by this classification— social, technical, social/technical, or none—was compared to the strategy actually used in the study, and performance consequences were compared with the consequences predicted by the theoretical framework. In each case group performance was found to change in the predicted direction. In those conditions where intervention was not indicated by the theory, performance declined subsequent to the intervention. Where either a social or technical intervention was indicated by the theory but where the actual intervention used was incongruent with that recommendation (e.g., interpersonal assistance for group members facing a technically complex task), performance declined subsequent to the intervention. However, where the intervention was congruent with task demands, performance improved subsequent to the intervention.

This review accomplished two things:

a. it supported the theoretical task typology and task-demands arguments presented here, and
b. it provided further support for our focus on the tasks as a powerful explanatory variable by reconciling what were previously thought to be contradictory findings (e.g., a particular intervention improving performance in one study but decreasing it in another).

A second, partial test of the need for an intervention-task fit was reported by Herold and Wolf (1977). Using two cells in our typology, low technical–low social and low-technical–high social complexity tasks, the performance and reactions of groups of MBA students and business executives were studied under theoretically appropriate and inappropriate leader decision-making strategies.

The experimental manipulation consisted of having half the leaders in each task condition act in a traditional, hierarchical fashion when confronted with a decision, while half were instructed to allow the group to participate in decision making.

Given our classification of tasks, participative decision-making should be an appropriate strategy where social complexities or process difficulties exist. This strategy should not be helpful for the performance of tasks having no needs for members to resolve process difficulties, and may in fact be detrimental, by distracting members from the task and focusing attention on social processes which are not task-relevant. Similarly, unilateral decision-making should be appropriate when the decision maker has all the relevant data and no social process issues exist which the group would be expected to work through. This style should not, however, be appropriate for a socially complex situation because it does not provide any means for meeting the social demands of the task. (Note that the traditional role of the supervisor as decision-maker is treated here as the "no-intervention" recommendation made earlier for the low technical–low social cell. . . .

Using the evaluation criteria of decision quality/rationality and decision acceptance, the following hypotheses were tested by the study:

1. *Decision acceptance or subordinate satisfaction with the decision is lowest under unilateral decision-making in the socially complex situation.* This hypothesis reflects the task-contingent view that it is not the decision-making strategy itself, but rather the inability of the particular strategy to address the social demands, that will lead to dissatisfaction.
2. *Decision quality is lowest under participative decision-making in the low technical–low social complexity task.* This again is a task-contingent hypothesis, since it proposes a conditional interaction between decision-making strategies and task attributes. The underlying logic is that focusing on social process when social complexity is low only

diverts energies from the task at hand and adversely affects performance.

. . . These hypotheses are especially pertinent to the Vroom and Yetton Contingency Model of Decision-Making.

Acceptance. As predicted, the percentage of dissatisfied group members in the unilateral-socially-complex condition (decision strategy inappropriate given the social complexity of the task) was significantly higher than for the other three conditions—73% vs. an average of 33% for all other conditions.

Quality. All groups in the two unilateral conditions made a high-quality decision, and 80% also did in the participative-socially-complex condition. However, only 20% of the groups using a participative strategy for the socially-simple problem made a high quality decision. As predicted, quality was significantly lower when the intervention strategy focused the group's attention on social process when the task was low in social complexity.

If we view leader decision-style training as but one of many intervention strategies which can be applied in pursuit of improved group effectiveness, then these findings are supportive of the position that to be effective, interventions into group process must be selected on a task-contingent basis. These findings also support the importance of the social and technical complexity dimensions for specifying these contingencies. Intervention strategies should be selected on the basis of whether or not they are congruent with the social and technical demands inherent in the task confronting the group. It is too often assumed that participation is universally preferred by group members to unilateral decision-making. These data suggest that dissatisfaction under conditions of unilateral decision-making occurs only when the task is of sufficient social complexity that unresolved social process issues are the probable cause of dissatisfaction. Even more important is the finding that inappropriate interventions, rather than merely being ineffective, actually decreased group effectiveness. This was the finding in the previously discussed reanalysis of previous studies (Herold, 1978), and its independent confirmation is reassuring. These findings have since been replicated using larger and more diverse samples of students and managers.

GROUP PROCESS: A MORE COMPLEX VIEW

[Summary: In this section we look at what should take place, given the task at hand. We must also consider factors which may affect what does take place when a group meets to perform a particular task. This focus represents a shift from analysis of the characteristics of tasks to an analysis of the characteristics of the group and its environment and involves consideration of the role of group members' abilities and motivation in influencing the level of group performance. The performance level attained by the group will be a function of how the ability-motivation combinations possessed by various group members are aggregated during the group's performance phase.

Figure 4 summarizes the stages of our analysis to this point. We start by analyzing the tasks and their demands as determinants of appropriate interaction processes required for group effectiveness. We must note, in addition, that what actually takes place during the group's interaction process is a function of both task demands and abilities and motivation of group members.

Note the arrow leading from task to the aggregation process, reinforcing the importance of the task in any analytic framework. The nature of the task often dictates how group member contributions will be combined to create the group response. Furthermore, Figure 4 proposes an effect of tasks on motivation. For example, task difficulty may affect the perceived relationship between individual and group efforts and task success. Furthermore, the attractiveness of the task and its subtasks may influence the types of outcomes and valences that individuals associate with task performance.

Another interdependency in our model is the effect that can be postulated to exist between aggregation processes, which translate the behavior of individual members into a group response, and individual member motivation. The means by which member contributions are combined will affect motivational levels of individuals. For example, where the task dictates that the group product is the sum of the individual

Figure 4.   The Aggregation of Member Contributions as Determined by Individual Ability-Motivation Levels, Determines Response to Task Demands

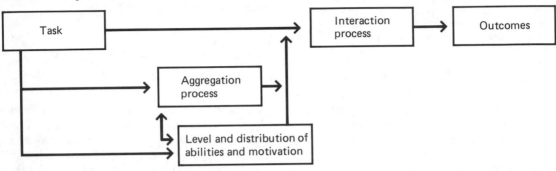

contributions, individuals could assume that the group is likely to succeed even without their help. For tasks where group productivity is determined by the productivity of its best member, individuals may assume that their contribution will not be the one likely to represent the group's performance.]—Eds.

Traditional Input Variables as They Affect Ability, Motivation and the Aggregation Process

Through consideration of individual member abilities and motivational levels and the process by which these are aggregated, we now have a convenient theoretical framework around which to include a host of traditionally researched input variables. In this section we shall demonstrate how these variables affect member motivation, member abilities, and the aggregation process. This demonstration will not include comprehensive summaries of research pertaining to each variable, nor will all possible input variables be considered.

Group norms.   Group norms—standards for members' behaviors—affect individual member motivational levels as well as the aggregation process. Norms influence the attractiveness of certain outcomes associated with a given level of performance, the probability that certain outcomes will follow from particular behaviors, and the probability that certain individual efforts will lead to the attainment of individual performance goals.

Norms may affect the aggregation process by dictating the combination and weighting of member contributions (e.g., opinions and contributions of high-status members may receive more weight), or by affecting the division of tasks into subtasks and the assignment of members to subtasks. Thus senior members may get first choice of subtasks regardless of their qualifications to perform them. Torrance (1954) found that in 3-man aviator groups, pilots, who enjoyed the highest status, were more successful in getting their opinions accepted while gunners, who enjoyed the lowest status, were least successful. The effects of status were more prominent in intact than in *ad hoc* groups. In other groups age, physical strength, past success, and wealth may influence the aggregation process. Note, however, that norms can affect aggregation processes only for those tasks in which group process determines the aggregation rule.

Group cohesiveness.   Perhaps more than is true of the other traditional variables in the group performance area, research concerned with group cohesiveness is of very little use if not combined with an understanding of the task contingencies involved.

As Cartwright (1968) noted, sources of attraction to groups are of two general types: those related to the attractiveness of the group and those related to the attractiveness of alternatives available to group members. One example of the former type is the appeal of the group's goals or tasks. Cohesiveness arising from this attraction would be expected to systematically increase the group's motivation to successfully complete the task at hand. It seems reasonable *not* to expect cohesiveness arising out of such other possible attractions as appeal of other participants and rewards of interaction to be systematically related to performance. In fact, the interaction which results from these other attractions may cause neglect of important task demands with subsequent reduction in group performance.

Cohesiveness which is due to the appeal of the group's tasks and goals may affect the attractiveness of attaining individual and group performance. For example, the attractiveness of meeting individual and group money-collection standards may be influenced by the degree to which members in a charity drive are attracted by the group goal of collecting money for a worthy cause. Member beliefs concerning the importance of their contribution and the probability of positive outcomes following successful individual and group performance would be similarly affected. On the other hand, cohesiveness which is a consequence of the attractiveness of other aspects ("they are all nice people," or, "it gets me out of the house") or which results merely from the lower attractiveness of other group memberships is likely to motivate behaviors aimed at maintaining group membership rather than performing at a high level.

Cohesiveness can also affect the aggregation process (when it is not predetermined) by influencing the degree to which group norms related to the aggregation process are enforced or by influencing the attractiveness associated with sanctions or rewards which follow norm compliance or violation.

Group size. Group size can be shown to affect the motivation, aggregation, and ability factors in our model. As group size increases, the availability, range, and distribution of abilities are also likely to increase. These changes have differential consequences for the potential productivity of groups performing different tasks. For conjunctive tasks, the likelihood of including a poor performer who will lower group productivity increases with group size. For disjunctive tasks, the likelihood of including a superior member who will improve group productivity increases with size. For additive tasks, total production should rise as people are added, though the relationship is by no means linear. For discretionary and divisible tasks, the relationships take different forms which may best be explained by the effects of size on the aggregation process.

For those tasks where groups can affect the task aggregation process, the process will most likely be affected by group size. As group size increases beyond some intermediate level, certain aggregation processes are ruled out and others are added (e.g., going from town meetings to elected councilmen as the size of a town increases). Similarly, the search process required to arrive at an optimal aggregation process ("who knows what?," "who should do what?," "whose opinion should receive what weight?") is likely to become too complex, with the group opting for simpler aggregation mechanisms. In general, as group size increases, coordination problems associated with marshaling the increased resources also increase and may outweigh potential benefits of the additional resources.

Increased group size is likely to decrease member motivation. The individual is likely to believe that his contribution to group success is reduced and his share of outcomes following from group success will decrease, and he may find fewer positive personal outcomes from performance of his role. Thus, except for cases where group size is so small that members fear the group will be unable to meet task demands, increased group size can often be expected to decrease individual member motivation.

Leadership. Leadership is not the primary focus of this [reading], but it is worth noting that much of the research on leader behavior is concerned with whether the behavior under investigation affects group members' abilities, motivation, or the group's aggregation process.

The research dealing with participative leadership is a good example of this concern. The leader who practices participative management is really affecting the group in three ways:

a. engaging in an aggregation process which allows all group members to input and assigning heavy weight to each member's contribution (contrast this with the autocratic leader who assigns full weight to his/her own contribution, or the consultative leader who assigns some variable weight to each input solicited from particular subordinates);

b. affecting member motivation by influencing certain key expectations (e.g., the relationship between individual contribution and group product) and by providing new, attractive outcomes (e.g., rewards inherent in the process of participation); and

c. affecting member abilities to the degree that their skills are improved as a function of having participated and learned about the content or process involved in the task.

One could now gain further understanding from findings, such as those reviewed earlier (Herold and Wolf, 1977), which show a decline in performance for some tasks under participative conditions. Namely, when the distribution of skills or knowledge favors one individual, optimum performance requires that full weight be assigned to that member's inputs. Participation under these conditions dilutes this best contribution by aggregating the contributions of less knowledgeable people, thus detracting from performance.

Completing the Model

In the last section we introduced some variables which have been the focus of mainstream research on groups. We argued that the effects of these variables on performance might best be understood through their impact on the group's abilities, motivation, and aggregation process. In this section we shall continue to expand the model we began in Figure 4 by inserting these traditional variables and by considering other interdependencies, influences, and feedback loops which are required to more completely depict the complexities of group performance. Figure 5 represents the more complete model.

In addition to inserting the traditional input variables and noting their effect on abilities, motivation and the aggregation process, we propose a direct influence of tasks on many of these input variables. Task characteristics may influence group cohesiveness and may be associated with certain behavioral norms.

The next set of relationships to be discussed are the feedback loops in our model, which represent the dynamic nature of group process. Much of the social-psychological literature concerning group performance assumes group interaction to be a one-time affair, with the group's life ending upon task completion. This may be due to the heavy reliance on short-lived laboratory groups for sources of data. However, the dynamic nature of group interaction is such that every process-performance episode or sequence of episodes may have profound effects on subsequent group interaction process and performance effectiveness. We shall discuss two types of such feedback processes: those related to group interaction process and those related to group performance outcomes.

If a group produces a product, their degree of success and the events associated with that success (e.g., environmental and interpersonal rewards)[2] will influence future group interaction processes by affecting individual member motivational levels, traditional input variables, future aggregation processes, and even to some extent member abilities. Members are likely to modify perceptions concerning their own efforts, the group's efforts, outcomes associated with individual and group performance, and the relationship between individual and group performance in view of events associated with a particular performance episode. Individuals' motivation may also be modified by changes in the "traditional" input variables brought about by group performance. For example, if we find that group cohesiveness increases with task performance success, that change in cohesiveness will affect future aggregation processes and motivational levels in the manner described earlier. Future aggregation processes can be influenced, if under the group's control, by the reinforcing value which the outcomes of a given performance episode have for affecting the group's reliance on similar processes in the future. These consequences of the group's outcomes are represented by the dashed feedback loops originating from the "outcomes" section of Figure 5.

The interaction process which leads to the creation of a group product can also have several feedback effects. Engaging in an interaction process and noting its outcomes may improve member skills (assessment of task demands,

Figure 5. A More Complete Model of the Determinants of Group Performance Effectiveness

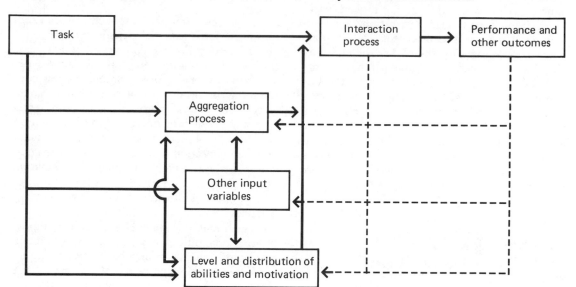

weighting of member resources, and performance-specific abilities) for future performance episodes. The experience of members during the performance phase can also influence their willingness to engage in particular aggregation processes in the future (e.g., groups frustrated by the time-consuming aspects of democratic process may be more reluctant to use it as an aggregation process in the future) as well as influencing the traditional input variables.

Group members' experiences from interaction also affect individual member motivational levels by influencing beliefs about outcomes available, the probability of their occurrence, and their attractiveness to group members. The quality of the interaction experience may change beliefs about the group's chances for success and may uncover new outcomes attainable as a function of group interaction. These various influences are again denoted with dashed feedback loops going from the "group interaction process" section to the affected elements in the model.

In summary, the earlier part of this [reading] dealt with analyzing the task so as to determine its technical and social demand characteristics, and the consequent process requirements which would meet these demand characteristics. The

latter section has tried to more fully represent the determinants of group performance, above and beyond what we know about the task and its required interaction process. This division is consistent with the argument that, by and large, information relevant to the task and to how the group plans to go about performing it (process) will prove uniquely useful in predicting group effectiveness. This view is supported by the data described earlier concerning appropriate and inappropriate process.

On the other hand, the "task only" approach is obviously an oversimplification of what really goes into a group's final product. We therefore presented a more complete representation of factors likely to affect group outcomes. As with any attempt to model behavioral phenomena, greater realism means greater complexity, which may mean lower utility. Our purpose here was to show where the various pieces might fit rather than suggesting that all these factors, influences, and relationships need to be considered every time one considers a particular group's performance.

The total model may prove most useful as a diagnostic checklist or road map which those interested in groups can apply in a given situation.

The model provides several diagnostic questions which can be asked when trying to work backwards from a particular observation of performance. What are the task demands? Is group process appropriate for these? Are the necessary abilities represented in the group? If they are, are they distributed in a fashion likely to lead to successful performance? Is member motivation a problem? If so, what are possible reasons for lack of motivation? Given these types of diagnostic questions and one's knowledge about a particular group and its environment, one ought to be able to isolate those aspects of the model which are most useful for the particular situation.

CHANGE STRATEGIES REVISITED—USING WHAT WE KNOW

Earlier we classified strategies used for changing group process and performance as being either social or technical in nature. We also noted that other strategies could be considered structural in that they aim at changing the context or environment within which the group operates. The social-technical distinction was claimed to be useful when an analysis of the group's task was all we had to go on.

Looking at our more complete model, we can now identify five distinct areas which, if they were targeted for change, would likely change the group's product or outcomes: the task itself; member motivation levels; member abilities; the group's aggregation process; and any of the traditional input variables thought to affect motivation, abilities, and aggregation processes. Given the diagnostic posture advocated in the previous section, we can now start thinking of change strategies as focusing on one or more of these targets for change, to be applied contingent on the perceived need for particular changes . . . In the remainder of this [reading], we shall briefly show how various approaches to improving the performance of groups may be analyzed according to the variable(s) in our model on which they have their major impact.

Social Approaches

Social process interventions, such as social skill training efforts, can be viewed as attempts to change certain skills and/or norms which guide the behavior of group members. Such approaches as laboratory or T-group training, process consultation, and interpersonal skill training can all be considered to fall in this category. An integral part of many such techniques is the examination of existing group norms and the encouragement of experimentation with new forms of behavior. These methods usually encourage the formation of new group norms related to issues such as risk-taking, openness, trust, and dealing with deviant behavior.

If such methods are effective in changing the interpersonal skills of group members, they might also cause a change in member motivation levels and/or aggregation processes. A change in the interpersonal climate could make interaction between group members more rewarding as well as influencing the manner in which member inputs will be solicited and combined.

Technical Approaches

Technical and procedural interventions into group process, like social approaches, can be conceived of as changing skill levels and distribution among group members as well as affecting motivation, aggregation processes, and group norms.

Almost all organizational training programs seek to alter technical skill levels. Many are straightforward attempts to change member ability levels, but some technical change strategies are aimed directly at the other change targets in our model. For example, Maier and his associates (e.g., Maier, 1967; Maier and Solem, 1952) have focused on training discussion leaders as a means of improving problem solving in groups. Part of this training calls for the discussion leader to counter early discouragement of minority views by soliciting and encouraging their expression. The leader thereby changes not only group norms but also the aggregation process by including inputs which previously might have received no weight in the group's deliberations.

Other procedural change attempts have focused on modifying task-related norms. Noting that anti-planning norms often govern the behavior of groups and are usually detrimental to the group's performance, both Shure et al. (1962) and Hackman et al. (1976) have shown that interventions aimed at encouraging groups to spend a portion of their time on planning activities can counteract such norms.

Research concerned with group decision rules, and the consequences of changing these (e.g., Davis, 1973), reveal that group performance can be affected through modification of the group's aggregation process. For example, a parliamentary procedure change from majority rule to a unanimity rule represents a major change in the aggregation rule used and probably in the outcome.

Structural Approaches

As noted earlier, structural changes are aimed not at changing the group's interaction process per se, but rather at changing the environment within which the group functions. These environmental changes may then lead to changes in individual behavior and group process. Perhaps because they are one step removed from actual member behavior, these change strategies have been largely ignored as sources for creating changes in group effectiveness.

One could probably conceive of structural changes which affect each of our five possible targets of change. We shall briefly mention only a few and show how they affect the task, motivational levels, and member abilities.

The organization can impact the group's task by changing the design of the task or by changing the organizational systems and technologies available for task performance. While considerable recent attention has been paid to the effects of *individual* task design on motivation and performance, . . . research on task designs likely to elicit commitment and effort on the part of *group* members has been lacking (Hackman and Morris, 1975). The way that group tasks are defined affects member motivation, the relevance of member skills, the aggregation processes likely to be

used, etc., and hence will affect group performance.

Group tasks can be altered by changing the technology available to the group for performing the task. Thus the introduction of a computerized management information system could change a previously technically complex task into a simple one. Other changes in resources, equipment, and information can also change the demands placed on the group by the task.

Member motivation levels can be influenced by most formal organizational systems and hence by changes in these systems. It is not hard to realize that organizational control, evaluation, reward, appraisal, and authority systems influence what group members do during the group's performance phase. Considerable research has been performed on the effects of such systems on individuals' motivation and performance, but little has been done to explore the potential of changes in such systems for changes in group products.

Finally, group effectiveness can be affected by alterations in member abilities brought about by changes in an organization's selection, placement, and retention practices. However, while much work has been done on selecting and matching individuals to jobs, little work has been done to systematically use group-level criteria for selecting individuals for work groups and for particular sub-tasks.

Summary

In the last section of this [reading] we presented a model from which one could derive a series of diagnostic questions concerning the likely determinants of group performance, and determine the most appropriate focus for creating change in the effectiveness of a given group. We have tried to emphasize that:

a. a considerable variety of change strategies is available to us;

b. these strategies have different purposes; and

c. they should be selected based on a diagnosed need—in this case, the diagnosis being aided by the model we have presented.

This last point is especially important, given the apparent propensity to engage in change efforts in a faddish, atheoretical manner. We have advocated a situation-contingent approach in which the task typology is used to make a broad determination of the social and/or technical issues likely to require attention. Further analysis may then determine the specific areas of difficulty (e.g., social interaction norms, technical skills, faulty aggregation process) within these two broadly defined areas. This analysis should suggest an aim for the intervention strategy (e.g., change performance-related norms). Once this aim has been established, particular strategies will suggest themselves while a host of other strategies will be eliminated. For example, if technical skills are deemed insufficient to meet technical task demands, strategies aimed at improving such skills should be considered while all others would be ruled out. However, if the problem is that interpersonal issues prevent the aggregation of member contributions in an optimal fashion, then a T-group or other social process intervention would be suggested. . . .

We also wish to emphasize the potential value of having such a wide variety of strategies available to us. Many of these have been under-utilized. We need to better explore the potential of all available strategies for creating change in the effectiveness of groups. We also need to recognize that even when changes are instituted for purposes other than to affect group process, the effect will often be to create major changes in the way groups go about performing their tasks.

NOTES

1. Individuals often experience a similar dilemma when trying to consciously attend to an automatic behavior such as dancing or tying a necktie, and find that it inhibits their performance.

2. Although our discussion has focused mostly on task performance as the product of the group's interaction process, our full model allows for other outcomes such as those covered by the broader definition of effectiveness offered by Hackman (1976) and discussed at the beginning of this [reading].

REFERENCES

Cartwright, D., "The nature of group cohesiveness," in D. Cartwright and A. Zander (eds.), *Group dynamics*, 3rd ed. New York: Harper & Row, 1968.

Davis, J. H., *Group performance*. Reading, Mass.: Addison-Wesley, 1969.

Davis, J. H., "Group decision and social interaction: A theory of social decision schemes," *Psychological Review*, 1973, 80, 97–125.

Hackman, J. R., "The design of self-managing work groups," Technical Report No. 11, Yale University, School of Organization and Management, New Haven, 1976.

Hackman, J. R., Brousseau, K. R., and Weiss, J. A., "The interaction of task design and group performance strategies in determining group effectiveness," *Organizational Behavior and Human Performance*, 1976, 16, 350–365.

Hackman, J. R. and Morris, C. G., "Group tasks, group interaction process, and group performance effectiveness: A review and proposed integration," in L. Berkowitz (ed.), *Advances in experimental social psychology*. New York: Academic Press, 1975.

Herold, D. M., "Towards an understanding of group motivation: An expectancy theory model of individuals' motivation to perform a group task," Technical Report No. M-76-8, Georgia Institute of Technology, College of Industrial Management, 1976.

Herold, D. M., "Improving the performance effectiveness of groups through a task-contingent selection of intervention strategies," *Academy of Management Review*, 1978.

Herold, D. M. and Wolf, G., "Effects of task contingent interventions on group performance and satisfaction." Paper presented at a meeting of American Institute for Decision Sciences, Chicago, October 19–22, 1977.

Katzell, R. A., Miller, C. E., Rotter, N. G., and Venet, T. G., "Effects of leadership and other inputs on group processes and outputs," *Journal of Social Psychology*, 1970, 80, 157–169.

Leavitt, H. A., "Applied organizational change in industry: Structural, technological and humanistic approaches," in J. G. March (ed.), *Handbook of organizations*. Chicago: Rand McNally, 1965, 1144–1170.

Maier, N. R. F., "Assets and liabilities in group problem solving: The need for an integrative function," *Psychological Review*, 1967, 74, 239–249.

Maier, N. R. F. and Solem, A. R. "The contribution of a discussion leader to the group thinking," *Human Relations*, 1952, 5, 277–288.

Shaw, M. E., "Some effects of problem complexity upon problem solution efficiency in different communication nets," *Journal of Experimental Psychology*, 1954, *48*, 211–217.

Shaw, M. E., *Group Dynamics: The Psychology of Small Group Behavior.* New York: McGraw Hill, 1971.

Shaw, M. E., "Scaling Group Tasks: A Method for Dimensional Analysis," JSAS Catalog of Selected Documents in Psychology, 1973, *3*, 8 (ms no. 294).

Shure, C. H., Rogers, M. S., Larsen, I. M., and Tassone, J., "Group planning and task effectiveness," *Sociometry*, 1962, *25*, 263–282.

Steiner, I. D., *Group process and productivity.* New York: Academic Press, 1972.

Torrance, E. P., "Some consequences of power differences on decision making in permanent and temporary three-man groups," *Research Studies*, State College of Washington, 1954, *22*, 130–140.

Zajonc, R. B., "The requirements and design of a standard group task," *Journal of Experimental Social Psychology*, 1965, *1*, 71–88.

16

A perspective on group decision making

Nina G. Hatvany
and Deborah Gladstein

Managers are always faced with decisions. Simon (1979, p. 500) says that "decision making is the heart of administration." Decision making spans many areas ranging from trivial issues to such vital questions as whether the organization should liquidate its assets. We are here concerned with major decisions about the organization's continued success or even survival. These become necessary when environmental opportunities and constraints emerge, such as new markets or governmental regulations, as well as when internal opportunities and problems occur, such as a new technological development or a strike.

The central element of such decisions is uncertainty. Uncertainty is characterized by incomplete or conflicting information concerning either the nature of the problem, the alternative courses of action open, the consequences of various actions, or the components of a successful solution. Uncertainty is typical of novel, nonroutine decisions, where standard operating procedures in response to particular contingencies have not been developed.

This paper focuses on the small group as the decision-making vehicle. It is assumed that group members have a high level of motivation as well as necessary skills and knowledge. It is further assumed that decisions are to be of good quality and are to be willingly implemented by group members. Our emphasis will be on group decision making done in formal meetings, since such decision making is more open to both scrutiny and change and since managers in organizations spend an estimated 50 percent of their time in such scheduled meetings (Mintzberg, 1973).

This article appears here for the first time. Copyright © 1982 by Nina G. Hatvany and Deborah Gladstein. Printed by permission.

In the first of five sections we cite some reasons that groups increasingly are used to make decisions in organizations. The second section briefly outlines a normative view of the decision-making process. The third section is a discussion of the factors, inherent in group decision making under uncertainty, that may interfere with the process suggested. The subject of the fourth section is the measures available to increase the quality of group decisions under uncertainty. The last section acknowledges the impossibility of achieving optimal decisions but concludes that group decision making per se is of great benefit to an organization. We argue that groups must not be viewed in isolation but rather in their organizational context. In this context, a new perspective on group behavior emerges. It is during group decision making that the vital organizational functions of communication, coordination, and control are realized.

THE NEED FOR GROUP DECISION MAKING

Whether by necessity or design groups increasingly are involved in organizational decision making. The use of groups alleviates some problems inherent in individual decision making. An individual has limited capacity to process information (Miller, 1956; Simon, 1959) and is further limited by his or her professional training, technical expertise, and perspective within the organization. In a group, the labor of gathering specialized information can be divided among members, and the information base is broadened. The subjective nature of individual probability estimates may shift toward greater objectivity when aggregated (Friedman, 1979).

Group decision making is also a very useful device for linking the planners and those who will have to implement the decision. This link serves the symbolic function of underlining the importance of various organizational constituencies (Pfeffer, 1980). It also serves the vital function of maintaining an accurate flow of information from the various organizational arenas to the planners and vice versa. In addition, representatives of groups outside the organization, such

as labor unions and citizen bodies, are increasingly demanding a role in organizational decision-making bodies (Steiner, 1972).

In sum, a group making decisions can increase the scope and accuracy of information brought to bear on a decision; it serves as a link between planning and implementing; and it includes, both actually and symbolically, various important constituencies inside and outside the organization. The key question is: How can groups make decisions that maximize effectiveness?

NORMATIVE DECISION-MAKING PROCEDURES FOR BOTH INDIVIDUALS AND GROUPS

It is imperative that the decision-making process begin with identification of either the problem or the opportunity faced. In many laboratory studies of decision making, a problem is given to individuals or groups. In the organizational context, however, problems are often indicated only by a few presenting symptoms. When a drop in profits occurs, there are usually multiple possible explanations. Before correct action can be taken, the cause of the problem must be identified—is it customer dissatisfaction, price, or poor distribution? Problem finding is of prime importance in effectively directing the search for an optimal solution (Pounds, 1969).

Classical models of rational choice specify procedures to be followed once the decision arena has been identified. They require that decision makers have complete knowledge of all the alternative solutions as well as the consequences or outcomes associated with each of the alternatives. Each outcome must then be compared against the particular value or linear combination of values that the decision maker is attempting to maximize.

Extensions of the classical model include discussions of decision making under risk, rather than certainty, where outcomes have a certain probability of occurring. The value of the outcome must then be multiplied by the probability of its occurrence, such that the best outcome will be one that maximizes the expected utility of the outcome. Further extensions discuss decision making under uncertainty, where probabilities are not known and must be estimated by the decision maker. Then "subjective expected utility" replaces simple utility in a decision maker's calculations (Edwards, 1954).

This ideal model is not one that can be followed by human beings with limited information-processing abilities, particularly in situations characterized by uncertainty (Simon, 1945; 1979). Not all the information about the alternatives and their consequences is available, nor can it all be examined at the start of problem solving. As decision making proceeds, new information may well change the parameters of the decision and must be taken into account (Friedman, 1979). In addition, there are enormous difficulties associated with generating alternatives and with estimating both the probabilities of outcomes and their utility. Typically, the decision maker generates a limited set of alternatives (Lindblom, 1959) and selects the first that exceeds some minimal level of utility, a practice termed satisficing (Simon, 1959).

Utility estimation is virtually impossible because it is so difficult to compare qualitatively different outcomes. Steinbruner (1974) illustrates this point with an example: the choice between love and duty is clearly a subject for a novel, but it is difficult to imagine theoretical analysis relieving the dilemma.

No current theory addresses or attempts to counter all these human limitations. Janis and Mann (1977), however, outline procedures for decision making that recognize human limitations by requiring that some, not all, of the alternatives be surveyed. These procedures require the assimilation of new information and address the important issue of implementing the decision made. The best decision is useless if it is not carefully implemented. This model, however, like the classical model, places little emphasis on identification of both problems and opportunities.

Normative models of decision making generally include four phases. First, the problem or opportunity is defined. Second, alternative solutions are generated and examined in terms both of their feasibility and expected consequences. Third, solutions are evaluated and a choice is made. Fourth, the choice is implemented. It is obvious that during the first two phases as much information as time and manpower permit should be gathered. Implicit in all four phases is the need to search for and be open to new information that may change the nature of the decision and hence call for a reiteration of the process.

The process outlined represents the optimal procedure. In the words of Simon (1979, p. 499) "If human decision makers are as rational as their limited computational abilities and their incomplete information permit them to be, then there will be a close relation between the normative and descriptive decision theory."

In general, groups should adhere to the same decision-making process as individuals but must additionally aggregate the opinions of each group member in a way that reflects some sensible scheme, such as equality or weighting based on expertise, seniority, and the like.

The decision-making processes of groups tend, however, to unfold in ways dictated by the patterns of interaction among group members. The four phases of decision making are frequently molded or distorted. Events present themselves and are interpreted as symptoms of underlying problems, but little careful thought or objectivity is accorded to problem definition. Often, only a limited amount of information is selectively gathered, and few alternatives are generated. The primary values or goals of the group and the scope of its mandate are sometimes not articulated, an omission that naturally complicates the process of alternative evaluation. In some cases, furthermore, alternative evaluation is not conducted according to a scheme that assesses all the alternatives generated and sensibly weights the opinions of group members. The following section addresses the question of why these inadequacies in group decision making occur.

INADEQUACIES IN GROUP DECISION MAKING

We propose that difficulties in following an ideal model of group decision making stem from a variety of intertwined causes, including unconscious and conscious mechanisms. The effects of these mechanisms are demonstrated in a range of behaviors, from poor organization to deliberate attempts to manipulate the decision-making process. We will discuss "groupthink," a dramatic example of inadequacies in group decision making.

Unconscious and Conscious Mechanisms

Wilfred Bion (1961), an exponent of the Tavistock school, has contributed one perspective on the causes of dysfunctions. Bion believes that there are two aspects to every group. One aspect is the "work group," which is concerned with task accomplishment, agenda setting, decision making, implementation, and so on. However, as a result of the other aspect of groups, the "basic assumption group," task accomplishment is not consistently effected. The basic assumption group consists of unconscious mechanisms that cause the group to act on more illogical needs, such as a desire for "flight" from an urgent and oppressive decision. These mechanisms interfere with work group functioning and are evidenced in ineffective and self-contradictory behavior.

Such behavior also results when feelings and hidden agendas remain unexpressed and are communicated indirectly, leading to conflict and hostility. If interactions reflect personal disagreements, rather than substantive discussion of alternatives and values, then the decision-making process may be adversely affected. Zand (1972) demonstrated this phenomenon by comparing groups characterized by a low level of trust or expression of feelings to groups with a high level of trust. In low-trust groups, in contrast to high-trust groups, interpersonal obstacles interfered with problem identification, and energy and creativity were diverted from work.

Some agendas are, however, quite conscious. For example, an individual may vociferously press an opinion in order to sway the group toward personal goals, rather than the group's goals or mandate. Several theorists take the view that the organization can be viewed as an arena in which conflict and struggle among different subunits or groups takes place (Cohen, March, and Olsen, 1972; Pfeffer, 1978; Tushman, 1977). Manipulation of others' opinions is easier the more ambiguous or uncertain the decision. It is the unformulated arenas, such as long-range plan-

ning, that are most amenable to political decision-making processes. There is every reason to suppose that if group members do not share a commitment to a clear organizational mission, group decisions may be a result of bargaining among members with parochial priorities.

It is such unconscious and conscious mechanisms that are the ultimate cause of ineffective behaviors observed in decision-making groups. Some examples of ineffective behaviors follow.

Lack of Organization

A group may be ineffective as a decision-making unit simply because it knows neither the correct steps to follow nor the best way to organize itself to follow those steps efficiently. For example, group members will often begin a meeting without an explicit plan of how to structure their activities. They start to work using shared though unexpressed strategies (Hackman and Morris, 1975). These implicit procedures may not be the most productive. They easily result in unstructured meetings where discussions fall into a rut; group members focus on one train of thought for long periods of time and so increase the likelihood that few alternatives will be generated (Delbecq, Van de Ven, and Gustafson, 1975). There is a tendency toward task avoidance and tangential discussion and, predictably, little feeling of accomplishment.

There is also a tendency toward "solution mindedness" among decision-making groups. A group will also often adopt a solution to its problem very early in discussion. Hoffman and Maier (1964) showed, for example, that after one potential solution to a problem had received a great deal of positive support, later solutions offered to the group had very little chance of being adopted. This approach reduces the information used in discussions, limits the number of alternatives generated, and may also result in inadequate problem definition.

Groups may neglect to plan and examine alternative solutions for several reasons. There is often a great deal of external pressure to produce answers. Deadlines and time constraints are an organizational reality that pushes the group toward those solutions that fit habitual directions of thinking or are achieved through limited search rather than efficient planning of time and strategy (March and Simon, 1958). Expediency is fostered by internal pressures as well. The group may be uncomfortable with a problem with no obvious answer, and so it will seek to relieve that discomfort by finding a quick solution. Finding a solution gives group members a pleasing sense of achievement. Unanimity and commitment to the solution may be so intense that evidence of failure virtually will be ignored (Salancik, 1977). Unfortunately, this method of decision making may become standard practice, thus limiting the effectiveness of the group.

Conformity to Group Norms

Uniformity in a broad array of practices and characteristics is frequently observed among the members of a group. This uniformity may be evident in dress and discussion procedures as well as in individual opinions and values. It often stems from conformity to group standards or norms.

Individuals conform to norms because they desire the rewards, such as friendship, help, and recognition, that group membership brings (Asch, 1952; Newcomb, 1954) and are aware that deviation typically brings rejection (Schachter, 1951). Initially, certain unwritten expectations, procedures, and values are adopted by group members (usually those already espoused by high-status members). As the group evolves into a functioning unit, some of these group norms will be modified and several will become more specific. Certain standard operating procedures are developed and members adopt predictable roles. Standardized decision-making routines and rigid role definition may lower flexibility and effectiveness in dealing with diverse problems.

Similarly, overt individual conformity to opinions perceived to be held by other group members may result in the suppression of conflict and in the expression of a limited range of opinions. In particular, group members may consciously avoid expressing feelings in discussion, or even actively deny them, because they see their expression as inappropriate or antithetical to the current business culture. This attitude denies the group access to important information: people's feelings as well as unpopular information and opinions. Unexpressed doubts make it likely that group members will feel no real commitment to the adopted solution. If resistance to or discomfort with a decision can be brought into the open, then either a new and perhaps superior decision can be made, or commitment to the early decision will be the result of true acceptance rather than simple overt compliance.

Systematic Bias in Information

The information available to all group members may deviate from objective reality because it is not articulated in meetings or simply because of the circumscribed nature of the group members' particular organizational reality. Information made available may be limited further if it is provided by only one member of the group. That individual may make errors in his or her processing of a diverse and extensive body of information. Those errors will then be adopted by the group as a whole as each member seeks to ascertain from other group members what are "correct" beliefs and behaviors (Festinger, 1954). In essence, the group becomes its members' social universe and has the capacity to mediate beliefs about the "true" state of the world.

Biased opinions may be reinforced by the arguments raised during group discussion. An example of this phenomenon is "group polarization" (Moscovici and Zavalloni, 1969). In studies on this process, individuals first indicate their position on an issue. They then discuss the issue in a group and attempt to reach consensus. If the majority of individuals initially holds an opinion that tends to one pole of the issue, individual judgments will often shift during the group discussion so that the final group opinion (as well as the mean of later private individual judgments) is more polarized than was the mean of the initial individual decisions. This group polarization may be explained by the interplay of conformity in both behaviors and beliefs.

Experimental results of this nature have been obtained repeatedly in experiments studying the degree of risk that will be taken to achieve a particular outcome. The "risky shift phenomenon" is the name coined for these results, since the group consensus reached after discussions is typically more risky than the mean of initial individual decisions. These kinds of shift have been demonstrated not only in laboratory settings but also in real-life settings. Such systematic bias may be strengthened when certain group members' opinions exert a disproportionate amount of influence.

Unclear Weighting of Individual Opinions and Values

While the contribution of all group members to the alternatives generated and to their evaluation should not necessarily be equal, one would suppose that members' contributions should be weighted in a systematic rather than a random manner. However, extroverted, dominant, socially aggressive individuals with superior social skills typically have a disproportionate influence on decisions (Hoffman and Clark, 1979). Steiner (1972) proposes several reasons for groups being unable to weight individual members' contributions appropriately: the unreliability of status as a predictor of the quality of members' input, the low level of confidence proficient members may have in their own ability, the social pressures of the incompetent majority on the competent minority, and finally, the difficulty of evaluating the quality of any member's contribution.

This deference to status, numbers, dominance, confidence, and other such factors may be at the unconscious level. Deference can be motivated by an individual's desire to look good or to garner resources for his or her own area within the organization. A group member may develop commitment to a solution because of personal and unique priorities and therefore argue forcibly for it, be closed to alternatives, and be dissatisfied if that solution is not accepted. This behavior would naturally affect the two phases of alternative generation and choice.

As a result of the implicit attention to status and power differentials or because of the several other processes discussed, group interaction can reduce the care taken in problem definition, limit the amount of information gathered as well as the number of alternatives examined, and diminish the objectivity with which the opinions of group

members are weighted. All these gaps are also likely to affect successful implementation. These deleterious consequences occur in addition to the consequences of the limitations of individual human decision-makers. These limitations have their most dramatic effects in decisions that lead to such major political fiascos as the Bay of Pigs.

Groupthink

Janis (1971) has studied the "groupthink" process, which exemplifies a group's inability to function effectively. He identifies a variety of activities by group members that adversely affect all phases of decision making. Janis cites as an example of groupthink the decision made by the president and his advisers to invade Cuba in 1961. The now famous Bay of Pigs fiasco was a result of poor decision making by this top foreign policy advisory group. President Kennedy commented in retrospect, "How could we have been so stupid" (p. 43). This decision was a result of the nondeliberate suppression of critical thoughts on the part of group members. As the group became more cohesive, the group members became more loyal to one another and felt greater compulsion to avoid creating dissension.

Behavioral symptoms of groupthink have been identified by Janis. An illusion of invulnerability arises among group members that leads them to become overoptimistic and willing to take extraordinary risks. They collectively construct rationalizations in order to discount warnings and other negative feedback. Victims of groupthink believe unquestioningly in the inherent morality of their ingroup and hold stereotyped negative views of the leaders of "enemy" groups; they apply direct pressure to any individual who momentarily expresses doubts about any of the group's shared illusions or who questions the validity of the arguments supporting a policy alternative favored by the majority. Each individual avoids deviating from what appears to be group consensus, keeps silent about misgivings, and even minimizes the importance of his or her doubts. Arthur Schlesinger blames his silence on the "circumstances of the discussion" (Janis, 1971, p. 46). Groups engaging in this process share an illusion of unanimity within the group concerning almost all judgments expressed by members who speak in favor of the majority view. Individual group members sometimes appoint themselves as mindguards to protect the leader and fellow members from adverse information that might break the complacency they all share about the effectiveness and morality of past decisions. Janis' findings are based on the retrospective accounts of observers and participants, but Tetlock (1979) shows that content analysis of public statements connected with the decisions Janis examined supports Janis's observations. Decision makers involved in policy decisions characterized by groupthink were, for example, more simplistic in their perceptions of policies and made more positive references to the United States and its allies (although they were not more negative about their opponents).

We see in the process of groupthink the series of interrelated processes that result from failure to gather sufficient information initially, inability to incorporate new information or learning into the decision, and poor evaluation of alternatives.

SUGGESTIONS FOR ALLEVIATING THE PROBLEMS INHERENT IN GROUP DECISION MAKING

At this stage, the pessimist may have despaired altogether of using groups to make decisions. Certainly, the phases of problem definition, alternative generation, and choice are more complex at the group level than at the individual level because coordination of individuals and aggregation of their information and judgments must take place. Nonetheless, research and experience have provided several ways of improving group decision making. These methods center on upgrading the quality of information gathered for problem definition and alternative generation and providing a scheme by which to evaluate alternatives. There is also a need for flexibility in procedures if groups are to deal effectively with a variety of complex decisions. A range of these aids, for all groups and especially for those dealing with uncertainty, will be discussed. The tentative nature of the research findings should be borne in mind.

Problem Definition

The first priority is for the group to define its problem area. This does not mean only defining the problem of the moment but also outlining the scope of decision making for the group: what areas it will work on, what role it will play, what opportunities as well as problems it will address. It is important that group members openly express their expectations as to the function of the group and its potential range of activity, so that there is agreement about group goals. Only after such agreement can the group begin to define the specific problems to be addressed in meeting the group's goals.

Organizing

Once the problems to be addressed have been formulated, the group must organize itself in order to solve them. Hackman, Brousseau, and Weiss (reported in Hackman and Morris, 1975) conducted an experiment in which groups performed various tasks. Some of the groups had to perform tasks in which members were interdependent and information was distributed unequally among members. Among groups working on such complex and uncertain tasks, those who discussed how to carry out the tasks prior to doing them performed better than those who did not. The implication of these findings is that groups engaged in complex decision making benefit from some planning of how to go about their task.

The question remains as to which strategies are the most effective in performing various tasks. For most tasks, discussion alone should yield some good ideas for strategies. We will cite some research that suggests ways to organize not only for decision making but also for fulfillment for the group members' emotional needs—what are often termed "maintenance functions." Some practices associated with fulfillment both of task functions and socioemotional needs follow.

Participation

A participative style of decision making allows all the group members to feel that they have an opportunity to influence the decision. The key here seems to be the opportunity and not the necessity or pressure to participate. Indeed, some nonparticipating group members are satisfied with decisions made by others, although it is important that they feel their opinion is reflected in the decision (Hoffman and Maier, 1964). Coupled with the members' ability to influence the decision is the requirement that the group leader or influential members not dominate the decision-making arena. The group should listen to minority opinions and permit conflict to occur. This requirement allows for greater creativity and accommodates the possibility that minority opinions may be superior to majority opinions. Such an approach, of course, is contingent on a resolution of differences (Hoffman, 1979).

Separation of Decision-Making Phases

In a similar but more structured vein, Osborn (1957) concludes that the separation of alternative generation from alternative evaluation is beneficial, as is having members first work on a problem individually and then in the group (Hoffman, 1979). Preliminary work by individuals presumably lessens the risk of a potentially good idea being evaluated or subjected to majority pressure before it has been fully articulated.

Clear Communication

It has been suggested that group norms supporting candor about opinions enhances group functioning by adding to the amount and accuracy of information available to group members. It is also beneficial to label feelings and separate them from perceptions and beliefs. This process diminishes defensiveness and unclear communications and stimulates healthy conflict.

Communication can also be improved with decentralized and flexible communication patterns among group members. These typically lead to better group performance and member satisfaction, under conditions of uncertainty, than do reliance on centralized control and standard operating procedures (Collins and Guetzkow, 1964; Tushman, 1979).

Allocating Roles

One means by which a group may facilitate both task and maintenance functions is to ensure that group members assume the roles that fulfill those functions. Schein (1969) identifies several functions that should be performed. These include: initiating—focusing the group on problem definition and performance strategy, clarifying—helping members to understand each other, summarizing—reviewing points made during the course of discussion, harmonizing—mediating conflict in the group, and gatekeeping—ensuring participation and preventing interruptions.

Janis (1972) suggests some roles to ensure that information contraindicative of a chosen course of action is considered by group members. These include a devil's advocate, who points out the negative aspects of a given choice as well as an individual whose function is to seek opinions from nonmembers. The roles outlined here may be performed by the formal leader of the group, an informal leader, or by several members of the group, on either a permanent or an ad hoc basis.

These prescriptions, however, may not be enough. Group members may learn how to make better decisions in theory or as individuals and yet be unable to implement their learning in the group. They may be unaware of their own behavior or fall prey to pressures to conform, which mitigate against their newly learned behaviors. Even if the group as a whole is informed of new techniques, simply being told that another method is better will not necessarily lead the group to change. Argyris's (1966) study shows a great discrepancy between what executives said constituted effective behavior in meetings and their actual behavior in meetings. Executives knew what to do, but somehow their behavior did not reflect that knowledge.

Process Consultation

Process consultation, with a consultant external to the group, may be helpful both in overcoming these obstacles and in dealing with unexpressed and obstructive feelings. Process consultation refers to "a set of activities on the part of the consultant which helps the client to perceive, understand, and act upon process events which occur in the client's environment" (Schein, 1969, p. 9). Process consultation takes many forms and includes improving the way in which the group works together and enhancing the quality of interpersonal relations within the group.

The process consultant can help the group become aware of its own behavior and norms by providing feedback on how feelings are dealt with, how participative the group is, how open members are in communicating their viewpoints, what the communication structure and level of expertise are, what roles various individuals adopt, how much planning occurs, and how decision making is helped and hindered. Feedback serves two purposes: it energizes the group around process issues and directs that energy toward reducing the gap between what ought to go on and what really goes on (Nadler, 1977).

Attention is focused on problems that are amenable to intervention and not on problems due to factors not under the control of the group. In addition to providing feedback, the process consultant aims to "develop durable group skills" (Burke and Hornstein, 1972, p. 55). These skills include diagnosing by the group of its own problems, giving itself feedback, and processing its own behavior. It does not mean that the group learns the "correct" way to function, but rather develops the capacity to organize according to the task at hand and subsequently to evaluate what it has done so that it can constantly improve.

Agenda Setting

Although the process consultant is unlikely to make structural interventions such as separating decision phases, these are important, as mentioned above. Agenda setting is helpful to structure the meeting. An agenda helps establish priorities and should include as separate phases problem definition, alternative generation, and alternative evaluation.

The agenda can detail the time to be allocated to each activity and the order in which the group's business should be handled. High-priority items should be dealt with first. The whole group should participate in making the agenda. It can be a powerful tool when used by individuals to secure their own desired outcomes rather than those on which the whole group decides.

After the agenda has been set and the group begins to make decisions and allocate responsibilities, it is important that the content of the meeting be kept on record and that individuals know precisely what their task is. Otherwise, valuable time and energy can be wasted. Dyer (1977) suggests the use of an "action summary." This is a record of the meeting that includes the decisions made, a statement of who is to do what, the date of completion for that work, and the dates on which progress is to be reported.

Techniques for Structuring Group Decision Making

Two techniques for structuring the decision-making process are the Nominal Group Technique (NGT) and the Delphi Technique. Although these techniques are usually considered as alternatives to groups in which members interact with one another, we are here assuming long-term groups, so these techniques are suggested for use during part of the group's history.

The Nominal Group Technique, as described by Van de Ven (1974), is a process designed to assure different processes for each phase of creativity, to balance participation among members, and to incorporate mathematical voting techniques in the aggregation of individual judgments. The techniques operates as follows:

1. silent generation of ideas in writing
2. round-robin feedback from group members to record each idea in a terse phrase on a flip chart
3. discussion of each recorded idea for clarification and evaluation
4. individual voting on priority ideas, with the group decision being mathematically derived through rank-ordering or rating

The Delphi Technique is more complex. It requires outside help but does not require that participants in the decision-making group meet face to face. It is a method for the systematic solicitation and collation of judgments on a particular topic through a set of carefully designed sequential questionnaires interspersed with summarized information and feedback of opinions derived from earlier responses.

The decision as to whether or not to use the Nominal Group Technique, or a mode that allows interaction, will depend on the interaction skills of the group and the characteristics of the decision, the situation, and of the group membership. Groups trained in effective group functioning perform better on decision-making tasks than those not trained (Hall and Williams, 1970).

Thus, the level of performance in the interacting group should be considered before any of the techniques are used. Stumpf, Freedman, and Zand (1979) conducted an experiment testing several combinations of design factors that may be considered for group judgments. They found that in situations requiring originality, interacting groups recommend less effective decisions than do other groups; yet in situations requiring acceptance but not originality, and where there is the possibility of intragroup conflict, nominal groups propose less effective decisions than interacting groups.

All of the techniques mentioned above are applicable to all decision-making groups. Additional difficulties, however, are inherent in decision making under uncertainty. Mathematical programming for multicriteria decision making has been developed and includes some interesting methods for having computers increase man's limited information-processing capacities and for making the qualitative quantitative. As Ackoff (1971) points out, "The elimination of every qualitative aspect of decision making is logically and methodologically impossible, but what is qualitative at one time is always subject to quantification at a later time" (p. 22).

MATHEMATICAL TECHNIQUES FOR DEALING WITH UNCERTAINTY

At the simplest level, the tool of a decision tree, or its close cousin, the preference tree (Tversky and Sattath, 1979), is helpful in modeling a problem, showing where information is known or where it is missing and may be needed, and per-

Figure 1.   The Decision Tree

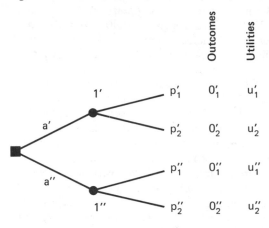

mitting simultaneous comparisons of alternatives. An example of this technique can be seen in Figure 1.

Here the □ is the decision node, under the control of the decision maker, and 0 is chance node, outcomes from which are unknown. The choice is between a' and a''. a' will result in $0'_1$ with a probability of p'_1, or in $0'_2$ with a probability p'_2 (Keeney and Raiffa, 1976). Of course in real uncertain decisions, all probabilities and consequences are not known, and the utilities or values associated with them are hard to determine. This method of modeling the decision nevertheless clarifies the choices under consideration and emphasizes the probabilistic nature of the problem so that the necessity for some quantification can be underlined for those who resist it (Keen, 1977). It shows where there is control and where there is high risk, and where information is and is not available. It gives some idea of the value of obtaining information and provides a simultaneous view of alternatives. The view or utilities associated with each consequence can be discussed if numerical values cannot be calculated.

The mathematical techniques developed by management scientists aid the decision-making process by helping to overcome behavioral limitations. One such method provides the decision makers with outcome alternatives and requests information on tradeoffs. Another keeps the feasible set of solutions down by eliminating solutions not as good as others with respect to objectives stated at the beginning. However, these methods are experimental (Keen, 1977) and can lead to computational headaches as the enormous number of variables and probabilities are considered.

Scenario Construction

Oxenfeldt, Miller, and Dickinson (1978) postulate that, given the changing environment and evolving values associated with uncertainty, mathematical techniques may be inappropriate. Other mechanisms, such as scenario writing about possible future outcomes, may be more helpful for speculating about the future. Scenario construction involves assuming that a certain outcome will occur and predicting in detail the results of such an outcome.

We suggest that scenario construction improves when decision makers view outside organizations as sets of standard operating procedures or, alternatively, as sets of political bargainers rather than as a single rational decision maker (Allison, 1971). Decisions in other organizations are, after all, often also made by groups who experience all the difficulties of achieving optimal decisions in the group setting.

Ackoff (1971) suggests that there should be not only one scenario of the future, but several alternative projections based on the different actions that organizations can take. These could include a projection based on an extrapolation of current trends; a "reactive" projection, where either no action by the organization or action only in response to crisis is assumed; and a "wishful" projection based on the assumption that an organization can and will "make things happen."

Although scenario construction is not a mathematical technique, it explicitly takes the uncertainty of the future into consideration, and its accuracy can be greatly enhanced with the use of mathematical forecasting tools.

Summary

Prescriptions for aiding groups in decision making can be only tentative. It is suggested that the group outline the problem and alternatives gen-erated, as well as the consequences and some estimate of the probability of their occurrence. In the process of aggregating probability estimates, the group will rectify some of the individual errors associated with forming these estimates. Once alternatives and probability estimates are calculated and any new information assimilated, the group must choose among alternatives. The choice is facilitated by some quantification of values and goals and by comparison of alternatives against those goals.

Decision makers need as much information as time and personnel permit about relevant portions of the environment and the organization. In addition, extensive information about the opinions, feelings, and goals of group members is required. Also, an aggregation of opinions will be superior if high weights are not given solely to the opinions of individuals with organizational power and status but also those of individuals with the expertise and resources relevant to the problem.

Groups can improve their skill in making decisions by using techniques to broaden the scope of information examined and to weight the opinions of group members in some systematic fashion. The reader should keep in mind the tentative nature of the results obtained by researchers investigating the techniques discussed in this paper. The proper use of many of these techniques is not fully understood. We do know that whatever techniques groups use, there is a limit to improvement in group decision making per se. There is, however, no limit to the benefits the organization may receive from decision making by groups.

AN ORGANIZATIONAL PERSPECTIVE

The Limits to Improvement in Group Decision Making

Decisions cannot always be correct. Under conditions of uncertainty, judgments are probabilistic. Inherent in probabilistic judgments is the possibility that events whose probable occurrence is predicted may not occur. Under such circumstances, judgments based on their occurrence will be incorrect.

In real-life organizational settings, we do not have a control group whose different decision about the same problem might let us evaluate the quality of a decision by another group. Is a decision that leads to a ghastly consequence necessarily a bad decision? It might not be; it might have been the best possible decision under difficult circumstances. We cannot make retrospective judgments about what might have been the best way of organizing or the best way to weight individual judgments.

Defining the "best" decision is always problematic. The following facts illustrate just a few problems. Economic models do not take into account what Koopmans (1964) strongly suggests is a highly valued outcome—the ability to postpone a choice. Likewise, cost-benefit analysis perhaps should compute not average costs and benefits but added costs and benefits, so as to encompass consideration of the organization's fixed costs. Time is a valuable commodity, and the search for and examination of information takes up time and effort. Organization members may be better used elsewhere. The marginal cost of additional time and information versus the benefit of a better decision must be considered. Finally, there is the problem of aggregating individual values and attendant utilities. This issue of aggregation when group decisions are made has received a good deal of attention from decision and value theorists and economists, but it is generally felt to be an unresolved problem within the classical framework (Minas and Ackoff, 1964).

Rather than focusing pessimistically on the difficulty experienced by individuals and more acutely by groups when making decisions about complex and uncertain problems, we will examine the important beneficial functions of decision making in groups. There are several such benefits both for individual group members and for the organization of which the group forms an integral part.

Benefits to Organization Members

Being a member of a group provides a variety of outcomes that are valued by individuals. Perceived benefits range from having needs for security and friendship met to gaining power and visibility. To the extent that these outcomes are not available elsewhere, they will enhance the attractiveness of the group for its members. In addition, the information that can be obtained from others in the group is valuable. Over time, individuals can learn a great deal from one another. Finally, as mentioned above, sharing decision making with others eases the individual's workload and lightens the responsibility for major decisions. The stress involved in making major decisions alone might contribute to poor decision making.

Benefits to the Organization

The advantages for the organization of having stable, formal groups with representation from several areas are enormous. Group meetings provide an arena for the interrelated functions of communication, coordination, and control.

Communication. In meetings, group members exchange valuable information about their own particular areas within the organization. This information may range from a discussion of present problems to anticipated future directions in strategy, resource availability, manpower, product development, and so on. Accessibility to this information not only helps groups make decisions but also enhances coordination among the various areas of a complex modern organization. Another advantage of group meetings is that information imparted there need be given only once and need not be repeated several times in several places.

In addition to being a forum for the distribution of information, group meetings are a place where acquaintances or even friends are made. An informal communication network develops from such friendships. This network is likely to facilitate problem solving in the future, when formal, hierarchical information channels can be bypassed in favor of a simple telephone call or visit. It has been shown that individuals who communicate about task-related issues enhance their own as well as organizational productivity (Roberts and O'Reilly, 1979; Tushman, 1977).

Group meetings provide not only an opportunity to share information and lay the groundwork for future information-sharing but also an arena for the dissemination and comprehension of the organization's mission. This understanding should emerge as the group discusses its goals and priorities. Knowledge by organization members of the central goals of the organization may have a valuable side effect. It results in greater congruence among the outcomes valued by group members in reference to decisions that affect the organization and hence eases the problem of aggregating the different values held by individual members.

Coordination. As organizational environments become increasingly turbulent and as the number of professional specializations proliferates within the organization, the need for coordination among areas of the organization increases (Lawrence and Lorsch, 1967). The interdependence of technical and functional specialists has created a need for some mechanisms by which information from various sources can be brought to bear on general organizational problems. Group meetings of specialists from various areas serves as an excellent formal method of coordination.

Once a decision is made, group meetings serve to monitor the implementation of the decision in the various areas of the organization. Thus, the fourth phase of decision making, implementation, is performed better than it could be by any one individual.

Control. Group meetings provide an opportunity for members to meet face-to-face and evaluate one another in action. Individuals can be observed in situations where they have to think in an orderly manner and perhaps answer difficult questions "on their feet." Group meetings might give a manager a better idea of whom he or she wants to send out to meet a client or give a presentation. The opportunity to see employees "in action" in public does not occur in one-on-one discussions.

In addition to the informal evaluation of performance and potential that goes on in group meetings, the fact that members are present when important decisions are formulated increases the

likelihood of their correct and successful implementation. Typically, when one individual solves a problem, he or she still has the task of persuading other organization members that his or her decision is correct. When groups solve such problems, a greater number of persons accept and feel responsible for making the solution work. In most cases, participation in making decisions also increases commitment to their implementation (Coch and French, 1948). The reason seems to be that participation in a decision increases the individual's "felt ownership."

Summary

The functions of communication, coordination, and control that are served by group decision making may well be more beneficial for the organization in the long term than are optimal decisions themselves. The best decision will prove inadequate if not carried out properly, and a poor decision may prove successful if effected by individuals who are knowledgeable about and committed to organizational goals. While the process of group decision making may be substantially improved, it may be most appropriate to take a broader focus and concentrate on capitalizing on the group as an arena for communication, coordination, and control. It is best not to view the group in isolation but in the context of the organization. Only then can such activities as "tangential discussions," which on the group level appear to inhibit the number of alternatives developed, be seen from the organizational perspective. For example, a tangential discussion may provide information for group members about another department or about how a colleague stands up under pressure.

We suggest that this kind of communication, coordination, and control have at least as much value as the benefit that accrues when the group generates one more alternative. These three functions lead to successful implementation of decisions and flexible response to rapidly changing environments. As one businessman observed, "Obviously there are meetings that waste time. But it's a mistake to say that meetings are a waste of time in business. Meetings *are* business" (cited by Meyer, 1979, p. 102).

REFERENCES

Ackoff, R. L. Frontiers of management science. *TIMS: The Bulletin*, 1971, *1*, 19–24.

Allison, G. T. *Essence of decision: Explaining the Cuban missile crisis.* Boston: Little, Brown, 1971.

Argyris, C. Interpersonal barriers to decision making. *Harvard Business Review*, March–April, 1966.

Asch, S. *Social psychology.* Englewood Cliffs, N.J.: Prentice-Hall, 1952.

Bion, W. R. *Experiences in groups.* London: Tavistock, 1961.

Burke, W. W., and Hornstein, H. A. *The social technology of organization development.* La Jolla, Calif.: University Associates, 1972.

Coch, L., and French, J. R. P., Jr. Overcoming resistance to change. *Human Relations*, 1948, *1*, 512–532.

Cohen, M. D., March, J. G., and Olsen, J. P. A garbage can model of organizational choice. *Administrative Science Quarterly*, 1972, *17*, 1–25.

Collins, B. E., and Guetzkow, H. *A social psychology of group processes for decision-making.* New York: Wiley, 1964.

Delbecq, A. L., Van de Ven, A. H., and Gustafson, D. H. *Group techniques for programming planning: A guide to nominal and Delphi processes.* Glenview, Ill.: Scott, Foresman, 1975.

Dyer, W. G. *Team building: Issues and alternatives.* Reading, Mass.: Addison-Wesley, 1977.

Edwards, W. The theory of decision making. *Psychological Bulletin*, 1954, *51*, 380–417.

Festinger, L. A theory of social comparison processes. *Human Relations*, 1954, *7*, 117–140.

Friedman, B. M. Optimal expectations and the extreme information assumptions of "rational expectations" macromodels. *Journal of Monetary Economics*, 1979, *5*, 23–41.

Hackman, J. R., and Morris, C. G. Group tasks, group interaction process, and group performance effectiveness: A review and proposed integration. In L. Berkowitz (ed.). *Advances in Experimental Social Psychology* (Vol. 8). New York: Academic Press, 1975.

Hoffman, L. R. Applying experimental research on group problem solving to organizations. *Journal of Applied Behavioral Science*, 1979, *15*, 375–391.

Hoffman, L. R., and Clark, M. M. Participation and influence in problem solving groups. In L. R. Hoffman. *The group problem solving process: Studies of a valence model.* New York: Praeger, 1979.

Hoffman, L. R., and Maier, M. R. F. Valence in the adoption of solutions by problem solving groups:

Concept, method, and results. *Journal of Abnormal and Social Psychology*, 1964, *69*, 264–271.

Janis, I. L. Groupthink. *Psychology Today*, November, 1971, 43–46, 74–76.

———. *Victims of groupthink.* Boston: Houghton-Mifflin, 1972.

Janis, I. L., and Mann, L. *Decision making: A psychological analysis of conflict, choice and commitment.* New York: Free Press, 1977.

Keen, P. G. W. The evolving concept of optimality. *Management Science*, 1977, *4*, 3.

Keeney, R. L., and Raiffa, H. *Decisions with multiple objectives: preference and value tradeoffs.* New York: Wiley, 1976.

Koopmans, T. C. On flexibility of future preference. In M. W. Shelly II and Glenn L. Bryan (eds.). *Human judgments and optimality.* New York: Wiley, 1964, 243–254.

Lawrence, P. R., and Lorsch, J. R. *Organization and environment.* Homewood, Ill.: Irwin, 1967.

Lindblom, C. The science of "muddling through." *Public Administration Review*, 1959, *19*, 78–88.

March, J. G., and Simon, H. A. *Organizations.* New York: Wiley, 1958.

Meyer, H. E. The meeting-goer's lament. *Fortune Magazine*, October 22, 1979, 94–102.

Miller, G. A. The magical number seven, plus or minus two. *Psychological Review*, 1956, *63*, 81–97.

Minas, J. S., and Ackoff, R. L. Individual and collective value judgments. In M. W. Shelly II and Glenn L. Bryan (eds.). *Human Judgments and Optimality.* New York: Wiley, 1964, 351–359.

Mintzberg, H. *The nature of managerial work.* New York: Harper & Row, 1973.

Moscovici, S., and Zavalloni, M. The group as polarizer of attitudes. *Journal of Personality and Social Psychology*, 1969, *12*, 125–135.

Nadler, D. A. *Feedback and organizational development: Using data-based methods.* Reading, Mass.: Addison-Wesley, 1977.

Newcomb, T. M. *Social psychology.* New York: Dryden, 1954.

Osborn, A. F. *Applied imagination* (rev. ed.). New York: Scribner's, 1957.

Oxenfeldt, A. R., Miller, D. W., and Dickinson, R. A. *A basic approach to executive decision making.* New York: AMACOM, 1978.

Pfeffer, J. *Organizational design.* Arlington Heights, Ill.: AHM Publishing, 1978.

———. Management as symbolic action: The creation and maintenance of organizational paradigms. In Larry L. Cummings and Barry M. Staw (eds.). *Research in Organizational Behavior*, Vol. 3. Greenwich, Conn.: Jai Press, 1980.

Pounds, W. F. The process of problem finding. *Industrial Management Review*, 1969, *11*, 1–19.

Roberts, K. H., and O'Reilly, C. A. III. Some correlates of communication roles in organizations. *Academy of Management Journal*, 1979, *22*, 42–57.

Salancik, G. R. Commitment and the control of organizational behavior and belief. In Barry M. Staw and Gerald R. Salancik (eds.). *New directions in organizational behavior*. Chicago: St. Clair Press, 1977.

Schachter, S. Deviation, rejection and communication. *Journal of Abnormal and Social Psychology*, 1951, *46*, 190–207.

Schein, E. H. Process consultation: Its role in organizational development. Reading, Mass.: Addison-Wesley, 1969.

Simon, H. A. *Administrative behavior.* New York: Free Press, 1945.

———. Theories of decision making in economics and behavioral sciences. *American Economic Review*, 1959, *49*, 253–283.

———. Rational decision making in business organizations. *American Economic Review*, 1979, *69*, 493–513.

Steinbruner, J. D. *The cybernetic theory of decision: New dimensions of political analysis.* Princeton, N.J.: Princeton University Press, 1974.

Steiner, I. D. *Group process and productivity.* New York: Academic Press, 1972.

Stumpf, S. A., Freedman, R. D., and Zand, D. E. Judgmental decisions: A study of interactions among group membership, group functioning, and the decision situation. *Academy of Management Journal*, 1979, *22*, 765–782.

Tetlock, P. E. Identifying victims of groupthink from public statements of decision makers. *Journal of Personality and Social Psychology*, 1979, *37*, 1314–1324.

Tushman, M. L. A political approach to organizations: A review and rationale. *Academy of Management Review*, 1977, *2*, 206–216.

———. Work characteristics and subunit communication structure: A contingency analysis. *Administrative Science Quarterly*, 1979, *24*, 82–98.

Tversky, A. and Sattath, S. Preference trees. *Psychological Review*, 1979, *86*, 542–573.

Van de Ven, A. H. *Group decision making and effectiveness: an experimental study.* Comparative Administration Research Institute, 1974.

Zand, D. E. Trust and managerial problem solving. *Administrative Science Quarterly*, 1972, *17*, 229–239.

III.B
Leadership

17

The supervisor as motivator:
His influence on employee
performance and satisfaction

Edwin A. Locke

It is widely recognized that supervisors can influence the "motivation" of their subordinates. However, the precise nature and mechanism of this influence (and its limitations) have not been clearly identified in the literature.

There are two interrelated aspects of motivation that must be considered in this context: satisfaction with the job (and supervisor) and work performance. Let us first consider how a supervisor can influence employee satisfaction.

THE SUPERVISOR AND SATISFACTION

An individual's degree of satisfaction with his job reflects the degree to which he believes (explicitly or implicitly) that it fulfills or allows the fulfill-

Source: Reprinted by permission of the publisher, from *Managing for Accomplishment,* edited by B. M. Bass, R. Cooper, and J. A. Haas (Lexington, Mass.: Lexington Books, D. C. Heath and Company), Copyright © 1970, D. C. Heath and Company.

Author's note: Preparation of this paper was facilitated by Grant No. 10542 from the American Institute for Research.

ment of his job values (Locke, 1969a). It follows that a supervisor can influence employee satisfaction by facilitating or blocking subordinate value attainment. There are two broad categories of job values over which a supervisor may have some control.[1]

1. Task values. Individuals have different degrees of intrinsic interest in different task activities. If a supervisor has any options with respect to task assignment, he can facilitate satisfaction by assigning workers tasks which they enjoy doing. Within limits he may even allow or promote restructuring of the job to increase its interest to the worker.

Furthermore, most employees have implicit or explicit performance goals in their work (quantity, quality, time limits, deadlines, quotas, budgets, etc.). Work goal achievement has been found repeatedly to be a major source of satisfaction on the job (Friedlander, 1964; Herzberg, 1966; Hoppock, 1935; Wernimont, 1966). A supervisor can either help or hinder his subordinates in the pursuit of their work goals and will affect their satisfaction accordingly.

A study of Hahn of several hundred Air Force officers found that when actions of superiors were judged to be responsible for causing a "good day on the job" these actions entailed work goal facilitation 33% of the time. When the actions of superiors were seen as causing a "bad day on the job," it was perceived to be caused by work goal blockage or hindrance 56% of the time.[2]

There is a crucial respect in which a supervisor has more *potential* for causing employee dissatisfaction than for causing satisfaction, as implied by the above data. A supervisor can help an employee attain his work goals but he cannot attain them for him. The subordinate himself must be at least *one* of the agents responsible for the accomplishment of his own work. However, the converse is not necessarily true. A supervisor can hinder or prevent goal attainment regardless of the actions of his subordinates—such as by refusing to give him the permission, or time, or facilities, money, helpers, authority, etc., needed to achieve them.

Similarly a supervisor can allow a subordinate to work on tasks which the subordinate finds intrinsically interesting but he cannot create interests himself. However, a supervisor can prevent an employee from working on tasks which interest him without the latter's consent or participation.

The above should not be taken as supporting Herzberg's (1966) theory of motivation as it now stands. Herzberg claims that supervision can cause only dissatisfaction with the job whereas task factors such as achievement can only cause satisfaction. Herzberg's supporting data, however, are virtually meaningless since his classification system confuses *events* (what happened) with *agents* (who made it happen). When incidents reported as causing satisfaction and dissatisfaction on the job are classified separately as to agent and event, it is found that the *same class of events* (namely, task-related events, such as achievement and failure) are seen as the main cause of *both* satisfaction and dissatisfaction, but that *different agents* are judged to be predominantly responsible for these events. The self is typically given credit for good day events (successes) while others (supervisors) are usually blamed for bad day events (failures). It must be added that the latter relationship is only statistical. Some individuals do blame themselves for failures and give others (partial) credit for their successes.[3] Furthermore, defensiveness could lead them to underestimate their actual degree of responsibility for failures.

2. Non-task values. A supervisor also administers rewards and punishments for performance, both directly and indirectly. He has direct control, for example, over the giving of praise and recognition for a job well done and of criticism for a poor job. By recommending or criticizing an employee to his own superiors, a supervisor can indirectly affect a subordinate's chances for raises and promotions.

Employees value supervisors who have influence in the organization (Mann and Hoffman, 1960; Pelz, 1952). Influence is what enables a supervisor to gain values for his subordinates from the organization, e.g., raises, promotions, time off, good equipment, better working conditions, etc.

Rosen (1969) found that two of the characteristics which best differentiated between the most and least-liked foremen in a furniture factory were the ability to "get things for his men" and to "organize the work." Since these workers were on a piece-rate incentive, there is little doubt that money was one thing a good foreman could help his men to get, especially if he knew how to organize the work.

There is an interconnection between task and non-task values in that the former can be a means to attaining the latter. By helping his subordinates attain high production, solve problems, and do competent work, a supervisor can help them make high earnings and gain promotions.

If an employee sees his supervisor as instrumental in gaining him important job values, he will not only like the job, he will like the supervisor as well. Employees also like supervisors who are "pleasant," "considerate" and "friendly" (Mann and Hoffman, 1960; Rosen, 1969; Vroom, 1964). At first glance these traits might seem to be completely unrelated to the idea of functional utility; but a closer look suggests otherwise. A supervisor may be described as unpleasant and inconsiderate because in the past he has blocked value attainment by subordinates or he projects the kind of personality that *would* do so if given the chance. An unfriendly supervisor is typically one who does not acknowledge or reward work or who unjustly condemns or punishes marginal work or who looks as though he might do these things.

Individuals also like people who are like themselves, with whom they have important traits in common. This too can be interpreted (partly) in functional terms. A supervisor who values the same things as his subordinates, for example, is more likely to be of benefit to them than one whose values are opposite to theirs.

The functional (utility) implications of being pleasant or having values similar to one's subordinates do not exhaust the reasons a supervisor could be liked. Individuals may value each other not only as a means to an end but as ends in themselves. The value in such a case is associated with the person rather than in what he can do for you. One can respond to a supervisor *qua* individual as well as *qua* supervisor.

A discussion of the reasons individuals value those who respond to them as persons is beyond the scope of this paper.[4] Suffice it to say that this principle is probably less crucial to an understanding of supervisor-subordinate relationships than is the principle of functional utility.

THE SUPERVISOR AND PERFORMANCE

A subordinate who likes his supervisor will desire to approach (interact with) him, to seek or take his advice, and/or (within limits) to do favors for him. There is nothing inherent in the fact of liking supervisor, however, that necessarily leads to high production.

A subordinate who dislikes his supervisor will want to avoid him, or persuade him to change his ways, or file a grievance against him or refuse to do favors for him or possibly quit the job altogether. There is nothing inherent in fact of disliking, however, that necessitates low production, although such a reaction is possible (if the employee sees it as an appropriate means of "getting even" with the supervisor and thinks he can get away with it).

In short there is no causal connection—divorced from the individuals' other values, his beliefs and expectations and his understanding of the total job—between satisfaction with the job or supervisor and productivity (for a detailed theoretical discussion of this issue, see Locke, 1969b).

I have argued previously (Locke, 1970) that the most direct motivational determinant of an individual's performance on the job is his specific performance goal or intention (Locke, Cartledge and Knerr, 1970). Let us now discuss the relationship between goals and performance.

GOAL CONTENT AND PERFORMANCE

Goals and values have two major attributes: content and intensity (Rand, 1966). The attribute of content pertains to the *what*, to the nature of the activity or end sought. The attribute of intensity pertains to the *how much*, to the importance of the goal or value in the individual's value hierarchy.

The effects of goal content are most fundamentally directive in nature. This is true with respect to both mental and physical action. If a (normal) individual's purpose is to think about how he will spend his next pay check, he will think of that topic rather than about something else. A man whose goal is to walk across the street will walk there rather than to another location.

This is not to claim that all goals lead to the activity or end specified by the goal. To attain a desired goal successfully an individual must possess sufficient ability and mental health and be given sufficient opportunity. Goal attainment may be prevented by lack of knowledge, capacity or determination on his part, or by external interference. Furthermore, goal conflicts may render efficacious action and efficacious thinking impossible.

Even when action is abortive or unsuccessful, it is typically set in motion and guided by some goal or intention. For example, a person who accidentally hits a shot out of bounds in tennis still intended to hit the ball, even if it did not go where he wanted it to go. Further, the degree of discrepancy between the place he intended to hit the ball and the place he did hit it might be only a matter of inches.

If an individual's goal is long range, or difficult, or complex, he may have to establish a series of *subgoals* and develop a coordinated *plan of action* in order to reach it. The *means* by which a goal can be attained may not be known initially and may have to be discovered. For this reason goals may indirectly stimulate creativity and the seeking of new knowledge. This was illustrated in a study done at General Electric by Stedry and Kay (1964; see also a study by Chaney, 1969). A group of foremen were assigned quantitative production goals with respect to both quantity and quality. Some of these who were assigned difficult goals, rather than simply exhorting their subordinates to work harder, made an effort to discover the causes of and to eliminate unproductive time. The latter procedure generally led to greater performance improvement than the former. A laboratory study by Eagle and Leiter (1964) found that individuals who had an intention to memorize certain materials did so more effectively if they developed a specific learning plan than if they simply "tried" to learn the material.

The pursuit of any goal requires action, whether it be mental or physical, and action requires effort. A second function of goal content, which is necessarily entailed in the directive function, is the *regulation of energy expenditure*. Different goals require different amounts of effort. More energy is required to run the marathon than to walk across the room; more mental concentration is needed to write a book than to write one's name. Typically, a person mobilizes an amount of energy that is appropriate to the perceived difficulty of the goal sought. For instance, Bryan and Locke (1967) found that when people are given different amounts of time to complete the same task, those given the shorter time limits worked faster than those given longer time limits. These authors noted that:

> Because the phenomenon [of adjusting effort level to the perceived difficulty of the task] is so much a part of our everyday life, it is often taken for granted and we do not always think about it consciously. But it can become particularly salient when errors of . . . [judgment] occur. For example, if a weight lifter's weights are secretly replaced by wooden blocks painted to resemble the real weights, he will be likely to jerk [them] right through the ceiling [on his first try] . . . (Bryan and Locke, 1967, p. 259).

Goal importance may also influence direction and level of effort by affecting the individual's degree of commitment to his goal. The greater a man's commitment, the longer he should persist at a task in the face of failure, fatigue and stress.

Most studies of the effect of goals have focused on the relationship of goal content to performance on simple laboratory tasks. (See Locke, 1968a, for a review.) In these tasks, performance could be influenced relatively directly by effort or choice; the acquisition of new knowledge and long range planning were not required. Two categories of studies have stressed the directing function of goals, while two other categories have stressed the energizing as well as the directing effects of goal content. Studies representative of each category are described below:

1. Intentions and response selection. In these studies, typified by the work of Dulany (1962, 1968) and Holmes (1967), subjects had to select (on each trial) one of a number of possible verbal responses and were "rewarded" or "punished" according to their choices. It was found that the individual's intentions with respect to responses were correlated as high as .94 with his actual responses, regardless of the "reinforcements" given for performance.

2. Intentions and task choice. In another group of studies subjects could choose, on each trial, the difficulty of the task they would work on and were offered various monetary incentives for succeeding at their chosen task. Correlations in the .70's and .80's were typically found between intentions with respect to future choices and actual choice distributions regardless of incentive condition (Locke, Bryan and Kendall, 1968).

3. Qualitatively different goals and performance. Two types of studies fall into this category. In one, all subjects worked on the same task but tried to minimize or maximize their scores on different performance dimensions on different trials. The interest was in whether subjects could modify their scores on the various dimensions as intended. Locke and Bryan (1969) found that subjects could lower their scores on two dimensions of automobile driving performance as intended 100% of the time. They also found that subjects committed fewer errors on an addition task when trying to minimize errors than when trying to maximize the number of problems correct.

In the second subcategory of studies only one performance dimension was involved (number of correct answers). Individuals trying to do "as well as possible" on a task were compared to those trying to reach difficult, quantitative goals. Subjects trying for the latter type of goal typically outperformed subjects trying for the former (Locke, 1968a; Mace, 1935). One effect of trying for specific hard goals is to prevent performance from dropping below one's previous best level more often than is the case with the abstract goal of "do your best" (Locke and Bryan, 1966).

4. *Goal level and performance level (output)*. Most studies of the effects of goals have focused on the relationship between the individual's level of aspiration (quantitative goal level) and his performance level on a task. A consistent finding has been that high, difficult goals lead to a higher level of performance than moderate or easy goals. The evidence thus far suggests that, provided the individual has the requisite ability, there is a positive, linear relationship between goal level and performance level (Locke, 1968a). No claim is made that this linear relationship would hold across all possible levels of goal difficulty; some goals are obviously impossible to reach.

Let us now summarize the findings with respect to goals and performance. The results indicate that on simple repetitive tasks goals usually lead to the behavior specified by the goal, or else to outcomes correlated with the intended goal. Goals guide performance by determining the direction or content of mental and/or physical action; as a result they energize action by leading the individual to mobilize the effort necessary to attain the goal.

It should be stressed that the above findings presuppose that the individual has really *accepted* (is actually committed to) the goal(s) in question. This issue will be discussed further below.

Considerable research evidence indicates that the effects of external incentives on action depend on the goal and intentions individuals set in response to them. For it has been found in a number of laboratory studies that: (a) when incentives do affect behavior, they also affect goals and intentions; (b) when differential goal-setting is controlled or partialled out, there is no relationship of incentive condition to choice behavior or to level of performance; and (c) partialling out or controlling incentive differences does not vitiate the relationship between goals and performance.

These findings are most well documented with respect to three external incentives: *money* (Locke, Bryan and Kendall, 1968); *feedback* regarding overall task performance ("knowledge of results," Locke, 1967, 1968b; Locke and Bryan, 1968, 1969; Locke, Cartledge and Koeppel, 1968); and so-called *verbal reinforcement* (Dulany, 1962, 1968; Holmes, 1967). There is some documentation with respect to three other incentives: *instructions* (Eagle, 1967; Locke, Cartledge and Koeppel, 1968); *time limits* (Bryan and Locke, 1967); and *participation* (Locke, 1968a; Meyer, Kay and French, 1965). Experimental evidence is still lacking for incentives such as competition, and praise and reproof. (See Locke, 1968a, for a theoretical analysis of these incentives.)

GOAL COMMITMENT AND PERFORMANCE

Very few studies have explored either the determinants or the effects of goal commitment. Theoretically, strength of goal commitment should be a function of the importance of the goal in the individual's value hierarchy. The importance of goal attainment should be a function of the importance of success and efficacy as ends in themselves and of the importance of the other values to which goal attainment leads (money, promotion) and/or of the disvalues which it avoids (lack of money, being fired, losing a promotion, etc.).

One procedure that may promote goal commitment is *participation* in the goal-setting process. A possible explanation for this is that making an overt agreement to strive for or attain a certain goal engages a value not previously engaged. It implies an overt test of one's *integrity:* (loyalty to one's stated values in action). Participation may also allow subordinates to choose tasks or methods of work which interest and challenge them to a greater extent than would be the case if supervisors made assignments on their own.

HOW THE SUPERVISOR INFLUENCES GOAL-SETTING

The implication of the above is that in order for a supervisor to influence the job performance of his subordinates, he must implicitly or explicitly influence the goals they set and/or their commitment to them. There are at least four ways he can try to do this, differing in degree of directness:

1. *Instructions.* The simplest and most direct method is to tell the subordinate what is expected of him on the job, not only with respect to the content of the work but also with respect to the speed or proficiency level desired.

The effect of instructions on performance will depend upon their content and upon whether or not the employee *accepts* them. When goals assigned by a supervisor (or experimenter) are judged to be unreasonable or impossible, they may be rejected by the individual and easier ones (overtly or covertly) substituted in their place. (See Stedry, 1960; Stedry and Kay, 1964.) Or barring this, the individual may leave the situation (e.g., job) altogether.

Whether or not an employee accepts an assigned goal will depend upon other factors as well; whether he believes the demands to be morally legitimate; whether he sees them as just in the context of his ability and the nature of the job; whether the goal is congruent with his personal preferences; his desire to help or hurt the supervisor; the anticipated outcomes of compliance and noncompliance; the amount of "pressure" exerted, etc.

A study at General Electric by Miller (1965) found that direct instructions to production workers to improve the quality of their work sometimes resulted in an initial improvement in performance; but this improvement was not maintained unless it was made clear that punishments (loss of income) would be administered for noncompliance with this request. In other words, the instructions had to be backed up by (the threat of) sanctions for them to be effective.

2. *Participation.* Rather than assigning goals to employees a supervisor may let his subordinates participate in the goal-setting process. It was mentioned earlier that such a procedure can enhance goal commitment by engaging the employee's integrity and his personal interests.

It must be stressed, however, that simply using the *method* of participation does not guarantee either increased job satisfaction or higher productivity as is often implied by advocates of the "human relations" approach to motivation. Its outcome will depend on such factors as: (a) the particular values of the employees (whether they want to participate); (b) the nature of the job (size of work group; need for rapid decisions); and (c) the content of the participation sessions. (The first factor is discussed in Vroom, 1964.)

With respect to the last point, a close examination of several experimental studies of participation by Locke (1968a) revealed that employees in the "participation" conditions were typically urged to aim for higher production goals than they had previously whereas employees in the "control" conditions received no such request. In other studies, supervisors of participation groups were given special training designed to correct their weaknesses and deficiencies (Chaney, 1969). In a recent field study Meyer, Kay and French (1965) found that the goals employees set (or failed to set) during conferences with their supervisors had far more influence on subsequent performance than participation as such.

3. *Rewards and punishments.* Money is the most widely used incentive in industry. Not only is it an incentive to take a job or to switch jobs, it may be an incentive to perform competently on the job. The effectiveness of money in motivating effective performance will depend on such things as: (a) how the incentive system is structured; (b) what the employee believes it is given (or withheld) for; and (c) the degree to which he values money (in comparison to other rewards).

Many years ago F. W. Taylor (1911) argued that ordinary piece-rate incentives were not optimal for increasing production because workers often failed to set their output goals as high as they were capable of achieving. A key element of Taylor's Scientific Management system was to assign workers specific (and high) production quotas and to make monetary bonuses (and remaining on the job) contingent upon their attaining these quotas. Locke, Bryan and Kendall (1968) found this method to produce higher output than offering piece-rate incentives alone in some recent laboratory studies.

Other studies have shown that the effectiveness of monetary incentives depends upon the degree to which workers believe that high effort and high performance will "pay-off" in higher earnings and on the degree to which they value money (Georgopoulos, Mahoney and Jones, 1957; Porter and Lawler, 1968). Dalton (in Whyte, 1955) found that incentive pay was not very effective for workers who valued the approval of their coworkers (which was contingent upon moderate to low production) more than maximizing earnings.

Praise and criticism are also commonly used incentives, but their effects on subsequent performance are far from simple. (See the review article by Kennedy and Willcatt, 1964.) A crucial determinant of the effect of praise is the subordinate's interpretation of what it *means*. If he interprets it to mean that his performance is adequate and he sees no other values to be gained by increasing production, it may be an incentive to maintain his present level of production. If the employee understands it to mean that if he keeps up the good work, he may be promoted, and he values promotion, it may encourage him to work even harder. If praise is seen as being insincere or manipulative in its intent, it may have no effect at all (or a negative effect) on performance.

The effects of criticism on subsequent performance also depend upon how the employee interprets it. For example, an individual may deliberately refrain from performance improvement after being criticized because it would be an implicit admission that the criticism was justified—which admission would threaten his self-esteem. Meyer, Kay and French (1965) found criticism by supervisors to inhibit subsequent performance improvement by subordinates because it produced defensiveness rather than constructive goal-setting.

Even if a man believed criticism to be justified (in the sense that performance was not up to the minimum requirements of the job), he would become apathetic if he believed that further improvement was totally impossible. Many individuals have implicit deterministic premises (to the effect

that certain abilities are impossible to acquire or that certain things are not open to their understanding or that certain personality traits or emotional reactions are beyond their control). Such premises can severely undercut a man's motivation to persist in the face of difficulty and failure.

Under certain conditions, criticism will spur a man on to greater efforts. The necessary conditions for such an effect are not yet known but they would no doubt include: (a) the individual's belief that his performance was, in fact, inadequate; (b) his conviction that he can do better; and (c) his desire to improve.

4. Setting an example. Some results reported by Cooper[5] suggest a relatively indirect way that supervisors may influence subordinate goals. He found positive correlations between the degree to which supervisors were rated by their superiors as "task oriented" and high work quality and low absence on the part of subordinates. Although several interpretations of these correlations are possible, the one suggested by Cooper is that employees implicitly adopted (some of) the work attitudes and standards of their supervisors.

It is not difficult to imagine how this might happen. A supervisor who comes late, who is frequently absent, who takes numerous coffee breaks, who is careless in his work and unconcerned with its outcome could not help but convey to a subordinate that the work is not very important, that he does not value it, and that low standards of performance are acceptable. (The employee may adopt such standards without any explicit purpose to do so, in the same way that a student may absorb or adopt the values of his teachers.)

Similarly, a supervisor who loves his job, who sets himself high standards and works to achieve them, who creates an atmosphere of dedication to hard work and high standards may help instill similar attitudes in his subordinates.

SATISFACTION WITH SUPERVISION AND PRODUCTIVITY

The foregoing discussion indicated that high production (ability and knowledge being equal) was the result of setting high or hard work goals. It follows that the supervisor with high producing subordinates (ability being equal) will be the one whose subordinates set and attain high goals.

A supervisor may try to achieve high production by direct instructions backed up by threats of punishment. If employees see no short-run alternative to accepting hard goals, high production may result. But such high production would be accompanied by low satisfaction with the job and with supervision to the degree that: (a) employees fail to achieve fully their hard goals or goal attainment fails to gain them just extrinsic rewards; (b) supervisors interfere with their task performance, and/or (c) the supervisors' pressures are perceived as excessive and/or illegitimate. In the long run, of course, such actions as the above may lead to increased absences, grievances and turnover, depending on the workers' other values and the job market (Locke, 1970).

Alternatively, a supervisor could offer positive incentives (monetary bonuses, recognition, increased responsibility) to employees who reached (or approached) high work goals. If high goals were set as a result, high production could occur. To the extent that the supervisor was perceived as helping his subordinates to achieve these goals and as giving just rewards for success, he would be liked. In this case, production and satisfaction with supervision would both be high.

An individual could also set high work goals on his own and not interact with his supervisor at all. If the person preferred to be left alone, high production would be accompanied by indifference toward the supervisor.

Many other patterns are possible. A supervisor might reward his subordinates for low production. If they actually set low goals as a result and personally valued low productivity, high satisfaction with supervision would accompany low production. Or, if a supervisor prevented his employees from achieving their work goals through interference and harassment, and then penalized them for their failure, low satisfaction and low production would result.

To repeat, there is no direct causal relationship between satisfaction with supervision (on the job) and productivity. The two effects are the results of different causes. Production level, to the degree that it is affected by motivation, depends (in the short run) upon the production goal the individual is actually trying for, *regardless of*

how or why he chose that goal. (The reasons why an employee has a particular goal, of course, have long range implications, since these factors determine how susceptible the goal is to change and under what conditions.) Satisfaction with supervision depends (in the short run) upon the degree to which the supervisor is perceived as achieving or helping the employee to achieve his work and other goals *regardless of the particular content (level) of these goals.*[6]

Satisfaction is an outcome of action and an incentive to further action; thus it fulfills a crucial motivational function. But a man's emotional reactions do not determine the content of his values, or his goals, or his knowledge, or his thinking (Locke, 1970).

CONCLUSION

A supervisor can contribute in important ways to an individual's satisfaction and his motivation to produce. But there is a fundamental respect in which he cannot "motivate" an employee. To perform adequately on a job, an individual must choose to pursue values; he must gain the knowledge needed to perform the work; he must set goals; he must expend effort. A supervisor can help fulfill an employee's desires but he cannot provide him with desires; he can offer him new knowledge or the chance to gain new knowledge but he cannot force him to learn; he can assign goals to a worker but he cannot compel him to accept those goals. In short, a supervisor's influence is *limited*; what he can accomplish depends not simply on his own actions but on the values, knowledge, and goals of his subordinates.

To put the matter more generally, man is not a passive responder to external stimulation but an active agent. He is not an effect of the actions of others but a cause in his own right.

NOTES

1. These categories are discussed in more detail in Locke (1970).

2. These percentages were computed from unpublished data supplied by Clifford P. Hahn of the American Institutes for Research.

3. Much of this data has been gathered and analyzed by Joseph Schneider of the University of Maryland in partial fulfillment of his Master's degree. The unpublished data of Hahn, some of which were referred to above, yielded similar results.

4. The basic psychological principle involved here was first discussed, to the author's knowledge, in N. Branden's "Self-esteem and Romantic Love," *The Objectivist*, 1967, VI, No. 12, 1–8.

5. R. Cooper, "Task-oriented Leadership and Subordinate Response," in B. M. Bass, R. Cooper, & J. A. Haas (Eds.) *Managing for accomplishment.* Lexington, Mass.: Heath-Lexington, 1970.

6. One important qualification must be made to this statement. If an individual's goals and values are irrational (anti-life) or if he has value conflicts, he will not derive the same quality or duration or intensity of pleasure from attaining them as compared with rational values. This issue is discussed in Locke (1969a) based on Rand (1964).

REFERENCES

Bryan, J. F., & Locke, E. A. Parkinson's law as a goal-setting phenomenon. *Organizational Behavior and Human Performance*, 1967, **2**, 258–275.

Chaney, F. B. Employee participation in manufacturing job design. *Human Factors*, 1969, **11**, 101–106.

Dulany, D. E., Jr. The place of hypotheses and intentions: An analysis of verbal control in verbal conditioning. In C. W. Eriksen (Ed.), *Behavior and awareness*, Durham, N.C.: Duke University Press, 1962, 102–129.

Dulany, D. E., Jr. Awareness, rules and propositional control: A confrontation with S-R behavior theory. In D. Horton and T. Dixon (Eds.), *Verbal behavior and general behavior theory*, Englewood Cliffs, N.J.: Prentice-Hall, 1968, 340–348.

Eagle, M. N. The effect of learning strategies upon free recall. *American Journal of Psychology*, 1967, **80**, 421–425.

Eagle, M., & Leiter, E. Recall and recognition in intentional and incidental learning. *Journal of Experimental Psychology*, 1964, **68**, 58–63.

Friedlander, F. Job characteristics as satisfiers and dissatisfiers. *Journal of Applied Psychology*, 1964, **48**, 388–392.

Georgopoulos, B. S., Mahoney, G. M., & Jones, N. W. A path-goal approach to productivity, *Journal of Applied Psychology*, 1957, **41**, 345–353.

Herzberg, F. *Work and the nature of man.* Cleveland: World Publishing Company, 1966.

Holmes, D. S. Verbal conditioning or problem solving and cooperation? *Journal of Experimental Research in Personality*, 1967, **2**, 289–294.

Hoppock, R. *Job satisfaction.* New York: Harper, 1935.

Kennedy, W. A., & Willcatt, H. C. Praise and blame as incentives. *Psychological Bulletin*, 1964, **62**, 323–332.

Locke, E. A. The motivational effects of knowledge of results: Knowledge or goal-setting? *Journal of Applied Psychology*, 1967, **51**, 324–329.

Locke, E. A. Toward a theory of task motivation and incentives. *Organizational Behavior and Human Performance*, 1968, **3**, 157–189. (a)

Locke, E. A. The effects of knowledge of results, feedback in relation to standards and goals on reaction time performance. *American Journal of Psychology*, 1968, **81**, 566–574. (b)

Locke, E. A. What is job satisfaction? *Organizational Behavior and Human Performance*, 1969, **4**, 309–336. (a)

Locke, E. A. Job satisfaction and job performance: A theoretical analysis. Unpublished manuscript. Washington, D.C.: American Institutes for Research, 1969. (b)

Locke, E. A. Studies of the relationship between satisfaction, goal-setting, and performance. *Organizational Behavior and Human Performance*, 1970, **5**, 135–158.

Locke, E. A., & Bryan, J. F. Cognitive aspects of psychomotor performance: The effects of performance goals on level of performance. *Journal of Applied Psychology*, 1966, **50**, 286–291.

Locke, E. A., & Bryan, J. F. Goal-setting as a determinant of the effect of knowledge of score on performance. *American Journal of Psychology*, 1968, **81**, 398–406.

Locke, E. A., & Bryan, J. F. Knowledge of score and goal difficulty as determinants of work rate. *Journal of Applied Psychology*, 1969, **53**, 59–65.

Locke, E. A., Bryan, J. F., & Kendall, L. M. Goals and intentions as mediators of the effects of monetary incentives on behavior. *Journal of Applied Psychology*, 1968, **52**, 104–121.

Locke, E. A., Cartledge, N., & Koeppel, J. The motivational effects of knowledge of results: A goal-setting phenomenon? *Psychological Bulletin*, 1968, **70**, 474–485.

Locke, E. A., Cartledge, N., & Knerr, C. Studies of the relationship between satisfaction, goal-setting and performance. *Organizational Behavior and Human Performance*, 1970, **5**, 135–158.

Mace, C. A. Incentives: Some experimental studies. Industrial Health Research Board (Great Britain), 1935, Report No. 72.

Mann, F. C., & Hoffman, L. R. *Automation and the worker.* New York: Holt, 1960.

Meyer, H. H., Kay, E., & French, J. R. P., Jr. Split roles in performance appraisal. *Harvard Business Review,* 1965, **43,** 123–129.

Miller, L. The use of knowledge of results in improving the performance of hourly operators. General Electric Co., Behavioral Research Service, 1965.

Pelz, D. C. Influence: A key to effective leadership in the first-line supervisor. *Personnel,* 1952, **3,** 209–217.

Porter, L. W., & Lawler, E. E. *Managerial attitudes and performance.* Homewood, Ill.: R. D. Irwin, 1968.

Rand, A. The objectivist ethics. In A. Rand (Ed.), *The virtue of selfishness.* New York: Signet, 1964, 13–35.

Rand, A. Concepts of consciousness. *The Objectivist,* 1966, **5**(9), 1–8.

Rosen, N. A. *Leadership change and work-group dynamics.* Ithaca, N.Y.: Cornell University Press, 1969.

Stedry, A. C. *Budget control and cost behavior.* Englewood Cliffs, N.J.: Prentice-Hall, 1960.

Stedry, A. C., & Kay, E. The effects of goal difficulty on performance. General Electric Co., Behavioral Research Service, 1964.

Taylor, F. W. *The principles of scientific management.* New York: Harper, 1911.

Vroom, V. H. *Work and motivation.* New York: Wiley, 1964.

Wernimont, P. F. Intrinsic and extrinsic factors in job satisfaction. *Journal of Applied Psychology,* 1966, **50,** 41–50.

Whyte, W. F. *Money and motivation.* New York: Wiley, 1955.

18

Leaders: Their behavior and development

W. Warner Burke

> Because of not daring to
> be ahead of the world, one
> becomes the leader of the world.
>
> —*The Way of Lao Tzu*

According to the late Ralph Stogdill, "A preoccupation with leadership occurs predominantly in countries with an Anglo-Saxon heritage" (Stogdill, 1974, p. 7). To use a current colloquial term, one might say that we in the Western world are "hung up" about leadership. The United States has the distinction of being

the country in which the first systematic studies of leadership were conducted. These studies began just prior to the World War I when researchers of that era were requested by the government to help find young men with leadership potential. Leadership research has increased continually from that time until now, and by 1970 it took 600 pages to fill Stogdill's *Handbook of Leadership.*

Even with all this interest (if not preoccupation) and enormous amounts of research, we still do not have a commonly accepted definition of leadership. Stogdill (1974) discusses ten different definitions. His own definition, however, appears to be the most acceptable: "the process [act] of influencing the activities of an organized group in its efforts toward goal setting and goal achievement" (p. 10). Although acceptable, Stogdill's definition is nevertheless limiting. One limitation is that he does not account for the possibility of an emergent leader in an unorganized setting. For the purposes of this paper, however, his definition should suffice. At the risk of being a bit too simplified, let us agree that leadership is the process of influencing the activities of others.

Since we cannot completely agree on a definition, it is also possible that even with all of our interest in and research about leadership we may not agree on whether we, after all, know very much. Some argue that despite four decades that produced approximately 3,000 publications of research and theory cited by Stogdill, the accumulated evidence tells us very little. The editors of a recent book on leadership and some of their chapter authors have been severely critical (McCall and Lombardo, 1978). Unfortunately, it is true that many, perhaps most, of the books and articles cited in Stogdill's bibliography are trivial. If, however, we consider the cumulative effect of many of these studies and look for patterns and consistencies across these publications, we may be able to find some substance. The last five years have produced research that sheds more light on our understanding of leadership, especially of what seems to be effective leader behavior.

The purposes of this paper are to (1) provide a summary of the leadership literature over the past five decades, (2) review more recent evidence and consider what seem to be reliable patterns and consistencies, and (3) apply what knowledge we have toward the selection and development of leaders.

Before proceeding further, we should make a qualification. Rarely in the literature is a distinction made between *leader* and *manager*. In this paper the terms are used interchangeably. According to Zaleznik, this equation of terms is mistaken. The title of Zaleznik's (1974) award-winning paper raises the question "Managers and Leaders: Are They Different?" His paper is an explanation of and rationale for his answer to the question, which is yes, of course. Zaleznik makes his differentiation across four dimensions—attitudes toward goals, conceptions of work, relations with others, and senses of self. [Table 1] is a summary of what Zaleznik considers the differences to be.

Managers enjoy relating with people, attain much of their sense of self from such activities, and work to maintain order. Leaders tend to be loners, risk takers, and visionaries. While we do not discount the possible validity of Zaleznik's argument, we will assume in this reading that managers and leaders exist in the same organization. We will consider both from a common developmental frame of reference. This combined

Table 1.   Differences Between Managers and Leaders (after Zaleznik)

Dimension for comparison	Managers	Leaders
Attitudes towards goals	Impersonal, reactive, passive	Personal, active
Conceptions of work	An enabling process of coordinating and balancing Limiting options	Projecting ideas into images that excite people Developing options
Relations with others	Prefer to work with people Relate according to roles	Prefer solitary activities Relate intuitively and empathically
Senses of self	Belong to their environment Depend on memberships, roles, etc., for identity	Feel separate from their environment Depend on personal mastery of events for identity

approach is not inconsistent with Zaleznik's distinctions, and we urge the reader to keep them in mind.

PAST RESEARCH AND THEORY

It cannot be stated with absolute certainty, but it would seem that the so-called great man theory of leadership influenced the direction of early research. The great man theory was based on the assumption that famous leaders of the past were successful because they possessed certain personal characteristics and that the most successful leaders had similar if not identical personal characteristics, for instance, great intelligence. For more than a quarter century, researchers, especially those in the United States, seemed to base their studies on this assumption. Studies from the 1920s through the early 1950s were largely correlational analyses. Researchers were interested in discovering what personal characteristics correlated significantly with leadership success. Practically every physical and personality trait one could imagine was correlated with leadership success, from how tall the leader was to how brave. Successful leadership was defined in a variety of ways. Most definitions took into account group performance under leadership or extent of influence the leader was able to exert on the followers.

A trait theory evolved gradually. Although based more on systematic studies of leadership, this theory seems similar to the historical great man theory. The trait theory held that successful leaders shared a certain combination of traits, mostly personality traits, that others did not have; or if others had them, they were of a lesser degree or of a different mix. Successful leaders were persons who probably had more intelligence, courage, verbal ability, and energy than most people. They were probably extroverted; greater risk takers; and, if we believe *The Way of Lao Tzu*, humble. Some studies tentatively indicated that some of these traits were *the* ones, but later studies would either qualify these earlier results (for example, leaders are typically more intelligent than followers, but not much more intelligent) or they would show no relationship whatsoever.

For decades ths search continued, but that unique combination of traits that would distinguish great leaders from mere mortals persistently eluded researchers. During the late 1940s and early 1950s psychologists and sociologists began to abandon the fruitless search for unique traits and to take different approaches to the study of leadership. They seemed implicitly to agree that no such combination existed, or if it did, that the research methodology they were limited to was not sophisticated enough to discover the combination.

Although the trait approach has lost favor, certain research results are worth noting because they reflect a certain uniformity of traits in leaders. The early trait research was atomistic. Later studies used more sophisticated research methodology, such as factor analysis, and began to show certain trait groupings. As Stogdill (1974) summarizes it, the average leader tends to be superior to the average follower in intelligence (but not significantly so), achievement and knowledge, dependability, and socioeconomic status. Leaders also tend to have more of a sense of humor than followers. Stogdill states that "a person does not become a leader by virtue of the possession of some combination of traits, but the pattern of personal characteristics of the leader must bear some relevant relationship to the characteristics, activities, and goals of the followers" (pp. 63–64). The *interaction* of the leader's personal characteristics, the needs and goals of the followers, and the situational demands is the key to understanding leadership (Burke, 1965).

After World War II researchers took a different approach. They observed and recorded the behavior of leaders and stopped measuring personality characteristics. Examining actual behavior was a more deductive approach. From their findings, researchers attempted to draw conclusions about what is leadership behavior and what is not.

As a result of observing many problem-solving groups and meticulously recording their behavior, Bales (1950) and his associates concluded that two categories of leader behavior were primary—*task-oriented* behavior and *socioemotional* behavior. Bales further concluded that ideally a group has two leaders, one who directs the task requirements and another who takes care of the group's socioemotional needs.

At about the same time that Bales was discovering these two categories of leader behavior, independent but similar findings were being made by researchers at Ohio State University. Hemphill (1950) conducted several factor analytic studies and identified two primary factors that clearly differentiate leader behavior from other behavior—*consideration* and *initiation of structure*. During the 1950s—primarily as a result of work emanating from these Ohio State leadership studies led by Hemphill, Halpin, Fleishman, and Stogdill, among others—numerous investigations were conducted to clarify the meaning of these two factors. Consideration came to mean person- or follower-oriented behavior, that is, behavior that showed consideration for followers' needs and goals and behavior by which the leader acknowledged the accomplishments of followers. Initiating structure was defined as letting followers know what is expected of them and what they can expect from the leader concerning the direction of and the boundaries for task accomplishment. Thus, consideration addressed the human element and initiation of structure addressed the task. Not surprisingly, multiple studies show that consideration and initiating structure interact to influence work group performance and satisfaction. The most effective leaders are high on both.

In the early 1960s the Ohio leadership studies and the work of Bales came to the attention of two psychologists, at the time faculty members at the University of Texas. Blake and Mouton thought that these two factors of leadership would not communicate very much to the average manager. They postulated that managers have two simultaneous concerns—a concern for production or results and a concern for people, their labels for the previously identified factors of leadership. They theorized that managers differ in their relative concern with the two. That is, some managers are more concerned with getting results than they are with people and vice versa. They graphically arranged these two concerns on 9 point scales. The juxtaposition on a graph resulted in what they called the managerial grid, a two-dimensional model that describes managerial style (Blake and Mouton, 1964). How these two concerns combine for a given manager determines his or her style of management. The greater the concern for production, the more autocratic the manager's style tends to be; the greater the concern with people, the more permissive the management style. Blake and Mouton argue that a manager who has a simultaneously high concern for both production and people (what they label a 9/9 style) is likely to be the most effective.

A contemporary of Blake and Mouton, Fred Fiedler, was developing during the late 1950s and early 1960s what he later called a contingency theory of leadership (Fiedler, 1967). His theory is that leadership is contingent on the personal characteristics of the leader and certain situational factors, the latter defined in terms of how much control the leader has over the situation. Fiedler divides leaders into two personality types—those who are task-motivated and those who are relationship-motivated. If these categories sound familiar it is because they are not unlike initiation of structure and consideration. Fiedler categorizes situations along three dimensions: (1) leader-member relations, ranging from good to poor; (2) task structure, from high structure to low (that is, the goal is either clear or ambiguous); and (3) the leader's position power, from strong to weak. The cumulative results of more than fifty separate research studies show once again an interactive effect. Task-motivated leaders perform best under conditions where the situation is either highly controllable by the leader (that is, good leader-member relations, high task structure, and strong position power) or under conditions of low control by the leader. The relationship-motivated leader outperforms the task-motivated one when the conditions are somewhere in between the two extreme conditions described as optimal for the task-motivated leader (Fiedler, 1974). Fiedler adduces evidence to support the argument that the effective leader is one who (a) is fortunate enough to obtain a position that optimizes the relationship between his or her style and the situation or (b) can rearrange the situation to match his or her personality. Fiedler is pessimistic about attempts to change the personal characteristics of a leader. He does not believe people are changeable or adaptable. He does not advocate training people to adopt 9/9 style (participative management) on Blake and Mouton's managerial grid. Successful leaders, according to Fiedler, are those who shape the situations in which they find themselves to match more effectively their personalities. He argues that it is far easier to change situations than personalities (Fiedler, 1976).

Hersey and Blanchard (1969) have developed what might be called a purely situational model; that is, they do not really consider the leader's personality or style as a significant variable except to the extent the leader is able to adapt his or her behavior to fit the demands of a particular situation. Using the same two dimensions—task and relationships are their terms—Hersey and Blanchard combine them much as do Blake and Mouton but limit their model to four quadrants rather than eighty-one combinations based on 9 point scales. Hersey and Blanchard's model of situational leadership follows:

Figure 1.   The Situational Leadership Model

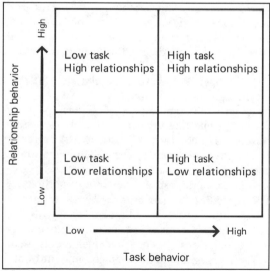

From P. Hersey and K. H. Blanchard, *Management of Organizational Behavior*, 3rd ed. Reprinted by permission.

Hersey and Blanchard argue that at times the leader should emphasize task and not emphasize relationships (lower right quadrant). In another situation, a leader's appropriate response might be to emphasize neither very much. The four quadrants of Figure 1 represent four relative emphases of the two dimensions. Hersey and Blanchard add that the primary factor for determining the degree of emphasis the leader places on these

two dimensions is the level of maturity of the followers. Defining maturity as followers knowing their jobs, they state that the higher the level of the followers' maturity, the less emphasis the leader should give to task and vice versa. If all followers are quite mature—their example is an R&D unit, a highly professional and competent group—then little emphasis is needed on either task or relationships.

Hersey and Blanchard conclude that the most successful leader is one who can adapt his or her style to handle different situational demands. The ideal leader should be able to behave equally adroitly in each of the four quadrants of their model.

There are at least two problems with the Hersey and Blanchard model. Evidence that directly supports their arguments is difficult to find. The other problem concerns the two dimensions they chose to promote their position. While it is quite reasonable to argue that a leader should adapt his or her behavior to deal effectively with different situations, it is difficult to imagine a situation in which ignoring both task requirements and relationships is appropriate. For a number of years the author chaired an academic department consisting of mature followers who knew their jobs—a situation that corresponds to Hersey and Blanchard's lower left quadrant. It is clear to the author that even with competent followers, he would have failed as a leader had he ignored giving task direction or failed to nurture faculty relationships. The point is that an effective leader should indeed adapt his or her behavior to situational demands, but the behavioral differences should vary on dimensions other than tasks and relationships.

Summary

Past evidence and thinking regarding leadership makes one thing clear. There is agreement in the literature that there are two aspects to leadership. Researchers, often working independently, recognize two functions, concerns, leader types, or dimensions that are essentially the same. The two may be called task and human relations, or structure and consideration, or other names, yet the consensual validation among these investigations is no small matter. There is still a debate among psychologists and sociologists, however, as to which is more valid, a contingency theory or a normative approach. Currently contingency theorists appear to have more support. It is widely held that under some conditions a task-oriented, directive leader is more effective while in other situations a relationship-oriented, people-directed leader is superior. Stogdill, however, concludes from his massive survey of leadership research that leaders who rate high in both structure and consideration are more successful, and recent evidence seems to support the normative conclusion, that is, that there is one best way to lead. Under most conditions a participative approach to a leader who integrates the two dimensions and does not use one at the expense of the other—is most effective.

CURRENT RESEARCH AND THEORY

In a study of 16,000 male managers from a variety of organizations in the United States, Hall (1976) found a difference between those who rose rapidly to top management ranks and those who rose slowly or not at all. Those who rose rapidly were more (a) participative (not permissive) in their managerial style, (b) open and solicitous of feedback when communicating with and relating to others, (c) prepared to involve their subordinates in decision making, (d) self-actualized, and (e) apt to utilize motivators as opposed to hygiene factors (Herzberg, 1966) in their motivational approach to subordinates, that is, to emphasize rewards related more to the work itself—opportunity to achieve—than to factors external to the work—pay, fringe benefits, etc. In a later study Donnell and Hall (1980) found essentially the same results with a group of approximately 1,000 female managers.

To summarize Hall's findings, we can list with a strong degree of statistical confidence these characteristics of successful managers:

- They are more concerned with the work and job itself than with the peripheral factors, such as fringe benefits.

- They are more likely to communicate openly and straightforwardly than to be secretive and political.

- They are more willing to confront other people regarding work-related issues than to ignore or suppress potential conflict.

- They are more likely to involve their subordinates in problem solving, planning, and decision making than to be unilateral.

- They are more concerned with getting results and achieving goals than with procedure and policy.

These findings may seem self-evident when successful managers are compared with less successful ones, but the findings are much more than obvious. First, these findings are based on sound, empirical evidence. Second, they are in general highly compatible with other evidence (Blumberg, 1969; Hollmann, 1976; Likert, 1967; and Marrow, Bowers, and Seashore, 1967). Last, the importance of these issues to the business community was confirmed recently when the *Wall Street Journal* found the Hall study worthy of front page coverage (August 22, 1978).

Janet Spence and Robert Helmreich (1978), psychologists at the University of Texas, have researched a different aspect of leadership. They developed questionnaires that reliably measure a person's (a) need for achievement, (b) degree of competitiveness, and (c) degree of integration of masculine and feminine characteristics, regardless of sex. The last is a measure of androgyny. Their studies of students working toward a master's in business administration (MBA), MBA alumni, and scientists points to consistent conclusions. Spence and Helmreich used, respectively, grade point average, amount of annual income, and number of mentions in *Science Citation Index* (an index of how influential one's research has been) as measures of success in the three groups. Their results showed that the more successful the individual (the higher the grade point average, income, and scientific influence) the more he or she tended to be high in need for achievement, low in competitiveness, and high in androgyny. A person who is high in androgyny is neither predominantly masculine (stereotypically analogous to task-directive behavior) nor feminine (analogous to people-oriented, nurturant behavior), but rather is high in both. Such a person suppresses neither behavior (analogous to the 9/9 style of management). Their findings suggest effective leaders possess a duality of masculinity and femininity rather than a bipolarity. Stated differently, masculinity and femininity are not opposite ends of a single continuum; rather, both feminine and masculine characteristics are present in all of us regardless of sex. Each of us can be characterized as both masculine and feminine. We can be seen as highly masculine, highly feminine, very high in neither, or highly masculine and feminine—androgynous.

The findings of Spence and Helmreich concerning androgyny are highly consistent with the leadership research that has been reported so far. Their findings underscore in quite another way the importance of the two key leadership attributes: *structure* and *consideration*. The abilities to define a task, to give concrete instructions about what must be done, and to direct its completion fall within traditional categories of masculine instrumental and assertive behavior. However, the abilities to be aware of the people who work for you, to be sensitive to their needs, and to be considerate of others in carrying out the leadership role are more generally categorized among the feminine characteristics of sensitivity, intuition, and caring. Hall discovered that successful managers are more disclosing and communicative and encourage more feedback than less successful ones. His findings reinforce the importance of "feminine" elements in the successful manager's behavior. Most men look for such behavior in male leaders. Certainly few successful male leaders reach positions of eminence without care and concern by their seniors.

From this research, we learn that the most successful manager and leader will be the person who has best command of a broad range of both feminine and masculine behaviors and can call on them as needed. We learn that people who are more rigidly tied to either masculine ("macho") or feminine (overly permissive-nurturant) behavior will be less successful. The successful manager (and perhaps the successful person in general) is one whose behavior is versatile—at times assertive or even aggressive and at other times caring and supportive.

Thus the work of Hall and of Spence and Helmreich add considerably to our understanding of the complicated mosaic of leadership. Their research findings also raise some important implications for the personal growth and learning of men and women with leadership potential. Their different socialization leads them to possess opposite if complementary strengths and limitations. Male managers are more likely to need help in developing interpersonal sensitivity and expressiveness. Female managers will need to cultivate assertiveness, the ability to instruct and direct, and an understanding of power. While large areas of training may overlap, it will be crucial to address these needs and crucial to assess performance by results and not by the extent to which the leader follows a strictly "masculine" method.

IMPLICATIONS FOR DEVELOPING LEADERS

Based on what we know so far about effective leadership we are in a position to delineate some steps for discovering and developing leaders.

1. Finding potential—what to look for. First, as Stogdill (1974) made clear, one should look for persons who are slightly more intelligent than the individuals who will be led. Second, the more a person is androgynous, the better the leadership potential. Third, above average ego strength is important. Although it may be more relevant to managers than to leaders, above average energy and general drive is crucial. Third, successful leaders are those who (a) have an above average need for power; (b) inhibit this need in socially desirable ways, that is, while they like to influence and control others they act more for the common good than for totally selfish purposes; (c) have an above average need for autonomy; (d) have a below average need for affiliation; and (e) enjoy organized activities, especially if they can shape them (McClelland, 1975; McClelland and Burnham, 1976). In short, successful leaders apparently enjoy if not have a strong need for influencing others. It seems reasonable to assume that the person who is good at influencing others likes the process.

In summary, one should look for these qualities in leaders.

- They are brighter than most.
- They are androgynous.
- They are above average in ego strength and drive.
- They like to influence others.
- They prefer autonomy.
- They are not necessarily interested in popularity.
- They enjoy organized work.

2. Personal development. Potential leaders should receive certain education and training. Leaders should receive relevant technical training and job skill development, for example, in finance, engineering, behavioral science, and so forth. They also should learn the basics of management—planning, budgeting, delegating, coaching, appraising and rewarding performance, and managing and conducting meetings. In order to manage meetings, potential leaders should learn about group dynamics is general and team development in particular. The importance of this training is obvious: leaders *lead* groups; they tend to manage activities and individuals. Finally, potential leaders need to learn the skills involved in participative management: how to (a) involve followers in decision making, (b) lead groups toward consensual decisions, (c) gain commitment to decisions so that implementation will follow quite naturally and quickly, and (d) promote collaboration and interdependence when conditions call for such behavior.

In summary, the personal development of potential leaders should include the following:

- technical and professional training
- management development
- participative management skill training
- education in group dynamics

3. Career development. Careers of potential leaders should be planned so to provide them mentors in the early stages. The so-called godfather system in Japanese organizations is essentially a mentor system with longstanding precedents. Researchers in the United States have found that mentors can significantly contribute to the future success of a leader (Lunding, Clements, and Perkins, 1978).

If the organization is a business, regardless of how large, an early entrepreneurial experience is beneficial to a potential leader's career. The opportunity to exercise his or her needs for power and autonomy in a situation where determinants of success are fairly clear provides unparalleled opportunities for learning and growth. If the organization is a nonprofit institution, the young leader can have a similar experience if given considerable autonomy to run his or her "own show." Size and complexity of this show is not nearly as important at having one in the first place.

Three other aspects of career development are also important. One is job rotation. Being able to broaden one's learning about various organizational tasks is invaluable for future leaders (Digman, 1978). A second aspect is feedback. Periodic feedback on how well one is performing on the job and within the organization overall will give the potential leader vital information about what areas he or she should pursue for future development. The third aspect is continuing education opportunities. Without these opportunities, a leader can develop his or her career only so far.

In summary, the career development paths or patterns of potential leaders should provide the following:

- mentors
- entrepreneurial (or equivalent) experience
- job rotation
- feedback on performance
- continuing education opportunities

RECAPITULATION

To review briefly, this paper summarizes the previous literature on leadership with an eye toward distilling what is of value for understanding and developing leaders. Early evidence and more current findings point to the importance of two dimensions or functions of any leader's behavior: task and follower relationships. There is agreement that the leader should emphasize both dimensions equally and strongly. The evidence also points to certain directions for the discovery and development of potential leaders. Because leaders display certain personal characteristics, among them need for power, and for the discovery process, they should receive training and education that emphasizes participative management training and education in group dynamics. Last, potential leaders' development is facilitated by mentors, opportunities for autonomous activities, breadth of job experiences, performance, feedback, and opportunities for continuing education.

Although our knowledge about the personal characteristics of successful leaders and about the constituents of effective leadership is relatively limited, we nevertheless have enough evidence to take certain steps. Despairing by saying either that leaders must apparently be born and not made or that the evidence is so trivial and contradictory that it is useless is neither warranted nor productive.

REFERENCES

Bales, R. F. *Interaction process analysis.* Reading, Mass.: Addison-Wesley, 1950.

Blake, R. R. and Mouton, J. S. *The managerial grid.* Houston: Gulf Publishing, 1964.

Blumberg, P. *Industrial democracy.* New York: Schocken Books, 1969.

Burke, W. W. Leadership behavior as a function of the leader, the follower, and the situation. *Journal of Personality*, 1965, *33*(11), 60–81.

————."Developing and selecting leaders: What we know." In W. B. Eddy and W. W. Burke (Eds.). *Behavioral science and the manager's role.* San Diego, Calif.: University Associates, 1980.

Digman, L. A. How well-managed organizations develop their executives. *Organizational Dynamics*, 1978, *7*(2), 63–80.

Donnell, S., and Hall, J. Men and women as managers: A significant case of no significant differences. *Organizational Dynamics*, 1980, *8*(4), 60–77.

Fiedler, F. E. *A theory of leadership effectiveness.* New York: McGraw-Hill, 1967.

————. "The contingency model: New directions for leadership utilization. *Journal of Contemporary Business*, 1974, Autumn, 65–80.

————. The leadership game: Matching the man to the situation. *Organizational Dynamics*, 1976, *4*(3), 6–16.

Hall, J. To achieve or not: The manager's choice. *California Management Review*, 1976, *18*(4), 5–18.

Hemphill, J. K. *Leader behavior description.* Columbus, Ohio: Ohio State University, Personnel Research Board, 1950 (mimeo).

Hersey, P., and Blanchard, K. H. *Management of organizational behavior.* Englewood Cliffs, N.J.: Prentice-Hall, 1969.

Herzberg, F. *Work and the nature of man.* Cleveland: World Publishing, 1966.

Hollman, R. W. Supportive organizational climate and managerial assessment of MBO effectiveness. *Academy of Management Journal*, 1976, *19*(4), 571.

Likert, R. *The human organization.* New York: McGraw-Hill, 1967.

Lunding, F. J., Clements, G. L., and Perkins, D. S. (Interviews). Everyone who makes it has a mentor. *Harvard Business Review*, 1978, *56*(4), 89–101.

McCall, M. W., and Lombardo, M. M., (Eds.). *Leadership: Where else can we go?* Durham, N.C.: Duke University Press, 1978.

McClelland, D.C. *Power: The inner experience.* New York: Irvington Publishers, 1975.

McClelland, D. C., and Burnham, D. H. Power is the great motivator. *Harvard Business Review*, 1976, *54*(2), 100–110.

Marrow, A. J., Bowers, D. G., and Seashore, S. E. *Management by participation.* New York: Harper & Row, 1967.

Spence, J. T., and Helmreich, R. L. *Masculinity and femininity: Their psychological dimensions, correlates, and antecedents.* Austin: University of Texas, 1978.

Stogdill, R. M. *Handbook of leadership: A survey of theory and research.* New York: Free Press, 1974.

Zaleznik, A. Managers and leaders: Are they different? *Harvard Business Review*, 1977, *55*(3), 67–78.

19

Decision making as a
social process: Normative and
descriptive models of leader behavior

Victor H. Vroom
and Arthur G. Jago

INTRODUCTION

Several scholarly disciplines share an interest in the decision-making process. On one hand, there are the related fields of operations research and management science, both concerned with how to improve the decisions which are made. Their models of decision making, aimed at providing a rational basis for selecting among alternative courses of action, are termed normative or prescriptive models. On the other hand, there have been attempts by psychologists, sociologists, and political scientists to understand the decisions and choices that people do make. March and Simon [6] were among the first to suggest that an understanding of the decision-making process could be central to an understanding of the behavior of organizations—a point of view that was later amplified by Cyert and March [1] in their behavioral theory of the firm. In this tradition, the goal is understanding rather than improvement, and the models are descriptive rather than normative.

Whether the models are normative or descriptive, the common ingredient is a conception of decision making as an information-processing activity, frequently one which takes place within a single manager. Both sets of models focus on the set of alternative decisions or problem solutions from which the choice is, or should be, made.

Source: From Victor H. Vroom and Arthur G. Jago, "Decision making as a social process: Normative and descriptive models of leader behavior," *Decision Sciences,* 5 (1974). Reprinted by permission of the publisher.

Authors' note: The research contained in this article was sponsored by the Organizational Effectiveness Research Program, Office of Naval Research (Code 452) under Contract to the senior author (No. N00014-67-A-0097-0027; NR 177-935). Reproduction in whole or in part is permitted for any purpose of the United States Government.

The normative models are based on the consequences of choices among these alternatives, the descriptive models on the determinants of these choices.

In this article, the authors take a somewhat different, although complementary, view of managerial decision making. They view decision making as a social process with the elements of the process presented in terms of events between people rather than events that occur within a person. When a problem or occasion for decision making occurs within an organization, there are typically several alternative social mechanisms available for determining what solution is chosen or decision reached. These alternatives vary in the person or persons participating in the problem solving and decision-making process, and in the relative amounts of influence that each has on the final solution or decision reached.

There are both descriptive and normative questions to be answered about the social processes used for decision making in organizations. The normative questions hinge on knowledge concerning the consequences of alternatives for the effective performance of the system. The dimensions on which social processes can vary constitute the independent variables, and criteria of the effectiveness of the decisions constitute dependent variables. Ultimately, such knowledge could provide the foundation for a specification of the social and interpersonal aspects of how decisions *should be* made within organizations.

Similarly, the descriptive questions concern the circumstances under which alternative social processes for decision making *are* used in organizations. The dimensions on which social processes vary become the dependent variables, and characteristics of the manager who controls the process and the nature of the decision itself provide the basis for the specification of independent variables.

Vroom and Yetton [10] provided a start to an examination of both normative and descriptive questions through an examination of one dimension of decision making—the extent to which a leader encourages the participation of his subordinates in decision making. Participation in decision making was a logical place to start since there is substantial evidence of its importance and of the circumstances surrounding different consequences of it [3] [9] [11].

The purpose of this article is twofold: (1) to provide a brief summary of the objectives, methods, and results of the research pertaining to both normative and descriptive models of decision processes used in organizations (described in detail in Vroom and Yetton [10]); (2) to describe some recent extensions of the previous work, including an empirical investigation designed to explore facets of decision-making not previously studied.

Vroom and Yetton concern themselves primarily with problems or decisions to be made by managers with a formally defined set of subordinates reporting to them. In each problem or decision, the manager must have some area of freedom or discretion in determining the solution adopted, and the solution must affect at least one of the manager's subordinates. Following Maier, Solem, and Maier [4], they further make a distinction between group problems and individual problems. If the solution adopted has potential effects on all immediate subordinates or some readily identifiable subset of them, it is classified as a group problem. If the solution affects only one of the manager's subordinates, it is called an individual problem. This distinction is an important one because it determines the range of decision-making processes available to the manager. Table 1 shows a taxonomy of decision processes for both types of problems. Each process is represented by a symbol (e.g., AI, CI, GII, DI) which provides a convenient method of referring to each process. The letters in the code signify the basic properties of the process (A stands for autocratic; C for consultative; G for group; and D for delegated). The roman numerals that follow the letter constitute variants on that process. Thus AI represents the first variant on an autocratic process: AII the second variant, and so on.

The processes shown in Table 1 are arranged in columns corresponding to their presumed applicability to either group or individual problems and are arranged within columns in order of increasing opportunity for the subordinate to influence the solution to the problem.

The discrete alternative processes shown in Table 1 can be used both normatively and descriptively. In the former use, they constitute discrete alternatives available to the manager or decision maker who presumably is motivated to choose that alternative which has the greatest likelihood of producing effective results for his organization. In the latter use, the processes constitute forms of behavior on the part of individuals which require explanation. In the balance of this paper, we will attempt to keep in mind these two uses of the taxonomy and will discuss them separately.

A NORMATIVE MODEL OF DECISION PROCESSES

What would be a rational way of deciding on the form and amount of participation in decision making to be used in different situations? Neither debates over the relative merits of Theory X and Theory Y [7], nor the apparent truism that leadership depends on the situation, are of much help here. The aim in this portion of the research is to develop a framework for matching a leader's behavior, as expressed in the alternatives presented in Table 1, to the demands of his situation. Any framework developed must be consistent with empirical evidence concerning the consequences of participation and be operational so that a trained leader could use it to determine how he should act in a given situation.

The normative model should provide a basis for effective problem solving and decision making by matching the desired decision process with relevant properties of particular problems or decisions to be made. Following Maier [5], the effectiveness of a decision is thought to be a function of three classes of outcomes, each of which may be expected to be affected by the decision process used. These are:

Table 1. Decision-Making Processes

For individual problems	For group problems
AI You solve the problem or make the decision yourself, using information available to you at that time.	**AI** You solve the problem or make the decision yourself, using information available to you at that time.
AII You obtain any necessary information from the subordinate, then decide on the solution to the problem yourself. You may or may not tell the subordinate what the problem is, in getting the information from him. The role played by your subordinate in making the decision is clearly one of providing specific information which you request, rather than generating or evaluating alternative solutions.	**AII** You obtain any necessary information from subordinates, then decide on the solution to the problem yourself. You may or may not tell subordinates what the problem is, in getting the information from them. The role played by your subordinates in making the decision is clearly one of providing specific information which you request, rather than generating or evaluating solutions.
CI You share the problem with the relevant subordinate, getting his ideas and suggestions. Then *you* make the decision. This decision may or may not reflect your subordinate's influence.	**CI** You share the problem with the relevant subordinates individually, getting their ideas and suggestions without bringing them together as a group. Then *you* make the decision. This decision may or may not reflect your subordinates' influence.
GI You share the problem with one of your subordinates and together you analyze the problem and arrive at a mutually satisfactory solution in an atmosphere of free and open exchange of information and ideas. You both contribute to the resolution of the problem with the relative contribution of each being dependent on knowledge rather than formal authority.	**CII** You share the problem with your subordinates in a group meeting. In this meeting you obtain their ideas and suggestions. Then, *you* make the decision which may or may not reflect your subordinates' influence.
DI You delegate the problem to one of your subordinates, providing him with any relevant information that you possess, but giving him responsibility for solving the problem by himself. Any solution which the person reaches will receive your support.	**GII** You share the problem with your subordinates as a group. Together you generate and evaluate alternatives and attempt to reach agreement (consensus) on a solution. Your role is much like that of chairman, coordinating the discussion, keeping it focused on the problem, and making sure that the critical issues are discussed. You do not try to influence the group to adopt "your" solution and are willing to accept and implement any solution which has the support of the entire group.

1. The quality or rationality of the decision.
2. The acceptance or commitment on the part of subordinates to execute the decision effectively.
3. The amount of time required to make the decision.

Space prevents an exposition of the empirical evidence concerning the consequences of participation, but the reader interested in these questions is referred to Vroom [9], and Vroom and Yetton [10, pp. 20–31] for a presentation of that evidence. Since the research program began, a number of normative models for choosing among alternative decision processes have been developed. Each revision is slightly more complex than its predecessor but, in the minds of both developers and users, also more accurate in forecasting the consequences of alternatives. Most of these models have been concerned solely with group problems (the right hand column in Table 1). In Vroom and Yetton [10] virtually all of the discussion of normative models is oriented toward group problems; although, in their discussion of further revisions and extensions of the model, they discuss the possibility of a model for both individual and group problems and present a tentative model which governs choice of decision processes for both types.

Figure 1 shows the latest version of a model intended to deal with both types of problems. Like previous models, it is expressed in the form of a decision tree. Arranged along the top of the tree are a set of eight problem attributes, expressed here in the form of simple Yes-No questions that a leader could ask himself about the decision-making situation he is presently confronting.[1] To use the model, one starts at the left-hand side of the tree and works toward the right-hand side, asking oneself the questions pertaining to any box that is encountered. When a nominal node is reached, a number will be found designating the problem type and one or more decision-making processes considered appropriate for that problem. Within each problem type there are both individual and group problems, and the feasible set of methods is different for each.

The decision processes specified for each problem type are not arbitrary. The specification of the feasible set of decision processes for each problem type is governed by a set of ten rules that serve to protect the quality and acceptance of the decision by eliminating alternatives that risk one or the other of these decision outcomes. These rules, consistent with existing empirical evidence concerning the consequences of participation, are shown in Table 2 in both verbal and set-theoretic form. It should be noted that the rules are of three distinct types. Rules 1 through 4 are designed to protect the quality or rationality of the decision; Rules 5 through 8 are designed to protect the acceptance of or commitment to the decision; and Rules 9 through 10 eliminate the use

of group methods for individual problems and vice versa. The decision tree is merely a convenient structure for applying these rules, and, once the problem type has been determined, the rules have all been applied. It can be seen that there are some problem types for which only one method remains in the feasible set, and others for which two, three, four, or even five methods remain in the feasible set.

When more than one method remains in the feasible set, there are a number of ways in which one might choose among them. One method, called Model A and discussed at length by Vroom and Yetton, uses the number of manhours required by the process of decision making. They argue that if the alternatives within the feasible set are equal in the probability of generating a rational decision which subordinates will accept, a choice among them based on the time requirement of each will be of maximum short-run benefit to the organization.

The basis for estimating the relative requirements in manhours for the alternatives given for group problems is simple. Vroom and Yetton argue that more participative processes require more time. Therefore, the ordering of the methods shown for group problems in terms of manhours is perfectly correlated with the degree of participation they permit (AI $<$ AII $<$ CI $<$ CII $<$ GII). However, the extension of the model to cover individual problems complicates this picture, since the decision process which provides greatest opportunity for subordinate influence, DI, is certainly less time consuming than GI, which requires reaching a solution which has the agreement of both superior and subordinate. While the differences in time requirements of the alternatives for individual problems is not nearly so great as the differences in the alternatives for group problems, we have assumed an ordering such that AI $<$ DI $<$ AII $<$ CI $<$ GI. The reader will note that the ordering of alternatives from left to right within the feasible sets for each problem type in Figure 1 reflects this assumption. Thus, for both group and individual problems, the minimum-manhours solution is assumed to be the alternative furthest to the left within the feasible set.

There are, however, other bases for choice within the feasible set. A manager may wish to

Figure 1. Decision-Process Flow Chart for Both Individual and Group Problems

A. Is there a quality requirement such that one solution is likely to be more rational than another?
B. Do I have sufficient info to make a high quality decision?
C. Is the problem structured?
D. Is acceptance of decision by subordinates critical to effective implementation?
E. If I were to make the decision by myself, is it reasonably certain that it would be accepted by my subordinates?
F. Do subordinates share the organizational goals to be attained in solving this problem?
G. Is conflict among subordinates likely in preferred solutions? (This question is irrelevant to individual problems.)
H. Do subordinates have sufficient info to make a high quality decision?

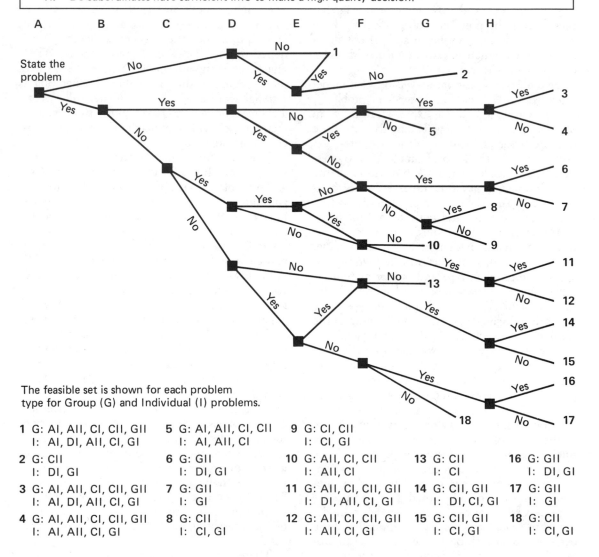

The feasible set is shown for each problem
type for Group (G) and Individual (I) problems.

1 G: AI, AII, CI, CII, GII
   I: AI, DI, AII, CI, GI

2 G: CII
   I: DI, GI

3 G: AI, AII, CI, CII, GII
   I: AI, DI, AII, CI, GI

4 G: AI, AII, CI, CII, GII
   I: AI, AII, CI, GI

5 G: AI, AII, CI, CII
   I: AI, AII, CI

6 G: GII
   I: DI, GI

7 G: GII
   I: GI

8 G: CII
   I: CI, GI

9 G: CI, CII
   I: CI, GI

10 G: AII, CI, CII
   I: AII, CI

11 G: AII, CI, CII, GII
   I: DI, AII, CI, GI

12 G: AII, CI, CII, GII
   I: AII, CI, GI

13 G: CII
   I: CI

14 G: CII, GII
   I: DI, CI, GI

15 G: CII, GII
   I: CI, GI

16 G: GII
   I: DI, GI

17 G: GII
   I: GI

18 G: CII
   I: CI, GI

Table 2. Rules Underlying the Normative Model

1. *The Leader Information Rule:* $A \cap \overline{B} \rightarrow \overline{AI}$

   If the quality of the decision is important and the leader does not possess enough information or expertise to solve the problem by himself, then AI is eliminated from the feasible set.

2. *The Subordinate Information Rule:* $A \cap \overline{H} \rightarrow \overline{DI}$
   (applicable to individual problems only)

   If the quality of the decision is important and the subordinate does not possess enough information or expertise to solve the problem himself, then DI is eliminated from the feasible set.

3a. *The Goal Congruence Rule:* $A \cap \overline{F} \rightarrow \overline{GII}, \overline{DI}$

   If the quality of the decision is important and the subordinates are not likely to pursue organization goals in their efforts to solve this problem, then GII and DI are eliminated from the feasible set.

3b. *The Augmented Goal Congruence Rule:* $A \cap (\overline{D} \cup E) \cap \overline{F} \rightarrow \overline{GI}$
   (applicable to individual problems only)

   Under the conditions specified in the previous rule (i.e., quality of decision is important, and the subordinate does not share the organizational goals to be attained in solving the problem) GI may also constitute a risk to the quality of the decision taken in response to an individual problem. Such a risk is a reasonable one to take only if the nature of the problem is such that the acceptance of the subordinate is critical to the effective implementation and prior probability of acceptance of an autocratic solution is low.

4a. *The Unstructured Problem Rule (Group):* $A \cap \overline{B} \cap \overline{C} \rightarrow \overline{AI}, \overline{AII}, \overline{CI}$

   In decisions in which the quality of the decision is important, if the leader lacks the necessary information or expertise to solve the problem by him-

self and if the problem is unstructured, the method of solving the problem should provide for interaction among subordinates. Accordingly, AI, AII, and CI are eliminated from the feasible set.

4b. *The Unstructured Problem Rule (Individual):* $A \cap \overline{B} \cap \overline{C} \rightarrow \overline{AII}$

   In decisions in which the quality of the decision is important, if the leader lacks the necessary information to solve the problem by himself and if the problem is unstructured, the method of solving the problem should permit the subordinate to generate solutions to the problem. Accordingly, AI and AII are eliminated from the feasible set.

5. *The Acceptance Rule:* $D \cap \overline{E} \rightarrow \overline{AI}, \overline{AII}$

   If the acceptance of the decision by subordinates is critical to effective implementation and if it is not certain that an autocratic decision will be accepted, AI and AII are eliminated from the feasible set.

6. *The Conflict Rule:* $D \cap \overline{E} \cap G \rightarrow \overline{AI}, \overline{AII}, \overline{CI}$
   (applicable to group problems only)

   If the acceptance of the decision is critical, an autocratic decision is not certain to be accepted and disagreement among subordinates in methods of attaining the organizational goal is likely, the methods used in solving the problem should enable those in disagreement to resolve their differences with full knowledge of the problem. Accordingly, AI, AII and CI, which permit no interaction among subordinates, are eliminated from the feasible set.

7. *The Fairness Rule:* $\overline{A} \cap D \cap \overline{E} \rightarrow \overline{AI}, \overline{AII}, \overline{CI}, \overline{CII}$

   If the quality of the decision is unimportant, but acceptance of the decision is critical and not certain to result from an autocratic decision, the decision process used should permit the subordinates to interact with one

(continued)

Table 2.   *(continued)*

another and negotiate over the fair method of resolving any differences with full responsibility on them for determining what is equitable. Accordingly, AI, AII, CI and CII are eliminated from the feasible set.

8. *The Acceptance Priority Rule:* $D \cap \overline{E} \cap F \rightarrow \overline{AI}, \overline{AII}, \overline{CI}, \overline{CII}$

    If acceptance is critical, not certain to result from an autocratic decision and if (the) subordinate(s) is (are) motivated to pursue the organizational goals represented in the problem, then methods which provide equal partnership in the decision-making process can provide greater acceptance without risking decision quality. Accordingly, AI, AII, CI, and CII are eliminated from the feasible set.

9. *The Group Problem Rule:* Group $\rightarrow$ $\overline{GI}, \overline{DI}$

    If a problem has approximately equal effects on each of a number of subordinates (i.e., is a group problem) the decision process used should provide them with equal opportunities to influence that decision. Use of a decision process such as GI or DI which provides opportunities for only one of the affected subordinates to influence that decision may in the short run produce feelings of inequity reflected in lessened commitment to the decision on the part of those "left out" of the decision process and, in the long run, be a source of conflict and divisiveness.

10. *The Individual Problem Rule:* Individual $\rightarrow$ $\overline{CII}, \overline{GII}$

    If a problem affects only one subordinate, decision processes which *unilaterally* introduce other (unaffected) subordinates as equal partners constitute an unnecessary use of time of the unaffected subordinates and can reduce the amount of commitment of the affected subordinate to the decision by reducing the amount of his opportunity to influence the decision. Thus, CII and GII are eliminated from the feasible set.

---

choose the most participative alternative that can be used while still producing rational and acceptable solutions to organizational problems. Such a position could be grounded in humanistic considerations, emphasizing the intrinsic value of participation, or on pragmatic considerations, such as the utility of participation in developing informed and responsible behavior [10]. A model based on these considerations is termed Model B.

The reader should note that both Models A and B are consistent with the rules which generate the feasible set. They merely represent different bases for choice within it. Model A chooses the method within the feasible set which is the most economical method in terms of manhours. Its choice is always the method furthest to the left in the set shown in Figure 1. Model B chooses the most participative method available within the feasible set, which is that method closest to the bottom of Table 1. Model A seeks to minimize manhours, subject to quality and acceptance constraints, while Model B seeks to maximize participation, subject to quality and acceptance constraints. Of course, when only one process exists within the feasible set, the choices of Model A and B are identical. Perhaps the best way of illustrating the model is to show how it works in sample situations. Following are a set of actual leadership problems,[2] each based on a retrospective account by a manager who experienced the problem. The reader may wish, after reading each case, to analyze it himself using the model and then to compare his analysis with that of the authors.

Case I: You are president of a small but growing Midwestern bank, with its head office in the state's capital and branches in several nearby market towns. The location and type of business are factors which contribute to the emphasis on traditional and conservative banking practices at all levels.

When you bought the bank five years ago, it was in poor financial shape. Under your leadership, much progress has been made. This progress has been achieved while the economy has moved into a mild recession, and, as a result, your prestige among your bank managers is very high. Your success, which you are inclined to attribute principally to good luck and a few timely decisions on your part, has, in your judgment, one unfortunate by-product. It has caused your subordinates to look to you for leadership and guidance in decision making beyond what you consider necessary. You have no doubts about the fundamental capabilities of these men but wish that they were not quite so willing to accede to your judgment.

You have recently acquired funds to permit opening a new branch. Your problem is to decide on a suitable location. You believe that there is no "magic formula" by which it is possible to select an optimal site. The choice will be made by a combination of some simple common sense criteria and "what feels right." You have asked your managers to keep their eyes open for commercial real estate sites that might be suitable. Their knowledge about the communities in which they operate should be extremely useful in making a wise choice.

Their support is important because the success of the new branch will be highly dependent on your managers' willingness to supply staff and technical assistance during its early days. Your bank is small enough for everyone to feel like part of a team, and you feel that this has and will be critical to the bank's prosperity.

The success of this project will benefit everybody. Directly, they will benefit from the increased base of operations, and, indirectly, they will reap the personal and business advantages of being part of a successful and expanding business.

Analysis:

A (Quality?) = Yes
B (Leader's Information?) = No
C (Structured?) = No
D (Acceptance?) = Yes
E (Prior Probability of Acceptance?) = Yes
F (Goal Congruence?) = Yes
G^3 (Conflict?) = No
H^3 (Subordinate Information?) = Yes

Synthesis:

Problem Type	14-Group
Feasible Set	CII, GII
Model A Behavior	CII
Model B Behavior	GII

Case II: You are regional manager of an international management consulting company. You have a staff of six consultants reporting to you, each of whom enjoys a considerable amount of autonomy with clients in the field.

Yesterday you received a complaint from one of your major clients to the effect that the consultant whom you assigned to work on the contract with them was not doing his job effectively. They were not very explicit as to the nature of the problem, but it was clear that they were dissatisfied and that something would have to be done if you were to restore the client's faith in your company.

The consultant assigned to work on that contract has been with the company for six years. He is a systems analyst and is one of the best in that profession. For the first four or five years his performance was superb, and he was a model for the other more junior consultants. However, recently he has seemed to have a "chip on his shoulder," and his previous identification with the company and its objectives has been replaced with indifference. His negative attitude has been noticed by other consultants, as well as by clients. This is not the first such complaint that you have had from a client this year about his performance. A previous client even reported to you that the consultant reported to work several times obviously suffering from a hangover and that he had been seen around town in the company of "fast" women.

It is important to get to the root of this problem quickly if that client is to be retained. The consultant obviously has the skill necessary to work with the clients effectively. If only he were willing to use it!

Analysis:

A (Quality?) = Yes
B (Leader's Information?) = No
C (Structured?) = No
D (Acceptance?) = Yes
E (Prior Probability of Acceptance?) = No
F (Goal Congruence?) = No
H^3 (Subordinate Information?) = Yes

Synthesis:

Problem Type	18-Individual
Feasible Set	CI, GI
Model A Behavior	CI
Model B Behavior	GI

Case III: You have recently been appointed manager of a new plant which is presently under construction. Your team of five department heads has been selected, and they are now working with you in selecting their own staffs, purchasing equipment, and generally anticipating the problems that are likely to arise when you move into the plant in three months.

Yesterday, you received from the architect a final set of plans for the building, and, for the first time, you examined the parking facilities that are available. There is a large lot across the road from the plant intended primarily for hourly workers and lower level supervisory personnel. In addition, there are seven spaces immediately adjacent to the administrative offices, intended for visitor and reserved parking. Company policy requires that a minimum of three spaces be made available for visitor parking, leaving you only four spaces to allocate among yourself and your five department heads. There is no way of increasing the total number of such spaces without changing the structure of the building.

Up to now, there have been no obvious status differences among your team, who have worked together very well in the planning phase of the operation. To be sure, there are salary differences, with your Administrative, Manufacturing, and Engineering Managers receiving slightly more than the Quality Control and Industrial Relations Managers. Each has recently been promoted to his new position, and expects reserved parking privileges as a consequence of his new status. From past experience, you know that people feel strongly about things which would be indicative of their status. So you and your subordinates have been working together as a team, and you are reluctant to do anything which might jeopardize the team relationship.

Analysis:

A	(Quality?)	= No
D	(Acceptance?)	= Yes
E	(Prior Probability of Acceptance?)	= No
G^3	(Conflict?)	= Yes

Synthesis:

Problem Type	2-Group
Feasible Set	GII
Model A Behavior	GII
Model B Behavior	GII

Case IV: You are executive vice president for a small pharmaceutical manufacturer. You have the opportunity to bid on a contract for the Defense Department pertaining to biological warfare. The contract is outside the mainstream of your business; however, it could make economic sense since you do have unused capacity in one of your plants, and the manufacturing processes are not dissimilar.

You have written the document to accompany the bid and now have the problem of determining the dollar value of the quotation which you think will win the job for your company. If the bid is too high, you will undoubtedly lose to one of your competitors; if it is too low, you would stand to lose money on the program.

There are many factors to be considered in making this decision, including the cost of the new raw materials and the additional administrative burden of relationships with a new client, not to speak of factors which are likely to influence the bids of your competitors, such as how much they *need* this particular contract. You have been busy assembling the necessary data to make this decision but there remain several "unknowns," one of which involves the manager of the plant in which the new products will be manufactured. Of all your subordinates, only he is in the position to estimate the costs of adapting the present equipment to their new purpose, and his cooperation and support will be necessary in ensuring that the specifications of the contract will be met. However, in an initial discussion with him when you first learned of the possibility of the contract, he seemed adamantly opposed to the idea. His previous experience has not particularly equipped him with the ability to evaluate projects like this one, so that you were not overly influenced by his opinions. From the nature of his arguments, you inferred that his opposition was ideological rather than economic. You recall that he was actively involved in a local "peace organization" and, within the company, was one of the most vocal opponents to the war in Vietnam.

Analysis:

A	(Quality?)	= Yes

B	(Leader's Information?)	= No
C	(Structured?)	= Yes
D	(Acceptance?)	= Yes
E	(Prior Probability of Acceptance?)	= No
F	(Goal Congruence?)	= No
H[3]	(Subordinate Information?)	= No

Synthesis:

Problem Type	8 or 9 individual
Feasible Set	CI, GI
Model A Behavior	CI
Model B Behavior	GI

TOWARD A DESCRIPTIVE MODEL

So far, we have been concerned only with normative or prescriptive questions. But, how do managers really behave? What decision rules underlie their willingness to share their decision-making power with their subordinates? In what respects are these decision rules similar to or different from those employed in the normative model?

The manner in which these questions are posed is at variance with much of the conventional treatment of such issues. Frequently, leaders are typed as autocratic or participative or as varying on a continuum between these extremes. In effect, autocratic or participative behavior is assumed to be controlled by a personality trait, the amount of which varies from one person to another. The trait concept is a useful one for summarizing differences among people, but allows no room for the analysis of intra-individual differences in behavior. Following Lewin's [2] classic formulation $B = f(P,E)$, we assumed that a leader's behavior in a given situation reflects characteristics of that leader, properties of the situation, and the interaction of the two.

Two somewhat different research methods have been used in studying the situational determinants of participative behavior. The first method [10, chapter 4] utilized what we have come to refer to as "recalled problems." Over 500 managers, all of whom were participants in management development programs, provided written descriptions of a group problem which they encountered recently. These descriptions ranged in length from one paragraph to several pages and covered virtually every facet of managerial decision making. Each manager was then asked to indicate which of the methods shown on the right hand side of Table 1 (AI, AII, CI, CII, GII) he had used in solving the problem. Finally, each manager was asked a set of questions concerning the problem he had selected. These questions corresponded to attributes in the normative model.

Preliminary investigation revealed that managers perceived the five alternatives as varying (in the order shown in Table 1) on a scale of participation but that the four intervals separating adjacent processes were not seen as equal. On the basis of the application of several scaling methods [10, pp. 65–71], the following values on a scale of participation were assigned to each process: AI = 0; AII = .625; CI = 5.0; CII = 8.125; GII = 10.

Using the managers' judgments of the status of the problems they described on the problem attributes as independent variables and the scale values of their behavior on the problem as a dependent variable, it is possible to use the method of multiple regression to determine the properties of situations, i.e., problems, which are associated with autocratic or participative behavior. It is also possible to insert the managers' judgments concerning their problems into the normative model and to determine the degree of correspondence between managerial and model behavior.

Several investigations have been conducted using this method—all of which have been restricted to group problems and the decision processes corresponding to them. The results are consistent with the view that there are important differences in the processes used for different kinds of problems. Specifically, managers were more likely to exhibit autocratic behavior on structured problems in which they believed that they had enough information, their subordinates lacked information, their subordinates' goals were incongruent with the organizational goals, their subordinates' acceptance of the decision was not critical to its effective implementation, and the prior probability that an autocratic decision would be accepted was high. Thus, many (but not all) of the attributes contained in the normative model had an effect on the decision processes which managers employed, and the directions of these effects are similar to those found in the model. However, it would be a mistake to conclude that the managers' behavior was always identical to that of the model. In approximately two thirds of the problems, nevertheless, the behavior which the manager reported was within the feasible set of methods prescribed for that problem, and in about 40% of the cases it corresponded exactly to the minimum manhours (Model A) solution.

Several observations help to account for differences between the model and the typical manager in the sample. First, as is apparent from an inspection of Figure 1, the normative model incorporates a substantial number of interactions among attributes, whereas no such interactions appeared in the results of the regression analysis. Second, the magnitude of the effects of two attributes pertaining to the acceptance or commitment of subordinates to decisions was considerably weaker in the descriptive than in the normative model, suggesting that these considerations play less of a role in determining how people behave. This inference was further supported by the fact that rules designed to protect the acceptance of the decision in the normative model were violated far more frequently than rules designed to protect decision quality.

The results of this research were supportive of the concept of intra-personal variance in leadership style and helped to identify some of the situational factors influencing leaders' choices of decision processes. There were, however, some key methodological weaknesses to this research. Limited variance in and intercorrelations among problem attributes restricted the extent to which situational effects could be determined with precision. Furthermore, the fact that subjects selected and scored their own problems may have led to confounding of individual differences and situational effects. Finally, since only one problem was obtained from each manager, it was impossible to identify interactions between person and situational variables, i.e., idiosyncratic rules for deciding when and to what extent to encourage participation by subordinates.

The methodological problems inherent in the use of "recalled problems" dictated a search for

another method with which to explore the same phenomenon. The technique selected involved the development of a standardized set of administrative problems or cases, each of which depicted a leader faced with some organizational requirement for action or decision making. Managers were asked to assume the role of leader in each situation and to indicate which decision process they would employ.

Several standardized sets of cases were developed using rewritten accounts of actual managerial problems obtained from the previous method. These sets of cases, or problem sets, were developed in accordance with a multi-factorial experimental design, within which the problem attributes were varied orthogonally. Each case corresponded to a particular combination of problem characteristics, and the entire set of cases permitted the simultaneous variation of each problem attribute. To ensure conformity of a given case or problem with the specifications of a cell in the experimental design, an elaborate procedure for testing cases was developed [10, pp. 97–101], involving coding of problems by expert judges and practicing managers.

This method showed promise of permitting the replication of the results using recalled problems with a method that avoided spurious effects stemming from the influence of uncontrolled variables on problem selection. Since the use of a "repeated measures design" permitted a complete experiment to be performed on each subject, the main effects of each of the problem attributes on the decision processes used by the subject could be identified. By comparing the results for different subjects, the similarities and differences in these main effects, and the relative importance of individual differences and of situational variables could be ascertained.

Vroom and Yetton worked exclusively with group problems and with an experimental design which called for thirty cases. The results, obtained from investigations of eight distinct populations comprising over 500 managers, strongly support the major findings from the use of recalled problems, both in terms of the amount of correspondence with the normative model and the specific attributes of situations which tended to induce autocratic and participative decision processes. Moreover, the nature of the methods used made it possible also to obtain precise estimates of the amount of variance attributable to situational factors and individual differences. Only 10% of the total variance could be accounted for in terms of general tendencies to be autocratic or participative (as expressed in differences among individuals in mean behavior on all thirty problems), while about 30% was attributable to situational effects (as expressed in differences in mean behavior among situations).

What about the remaining 60% of the variance? Undoubtedly, some of it can be attributed to errors of measurement, but Vroom and Yetton were able to show that a significant portion of that variance can be explained in terms of another form of individual differences, i.e., differences among managers in ways of "tailoring" their approach to the situation. Theoretically, these can be thought of as differences in decision rules that they employ concerning when to encourage participation.

A FOLLOW-UP INVESTIGATION

The descriptive results reported thus far are but a cursory account of the previous work of Vroom and Yetton [10]. The territory which they explored, however, represents only one-half of the domain originally mapped out in the introductory section of this article. As we have pointed out repeatedly, all of their empirical investigations dealt exclusively with group problems. The extended model (Figure 1), including both individual and group problems, was the focus of the follow-up investigation reported here. The questions to be answered concerned differences between descriptive models of behavior on group versus individual problems, and the extent of manager agreement with the yet-untested extension of the normative model.

Since the use of standardized cases in testing the group model provided consistent and richer data than use of recalled problems, only standardized cases were employed in this investigation. Like previous problem sets, a new set of cases was constructed, drawing from those group problems included in previous sets and individual problems rewritten from a large sample of actual decision-making situations.

If each of the eight dichotomous attributes (Figure 1) were varied independently for both group and individual problems, 2^9 or 512 unique combinations of attribute characteristics could be generated. To reduce the size to a workable number of combinations to be included in the revised problem set, a number of "nesting" procedures dictated by obvious interrelationships among the attributes were used. Five principles, the first three of which were employed by Vroom and Yetton [10] in previous sets, convey these procedures:

Principle 1: Leader's information *(B)*, problem structure *(C)*, and subordinates' goal congruence *(F)* are varied only when there is a quality requirement *(A)* to the problem.

Principle 2: Problem structure *(C)* is varied only when the leader does not have sufficient information *(B)* to make a high-quality decision.

Principle 3: The prior probability of acceptance of an autocratic solution *(E)* is varied only when acceptance of the decision by subordinates is critical for effective implementation *(D)*.

Principle 4: Subordinate information *(H)* is varied only in individual problems having a quality requirement *(A)*.

Principle 5: Conflict among subordinates *(G)* is varied only in group problems.

The rationale for the first three of these procedures is discussed by Vroom and Yetton [10, pp. 95–97]. Principle 4 reflects the irrelevance of subordinate information to the effectiveness of decisions lacking a quality requirement, and the irrelevance of subordinate information to the behavior of the normative model for group problems. Similarly, Principle 5 is based on the fact that potential conflict or disagreement among a set of subordinates is both difficult to manipulate in problems affecting only a single subordinate and irrelevant to the behavior of the model on individual problems.

The applications of these five nesting principles reduced the number of problem cases required from 512 to 81. These 81 cells in the experimental design represented 72 cases in which there was a quality requirement (36 group, 36 individual) and 9 cases without a quality requirement. This number was further reduced by 50 percent sampling of the cells having a high-quality requirement, the cells chosen being balanced with respect to the remaining variables. In addition to the sampling, three individual problems with low-quality requirements were included to decrease the high-low ratio for this attribute. Although confounding some higher-order interactions, this process reduced the number of standardized problems required to 48 (24 group and 24 individual problems), while retaining the desirable property that certain main effects are orthogonal.

Cases thought to meet the specifications of the above design were coded on each attribute by expert judges and managers in a manner similar to that of problems used in previous problem sets. Those with ambiguous status on any attribute were revised until criteria for their inclusion in a given cell in the experimental design were met. When all 48 problems or cases had been selected, they were assigned numbers in accordance with a random process and administered to subjects, all of whom were practicing managers.

The managers studied were all participants in a management development program in which the senior author played an instructional role. The program was similar to that described in Vroom and Yetton [10, chapter 8]. In working on the problem set, each manager was asked to assume the role of leader in each of the 48 situations and to indicate the decision process (from the two columns in Table 1) that he would use in each situation. Each knew that he would receive an individualized computer printout representing an analysis of his leadership style, but was naive with regard to the model, problem attributes, or the basis for construction of the problem set.

Managers in three distinct management development programs were studied using this method. The three populations varied most obviously in the heterogeneity of the managerial jobs performed by the participants. A brief description of each population follows:

Population 1 (P1)—High Heterogeneity.
N = 30

. . . highly diverse group, one-half of whom were managers from business firms. The industries they represented included oil, steel, pulp and paper, aircraft, and banking; and their locations included Greece, Iran, Switzerland, Egypt, and the United States. The other half were military officers from the Air Force, Army, Marines, and Navy; and their functions ranged from publications to research and development.

Population 2 (P2)—Moderate Heterogeneity.
N = 40

. . . group of middle managers from a large industrial corporation producing a wide variety of electrical products. The managers came from many operations of the company including space products, environmental systems, steam turbines, and consumer products. Their functions within these operations included manufacturing, engineering, finance, marketing, and employee relations.

Population 3 (P3)—Low Heterogeneity.
N = 28

. . . group of department heads from the research center of a large public utility specializing in tele-communications.

Discrimination Between Group and Individual Problems

Of foremost importance was whether the managers' behavior would reflect the distinction between group and individual decision-making situations. Since CII and GII are decision-making processes applicable only to group problems, their use on individual problems would indicate that managers do not discriminate between these types of situations. Use of GI and DI on group problems would indicate a similar confusion. The mean frequency of decision process choices on the 24 group and 24 individual cases (Table 3), suggests that managers do discriminate between the two types of problems. The average manager chose, for group problems, processes that are designed for exclusive use in individual problems only 0.25 times in 24. He chose group decision-making processes for individual problems less than 0.80 times in 24. This data provides strong support for the fact that managers implicitly dis-

Table 3.   Mean Frequency of Process Choice on Group and Individual Problems (N = 98)

Process	Group problems	Individual problems	Difference[1]
AI	3.24	4.62	$p < .001$
AII	2.48	2.11	ns
CI	4.05	5.99	$p < .001$
CII	7.50	0.47	$p < .001$
GI	0.09	6.30	$p < .001$
GII	6.48	0.31	$p < .001$
DI	0.16	4.20	$p < .001$

[1]Repeated measures T-Test (two-tailed)

tinguish group from individual problems, a distinction that is basic to the broader structure of the normative model.

The data in Table 3 also suggests that managers behave more autocratically in situations affecting only one subordinate than in situations affecting a group. Use of AI and CI, comparatively autocratic processes common to both the group and individual models, is significantly greater on individual than on group problems. Consequently, use of the more participative processes relevant to group situations (CII and GII) is greater than the use of the more participative processes (GI and DI) relevant to interaction with single subordinates.

Individual and Situational Main Effects

Using standardized cases, Vroom and Yetton [10] were able to attribute 30% of the variance in participation on group problems to situational determinants. The use here of standardized individual problems also lends itself to such analysis. Before fitting a linear model to the data, however, the newly included decision processes, GI and DI, required assignment of values on a scale of participation. Using the same scaling technique employed for group processes, GI was assigned a value of 8.125 and DI a value of 10.

These values can now be used in an effort to calculate the amount of variance in decision processes attributable to the problem and to the individual manager. The analysis, which treats problem and individual as nominal variables, was identical to that used by Vroom and Yetton [10]. It was carried out separately for group and individual problems and for each of the three populations. Table 4 reports the results.

The data on group problems clearly replicates the earlier finding of Vroom and Yetton. Situational differences account for about 35% of the variance in managers' behavior, while individual differences account for a much lower 12%. Thus, the amount of influence of situational factors in determining choice of a leadership method on

Table 4.   Percent Total Variance Attributable to Problem and Individual Differences

	Group problems				Individual problems			
	P1	P2	P3	ALL	P1	P2	P3	ALL
Due to Problem	31.0%	39.6%	45.8%	34.7%	39.7%	49.2%	50.6%	44.0%
Due to Individual	11.4%	7.3%	7.4%	11.7%	7.7%	8.8%	5.3%	8.7%

group problems is roughly three times the influence of individual differences. This ratio is even higher when one looks at individual problems, where the influence of situational factors appears to be roughly five times the influence of individual differences.

The amount of variance attributable to individual differences and to shared situational effects might be expected to vary with the homogeneity of the roles carried out with the populations studied. If the nature of the work performed has anything to do with the development of a leadership style, as reflected in behavior on the standardized cases, then one would expect to find that managers performing more homogeneous roles would be less different from one another. A comparison of the proportion of explained variance attributable to individuals and to situations for the three populations strongly supports this prediction. In fact, the ratio of shared situational effects to individual effects for P3, the most homogeneous population studied, is 9.6 to 1 for individual problems, compared with 5.6 and 5.2 for P2 and P1, respectively. For group problems, the ratio for P3 is 6.2, compared with 5.4 and 2.7 for P2 and P1, respectively.

Problem Attributes as Determinants of Behavior

The results shown in Table 4 corroborate Vroom and Yetton's earlier findings with respect to the relative importance of situational factors and traits of authoritarianism-participation in determining decision processes used on group problems. It also extends those conclusions to individual problems with an indication that situational variables play an even stronger role relative to traits.

However, the results presented so far do not indicate what situational variables are important in influencing behavior on standardized cases. The experimental design underlying the problem set makes it possible to assess the direction and magnitude of the effect of the eight problem attributes in determining the decision process used by the 98 managers studied.

Two methods were used in the analyses of the data:

(1) *The main effects* of each problem attribute were computed by subtracting the mean scale value of the decision processes used on all problems selected to represent a low value of the attribute from the mean scale value of the decision processes on all problems selected to represent a high value of that attribute. Since the method of scaling the decision processes accords larger scores to more participative processes, a positive value for the main effect of a given attribute indicates a tendency for that attribute to result in use of more participative methods by a typical manager.

Calculations of main effects of attributes were made separately for group and individual problems. The number of problems representing high and low values of each attribute is given by the experimental design. It should be noted that calculations of main effects of some attributes were based on less than the entire set of problems, due to the use of the nesting principles mentioned above.

(2) *Multiple regressions* were performed separately for behavior on group and individual problems. Level of participation was the dependent variable, and problem attributes were the independent variables. A value of 1 was given to the problem attribute if the attribute was present, and −1 if the attribute was absent from the problem. When one variable was nested within another, assumptions had to be made to permit a complete specification of all attributes for all problems. (This requirement of multiple regression distinguishes it from the previous method in which main effects could be based on only a subset of the cases.) The assumptions used follow directly from the nesting principles discussed earlier.[4]

The principle advantage of the second method is its usefulness in determining the proportion of situational variance attributable to the influence of each problem attribute.[5] The results from both methods are shown in Table 5.

All but one of the mean main effects have the same sign for both group and individual problems. Furthermore, the signs are consistent with the direction of effect on attributes of the behavior of Model A in all but two of the fourteen effects studied. Subjects tended to show more participation on problems in which the leader lacked relevant information, particularly if the problem was also unstructured. They showed more partic-

Table 5.   Main Effects of Problem Attributes and Their Contribution to Situational Variance

Problem attributes	Group problems			Individual problems		
	Mean main effect[1]		% Situational variance	Mean main effect[1]		% Situational variance
Quality requirement	1.72	(1.46)[2]	5.6%	−0.45	(1.01)[2]	1.2%
Leader's information	−0.44	(−3.44)	0.4	−1.67	(−3.23)	3.2
Structure	−1.69	(−5.00)	7.5	−0.83	(−1.88)	1.4
Importance of acceptance	0.65	(3.36)	1.1	1.90	(2.27)	5.7
Prior probability	−2.44	(−6.72)	20.6	−0.94	(−5.63)	2.4
Goal congruence	0.46	(0.97)	0.4	3.51	(2.85)	40.8
Conflict	−1.30	(0.42)	8.4	—	—	—
Subordinate information	—	—	—	0.87	(1.46)	5.0

[1]Main effects are significantly different from zero at the .001 level or beyond (two-tailed T-test).
[2]Figures in parentheses show main effects calculated for Model A's behavior on same problems.

ipation on problems that required subordinate acceptance than on problems that did not, especially when they lacked the expert, legitimate, or referent power to gain that acceptance from an autocratic decision. Finally, managers were found to show more participation when subordinates shared organizational goals than when they did not.

The one problem attribute which appears to have a differential effect on the two types of problems is attribute A—the existence of a quality requirement. The same set of managers tended to encourage a greater degree of participation by their subordinates on group problems with a quality requirement and on individual problems without a quality requirement. Additional examination of the frequency of use of each decision process on problems with high and low quality requirements indicates that the effects of this problem attribute are not linear across the participation scale, particularly for individual problems. The existence of a quality requirement militates against the use of AI for group problems and against the use of both AI and DI for individual problems. CI is the modal style for the individual problems with a quality requirement while CII is the modal process for group problems.

Two other attributes were varied only within one set of 24 problems and provided no basis for comparison of group and individual problems. As found previously by Vroom and Yetton, managers responded to potential conflict and disagreement among subordinates by becoming more autocratic on group problems. In this respect, they differed from Model A, which showed a small but positive effect. They also responded to a high level of subordinate information and expertise by becoming more participative on individual problems. The latter is a new finding but not an unexpected one.

While the direction of the main effects of the comparable problem attributes are similar, their magnitudes are not. The contribution of each attribute, considered alone, to the explanation of situational variance is also shown in Table 5.[6]

Prior probability of acceptance of an autocratic decision (attribute E) is the most important determinant of participation on group problems, explaining 20.6% of the situational variance. However, it explains only 2.4% of that variance for individual problems. Apparently, the degree to which a leader possesses enough power to gain acceptance of his own decision is more relevant to his handling of matters affecting the entire system under his direction than to matters affecting only a single subordinate. It is possible that the greater time required for the more participative approaches to group problems, relative to those for individual problems, limits their use to situations in which the leader cannot gain acceptance of his own ideas. "If you can sell your own solution, then sell it—you save time that way" is more consistent with managers' behavior on group problems than on individual problems. It also is interesting to note that this difference is consistent in direction with the main effects for Model A, also shown in the table.

A second problem attribute to possess markedly different explanatory power for group and individual problems is goal congruence (attribute G). It accounts for an overwhelming 40.8% of the problem variance in decision processes for individual problems but less than one-half of 1% of the variance for group problems. The set of managers studied were extremely reluctant to delegate problems to subordinates who did not share the goals to be achieved. (DI was used in only 0.3% of such instances.) However, they did not exhibit the same reluctance to use the GII process in situations of low mutual interest. Conceivably, the fact that an entire set of subordinates does not share the goals to be achieved in a problem which affects them all constitutes a signal to many managers for the use of participative methods in order to effect a greater rapprochement with system objectives. On the other hand, alienation of a single subordinate constitutes a less serious problem. He can typically be replaced or "brought into line" at a later time. The results shown as main effects for Model A are similar in direction, but the difference is not nearly as large.

Agreement with the Normative Model

Effects of the problem attributes on the behavior of 98 managers reported in Table 5 bear reasonable similarity to the role of the attributes in the normative model. A comparison of Model A main effects of each problem attribute with the observed values reveals that similarity. Indeed, the directions of main effects calculated for Model A are identical to those shown for the behavior of the managers for 12 of 14 comparisons. Even the two main effects with a different sign are instructive.

A more accurate indication of similarity between the behavior of the model and that of the managers studied may be seen by examining the frequency with which their choices of decision processes were in agreement with the feasible set, Model A, and Model B choices. These data, along with certain other aggregate indices of behavior, are shown in Table 6.

It can be seen that agreement with all three indices shows significantly higher agreement between the normative model and managers' behavior on individual problems than on group problems. For example, the number of instances of agreement with the feasible set is 16.34 (68%)[7] for group problems but 19.81 (or 82.5%) for individual problems.

This difference cannot be attributed to the number of feasible responses for group and individual problems. Indeed, a random assignment of decision processes in each subset of problems would yield the same expected agreement with the feasible set—9.57, or about 40%, for both individual and group problems. However, an inspection of the structure of the model shown in Figure 1 reveals another possible basis for the difference in agreement rates for individual and group problems. It will be noted that GII—the most participative process for group problems—stands alone within the feasible set for 5 of the 18 types of group problems. However, there are none of the 18 types of individual problems for which DI—the most participative method for individual problems—stands alone. If a given manager found the loss of control inherent in either delegation or group decision making threatening, and never employed either process in the 48 cases, he would automatically violate the feasible set on five group problems but would not necessarily exhibit any rule violations on individual problems.

For both kinds of problems, agreement with Model A exceeds agreement with Model B, although the difference for group problems does not reach conventional levels of statistical significance. Larger differences were found by Vroom and Yetton for their population of over 500 managers. It is likely that the substantially higher level of participation on group problems for the populations reported here prevents the replication of these results.

The fourth row in the table shows mean level of participation (MLP) for Model A, Model B, and for the 98 managers studied. It is worth not-

Table 6.   Managers' Agreement with the Normative Model

	Short-term Model (A)		Developmental Model (B)		Managers' behavior			
	Group	Ind.	Group	Ind.	Group	Ind.	Diff[1] rGrp., Ind.	Grp., Ind.
Agreement with feasible set	24	24	24	24	16.34	19.81	0.25**	$p < .001$
Agreement with Model A	24	24	9	9[2]	7.78	10.59	0.17	$p < .001$
Agreement with Model B	9	9[2]	24	24	7.29	9.34	0.27**	$p < .001$
MLP[3]	4.43	4.09	9.30	8.13	6.25	5.47	0.71**	$p < .001$
Mean within-person variance	18.84	15.92	0.82	3.91	12.19	12.53	0.51**	ns

**Correlations significant at .01 level or beyond.
[1]Repeated measures T-test (two-tailed).
[2]These values reflect the fact that there are 9 group and 9 individual problems that have feasible sets which contain one alternative that satisfies both the Model A and Model B requirement.
[3]Mean level of participation (MLP) is the mean scale value of selected decision processes.

ing that managerial behavior tends to be more participative than Model A but more autocratic than Model B. Of perhaps greater interest is the fact that the behavior of managers and that of both models is more autocratic on individual than on group problems.

The final row in the table shows the average within-person variance in behavior across problems for the managers studied and the variance for the two models. Managerial behavior exhibits less variance across situations than Model A but substantially more variance than the highly participative Model B.

The second column from the right shows correlations between various indices of behavior on group and individual problems. Managers who use participative methods on group problems also tend to be more participative on individual problems. In fact, the correlation of 0.71 between MLP on group and individual problems, each based on 24 problems, approaches Vroom and Yetton's estimate of 0.81 for the reliability of a 30-problem test using solely group problems. This finding clearly refutes a speculation which launched the inquiry into the relationship between behavior on group and individual problems. In an ear-

lier phase of the research, several managers who received feedback based on group problems depicting their behavior as autocratic relative to their peers insisted that, while they were opposed to group meetings for the purpose of making decisions, they really believed in delegation. Such an assertion is inconsistent with the correlation and mean difference of power sharing on the two types of problems.

The correlation between variance in behavior on group and individual problems is likewise supportive of consistency in style in dealing with these two kinds of problems. Those who exhibit variety in their approaches to dealing with group problems also exhibit variety in their approach to individual problems, to a degree which comes close to the reliability of this property within group problems alone.

There is also a tendency for managers whose behavior is consistent with the model for group problems to behave consistently with the model for individual problems. However, the correlation reported for the three indices of agreement with the normative model are both smaller in magnitude and smaller in relation to estimated reliabilities than the previous two coefficients.

When a manager's behavior is outside the feasible set of alternatives for a given problem, his choice of decision process violates at least one of the ten rules described earlier. Identification of the relative frequency of violations of each of those rules provides a clearer understanding of the bases of agreement or disagreement with the normative model.

Table 7 shows (1) the rules; (2) the number of applicable group and individual problems to each rule, i.e., the maximum number of times each rule could be violated in the 48-case problem set; (3) the mean observed probability of violation[8] of each rule; and (4) an expected probability of rule violations,[9] assuming a random assignment of choices consistent with the total frequency distribution of choices. The difference between expected and observed (Expected-Observed) can be taken as evidence of discrimination between problems to which the rule is applicable and problems to which the rule is not applicable. A positive difference is indicative of discrimination consistent in direction with the model and a negative difference indicative of discrimination opposite in direction to the model.

The weighted average of rule violations for group and individual problems shows that rules tend to be violated less than half as frequently on individual as on group problems. This finding is consistent with the previous observation of substantially greater agreement with the feasible set on individual problems. Nonetheless, a comparison of weighted averages with expected probabilities shows greater-than-expected conformity with the rules of the model for *both* kinds of problems. This global indicator of consistency with the model is perhaps less revealing than a detailed examination of the results for each rule. Vroom and Yetton [10, pp. 147–149] had previously found that acceptance rules (5–8) had generally

Table 7. Comparison of Observed and Expected Probability of Rule Violation (N = 98)

	Rule	Applicable cases (Grp., Ind.)	Group problems Obs.	Exp.	Diff.[1]	Individual problems Obs.	Exp.	Diff.[1]
1	$A \cap \bar{B} \to \overline{AI}$	(12, 12)	.037	.135	$p < .001$	.025	.193	$p < .001$
2	$A \cap \bar{H} \to \overline{DI}$	(0, 9)	—	—	—	.026	.175	$p < .001$
3A	$A \cap \bar{F} \to \overline{GII}, \overline{DI}$	(9, 9)	.260	.270	ns	.003	.175	$p < .001$
3B	$A \cap (\bar{D} \cup E) \cap \bar{F} \to \overline{GI}$	(0, 6)	—	—	—	.092	.262	$p < .001$
4A	$A \cap \bar{B} \cap \bar{C} \to \overline{AI}, \overline{AII}, \overline{CI}$	(6, 0)	.284	.407	$p < .001$	—	—	—
4B	$A \cap \bar{B} \cap \bar{C} \to \overline{AI}, \overline{AII}$	(0, 6)	—	—	—	.128	.281	$p < .001$
5	$D \cap \bar{E} \to \overline{AI}, \overline{AII}$	(8, 8)	.079	.238	$p < .001$	.131	.281	$p < .001$
6	$D \cap \bar{E} \cap G \to \overline{AI}, \overline{AII}, \overline{CI}$	(4, 0)	.263	.407	$p < .001$	—	—	—
7	$\bar{A} \cap D \cap \bar{E} \to \overline{AI}, \overline{AII}, \overline{CI}, \overline{CII}$	(2, 2)	.765	.730	ns	.087	.530	$p < .001$
8	$D \cap \bar{E} \cap F \to \overline{AI}, \overline{AII}, \overline{CI}, \overline{CII}$	(3, 3)	.466	.730	$p < .001$	.320	.530	$p < .001$
9	Group $\to \overline{GI}, \overline{DI}$	(24, 0)	.011	.224	$p < .001$	—	—	—
10	Ind. $\to \overline{CII}, \overline{GII}$	(0, 24)	—	—	—	.032	.307	$p < .001$
	Weighted average	(68, 79)	.138	.280	$p < .001$	.061	.266	$p < .001$

[1]T-Test (one-tailed)

higher observed probabilities of rule violations than quality rules (1–4). With few exceptions, the same results were obtained here, but the inclusion of expected rates of violation for each rule as a standard of comparison reveals that acceptance rules (due to a greater inclusiveness in processes eliminated) are expected to have higher violation rates.

A more appropriate basis for determining consistency between a rule and managerial behavior is the degree of difference in behavior between those problems to which the rule is applicable and behavior on the entire set of problems. A comparison of expected and observed rates of violation of rules relevant to individual problems shows substantial evidence that these managers are tending to make the kinds of discriminations made in the rules. Observed values are always significantly less than expected values. When comparing across rules, it is evident that rule 8 is the only rule relevant to individual problems which is violated with some notable frequency. This rule prohibits use of processes other than GI and DI when the acceptance by an individual subordinate of a decision is critical, when the prior probability of his acceptance of an autocratic decision is low, and when the subordinate shares the goals to be obtained.

A similar comparison for group problems tells a quite different story. For two of the eight rules, the difference between observed and expected values is not significant. Rule 7, the Fairness Rule, is, in fact, violated slightly more frequently than expected, based on random choices, and Rule 3a is violated almost as frequently as expected. A recomputation of the weighted average of observed probability of rule violations for group problems eliminating Rules 3a and 7 yields a value of 0.096. While still greater than the observed probability for individual problems (0.061), this calculation shows that, in large measure, the disparity between agreement with the feasible set on group versus individual problems can be attributed to managers' inappropriate use of the GII process, i.e., their reluctance to use the GII process on problems which are essentially matters of fairness and equity (Rule 7), and their willingness to use GII on problems where their subordinates do not share the goals of the organization (Rule 3a).

DISCUSSION AND SUMMARY

In this paper a normative model of social processes for decision making was presented. This model represented a slightly elaborated and refined version of a model presented in Vroom and Yetton [10]. We share the previous authors' view that such models are far from perfect but can serve a useful function in stimulating research which, in time, will be reflected in better models.

The latter half of this paper was devoted to questions related to how managers do select decision processes—to the factors which influence the degree to which they share their decision-making power with their subordinates. In pursuing these questions, we also relied heavily on the previous work of Vroom and Yetton by using a set of standardized cases selected in accordance with an experimental design. Each case depicted a leader faced with a problem to solve, and subjects were asked to assume his role and to select from a specified list of decision processes the one they would employ. The major difference from Vroom and Yetton was in the nature of the experimental design used in the construction of the "problem set." Whereas Vroom and Yetton's design utilized 30 "group problems" and five decision processes, the design used here provided for seven decision processes and 24 group and 24 individual problems. This design permitted the additional exploration of relationships between behavior on each kind of problem, and of the consistency of the behavior on the latter with the normative model.

The results are supportive of previous conclusions drawn by Vroom and Yetton but augment them in several significant ways. The managers studied do make the discrimination between group and individual problems required by the normative model and select from the appropriate class of decision methods for each problem. Furthermore, the role that the problem attributes play in affecting managers' behavior on the two kinds of problems are distinct in several respects. Therefore, a descriptive model to account for the circumstances under which managers share their decision-making power with subordinates must incorporate a distinction between group and individual problems and the differences in the effects of problem attributes on each kind of problem.

Agreement between the normative model and managers' behavior is substantially higher for individual problems than for group problems, although both exceed chance. The principal bases for deviations from the model on group problems lie in the circumstances surrounding the use of group decision making (GII). Managers are exceedingly reluctant to employ GII on problems without a quality requirement but involving substantial components of fairness and equity and, consequently, exhibit higher-than-expected violations of Rule 7. On the other hand, they make greater use of GII in problems with a quality requirement when the interests of subordinates do not coincide with organizational goals—a use that is prohibited by Rule 3a in the model. The disagreement with the normative model for individual problems is, in large measure, due to a reluctance to employ participative methods (DI and GI) as a means of obtaining needed commitment to a course of action from a subordinate.

The results presented here provide further evidence against the explanatory power of a trait of authoritarianism-participation in accounting for the decision process used by managers. While managers who tend to employ power-equalization methods on group problems also tend to use such methods on individual problems ($r = .71$), there is wide variance in the processes used in different situations. The variance in behavior that can be attributed to situational characteristics is many times larger than the variance that is attributable to individual differences. From these results, it makes substantially more sense to talk about autocratic and participative situations rather than autocratic and participative managers. The results presented reinforce the earlier conclusion of Vroom and Yetton from their investigation of group problems and suggest that a similar but stronger conclusion can be drawn with respect to individual problems. [It makes] substantially more sense to talk about autocratic and participative situations rather than autocratic and participative managers. The results presented reinforce the earlier conclusion of Vroom and Yetton from their investigation of group problems and suggest that a similar but stronger conclusion can be drawn with respect to individual problems.

Finally, the results presented indicate that the relative explanatory power of situational and individual difference variables is probably not independent of the similarity in roles performed by the managers in the population. The greater the homogeneity within the population, the smaller the proportion of variance attributable to mean differences among managers, and the greater the tendency to respond in a similar fashion to situational demands. The obvious implication is that the nature of the role occupied by the manager shapes his leadership style, but the manner in which this occurs is a subject for further investigation.

NOTES

1. For a detailed definition of these attributes and of criteria to be used in making Yes-No judgments, see Vroom and Yetton [10, pp. 21–31].
2. For additional problems and their analysis, see Vroom and Yetton [10, pp. 40–44].
3. The question pertaining to this attribute is asked in the decision tree but is irrelevant to the prescribed behavior.
4. The assumptions used for this purpose are as follows: (1) $A = -1 \rightarrow B = 1$, $C = 1$, $F = 1$; (2) $B = 1 \rightarrow C = 1$; (3) $D = -1 \rightarrow E = 1$ and (4) $A_I = -1 \rightarrow H = 1$.
5. The regression method (Overall and Spiegel [8, pp. 315–317]) derives main effect estimates from an additive (no interaction) model and includes interaction parameters only to evaluate deviation from the additive model. Overall and Spiegel claim this method is appropriate when the problem is conceived as a multiclassification factorial design, but computational difficulties, or unequal cell frequencies, prevent employment of conventional analysis of variance techniques. No findings relevant to interactions among problem attributes is presented here, although data concerning such interactions for group problems is presented in Vroom and Yetton [10].
6. The experimental design and the method of coding attributes for the regressions result in some multicollinearity among independent variables. It appears, however, that any confounding is negligible, since only variables with very low main effects are affected. Since the experimental design and coding method were consistent for group and individual problems, multicollinearity does not contribute to the observed differences between the two types of problems.

7. This figure is comparable to the 69.7% agreement reported by Vroom and Yetton for 551 managers on 30 group problems.

8. Probabilities of violation of a given rule are calculated by dividing the frequency of violation by the frequency of applicability of the rule within the 48-case problem set. This transformation permits comparisons to be made across rules [10, pp. 146–147].

9. Expected probabilities of rule violations were based on random assignment of process choices constrained only by the mean distribution of decision processes in each subset of 24 problems. These probabilities reflect the rule violations expected of a person who maintained the mean frequency of use of each process but who did not discriminate among problems in his allocation of processes.

REFERENCES

[1] Cyert, R. M., and J. G. March, *A Behavioral Theory of the Firm*, Englewood Cliffs, N.J.: Prentice-Hall, 1963.

[2] Lewin, K., "Frontiers in Group Dynamics," *Field Theory in Social Science*, edited by D. Cartwright (New York: Harper, 1951), pp. 188–237.

[3] Lowin, A., "Participative Decision Making: A Model, Literature Critique, and Prescriptions for Research," *Organizational Behavior and Human Performance*, 3, 1968, pp. 68–106.

[4] Maier, N. R. F., A. R. Solem, and A. A. Maier, *Supervisory and Executive Development: A Manual for Role Playing*, New York: Wiley, 1957.

[5] Maier, N. R. F., "Problem-solving Discussions and Conferences," *Leadership Methods and Skills*, New York: McGraw-Hill, 1963.

[6] March, J. G., and H. A. Simon, *Organizations*, New York: Wiley, 1958.

[7] McGregor, D., *The Human Side of Enterprise*, New York: McGraw-Hill, 1960.

[8] Overall, J. E., and D. K. Spiegel, "Concerning Least Squares Analysis of Experimental Data," *Psychological Bulletin*, 72, 1969, pp. 311–322.

[9] Vroom, V. H., "Industrial Social Psychology," *Handbook of Social Psychology*, edited by G. Lindzey and E. Aronson (Reading, Mass.: Addison-Wesley, 1970), 5, pp. 196–268.

[10] Vroom, V. H., and P. W. Yetton, *Leadership and Decision-Making*, Pittsburgh: University of Pittsburgh Press, 1973.

[11] Wood, M. T., "Power Relationships and Group Decision Making in Organizations," *Psychological Bulletin*, 79, 1973, pp. 280–293.

III.C
Conflict

20
Organizational conflict

Kenneth W. Thomas

. . . Much of the ambivalence toward conflict in the field of organizational behavior appears to come from two contrasting themes. The first involves coordination and efficiency. Viewed from this perspective, organizational conflict can be interpreted as the mutual interference of different parts of the organization, similar to the friction which interferes with the smooth functioning of a machine—as a breakdown in the coordination of parts which interferes with the machine's efficiency. In fact, March and Simon (1958, p. 112) defined conflict as "a breakdown in standard mechanisms of decision making."

The second and more recent theme sees conflict as playing a central role in organizational innovation and adaptation. From this perspective, conflict can be interpreted as a critical questioning of the status quo—of prevailing ideas, policies, procedures, etc. For example, after reviewing a number of studies on group decision making, Hall (1971), p. 88) stated that "conflict, effectively managed, is a necessary precondition for creativity." Lack of open disagreement

in a decision-making group can be viewed as inviting poor decisions—a phenomenon called group-think. . . . In the same vein, Robbins (1974) noted that the failures of organizations like the Penn Central Railroad and Studebaker have been attributed to too much harmony, and argued that conflict within top management is essential to organizational change, adaptation and survival.

Obviously, each of these two themes makes valid points, but is part of a larger picture. Organizational ambivalence toward conflict is to some degree a reflection of tensions between the organization's needs for reasonable degrees of both efficiency and innovation.

If conflict is important to the organization, it is equally vital to the individual manager. Recent studies indicate that conflict management is both a frequent and an important managerial activity. In a recent survey, top and middle managers reported spending about 20 percent of their time dealing with some form of conflict (Thomas and Schmidt, 1976). Furthermore, they indicated that conflict management skills had become more important to their performance during the past ten years, and were highly interested in learning more about conflict and its management. . . .

Source: Reprinted with permission from *Organizational Behavior,* edited by Steven Kerr. Grid Publishing, Inc., Columbus, Ohio, 1979.

Putting Conflict in a Context

. . . The definition of conflict has been a controversial topic among researchers. Pondy (1967, p. 298) observed that definitions of conflict have varied over the following aspects of the conflict process:

> (1) *Antecedent conditions* (for example, scarcity of resources, policy differences) of conflictful behavior, (2) *affective states* (e.g., stress, tension, hostility, anxiety) etcetera, (3) *cognitive states* of individuals (i.e., their perception or awareness of conflictful situations) and (4) *conflictful behavior,* ranging from passive resistance to overt aggression.

Rather than arguing for one of these specific definitions, Pondy recommended that the term conflict be used in a more general way to refer to the entire process which includes all these phenomena.

However, this general meaning needs to be defined more precisely in order to distinguish conflict from such other processes as decision making. . . .

Conflict can occur between any units or parties—supervisor and subordinate, companies and unions, between peers, departments or other groups, or between organizations. Rather than broadly reviewing research and theory from these different areas, this [reading] will attempt to pre-sent a more integrated treatment of conflict from a somewhat narrower perspective. The [reading] will focus upon the relevance of selected theory and research for the manager who has responsibility for the performance of an organizational unit. Furthermore, our focus will be upon conflicts occurring *within* the system under the manager's supervision—whether a work group, division, or an entire organization. The [reading] will focus upon theory and research relevant to the manager's need to evaluate the effects of conflicts within his or her unit, diagnose the sources and dynamics of those conflicts, and intervene to manage conflicts when intervention is appropriate. . . .

A useful point of departure is the model of interdepartmental conflict developed by Walton and Dutton (1969), shown in Figure 1. Contextual and personality factors are shown as shaping various attributes of the relationship between departments, which in turn produce consequences for the organization's effectiveness. Higher executives are seen as responding to those consequences by modifying contextual and personality factors bearing upon the relationship—through allocation of resources, transfers of personnel, creating new policies, etc. In addition, the parties directly involved in the relationship are seen as engaging in efforts to manage their own interface.

Figure 2 shows a revision of the Walton and Dutton model which will serve as an organizing

Figure 1. The Walton and Dutton Model of Interdepartmental Conflict

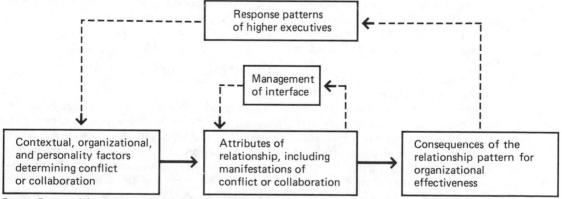

Source: Reprinted from "The Management of Interdepartmental Conflict: A Model and Review," by Richard E. Walton and John M. Dutton. Published in *Administrative Science Quarterly,* Vol. 14, #1 by permission of *The Administrative Science Quarterly.* Copyright © 1969 by Cornell University.

Figure 2.   Revised Model: The Manager's Role in Managing Intra-System Conflict

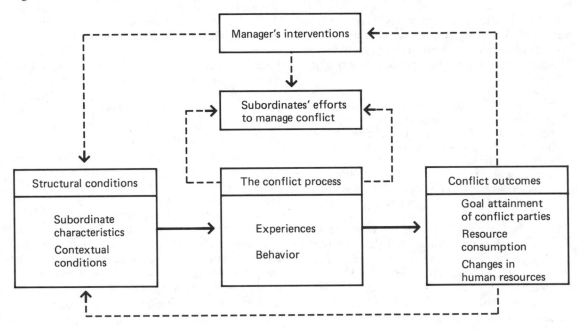

device for the rest of this [reading]. Since we are concerned with a manager's handling of conflict within his or her unit at any organizational level, the term "manager" has replaced "higher executives." Furthermore, since conflict is defined as a process (or series of events), the model focuses upon the conflict process rather than "attributes of relationship." Both the internal experiences of the conflicting parties and their externally visible behaviors are identified as important parts of this process. Subordinate characteristics and contextual conditions are labeled as "structural conditions" to distinguish them from the conflict process which they influence.

Conflict consequences are referred to as the "outcomes" of the conflict process, and are broken down into three major dimensions: goal attainment by the conflicting parties, resource consumption, and changes in human resources. These outcomes are seen as altering structural conditions directly, as well as shaping the manager's conflict management interventions into the system.

Finally, two varieties of these interventions are identified. The manager may make *structural* in-

terventions which change the characteristics of subordinates and the context in which they interact, as in the Walton and Dutton model. In addition, the manager may make *process* interventions by becoming directly involved in the sequence of events in an ongoing conflict episode—by trying to influence the experiences (perceptions, feelings) and/or behaviors of subordinates. As shown in the revised model, these process interventions augment efforts of subordinates to manage their own conflicts.

CONFLICT BEHAVIORS

The most visible aspects of conflict are behaviors used by the parties in attempting to cope with a conflict. These behaviors often provide the means for the manager to identify and begin diagnosing a conflict situation. Accordingly, conflict behaviors will be reviewed before discussing the other elements of Figure 2.

Until the mid-1960s, most research on organizational conflict attempted to classify conflict behaviors along a single dimension, such as co-operative-competitive, or cooperative-conflict-ful. These relatively simple classifications have a common-sense appeal. However, more recent research suggests that no single dimension can capture the range of behavioral alternatives which are available to conflict parties.

A Two-Dimensional Framework

. . . Blake and Mouton in *The Managerial Grid* (1964) described five management styles in terms of two underlying attitudes of the manager: concern for production and concern for people. Each style was assigned a preferred behavior for handling conflict with subordinates, resulting in a list of five conflict behaviors: suppression, confrontation, compromise, avoiding, and smoothing.

In the last fifteen years, a number of variations on this scheme for classifying conflict behaviors have appeared which attempt to extend it beyond the supervisor-subordinate relationship. The version shown in Figure 3 was developed by Thomas (1976). Rather than classifying behaviors according to a party's personality (i.e., values or style), this framework considers the party's intentions in a given conflict situation, intentions which may or may not relate to supervisory goals such as production. The two underlying dimensions of intention in this scheme are

a. *cooperativeness*—attempting to satisfy the other party's concerns; and

b. *assertiveness*—attempting to satisfy one's own concerns.

As shown in Figure 3, five behavioral intentions, or conflict-handling modes, are plotted on these two dimensions. *Competing* (assertive, uncooperative) is an attempt to attain one's own concerns at the other party's expense, usually by overpowering the other—for example, through argument, authority, threats, or physical force. By contrast, *accommodating* (unassertive, cooperative) satisfies the other's concerns at the neglect of one's own. *Avoiding* (unassertive, uncooperative) neglects both one's own and the other's concerns by sidestepping or postponing the raising of conflict issues. *Collaborating* (assertive, co-

Figure 3. A Two-Dimensional Model of Conflict Behavior

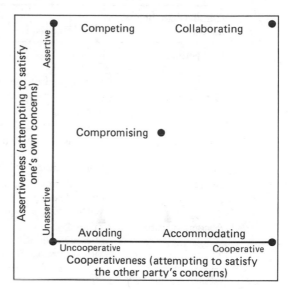

Source: Adapted from Thomas L. Ruble and Kenneth W. Thomas, "Support for a Two-Dimensional Model of Conflict Behavior," *Organizational Behavior and Human Performance*, 16 (1976), p. 145, Figure 1. Copyright © 1976 by Academic Press, Inc. Reprinted by permission.

operative) is an attempt to fully satisfy the concerns of both parties. The remaining mode, *compromising*, is intermediate in both assertiveness and cooperativeness. Compromising seeks partial satisfaction for both parties through a middle-ground position which represents some mutual sacrifice. Compromising is thus intermediate between competing and accommodating in that it yields some concessions, but also extracts some concessions from the other. Likewise, it seeks more joint satisfaction than avoiding, but less than the complete mutual satisfaction which collaborating seeks. Table 1 presents other terms from the conflict literature which have been used to label each of these five conflict-handling modes, along with representative proverbs.

A key feature of many two-dimensional models of conflict behavior is the identification of collaboration, or problem-solving, as an attractive alternative in many conflict situations. Collaboration involves the following steps:

TABLE 1.   The Five Conflict-Handling Modes

Conflict-handling modes	Related terms	Proverbs[a]
Competing	Forcing Conflictful Moving against the other	Put your foot down where you mean to stand.
Collaborating	Problem solving Integrating Confronting	Come let us reason together.
Compromising	Splitting the difference Sharing Horse-trading	You have to give some to get some.
Avoiding	Moving away from the other Losing-leaving Withdrawing	Let sleeping dogs lie.
Accommodating	Yielding-losing Friendly helping Moving toward the other	It is better to give than to receive.

[a]Lawrence and Lorsch, 1967.

1. confronting the conflict.
2. identifying the underlying concerns of the two parties.
3. posing the conflict as a problem: namely, is there a way that both parties' concerns can be satisfied?
4. problem solving to find alternatives which would satisfy both parties; and
5. selecting the most jointly satisfactory alternative.

An Example: Sales and Production

As an illustration of the conflict modes, consider the following case. (We will refer back to this example throughout the [reading].) A Production Manager has been frustrated by unexpected special orders from Sales which upset the efficiency of his operation. If he had had advance knowledge of these orders, he could have scheduled his production runs more efficiently to minimize the down time required to retool. So far, he has *avoided* raising the issue. In an article in a trade journal, however, he finds that another company requires its Sales staff to give Production advance notice of all pending sales orders through a fairly detailed weekly questionnaire. The Production Manager now raises the issue and shows the questionnaire to his counterpart in Sales, who refuses to cooperate: "That questionnaire will take two hours a week which my salespeople don't have! They are already snowed under with paperwork!"

At this point the Production Manager could *compete* by arguing the need for greater efficiency, attempting to enlist the support of the Vice President of Operations, etc. Instead he might *accommodate*, recognizing that the questionnaire would impose a hardship on Sales. Or he might attempt a *compromise*, proposing for example that Sales fill out the questionnaire every two or three weeks. All three of these options preserve a win-lose relationship between the concerns of Sales and Production—one's gains are considered the other's losses.

In contrast, a *collaborative* strategy would be to initiate a joint search for a new alternative which would give Production advance warning on special orders without increasing the amount of Sales' time lost to paperwork. If the two managers put their heads together they might reach agreement over what exactly is the core of the information which Production needs, finding perhaps that most of the questionnaire's information is not important. They might also find ways to reduce Sales' existing paperwork, and uncover ways to transmit information to Production which are more efficient than a questionnaire—for example, an occasional telephone call. Such alternatives might more fully satisfy the joint concerns of the two departments than would compromise, competition, or accommodation.

Integrative and Distributive Dimensions

More insight into this example and into the five conflict-handling modes can be gained by introducing two additional behavioral dimensions which were first identified by Walton and McKersie (1965) in the context of labor-management bargaining—an integrative dimension and a distributive dimension (see Figure 4). Speaking generally, any conflict outcome can be viewed in terms of

a. the total satisfaction of the two parties' concerns and
b. the division of that satisfaction between the two parties.

The *distributive* dimension represents a party's intentions with respect to the proportion of satisfaction going to each party—who gets what portion of the pie. Along this dimension, competing represents extreme taking, accommodating represents extreme giving, and the other modes are intermediate. As noted above, competing, compromising, and accommodating focus on the win-lose aspects of a conflict, assuming that there is a fixed and limited degree of satisfaction and dissatisfaction (winning and losing) which must be allocated between the two parties.

In contrast, the *integrative* dimension is concerned with determining the total degree of satisfaction for both parties—the size of the total pie. Along this dimension, collaborating attempts to enlarge the pie by finding an alternative which enables both parties to satisfy their concerns completely; avoiding reduces the size of the pie by neglecting the concerns of both parties, and the other modes are intermediate.

Figure 4. Integrative and Distributive Dimensions of Conflict Behavior

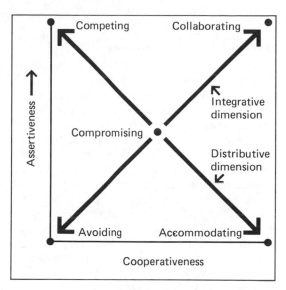

Source: Reprinted with permission of authors and publisher from Kilmann, R. H., and Thomas, K. W. "Interpersonal conflict-handling behaviors as reflections of Jungian personality dimensions." *Psychological Reports,* 1975, 37, 971–980, Figure 1.

Meaningfulness of the Two-Dimensional Framework

The classification of conflict-handling modes described above provides a rich framework for capturing different behavioral dimensions in a conflict situation. A study by Ruble and Thomas (1976) provided evidence that the scheme is also meaningful to individuals in conflict situations. The study assessed the emotional connotations which individuals attach to different events, concepts, or things. In both actual and hypothetical conflict situations, individuals were found to perceive the five conflict-handling modes in terms of two separate dimensions—dynamism (strength and activity) of the mode and evaluative approval (good vs. bad) of the mode. Perceptions of dynamism corresponded to assertiveness, while evaluative approval tended to correspond to cooperativeness. Thus there is evidence that individuals in conflict situations respond emotionally to behaviors in ways that parallel the basic dimensions of this classification scheme. . . .

THE CONFLICT PROCESS[1]

Having discussed conflict behaviors, we should next consider the larger conflict process of which behavior is only one part. The conflict process is the sequence of events which occur over time in a conflict. In the earlier example of Sales and Production, the Production Manager felt his efficiency goals to be frustrated, concluded that his frustration was due to unexpected orders from Sales, and made a proposal to the Sales Manager, who initially refused to go along. To complete this scenario, let's assume that the Production Manager perceives the Sales Manager's refusal as unreasonable, begins arguing competitively for his questionnaire, meets continuing resistance, and eventually gives up (accommodates).

Figure 5 shows a *process model* of conflict—a model of the major events in the conflict process between two parties. This model was developed by Thomas (1976) in a review of the conflict literature, and builds upon features from earlier models by Pondy (1967) and Walton (1969). As shown in the figure, conflict in a relationship tends to occur in cycles or episodes. Each episode is influenced by the outcomes of previous episodes and sets the stage for future episodes. Five major events are identified within a given episode, as seen from the point of view of each of the parties: frustration, conceptualization, behavior, the reaction of the other party, and an outcome.

. . .

In keeping with our definition of conflict, a conflict episode begins when one party (in our example the Production Manager) experiences or anticipates the frustration of a concern by a second party (Sales is perceived as hindering the Production Manager's efficiency). If dealt with consciously, party one will then conceptualize the conflict situation, formulating some ideas about the conflict issue (advance information on special orders), about alternatives available to deal with it (a weekly questionnaire), about the intentions

Figure 5. A Process Model of Conflict Episodes

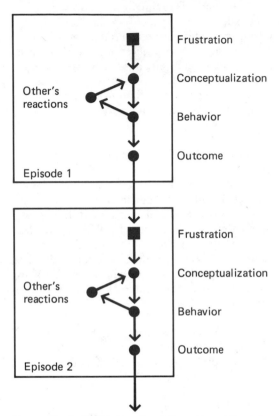

Source: Handbook of Industrial and Organizational Psychology (Marvin D. Dunnette, ed.), p. 895. Copyright © 1976 Rand McNally College Publishing Company. Used by permission of Houghton Mifflin Company.

of party two, and so on. Based upon this conceptualization, party one engages in behavior toward party two (proposing the questionnaire). Party two then reacts to this behavior (refusal). The loop in Figure 5 represents the effects on the party of the other party's behavioral reaction, which may lead party one to a reconceptualization of the situation and new behavioral tactics (arguing), leading to more reactions from party two (continued resistance). Thus party one's initial behavior may produce a prolonged interaction between the two parties. The episode ends when interaction over the conflict issue stops (the Production Manager gives up). At this point, various conflict outcomes (described by Pondy, 1967, as the *conflict aftermath*) occur.

Some basic events within this conflict process will be discussed below in more detail, followed by a discussion of possible managerial interventions into the process.

Frustration

Conflict researchers have traced conflicts to a wide variety of frustrated concerns: performance goals, promotion, power, scarce economic resources, behavioral norms and expectations, rules and agreements, values, strongly-held beliefs, status, autonomy, and a large number of personal needs. Conflicts can be traced to the frustration of anything which individuals or groups care about.

Accordingly, one important dimension of conflict outcomes is the degree to which a party's concerns have been satisfied. As shown in Figure 5, residual frustration from a previous conflict episode is likely to cause subsequent episodes. In the example of Sales and Production, the conflict has not been resolved for the Production Manager, who remains frustrated by the lack of advance information on special orders. Although he has accommodated to end the present conflict episode, his continuing frustration will probably lead him to raise the issue again in some form. Until then, the conflict remains in what Pondy (1967) called a *latent stage*.

A given conflict can be said to be *resolved* when no residual frustration remains concerning the issue in question. Follett (1941) argued some time ago that only an *integrative* (collaborative) outcome produces true resolution of a conflict issue. With compromise, accommodation, domination by one party, or avoidance, frustration appears to spawn future episodes.

It is important to realize that the experience of frustration is an emotion which may or may not be accompanied by an intellectual awareness of its source. Anxiety, anger, and depression are all possible reactions to potential or present frustration. Very often the conflict parties and their supervisor will be aware of these emotions *before* they become aware of what has caused them.

Conceptualization

Each party's conceptualization of the conflict situation is inherently subjective. For practical purposes, there is no such thing as an objective conceptualization of a conflict. . . . People generally perceive situations in terms of their own concerns and from the vantage point of the limited information they have. This is as true for the manager as for the subordinates who are directly involved. Gathering information and considering other points of view can lead to a more comprehensive understanding of the conflict, which is likely to be more useful for problem-solving. Yet making the effort to understand takes time and energy. The conflicting parties may decide to stop this effort at differing points, depending upon a number of factors, including time pressures and various psychological characteristics (cf. Louis, 1977). No matter how early this process stops—no matter how distorted, simplified, or inaccurate a party's understanding of the conflict situation is—each party's conceptualization forms the basis for subsequent efforts to cope with the conflict. This fact has important implications for the manager, who must understand the parties' conceptualizations of the conflict in order to understand, predict, and effectively intervene to change behavior.

The conflict issue. An important part of each party's conceptualization is the definition of the conflict issue—what the conflict is about. The definition of a conflict issue involves some assessment of the primary concerns of the two parties: "I think we should diversify our product line, but the Vice President wants to stick to our best selling products," "I'd like to talk at meetings, but George wants to dominate the discussion," and so on.

A conflict party may define the issue in a number of ways: there is no one "correct" definition. Thomas (1976) suggested three dimensions along which definitions differ: egocentricity, insight into underlying concerns, and the size of the issue. Each of these dimensions is likely to have important effects upon subsequent behavior.

Egocentricity is the degree to which a party defines the issue in terms of his or her own concerns alone. In our Sales-Production example, the Production Manager could have defined the issue egocentrically as: "I need Sales to fill out this questionnaire, but the Sales Manager won't agree to do it." The opposite of an egocentric definition is one which shows an appreciation of the other party's concern: "I need Sales to fill out this questionnaire, but the Sales Manager can't spare the time." Egocentric definitions of an issue, because they contain no information about the other party's concerns, make the other's position seem arbitrary and without merit. Accordingly, they make cooperation less likely.

A related but more general dimension is *insight into underlying concerns,* which involves a party's depth of understanding of the reasons for the two parties' positions. The most superficial level of insight only notes the positions of the parties on the issue being contested: "I want the questionnaire filled out, and he doesn't." A deeper appreciation would identify the more basic concerns of the two parties which have caused them to take these positions: "I need advance warning of special sales, but Sales is too busy to devote much time to providing this information." More insightful definitions of issues contain enough information about the parties' concerns to allow them to begin a collaborative search for an integrative outcome. In contrast, superficial definitions often serve to draw battle lines over one party's proposal. Filley (1978) observed that:

> . . . conflicts frequently occur about two solutions with no discussion or identification of the goals involved. This "my way (solution) versus your way (solution)" leads naturally to power-oriented [competitive] behavior.

A number of researchers have noted that it is often difficult and time consuming to identify underlying concerns in a conflict. As mentioned earlier, conflicting parties occasionally respond to frustrations without knowing their sources at a conscious level. Walton (1969) remarked that personal, emotional concerns tend to be seen as less acceptable than task-related concerns and are therefore less likely to be recognized or acknowledged by the parties. Frustrations of emotional concerns may be expressed through task-related issues, which are sometimes called *umbrella issues*

or *goblet issues* (Walton, 1969; Schutz, 1958b). The less acceptable underlying concerns are often referred to as *hidden agendas.* Goblet issues may appear irrational or mystifying to the manager and may be impossible to resolve without getting at underlying emotional concerns; this may require a skilled consultant.

The last dimension of a conflict issue, the *size* of the issue, was originally discussed . . . in the context of international conflict. He observed that wars are usually fought over "large" issues, which are difficult to resolve in any other way. Therefore, he recommended that conflict managers help parties perceive the conflict issue in smaller terms. Issues are made larger when they are conceptualized as involving large groups, a large number of events, abstract principles, or as setting a precedent for future interaction. In our conflict example, the Production Manager could conceptualize the conflict as large by viewing it as a conflict between two entire departments (rather than between two managers), as involving the general issue of cooperation by Sales (instead of advance warning on special orders), as involving the general principle of efficiency (rather than specific time for retooling), as settling this issue "once and for all" (rather than reaching an interim agreement), and as showing Sales that they can't push Production around (rather than confining discussions to the substance of the issue). With all that at stake, the Production Manager might well decide to "fight to the last man."

Attributions of the other's intent.   Each party's perception of the other party's behavior has an effect upon both strategic thinking and feelings toward the other party. Thomas and Pondy (1977) pointed out that the other party's behavior can often be interpreted in a number of ways. Strictly speaking, the five conflict-handling modes discussed earlier are not behaviors, but strategies or intentions. For example, if the Sales Manager tells the Production Manager that his position doesn't make sense, that is behavior. However the Production Manager, in order to know how to respond to this behavior, needs to come to some conclusion about the Sales Manager's intentions in making that remark. Was it a competitive tactic to undermine the Production Manager's position or to insult his intelligence? Or was it a collaborative attempt by the Sales Manager to provide feedback on an unsuccessful communication attempt? The Production Manager's response will probably depend heavily upon which of these intentions he attributes to the other party.

There appear to be strong biases in conflict parties' attributions of each other's intentions. Thomas and Pondy (1977) asked sixty-six managers to recall a recent conflict, to state which conflict-handling mode had been used by themselves and by the other party, and to describe the behaviors used to carry out these modes. Results are shown in Figure 6. Differences between perceptions of own and others' modes are striking. Parties tended to see themselves as cooperative—most frequently as collaborative. In contrast, they tended overwhelmingly to see the other's behavior as competitive. When asked to describe the specific behaviors used by both parties, individuals tended to describe their own behavior in very reasonable terms ("informing," "suggesting," "reminding"), and to describe the other party's behavior as unreasonable ("demanding," "refusing," etc.).

Thomas and Pondy suggested that four perceptual factors may contribute to this bias:

1. Both parties tend to be more aware of the reasons behind their own behavior than of the considerations behind the other's behavior. Frustrating behavior from the other party therefore tends to look more arbitrary and unreasonable than their own behavior.

2. Parties have some need to view their own behavior in positive (i.e., cooperative) terms.

3. Because they are threatening, competitive acts by the other party are more likely to be noticed and remembered by a party than are cooperative gestures, leading to an exaggerated impression of the other party's competitiveness.

4. Each party is less able to notice competitive or aggressive mannerisms in their own behavior than in the other's behavior, since they are unable to see their own facial expressions, less able to hear their own intonations when talking, etc.

. . .

PROCESS INTERVENTIONS

As shown earlier in Figure 2, one way in which the manager may manage conflict is to become directly involved in the ongoing sequence of events which has just been described. Kilmann

Figure 6. Percentages of 66 Executives Attributing Each Conflict Handling Mode to Self and to the Other Party.

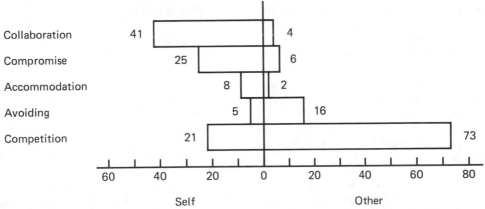

Source: From Kenneth W. Thomas and Louis R. Pondy, "Toward an Intent Model of Conflict Management Among Principal Parties," *Human Relations*, 30 (1977), p. 1094, Figure 1. Reprinted by permission.

and Thomas (1978) identified two broad classes of these process interventions—consciousness raising and interaction management.

Consciousness-raising interventions are directed at changing the internal experiences of the parties—the frustrations and conceptualizations which shape their behavior. The manager may help subordinates clarify the nature and sources of frustrations so they can be dealt with. This may involve surfacing hidden agendas and, in general, helping to "sort through the emotional underbrush" (Walton, 1969) to find underlying issues. With respect to the parties' conceptualizations, the manager can help define a given conflict in new ways and help them reinterpret and understand each other's behavior. As noted above, changes in conceptualization can influence each party's perception of the stakes involved, the possibilities for integrative outcomes, and the reasonableness and intentions of the other party. The manager can also direct attention to different potential conflict issues, thus helping to set priorities among issues which need to be addressed.

Interaction management interventions are directed at the overt behaviors used by the parties during the conflict. The manager can intervene into ongoing conflict interchanges at meetings, for example, acting as a referee to stop unfair behavior or personal attacks, rewording the parties' statements to make them less provocative, seeing that parties understand and have a chance to reply to each others' comments, and so on. In this manner, the manager may be able to control the level of escalation or de-escalation of competitive tactics, and steer behavior toward desired conflict modes. By his or her own behavior, the manager may also provide a model of the behavior desired.

Many specific process intervention techniques have been discussed in the literature on conflict management. Because of space limitations we shall focus here on two of the most interesting interventions which have been successfully used in organizations.

Intergroup Confrontation

This intervention has been used successfully in a number of cases where escalated competitive relations between groups have begun to interfere with the work relationship—between departments, between headquarters and field personnel, between labor and management, etc. A relatively standardized design for this intervention has evolved. According to Beckhard (1969), this design involves the following steps:

1. Leaders or members of the conflicting groups are assembled for the purpose of getting agreement on the fact that they have a common stake in reducing tension and frustration between them and in finding ways to increase productivity and collaboration in their relationship. Some commitment to the process is thus obtained.

2. Separately, each group is then asked to develop a list which describes their attitudes toward the other group—including the exasperating things which the other group does. This step serves to surface and clarify frustrations of the two groups.

3. While still separated, the groups are asked to develop another list—their guesses about what the other group is writing about them. This step starts the group thinking about the effects which their own behavior may have had on the other group.

4. The two groups are then brought together to share their lists. Importantly, the groups are not allowed to interact during this step. Each group (or a spokesperson for each group) simply presents and explains their lists to the other group. Thus, each group is required to listen to the frustrations and perceptions of the other group without engaging in argument or other tactics which might close off information and continue the conflict escalation.

5. The groups then return to their separate locations to react to the lists, including the inevitable differences between the (usually favorable) view each group has about its own behavior and the (usually negative) perceptions of that same behavior by the other group. Each group is also asked to develop a list of issues which should receive priority attention from both groups. Removed from the heat of interaction, the groups have time to sort through the dif-

ferences that now appear secondary or seem to be due to misunderstandings, and to identify underlying issues which are most critical.

6. The groups then get together to compare these lists, agree on a common list of issues, and decide which of these are most important.

7. Now that the groups' attention is focused upon a common set of problems, the groups are asked to begin the task of finding solutions to these problems together.

. . .

STRUCTURAL CONDITIONS

The conflict process described earlier does not occur in a vacuum. Conflicts occur within a framework of conditions which generate frustrations, constrain outcomes, and otherwise influence the course of conflict episodes. As noted in our description of the conflict process, the parties' perceptions and conceptualizations may lead them to interpret conditions in different ways. Therefore these conditions do not automatically or consistently affect the parties' behavior. Nevertheless, we can speak of these conditions as exerting general forces on the parties which tend to push conflict episodes in specific directions.

As shown in Figure 2, conditions which shape the conflict process include the internal structuring of the conflict parties (their personal characteristics) as well as the context in which they interact. To a large extent, these conditions are shaped by managerial actions and decisions. It is therefore important that the manager understand the effects of these conditions upon conflict episodes and their outcomes.

For example, we might gain more insight into why the Production-Sales conflict episode occurred as it did if we learned more about the situation in which it occurred. Investigating, we learn that a temporary downturn in business has forced a freeze in new hiring in both departments, which has made it especially difficult for the understaffed Sales force to meet its responsibilities. With declining profits, there has been increasing pressure upon both departments to increase performance—pressure for increasing sales and for greater production quantity and efficiency. Though there are no fixed policies which specify that Sales must furnish advance notice on special orders, the unexpected arrival of these orders in Production has become a sore point for Production foremen, who have been pressuring the Production Manager to do something about it. (The trade journal article about the questionnaire was, in fact, given to the Production Manager by one of his foremen.) The Vice President of Operations, who is the immediate supervisor of both department managers, has a reputation for being hard-nosed and assertive and has encouraged similar behavior among his subordinates. The Sales Manager, who has a similar reputation, appears to have more influence with the Vice President than does the Production Manager, which gives him more informal power than the other department heads.

In this section we shall review several structural conditions related to this example which have been shown to impact upon conflict episodes. Then the following section will consider ways in which structural conditions can be influenced to manage conflict.

. . .

Social Pressures

Conflicting parties interact within a framework of social forces—within a structure of social roles, expectations and norms which constrain behavior.

Informal rules. The organization or subsystem of which the conflict parties are members is likely to have informal rules and standards about "proper" ways of dealing with conflict. These rules vary from organization to organization, and from department to department within an organization, and are part of the organization's climate. These informal rules often discourage types of escalated competition within the organization which would be extremely disruptive—kinds of coercion and violence, for example. They may also prescribe ideal modes of conflict behavior. Collaborative problem-solving may be valued in one department of a company, while competitive behavior is more respected in another.

As shown in the Sales-Production example, the manager of an organizational system or subsystem has some influence over these standards of behavior. In one study of interdepartmental conflict, Thomas and Walton (1971) found that more collaboration and accommodation were reported under managers who were seen as emphasizing cooperation.

Constituent pressure. Another set of social forces comes into play when a conflict involves groups rather than individuals—for example, two departments. In a number of laboratory experiments, Blake and Mouton (1961) observed that intergroup conflicts tend to draw each group together, increasing cohesion, solidifying the group's leadership structure, and mobilizing it toward the common purpose of dealing with the other group.

In such conflicts, the members of each group are likely to feel like representatives of their group and to be aware that their behavior toward the other group may make them heroes or "goats" in their own group. Accordingly, each party may feel increased pressure to defend the group's position on the conflict issue, taking a hard line to demonstrate loyalty to the group and to try to win a victory. The Production Manager in our example appears to be under such pressures from his foremen.

The Blake and Mouton studies also found that group members tended to have high opinions of the merits of their own position and low opinions of the other group's position. Accordingly, they tended to be relatively unaware of similarities in the two groups' positions and to have unrealistically high demands and expectations. These conditions are likely to aggravate group demands of strongly competitive behavior from the group's representatives, making it difficult to engage in collaboration, compromise, or other modes.

Conflict of Interest

A conflict of interest occurs to the extent that concerns of the conflicting parties are mutually incompatible. Some degree of conflict of interest occurs whenever integrative outcomes are not possible. In these situations, satisfaction of one party's concern means some degree of frustration for the other party.

Conflict of interest can be created by a variety of situational constraints. Budget limitations usually make it necessary to ration organizational expenditures, creating conflict of interest between different budget units. The fact that only one person can be promoted to a given position leads to conflict of interest among people who aspire to the same position. Limits on time available for committee meetings can create conflict of interest among advocates for different agenda items.

In these examples, conflict of interest occurs because there are insufficient resources to meet both parties' concerns at the same time. To some extent, then, the degree of conflict of interest within an organizational system depends upon the resources available to the organization at any point in time. Cyert and March (1963) noted that intraorganizational conflict is reduced during periods of relative prosperity, when the organization accumulates a surplus of resources. This *organizational slack* can be used to reduce conflict of interest by providing more money for projects, creating new positions for promotions, hiring more people, and so on. Conversely, conflict of interest tends to be greatest during periods of organizational decline. In our example a business downturn has reduced the Sales force, making it increasingly difficult for Sales to meet its own objectives and simultaneously attend to requests from Production. Apparent conflict of interest has thus been created on the issue of supplying advance information to Production.

Research in a number of settings strongly suggests that conflict of interest is linked to uncooperative behavior. In a classic study, Sherif and Sherif (1956) created conflict of interest between groups in a boys' camp by establishing competitive sporting events for a desirable prize to be awarded on a group basis. The result was hostility and uncooperative behavior between the groups—ranging from hostile and assertive (competitive) behavior to avoidance—which continued well after the sporting events were concluded.

Deutsch (1949) created conflict of interest within classroom groups by announcing that grades on group problem solving tasks would be awarded to individuals on the basis of their relative contributions—thus rationing the number of high grades within each group. In contrast, *commonality of interest* was created within other groups by announcing that all group members would get identical grades on the basis of solutions arrived at by their total group. The groups with greater conflict of interest showed much less interpersonal coordination and teamwork during discussions. Quality of solutions and enjoyment of the experience were considerably lower under the conflict of interest condition.

More recently, conflict researchers have proposed that specific forms of uncooperative behavior produced by conflict of interest in organizations depend upon two other situational conditions—the stakes involved and interdependencies between the parties.

Stakes. Thomas (1976) observed that a party's assertiveness in a conflict situation is likely to depend upon the stakes involved. Since the more assertive conflict modes (competing and collaborating) require a greater investment of time and energy, these behaviors are more likely to be reserved for issues which are important to a party. Accordingly, Thomas predicted that conflict of interest and stakes in a conflict situation will tend to interact to shape behavior, as shown in Figure 7. High conflict of interest is likely to produce competition when a party has a great deal at stake. This appears to be the case in our Production-Sales example, where pressures from top management have increased the stakes for both parties. When there is conflict of interest with little at stake, the situation may be experienced as a minor annoyance to be neglected (avoided) in favor of more important issues. Collaboration can be expected to occur when there is commonality of interest on important issues. On issues involving commonality of interest which are less important, one party may defer (accommodate) to the other party's wishes. Since there is commonality of interest, the party has little to lose in relying upon the other party and devoting his or her own attention to matters having a higher priority. Compromise might be expected in situations which are more intermediate in terms of stakes and conflict of interest.

Figure 7. Predominant Conflict-Handling Behaviors Used by a Party as a Function of Stakes and Conflicts of Interest

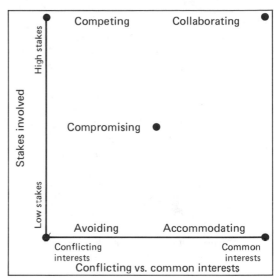

Source: Handbook of Industrial and Organizational Psychology (Marvin D. Dunnette, ed.), p. 922. Copyright © 1976 Rand McNally College Publishing Company. Used by permission of Houghton Mifflin Company.

Interdependence. Competing was described earlier as attempting to win the satisfaction of one's own concerns at the other party's expense. Based in part upon a review of previous conflict terminology, Schmidt and Kochan (1972) argued the importance of distinguishing between two kinds of competitive behavior. The first kind involves parallel striving while the second involves mutual interference. Both behaviors are seen as responses to conflict of interest (presumably under conditions of high stakes as well). However, Schmidt and Kochan proposed that the two kinds of behavior occur when different forms of interdependence exist between the conflict parties.

Parallel striving occurs when both parties are dependent upon some third entity for important resources. With parallel striving, both parties exert their efforts rather independently of each other to obtain those resources: two candidates for promotion may try to outperform each other to impress the manager who will make the decision, or two department heads may seek to demonstrate the merits of their budget proposals to their supervisor in order to receive a majority of funds.

In contrast, *mutual interference* occurs when a party more directly blocks the other party's progress toward his or her goal. Schmidt and Kochan observed that this sort of behavior tends to occur when activities of the two parties are more directly interdependent, giving each party the opportunity to obstruct the other. Two parties may withhold agreement and argue over a course of action (as in our example); a Maintenance supervisor may threaten to withhold service from Production until a Production Manager complies with his wishes, and so on.

The distinction between these two forms of competitive behavior is potentially very important to the manager of an organizational system—especially when the conflict issues relate directly to organizational goals. Parallel striving often spurs increased effort toward organizational goals, while mutual interference often interferes with each party's efforts to reach those goals. However, the manager does not usually have the option of eliminating the task interdependencies among subordinates which create mutual interference. In fact, conflict of interest and task interdependencies are usually necessary to achieve organizational effectiveness and are deliberately designed into most organizations. Different concerns which are important to the organization tend to be incorporated into the responsibilities of specialized positions or departments, in order that they will be pursued vigorously. Special units are sometimes created solely to provide checks and balances for other units—such as the Quality Control function with respect to Production. Organizational personnel are often hired, or committees formed, to ensure that spokespersons for different viewpoints are present. Procedures are frequently designed so that unilateral decisions cannot be made on issues which affect the concerns of other departments, insuring that confrontations occur on those issues. Finally, limits on organizational resources inevitably require that difficult priorities be established between departments and projects.

Power and Status

. . . Individuals and groups obtain power and status from a number of sources. The relative power and status of two parties has an impact on their conflict behaviors. Walton (1969) observed that parties may be unassertive in dealing with higher-power parties out of deference or fear of punishment, while finding it easy to ignore or dominate lower-power parties. In our example, the Sales Manager's greater power within the organization may make it easier for him to dismiss the Production Manager's requests. Accordingly, Walton argued that collaboration in conflict situations is most likely to occur when parties are of roughly equal power.

In a study of power and conflict in the classroom, Jamieson and Thomas (1974) found that students from high school through graduate school reported using more avoiding than any other mode during disagreements with teachers. Although other factors may be involved, this avoidance appeared largely due to differences in power.

In other studies, researchers have found that higher-status individuals and departments resent and resist demands or requests by lower-status parties. It is important, therefore, that organizational concerns be assigned to people who have sufficient status to assert such concerns effectively.

Organizational Policy

Existing policies and procedures are often the outcomes of prior conflicts. Cyert and March (1963) argued that organizational policies can frequently be understood in terms of political struggles among competing interest groups within the organization. Such struggles (conflicts) serve to set overall priorities and to decide between alternative course of action.

Although Cyert and March were mainly concerned with top management decisions, policies and rules serve much the same functions at all organizational levels. Rules tend to be created in response to sensitive issues between parties. If

Sales and Production continually conflict over the amount of lead time Production must have on special orders, then it is likely that a rule will emerge to cover this issue. The rule may be a formal agreement between the parties, or an informal set of expectations, or it may be imposed by a superior. However derived, effective rules save time and energy which would have to be invested in settling each case as it arises. In time, the behavior prescribed by the rule may become automatic, so that the parties no longer conceptualize relevant situations as a conflict. Sales, for example, may simply tell customers that certain lead times are required.

STRUCTURAL INTERVENTIONS

Unlike process interventions, which are directed at events in a single ongoing episode, structural interventions change conditions which are likely to have continuing impacts on conflicts within the manager's system. Kilmann and Thomas (1978) divided structural interventions into two broad categories: selection and training, and contextual modification.

Selection and training interventions alter intrasystem conflicts by making relatively stable changes in the characteristics of people within that system. One approach is through the selection of people who fill the positions—through recruiting, screening, promotion, placement, and transfer decisions. For example, questions about cooperative behavior are common in reference letters and performance appraisals. Severe personality clashes may be dealt with through transfers. Occasionally, work groups have been formed on the basis of personal compatibilities—for example, some submarine crews during World War II (Schutz, 1958a) and, more recently, some problem-solving task forces (Kilmann, 1977; Mitroff, Barabba and Kilmann, 1977). In contrast, training interventions attempt to produce lasting changes in individuals who have already been selected or placed—through initial orientation programs, educational programs directed at cognitive learning about conflict and other topics, experiential courses or workshops which allow individuals to practice new conflict behaviors and skills, job rotation practices to broaden an individual's perspective, and so on.

Contextual modification interventions change important features of the context in which the parties interact. Through formal authority, the manager may exert influence over conflict of interest, conflict stakes, policies, power and interdependencies by changing incentive systems, procedures, formal responsibilities and titles of the parties, etc. The manager may also create a range of integrating mechanisms to help manage conflicts and increase coordination between subsystems. Less formally, the manager may be able to shape the social pressures which bear upon conflicting parties by helping to change informal rules and expectations within the system.

As with process interventions, a large number of structural intervention techniques exist to manage conflict. We shall discuss three of the most common structural interventions.

1. Policy Decisions

In most of the process interventions described earlier the manager played the role of a *mediator*— someone who helps the conflict parties reach their own decision. However, through the use of formal authority, the manager may often act as an *arbitrator*, imposing a settlement by making a policy decision which is binding upon subordinates, thus terminating the conflict episode. Although there are advantages to this procedure, there are also some risks. Subordinates may not accept decisions believed to be unfair or which they feel they have had no say about. To the extent that a conflicting party continues to feel frustrated, the underlying conflict may recur in other forms.

2. Superordinate Goals

Superordinate goals are goals which are highly desired by both parties and which cannot be attained by either party's individual efforts (Sherif, 1958). They encourage active collaboration since they involve both commonality of interest and high stakes. In the boys' camp study mentioned earlier, Sherif and Sherif (1956) were able to reverse hostile and uncooperative relations between groups by giving them tasks which involved a superordinate goal. The experience of collaborative effort between groups created generalized feelings of good will which continued long after the task was concluded.

It might appear that all organizational members have superordinate goals—namely, the performance of their organizational system. However, organizational performance is likely to be affected by many factors other than the efforts of individual parties, and parties are frequently rewarded for individual goal attainment rather than for overall system performance. Superordinate goals are likely to be more compelling when tied directly to collaborative efforts of the parties and when they are either intrinsically important to the parties or systematically rewarded by the organization. For example, group incentive plans have been used to encourage collaboration among work group members by tying individual rewards to overall group performance. Such plans seem most appropriate when there is high task interdependence among the parties.

3. Training

Finally, the manager may recommend that subordinates undergo training in conflict management skills. University extension programs and a number of consulting firms offer regular workshops in conflict management. There are also a number of training aids available to Personnel departments to help in conducting in-house programs—films, role plays, instruments for assessing conflict behavior, and complete training packages. One fairly comprehensive package contains films, role plays, diagnostic instruments and other materials which cover the following topics: positive and negative effects of conflict, sequence of events in a conflict episode, alternative conflict-handling behaviors and their uses, dynamics of intergroup conflicts, escalation and de-escalation, and basic mediation strategies (Schmidt, Thomas, Millgate and Olson, 1974).

. . .

NOTE

1. Much of this section is based upon Thomas (1976).

REFERENCES

Beckhard, Richard, *Organization development: Strategies and models.* Reading, Mass.: Addison-Wesley, 1969.

Blake, Robert R. and Mouton, Jane S., "Reactions to intergroup competition under win-lose conditions," *Management Science,* Vol. 7, 1961, 420–435.

Blake, Robert R. and Mouton, Jane S., *The Managerial Grid.* Houston: Gulf Publishing, 1964.

Cyert, Richard M. and March, James G., *A behavioral theory of the firm.* Englewood Cliffs: Prentice-Hall, 1963.

Deutsch, Morton, "An experimental study of the effects of cooperation and competition upon group process," *Human Relations,* Vol. 2, 1949, 199–231.

Filley, A. C., "Some normative issues in conflict management," *California Management Review,* Vol. 20, 1978.

Follet, Mary Parker, *Creative Experience.* London: Longmans, Green & Co., 1941.

Hall, Jay, "Decisions, decisions, decisions," *Psychology Today,* Vol. 5, November, 1971, 51–54, 86–87.

Jamieson, David W. and Thomas, Kenneth W., "Power and conflict in the student-teacher relationship," *Journal of Applied Behavioral Science,* Vol. 10, 1974, 321–336.

Kilmann, Ralph H., *Social systems design: Normative theory and the MAPS design technology.* New York: Elsevier, 1977.

Kilmann, Ralph H. and Thomas, Kenneth W., "Four perspectives on conflict management: An attributional framework for organizing descriptive and normative theory," *Academy of Management Review,* Vol. 3, 1978, 59–68.

Lawrence, Paul H. and Lorsch, Jay W., *Organization and environment: Managing differentiation and integration.* Homewood, Ill.: Richard D. Irwin, 1969.

Louis, Meryl R., "How individuals conceptualize conflict: Identification of steps in the process and the role of personal/developmental factors," *Human Relations,* Vol. 30, 1977, 451–467.

March, James G. and Simon, Herbert A., *Organizations.* New York: John Wiley & Sons, 1958.

Mitroff, Ian I., Barabba, Vincent P., and Kilmann, Ralph H., "The application of behavioral and philosophical technologies to strategic planning: A case study of a large federal agency," *Management Science*, Vol. 23, 1977, 44–58.

Robbins, Stephen P., *Managing organizational conflict: A nontraditional approach*. Englewood Cliffs, N.J.: Prentice-Hall, 1974.

Ruble, Thomas L. and Thomas, Kenneth W., "Support for a two-dimensional model of conflict behavior," *Organizational Behavior and Human Performance*, Vol. 16, 1976, 143–155.

Schmidt, Stuart M. and Kochan, Thomas A., "Conflict: Toward conceptual clarity," *Administrative Science Quarterly*, Vol. 17, 1972, 359–370.

Schmidt, Warren H., Thomas, W., Millgate, Irvine H., and Olson, Richard F., *The management of conflict*. Tuxedo, N.Y.: Xicom, Inc., 1974.

Schutz, William C., "The interpersonal underworld." *Harvard Business Review*, Vol. 36, July–August, 1958, 123–135(b).

Sherif, Muzafer, "Superordinate goals in the reduction of intergroup conflict," *The American Journal of Sociology*. Vol. 63, 1958, 349–356.

Sherif, Muzafer and Sherif, Carolyn W. *An outline of social psychology* (rev. ed.). New York: Harper and Brothers, 1956.

Thomas, Kenneth W., "Conflict and conflict management," in M. D. Dunnette (ed.), *Handbook of industrial and organizational psychology*. Chicago: Rand McNally, 1976.

Thomas, Kenneth W., and Pondy, Louis R., "Toward an 'intent' model of conflict management among principal-parties," *Human Relations*, Vol. 30, 1977, 1089–1102.

Thomas, Kenneth W. and Schmidt, Warren H., "A survey of managerial interests with respect to conflict," *Academy of Management Journal*, Vol. 19, 1976, 315–318.

Thomas, Kenneth W. and Walton, Richard E., "Conflict-handling behavior in interdepartmental relations." Research Paper No. 38, Division of Research, Graduate School of Business Administration, UCLA, 1971.

Walton, Richard E., *Interpersonal peacemaking: Confrontations and third party consultation*. Reading, Mass.: Addison-Wesley, 1969.

Walton, Richard E. and Dutton, John M., "The management of interdepartmental conflict: A model and review," *Administrative Science Quarterly*, Vol. 14, 1969, 73–84.

Walton, Richard E. and McKersie, Robert B., *A behavioral theory of labor negotiations: An analysis of a social interaction system*. New York: McGraw-Hill, 1965.

Mechanisms for Organizational Design

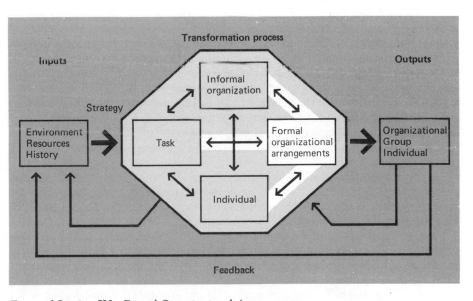

Focus of Section IV—Formal Organizational Arrangements

INTRODUCTION

To this point we have looked at individual motivation and decision making and at the impact of groups on individuals and on leadership considerations within groups. We have yet to consider the nature of the interaction between groups or subunits within organizations, nor have we considered the context in which groups operate. This section will deal with the formal context within which individuals and groups operate. We will postpone consideration of intergroup and political behavior until we reach Section V.

Individuals and groups operate within the formal or prescribed organization. Formal organizational arrangements provide constraints and opportunities within which individuals operate. It is useful to analyze formal organizational arrangements at several levels. The most basic questions are: what is the *formal configuration* of the organization—is it organized by function, product, service, or client? How differentiated or specialized is the organization? Are there, for instance, distinct sales and marketing departments or do the same individuals work on both functions? A second set of questions is: *within subunits*, what is the extent of rules and regulations, who makes decisions, how frequently are individuals evaluated, how formal are role definitions and task requirements? A final series of questions is: what formal mechanisms exist to coordinate the *various subunits*? To what extent, for example, are there formalized planning and control systems, individuals assigned liaison duties, management information systems, and formal career systems developed to facilitate the coordination between units? These, as well as physical location and architecture, are all aspects of the formal organization. Organizational arrangements are a powerful determinant of behavior in that they provide the premises within which people make decisions, they directly affect the flow and distribution of information, and they provide the formal authority to call for and implement decisions.

These three levels of analyses suggest some basic decisions to be made about organizational design: 1) what is the organization's basic configuration, and what are the relevant subunits; 2) what are the optimal structures for these different subunits; and 3) how are the subunits to be linked together? The initial question can only be answered with reference to the organization's external environment and to its strategy (see Reading 5, Section I, by MacMillan). The two final sets of decisions can be made by focusing attention on the organization's work requirements and its history.

In this section we will address these questions: 1) why is it that similar units (for instance, manufacturing or research projects) facing similar tasks have different performance levels and 2) why is it that effective subunits do not necessarily produce an effective product (for instance, effective marketing and R&D units that produce commercially unsuccessful products)? Our premise is that organizational arrangements have an important impact on organizational, group, and individual performance; that there is no one best set of organizational arrangements; and that management must, therefore, explicitly choose a set of organizational arrangements to meet individual and task requirements. The design literature does not suggest definitive solutions to the structure problem; it does, however, yield a feasible set of alternatives from which management ought to choose. We shall postpone the discussion of organization design over time until Section V.

ORGANIZATIONAL ARRANGEMENTS AND THE CONGRUENCE MODEL

Organizational arrangements are an important component of the congruence model because they can be manipulated easily by management and because they have direct impact on both individuals and groups. Organizational arrangements are, however, extremely complex and require that the several levels of analysis be balanced (for example, in order to work, a matrix structure requires a number of consistent reward and control mechanisms). As with the other components of the model, organizational arrangements can have both positive and negative effects— they can work to facilitate or hinder task accomplishment and organizational effectiveness.

The model suggests that several fits must be examined. First, there is the *organization arrangement–task fit.* The following questions emerge: To what extent do formal organizational arrangements facilitate task accomplishment? To what extent do subunits attend to and deal with environmental complexity? To what extent are the subunits themselves organized to take advantage of in-house expertise? To what extent do formal mechanisms exist to facilitate coordination across subunits?

Second is the *organization arrangement–individual fit.* Two questions arise: To what extent do the reward and control systems along with the flow of work meet the needs of the organization's employees? To what extent does the formal organization help generate a psychological contract that both the employees and the organization can fulfill?

Last, the *organization arrangement–informal organization* fit addresses the consistency between the goals and objectives of the formal and informal systems. The fundamental question here is whether the formal and informal organizations complement or are in conflict with each other.

ORGANIZATION ARRANGEMENTS AND ORGANIZATIONAL EFFECTIVENESS: AN OVERVIEW

An organization must have a structure that permits it to attend effectively to uncertainty. Organizations can deal with uncertainty by developing specialized units to deal with distinct sources of uncertainty (for instance, the division of labor). This differentiation is, of itself, a source of work-related uncertainty because the specialized units themselves must be coordinated. Management must analyze different sources of uncertainty to make several explicit design choices. First, based on an external analysis and on strategic considerations, a decision about the core configuration of the organization must be made. Management must then structure the subunits to reflect their unique work requirements. Last, work interdependence requirements must be analyzed and an appropriate set of integrating mechanisms chosen.

In this approach to design form must fit function. Design decisions must be made at several levels of analysis. Each decision is based on an analysis of relevant work requirements, and each decision must be consistent with the others (that is, internally consistent reward, control, measurement systems). Because of the number of design alternatives, this approach will not yield an optimal design; rather, it will yield a feasible set of design alternatives. The choice of organizational arrangements must be made in conjunction with an awareness of history and precedent. Part of the design problem is to ensure that the organization's individuals and the informal organization work congruently with formal arrangements to get the work accomplished. Analyses of these organization components is vital to good organizational design.

THE READINGS IN SECTION IV

The readings in this section are organized into two parts. Part IV.A (Readings 21 and 22) presents some basic concepts and several complementary frameworks for the analysis of organizational design. Tushman and Nadler give a synthesis and review of the design literature in Reading 21. They argue that information processing concepts provide an economical and useful approach to the design question. In Reading 22, Duncan provides a different, though consistent, approach to organization design. Duncan's method uses decisional analysis.

Part IV.B (Readings 23–28) provides detail on a range of coordination and control mechanisms. In Reading 23, Galbraith discusses several design strategies by which to achieve coordination. He argues that the choice of an integrating mechanism must be based on work requirements and that organizations should minimize the costs of coordination. In Reading 24, Lorange and Vancil provide rich description and insight into designing planning systems. Todd's article (Reading 25) addresses the problem of assessing subunit performance once larger plans are in place. Todd discusses a way to link management control systems to individual, group, and organizational levels of analysis. In Reading 26, Hatvany and Pucik analyze Japanese organizations and attribute their effectiveness to thorough analysis of the interrelations between structure, control, reward, career and individual selection, and socialization. In Reading 27, Lawrence, Kolodny, and Davis expand on Galbraith's earlier mention of matrix organizations. They discuss some of the dilemmas and realities of matrix organizations, perhaps the most complex and costly mechanism to achieve coordination and control.

Together these readings provide a coherent set of concepts, models, and tools for thinking about organization design at a given point in time. Later, Section V will address the questions of organization design over time, political dynamics in organizations, and implementation. In that last section, we move from a static approach to organizations to an approach that focuses on dynamics and change.

21

Information processing
as an integrating concept
in organizational design

Michael L. Tushman
and David A. Nadler

A basic goal of organizational research has been to discover what kinds of organizational designs or structures will be most effective in different situations. Ever since Burns and Stalker [4] presented the idea that different approaches to structuring organizations might have differential effectiveness under varying conditions, much work has been done attempting to identify the critical contingencies of design. The generally accepted view of organizational design that has evolved is that the structure of an organization should match or fit characteristics of certain variables both inside and outside the organizational system.

The central research question in design has been to identify variables that will enable re-

Source: From Michael L. Tushman and David A. Nadler, "Information processing as an integrating concept in organizational design," *Academy of Management Review*, 3 (1978), pp. 613–624. Reprinted by permission of the publisher.

Author's note: The authors would like to thank Jay Galbraith, University of Pennsylvania, for his constructive comments and insights. Also, an anonymous reviewer of this journal has been particularly helpful.

searchers to make consistent and valid predictions of what kinds of organizational structures will be most effective in different situations. The attempt to identify critical contingent variables has led to the investigation of issues such as the technologies of an organization [14, 21, 27, 30, 46], the nature of the environment in which the organization must function [8, 9, 10, 23, 26], and the nature of interdependencies that exist among the units within an organization [1, 37, 43].

While research on contingent approaches to design has been fruitful, there remain both contradictory results [27, 29, 36], as well as a lack of clarity regarding the concept of congruence or fit. This article uses information processing ideas to synthesize the design/structure literature and to clarify the concept of congruence.

This article builds on the view of organizations as information processing systems facing uncertainty and extends this concept to develop a conceptual model for organizational design and structure. Information processing refers to the gathering, interpreting, and synthesis of information in the context of organizational decision making. This article distinguishes between information and data. Information refers to data which are relevant, accurate, timely and concise. As information must effect a change in knowledge, data may or may not be information, and data processing may or may not be information processing. Such a model should serve to integrate much existing research, while stimulating future research aimed at testing the validity and applicability of the model. The approach to developing the model is the presentation of a number of propositions about organizations, uncertainty, and information processing. In each case, some relevant research is noted. From these propositions, a conceptual model of organizational structure is developed. Based on this model, implications for research and practice are identified.

WORKING ASSUMPTIONS

There are many different ways of thinking about organizations; each approach is built on different assumptions about how organizations are structured and how they function. It is important to clarify working assumptions which underlie the analysis and to make clear the particular perspective from which organizations will be viewed.

A basic assumption is that organizations are open social systems which must deal with work-related uncertainty [20, 37, 44]. There are several sources of uncertainty to which organizations must respond. Since organizations are dependent on inputs from the larger environment, and since this environment is at least potentially unstable, the organization must be able to track and cope with environmental-based uncertainty [25, 44]. Within the organization, subunits must be able to deal with problem solving and coordination problems associated with different tasks and with different amounts of task interdependence [23, 43].

If organizations must deal with these several sources of work-related uncertainty, a critical task of the organization is to facilitate the collection, gathering, and processing of information about how different components of the organization are functioning, about quality of outputs, and about

conditions in external technological and market domains. In short, organizations must develop information processing mechanisms capable of dealing with both external and internal sources of uncertainty [47].

A second assumption follows from this logic: organizations can fruitfully be seen as information processing systems. Given the various sources of uncertainty, a basic function of the organization's structure is to create the most appropriate configuration of work units (as well as the linkages between these units) to facilitate the effective collection, processing and distribution of information [9, 12, 25]. In this context, information as gathered and processed by the organization's structure will be broadly defined to include: plans, work standards, budgets, feedback on performance, inventory levels, external technical and market conditions, etc.

A third assumption is that organizations can be viewed as composed of sets of groups or departments (referred to here as subunits). As organizations grow, they differentiate; to realize economies of scale and benefits of specialization, subunits are created which have specialized tasks and/or deal with specific aspects of the organization's task environment [20, 23, 37]. At the same time, these subunits are interdependent to varying degrees and must share scarce resources—their activities must be linked together [23, 43]. This perspective on organizational structure implies a need to shift attention to the subunit level of analysis. Rather than asking what should be the structure of a particular organization, more appropriate questions are: (a) What are the optimal structures for the different subunits within the organization (e.g. R&D, sales, manufacturing); (b) What structural mechanisms will facilitate effective coordination among differentiated yet interdependent subunits?

These three working assumptions represent one way of conceptualizing organizations. We shall look at organizations as open social systems which must cope with environmental and organizationally based uncertainty. Organizational structure must perform the major functions of facilitating the collection of information from external areas as well as permitting effective processing of information within and between subunits which make up the organization. The basic unit of analysis will be the subunit; the basic structural problem is to design subunits and relations between subunits capable of dealing with information processing requirements faced during task execution. Finally, this approach to structure directs attention away from a static approach to structure towards a more dynamic approach to the structuring of organizations over time.

AN INFORMATION PROCESSING MODEL

Information processing ideas provide a way of organizing much of the structure/design literature. Given the previous set of assumptions, the basic features of a model will be presented by developing a series of propositions, with relevant research.

P1: *The tasks of organizational subunits vary in their degree of uncertainty.*

Uncertainty is defined as the difference between information possessed and information required to a complete a task [7, 12]. If they so vary, the nature of a subunit's work will be a major determinant of the amount of uncertainty with which it must deal. Three sources of work related uncertainty, and therefore of information processing requirements, will be discussed: subunit task characteristics, subunit task environment, and inter-unit task interdependence.

Subunit Task Characteristics

Task characteristics have been an important concern to organizational structure researchers [24]. While the results of this research have not always been consistent (regarding methods or unit of analysis) or convergent [2, 17], a review of the task literature indicates that task predictability is a thread which links the various studies together. Galbraith [12] suggests that tasks differ in their amount of predictability and thus in the amount of uncertainty which the unit must deal with during task execution.

Task complexity and intra-unit task interde-

pendence are each sources of uncertainty and of information processing requirements [27]. For example, routine tasks or tasks with a minimal amount of intra-unit interdependence can be preplanned, and their information processing requirements are minimal. Complex tasks, tasks that are not well understood, or tasks which involve reciprocal interdependence, can not be preplanned and are associated with greater uncertainty [25, 37]. There is substantial literature to support this uncertainty-based approach to subunit task characteristics [14, 30, 35, 42, 43]. As an example, an intensive care nursing subunit (complex task with substantial intra-unit interdependence) faces much greater information processing requirements than does a rehabilitation-oriented nursing subunit (i.e. more routine task and less interdependence among the nurses).

Subunit Task Environment

The task environment has been a much used, yet ill defined and hotly debated term [39]. The reviews by Downey and Slocum [7] emphasize a perceptual orientation by suggesting that the task environment be defined as those external actors which are attended to by organizational members. The environment is generally seen as a source of uncertainty, since areas outside the organization (or subunit) are not under the unit's control and are therefore potentially unstable [20, 37, 44].

While the number of dimensions affecting perceived environmental uncertainty is huge [19], Duncan [8] found that a static/dynamic dimension is a particularly important contributor to perceived uncertainty: the more dynamic or changing the environment, the greater the uncertainty faced by the focal unit. For instance, subunits facing a stable environment can develop rules or standard operating procedures (SOP) to deal with their environment. If subunits face a changing environment, then fixed rules and SOPs will not be able to deal effectively with the substantial environmental uncertainty. Much of the literature supports this uncertainty based approach to the task environment [8, 9, 18, 23, 26, 28].

Inter-Unit Task Interdependence

Task characteristics and task environment are sources of uncertainty for organizational subunits which have important implications for the design of subunit structure. A third source of uncertainty with even broader structural implications is the degree to which a subunit is dependent upon other subunits in order to perform its task effectively. The amount of task interdependence that exists between differentiated subunits is associated with the need for effective coordination and joint problem solving. Task interdependence is thus another important source of work-related uncertainty.

A subunit performing a task which is fairly autonomous has little need for information from or collaboration with other areas. If the subunit's task is changed so that it is dependent upon the work of other units, the need for joint coordination and effective problem solving increases, and the subunit must cope with increased amounts of work related uncertainty. Thompson [37] provides a classification of types of interdependence that might characterize relationships among subunits. In order of increasing complexity, the types of interdependence are: pooled, sequential, and reciprocal. As the type of interdependence becomes more complex, coordination and mutual problem solving demands increase [13, 25]. While there is relatively little research focusing on inter-unit task interdependence, Van de Ven et al. [43], Lawrence and Lorsch [23], Aiken and

Hage [1], have reported evidence to support the relationship between the type of interdependence and problem solving complexity. In all, theory and research suggest that the more complex the inter-unit task interdependence, the greater the task associated uncertainty which must be dealt with by respective subunits.

In summary, three factors combine to influence the degree of uncertainty which organizational subunits face. As the task becomes less routine or involves more substantial intra-unit task interdependence, as the task environment becomes more unstable, and as inter-unit task interdependence becomes more complex, subunits must cope with increased amounts of work-related uncertainty (see Figure 1).

P2:   *As work related uncertainty increases, so does the need for increased amounts of information, and thus the need for increased information processing capacity.*

Where the nature of the subunit's work is highly certain, small amounts of information are sufficient—perhaps in the form of fixed standards, formal operating procedure, or rules. Little new information or information processing are required during task performance. Thus, the need for continual monitoring, feedback, and adjustment is minimal, and the information processing requirements for the subunit are relatively small. Where the nature of the unit's work is highly uncertain, need for the constant flow of information increases among role occupants. Under these

Figure 1.   Sources of Uncertainty and of Information Processing Requirements

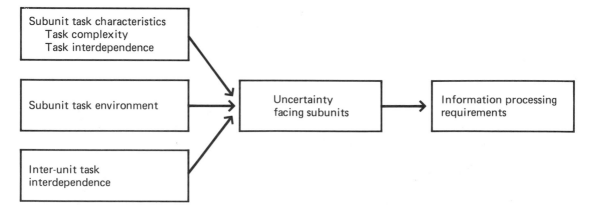

more uncertain conditions, new information becomes important; there are needs for mutual adjustment; and information exchange among components of the interdependent task is essential [9, 15, 23, 43, 47].

Thus, as the amount of uncertainty which a subunit faces increases, so too does the need for increased information processing capacity. In short, the greater the uncertainty faced by the subunit, the greater are its information processing requirements. Similarly, the greater the uncertainty faced by a set of subunits, the greater are the information processing requirements for the whole organizational structure.

P3: *Different organizational structures have different capacities for effective information processing.*

Structural conditions affect the subunit's ability to attend to and deal with uncertainty. Effective information processing includes the collection of appropriate information, the movement of information in a timely fashion, and its transmission without distortion. Effective information processing also implies the ability to handle needed quantities of information according to these criteria. Two dimensions of subunit structure affects its information processing capacity: The organismic-mechanistic nature of the subunit's structure, and the nature of coordination and control mechanisms which work to tie interdependent units together (e.g. control, planning, or reward systems). To simplify the discussion of subunit structure, the concepts of organismic and mechanistic structure are used. These structural terms will be a shorthand way of referring to a larger set of structural variables which frequently covary including: formalization, centralization, leadership style, degree of participation, lateral and vertical communication, and distribution of power and control [23, 27]. These two basic structural dimensions will be discussed in greater detail below.

Organismic and Mechanistic Structures—Research indicates that organismic structures are able to deal with greater amounts of uncertainty than mechanistic structures [3, 9, 35]. Why should this be? One way of thinking about the impact of subunit structure on information processing capacity is by focusing on the impact of subunit structure on patterns of communication.

Subunit structure has an important impact on the subunit's ability to process information and deal with uncertainty. Highly connected (organismic) communication networks permit efficient use of individuals as problem solvers since they increase the opportunity for feedback and error correction and for the synthesis of different points of view. Because highly connected networks are relatively independent of any one individual, they are less sensitive to information overload or saturation than more limited networks. Finally, highly connected networks tend to be associated with less formality, less attention to rules and regulations, and greater peer involvement in decision making [32, 35]. Since each of the above is related to a subunit's ability to deal with uncertainty, organismic communication networks have a greater ability to deal with work related uncertainty than do more hierarchical or mechanistic communication networks. A number of studies have reported results which support this logic [9, 15, 33, 34, 43].

While organic structures are able to deal effectively with greater amounts of uncertainty than more mechanistic structures, there are costs associated with this increased information processing capacity. Organismic structures consume more time, effort, energy, and are less amenable to managerial control. Thus, the benefits of increased information processing capacity must be weighed against the costs of less control and potentially increased reponse time [12, 33, 38].

Mechanisms for Coordination and Control—The organismic or mechanistic structuring of subunits provides them with different capacities to process information. When considering collections of subunits, the focus must shift to structures that exist to link together or coordinate activities of interdependent subunits.

These structures for linking (to be called coordinating and control mechanisms) include a range of different elements including rules and procedures, planning and control systems, and specific coordinating units such as product teams or task forces. In general, the more complex, elaborate, and comprehensive the coordination and control mechanisms are, the greater the ability to process information and deal with inter-unit uncertainty. As these coordination and control mechanisms become more complex, they also become more costly in the terms of time, energy, resources, and managerial control [12, 23, 43].

Galbraith [12, 13] proposed a range of coordination and control mechanisms. Based on his work, it is possible to construct a continuum of these mechanisms on the basis of cost, complexity, and capacity to process information (see Figure 2). Note that after joint planning there are alternative mechanisms to increase information processing capacity. Formal information or communication systems are most amenable when information is quantifiable or formal in nature (e.g. scheduling, forecasting), while lateral relations are most appropriate for information which is less quantifiable (e.g. informal communication). Thus, there are two complimentary approaches to achieve substantial inter-unit information processing capacity; one is more mechanistic in nature, the other more organismic.

Designing to Obtain Information Processing Capacity—From the previous discussion, designing a structure to obtain an optimal capacity to deal with work-related uncertainty involves two discrete issues. The first is structuring the subunit along organismic or mechanistic lines to obtain desired intra-unit information processing capacity. The second is creating coordination and control mechanisms which link units to obtain the desired inter-unit information processing capacity.

As units become more organismic, they have higher information processing capacity, but coordination costs within the unit may also increase (e.g. time spent on decision making). As coordination and control mechanisms become more complex, the total system has increased information processing capacity, but again increased costs are incurred in supporting these mechanisms. From these ideas, the basic design problem is to balance the costs of information-processing capacity against the needs of the subunit's work— too much capacity will be redundant and costly; too little capacity will not get the job done.

P4: *Organizations will be more effective when there is a match between information processing requirements facing the organization and information processing capacity of the organization's structure.*

One major criticism of contingency research is its lack of clarity as to what constitutes a fit or match between task dimensions and organizational structure [29]. Proposition 4 introduces information processing ideas as an intermediate step to define more explicitly the concept of fit. Thus, a subunit's information processing capacity (partially determined by its structure) must be capable of dealing with the information processing requirements of its work.

Proposition 4 can be derived from the basic open systems idea of requisite variety [44]. This idea suggests that if work units are to make order out of uncertainty, they must match highly uncertain conditions with complex information processing structures. Conversely, the less uncertainty faced by a subunit, the less its information processing requirements, and therefore its information processing mechanisms need not be complex. It follows that to be effective, subunits must match information processing capacity with information processing requirements [9, 12, 29].

Figure 2.   Mechanisms for Coordination and Control

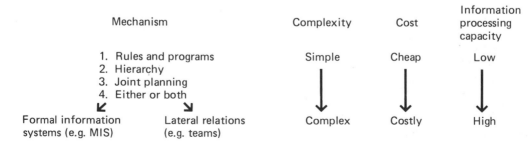

Figure 3. Relationships Between Information Processing Capacity and Information Processing Requirements

Information processing requirements	Information processing capacity	
	High	Low
Extensive	Match A	Mismatch B
Minimal	Mismatch C	Match D

The relationships between information processing capacity and requirements are diagrammed in Figure 3. Hypothetically high performing organizations are those which match capacity to requirements. Mismatch in capacity and requirements should be associated with lower organizational performance.

For example, in cell B, information processing capacity is not sufficient to deal with the uncertainty generated during the task (e.g. the extensive use of formal rules and regulations in R&D laboratories). Decisions will therefore be made with a less than optimal amount of information. It is also possible to have too much information processing capacity for the task's requirements. In this case (Cell C), the extra information processing capacity is redundant and costly in terms of time, effort, and control (e.g. the extensive use of horizontal communication where tasks are simple and weakly interdependent).

While relatively little research has been done to directly test this basic hypothesis, substantial literature can be seen as supportive of this matching idea. If information processing capacity must match information processing requirements, then effective subunits with complex tasks or those facing a changing environment should have more organismic structures than those subunits facing routine tasks or stable environmental conditions.

In support of the task-structure hypothesis, Hage and Aiken [14] found that psychiatric agencies (non-routine) were more organismic than were case work agencies (routine). Similarly, Woodward [46] found that successful organiza-tions with relatively complex tasks were less mechanistic than successful organizations with more routine tasks. Other studies with supportive results include Whitley and Frost [45], Perrow [31], Freeman [11], and Hickson et al. [16].

In support of the environment-structure hypothesis, Duncan [9] found that successful subunits in a changing environment had organismic structures while successful subunits facing stable environmental conditions had more mechanistic structures. Other studies with supportive results include Lawrence and Lorsch [23], Burns and Stalker [3], Connolly [6], Miller [26], and Neghandi and Reimann [28].

Not all of the research is supportive of ideas behind Proposition 4. Studies by Pennings [29] and Mohr [27] are frequently cited as providing counter evidence to the matching hypothesis. Pennings [29] found no relationship between environmental conditions and the degree of participation or power sharing in a set of brokerage offices (a relatively complex task). As the model suggests that subunit task characteristics *and* task environment are associated with subunit structure, Penning's results can be used to support the core association between work-related uncertainty, subunit structure, and effectiveness. Penning's [29] research *does* suggest that task characteristics have a more powerful impact on subunit structure than does task environment.

Mohr [27] hypothesized that subunit task characteristics (task complexity and task interdependence) would be associated with supervisory style (a proxy for subunit structure). In support of the information processing model, he found weak support for the task complexity hypothesis, yet substantially stronger support for the impact of task interdependence on subunit structure (e.g. the greater the interdependence, the greater the use of a democratic supervisory style). But the congruence hypothesis (that is, the link between performance and congruence) was supported only for task interdependence. Both studies can be seen as supportive of information processing logic and partially supportive of Proposition 4. They do underscore the need for future research to specify the differential impacts of subunit task characteristics, task environment, and task interdependence on subunit structure and effectiveness.

At the inter-unit level of analysis, the information processing approach suggests that the more complex the interdependence, the greater the information processing requirements. If so, then Proposition 4 would suggest that high performing units facing complex interdependence with other areas should utilize more complex coordination and control mechanisms, while high performing units with small amounts of interdependence should utilize simple coordination and control mechanisms. Compared to the task and environmental areas, relatively little literature speaks to this hypothesis, but Lawrence and Lorsch [23], Aiken and Hage [1], Khandwalla [21], and Van de Ven et al. [43] found that subunits facing substantial interdependence with other areas used complex coordination devices over and above more simple mechanisms. Units facing only limited amounts of interdependence used only simple coordination devices. This pattern of results was accentuated for high performing organizations in both the Lawrence and Lorsch [23] and Khandwalla [21] studies.

P4A: *Due to the alternative modes of achieving integration, the choice of coordinating and control mechanisms will not be deterministic.*

The theory and research and coordinating and control mechanisms suggest that more simple mechanisms should be utilized to the fullest possible extent; given their greater cost, the more complex integrating mechanisms should be used only for residual interdependence [13, 23]. Given several alternative means to achieve greater information processing capacity between subunits (see Figure 2), complete specification of the most appropriate set of coordinating and control mechanisms (formal systems, lateral relations, or both) will be contingent on the nature of the task and other organizational conditions (e.g. managerial values). In short, there will be no one-to-one correspondence between information processing requirements and information processing capacity.

Instead of a structural imperative, Proposition 4A suggests an alternative contingency mode. A consideration of subunit task uncertainty does not lead to a unique structural solution; rather, it leads to a feasible set of structural alternatives

from which the organization (or its dominant elite) must choose [4, 13, 37]. Consistent with Child's [5] work on strategic choice, organizational structure can be seen as a result of the nature of subunit work related uncertainty *and* the nature of the organization's decision making elite's values [4].

P5: *If organizations (or subunits) face different conditions over time, more effective units will adapt their structures to meet the changed information processing requirements.*

Proposition 4 is, by itself, a static hypothesis. What are the structural implications of changing work demands (e.g. due to environmental conditions or the phase of a program)? The information processing approach suggests that the organization (or subunit) must adapt to varying information processing demands. Research supports this approach to the structuring of organizations over time.

At the organizational level of analysis, Utterback and Abernathy [41] found that structure of production organizations was dependent on the stage of the product's development. They found that in the idea or initial development stage, more organic/flexible structures were most appropriate, but that mechanistic structures were most appropriate in the product's implementation or diffusion stages. Illustrating this process approach to structure from a different angle, Chandler [4] found that one set of more successful organizations was able to cope with changing technological and market conditions by adaptation of structures.

At the project or departmental level of analysis, Duncan [9] found that successful subunits will adapt their structures to cope with different degrees of work related uncertainty. Zaltman et al. [47] and Utterback [40] reviewed the innovation and organization literatures and suggest that as projects or departments move through problem solving phases, different structural forms are appropriate. More specifically, Zaltman et al. [47] suggest that organismic structures are appropriate in early stages of a project, while more mechanistic structures are most appropriate during implementation stages.

In all, Proposition 5 suggests that not only may

different subunits have different structures, but that the same subunit may have different structures over time. This process approach to structure directs attention away from a static approach to structure towards a more dynamic approach to structuring organizations over time.

The five propositions form the basis of an information processing approach to organizational structure (see Figure 4). The basic notion is that subunits face different amounts of work-related uncertainty and that to be successful, they must match information processing capacity to information processing requirements. Since different structures have different information processing capabilities, subunits can deal with work related uncertainty with appropriate structural arrangements. Thus, the essence of organizational design is: subunits must choose from a feasible set of structural alternatives, a particular set of organizational arrangements, to most effectively deal with their information processing requirements. Finally, since an organization's (or subunit's) information processing requirements are likely to change over time, the task of organizational structuring or design will never be fully accomplished.

SUMMARY

The concept of information processing as well as the model of structural conditions associated with organizational effectiveness have implications for both research and practice. While various components of the information processing model have been derived from previous research, the model's central hypothesis remains to be fully tested. Research needs to be done to test whether organizational effectiveness is indeed associated with the fit or match between the information processing requirements facing an organization (and its subunits) and the information processing capacity of its structure.

Future research could focus on the relative impact of task characteristics, task environment, and task interdependence on subunit structure, the differential effectiveness of alternative mechanisms of coordination and control, and on the impact of managerial decision making on the choice of organization structure. Finally, future research could focus on the evolution of structure over time and the existence of mechanisms other

Figure 4. The Information Processing Model

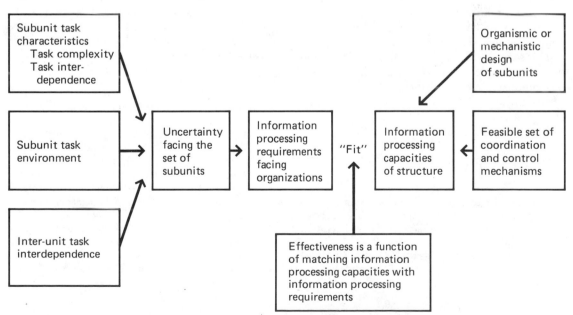

than structure for increasing subunit information processing capacity (e.g. special boundary roles or organizational climate).

More pragmatically, the information processing model holds promise as a tool for the problem of designing organizations. The model implies that design should first consider the composition and structure of organizational subunits and then consider appropriate mechanisms for linking those units together. The model implies a number of specific steps in designing an organization's structure. The first step is an identification of the most critical information processing needs and the formation of subunits around those needs. Thus, organizational roles with the highest need for information processing would be grouped together in subunits (a methodology for implementing this aspect of design is presented in Kilmann and McKelvey [22]). Second, those subunits would be structured along organismic or mechanistic lines according to the degree of uncertainty that each faces. Third, groups of subunits would be linked together with coordination and control mechanisms. The complexity of these mechanisms would be influenced by the amount of task interdependence among the subunits. Finally, this model suggests that the task of organizational design is never fully accomplished. As information processing requirements change, so too must the organization's structure.

Both research and practice can benefit from a comprehensive integrating model of organizational structure and design. The information processing model is one approach. This approach has promise, but its ultimate effectiveness remains to be determined by further exploration and research.

REFERENCES

[1] Aiken, M., and J. Hage. "Organizational Interdependence and Intra-Organizational Structure," *American Sociological Review*, Vol. 33 (1968), 912–930.

[2] Aldrich, H. "Technology and Organization Structure," *Administrative Science Quarterly*, Vol. 17 (1972), 26–43.

[3] Burns, T., and G. Stalker. *The Management of Innovation* (London: Tavistock Press, 1966).

[4] Chandler, A. *Strategy and Structure* (Cambridge, Mass.: M.I.T. Press, 1962).

[5] Child, J. "Organization Structure, Environment, and Performance: The Role of Strategic Choice," *Sociology*, Vol. 6 (1972), 1–22.

[6] Connolly, T. "Communication Nets and Uncertainty in R&D Planning," *IEEE Transactions on Engineering Management*, Vol. 22 (1975), 50–54.

[7] Downey, K., and J. Slocum, "Uncertainty: Measures, Research, and Sources of Variation," *Academy of Management Journal*, Vol. 18 (1975), 562–578.

[8] Duncan, R. "Characteristics of Organizational Environments," *Administrative Science Quarterly*, Vol. 17 (1972), 313–327.

[9] Duncan, R. "Multiple Decision Making Structure in Adapting to Environmental Uncertainty," *Human Relations*, Vol. 26 (1973), 273–291.

[10] Emery, F., and E. Trist. "The Causal Texture of Organizational Environments," in Hill and Egan (Eds.), *Readings in Organizational Theory* (Boston: Allyn Bacon, 1965), pp. 435–447.

[11] Freeman, J. "Environment, Technology, and the Administrative Intensity of Organizations," *American Sociological Review*, Vol. 38 (1973), 750–763.

[12] Galbraith, J. *Designing Complex Organizations* (Reading, Mass.: Addison-Wesley, 1973).

[13] Galbraith, J. *Organizational Design* (Reading, Mass.: Addison-Wesley, 1977).

[14] Hage, J., and M. Aiken. "Routine Technology, Social Structure, and Organizational Goals," *Administrative Science Quarterly*, Vol. 14 (1969), 366–377.

[15] Hage, J., M. Aiken, and C. B. Marrett. "Organization Structure and Communication," *American Sociological Review*, Vol. 36 (1971), 860–871.

[16] Hickson, D., D. Pugh, and D. Pheysey. "Operations Technology and Organization Structure," *Administrative Science Quarterly*, Vol. 14 (1969), 378–397.

[17] Hrebiniak, L. "Jobs Technology, Supervision, and Work Group Structure," *Administrative Science Quarterly*, Vol. 19 (1974), 395–411.

[18] Huber, G., M. O'Connell, and L. Cummings. "Perceived Environmental Uncertainty: Effects of Information and Structure," *Academy of Management Journal*, Vol. 18 (1975), 725–740.

[19] Jurkovich, R. "A Core Typology of Organization Environments," *Administrative Science Quarterly*, Vol. 19 (1974), 380–410.

[20] Katz, D., and R. Kahn. *The Social Psychology of Organizations* (New York: Wiley Co., 1966).

[21] Khandwalla, P. "Mass Output Orientation and Organizational Structure," *Administrative Science*

Quarterly, Vol. 19 (1974), 74–98.

[22] Kilmann, R., and B. McKelvey. "Organization Design: A Participative Multivariate Approach, *Administrative Science Quarterly,* Vol. 20 (1975), 24–36.

[23] Lawrence, P., and J. Lorsch. *Organizations and Environment* (Cambridge: Harvard University Press, 1967).

[24] Lynch, B., "An Empirical Assessment of Perrow's Technology Construct," *Administrative Science Quarterly,* Vol. 19 (1974), 338–356.

[25] March, J., and H. Simon. *Organizations* (New York: Wiley Co., 1958).

[26] Miller, R. *Innovations, Organization, and Environment* (Sherbrooke, England: University of Sherbrooke Press, 1971).

[27] Mohr, L. "Organization Technology and Organization Structure," *Administrative Science Quarterly,* Vol. 16 (1971), 444–459.

[28] Neghandi, A., and B. Reimann. "Task Environment, Decentralization, and Organizational Effectiveness," *Human Relations,* Vol. 26 (1973), 203–214.

[29] Pennings, J. "The Relevance of the Structural-Contingency Model for Organizational Effectiveness," *Administrative Science Quarterly,* Vol. 20 (1975), 393–410.

[30] Perrow, C. "Hospitals," in J. March (Ed.), *Handbook of Organizations* (Chicago: Rand McNally, 1965).

[31] Perrow, C. *Complex Organizations* (San Francisco: Scott-Foresman, 1972).

[32] Price, J. *Organization Effectiveness: An Inventory of Propositions* (Homewood, Ill.: R. D. Irwin Co., 1968).

[33] Shaw, M. "Communication Networks," in L. Berkowitz (Ed.), *Advances in Experimental Social Psychology* (New York: Academic Press, 1964).

[34] Smith, C. G. "Consultation and Decision Process in a R&D Laboratory," *Administrative Science Quarterly,* Vol. 15 (1970), 203–215.

[35] Snadowsky, A. "Communication Network Research: An Examination of Controversies," *Human Relations,* Vol. 25 (1972), 283–306.

[36] Steers, R. "Problems in the Measurement of Organizational Effectiveness," *Administrative Science Quarterly,* Vol. 20 (1975), 546–558.

[37] Thompson, J. D. *Organizations in Action* (New York: McGraw-Hill, 1967).

[38] Thompson, J. D., and A. Tuden. "Strategies, Structures, and Processes of Organizational Decision," in J. D. Thompson et al. (Eds.), *Comparative Studies in Administration* (Pittsburgh: University of Pittsburgh Press, 1959).

[39] Tosi, H., R. Aldag, and R. Storey. "On the Measurement of the Environment," *Administrative Science Quarterly,* Vol. 18 (1973), 27–36.

[40] Utterback, J. "The Process of Technological Innovation Within the Firm," *Academy of Management Journal,* Vol. 14 (1971), 75–88.

[41] Utterback, J., and W. Abernathy. "A Dynamic Model of Process and Product Innovation," *Omega,* Vol. 3 (1975), 639–656.

[42] Van de Ven, A., and A. Delbecq. "A Task Contingent Model of Work Unit Structure," *Administrative Science Quarterly,* Vol. 19 (1974), 183–197.

[43] Van de Ven, A., A. Delbecq, and R. Koening. "Determinants of Coordination Modes Within Organizations," *American Sociological Review,* Vol. 41 (1976), 322–338.

[44] Weick, Karl. *The Social Psychology of Organizing* (Reading, Mass.: Addison-Wesley Co., 1969).

[45] Whitley, R., and P. Frost. "Task Type and Information Transfer in a Government Research Lab," *Human Relations,* Vol. 25 (1973), 537–550.

[46] Woodward, J. *Industrial Organizations* (London: Oxford Press, 1965).

[47] Zaltman, G., R. Duncan, and J. Holbek, *Innovation and Organizations* (New York: Wiley Co., 1973).

22
What is the
right organization structure?

Robert Duncan

Organization design is a central problem for managers. What is the "best" structure for the organization? What are the criteria for selecting the "best" structure? What signals indicate that the organization's existing structure may not be appropriate to its tasks and its environment? This article discusses the purposes of organization structure and presents a decision tree analysis approach to help managers pick the right organization structure.

THE OBJECTIVES OF ORGANIZATIONAL DESIGN

What is organization structure and what is it supposed to accomplish? Organization structure is more than boxes on a chart; it is a pattern of interactions and coordination that links the technology, tasks, and human components of the organization to ensure that the organization accomplishes its purpose.

An organization's structure has essentially two objectives: First, it facilitates the flow of information within the organization in order to reduce the uncertainty in decision making. The design of the organization should facilitate the collection of the information managers need for decision making. When managers experience a high degree of uncertainty—that is, when their information needs are great—the structure of the organization should not be so rigid as to inhibit managers from seeking new sources of information or developing new procedures or methods for doing their jobs. For example, in developing a new product, a manufacturing department may need to seek direct feedback from customers on

how the new product is being accepted; the need to react quickly to customer response makes waiting for this information to come through normal marketing and sales channels unacceptable.

The second objective of organization design is to achieve effective coordination-integration. The structure of the organization should integrate organizational behavior across the parts of the organization so it is coordinated. This is particularly important when the units in the organization are interdependent. As James Thompson had indicated, the level of interdependence can vary. In *pooled interdependence* the parts of the organization are independent and are linked together only in contributing something to the same overall organization. In many conglomerates, the divisions are really separate organizations linked only in that they contribute profits to the overall organization. Simple rules—procedures—can be developed to specify what the various units have to do. In *sequential interdependence,* however, there is an ordering of activities, that is, one organizational unit has to perform its function before the next unit can perform its. For example, in an automobile plant manufacturing has to produce the automobiles before quality control can inspect them. Now such organizations have to develop plans to coordinate activities; quality control needs to know when and how many cars to expect for inspection.

Reciprocal interdependence is the most complex type of organizational interdependence. Reciprocal interdependence is present when the output of Unit A become the inputs of Unit B and the outputs of B cycle back to become the inputs of Unit A. The relationship between the operations and maintenance in an airline is a good example of this type of interdependence. Operations produces "sick" airplanes that need repair by maintenance. Maintenance repairs these planes and the repaired planes become inputs to the operations division to be reassigned to routes. When reciprocal interdependence between organization

Source: Reprinted, by permission of the publisher, from *Organizational Dynamics,* Winter 1979, © 1979 by AMACOM, a division of American Management Associations. All rights reserved.

units is present, a more complex type of coordination is required. This is coordination by feedback. Airline operations and maintenance must communicate with one another so each one will know when the planes will be coming to them so they can carry out their respective functions.

Organizational design, then, is the allocation of resources and people to a specified mission or purpose and the structuring of these resources to achieve the mission. Ideally, the organization is designed to fit its environment and to provide the information and coordination needed.

It is useful to think of organization structure from an information-processing view. The key characteristics of organizational structure is that it links the elements of the organization by providing the channels of communication through which information flows. My research has indicated that when organizational structure is formalized and centralized, information flows are restricted and, as a consequence, the organization is not able to gather and process the information it needs when faced with uncertainty. For example, when an organization's structure is highly centralized, decisions are made at the top and information tends to be filtered as it moves up the chain of command. When a decision involves a great deal of uncertainty, it is unlikely therefore that the few individuals at the top of the organization will have the information they require to make the best decision. So decentralization, that is, having more subordinates participate in the decision-making process, may generate the information needed to help reduce the uncertainty and thereby facilitate a better decision.

ALTERNATIVE ORGANIZATIONAL DESIGNS

The key question for the manager concerned with organizational design is what are the different structures available to choose from. Contingency theories of organization have shown that there is no one best structure. However, organization theorists have been less clear in elaborating the decision process managers can follow in deciding which structure to implement.

In discussing organization design, organization theorists describe structure differently from the way managers responsible for organization design do. Organizational theorists describe structure as more or less formalized, centralized, specialized, or hierarchical. However, managers tend to think of organizational structure in terms of two general types, the *functional* and the *decentralized.* Most organizations today are either functional or decentralized or some modification or combination of these two general types. Therefore, if we are to develop a heuristic for helping managers make decisions about organization structure, we need to think of structures as functional or decentralized and not in terms of the more abstract dimensions of formalization, centralization, and so on, that organizational theorists tend to use.

ORGANIZATIONAL ENVIRONMENT AND DESIGN: A CRITICAL INTERACTION

In deciding on what kind of organization structure to use, managers need to first understand the characteristics of the environment they are in and the demands this environment makes on the organization in terms of information and coordination. Once the environment is understood, the manager can proceed with the design process.

The first step in designing an organization structure, therefore, is to identify the organization's environment. The task environment constitutes that part of the environment defined by managers as relevant or potentially relevant for organizational decision making. Figure 1 presents a list of environmental components managers might encounter. Clearly, no one organization would encounter all these components in decision making, but this is the master list from which organizational decision makers would identify the appropriate task environments. For example, a manager in a manufacturing division could "define an environment consisting of certain personnel, certain staff units and suppliers, and perhaps certain technological components. The usefulness of the list in Figure 1 is that it provides a guide for decision makers, alerting them to the

Figure 1.   Environmental Components List

Internal environment	External environment
Organizational personnel component —Educational and technological background and skills —Previous technological and managerial skill —Individual member's involvement and commitment to attaining system's goals —Interpersonal behavior styles —Availability of manpower for utilization within the system	Customer component —Distributors of product or service —Actual users of product or service
	Suppliers component —New materials suppliers —Equipment suppliers —Product parts suppliers —Labor supply
Organizational functional and staff units component —Technological characteristics of organizational units —Interdependence of organizational units in carrying out their objectives —Intraunit conflict among organizational functional and staff units —Intraunit conflict among organizational functional and staff units	Competitor component —Competitors for suppliers —Competitors for customers
	Sociopolitical component —Government regulatory control over the industry —Public political attitude toward industry and its particular product —Relationship with trade unions with jurisdiction in the organization
Organizational level component —Organizational objectives and goals —Integrative process integrating individuals and groups into contributing maximally to attaining organizational goals —Nature of the organization's product service	Technological component —Meeting new technological requirements of own industry and related industries in production of product or service —Improving and developing new products by implementing new technological advances in the industry

elements [of] the environment they might consider in decision making.

Once managers have defined the task environment, the next step is to understand the state of that environment. What are its key characteristics? In describing organizational environments, we emphasize two dimensions: simple-complex and static-dynamic.

The simple-complex dimension of the environment focuses on whether the factors in the environment considered for decision making are few in number and similar or many in number and different. An example of a *simple* unit would be a lower-level production unit whose decisions are affected only by the parts department and materials department, on which it is dependent

for supplies, and the marketing department, on which it is dependent for output. An example of a *complex* environment would be a programming and planning department. This group must consider a wide variety of environmental factors when making a decision. It may focus on the marketing and materials department, on customers, on suppliers, and so on. Thus this organizational unit has a much more heterogeneous group of environmental factors to deal with in decision making—its environment is more complex than that of the production unit.

The static-dynamic dimension of the environment is concerned with whether the factors of the environment remain the same over time or change. A *static* environment, for example, might be a production unit that has to deal with a marketing department whose requests for output remain the same and a materials department that is able to supply a steady rate of inputs to the production unit. However, if the marketing department were continually changing its requests and the materials department were inconsistent in its ability to supply parts, the production unit would be operating in a more *dynamic* environment.

Figure 2 provides a four-way classification of organizational environments and some examples of organizations in each of these environments. Complex-dynamic (Cell 4) environments are probably the most characteristic type today. These environments involve rapid change and create high uncertainty for managers. The proper organizational structure is critical in such environments if managers are to have the information necessary for decision making. Also, as organi-

zations move into this turbulent environment, it may be necessary for them to modify their structures. For example, AT&T has moved from a functional organization to a decentralized structure organized around different markets to enable it to cope with more competition in the telephone market and in communications. This change in structure was in response to the need for more information and for a quicker response time to competitive moves.

STRATEGIES FOR ORGANIZATIONAL DESIGN

Once the organization's environment has been diagnosed, what type of structure the organization should have becomes the key question.

Figure 2. Classification of Organizational Environments

	Simple	**Complex**
	Low perceived uncertainty	Moderately low perceived uncertainty
Static	Small number of factors and components in the environment Factors and components are somewhat similar to one another Factors and components remain basically the same and are not changing *Example:* Soft drink industry 1	2 Large number of factors and components in the environment Factors and components are not similar to one another Factors and components remain basically the same *Example:* Food products
	Moderately high perceived 3 uncertainty	4 High perceived uncertainty
Dynamic	Small number of factors and components in the environment Factors and components are somewhat similar to one another Factors and components of the environment are in continual process of change *Example:* Fast food industry	Large number of factors and components in the environment Factors and components are not similar to one another Factors and components of environment are in a continual process of change *Examples:* Commercial airline industry Telephone communications (AT&T)

Simple Design Strategy

When the organization's environment is relatively simple, that is, there are not many factors to consider in decision making, and stable, that is, neither the make-up of the environment nor the demands made by environmental components are changing, the information and coordination needs for the organization are low. In such circumstances, a *functional organization structure* is most appropriate.

A key characteristic of the functional organization is specialization by functional areas. Figure 3 presents a summary of this structure's strengths and weaknesses. The key strengths of the functional organization are that it supports in-depth skill development and a simple decision-communication network. However, when disputes or uncertainty arises among managers about a decision, they get pushed up the hierarchy to be resolved. A primary weakness of the functional organization, therefore, is that when the organization's environment becomes more dynamic and uncertainty tends to increase, many decisions move to the top of the organization. Lower-level managers do not have the information required for decision making so they push decisions upward. Top-level managers become overloaded and are thus slow to respond to the environment.

Organizational Design Dilemma

The organizational designer faces a dilemma in such situations. Designs can be instituted that *reduce* the amount of information required for decision making. Decentralization is the principal strategy indicated. Or organizations can develop more lateral relations to *increase* the amount of information available for decision making.

A decentralized organization is possible whenever an organization's tasks are self-contained. Decentralized organizations are typically designed around products, projects, or markets. The decentralized healthcare organization in Figure 4 is organized around product areas (Medical and Dental) and market area (International). Each division has all the resources needed to perform its particular task. For example, Medical Products (Figure 4) has its own functional organization consisting of production, marketing, and R&D to carry out its mission. The information needed by Medical Products Division's managers is re-

Figure 3.   Characteristics of the Functional Organization

Organizational functions	Accomplished in functional organization
Goals	Functional subgoal emphasis (projects lag)
Influence	Functional heads
Promotion	By special function
Budgeting	By function or department
Rewards	For special capability

Strengths	Weaknesses
1. Best in *stable* environment	1. Slow response time
2. Colleagueship ("home") for technical specialists	2. Bottlenecks caused by sequential tasks
3. Supports in-depth skill development	3. Decisions pile at top
4. Specialists freed from administrative / coordinating work	4. If multiproduct, product priority conflict
5. Simple decision/communication network excellent in small, limited-output organizations	5. Poor interunit coordination
	6. Stability paid for in less innovation
	7. Restricted view of whole

Figure 4.   Decentralized Organization

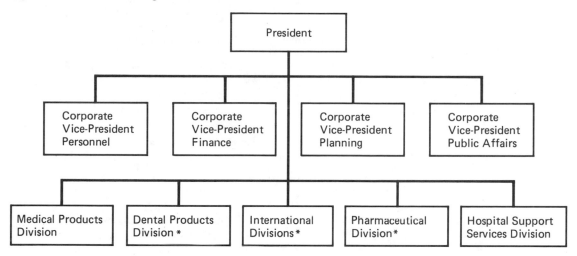

duced because they have organized around a set of common medical products, and they don't have to worry about dental, pharmaceutical, or hospital support services or products.

In the decentralized organization, managers only have to worry about their own products or services; they have the resources to carry out these activities, and they don't have to compete for shared resources or schedule shared resources. There is also a full-time commitment to a particular product line. The decentralized structure is particularly effective when the organization's environment is very complex, that is, there are a large number of factors to be considered in decision making, and the environment can be segmented or broken down into product or market areas around which the organization can structure itself. For example, the health products organization (Figure 4) probably started out as a functional organization. However, as its product line increased, it undoubtedly became more difficult for one manufacturing unit to have the expertise to produce such a wide range of products efficiently and to handle the diversity of information needed to do it. It would also be difficult for one marketing unit to market such a diverse group of products; different kinds of information and skills would be required to sell the different products. Segmenting this complex environment into product areas facilitates increased specialization. As

a result, divisional managers need less information than if they had to deal with all the products and services of the corporation.

Figure 5 summarizes the characteristics and the strengths and weaknesses of the decentralized organization. Decentralized organizations face several problems. For example, it is sometimes difficult to decide what resources are to be pooled in a corporate staff to be used to service the entire organization. If the divisions are very different from one another in terms of products, customers, technology, and so on, however, it becomes very difficult to staff a corporate services unit with the diverse knowledge needed to be able to help the divisions. A restricted approach to innovation is another problem decentralized organizations may encounter. Because each division is organized around a particular product or geographic area, each manager's attention is focused on his or her special area. As a result, their innovations focus on their particular specialties. Managers don't have the diverse information needed to produce radical innovations.

One major liability of decentralized organizations is their relative inability to provide integration-coordination among the divisions, even when their interdependence increases. When divisions are relatively autonomous and have only pooled interdependence, there is not much need for coordination. However, when uncertainty in-

Figure 5. Characteristics of the Decentralized Organization

Organizational functions	Accomplished in decentralized organization
Goals	Special product emphasis (technologies lag)
Influence	Product, project heads
Promotion	By product management
Budgeting	By product, project, program
Rewards	For integrative capability

Strengths	Weaknesses
1. Suited to fast change	1. Innovation/growth restricted to existing project areas
2. High product, project, or program visibility	2. Tough to allocate pooled resources (i.e., computer, lab)
3. Full-time task orientation (i.e., dollars, schedules, profits)	3. Shared functions hard to coordinate (i.e., purchasing)
4. Task responsibility, contact points clear to customers or clients	4. Deterioration of in-depth competence—hard to attract technical specialists
5. Processes multiple tasks in parallel, easy to cross functional lines	5. Possible internal task conflicts, priority conflicts
	6. May neglect high level of integration required in organization

creases and the divisions have to work together because of increased either sequential or reciprocal interdependence between the units, decentralized organizations have no formal mechanisms to coordinate and resolve the increased needs for information.

Since today's organizational environments are becoming more complex and interdependent, large decentralized corporations are finding that the need to integrate has increased for at least five reasons:

1. The increased level of regulation organizations face requires more and more coordination across divisions to be sure that all regulatory requirements are being met. For example, crackdowns by the SEC on illegal foreign payments and the increased liabilities of boards of directors have required organizations to have better control systems and information sources to enable their headquarters staff groups to know what's going on in the divisions. Affirmative action requirements have required that divisions share information on how they are doing and where possible pools of affirmative action candidates may be found.

2. Organizational environments are changing, and this can lead to a requirement of more coordination across divisions. New customer demands may require what were previously autonomous divisions to coordinate their activities. For example, if the International Group in the health products company mentioned earlier faces a demand to develop some new products for overseas, it may be necessary to provide a means by which the Medical Products and Pharmaceutical Divisions can work in a coordinated and integrated way with International to develop these new products.

3. Technological changes are placing more emphasis on increased interaction among divisions. More and more, computer systems and R&D services are being shared, thus compelling the divisions to interact more with one another.

4. The cost of making "wrong" strategic decisions is increasing in terms of both sunk costs and losses because of failure to get market share. Since such "wrong" decisions sometimes result from a lack of contact between divisions, it emphasizes the need to have more coordination across divisions and more sharing of information. For example, AT&T has just recently begun to market telephone and support equipment to counter the competition of other suppliers of this equipment that have entered the market. To do this AT&T has organized around markets. It has also increased the opportunities for interaction among these market managers so they can share information, build on one another's expertise and competence, and ensure required coordination.

5. Scarce resources—for example, capital and raw materials—will require more interaction among divisions to set overall priorities. Is a university, for example, going to emphasize its undergraduate arts program or its professional schools? By setting up task forces of the deans of the schools, the university might be able to identify opportunities for new innovative programs that could benefit the entire organization. New programs in management of the arts—museums, orchestras, and so on—could draw on the expertise of the arts department and the business school and would not require a lot of new venture capital.

For a number of reasons, then, there is a need for increased coordination among divisions in decentralized organizations. Given the decentralized organization's weakness, organizational designers need to implement the second general design strategy, increasing the information flow to reduce uncertainty and facilitate coordination.

Lateral Relations: Increasing Information Available for Decision Making

Lateral relations is really a process that is overlaid on an existing functional or decentralized structure. Lateral relations as a process moves decision making down to where the problem is in the organization. It differs from decentralization in that no self-contained tasks are created.

Jay Galbraith has identified various types of lateral relations. *Direct contact*, for example, can be used by managers of diverse groups as a mechanism to coordinate their different activities. With direct contact, managers can meet informally to discuss their common problems. *Liaison roles* are a formal communication link between two units. Engineering liaison with the manufacturing department is an excellent example of the liaison role. The engineer serving in the liaison role may be located in the production organization as a way of coordinating engineering and production activities.

When coordination between units becomes more complex, an *integrator role* may be established. Paul Lawrence and Jay Lorsch have indicated that the integrator role is particularly useful when organizational units that must be coordinated are differentiated from one another in terms of their structure, subgoals, time, orientation, and so on. In such situations, there is the possibility of conflict between the various units. For example, production, marketing, and R&D units in an organization may be highly differentiated from one another. Marketing, for example, is primarily concerned with having products to sell that are responsive to customer needs. R&D, on the other hand, may be concerned with developing innovative products that shape customer needs. Production, for its part, may want products to remain unchanged so that manufacturing setups don't have to be modified. Obviously there are differences among the three units in terms of their subgoals. The integrator role is instituted to coordinate and moderate such diverse orientations. The integrator could be a materials manager or a group executive whose additional function would be to coordinate and integrate the diverse units in ways that meet the organization's common objectives.

To be effective as an *integrator*, a manager needs to have certain characteristics. First, he needs wide contacts in the organization so that he possesses the relevant information about the different units he is attempting to integrate. Second, the integrator needs to understand and share, at least to a degree, the goals and orientations of the different groups. He cannot be seen as being a partisan of one particular group's perspective. Third, the integrator has to be rather broadly trained technically, so that he can talk the language of the different groups. By being able to demonstrate that he has some expertise in each area, he will be viewed as more credible by each group and will also be better able to facilitate information exchange between the units. The integrator can in effect become an interpreter of each group's position to the others. Fourth, the groups that the integrator is working with must trust him. Again, the integrator is trying to facilitate information flow and cooperation between the groups and thus the groups must believe that he is working toward a solution acceptable to all the groups. Fifth, the integrator needs to exert influence on the basis of his expertise rather than through formal power. The integrator can provide information and identify alternative courses of action for the different units as they attempt to coordinate their activities. The more he can get them to agree on solutions and courses of action rather than having to use his formal power, the more committed they will be to implementing the solution. Last, the integrator's conflict resolution skills are important. Because differentiation between the units exists, conflict and disagreement are inevitable. It is important, therefore, that confrontation is used as the conflict resolution style. By confrontation we mean that parties to the conflict identify the causes of conflict and are committed to adopting a problem-solving approach to finding a mutually acceptable solution to the conflict. The parties must also be committed, of course, to work to implement that solution.

When coordination involves working with six or seven different units, then task forces or teams can be established. Task forces involve a group of managers working together on the coordination problems of their diverse groups. For example, in a manufacturing organization, the marketing, production, R&D, finance, and engineering managers may meet twice a week (or more often when required) to discuss problems of coordination that they may be having that require their cooperation to solve. In this use a task force is a problem-solving group formed to facilitate coordination.

The matrix type of structure is the most complex form of lateral relations. The matrix is typically a formal structure in the organization; it is not a structure that is often added temporarily to an existing functional or decentralized structure.

As Lawrence, Kolodny, and Davis have indicated in their article "The Human Side of the Matrix" (*Organizational Dynamics*, Summer 1977) [Reading 27], there are certain key characteristics of a matrix structure. The most salient is that there is dual authority, that is, both the heads of the functions and the matrix manager have authority over those working in the matrix unit.

The matrix was initially developed in the aerospace industry where the organization had to be responsive to products/markets as well as technology. Because the matrix focuses on a specific product or market, it can generate the information and concentrate the resources needed to respond to changes in that product or market rapidly. The matrix is now being used in a variety of business, public, and health organizations. Figure 6 provides a summary of the characteristics and strengths and weaknesses of the matrix form of organization.

The matrix structure is particularly useful when an organization wants to focus resources on producing a particular product or service. The use of the matrix in the aerospace industry, for example, allowed these organizations to build manufacturing units to [produce] particular airplanes, thus allowing in-depth attention and specialization of skills.

Matrix organizations, however, are complicated to manage. Because both project managers and traditional functional area managers are involved in matrix organizations, personnel in the matrix have two bosses, and there is an inherent potential for conflict under such circumstances. As a result, the matrix form of lateral relations should only be used in those situations where an organization faces a unique problem in a particular market area or in the technological requirements of a product. When the information and technological requirements are such that a full-time focus on the market or product is needed, a matrix organization can be helpful. Citibank, for example, has used a matrix structure in its international activity to concentrate on geographic areas. Boeing Commercial Airplane has used the matrix to focus resources on a particular product.

Lateral relations require a certain organizational design and special interpersonal skills if this process for reducing uncertainty by increasing the information available for improving co-

Figure 6. Characteristics of the Matrix Organization

Organizational functions	Accomplished in matrix organization
Goals	Emphasis on product/market
Influence	Matrix manager and functional heads
Promotion	By function or into matrix manager job
Budgeting	By matrix organization project
Rewards	By special functional skills and performance in matrix

Strengths	Weaknesses
1. Full-time focus of personnel on project of matrix	1. Costly to maintain personnel pool to staff matrix
2. Matrix manager is coordinator of functions for single project	2. Participants experience dual authority of matrix manager and functional area managers
3. Reduces information requirements as focus is on single product/market	3. Little interchange with functional groups outside the matrix so there may be duplication of effort, "reinvention of the wheel"
4. Masses specialized technical skills to the product/market	4. Participants in matrix need to have good interpersonal skills in order for it to work

ordination is going to be effective. From a design perspective, four factors are required:

1. The organization's reward structure must support and reward cooperative problem solving that leads to coordination and integration. Will a manager's performance appraisal, for example, reflect his or her participation in efforts to achieve coordination and integration? If the organization's reward system does not recognize joint problem-solving efforts, then lateral relations will not be effective.

2. In assigning managers to participate in some form of lateral relations, it is important that they have responsibility for implementation. Line managers should be involved since they understand the problems more intimately than staff personnel and, more importantly, they are concerned about implementation. Staff members can be used, but line managers should be dominant since this will lead to more commitment on their part to implementing solutions that come out of lateral relations problem-solving efforts.

3. Participants must have the authority to commit their units to action. Managers who are participating in an effort to resolve problems of coordination must be able to indicate what particular action their units might take in trying to improve coordination. For example, in the manufacturing company task force example mentioned earlier, the marketing manager should be able to commit his group to increasing the lead time for providing information to production on deadlines for delivering new products to customers.

4. Lateral processes must be integrated into the vertical information flow. In the concern for increasing information exchange *across* the units in the organization there must be no loss of concern for vertical information exchange so that the top levels in the organization are aware of coordination efforts.

Certain skills are also required on the part of participants for lateral relations to work:

1. Individuals must deal with conflict effectively, in the sense of identifying the sources of

conflict and then engaging in problem solving to reach a mutually acceptable solution to the conflict situation.

2. Participants need good interpersonal skills. They must be able to communicate effectively with one another and avoid making other participants defensive. The more they can learn to communicate with others in a descriptive, non-evaluative manner the more open the communication process will be.

3. Participants in lateral relations need to understand that influence and power should be based on expertise rather than formal power. Because of the problem-solving nature of lateral relations, an individual's power and influence will change based on the particular problem at hand and the individual's ability to provide key information to solve the problem. At various times different members will have more influence because of their particular expertise.

Lateral relations, then, is a process that is overlaid onto the existing functional or decentralized organization structure. Lateral relations requires various skills, so it is imperative that an organization never adopts this approach without training the people involved. Before implementing lateral relations team building might be used to develop the interpersonal skills of the participating managers. These managers might spend time learning how to operate more effectively in groups, how to improve communication skills, and how to deal with conflict in a positive way so that it does not become disruptive to the organization.

The Organizational Design Decision Tree

We have discussed the different kinds of organization structure that managers can implement. We are now prepared to identify the decision-making process the manager can use in selecting the appropriate structure to "fit" the demands of the environment. Figure 7 presents a decision tree analysis for selecting either the functional or decentralized organization structure. This decision analysis also indicates when the existing functional or decentralized organization structure

should be supplemented with some form of lateral relations in the form of a task force or team or a matrix. In general, an organization should use one of the simpler forms of lateral relations rather than the more complex and expensive matrix. In using this decision tree, there are a number of questions that the designer needs to ask.

The first question is whether the organization's environment is *simple*, that is, there are few factors to consider in the environment, or *complex*, that is, there are a number of different environmental factors to be considered in decision making. If the environment is defined as *simple*, the next question focuses on whether the environmental factors are *static*, that is, remain the same over time, or are *dynamic*, that is, change over time. If we define the environment as static, there is likely to be little uncertainty associated with decision making. In turn, information requirements for decision making are low. In this simple-static environment, the functional organization is most efficient. It can most quickly gather and process the information required to deal with this type of environment.

At this point the question might be raised, are there any organizational environments that are in fact both simple and static or is this a misperception on the part of the managers that oversimplifies the environment? There may be environments like this, but the key is that these environments may change, that is, they may become more dynamic as the marketplace changes, as resources become scarce, or the organization's domain is challenged. For example, the motor home/recreational vehicle industry was very successful in the early 1970s. Its market was relatively homogeneous (simple) and there was a constantly high demand (static) for its products. Then the oil embargo of 1973 hit, and the environment suddenly became dynamic. The industry had a very difficult time changing because it had done no contingency planning about "what would happen if" demand shifted, resources became scarce, and so on. The important point is that an organization's environment may be simple and static today but change tomorrow. Managers should continually scan the environment and be sensitive to the fact that things can change and contingency planning may be useful.

Figure 7. Organizational Design Decision Tree Heuristic

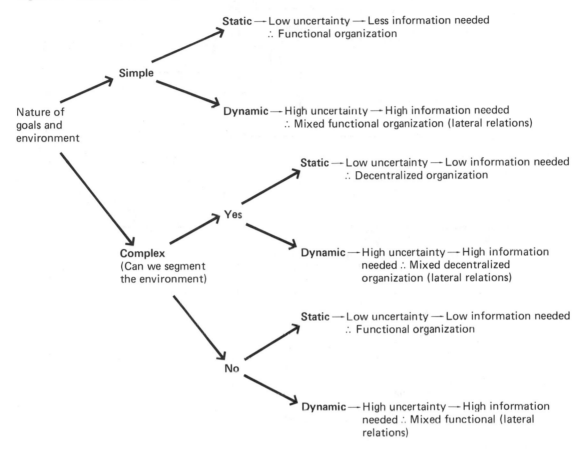

If this simple environment is defined as dynamic, with some components in the environment changing, some uncertainty may be experienced by decision makers. Thus information needs will be greater than when the environment was static. Therefore, in this simple-dynamic environment the mixed functional organization with lateral relations is likely to be the most effective in gathering and processing the information required for decision making. Because the organization's environment is simple, the creation of self-contained units would not be efficient. It is more economical to have central functional areas responsible for all products and markets as these products and markets are relatively similar to one another. However, when un-

certainty arises and there is need for more information, some form of lateral relations can be added to the existing functional organization.

Figure 8 shows the functional organization of a manufacturing organization. The organization suddenly may face a problem with its principal product. Competitors may have developed an attractive replacement. As a result of this unique problem, the president of the firm may set up a task force chaired by the vice-president of sales to develop new products. The task force consists of members from manufacturing, sales, research, and engineering services. Its function, obviously, will be to develop and evaluate suggestions for new products.

If the organization's environment is defined by

Figure 8. Functional Organization with Task Force

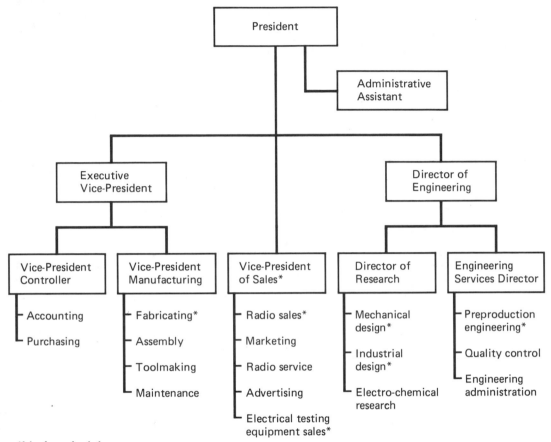

*Members of task force

the managers as complex, that is, there are a large number of factors and components that need to be considered in decision making, the next question to ask is, can the organization *segment* its environment into geographic areas, market, or product areas? If the environment is defined as segmentable, then the next question focuses on whether the environment is static or dynamic. If the environment is defined as static, there is going to be low uncertainty and thus information needs for decision making are not going to be high. Thus, in the complex-segmentable-static environment, the decentralized organization is most appropriate, and the health products organization discussed earlier is a good example of this. The organization can break the environ-

ment apart in the sense that it can organize around products or markets, for example, and thus information, resources, and so forth, are only required to produce and market these more homogeneous outputs of the organization.

In the complex-segmentable-dynamic environment there is a change in the components of the environment and the demands they are making on the organization, or in fact the organization has to now consider different factors in the environment that it had not previously considered in decision making. Uncertainty and coordination needs may be higher. The result is that decision makers need more information to reduce uncertainty and provide information to facilitate coordination. The mixed decentralized organi-

Figure 9. Decentralized Organization with Lateral Relations

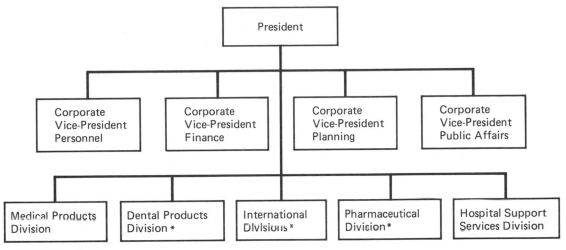

*Members of task force

zation with lateral relations is the appropriate structure here.

Figure 9 presents the design of a multidivision decentralized health products organization. Some form of lateral relations may be added to this structure to help generate more information. For example, the International Division may be attempting to develop new products but may be encountering problems, with the result that the entire organization, stimulated by the president's concern, may be experiencing uncertainty about how to proceed. In such a situation, a task force of the manager of the International Group and the Dental Group and the Pharmaceutical Group might work together in developing ideas for new products in the International Division. The lateral relations mechanism of the task force facilitates information exchange *across* the organization to reduce uncertainty and increase coordination of the efforts of the divisions that should be mutually supportive. By working together, in the task force, the division managers will be exchanging information and will be gaining a better understanding of their common problems and how they need to work and coordinate with one another in order to solve these problems.

If the organization's complex environment is defined by managers as nonsegmentable, the functional organization will be appropriate be-

cause it is not possible to break the environment up into geographic or product/service areas.

In effect, there simply might be too much interdependence among environmental components, or the technology of the organization may be so interlinked, that it is not possible to create self-contained units organized around components of the environment.

A hospital is a good example of this organization type. The environment is clearly complex. There are numerous and diverse environmental components that have to be considered in decision making (for example, patients, regulatory groups, medical societies, third-party payers, and suppliers). In the complex-nonsegmentable-static environment, environmental components are rather constant in their demands. Thus here the functional organization is most appropriate.

However, the functional organization, through its very specific rules, procedures, and channels of communication, will likely be too slow in generating the required information. Therefore, some form of lateral relations may be added to the functional organization. Figure 10 presents an example of an aerospace functional organization that uses a matrix structure for its airplane and missile products divisions. The matrix structure provides in-depth concentration of person-

Figure 10. Functional Organization with Matrix

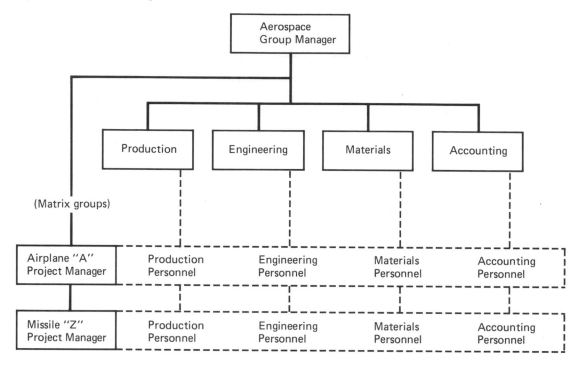

nel and resources on these different product areas, each of which has its own very unique information and technological requirements.

SYMPTOMS OF INAPPROPRIATE ORGANIZATIONAL STRUCTURE

The key question at this point is "So what?" What are the costs to an organization if it is using the wrong structure, given its product/service and the environment in which it operates? In order to be effective, an organization needs to attain its goals and objectives, it needs to adapt to the environment, and last, it should be designed in such a way that its managers experience low role conflict and ambiguity.

Therefore, there are certain kinds of information the manager responsible for organizational design should be sensitive to in monitoring whether the appropriate structure is being used. While using the appropriate structure may have

some direct impact on the organization's ability to attain its goals, its biggest impact will probably be on the adaptability of the organization and the role behavior of its managers.

Certain kinds of symptoms regarding ineffective adaptability may occur. For example:

• Organizational decision makers may not be able to anticipate problems before they occur. There may be a tendency in the organization to wait until problems occur and then react to them because the organization simply does not have enough information to develop contingency plans.

• Decision makers may err in trying to predict trends in their decision environment. Without proper coordination across divisions, the organization may lose control over the relationship between its internal functioning and its environment.

• The organization may not be able to get key information for decision making to the right place for effective decision making. For example, division managers from different product groups may have information that quality and liability standards on their respective products are unrealistically high. However, because of decentralization and lack of effective coordination through some form of lateral relations, this information may not get to the staff groups in the organization that are responsible for setting corporate policy in this area.

• The organization, having identified a problem vis-à-vis its environment, may simply not be able to take corrective action quickly enough.

Symptoms of poor fit between structure and environment may also show at the level of the individual in terms of some increase in either role conflict or role ambiguity. It is important, therefore, that the organization monitor the level of role conflict and role ambiguity among its managers and the resulting stress they experience so the system has a baseline for comparison. If there is a significant increase from this baseline in conflict and ambiguity and stress, then the organization may consider that the increase is a symptom of an organizational design problem. For example:

• Individuals may be experiencing increased role conflict. This may occur when the organization is implementing a functional organization in a dynamic environment. The environment may be changing and the individuals may be required to make quick responses to this changing environment. Having to wait for new policy changes to come down the hierarchy may delay the organization from responding appropriately. Decision makers at the top of the organization will also suffer from role conflict when the environment is changing rapidly. In the functional organization, when new situations occur they are referred to higher levels of the organization for decision and action. The result is that top-level decision makers become overloaded and the organization's response to the environment slows down. In a dynamic environment, the functional organization constrains the decision-making adaptation process.

• Individuals in the organization also may experience increased role ambiguity—they may be unclear as to what is expected of them in their roles. For example, role ambiguity is likely to occur when the decentralized organization is implemented without some effective use of lateral relations. Individuals may feel they don't have

the information needed for decision making. Divisional managers may not know what the corporate staff's policy is on various issues, and corporate staff may have lost touch with the divisions.

These are the kinds of information managers should be aware of as indicators of dysfunctional organization design. These data can be collected in organizational diagnosis surveys that we have developed so that a more systemic monitoring of structure exists just as we monitor organizational climate. As fine tuning the organization's design to its environment becomes more critical organizations will begin to monitor their organizational design more systematically.

SUMMARY

What are the advantages to managers in using the design decision tree? There appear to be several:

1. It provides a *broad framework* for identifying the key factors a manager would think about in considering an organizational design. For example: What is our environment? What different structural options do we have?

2. It forces the manager to *diagnose* the decision environment. What is our environment like? How stable is it? How complex is it? Is it possible to reduce complexity by segmenting the environment into product or geographical subgroups?

3. It causes managers to think about how *much interdependence* there is among segments of the organization. How dependent on one another are different parts of the organization in terms of technology, services, support, help in getting their tasks completed? The decision points in the heuristic force managers to question themselves about what other parts of the organization they need to coordinate their activities with, and then to think about how to do it.

4. Once the organization is in either a functional or decentralized structure, the decision tree points out what can be done to meet *the increased needs for information* through the use of lateral relations. Lateral relations provide a mechanism for supplementing the existing structure to facilitate dealing with the organization's increased needs for information and coordination.

Managers in a variety of organizations have commented that the decision tree gives them ". . . a handle for thinking about organizational design so we can tinker with it, fine tune it and make it work better. We don't have to be coerced by structure. We now have a better feel for when certain structures should be used and for the specific steps we can take to make a given structure work."

SELECTED BIBLIOGRAPHY

For a general background on organization theory as it applies to design, see James Thompson's *Organizations in Action* (McGraw-Hill, 1967) and Paul Lawrence and Jay Lorsch's *Organization and Environment* (Irwin, 1967). For a specific treatment of organizational design see Jay Galbraith's *Organizational Design* (Addison-Wesley, 1977) and (with Dan Nathanson) *Strategy Implementation: The Role of Structure and Process* (West Publishing, 1978). The Autumn 1977 *Organizational Dynamics* issue was devoted principally to design.

Two articles are particularly helpful—Jay Lorsch's "Organizational Design: A Situational Perspective" pp. 2–14 and Jeffrey Pfeffer and Gerald Salancik's "Organizational Design: The Case for a Coalitional Model of Organizations." pp. 15–29. For a focus on the learning process regarding design see Robert Duncan and Andrew Weiss's "Organizational Learning: Implications for Organizational Design" in Barry Staw's (ed.), *Research in Organizational Behavior* (JAI Press, 1978). For an excellent discussion of matrix organizations see Paul Lawrence, Harvey Kolodny, and Stan Davis' "The Human Side of the Matrix" (*Organizational Dynamics*, Summer 1977). pp. 43–61.

Business Week and *Fortune* magazines provide numerous excellent discussions of organizations facing design problems. For example, see "Behind the Profit Plunge at Heublein" (*Business Week*, July 4, 1977) pp. 64–65 and "Selling is No Longer Mickey Mouse at AT&T" (*Fortune*, July 17, 1978). pp. 84–104.

For an excellent discussion of organizational diagnosis see Marvin Weisbord's *Organizational Diagnosis* (Addison-Wesley, 1978).

23
Information
processing model

Jay R. Galbraith

In this [reading] the basic model is created and the overall structure of the framework is outlined. . . . Of necessity, the remainder of the [reading] is fairly abstract. The purpose is to conceive of organizations as information-processing networks and to explain why and through what mechanisms uncertainty and information relate to structure. In order to accomplish this explanation, the basic bureaucratic mechanical model is created. The value of the model is not that it describes reality but that it creates a basis from which various strategies are formed to adapt the bureaucratic structure for handling greater complexity.

MECHANISTIC MODEL

In order to develop the model and the design strategies, assume that we have a task which requires several thousand employees divided among

Source: Jay Galbraith, *Designing Complex Organizations*, © 1973, Addison-Wesley Publishing Company, Inc., Chapter 2, "Information Processing Model," pages 8–19. Reprinted with permission.

many subtasks. For example, the task of designing and manufacturing an aircraft or space capsule requires a group to design the capsule, a group to design the manufacturing methods, a group to fabricate parts and components, a group to assemble the parts, and a group to test the completed unit. The result is a division of labor which involves considerable interdependence and therefore coordination among the groups. The workflow is shown schematically in Figure 1.

In order to complete the task at a high level of performance, the activities that take place in the various groups must be coordinated. The behavior of the product design engineer must be consistent with the behavior of the process design engineers, etc. Although the behavior of several thousand people must be coordinated, it is impossible for all of them to communicate with each other. The organization is simply too large to permit face-to-face communication to be the mechanism for coordination. The organization design problem is to create mechanisms by which an integrated pattern of behavior can be obtained across all the interdependent groups. In order to see what these mechanisms are and the conditions under which they are appropriate, let us start with a very predictable task and slowly increase the degree of task uncertainty.

First we have a task, like the one represented in Figure 1, in which there is a high degree of division of labor, a high level of performance, and relatively large size. A good deal of information must be processed to coordinate the interdependent subtasks. As the degree of uncertainty increases, the amount of information processing during task execution increases. Organizations must evolve strategies to process the greater amount of information necessary to maintain the level of performance. Let us follow the history of a fictitious organization performing the task represented in Figure 1 and observe the mechanisms that are created to deal with increasing information loads caused by increasing task uncertainty.

Rules, Programs, Procedures

The simplest method of coordinating interdependent subtasks is to specify the necessary behaviors in advance of their execution in the form of rules or programs.[1] In order to make effective use of programs, the organization's employees are taught the job-related situations with which they will be faced and the behaviors appropriate to those situations. Then as situations arise daily, the employees act out the behaviors appropriate to the situations. If everyone adopts the appropriate behavior the resultant aggregate response is an integrated or coordinated pattern of behavior.

The primary virtue of rules is that they eliminate the need for further communication among the subunits. If an organization has hundreds of employees, they cannot all communicate with each other in order to guarantee coordinated action. To the extent that the job-related situations can be anticipated in advance and rules derived from them, integrated activity is guaranteed without communication. These rules and programs perform the same functions for organizations that habits perform for individuals. They eliminate the need for treating each situation as new. The amount of communication and decision making is reduced each time a situation is repeatedly encountered. In addition, rules provide a stability to the organization's operations. As people come and go through an organization, the rules provide a memory for handling routine situations.

The best example of a programmed task is the automobile assembly operation. Each employee learns a specific set of behaviors for each possible situation he will face, e.g., station wagon, convertible, deluxe sedan, standard sedan, etc. For assembly operations the programs and procedures are created by engineers. In other situations individuals simply program themselves. That is, after confronting the same situation many times, individuals coordinate their behavior by following the same approach as in the past. Many standard operating procedures arise in this manner.

The use of rules and programs as coordination devices is limited, however. It is limited to those job-related situations which can be anticipated in advance and to which an appropriate response can be identified. As the organization faces new and different situations, the use of rules must be supplemented by other integrating devices.

Figure 1.   Horizontal Workflow Across a Functional Division of Labor

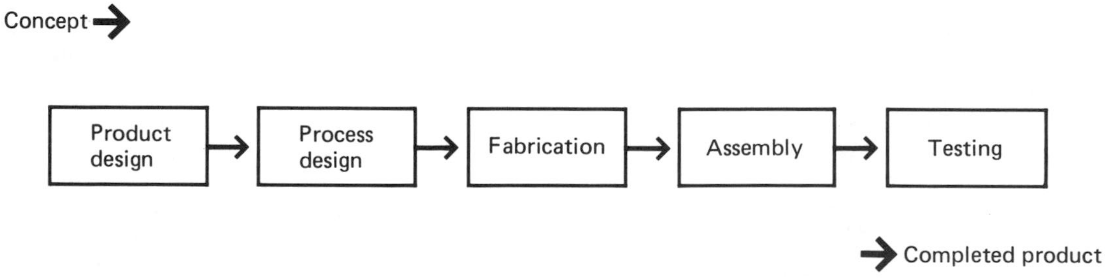

Concept →

Product design → Process design → Fabrication → Assembly → Testing

→ Completed product

Hierarchy

As the organization that depends on rules encounters situations it has not faced before, it has no ready-made response. When a response is developed for the new situation it must take into account all the subtasks that are affected. The information collection and problem solving activities may be substantial. To handle this task new roles are created, called managerial roles, and arranged in a hierarchy as shown in Figure 2.[2] The occupants of these roles handle the information collection and decision making tasks necessitated by uncertainty.

Then as unanticipated events arise, the problem is referred to the manager who has the information to make a new decision. In addition, the hierarchy is also a hierarchy of authority and reward power, so that the decisions of the role occupants are effective determinants of the behavior of the task performers. In this manner the hierarchy of authority is employed on an exception basis. That is, the new situation, for which there is no preplanned response, is referred upward in the hierarchy to permit the creation of a new response. Since the process we are describing remains rather mechanical, the new situation is referred upward in the hierarchy to that point where a shared superior exists for all subunits affected by the new situation. For example, in Figure 2, if a problem arises during testing which requires product design work, it is referred to the general manager. If a situation arises affecting assembly and fabrication, it is referred to manager No. 2.

It is important to point out that the hierarchy is employed *in addition to, not instead of,* the use of rules. That is, the rules achieve coordination for the uniform and repetitive situations, whereas the new and unique situations are referred upward. This combination guarantees an integrated coordinated organizational response to the situations which the organization faces.

The weakness of hierarchical communication systems is that each link has a finite capacity for handling information. As the organization's subtasks increase in uncertainty, more exceptions arise which must be referred upward in the hierarchy. As more exceptions are referred upward, the hierarchy becomes overloaded. Serious delays develop between the upward transmission of information about new situations and a response to that information downward. In this situation, the organization must develop new processes to supplement rules and hierarchy.

Targeting or Goal Setting

As task uncertainty increases, the volume of information from the points of action to points of

Figure 2.   Hierarchical Organization Structure

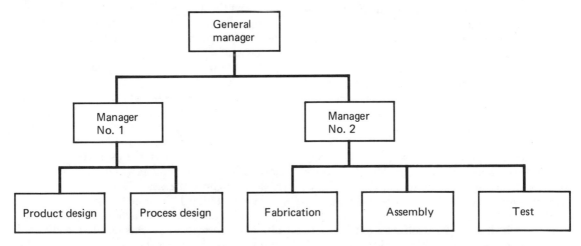

decision making overload the hierarchy. In this situation it becomes more efficient to bring the points of decision down to the points of action where the information originates. This can be accomplished by increasing the amount of discretion exercised by employees at lower levels of the organization. However, as the amount of discretion exercised at lower levels of the organization is increased, the organization faces a potential behavior control problem. That is, how can the organization be sure that the employees will consistently choose the appropriate response to the job-related situations which they will face?

In order to increase the probability that employees will select the appropriate behavior, organizations make two responses to deal with the behavior control problem.[3] The first change involves the substitution of craft or professional training of the work force for the detailed centralized programming of the work processes.[4] This is illustrated by a comparison between manufacturing industries and construction industries. In mass production, the work processes that are planned in advance are:

1) the location at which a particular task will be performed
2) the movement of tools, of materials and of workers to this work place and the most efficient arrangement of these workplace characteristics
3) sometimes the particular movements to be performed in getting the task done
4) the schedules and time allotments for particular operations
5) inspection criteria for particular operations.

In construction all these characteristics of the work process are governed by the worker in accordance with the empirical lore that makes up craft principles.[5]

These two descriptions represent a shift from control based on supervision and surveillance to control based on selection of responsible workers. Workers who have the appropriate skills and attitudes are selected.

Professionalization by itself may not be sufficient to shift decision making to lower levels of the organization. The reason is that in the presence of interdependence, an alternative which is based on professional or craft standards may not be best for the whole organization. Thus alternatives which are preferred from a local or departmental perspective may not be preferred from a global perspective. The product design that is technically preferred may not be preferred by the customer, may be costly to produce, or may require a schedule which takes too long to complete. In order to deal with the problem, organizations undertake processes to set goals or targets to cover the primary interdependencies.

An example of the way goals are used can be demonstrated by considering the design group responsible for an aircraft wing structure. The group's interdependence with other design groups is handled by technical specifications elaborating the points of attachment of the wing to the body, forces transmitted at these points, centers of gravity, etc. The group also has a set of targets (not to be exceeded) for weight, design man-hours to be used, and a completion date. They are given minimum stress specifications below which they cannot design. The group then designs the structures and assemblies which combine to form the wing. They need not communicate with any other design group on work related matters if they and the interdependent groups are able to operate within the planned targets.

Thus goal setting helps coordinate interdependent subtasks and still allows discretion at the local subtask level. Instead of specifying specific behaviors through rules and programs, the organization specifies targets to be achieved and allows the employees to select behaviors appropriate to the target.[6]

The ability of the design groups to operate within the planned targets, however, depends partly on the degree of task uncertainty. If the task is one that has been performed before, the estimates of man-hours, weight, due date, etc., will probably be realized. If it is a new design involving new materials, the estimates will probably be wrong. The targets will have to be set and reset throughout the design effort.

The violation of planned targets usually requires additional decision making and hence additional information processing. The additional information processing takes place through the hierarchy in the same way that rule exceptions were handled. Problems are handled on an exception basis. They are raised to higher levels of the hierarchy for resolution. The problem rises to the first level at which a shared superior exists for all affected subunits. A decision is made, and the new targets are communicated to the subunits. In this manner the behavior of the interdependent subunits remains integrated.

However, as the organization performs more uncertain tasks, such as designing and building a 747 jumbo jet, the hierarchical channels become overloaded once again. The organization does not have the information to estimate how many man-hours are needed to design the new titanium wings. How much weight will the wings require? Will it take 9 months, a year, or 18 months to complete the design? The information necessary to make these decisions can only be discovered during the actual design. The decisions must be made and remade each time new information is discovered. The volume of information processing can overwhelm an organization behaving in the mechanical fashion outlined in this chapter. The organization must adopt a strategy to either reduce the information necessary to coordinate its activities or increase its capacity to process more information. In the next section these strategies are identified and integrated into the framework. . . .

DESIGN STRATEGIES

The ability of an organization to successfully coordinate its activites by goal setting, hierarchy, and rules depends on the combination of the frequency of exceptions and the capacity of the hierarchy to handle them. As task uncertainty increases, the number of exceptions increases until the hierarchy is overloaded. Then the organization must employ new design strategies. Either it can act in two ways to reduce the amount of information that is processed, or it can act in two ways to increase its capacity to handle more information. An organization may choose to develop in both of these ways. The two methods for reducing the need for information and the two methods for increasing processing capacity are

shown schematically in Figure 3. The effect of all these actions is to reduce the number of exceptional cases referred upward into the organization through hierarchical channels.

Creation of Slack Resources

An organization can reduce the number of exceptions that occur by simply reducing the required level of performance. In the example of the wing design, the scheduled time, weight allowance, or man-hours could be increased. In each case more resources could be consumed. These additional resources are called slack resources.[7]

Slack resources are an additional cost to the organization or the customer. However, the longer the scheduled time available, the lower the likelihood of a target being missed. The fewer the exceptions, the less the overload on the hierarchy. Thus the creation of slack resources, through reduced performance levels, reduces the amount of information that must be processed during task execution and prevents the overloading of hierarchical channels. Whether the organization chooses this strategy depends on the relative costs of the other three strategies for handling the overload.

Creation of Self-Contained Tasks

The second method for reducing the amount of information processed is to change from the functional task design to one in which each group has all the resources it needs to perform its task. In the example of the 747, self-contained units could be created around major sections of the aircraft—wing, cabin, tail, body, etc. Each group would have its own product engineers, process engineers, fabricating and assembly operations, and test facilities. In other situations, groups can be created around product lines, geographical areas, projects, client groups, markets, etc., each of which would contain the input resources necessary for the task.

The strategy of self-containment shifts the basis of the authority structure from one based on input, resource, skill, or occupational categories, to one based on output or geographical cate-

Figure 3. Organization Design Strategies

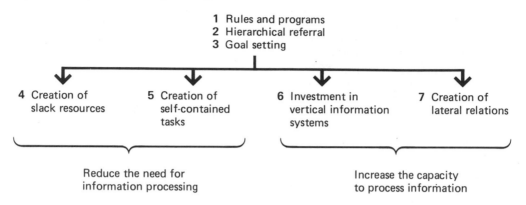

gories. The shift reduces the amount of information processing through several mechanisms—two are described here.

First, it reduces the amount of output diversity faced by a single collection of resources. For example, a professional organization with multiple skill specialties that provides service to three different client groups must schedule the use of these specialties across three demands for their services and determine priorities when conflicts occur. But if the organization changes to three groups, one for each client category, each with its own full complement of specialties, the schedule conflicts across client groups disappears, and there is no need to process information to determine priorities.

The second source of information reduction occurs through a reduced division of labor. The functional or resource specialized structure pools the demand for skills across all output categories. In the example above, each client generates approximately one-third of the demand for each skill. Since the division of labor is determined by the extent of the market, the division of labor must decrease as the demand decreases. In the professional organization, each client group may have generated a need for one-third of a computer programmer. The functional organization would have hired one programmer and shared him across the groups. In the self-contained structure, there is insufficient demand in each group for a programmer, and so the professionals must do their own programming. Specialization is reduced but

there is no problem of scheduling the programmer's time across the three possible uses for it.

Thus the first two strategies reduce overloads on the hierarchy by reducing the number of exceptions that occur. The reduction occurs by reducing the level of performance, diversity of output, or division of labor. According to the theory put forth earlier, reducing the level of performance, etc., reduces the amount of information required to coordinate resources in creating the organization's services or products. In this way, the amount of information to be acquired and processed during task execution, and as a consequence the amount of task uncertainty, is reduced.

In contrast, the other two strategies take the required level of information as given, and create processes and mechanisms to acquire and process information during task execution.

Investment in Vertical Information Systems

The organization can invest in mechanisms which allow it to process information acquired during task performance without overloading the hierarchical communication channels. The investment occurs according to the following logic. After the organization has created its plan or set of targets for weight, stress, budget, and schedule, unanticipated events occur which generate exceptions requiring adjustments to the original plan. At some point when the number of exceptions becomes substantial, it is preferable to generate a new plan rather than make incremental changes in the old one with each exception. The issue is then how frequently plans should be revised—yearly, quarterly, or monthly? The greater the uncertainty, the greater the frequency of replanning. The greater the frequency of replanning, the greater the resources, such as clerks, computer time, input-output devices, etc., required to process information about relevant factors.

Providing more information more often may simply overload the decision maker. Investment may be required to increase the capacity of the decision maker by employing computers, various man-machine combinations, assistants-to, etc. The cost of this strategy is the cost of information processing resources.

The investment strategy is to collect information at the points of origin and direct it, at appropriate times, to the appropriate places in the hierarchy. The strategy increases the information processing at planning time while reducing the number of exceptions which have overloaded the hierarchy.

Creation of Lateral Relations

The last strategy is to selectively employ lateral decision processes which cut across lines of authority. The strategy moves the level of decision making down to where the information exists rather than bringing it up to the points of decision. It decentralizes decisions but without creating self-contained groups. Several mechanisms are employed. The number and types depend upon the level of uncertainty.

The simplest form of lateral relation is direct contact between two people who share a problem. If a problem arises in testing (see Figure 2), the manager of test may contact the manager of assembly and secure the necessary change. Direct contact avoids the upward referral to another manager and removes overloads from the hierarchy.

In some cases there is a large volume of contact between two subtasks such as process design and assembly. Under these circumstances a new role, a liaison role, may be created to handle the interdepartmental contacts.

As tasks of higher uncertainty are encountered, problems are detected in testing which require the joint efforts of product and process design, assembly, and testing. Rather than refer the problem upwards, managers of these areas form a task force or team to jointly resolve the issue. In this manner interdepartmental group problem solving becomes a mechanism to decentralize decisions and reduce hierarchical overloads.

As more decisions and more decisions of consequence are made at lower levels of the organization through interdepartmental groups, problems of leadership arise. The response is the creation of a new role, an integrating role.[8] The function of the role is to represent the general manager in the interdepartmental decisions for a particular brand, product line, project, country, or geographical unit. These roles are called product managers in commercial firms, project managers in aerospace, and unit managers in hospitals.

After the role is created the issue is, how much and what kind of influence does the role occupant need in order to achieve integration for the project, unit, or product. Mechanisms from supporting information and budget control all the way to dual reporting relations and the matrix design are employed under various circumstances. . . .

In summary, lateral relations permit the moving of decisions to lower levels of the organization and yet guarantee that all information is included in the process. The cost of the strategy is the greater amounts of managerial time that must be spent in group processes and the overhead expense of liaison and integrating roles.

Choice of Strategy

Four strategies have been briefly presented. The organization can choose to follow one or some combination of several if it chooses. It will choose that strategy which is least expensive in its environmental context.

It is important to note that the four strategies are hypothesized to be an exhaustive set of alternatives. That is, if the organization is faced with greater uncertainty, due to technological change, higher performance standards, increased competition, or diversified product line to reduce dependence, the amount of information processing is increased. *The organization must adopt at least one of the four strategies when faced with greater uncertainty.* If it does not consciously choose one of the four, then the first, reduced performance standards, will happen automatically. The task information requirements and the capacity of the organization to process information are always matched. If the organization does not consciously match them, reduced performance through budget overruns or schedule overruns will occur in order to bring about equality. Thus the organization should be planned and designed simultaneously with the planning of the strategy and resource allocations. But if the strategy involves introducing new products, entering new markets, etc., then some provision for increased information must be made. Not to decide is to decide, and it is to decide upon slack resources as the only strategy for removing hierarchical overload.

SUMMARY

This [reading] has introduced the basic theory [of the information processing model]. . . . Starting from the observation that uncertainty appears to make a difference in type of organization structure, it was postulated that uncertainty increased the amount of information that must be processed during task execution. Therefore perceived variation in organization form was hypothesized to be variation in the capability of the organization to process information about events that could not be anticipated in advance.

Uncertainty was conceived as the relative difference in the amount of information required and the amount possessed by the organization. The amount required was a function of the output diversity, division of labor, and level of performance. In combination the task uncertainty, division of labor, diversity of output, and level of performance determine the amount of information that must be processed.

Next the basic, mechanistic, bureaucratic model was introduced along with explanations of its information processing capabilities. It was shown that hierarchical communication channels can coordinate large numbers of interdependent subtasks but have a limited capacity to remake decisions. In response four strategies were articulated which either reduced the amount of information or increased the capacity of the organization to process more information. The way to decrease information was to reduce the determinants of the amount of information: performance levels, diversity, and division of labor. The strategies to increase capacity were to invest in the formal, hierarchical information process and to introduce lateral decision processes. Each of these strategies has its effects and costs. . . .

NOTES

1. James G. March and Herbert A. Simon, *Organizations* (New York: John Wiley, 1958), pp. 142–150.

2. For a more detailed discussion of hierarchical arrangements, see James C. Emery, *Organizational Planning and Control Systems* (New York: Macmillan, 1969), pp. 11–12.

3. There are two aspects to this problem. First, individuals may choose behaviors which are ineffective because they do not have the information or knowledge to make a rational choice. This is the cognitive problem addressed here. The other aspect is that individuals may have goals which are different from organizational goals. Processes for dealing with this problem have been discussed already in this series. See Richard Beckhard, *Organization Development: Strategies and Models* (Reading, Mass.: Addison-Wesley, 1969), pp. 35–40.

4. Arthur Stinchcombe, "Bureaucratic and Craft Administration of Production: A Comparative Study," *Administrative Science Quarterly*, September 1959, pp. 168–187.

5. Ibid., p. 170.

6. Here again there are motivation questions. How difficult should the goals be? Should incentives be attached to them? Should the manager participate in setting them? See John Campbell, Marvin Dunnette, Edward Lawler, III, and Karl Weick, Jr., *Managerial Behavior, Performance and Effectiveness* (New York: McGraw-Hill, 1970), Chapter 15.

7. James G. March and Herbert A. Simon, *Organizations* (New York: John Wiley, 1958); and Richard Cyert and James G. March, *A Behavioral Theory of the Firm* (Englewood Cliffs, N.J.: Prentice-Hall, 1963).

8. Paul Lawrence and Jay Lorsch, *Organization and Environment* (Boston: Division of Research, Harvard Business School, 1967), Chapter 3.

Peter Lorange and Richard F. Vancil

Every business carries on strategic planning, although the formality of that process varies greatly from one company to the next. Conceptually, the process is simple: managers at every level of a hierarchy must ultimately agree on a detailed, integrated plan of action for the coming year; they arrive at agreement through a series of steps starting with the delineation of corporate objectives and concluding with the preparation of a one- or two-year profit plan. However, the *design* of that process—deciding who does what, when— can be complex, and it is vital to the success of the planning effort.

A strategic planning system is nothing more than a structured (that is, designed) process that organizes and coordinates the activities of the managers who do the planning. No universal, off-the-shelf planning system exists for the simple and obvious reason that companies differ in size, diversity of operations, the way they are organized, and managers' style and philosophy. An effective planning system requires "situational design"; it must take into account the particular company's situation, especially along the dimensions of size and diversity.

While providing in this article some guidelines for designing strategic planning systems, we caution the reader to recognize that, for the reasons just stated, such generalizations can be treacherous. We do not aspire to prescribe a planning system for your organization; you must do the tailoring.

But some useful generalizations are possible, particularly in distinguishing between large companies and small ones and between highly diversified companies and less diversified ones. Size and diversity of operations generally go hand-in-hand, although exceptions to that rule are com-

mon. Several of the large airlines, for example, are in one business, and a number of mini-conglomerates with sales of less than $100 million have divisions in disparate industries. For convenience here, we shall talk about companies as "small" or "large," defining those labels in terms of the typical characteristics shown in *Exhibit 1*.

While your company may not neatly match either set of characteristics, an understanding of why an effective strategic planning system is different in these two types of companies may enable you to design a system that fits your situation. We should note that the characteristics of small companies also describe a "typical" division in a large, diversified business. Therefore, division managers in such companies can follow our discussion at two levels simultaneously: (1) in their role as a part of the corporate planning process, and (2) in their strategic planning role for their own "small" businesses.

There are six issues on which a choice must be made while designing a strategic planning system. With each issue the proper choice for large companies will be different in most cases from the one for small companies. The issues are: communication of corporate performance goals, the goal-setting process, environmental scanning, subordinate managers' focus, the corporate planner's role, and the linkage of planning and budgeting. We shall describe each of these issues in turn and briefly discuss why the design choice differs in the two corporate settings.

COMMUNICATION OF CORPORATE GOALS

A common roadblock in designing a formal planning system occurs when second-level managers ask headquarters for guidelines to focus the preparation of their strategic plans. These managers, uncertain how to tackle the assignment, may ask,

Exhibit 1.   Characteristics of "Small" and "Large" Companies

	"Small" companies	**"Large" companies**
Annual sales	Less than $100 million	More than $100 million
Diversity of operations	In a single industry	In two or more different industries
Organization structure	Functional departments	Product divisions
Top executives' expertise in industries in which company operates	Greater than that of functional subordinates	Less than that of divisional subordinates

implicitly or explicitly, "Tell us where you want us to go and the performance you expect from us, and we'll give you a plan of how to achieve it." These questions are not unreasonable, but acceding to them may violate the very purpose for undertaking strategic planning. To determine how goals should be communicated and how specific they should be is an important matter in planning system design.

When the president of a *small company* (or the general manager of a division of a diversified company) initiates the strategic planning process, he shares with his functional subordinates his thoughts about the objectives and strategy of the business. In most situations, however, he does not make explicit his performance goals. Instead, he asks his functional managers to devise a set of action programs that will implement the strategy of the business in a manner consistent with its objectives. In a pharmaceutical company that we observed, the R&D, manufacturing, and marketing functions jointly proposed a series of possible programs for developing various new drugs and modifying existing ones. But often, of course, this "programming" process involves only a single department.

Usually, the managers concerned realize that there is no need to anticipate the results of their planning efforts by trying to establish goals before establishment and evaluation of the programs. This would be time-consuming and burdensome and might also create false expectations among the functional managers.

The programming process is oriented much more toward analysis of alternative actions than toward establishment of corporate goals, primar-

ily because the functional managers involved in programming tend (properly) to have a parochial point of view. They have a somewhat shorter time horizon than the president and focus their attention on their own areas of the business. The president is the one who selects the action programs for achieving the goals he has set for the business. Functional managers do not need to know the president's performance goals, only that he wants the managers to recommend the best set of programs.

Because of its action orientation, the programming process usually lacks continuity from one year to the next. The objectives and strategy of the business may remain the same, but each year it is necessary to reexamine all existing programs and try to devise new ones. As a consequence, even though the programming activity commonly uses a three- to five-year time horizon, management pays little attention to the tentative goals established in the preceding year. Instead, the focus is on the current situation, the best set of action programs now, and the development of an achievable goal for the forthcoming year.

The diversity of the portfolio of businesses in *large companies* is often so great that it limits top management's capacity for in-depth perception and familiarity with each business. Consequently, management has to rely on the relatively unconstrained inputs from the divisions.

Division managers do heed corporate guidance in the form of broad objectives, but as a rule top management should delay development of a statement of performance goals for the corporation. Usually, a division manager is in a better position to assess the potential of his own business if he is unbiased by corporate expectations. Delay also permits the top executives to change their approach to the task. In the absence of a formal strategic planning process, top management may have developed explicit goals for itself; but it cannot be sure of the appropriateness of the goals when viewed in the context of a set of independently arrived-at divisional goals. Divisional recommendations stimulate a better job of corporate goal setting.

GOAL-SETTING PROCESS

From the division manager's viewpoint, should he or corporate management set the division's goals? This issue is sometimes cast as a choice between "top-down" and "bottom-up" goal setting. Actually, of course, management at both levels must agree on divisional goals. An important issue, however, remains: Which level in the hierarchy should initiate the process? In a homogeneous company, the same issue arises concerning the general manager and functional managers. The design of the planning system can strongly influence how this issue is resolved.

The goals that emerge from the programming process in a *small company* are tied to an approved set of action programs. Until the president has decided on the programs, no functional manager can set goals for his sphere of activity. Selection of a set of action programs, therefore, more or less automatically determines the performance goals for each functional unit. In many small companies—such as the pharmaceutical concern we spoke of—a "package" of action programs spells out the functional goals for every department, because of the interdependence of all the departments.

In a sense then, functional goal setting is a top-down process. The functional managers propose action programs, but the president with his business-wide perspective determines the programs and goals for his functional subordinates.

In a *large company* with a relatively diversified group of businesses, "capacity limitations" at the corporate level dictate a more or less bottom-up approach. The divisions initiate much of the goal setting, since it requires intimate knowledge of the industry-specific set of business conditions.

Establishing an effective corporate-divisional goal-setting climate in a large company is not easy. For the first year or two of a formal planning effort, the best approach in most situations is to allow the initiative for recommending divisional goals to rest with the division manager. This approach gives him support in running his business and encourages strategic thinking at the divisional level.

Later, after the corporate and divisional managers have gained experience in hammering out a mutually agreeable set of divisional goals, the division manager's annual proposal for divisional goals will become more constrained than in the early years. In a divisionalized, consumer goods manufacturer we know of, the first years of carrying on the planning process were viewed frankly as a learning experience for division managers in making plans operational as well as for top management in learning to appreciate the strategic problems of each business of the company.

The cumulative experience of negotiating the goal setting over the years improves the effectiveness of the process. Corporate management can help nurture this development by creating a system that maintains a proper top-down/bottom-up balance. One way to achieve this balance is by withholding an explicit statement of corporate goals for the first year or two, while requiring the division manager to recommend goals for his division.

ENVIRONMENTAL SCANNING

A strategic planning system has two major functions: to develop an integrated, coordinated, and consistent long-term plan of action, and to facilitate adaptation of the corporation to environmental change. When introducing and developing such a system, companies commonly concentrate on its integrative aspects. The design of the system, however, must also include the function of environmental scanning to make sure that the planning effort also fulfills its adaptive mission.

Corporate management, of course, provides subordinates with a set of forecasts and assumptions about the future business environment. Since each manager, initially at least, draws the strategic plans for his sphere of responsibility more or less independently of his counterparts, all managers must have access to the same set of economic and other environmental forecasts.

Environmental scanning in *small companies* is a strategically oriented task that can go far beyond the mere collection of data about markets, competitors, and technological changes. A company that, for example, enjoys a large share of the market for a product used by middle- and upper-income teenagers and young adults may devote considerable effort in analyzing demographic trends and changes in per capita income. A fairly accurate forecast of market size five years hence is possible to make and would be useful in appraising the potential for the company's growth.

The task of monitoring detailed environmental changes in *large companies* is too difficult to be performed by top management alone. Division management, therefore, is expected to study the external environment that may be relevant to their particular businesses. In these circumstances, headquarters typically provides only a few environmental assumptions—mainly economic forecasts.

Environmental scanning may play another important role in large companies that are interested in diversification through acquisitions. In one diversified electronics and high-technology company that set out to decrease its dependence on defense contracts, the vice president in charge of planning spent most of his time searching for acquisition opportunities. After establishing close ties with the investment community and certain consultants, he spread word of his company's intentions.

SUBORDINATE MANAGERS' FOCUS

In a strategic planning effort, where should the second-level managers direct their attention? What roles do the division manager, functional manager, and top management play? We shall consider these questions in terms of whether plans should be more quantitative or more qualitative, more concerned with financial detail or with strategic analysis.

Preparation of a functionally coordinated set of action programs for a *small company* may require a great deal of cross-functional communication. Much of this interchange is most efficiently expressed in dollar or other quantitative terms, such as numbers of employees, units of product, and square feet of plant space. Use of financial or quantitative data is appropriate for two reasons: (1) it helps each functional manager understand the dimensions of a proposed program and forces him to think through the implications of executing it; (2) it permits the president to select more confidently the set of programs to be implemented. The pharmaceutical company previously referred to, for instance, focuses on the funds flows that might be expected from the various strategic programs suggested by the functional departments.

In practice, the financial and quantitative aspects of functional planning become progressively detailed as the programming process continues, culminating in very specific plans that constitute the operating budget.

In a diversified *larger company*, top management wants each division to adopt a timely strategic outlook and division management to focus primarily on achieving that outlook. Particularly during the early years of the planning program, division managers should be permitted to develop as much financial detail in support of their proposals as they think desirable. As a result, they may generate more financial detail than necessary for strategic business planning. After a year or two, therefore, the corporate requirements for financial detail to support division proposals should be made explicit—and should be explicitly minimal.

Division managers should be asked to shift the focus of their efforts to identification and analysis of strategic alternatives, using their expertise to estimate quickly the financial implications. This focus has been a goal from the beginning, of course, but it is difficult to achieve at the outset. Failing to shift the focus is an even greater danger; the planning activity becomes a "numbers game" and never achieves its purpose.

Considering that the division manager may never have seen, much less prepared, long-range financial projections for his business, drawing them up should be a useful activity. Such projections help him lengthen the time horizon of his thinking; they oblige him to make his intuitive economic model of the business more explicit, which in turn enables him to forecast changes in financial performance. As a result, a division manager's initial planning efforts tend to be financially oriented and, in many respects, analogous to long-range budgeting. Corporate management should design the requirements of the system to mitigate the pressures that initiation of formal planning poses for a division manager.

One important caveat for the chief executive of a large company: he should never allow himself to get so involved in the development of business plans that he assumes the division managers' planning job. A situation that we investigated concerned the newly appointed president of a multinational company in the consumer products business, whose experience was mainly in marketing. He could not resist "helping" one of his divisions develop a detailed, more aggressive marketing plan. Such interference often inhibits the division from coming up with a realistic plan to which it can commit itself. In this case, quiet resistance effectively shelved the president's ideas.

CORPORATE PLANNER'S ROLE

A major issue in the design of the planning system is where the corporate planner fits. Strategic planning is a line management function; a sure route to disaster is to have plans produced by staff planners and then issued to line-managers. Strategic planning is essentially a people-interactive process, and the planner is only one in the cast of characters involved. If the process is to function effectively he must clearly understand his proper role. The corporate planner's function in small and large companies is quite different.

In *a small company* (or a product division of a large company), the planner performs the function of staff planning assistant to the president (or the general manager). While coordinating the planning activities of the functional managers, he concerns himself with the president's problem of selecting the best set of action programs. Only the president—and his planning assistant—has

a business-wide perspective of the choices, and the assistant must do the bulk of the analysis.

Cast in this role, the planner may become a very influential member of the president's (or the general manager's) executive team. If he uses his power sensitively, he need not lose effectiveness with his peers running the functional departments. They can appreciate the necessity for cross-functional analysis of program alternatives. Managing the planning process is an almost incidental role for the assistant, since he merely formalizes the analysis that leads to a coordinated set of action programs.

In *a large company*, the corporate planner's organizational status can have significant symbolic value in conveying to division managers the importance of formal strategic planning and the difference between it and conventional budgeting. The planner's role initially is that of a catalyst, encouraging line managers to adopt a strategic orientation. He helps corporate management do a better job of resource allocation among the divisions, partly by assisting the division managers in strategic planning for their businesses. But he must not succumb to the temptation to become more involved in formulating the plans, or he may lose his effectiveness.

System maintenance and coordination is the planner's primary function as the planning effort matures; he monitors its evolution and maintains consistency. His tasks differ greatly from the mainly analytical role of the planner in the small company.

LINKAGE OF PLANNING AND BUDGETING

The steps in a typical planning system represent an orderly, gradual process of commitment to certain strategic alternatives. Each step is, theoretically at least, linked to those preceding. In financial terms, this linkage may be quite explicit; for instance, a division's profit forecast prepared in the first planning cycle may become the profit commitment for next year's operating budget. Although few companies expect to achieve this financial linkage in narrowing the choices, all the parties involved in the process should understand the intended relationship between the cycles.

How fast this narrowing should be is a situational design question that depends on the particular corporate setting. A tight linkage between planning and budgeting indicates that more strategic commitments have been made at an earlier stage. A loose linkage, on the other hand, implies that the narrowing process is slower and will occur mainly late, in the budgeting stage of the process.

Exhibit 2 shows examples of slow versus rapid narrowing profiles. Notice that a company that does little narrowing in the early stages faces the task of considering a large number of strategic issues in the budgeting stage. This implies that either the company is equipped with an adequate organization to process an immense and "peaky" budgeting workload, or it will neglect some choices altogether, with the likely result that the quality of its allocation decisions suffers.

A *small company* with little diversity in its operations may wish to adopt an early or rapid narrowing process, since the functional and corporate executives involved are thoroughly familiar with the strategy of the few businesses in question. Then functional managers can proceed directly to the development of action programs to continue implementation of that strategy. Quantitative financial linkage between the selected programs and the resulting budgets is feasible, and "tight" linkage of this type is common practice.

In *a large company,* linkage is usually looser and the narrowing process more gradual. During the start-up phase top management should give division managers plenty of time to devote to strategic thinking about their businesses—but the lower-level executives must remember to differentiate that activity from long-range budgeting, with its related requirement of divisional performance fulfillment.

As the system matures, however, management can gradually accelerate the narrowing process without jeopardizing the creative aspect of planning. A natural result of this progress is a more precise definition of the linkage between the planning cycle and the budgeting cycle. A large producer of heavy equipment we know of, for instance, has "tightened up" the linkage between planning and budgeting. The top executives believe that this development is a natural consequence of their increasingly cohesive strategic points of view.

EVOLVING SYSTEMS

In sum, significant differences exist between the planning procedures used in the two types of companies we have examined. The issues that management must address, and our attempt to

Exhibit 2.   Slow versus Rapid Narrowing Profiles in the Planning Process

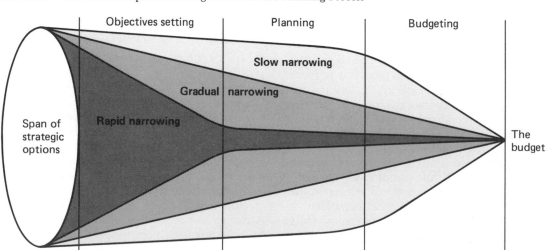

Exhibit 3.   Approaches to Planning System Design Issues

	Situational settings		
	"Small" companies	"Large" companies	
Issues		New planning system	Mature planning system
Communication of corporate goals	Not explicit	Not explicit	Explicit
Goal-setting process	Top-down	Bottom-up	"Negotiated"
Corporate-level environmental scanning	Strategic	Statistical	Statistical
Subordinate managers' focus	Financial	Financial	Strategic
Corporate planner's role	Analyst	Catalyst	Coordinator
Linkage of planning and budgeting	Tight	Loose	Tight

delineate what is good practice in small and large companies, are summarized in *Exhibit 3.*

In companies that are not very diversified and are functionally organized—as well as product units of diversified corporations—top management carries on the strategic thinking about the future of the business. In such companies, a formal process to help organize that reflective activity is frequently unnecessary, in view of the few managers involved. Instead, formal strategic planning focuses on the development and review of innovative action programs to implement the strategy. The planning system reflects that focus: goal setting is top-down, linkage to the budget is tight, and the staff planning officer plays a major role as cross-functional program analyst and environmental scanner.

In companies that operate in several industrial sectors and are organized into product divisions, initiating a formal strategic planning process is a major task. The first year or two of such an effort must be viewed as an investment in fostering a planning competence among division managers; the payoff in better decisions at the corporate level must wait until the system matures.

If the planning system is to survive as more than an exercise in pushing numbers into the blank spaces on neatly designed forms, it must evolve rapidly along several dimensions. A mature system, however, can be invaluable, helping both corporate and divisional executives make better and better-coordinated strategic decisions.

Any company—indeed, any organization—is a dynamically evolving entity whose situational setting is subject to change. Accordingly, to remain effective, the design of the planning process is a continuous task requiring vigilance and insight on the part of management.

25

Management control systems:
A key link between strategy,
structure and employee performance

John Todd

The failure of large corporations such as Franklin National Bank, Du Pont Walston, and Equity Funding in the 1970s has dramatically emphasized the need for managerial control. Such control can be exercised in a number of ways. A manager can exert a measure of personal control by giving orders, making decisions, and keeping an eye peeled. Such methods, however, tend to be inadequate because of the physical limitations on what a person can do. The chief executive of Franklin National Bank found that this style of management, which reflected his belief that every organization is but the shadow of one man, did not allow him to maintain adequate control. The result was a disastrous combination of bad loans and losses on bonds and foreign exchange.

The most promising alternative to personal control by managers is a management control system (MCS). In considering MCSs it is important to think in terms of potential control rather than automatic control. Traditionally, MCSs have been equated with a collection of financial, accounting, and budgeting procedures, and the yardsticks for measuring their effectiveness have been the timeliness and understandability of printed reports. From this viewpoint, in their relationships to MCS managers tend to be little more than passive recipients of historical reports. It is imperative to define a firm's MCS in such a way as to recognize the greater potential control that active managerial participation can provide.

An MCS can be viewed as a sequentially integrated series of steps. Goals for the organization and its employees need to be set, results need to be measured, and managerial action needs to be taken in response to those results. These steps are shown in the accompanying diagram, with the solid linking lines indicating the basic control steps.

As [Figure 1] shows, the evaluation of results normally takes into account both expected and actual results. The action step then attempts to reinforce satisfactory performance with rewards or to correct unsatisfactory performance with penalties or training. The managerial response may also include a revision of goals to reflect changed expectations as a result of recent experience.

Every manager has a responsibility for the execution of the basic MCS steps shown in the diagram. Within this framework, however, the ways in which the managerial control functions are conducted can vary tremendously. This article deals particularly with managerial control options that have a demonstrable positive correlation with employee performance.

THE NEED FOR
A NEW MCS MODEL

In the early years of professional management, there was little concern about undesirable side effects of management control systems. Classical management theory assumed that employees were rational, economic men and would therefore conform to managerially defined expectations. Any attendant morale or turnover problems were usually considered the responsibility of personnel specialists, not of line managers.

The Hawthorne experiments a half-century ago unearthed dysfunctional employee practices that the company's control system had failed to prevent—or even detect. The researchers ex-

Figure 1.

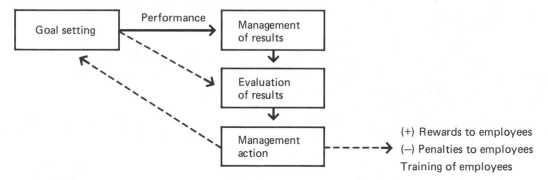

plained this in terms of management's sole concern which the technical system and corresponding neglect of the social system. When work standards ran counter to employee-defined norms, the work group was able to develop elaborate ways of dealing with the perceived threat to the social system. Fritz Roethlisberger, one of the principal researchers, later wrote of the "vicious-cycle syndrome" he had observed at Hawthorne as well as at other companies.

> The breakdown of rules begot more rules to take care of their breakdown or the breakdown of close supervision encouraged the use of still closer methods of supervision and, as a result, the continuous search and invention of new control systems to correct for the limitations of previous ones.

Other unanticipated problems have stemmed from control systems. Employees have often expressed resentment and hostility toward systems that set unrealistic goals, that demand excessive paperwork, that improperly measure performance, that fail to reward good performance, that do not allow for employee participation, and so on. Employees have often responded with actions as well as words. They have followed the rules, "done it by the books," for example, even though they knew the rules were a mistake, in order to show up the persons who designed the systems. In other words, they practiced malicious obedience. In numerous instances, corporate long-run success has been subordinated to short-run quantitative results because of pressure from the con-

trol system. Maintenance of both physical and human assets may be neglected in order to meet current cost budgets, and high-pressure tactics may be used to meet sales quotas.

One of the most spectacular instances of negative byproducts of a control system was the Equity Funding scandal. In that company, top management set goals for subordinate managers that were impossible to meet by legitimate means. Employees reacted to this pressure by "manufacturing on paper" millions of dollars of assets and profits; this was the only way they could keep their high-paying jobs. In another similar case, the Boy Scouts of America revealed that membership figures coming in from the field had been falsified, thereby vastly overstating the total. Field personnel had responded to the pressures of a national membership drive by providing false data; it had been easier to report new members than to enroll them. In short, as these two instances illustrate, organizational control systems can generate unintended and unfortunate consequences.

Although it is important for managers to be aware of these potential pitfalls of control systems, it is even more important that they have positive guidelines for the design and implementation of these systems. The potential of management control systems as a stimulant and a motivator has received far less attention than their effects as a constraint on employee behavior. Managers should consider MCSs as complementary to leadership, organizational design, and other positive means of direction and control.

CORPORATE STRATEGY AND THE MCS

As other writers have noted, it is important to tie together the strategy of an organization and its internal structure. Departmental and individual goals, performance measures, and managerial response to deviations, all need to be tailored to the strategy and structure of the particular organization. Management control must be linked to a planning base—to the basic question, "What are we trying to do?" Only after the competitive and strategic requirements of the organization are defined can effective work goals for employees be developed.

In addition, just as corporate strategy must be continually revised in response to environmental or resource changes, there must be a corresponding updating of control processes. Flexibility is particularly critical in rapidly changing situations such as those that characterize short product-life cycles. A standard five-year plan may be an inappropriate control for products that are likely to grow, mature, and decline at irregular intervals in a short time frame.

In addition to the need for an MCS to be integrated with the corporate strategy and responsive to change in the environment, a well-constructed MCS will be particularly useful to a manager if it takes into account the personal job goals and other personal characteristics of employees, such as abilities and attitudes. The most publicized "misfits" in organizations have been young people with their demands for jobs more closely attuned to their personal goals of "meaningfulness" and "humaneness." The desire for a more responsive work environment, however, extends far beyond youthful workers. In a recent survey, while two out of three workers expressed a willingness to work harder if their pay were correspondingly increased, an almost equal number said they would work harder if they "had more say about the kind of work they did and the way they did it." Clearly, then, top management can develop a more effective MCS if the personal goals of operating managers are considered. The operating managers, in turn, can be more effective if they also consider the personal objectives of their subordinates as they develop appropriate MCSs for their operating areas.

EFFECT OF AN MCS ON EMPLOYEE PERFORMANCE

With such considerations in mind, two studies were undertaken in an attempt to identify the most important characteristics of a management control system relative to employee performance. In the first study, two offices of an accounting firm were compared on differences between their MCSs and the relationship of these differences to employee performance. Since the strategy and structure of the two offices were approximately the same, the study could focus directly on the interaction between the MCS and employee performance. The second study considered how the employees of three national sales organizations perceived their firm's MCSs and then related their perceptions to individual performance.

MCS's Effects in an Accounting Firm

From among several offices operated by the firm, two were chosen for comparative study. The two offices, identified here as A and B, were similar in type of operation, and each had approximately 75 professional staff employees.

Over a five-year period, the two offices showed a significant difference in performance. [Figure 2] below shows the changes in volume of business in terms of index numbers. (The first-year base amount is 1.00; a larger number represents the extent of growth over that amount.) Since the output of an accounting firm is the chargeable time of its employees, firm officials considered gross billings (called volume of business) to be the single best measure of performance for these two offices.

As [Figure 2] shows, beginning with the third year, Office A far outdistanced Office B in performance. Office A showed steady and impressive growth, while Office B showed practically none. Officials at the firm's home office also considered Office A to be much stronger in relation to com-

Figure 2.

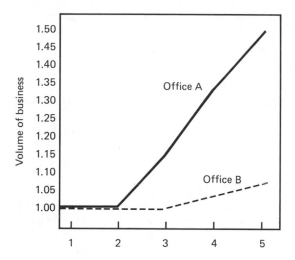

peting firms in its geographic area than Office B in its area. Thus the superiority of Office A is shown by both objective indicators and professional evaluations.

This study focused on the differences between the MCS in offices A and B, as revealed in questionnaires and in extensive interviews with employees. From these questionnaires and interviews, a number of findings and conclusions were developed.

Results of the Study

A statistical analysis of the responses on the questionnaire revealed three basic factors in the employees' perceptions of the MCS. Underlying each factor were a number of questions that respondents tended to answer in a similar manner. The three factors were:

1. Clarity of the control system.
2. Strength of the performance-rewards relationship.
3. Amount of individual control and influence.

The fact that these central features emerged in the way respondents described the firm's control system is less significant than the fact that these three features also distinguished between high and low performance. The employees in the more successful office described their management control system differently from the employees in the less successful office on these factors.

Beyond the correlation of each of the MCS factors with office performance, there is a larger theme in the findings. Each characteristic seems to contribute toward a person's general sense of control over the job situation—the ability to control the job outcomes that will be achieved through personal effort. To be successful in their quest for valued job outcomes, employees need not only an assignment of authority (individual control and influence) but also an understanding of the means and ends of their mission—that is, how it can best be done (clarity) and how it can help them accomplish their individual goals (performance-rewards relationship). Thus in this sense, each control system characteristic is important in the development of an employee's overall sense of control over the job environment. The following description of each control system characteristic is taken from the analysis of the questionnaire results and interview data.

1. Clarity of the control system.   Employees in Office A viewed the management control system as having greater clarity than did the employees of Office B. This factor encompassed both the goal-setting and performance-evaluation processes of management control. It included reports about employees' feelings about how well they understood the goals their manager expected them to achieve as well as the importance the manager placed on these goals. It also included reports about the clarity with which the employees understood their superior's evaluation of the work. Although these elements were considered separately in the questionnaire, statistical analysis showed them to be closely related.

Interestingly, the two offices had officially adopted the same goal-setting and performance-evaluation procedures. Each employee was assigned to professional engagements (that is, jobs) by his or her manager, and a standard evaluation report was prepared for each person after each job was completed. The performance evaluation report also was supposed to be reviewed with the employee who had completed the job. Within the frame of these general policies, however, there was a great difference in the manner of execution. One Office A employee described the process of goal setting and performance evaluation in these words:

> Once the job assignments are made, and prior to going to the client's office, I review the previous year's workpapers and have at least one conference with my boss. We discuss any particular questions I might have about the procedures to be followed, and also both our observations and expectations about the job. On jobs that I've not been assigned to previously, the manager provides an extensive orientation to the client's business and personnel. The manager usually spends at least the first day at the job, helping me get familiar with the situation and making contact with client personnel. After that, we usually have weekly discussions, except when I need his help more often. . . . I get good feedback from him as we go along about his evaluation of the work, and then we have one indepth, windup session at the end of the job. In an informal way, we discuss strengths and deficiencies on the job. Although there usually are no surprises, it's nice to have everything out on the table at one time and get an overall evaluation.

The same processes in Office B were described by two employees in sharply contrasting terms. Said the first:

> I could do a better job if I could get more information. About all I usually have is last year's workpapers and a budget. The manager meets with the client, but I usually don't know what it is about. I have to find out everything by digging it out. I don't hear much from the manager, except about problems with the budget. He does a complete review of the workpapers at the end of the job and does quite a lot of work himself clearing up any problems. By then, I'm usually on another job and never get to see the final product. So, I don't get to see a whole job through to the finish and see all the pieces put together.

And in the words of the second Office B employee:

> There is a lot of discontent here because we have no way to find out how we stand in relation to others. "Doing about right" is the most common comment we hear in our performance evaluations.

The difference in the two offices, illustrated in these comments, reflects the skill of the managers and the amount of effort they expended on seeing that their subordinates had clear goals as well as feedback about their performance. In Office A, top managment insisted that all managers clearly spell out their expectations and evaluations to subordinates. Roles and responsibilities for each project were defined and communicated, and role playing and other training aids were used to help managers develop expertise in the planning and evaluation activities. In Office B, on the other hand, top managers only paid lip-service to the official company policies on goal setting and employment evaluation; they were still emotionally attached to the traditional pattern of having the manager deal with the client on all important items and restricting the employees to routine duties. With this approach, top management saw little need for sharing information with employees.

2. Performance-rewards relationship. One of the critical functions of a control system is to provide employees with reasons why they should work hard toward the achievement of organizational goals. In the current study, employees of Office A perceived a stronger link between successful job performance and valued job outcomes than did employees in Office B.

In public accounting, one of the most valued job outcomes is promotion into management. Office A employees shared the perception that superiors had achieved their positions through merit and that they too had a good chance to be promoted on the same basis. One staff member said: "Promotions here are not a matter of luck. You get ahead by hard work and competence." Top managers in Office A emphasized the dual responsibilities—technical and managerial—required of subordinates; at the same time they also offered encouragement and support to staff members who needed to develop in one or both of these areas. There was little doubt in the minds of staff members that top management was carefully monitoring their performance on both levels and that promotion decisions were clearly related to performance.

Not so in Office B, where the promotion system was perceived as a zero-sum game and the link between promotions and superior performance was somewhat tenuous. For example, no promotions into management had been made in the preceding year. According to the professional employees in the office, at least three individuals were well qualified; yet, because not all could be promoted, none had been promoted. Such an organization tends to end up with only the employees who are willing to stick it out. Here, too, the Peter Principle can be seen to function, with the remaining employees eventually being allowed to rise to their level of incompetence.

3. Individual control and influence. In the accounting firm study, questionnaire items that measured this characteristic asked about the degree of individual control and influence in establishing job goals and doing the work, as well as the innovation required and discretion used in the employee's work. Although the questions covered a broad area, employee answers were so consistent that it was decided to combine them into one index. Overall, the questions seemed to measure the extent to which employees felt they could control and influence their current work. Here is a typical comment by an Office A staff member.

> This is a professional firm. You are very much on your own after proving yourself in the first two years. You get a lot of responsibility early. It's good to be able to work without someone looking over my shoulder, but I can also ask someone for help if I need it.

Management in Office A was concerned about the need for organizational growth and recognized the need to create an environment within which employees could develop and unleash their abilities. Top managers believed that the biggest constraint to future growth of the office was the limited number of employees who could take on more responsibility. In order to build that future

leadership, management was committed to giving each employee an opportunity to go "as far as he can on his own," consistent with the professional standards that govern all accounting firms.

Job assignments on Office A projects were usually made in modular form, that is, by areas of responsibility rather than by specialized task, which was the traditional method. The assignment of full responsibility for the audit inventory, for example, allowed the accountant to see the whole inventory picture, from verification of quantities to valuation of the inventory. In contrast, the traditional specialist might be restricted to the physical inventory count or to testing mathematical computations without ever understanding the relationship of this work to other audit steps. A staff member described the modular approach in this way:

> There are twelve problem accounts on the job. Each staff member is assigned responsibility for researching the theory, writing up the audit program, and doing the work on certain of those accounts. We [the staff members] are the ones who know the most about the account—not the senior or the manager. Each of us has a meaningful job.

Records were kept of the modular assignments so that all inexperienced employees could gain experience on diversified jobs. This allowed employees and management to match interests and skills in a variety of jobs, as a prelude to specialization later on in the employees' careers. This initial career planning was ongoing, with new inputs from each employee, from performance records, and from environmental changes. The amount of influence exercised by employees was substantial, as management recognized the importance of individual commitment for an effective professional career.

In contrast, Office B employees more often spoke of "being controlled" rather than of "being in control." They expressed their feelings in these words:

> This organization is too rigid in terms of responsibility and assignments, which are tied too closely to seniority. Scheduling should be more

responsive to the individual's needs and experience. They should give more personal consideration when it comes to job assignments. We are human beings, not just things they bill out at $20 an hour.

Management's life is directed toward work and work alone. It seems that a person should live to work and nothing more. Those that stay with the firm are those hard, ambitious workers who only have time for work in their life. There doesn't seem to be a place for a person like myself who wants to do a good job and enjoy life too.

There is no apparent master plan with someone looking out for your interests. For example, there seems to be no link between evaluation of needed experience and job assignments. I definitely have no influence on job assignments.

This comparison of perceived individual control and influence in the two offices supported the theory that the amount of control in an organization is not a fixed sum. In other words, as employees believe they control more of their work, managers should in turn gain more control in accomplishing organizational objectives. Employee perceptions of greater individual control and influence should be associated with more achievement because of greater employee involvement and motivation.

The study demonstrated the importance of the employees' sense of control as a predictor of performance. Employees of high-performing Office A expressed the conviction that they had greater control over their situation, in terms of being able to act effectively for the accomplishment of both organizational and individual goals, than did lower-performing Office B. The employees in Office A expressed their sense of control in terms of rewards, job definition, and performance standards and evaluation. Here are three very brief statements that exemplify their sense of control in these areas.

There are rewards I value if I perform well.

I have considerable influence and control in the definition and accomplishment of my job.

I know what is expected of me and how well I am doing.

Office B is taking steps to implement a new control process similar to that in Office A. Short-ly after the conclusion of this study, Office B's managing partner accepted retirement. Although his early leadership had helped develop the office, his autocratic control methods initiated a vicious circle of inadequate employee development, high employee turnover, failure to adapt to new environmental forces, and limited business growth.

MCS's Effects in a Sales Organization

A later study by Charles Futrell involved the total sales staff of two national pharmaceutical companies and one national hospital supply company. A total of 413 salesmen were surveyed using a questionnaire containing the same control system questions used earlier in the accounting firm study. Subsequently, the replies to the questions and the performance rating for each salesman were matched.

Statistical analysis showed that all three of the control system characteristics listed above were correlated significantly with job performance. Those salesmen who perceived a high degree of clarity in their company's control system tended to have a better performance record. Likewise, the same relationship was found between job performance and the other two control system characteristics: The best performers tended to see a strong link between performance and rewards, to feel that they knew what was expected of them, and to believe they had influence and control over the accomplishment of their tasks.

One significant variation in the results of this study from the accounting firm study was the order in which the three characteristics were associated with individual performance. The performance-rewards relationship characteristic showed the strongest association with performance for the salesmen, whereas it had been the weakest characteristic for the accountants. Although the studies did not explain this difference, we can hypothesize that economic motivation was stronger for the salesmen than for the accountants, while the accountants were oriented more toward professional factors than the salesmen. For example, the characteristic most strongly related to performance for the accountants was "clarity," a relationship that reflects both the complex work they were doing and their personal need for precise feedback.

Although the overall finding in both studies were consistent, the proof of causality is not clear-cut. There might even be a reciprocal relationship between performance and the control system characteristics. The control system may affect performance, and performance may also influence employees' perceptions of the control system. The strong association of the three MCS characteristics and performance deserves the careful consideration of managers, however, particularly since they can directly influence each of the characteristics.

DEVELOPING MCSs WITH A LINK TO EMPLOYEES

Just as managing can never be a programmed activity, there can be no simple program to create ideal MCSs. No "chrome package" applied piecemeal to an organization will have an impact if employees receive contradictory signals from one day to the next. In short, an effective approach requires integrated action on several dimensions of management control.

The first step for a manager who is reviewing the effectiveness of his or her MCS to take is to determine the demands and rewards of the company's MCS in relation to the goals and capabilities of the employees who work for it. MCSs offer the most direct tool available to managers who want to integrate their employees emotionally into the mainstream of their organizations. Employee interviews and surveys will often provide managers with a very different picture of their MCS than they expected. This diagnosis can serve as a basis for the development of an action plan.

Second, a manager ought to devote more attention to the design and implementation of key MCS characteristics, such as clarity and the performance-rewards relationship.

Clarity

The ambiguity perceived by employees in the accounting firm's Office B is not unique. Many managers fail to meet their responsibilities for setting clear goals and providing adequate feedback. One pervasive warning signal of managerial dysfunction in organizational life today is the lack of clarity about the expectations of organizations and their employees.

The causes may range from poor communication to a dislike for "playing God" in appraisals. In a study by the author, employees were particularly critical of a company policy that required that the annual appraisal interview be conducted by someone other than the immediate supervisor; the interviewers conducting these appraisals usually could not go beyond prepared comments in their efforts to help employees understand how they might improve their ratings, and employees typically came away frustrated at this lack of clarity.

As noted earlier, employees want and need to know what is expected of them, as well as how well they are doing in meeting organizational expectations. One of the study participants said:

> We should be treated as intelligent, capable businessmen, interested in tackling problems we will be involved in. Don't hold the cards so close that no one knows what the game is.

This comment suggests why managers should keep their subordinates informed of organizational goals and expectations. All important standards of performance should be communicated, not just one or two bottom-line goals. Managers should focus on general priorities that will help employees in making decisions that involve trade-offs, such as efficiency versus morale or cost control versus customer satisfaction. Overlooking these gray areas in the goal-setting process means suboptimum results and dissatisfaction.

Although clarity is the objective of this process, managers should be aware that too much preciseness may stifle employee initiative. In Office B, for example, the restriction of employees to limited, routine work had a negative effect on performance and development. Clarity is not synonymous with having managers make all the decisions.

Beyond the determination of expectations, there should be a commitment to help employees understand how they are doing. Performance evaluations are undoubtedly one of the most underutilized and misused tools in management today. Reports of two-minute appraisal interviews abound. "I've got to go to a meeting in a couple of minutes," the appraiser announces, "so I'm not going to play around. You're doing about as well as expected, and you'll get a fair raise this year."

Managers have a responsibility to provide subordinates with candid and constructive feedback. With professional employees, such as accountants, feedback is doubly important because an evaluation of their results are somewhat subjective and because they tend to have a strong need for achievement. For those who are not professionals, feedback is a means of reinforcing desired behavior, as demonstrated in a number of experiments at Emery Air Freight and at other companies. Used correctly, performance evaluation helps both managers and subordinates to understand their past performance as well as their expectations—an important accomplishment.

Performance-Rewards Relationship

Of primary importance in the performance-rewards relationship is the need to ascertain what each employee wants from his job. This determination, as well as the feasibility of fulfilling these wants, can be settled as part of a psychological contract between a manager and his or her subordinates. The term psychological contract denotes a commitment that, in addition to any monetary agreement, the manager will attempt to provide opportunities for satisfaction of the subordinate's other needs and wants. The inherent prerequisite to any such contract is that the subordinate be free to communicate these needs and wants.

Another important step is to set up a system that will respond to individual and group expectations, consistent with the accomplishment of organizational objectives. This system may dispense extrinsic rewards, such as money and fringe benefits, as well as intrinsic outcomes, such as greater responsibility and meaningfulness of work. Managers should broaden the concept of reward systems to include all job outcomes, not just monetary and promotional rewards. An accountant expressed his reason for seeking another job in

these terms: "In two years I can probably get the promotion. But I look at what the people at that level are getting—more money and more headaches. Is that all I can expect?" This suggests that job design should join more traditional rewards as a means of responding to employee expectations and aspirations. The variety and challenge of work itself can be particularly significant.

According to the study findings, which showed that rewards are linked with individual and office performance, the link should at least, in part, be contingent upon employee success. This finding is consistent with the expectancy theory of motivation, which says that employee efforts reflect a combination of the attractiveness of probable results and the likelihood that those results will be achieved. Managers must demonstrate that rewards are based on performance. An employee whose past efforts have been rewarded is likely to feel that future efforts will also be rewarded. Bonus systems offer one means of rewarding outstanding performance, although their effectiveness can be no better than the predetermined goals on which they are based. In recent years we have seen the expansion of bonus systems to such unusual situations as police work. Other organizations have emphasized cost efficiency through group incentive plans, such as the Scanlon plan. These applications are illustrative of the flexibility available to managers who want to set up new performance-rewards links.

Individual Control and Influence

For managers, individual control and influence may present the greatest challenge as well as the greatest opportunity. The means of developing this characteristic will vary from organization to organization. As examples of positive action, the following suggestions were appropriate for the accounting firm:

1. Allow more diversity in the personal and professional growth and career paths of employees. A common perception among employees in many organizations is that they are considered to be little more than technical robots that should be developed in a lock-step. Often, the means and the ends of subordinate development duplicate the manager's career path because of his or

her attitude that "I came up this way and you must also." In the accounting profession, there is ample opportunity to provide varied career paths since there are always clients and types of work that will provide opportunities to employees with different career interests.

2. Allow employees more influence in determining the particular projects they will work on and how those projects will be completed. Although the manager, because of his broader perspective, has the primary responsibility for employee assignments, he should take into account employee interests and developmental needs. One employee suggested: "Scheduling should include an evaluation of the experience needed and whether or not it would be a challenge to the individual."

3. Develop better channels of communication upwards so that employee feelings, attitudes, and wants can be heard and dealt with more effectively. This should include a provision for appeals whenever an employee believes a decision by a superior unduly curtails personal goals. In some offices, this may just be a matter of making management's open-door policy more specific, to assure employees that they can appeal assignments, evaluations, and other perceived injustices. For others, such as those in Office B, it may mean developing new policies and procedures of improved group and individual upward communication. Because of the many professional demands on top management, an ombudsman or employee counselor may be warranted in some offices to act as staff spokesman to management.

In the accounting firm, each of these factors contributed toward the employees' sense of control over their jobs and in making the what, how, where, and when of their jobs more compatible with their personal interests and values. These and similar steps are needed in many organizations if they are to develop greater employee motivation and self-control.

Although we have considered the three characteristics separately, an integrated approach is obviously more desirable. Despite statistical independence, in the real world there is considerable overlap among the various measures. There may even be conflicting signals, at times, for two basic human needs—independence and support—underlie much of the problem in matching

the organizations with its employees. The simultaneous gratification of these needs in an organizational context requires a skillful balance of organizational mechanisms within the MCS.

The Du Pont Walston failure has been attributed to the loss of many productive and experienced employees. One of the employees who left explained his reason: "What got us was the way things were presented. Rather than creating a desire to do something, management told us we must do it." This is another example of keeping a tight rein, to the extent of frustrating the employee's need for independence.

It is not just a matter of delegating authority to subordinates, however, even though it may be a step in the right direction. To use an analogy, most of us would not relish the "freedom" of playing tennis on top of the World Trade Center without some "support" (such as a very heavy screen around the court). In a similar way, most employees recognize the importance of organizational support in planning and coordinating their efforts toward valued goals.

Another study was conducted in a large U.S. corporation that prided itself on hiring the best M.B.A.s and turning them loose to make profits for the organization. The study in one of the corporation's newer divisions showed widespread disenchantment among this group, referred to as the young tigers, largely because they had lots of freedom but no organizational direction and support in a field where technical expertise was important. They found themselves in a professional role doing an unprofessional job because they were not even sure of what they were supposed to do. One of the top managers of the company expressed management's attitude toward the problem: "I just don't understand the young tigers. I don't have time to wipe their noses for them. They're big boys now, and they should be able to figure out things for themselves."

In the face of a deteriorating situation in this division, the corporation replaced the managerial team with men who better understood the conflict found in most people over the degree of independence desired. As this experience with young professionals showed, the creation of a management control system with the proper blend of support and independence is an important requisite for youthful managers.

CONCLUSIONS

It is time to bring management control systems into the mainstream of managerial action. Overemphasis on financial figures and techniques has often obscured the real value of these MCSs to management. As a key link between the strategy and structure of the organization and its operating personnel, the MCS can serve functions of interpretation, direction, integration, and inspiration. The primary focus in these pages has been on the link between the MCS and the employees, as there has been less attention to this link than to the others. The key requirement is to consider employees along with organizational strategy and structure in developing an organization's management control system. The working model might take the form of [Figure 3]. This model can help managers keep in mind the importance of tailoring their management control system to the particular situation at hand, which includes not only organizational variables but also employee variables.

The interactive influence of control systems and employees on performance can best be understood by considering three characteristics of control systems. These are:

1. Clarity of management's expectations and evaluation of employees.
2. Strength of performance—rewards link for employees.
3. Employee influence on and control over their work.

These three characteristics represent major decision points in any management control system. Managers have options on each of the characteristics in the design and implementation of a control system. With these options, systems that appear theoretically comparable can be made to vary widely. As shown in the accounting firm, control systems that are similar on paper can be implemented in different ways, with results ranging from an autocratic, closed-loop system to a participative, group-oriented system.

In the primary study, comparing two offices of one accounting firm, the office with the control system that had greater clarity, performance-rewards link, and employee influence performed better than did the other office. Even though the same association of control system characteristics and performance was found in the study of sales organizations, it is important to remember from contingency theory that different degrees of one or more of the characteristics may better fit different situations. For example, the performance-rewards relationship was the most important control system characteristic for the salesmen, whereas it was the least important for the accountants. Managers in the two situations should therefore set different weights on these three common MCS characteristics in planning their overall approach to improved management control.

The MCS model provides flexibility for tailoring the managerial response to the strategy, structure, and employees of a particular situation. Using this tool, managers can keep their approach to operational control consistent with other variables in the organization.

Figure 3.

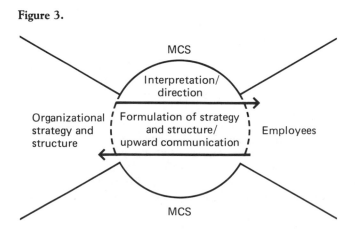

Nina G. Hatvany
and Vladimir Pucik

Productivity increases in Japan have been two to three times greater than increases in the United States over the past three decades. Absenteeism among employees in most Japanese companies is low, turnover rates are about half the American figures, and commitment to the firm is high (Glazer, 1976; Cole, 1979). Certainly, the productivity increases result not only from management practices in Japanese firms but also from overall economic and sociohistorical conditions specific to Japan. Japan's productivity growth has probably been raised as much by massive capital investments per worker (Denison and Chung, 1976) as by effective labor management. Nevertheless, the fact that many Japanese companies have developed management practices associated with high productivity and low turnover and absenteeism rates has received a great deal of attention in the popular press as well as in the recent empirical organizational literature (Marsh and Mannari, 1976; Pascale, 1978).

Past attempts to examine management in Japan have, however, been very seldom related to more universal organizational theories. Rather, they concentrated on confirming or disconfirming the existence of supposedly unique characteristics of workers and companies in Japan, such as permanent employment, "bottom-up" decision making, and the like. These characteristics were analyzed in isolation from other structural and process variables in organizations. The following discussion, by contrast, is an attempt to introduce

a model of the Japanese management system, a model based on fairly universal elements suitable for a comparative review.

THE MODEL OF THE JAPANESE MANAGEMENT SYSTEM

Our interpretation of "Japanese management" [Figure 1] centers on what we believe is the basic management paradigm in large Japanese companies, namely the focus on human resources (Tsurumi, 1977; Clark, R., 1979). As an amalgamation of shared rules and common intuition (Kuhn, 1970), this paradigm reflects an explicit preference for the maximum utilization of available human resources in the firm, both blue-collar and white-collar, as well as an implicit understanding of how an organization ought to be managed.

The focus on human resources translates into three main interrelated strategic thrusts. First, an internal labor market is created to secure a labor force of the desired quality and to induce the employees to remain in the firm (Pucik, 1979). Second, a company philosophy is articulated that expresses concern for employee needs and emphasizes cooperation and teamwork in a "unique" environment (Ouchi and Jaeger, 1978). Third, close attention is given both to hiring people who will fit well with the values of the particular company and to integrating employees into the company at all stages of their working life (Rohlen, 1974). These general strategies are translated into specific management techniques. Emphasis is placed on continuous development of employee skills; formal promotion is of secondary importance. Employees are evaluated on a multitude of criteria rather than only on individual "bottom-line" contribution. The work is structured in such a way that it may be carried out by groups oper-

Source: This article appears here for the first time. Copyright © 1982 by Nina G. Hatvany and Vladimir Pucik. Printed by permission.

Authors' note: The authors would like to thank Koya Azumi, Mitsuyo Hanada, Blair McDonald, Bill Newman, Bill Ouchi, Hans Pennings, Tom Roehl, Michael Tushman, and others for their helpful comments on earlier drafts of this paper. We are grateful to Citibank, New York, and the Japan Foundation, Tokyo, for their financial support of the work in the preparation of this paper.

Figure 1.   The Japanese Management System

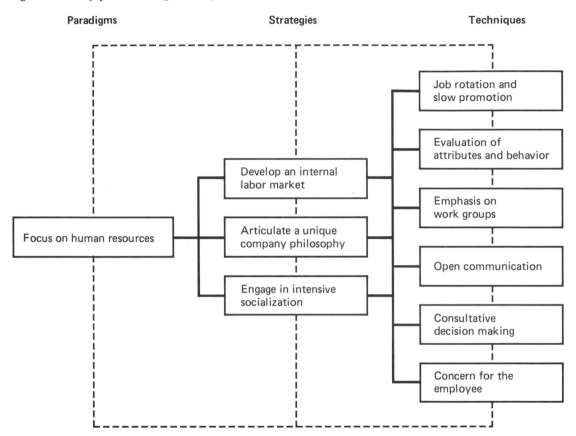

ating with a great deal of autonomy. Open communication is encouraged, supported, and rewarded. Information about pending decisions is circulated to all before the decisions are actually made. Active, observable concern for every employee is expressed by supervisory personnel (Rohlen, 1974; Clark, R., 1979).

Strategies

1. The organization as an internal labor market. In large Japanese companies it has become the rule that a male employee will be hired just after graduation from high school or university with the expectation of retaining him for the rest of his working life (Yoshino, 1968). The policy of lifetime employment is not extended to fe-

males, who are generally expected to leave the company and the job market once they are married. The temporary nature of the female work force, as well as the use of part-time workers, gives employers flexibility in adjusting the size of their workforce and in adapting to current economic conditions while still maintaining employment for regular male workers. The widespread use of subcontracting serves a similar purpose. Even during the recession in the mid 1970s, layoffs of regular workers were exceptional (Rohlen, 1979).

Such a set of employment practices that price and allocate labor according to intraorganizational rules and procedures rather than according to external demand and supply conditions is described in the economic literature as an internal labor market (ILM) (Doeringer and Piore, 1971). ILMs often develop in response to a scarcity of specific skills on the open labor market. Such a scarcity occurred in Japan as rapid industrialization took place in the 1920s, when a limited pool of skilled workers was available (Taira, 1970; Dore, 1973). Firms had to invest a great deal in training and naturally then attempted to discourage turnover by offering premium wages to senior workers. At the same time, when skills are learned on the job, they are largely company specific; the employees cannot realize their full value outside the firm, and interfirm mobility is discouraged even further (Becker, 1964).

Young Japanese workers at early stages of their careers are underpaid relative to what they contribute (Cole, 1971). They are compensated for underpayment at later stages in their tenure within the firm; the wages of the most senior workers may surpass the pay of the new hires by 200–400 percent, depending on the company (Haitani, 1978). However, this kind of wage system does not preclude the existence of additional merit differentials within older age groups. The seniority benefits and the lack of alternative employment opportunities at comparable wage levels for workers with prior experience, as well as the insufficiency of public welfare, again make an employee both unwilling and unable to move (Pucik, 1979). The widespread practice of long-term employment naturally results in a low unemployment rate and low interfirm mobility (Cole, 1979).

2. Articulated and unique company philosophy. Many chief executives of major Japanese firms have written books expressing their philosophy of work and management. These philosophies frequently describe the firm as a family, unique and distinct from any other firm.

Among the norms of "family" life, *wa,* harmony, is the single most popular component in company philosophies. The concept of *wa* expresses a "quality of relationship. . . . Teamwork comes to mind as a suitable approximation" (Rohlen, 1974, p. 74). *Wa* is the watchword for developing the group consciousness of the employees and enhancing cooperation within the work group. This "family" is a social group into which one is carefully selected, but which, as in a real family, one is not supposed to leave, even if one becomes dissatisfied with this or that aspect

of "family" life. However, the cultivation of a sense of uniqueness provides an ideological justification of the limited possibilities for interfirm mobility.

Reciprocally, the commitment of the "family" to the employee is expressed in company policies of avoiding layoffs and providing the employee with a whole range of supplementary welfare benefits. If companies did not provide reasonable employment security, they would find it nearly impossible to foster team spirit and cooperation (Williamson and Ouchi, 1980). The ideal is to reconcile two objectives: pursuit of profits and perpetuation of the company as a group. The employees are asked to devote substantial effort to the company's well-being. In return a profitable company is expected to contribute generously to the welfare of employees.

3. Intensive socialization. The development of cohesiveness within the firm is a major focus of personnel policies in a Japanese firm throughout the whole working life of an employee. In the initial screening process, young graduates are not favored solely because of structural features of the internal labor market in the firm. " 'Virgin' work forces are preferred for the reason that they can be readily assimilated into each company's unique environment as a community" (Hazama, 1979, p. 148). The basic criteria for hiring are moderate views and a harmonious personality. Ability on the job is obviously also a requirement, but at the same time applicants may be eliminated during the selection process if they arouse the suspicion that they cannot get along with people, possess radical views, or come from an unfavorable home environment (Rohlen, 1974). It is only natural that since new hires are expected to remain with the company a long time, even top executives often are closely involved in their interviewing and assessment. To encourage recruits into the company, employees' and teachers' referrals are frequently solicited.

The socialization process begins with the initial training program, which may last up to six months and is geared toward familiarizing new employees with the company. During the course of the program, the recruits learn about the business philosophy of the firm and experience work on the factory floor as well as in the showrooms

(Kim, 1979). They are expected to assume the identity of "company men"; their vocational specialization is of secondary importance. Both careful screening and introductory training are designed to develop the homogeneity of the people in the firm.

In addition to this initial socialization, a "resocialization" (Katz, 1980) takes place each time employees enter new positions, since they have to familiarize themselves with a new set of people and tasks. Employees are transferred for two main reasons. First, they are assigned to new positions to learn additional skills in on-the-job training programs. Second, periodic transfers are part of a long-range experience-building program, through which the organization grooms its future managers (Yoshino, 1968). While employees rotate semilaterally from job to job, they become increasingly socialized into the organization and immersed in the company philosophy and culture. The emergence of a maverick executive is thus a rare occurrence (Ouchi and Jaeger, 1978).

Techniques

Because one component reinforces the other, our model should be interpreted from a strictly causal perspective. The strategies that reflect management's focus on human resources are closely interrelated, as are all the specific techniques derived from management's basic paradigm.

1. Job rotation and slow promotion. Under conditions of lifetime employment, the hierarchical structure of organizations makes vacancies in higher positions emerge sequentially as each cohort moves a step closer toward retirement. Rapid promotion is thus unlikely unless an organization expands dramatically. This limited upward mobility is another element that encourages lateral job rotation in Japanese organizations. Although promotion is slow, carefully planned lateral job transfers add substantial flexibility to job reward and recognition. Not all jobs at the same hierarchical level are equal in their centrality or importance to the organization's activity (Schein, 1971). By assigning individuals to jobs that are at the same level but vary in their centrality, the organization can discriminate among

individuals who, within the formal system, share the same status, same salary, and same privileges (Rohlen, 1974). This informal recognition system has the effect of providing or withholding opportunities to learn skills required for future formal promotions.

An additional feature adding flexibility to the promotion systems of many Japanese firms is the emergence of a dual promotion ladder (Haitani, 1978). Promotion in status is based on the results of past evaluations and seniority within the firm; promotion in position is based on evaluation results and the availability of vacancies in the level above. Therefore, even if immediate upper-level positions are blocked by a cohort of seniors, promotion in status will provide an employee with more respect and money. Conversely, a position of responsibility can be assigned to an outstanding employee who does not fulfill the seniority requirements for promotion in status (Tsurumi, 1977).

Besides its relevance for promotion, job rotation is also facilitated by the necessity of in-house training in an ILM, where hiring of outsiders is avoided. This training is typically on-the-job, which is usually highly economical and does not require great administrative expenses (Williamson, 1975). The emphasis on job rotation creates an environment in which an employee becomes a generalist, rather than a specialist, in any functional area. These general skills are, however, for the most part still unique to the organization (Becker, 1964; Hazama, 1979). In this way, lifetime employment and non-specialized career path mutually reinforce one another in reducing interfirm mobility.

2. Evaluation of attributes and behavior. Employee evaluations are usually conducted on an annual or semiannual basis. The evaluation criteria include not only "bottom-line" performance measures on the individual and especially the team level but also various desirable personality traits and behaviors, such as creativity, emotional maturity, and cooperation with others (Hazama, 1979). In most companies, personality and behavior, rather than output, are the key criteria (Ouchi and Jaeger, 1978), yet the difference is often merely symbolic. Output measures may be translated easily into attributes such as leadership ability, technical competence, relations with others, and judgment. In this way, the employee is not made to feel that the "bottom-line," which may sometimes be beyond his or her control, is the key dimension of the evaluation. Occasional mistakes, particularly for lower-level employees, are considered part of the learning process (Tsurumi, 1977). In addition, the slow promotion system allows for careful judgments to be made even on such subjective criteria as the personality traits of honesty and seriousness (Ouchi and Jaeger, 1978). At the same time, evaluations do discriminate clearly among employees, since each employee is compared to other members of an appropriate group and ranked accordingly.

Because group performance is also a focus of evaluation, peer pressure on an individual to contribute sufficiently to the group's performance becomes an important mechanism of performance control. Long tenure, friendship ties, and informal communication networks enable both superiors and peers to have a very clear sense of the employee's performance and potential relative to others.

3. Importance of work group. Not only evaluation but many other company policies revolve around groups. Tasks are assigned to groups rather than to individuals (Rohlen, 1974). Group cohesion is stimulated by the delegation of responsibility to work groups as well as by other job design features, such as job rotation and group-based performance feedback. Work-group autonomy is enhanced by not using experts to solve operational problems for specific groups. Such action would be regarded as outside interference, and the result would be to undermine morale and leadership (Rohlen, 1974).

In most work settings, however, work-group autonomy is retained within clearly defined limits because the company carefully coordinates team activities and controls the training and evaluation of members, the size of the group, the amount of job rotation, and sometimes even the speed and amount of production (Cole, 1979). Yet within these limits, teamwork is not just part of a company's articulated philosophy, but forms the basic fabric of the work process. Job rotation is encouraged not only to develop each employee's

skills, but also to avoid production losses for the group when one or more workers are absent due to illness. As noted above, having group performance be a focus of evaluation also facilitates cooperation, since members work toward the same goals. Not surprisingly, these elements of job design are similar to those employed in work-group job enrichment programs in the United States (Hackman, 1977).

4. Open communication. Both the emphasis on team spirit in work groups and the network of friendships that employees develop during their long tenure in the organization encourage the extensive face-to-face communication reported in several studies involving Japanese companies (for instance, Pascale, 1978). Open communication is also an inherent part of the Japanese work setting. Work spaces are open and crowded with individuals at different levels in the hierarchy. Subordinates can do little that the supervisor is not aware of and vice-versa. Even high-ranking office managers seldom have separate private offices. Partitioned spaces, cubicles, and small rooms are used as special areas for conferences with visitors or for small discussions within the staff (Rohlen, 1974). In factories, the foreman is constantly on the floor discussing problems, helping with pieces of work, talking to outsiders, and instructing the inexperienced. Even senior plant managers spend as much time as possible on the floor (Rohlen, 1974).

Open communication is not limited to the vertical exchanges often emphasized in the literature (for instance, Nakane, 1970). Job rotation stimulates the emergence of extensive informal lateral communication networks in the organization. Without these networks, the transfer of much job-related information would be impossible. Although not included in written operational procedures, their use is implicitly authorized by the formal control system as a legitimate tool to get things done (Pucik, 1979).

5. Consultative decision making. The extensive face-to-face communication observed in Japanese companies is sometimes confused with participative decision making. However, data from Pascale's (1978) study indicate that the extent of face-to-face communication bears no relationship to employees' perceptions of their level of participation in decision making. The usual procedure for management decision making is for a proposal to be initiated by a middle manager, most often under the directive of top management (Hattori, 1977). This middle manager will engage in informal discussion and consultation with peers and supervisors. When all are familiar with the proposal, a request for a decision is made formally. Because of the earlier discussions, it is almost inevitably ratified, often in a ceremonial group meeting. The ratification does not indicate unanimous approval but does imply unanimous consent to its implementation.

". . . The manager will not decide until others who will be affected have had sufficient time to offer their views, feel they have been fairly heard, and are willing to support the decision even though they may not feel that it is the best one" (Rohlen, 1974, p. 308). This kind of decision making is *not* participative in the American sense of the word, which implies frequent group meetings and negotiation between manager and subordinates, nor is it "bottom-up," as suggested, for example, by Drucker (1975). This decision making is rather a "top-down" or interactive consultative process, especially when long-term planning and strategy are concerned (Kano, 1980). Although the locus of responsibility may appear ambiguous to outsiders (Tsuji, 1968; Yoshino, 1968), it is quite clear within the organization, especially at the upper levels (Clark, R., 1979).

6. *Concern for the employee.*   Informal communication not only facilitates decision making but also forms a channel to express management concern for the well-being of the employees. Managers invest a great deal of time in talking to employees about everyday matters. Indeed, the quality of relationships with subordinates is an important part of their evaluation (Cole, 1971). Managers thus develop a feeling for an employee's personal needs and problems as well as for his or her performance. Obviously, this intimate knowledge of each employee is facilitated by the employee's long tenure, but managers do consciously and explicitly attempt to get to know their employees and place a premium on having time to talk.

Deepening the company's involvement with employees' lives is the sponsoring of various cultural, athletic, and other recreational activites, resulting in a heavy schedule of company social affairs (Rohlen, 1974). The company allocates substantial financial resources to pay for benefits that are given all employees, such as a family allowance and various commuting and housing allowances. Furthermore, there are various welfare systems that "penetrate into every crack of workers' lives" (Hazama, 1971, p. 43). These range from company scholarships for employees' children to credit extension, savings, and insurance. Thus, employees perceive their own welfare and the financial welfare of their company as being identical (Tsurumi, 1977).

In this sense, the reciprocal relationship between the employee and the organization is especially important. The Japanese management system is based on the understanding that, in return for the employee's contribution towards the company's growth and well-being, the profitable firm will provide a stable and secure work environment and protect the employee's welfare even during a period of economic slowdown. We propose, however, that there is nothing uniquely Japanese in this exchange.

THE COMPARATIVE PERSPECTIVE

Twenty years ago, when Japan's economic growth first caught the attention of management experts, it was widely believed that the modernization of the Japanese economy would force radical changes in the traditional management methods in the direction of the modern American management style (Harbison and Myers, 1959). It was assumed that workers' loyalty is a remnant of feudalistic customs, that lifetime employment leads to featherbedding and wasteful allocation of labor, that slow promotion demotivates good managers, and that consensual decision making is time-consuming and inefficient. The expected shift to greater interfirm mobility and intrafirm conflict did not occur, and Japanese companies nevertheless continued to exhibit strong productivity gains.

The explanation for Japan's success is now often sought in personality traits, either inherently characteristic of Japanese people or induced by their cultural traditions (Tsuda, 1979; Clark, G., 1979). It is asserted that were it not for these personality traits, Japanese management practices could not survive. However, one of the principal causes of many researchers' claims about the unique character of the Japanese management system is the lack of integration of findings from studies of Japanese organizations with organizational theories developed outside Japan. As Cyert and March (1963) observe: "An organization is unique when we fail to develop a theory which would make it nonunique" (p. 287).

As a first step toward such a theory, we propose to highlight the relationship of the various so-called Japanese management strategies and techniques with positive work outcomes, such as commitment to the organization and productivity. Our review is not intended to be exhaustive but rather to suggest the feasibility of integrating findings from Japan with more general concepts. We therefore focus exclusively on relationships that may be derived from observations of behavior in non-Japanese settings.

Concern for Human Resources, Commitment, and Productivity

The internal labor market (ILM) and its relationship to commitment is a convenient starting point for our discussion. The guarantee of job security implicit in an ILM is a marked departure from conventional American managerial assumptions about the need to retain flexibility in the size of the work force so as to respond effectively to cyclical variations in demand. It is also often thought that institutionalized labor security deprives the manager of the ultimate weapon with which to control subordinates' behavior—the threat of firing. However, other more subtle forms of control are still available in an ILM, such as placement in a dead-end position or one of low centrality.

Moreover, job security has advantages for the organization. One, for example, is the reduction of employee hostility to the introduction of labor-saving technology or to organizational changes. Employees know that they may be transferred to new jobs, but do not fear losing their jobs altogether. Another is the suggestion by Hall (1976) and Salancik (1977) that long tenure is positively associated with commitment to the organization.

High commitment is elicited also by actions expressing the company's concern with the employees' welfare. Data presented by Steers (1977) indicate that an employee's level of commitment is related strongly, among other things, to (1) feelings of personal importance to the organization, which are based upon actions of that organization over time, and (2) the extent to which the organization is seen as dependable in carrying out its commitments to the employee.

The link between commitment and other behavioral outcomes is complex. Porter, Steers, Mowday, and Boulian (1974) assert that high commitment reduces turnover. High commitment in conjunction with binding choice also leads to high satisfaction (Salancik and Pfeffer, 1978). The results of four studies connecting labor market structure and commitment (Blauner, 1964; Marsh and Mannari, 1976; Ouchi and Jaeger, 1978; Cole, 1979) confirm these predictions in general. Analysis across age groups, years of tenure, level of education, and position in the hierarchy consistently displays significant differences in the concomitant variance of commitment and turnover for employees who work in an ILM setting and those who do not. The proper interpretation of available data is, however, complicated by the fact that commitment is a multifaceted variable comprising acceptance of the organization's goals and values, willingness to exert effort on behalf of the organization, and desire to maintain membership in the organization (Steers, 1977). One can assume that all these facets do not always pull in the same direction. For that reason, high commitment per se may have only a tenuous impact on performance. Additional organizational measures may be necessary to transform this commitment into a productive effort.

A philosophy that is both articulated and enacted may facilitate such a transformation because it presents a clear picture of the organization's goals, norms, and values. Familiarity with the goals of an organization provides direction for individuals, guides their actions, sets constraints on their behavior, and enhances their motivation (Scott, 1966). In fact, the strategy of disseminating an articulated company philosophy has been adopted by a number of American companies. As Peters (1978) points out, the biographies of many industrial leaders stress their quest to give operational force and meaning to their goals.

Not only does an articulated philosophy provide guidance in interpreting the organization's goals, but Ouchi and Price (1978) further suggest that an organizational philosophy may be regarded as an elegant informational device for providing a form of control at once all-pervasive and effective. Such a philosophy presents a basic theory of how the firm should be managed; the manager can use the philosophy for guidance in any situation. The benefits of an articulated company philosophy are lost, however, if it is not properly communicated to employees or not visibly supported in management's behavior. Therefore, ensuring that employees have understood the philosophy and seen it in action is one of the primary functions of the company's socialization effort.

As we pointed out earlier, employees are selected partly on the basis of their perceived ability to fit in with the company values and philosophy. This congruence of individual needs and goals and organizational goals facilitates the motivation of employees both to remain in the organization and to be productive (Lawler, 1973; Ouchi, 1980). In addition, the stringency of entry requirements means that employees tend to rationalize the effort that they exerted in order to enter the organization by feeling a high degree of commitment to the organization and satisfaction with their membership in it (Aronson and Mills, 1959; Salancik, 1977).

As employees remain in the organization over an extended period of time they tend to adopt the existing positive values, attitudes, and performance levels of their coworkers. This is partly a function of conformity to group pressures and norms in order to avoid social rejection as a deviant organization member (Asch, 1951; Schachter, 1951); it also reflects the behavior modeling and learning that occurs as the very young employee enters into and continues to develop within the organization (Bandura, 1969). Acknowledging the enormous impact of groups both directly, by the enforcement of norms, and indirectly, by affecting the beliefs and values of the members (Hackman, 1976), the organization devotes far greater attention to structural factors that enhance group motivation and cooperation than to the motivation of individuals.

The employee internalizes the values and objectives of the company, becomes increasingly committed to it, and learns the formal and informal rules and procedures, particularly through the process of job rotation. Eventually the individuals can be relied on to do their best for the organization in a variety of different situations. Research by Edstrom and Galbraith (1977) shows that an organization may actively use this effect of socialization. They examined a multinational organization in which the subunit decision-making environment varies enormously, yet which requires some degree of coordination and uniformity. The company transfers managers; seasoned managers are assigned on a rotating basis to new slots around the company. A well-socialized manager who has performed various functions and worked in several company locations is familiar both with the needs of the organization and the appropriate course of action in a variety of situations.

Each transfer also increases the chances for the employee to find a niche in the organization for which he or she is especially well suited. This fit between the ability of the employee and the requirements of the job encourages the expenditure of effort (Nadler and Lawler, 1977). Furthermore, job rotation facilitates the development of informal communication networks, which help in coordinating the flow of work across functional areas and in the speedy resolution of problems (Tushman, 1977; Roberts and O'Reilly, 1979). Finally, job rotation "unfreezes" individuals from being unresponsive to the demands of their jobs (Katz, 1980).

We have pointed out that job rotation is closely linked to the promotion system and mediates some of its restrictions on upward mobility. Although one may argue that deferred promotion may be a source of frustration to highly promising employees, several positive influences ought to be noted as well. First, no particular individual is discriminated against; promotion rules are the same for all "relevant others" and thus perceived as fair or "equitable" (Adams, 1965). Second, deferral may have positive motivational consequences. The public identification of "losers," who are in the majority when compared to "winners" in any hierarchical organization, is deferred. This system fosters excellence and prolonged competition because the losers—still hoping to beat the odds—struggle to do well.

The evaluation system in a Japanese company has several facets that may enhance organizational effectiveness. Because evaluations are based on the observations made by managers during their frequent, regular interactions with subordinates, the cost of such an evaluation system is relatively low (Williamson, 1975). The evaluation system, in conjuction with the ILM arrangements, has another interesting effect. Employees are not formally separated according to their ability until late in their tenure. Ambitious workers who seek immediate recognition therefore must engage in activities that will get them noticed. Bottom-line performance is not adequate since it is not a focus of managerial evaluation. The system encourages easily observable behavior that demonstrates willingness to exert substantial effort on behalf of the organization (Akerlof, 1976; Miyazaki, 1977).

It is often said that the emphasis on long-term objectives in Japanese organizations sets their market strategy apart from that of their United States counterparts (for example, Drucker, 1975; Tsurumi, 1976). A long-term perspective is indeed encouraged by the internal evaluation system. When behavior replaces bottom-line performance as the focus of evaluation, means as well as ends may be assessed. Such assessment may lead to a better match between the direction of employee efforts and company objectives (Levinson, 1976). In addition, aversion to risk is minimized and creativity facilitated, both by the assumption of permanent job tenure and by the tolerance of honest mistakes in the evaluation process. This combination of security and incentives for challenging assignments creates what Pelz (1967) characterizes as a "creative challenge," an environment suitable for innovation.

Basing performance evaluation and rewards on work group performance, such that all group members share the consequences of their efforts, tends to increase productivity as well as the level of mutual aid and tutoring (Wodarski, Hamblin, Buckholdt, and Ferritor, 1973). In general, the group can assist in developing job-relevant knowledge and skills in three ways: by direct instruction, by providing feedback about behavior, and by serving as models of correct or appropriate behavior (Hackman, 1976). Another benefit is that being in close proximity to others increases physiological arousal and can enhance performance, particularly on routine tasks (Zajonc, 1965). Also, peers in work groups can make assessments of an individual's performance based on information that only they possess (Kane and Lawler, 1978), and hence can exert powerful control over an individual's career path. An individual who recognizes this fact may attempt to be as productive as possible.

The structuring of tasks around groups serves a dual function: it not only enhances performance but also controls stimuli that are directly satisfying, such as acceptance, esteem, and a sense of identity (McClelland, 1961).

Satisfaction with group membership tends to reinforce itself in that the expectation of interaction with another individual tends to increase one's liking for that individual (Darley and Berscheid, 1967), as do proximity to another individual and increased information about him or her (Berscheid and Walster, 1969). The translation of organizational membership into membership in a small group seems to be characterized in general by higher job satisfaction, lower absence rates, lower turnover rates, and fewer labor disputes (Porter and Lawler, 1964). Finally, it has been found that jobs which are integrated with the work activities tend to be associated with more commitment to the organization (Salancik, 1977) since they involve demands from salient others.

Like so many other tasks in Japanese organizations, decision making is structured to involve the whole group rather than only a few individuals. We have already expressed the opinion that one should not assume consensual decision making in Japanese firms is participative. People outside the core group of decision makers merely express their consent to the proposed course of action. They do not participate; they do not feel ownership of the decision. The early communication of the proposed changes, however, helps to reduce uncertainty in the organization (Thompson, 1967). In addition, prior information on upcoming decisions provides employees with an opportunity to rationalize and accept the outcomes (Janis and Mann, 1977).

Another interpretation is suggested in Weick's (1969) critique of participative decision making. He argues that classic participation may result in compromise and destruction of the polarized responses that aid organizational adaptation to a changing environment. He proposes that a decision-making procedure permitting alternate expression of polarized responses would be more suitable for adaptation. Weick's notion is close to the Japanese style of consensus, in which the opposing party is willing to go along, because his or her point of view may prevail the next time around (Hattori, 1977).

Constraints on Adoption

It is often said that the high productivity in many Japanese companies is due in large degree to the unique cultural characteristics of the Japanese people. Certainly, societal norms about work in organizations are an important constraint. However, the measures management uses to elicit diligence in workers reveal a similarity in the characteristics of Japanese and American workers (Cole, 1979). It seems the psychological traits of Japanese people are an insufficient explanation of Japan's success in fostering productivity.

It is sometimes proposed that a "negotiated environment" or a position of market dominance is essential for resistance to economic fluctuations and the attendant ability to provide stable employment. Further, the opportunities for interfirm mobility are greater in the United States and thus perhaps less conducive to the development of an internal labor market. In addition, the American employee is less reliant on the company for his or her welfare in a country where the welfare transfers are mediated through the government and not through individual companies. It may seem that these factors together with the dominance

of craft-based unions in the United States (versus enterprise-based unions in Japan) preclude the emergence of organizations using strategies and techniques as described above.

This paper focuses on employment practices in large Japanese companies. Although it is true that similar practices are also in evidence in small companies, their emphasis on permanent employment is less pronounced because most of the smaller companies are vulnerable to drops in economic activity (Cole, 1979). Thus, in Japan as well as in other countries, the ability of the organization to control at least some sources of uncertainty in its environment may be an important factor influencing the feasibility of a given set of management techniques.

Nevertheless, market imperfections and transaction costs make an ILM a feasible alternative to other forms of employment contracts even for firms that do not enjoy the position of market dominance (Williamson, 1975). Moreover, the opportunities for interfirm mobility and a government-supported welfare system have not precluded the development of ILM organizations in the United States or in Western Europe (Doeringer and Piore, 1971; Mace, 1979). It may be that certain aspects of the ILM are emphasized to a lesser extent in the United States, but clearly the ILM concept is not an all-or-none proposition.

The argument made with respect to craft-based versus enterprise unions is also countered by the evidence. The successful application of the outlined management practices is possible even in union-organized plants in countries such as Britain, known for her militant craft-based unionism (Takamiya, 1979). In our interpretation, the existence of enterprise unions is an effect, rather than a cause, of the mutually beneficial relationship between the employee and the company.

Our "universalist" position is empirically supported not only by the relative ease with which the "imported" management techniques are introduced in Japanese subsidiaries abroad (Johnson and Ouchi, 1974; Takamiya, 1979) but also by several recent studies that demonstrate the existence of similar organizational patterns in Western companies (for example, Tsurumi, 1977;

Ouchi and Jaeger, 1978; Zager, 1978). Several of the latter companies are among the largest of American corporations, with a record of innovation, growth, and high employee morale. Description of these companies in the literature generally focuses on the practice of providing long tenure for employees. Other strategies and techniques, such as the articulation of company philosophy, job rotation, and consultative decision making, are also used (Ouchi and Jaeger, 1978; Ouchi and Johnson, 1978; Wilkins, 1978). We still know very little, however, about communication patterns in these organizations, the role of the work groups, and other features that are important in Japanese settings.

CONCLUSION

We have proposed an alternative to the traditional model of the Japanese management system. Our model is based on elements and relationships that are not unique to any one culture. The strategies and techniques we have reviewed constitute a remarkably well-integrated system. The management practices are highly congruent with the way tasks are structured, with the goals of individual members, and with the climate of the organization. Such good fit is expected to result in a high degree of organizational effectiveness or productivity (Nadler and Tushman, 1977).

In essence, it follows from our model that the successful adaptation of so-called Japanese management methods in the United States is quite feasible. If these methods are to be implemented rapidly, certain environmental changes (changes in tax laws, in antitrust regulations, and so forth) are desirable. Such changes would make it easier for organizations to focus on long-term utilization of human resources. We believe changes are essential in management's thinking about the nature of the relationship between the employee and the organization; otherwise desirable environmental changes will not come about. We further believe that without such change the United States is going to fall ever further behind in the race among nations for increased productivity.

REFERENCES

Adams, J. S. Inequity in social exchange. In L. Berkowitz (ed.). *Advances in experimental social psychology.* New York: Academic Press, 1965.

Akerlof, G. A. The economics of caste and of the ratrace and other woeful tales. *Quarterly Journal of Economics,* 1976, 4, 599–617.

Aronson, E., and Mills, J. The effect of severity of initiation on liking for a group. *Journal of Abnormal and Social Psychology,* 1959, 59, 177–81.

Asch, S. E. Effects of group pressure upon the modification and distortion of judgments. In H. Guetzkow (ed.). *Groups, Leadership and Men.* New Brunswick, N.J.: Rutgers University Press, 1951.

Bandura, A. *Principles of behavior modification.* New York: Holt, Rhinehart and Winston, 1969.

Becker, G. *Human capital.* New York: National Bureau of Economic Research, 1964.

Berscheid, E., and Walster, E. *Interpersonal attraction.* Reading, Mass.: Addison-Wesley, 1969.

Blauner, R. *Alienation and freedom: The factory worker and his factory.* Chicago: University of Chicago Press, 1964.

Clark, G. Group instinct is key to Japan's success. *The Japan Economic Journal,* October 23, 1979.

Clark, R. C. *The Japanese company.* New Haven, Conn.: Yale University Press, 1979.

Cole, R. E. *Japanese blue collar: The changing tradition.* Berkeley, Calif.: University of California Press, 1971.

———. *Work, mobility and participation.* Berkeley, Calif.: University of California Press, 1979.

Cyert, R. M., and March, J. G. *A behavioral theory of the firm.* Englewood Cliffs, N.J.: Prentice-Hall, 1963.

Darley, J. M., and Berscheid, E. Increased liking as a result of the anticipation of personal contact. *Human Relations,* 1967, 20, 29–40.

Denison, E. F., and Chung, W. K. *How Japan's economy grew so fast.* Washington, D.C.: Brookings Institution, 1976.

Doeringer, P., and Piore, M. *Internal labor markets and manpower analysis.* Lexington, Mass.: D. C. Heath, 1971.

Dore, R. P. *British factory—Japanese factory.* Berkeley, Calif.: University of California Press, 1973.

Drucker, P. Economic realities and enterprise strategy. In Ezra F. Vogel (ed.). *Modern Japanese organization and decision-making.* Berkeley, Calif.: University of California Press, 1975.

Edstrom, A., and Galbraith, J. R. Transfer of managers

as a coordination and control strategy in multinational organizations. *Administrative Science Quarterly*, June, 1977, *22*, 248.

Glazer, N. Social and cultural factors in Japanese economic growth. In Hugh Patrick and Henry Rosovsky (eds.). *Asia's new giant*. Washington, D.C.: Brookings Institution, 1976.

Hackman, J. R. Group influences on individuals. In Marvin D. Dunnette (ed.). *Handbook of industrial and organizational psychology*. Chicago: Rand McNally, 1976, 1455–1515.

———. Designing work for individuals and for groups. In J. R. Hackman, E. E. Lawler, and L. W. Porter (eds.). *Perspectives on behavior in organizations*. New York: McGraw-Hill, 1977, 242–256.

Haitani, K. Changing characteristics of the Japanese employment system. *Asian Survey*, 1978, *10*, 1029–1045.

Hall, D. T. *Careers in organizations*. Santa Monica, Calif.: Goodyear, 1976.

Harbison, F., and Myers, C. A. *Management in the industrial world: An international analysis*. New York: McGraw-Hill, 1959.

Hattori, J. A proposition on efficient decision-making in the Japanese corporation. *Management Japan*, Autumn 1977, *10*, 14–23.

Hazama, H. Characteristics of Japanese-style management. *Japanese Economic Studies*. Spring-Summer, 1979, 110–173.

Janis, I. L., and Mann, L. *Decision Making*. New York: Free Press, 1977.

Johnson, R. T. and Ouchi, W. G. "Made in America (Under Japanese Management)." *Harvard Business Review*, 1974, *52(4)*, 61–69.

Kane, J. S., and Lawler, E. E., III. Methods of peer assessment. *Psychological Bulletin*, 1978, *85*, 555–586.

Kano, T. Comparative study of strategy, structure and long-range planning in Japan and in the United States. *Management Japan*, Spring 1980, *11(1)*, 20–34.

Katz, R. Time and work: Towards an integrative perspective. In B. M. Staw and L. L. Cummings (eds.). *Review of research in organizational behavior*, Greenwich, Conn.: Jai Press, 1980.

Kim, K. The Japanese collective management system. Unpublished term paper. Columbia University Graduate School of Business, Spring, 1977.

Kuhn, T. *The structure of scientific revolution* (2nd edition). Chicago: University of Chicago Press, 1970.

Lawler, E. E. *Motivation in work organizations*. Monterey, Calif.: Brooks/Cole, 1973.

Levinson, H. Appraisal of what performance. *Harvard Business Review*, 1976, *4*, 30–46.

McClelland, D. C. *The achieving society*. Princeton, N.J.: Van Nostrand, 1961.

Mace, J. Internal labor markets for engineers in British industry. *British Journal of Industrial Relations*, 1979, *17(1)*, 50–63.

Marsh, R. M., and Mannari, H. *Modernization and the Japanese factory*. Princeton, N.J.: Princeton University Press, 1976.

Miyazaki, H. The rat race and internal labor markets. *The Bell Journal of Economics*, 1977, *2*, 394–418.

Nadler, D. A., and Lawler, E. E. Motivation—A diagnostic approach. In J. R. Hackman, E. E. Lawler, and L. W. Porter (eds.). *Perspectives on behavior in organizations*. New York: McGraw-Hill, 1977, 85–98.

Nakane, Ch. *Japanese society*. Berkeley, Calif.: University of California Press, 1970.

Ouchi, W. G. Markets, bureaucracies and clans. *Administrative Science Quarterly*, 1980, *25*, 129–140.

Ouchi, W. G., and Jaeger, A. M. Type Z organization: Stability in the midst of mobility. *Academy of Management Review*, 1978, *2*, 305–314.

Ouchi, W. G., and Johnson, J. B. Types of organizational control and their relationship to emotional well-being. *Administrative Science Quarterly*, 1978, *2*, 293–317.

Ouchi, W. G., and Price, R. L. Hierarchies, clans and theory Z: A new perspective on organization development. *Organizational Dynamics*, 1978, Autumn, 25–44.

Pascale, R. T. Communication and decision making across cultures: Japanese and American comparisons. *Administrative Science Quarterly*, 1978, *1*, 91–110.

Pelz, D. C. Creative tensions in the research and development climate. *Science*, 1967, *194*, 160–165.

Peters, T. J. Symbols, patterns and settings: An optimistic case for getting things done. *Organizational Dynamics*, 1978, Autumn, 3–31.

Porter, L. W., Steers, R. M., Mowday, R. T., and Boulian, P. V. Organizational commitment, job satisfaction and turnover among psychiatric technicians. *Journal of Applied Psychology*, 1974, *59*, 603–609.

Porter, L. W., and Lawler, E. E. The effects of "tall" versus "flat" organization structures on managerial job satisfaction. *Personnel Psychology*, 1964, *17*, 135–148.

Pucik, V. Lifetime employment in Japan: An alternative to the "culture-structure" causal model. *Journal of International Affairs*, 1979, *1*, 158–161.

Roberts, K., and O'Reilly, C. Some correlations of communication roles in organizations. *Academy of Management Journal*, 1979, *22*, 42–57.

Rohlen, T. *For Harmony and Strength*. Berkeley, Calif.: University of California Press, 1974.

———. "Permanent employment" faces recession,

slow growth and an aging work force. *The Journal of Japanese Studies*, Summer, 1979, 235–272.

Salancik, G. R. Commitment and the control of organizational behavior and belief. In B. M. Staw and G. R. Salancik (eds.). *New Directions in Organizational Behavior*, Chicago: St. Clair Press, 1977.

Salancik, G. R., and Pfeffer, J. A social information processing approach to job attitudes and task design. *Administrative Science Quarterly*, 1978, *2*, 224–253.

Schachter, S. Deviation, rejection and communication. *Journal of Abnormal Social Psychology*, *1951*, 46, 190–207.

Schein, E. H. The individual, the organization and the career: A conceptual scheme. *Journal of Applied Behavioral Science*, 1971, *7*, 401–426.

Scott, W. E. Activation theory and task design. *Organizational Behavior and Human Performance*, 1966, 1, 3–30.

Steers, R. M. Antecedents and outcomes of organizational commitment. *Administrative Science Quarterly*, 1977, *1*, 46–56.

Taira, K. *Economic development and labor market in Japan*. New York: Columbia University Press, 1970.

Takamiya, M. Japanese Multinationals in Europe: Internal operations and their public policy implications (discussion paper), Berlin: International Institute of Management, 1979.

Thompson, J. D. *Organizations in action*. New York: McGraw-Hill, 1967.

Tsuda, M. Japanese Style Management, Japanese Economic Studies, 1979, *7(4)*, 3–32.

Tsuji, K. Decision-making in the Japanese government: A study of ringisei. In R. E. Ward (ed.). *Political development in modern Japan*. Princeton, N.J.: Princeton University Press, 1968.

Tsurumi, Y. *The Japanese are coming*. Cambridge, Mass.: Ballinger, 1976.

——— . *Multinational management: Business strategy and government policy*. Cambridge, Mass.: Ballinger, 1977.

Tushman, M. L. Special boundary roles in the innovation process. *Administrative Science Quarterly*, 1977, *22*, 587–605.

Weick, K. E. *The social psychology of organizing*. Reading, Mass.: Addison-Wesley, 1969.

Wilkins, A. L. Interpreted organizational history: Myths, legends and organizational solidarity. Dissertation proposal prepared for field oral examination, Stanford University, June, 1978.

Williamson, O. E. *Market and hierarchies: Analysis and antitrust implications*. New York: Free Press, 1975.

Williamson, O. E., and Ouchi, W. G. Efficient boundaries. Paper presented at the Conference on the Economics of Organization. Berlin. Summer, 1980.

Wodarski, J. S., Hamblin, R. L., Buckholdt, D. R., and Ferritor, D. E. Individual consequences versus different shared consequences contingent on the performance of low-achieving group members. *Journal of Applied Social Psychology*, 1973, *3*, 276–290.

Yoshino, M. *Japan's managerial system*. Cambridge, Mass.: MIT Press, 1968.

Zajonc, R. B. Social facilitation. *Science*, 1965, *149*, 269–274.

Zager, R. Managing guaranteed employment. *Harvard Business Review*, 1978, *3*, 103–115.

27

The human side of the matrix

Paul R. Lawrence,
Harvey F. Kolodny, and Stanley M. Davis

Matrix management and organization have become increasingly common in recent years. If we were pressed to pick one word that characterizes the potential of the matrix organization, it would have to be flexibility. The matrix structure offers the potential of achieving the flexibility that is so often missing in conventional, single-line-of-command organizations and of reconciling this flexibility with the coordination and economies of scale that are the historic strengths of large organizations. (See [Figure 2] on the next page for the basic elements of matrix design.)

Now that the use of the matrix structure is so widespread, it has become apparent that it calls for different kinds of managerial behavior than are typical in conventional line organizations. This article will identify the key management roles in a matrix organization and describe the essential aspects called for in each of them.

Envision the matrix structure as a diamond. The general executive, who heads up the matrix, is at the top of the diamond. The matrix bosses, or matrix managers, who share common subordinate(s), are on the sides of the diamond. The person at the bottom is the 2-boss manager.

TOP LEADERSHIP

The top leadership is literally atop, or outside of, the matrix organization. This is not generally appreciated. Even in totally matrix organizations, the top executives are not *in* the matrix. Despite this, however, they are *of* it: It is the top leaders who oversee and sustain the balance of power.

In a corporationwide matrix, the top leaders are the chief executive and a few other key in-

Source: Reprinted by permission of the publisher, from *Organizational Dynamics,* Summer 1977, © 1977 by AMACOM, a division of American Management Associations. All rights reserved.

Figure 1.

dividuals; in a product group or a division matrix, the top leader is the senior manager. This individual does not share power with others and there is no unequal separation of authority and responsibility. Formally, the role itself is the same as in any traditional organization. What distinguishes it from the traditional top slot is the leadership process as it is applied to the people in the next levels down.

The top leader is the one who must "buy" the matrix approach. He must be convinced of its merits to the point that he believes it is the best (although not necessarily the ideal) of all alternative designs. He must also "sell" it; he must be very vocal and articulate in developing the concept and arousing enthusiasm for it among the ranks.

One of the several paradoxes of the matrix approach, then, is that it requires a strong, unified command at the top, to ensure a balance of power at the next level down. In some senses this is the benevolent dictator: "You will enjoy democracy (shared power), and I will enjoy autocracy (ultimate power)"; or "I'm OK, you're OK; but I'm still the boss."

Balancing power as a top leader therefore calls for a blend of autocratic and participative leadership styles. A clear example of this comes from

Figure 2.

Essential Characteristics of Matrix Organization

- The identifying feature of a matrix organization is that some managers report to two bosses rather than to the traditional single boss—there is a dual rather than a single chain of command.
- Firms tend to adopt matrix forms when it is absolutely essential that they be highly responsive to two sectors, such as markets and technology; when they face uncertainties that generate very high information processing requirements; and when they must deal with strong constraints on financial and/or human resources. The matrix form can help provide flexibility and balanced decision making but at the price of complexity.
- Matrix organization is more than matrix structure. It must also be reinforced by matrix systems such as dual control and evaluation systems, by matrix leadership behavior that operates comfortably with lateral decision making, and by a matrix culture that fosters open conflict management and a balance of power.
- Most matrix organizations assign dual command responsibilities to functional departments (marketing, production, engineering, and so on) and to product/market departments. The former are oriented to specialized resources while the latter focus on outputs. Other matrix organizations are area-based departments for either products or functions.
- Every matrix organization contains three unique and critical roles: the top manager who heads up and balances the dual chains of command; the matrix bosses (functional, product, or area) who share subordinates; and the 2-boss managers who report to two different matrix bosses. Each of these roles has its own unique requirements.
- The matrix organization started in aerospace companies, but now firms in many industries (chemical, banking, insurance, package goods, electronics, computer, and so on) and in different fields (hospitals, government agencies, professional organizations) are turning to different forms of the matrix structure.

Bastien Hello, head of the B-1 bomber division at Rockwell International. *The New York Times* called his project the most costly and complex plane project in history. In an interview he said:

Today I have some formidable people working for me. When you have a group like that, you have two choices, running a Captain Bligh operation, or a Mr. Roberts operation. I would call one autocratic, the other group therapy.

If I have to lean in one direction, I would shave a little closer to group therapy. It's not because I, and the fellows who work for me, don't have autocratic tendencies. We do. But if you're going to keep everybody working in the same direction, you've got to have group participation in the decisions.

So I like to get my team of managers together and thrash out problems with them, and I like to hear all sides. It's not that I'm a goodie goodie about it; there *is* malice aforethought to it.

Once they have participated in and agreed to the decision, you can hold their noses right to it. It's not that I like group sessions—I don't, they're painful—but they do bring the team along. And once you get them signed up, *then* you become autocratic about it.

The general executive of a matrix organization has the unique role of heading up both of its dual command structures, administrative and technical. As we understand this role, it involves three unique aspects: *power balancing, managing the decision context,* and *standard setting*. These three processes, while of concern to any top executive, take on a very special importance in a mature matrix organization. The reason for this importance is not hard to find. It stems directly from three basic reasons as to why a matrix can be a desirable organizational form.

1. The existence of dual pressures calls for balanced decision making that considers both as-

pects simultaneously. The general executive's critical role in achieving such decision making is to establish and sustain a reasonable balance of power between the two arms of the matrix.

2. The second necessary condition for a matrix organization to be effective is that a very high volume of information be processed and focused for use in making key decisions. If the organization is to cope with such an information processing load, the top leader must be only one among several key decision makers—he must delegate. However, he cannot delegate to other decision makers the job of setting the stage; he must himself manage the decision context.

3. Last, the top executive must set the standards of expected performance. Others contribute to this process, but unless the top individual has high expectations for the organization, it is unlikely that the matrix organization will respond adequately to the environmental pressure for resource redeployment, which we have identified as a third necessary condition for a matrix organization. Let us look at each of these three special aspects of the top leader's role in the matrix organization in more detail.

Power Balancing

The power balancing element of the general executive's role is, in our experience, vital to mature matrix organization performance. Any general manager must of course pay attention to this process, but it is uniquely critical in matrix organizations. If we contrast the pyramid diagram of a conventional hierarchy and the matrix diamond diagram, we have a clue as to why this is true. The diamond diagram, unlike the pyramid, is inherently unstable. For the structure to remain in place despite environmental pushing and pulling that lead to changed administrative and technical requirements, its emphasis and activities must be constantly rebalanced by hands-on top leadership. The analogy is crude but relevant. Managers in a leadership role are usually quite explicit about this requirement of their job. The "tuning" of a matrix organization needs continuing attention.

The basic methods that general executives use to establish a power balance are both obvious and important. The two arms of a matrix organization are, first of all, usually described in the formal documents that establish the structure as being of equal power and importance. The top executive uses every possible occasion to reinforce this message, and one way that is often used is by establishing dual budgeting systems and dual evaluation systems.

Most mature matrix organizations adopt dual budgeting systems, in which a complete budget is generated within each arm of the matrix. As with a double-entry accounting system, the dual budgets count everything twice—each time in a different way and for a different purpose. Functional budgets are primarily cost budgets—unless the functions sell their services outside. The budgets begin with product- and business-area estimates of work required from each functional area, usually expressed in manhours and materials requirements. Functional groups then add indirect and overhead costs to these direct hours and come up with an hourly rate for services to the product or business managers.

Product or business units accept these rates or challenge them, sometimes by threatening to buy from the outside. This is the time when the difference in outlook is most striking. Business units, for example, have little sympathy for functional desires to hold people in an overhead category for contingencies or for the development of long-term competence. A business unit is hard pressed to see the need to develop competence that may be required three years hence, or for another business when its own central concern is with short-term profit and loss. When the rates are approved for all the different functions, the product or business units develop their own profit and loss budgets for each of their product lines.

The parallel accounting systems provide independent controls that are consistent with the characteristic of the work in each type of unit and that recognize the partial autonomy of each organizational subunit. Each unit has the means to evaluate its own performance and to be evaluated independent of others. The CEO of one organization described the dual control systems in his organization as follows:

> The accounting system matches the organization precisely; so that's an aspect the product

manager and I don't have to talk about. He can see how he's doing himself. When resources seem to be a problem, then I must get involved.

Both product managers and functional managers get accounting evaluations. The functional shops have budgets but little spending money. They have a cost budget, but in theory it's all released into the projects. From the functional side, the accounting system locates and isolates unused capacity. As soon as the task requirement disappears the excess capacity turns up. The functional shop then has a "social" problem. The key thing is that the excess turns up immediately. There is no place to hide. Matrix is a free organization, but it's a tough organization.

With dual budgets, some interesting possibilities arise in achieving flexibility or organizational response. In the aforementioned organization, the CEO resolved an internal dispute: A product group was lobbying for control of repair and overhaul contracts on products in the field that it had developed and sold over the protests of a functional group that had always managed the organization's field repair and overhaul activity. In the resolution of the dispute, the function remained in charge of the activity, but the product group was credited with the profits from all repair and overhaul contracts on its products. Both sides were satisfied.

Dual personnel evaluation systems go hand in hand with dual budgeting to help sustain a power balance. If a person's work is to be directed by two superiors, in all logic both should take part in that person's evaluation. Occasionally, the duality is nothing more than a product or business group sign-off of an evaluation form prepared by the functional boss. At other times, the initiative comes from the other side, primarily because the individual involved may have been physically situated within the product or business unit and had limited contact with the functional unit during the period covered by the evaluation.

Regardless of the particular system design, the person with 2-bosses must know that both have been a part of the evaluation if that person is to feel committed to consider both orientations in his activities. For this reason many matrix organizations insist that both superiors sit in on the evaluation feedback with the employee and that both advise the employee of salary changes so that rewards will not be construed as having been secured from only one side of the matrix.

These basic formal arrangements for setting up a reasonable balance of power are essential in a mature matrix, but they are seldom sufficient. Too many events can upset the balance, and a loss of balance needs to be caught by the general manager or it can degenerate into a major power struggle and even an ill-advised move away from the matrix organization. The matrix can be thrown off balance in many ways, but a common cause of a loss of balance is a temporary crisis on one side of the matrix structure that is used as an excuse for mobilizing resources in that direction. Up to a point such a reaction to a true crisis is certainly appropriate, but it can be the start of a lasting imbalance unless it is corrected by the general manager.

A more lasting source of instability arises from the fact that product- and business-area managers manage a whole business and thereby have that special mystique associated with bottom-line responsibility. This is a source of power. They are seen as the sources of revenue—the people who make the cash register ring. The general manager needs to be alert to this one-sided source of power to avoid its unbalancing potential. The profit center manager is often tempted to argue that he must have complete control over all needed resources, but this argument has no place in a matrix organization.

Given the inherent power instability of the matrix, the general managers of mature matrix organizations use a wide variety of supplemental ways to maintain the balance of the matrix. These methods are not new, but they are worth remembering as especially relevant for use in a matrix. Here are five such means:

1. Pay levels, as an important symbol of power, can be marginally higher on one side of the matrix, thus acting as a countervailing force.

2. Job titles can be adjusted between the two sides as a balancing item.

3. Access to the general manager at meetings and informal occasions is a source of power that can be controlled as a balancing factor.

4. Situation of offices is a related factor that carries a status or power message.

5. Reporting level is a frequently used power-balancing method. For instance, product man-

agers can report up through a second-in-command while functional managers report directly to the general manager.

We have talked about the unbalancing potential possessed by profit center managers. But this imbalance of potential fluctuates from situation to situation. In many cases, the organization traditionally gave top priority to the functional side. Here the general manager employs his stratagems to shore up the prestige and position of the business-area or product managers and to make them in fact as well as in name the equals of the functional managers.

Managing the Decision Context

There is no substitute in a matrix organization for the sensitive management of the decision context by the top leadership. The existence of a matrix structure is an acknowledgment that the executive leaders cannot make all the key decisions in a timely way. There is too much relevant information to be digested, and too many points of view must be taken into account. But the general manager must set the stage for this decision making by others. He must see that it happens.

We have already seen that dual environmental pressures and complexity make conflict inevitable. To cope with this situation, the top manager must sponsor and act as a model of a three-stage decision process:

1. The conflicts must be brought into the open. This is fostered in the matrix structure, with its dual arms; but beyond this, the given manager must reward those who bring the tough topics to the surface for open discussion.

2. The conflicting positions must be debated in a spirited and reasoned manner. Relevant lines of argument and appropriate evidence must be presented. The executive manager's personal behavior has to encourage this in others.

3. The issue must be resolved and a commitment made in a timely fashion. The leader cannot tolerate stalling by others or passing the buck up the line.

All these decision processes call for a high order of interpersonal skills and a willingness to take risks. They also call for a minimum of status differentials from the top to the bottom ranks. Top leaders can favorably influence these factors by their own openness to dissent and willingness to listen and debate. One of the noticeable features of most leaders of matrix organizations is the simplicity of their offices and the relative informality of their manner and dress. The key point here is that this behavior must start at the top as part of setting the decision context.

Standard Setting

The leadership of matrix organizations is where high performance standards start. We earlier identified environmental pressures for high performance as a necessary condition for matrix organizations. But it is all too easy for organizational members to insulate themselves from these outside pressures. The general executive in a mature matrix organization internalizes the outside pressures and articulates them in the form of performance standards. Each subsystem on both sides of the matrix structure will of course be making its own projections and setting specific targets for higher review. But the overall level of aspiration in the organization begins with the general executive. This is a duty, as we said before, that he cannot afford to delegate.

THE MATRIX BOSS

The matrix organization boss shares subordinates in common with another boss. As matrices evolve, this means that the matrix structure boss will find himself positioned on one of the dimensions in the power balance. Whether the dimension is the one that is given or the one that is grown can make a significant difference for the perspective that evolves. Since one of the most typical evolutions is from a functional structure through a project overlay to a business-function balance, let us examine the matrix-boss role for each of these two dimensions in detail. The same lessons, however, apply to matrix structure bosses who are in charge of areas, markets, services, or clients.

The Functional Manager

One of the greatest surprises of the matrix organization form comes in the changing role of functional managers. In a functional organization, managers have authority over the objectives of their function, the selection of individuals, the priorities assigned to different tasks, the assignment of subordinates to different tasks and projects, the evaluation of progress on projects, the evaluation of subordinates' performance, and decisions on subordinate pay and promotions. They consult or take direction only from their boss in these matters, but much of the function is self-contained.

In a matrix organization, by contrast, none of these responsibilities is the sole responsibility of the functional manager. He must share many of the decisions with program or business managers or other functional managers at his level. Many matrix structures require dual sign-offs on performance evaluations and on pay and promotion decisions. Even when this is not so, consultation on these matters with others is essential for the effective functioning of the matrix and the power balance discussed previously. Tasks, assignments, and priority decisions have to be shared with business managers and indeed often come about as the result of decisions made by project or business teams. Even a function's objectives are partially determined by the resource demands of projects and businesses. The functional manager in his matrix role is responding in areas in which he has traditionally been the initiator. A manufacturing manager, for example, struggled against and for several years resisted the notion that many of the plant managers who reported to him had to set their goals in response to a business team's needs and that review of goal accomplishment, from a time point of view, was the business manager's and team's responsibility. He had difficulty in understanding that his responsibility was to review goal accomplishment from the point of view of a functional specialty.

Thus, for the functional manager, a matrix organization is often experienced as involving a loss of status, authority, and control. He becomes less central and less powerful as parts of his previous role as initiator move from the function to the business manager. The ultimate example of

this is the increased confrontation of functional managers by their functional subordinates, who are now also members of a business team that provides the legitimate need and social support for such upward initiation and confrontation. For managers who have been in relative control of their domain, this is a rude awakening that can create initial hostility and a quite predictable resistance to a matrix form of management.

As a matrix organization matures, however, functional managers adapt to these changes, and they find the role not only tolerable but highly challenging. Even though in matrix organizations it is the business managers who tend to control the money that buys human resources, functional managers must engage in very complex people planning.

They must balance the needs of the different product lines and/or businesses in the organization, they must anticipate training needs, and they must handle union negotiations if layoffs or promotions are involved. They must also administer support staff (supervisors, managers, secretaries, clerks) and accompanying resources (equipment, facilities, space, maintenance), many of which must be shared with the business units.

To accomplish this with any degree of efficiency, functional managers must balance workloads to avoid excessive peaks and valleys in resources. They must do this in any organization, but in a matrix, business managers act with relative autonomy, and functional managers cannot be effective by holding to some central plan prepared primarily for budget purposes. It is imperative that they know the producer- and business-workload projections and changes well in advance; that they negotiate constantly with these managers to speed up, slow down, schedule, plan, and replan the pace and amount of their activities. In other words, they must go to the business unit managers and be *proactive* if they are to manage their functions effectively.

Some comments from managers in two matrix organizations serve to underscore this need for proactive behavior:

> Functional managers have to learn that they're losing some of their authority to product units, and they will have to take direction from the product bosses. They have to segment their work

along product lines, not functional lines, and they must be willing to establish communication channels with product units.

Functional managers have to learn to become more aware of the impact of their decisions on our product market success and become more responsive to the product organization needs that reflect the market. They have to remove their blinders and look around them while they turn the crank.

One functional manager concurred heartily:

We have to learn to serve as well as dictate; become more customer-oriented—where the customer is the product line. We must realize that the function's mission is to perform the function and prove that the function is the best available. There is a burden of proof in matrix that did not exist in functional organization.

The Business Manager

As we have pointed out, in a matrix organization various functional specialists are brought together in temporary (project) or permanent (business or product) groupings. These groups are led by product or business managers who have the responsibility for ensuring that the efforts of functional members of the team are integrated in the interest of the project or business. In this regard they have the same responsibilities as a general executive; their objective is project accomplishment or the long-term profitability of a business.

However, in a matrix organization these business managers do not have the same undivided authority as does the general executive. People on the team do not report to them exclusively since many also report to a functional manager. Thus, as many such managers have complained, "We have all the responsibility and little of the required authority."

Top leaders in traditional organizations have the benefit of instant legitimacy because people understand that reporting to them means being responsive to their needs. This is because their boss not only has formal title and status, but influences their performance evaluation, their pay,

their advancement, and, in the long run, their careers. In a matrix organization these sources of authority are shared with functional managers, thus lessening, in the eyes of team members, the power of the project or business manager. He does not unilaterally decide. He manages the decision process so that differences are aired and tradeoffs made in the interest of the whole. Thus he is left with the arduous task of influencing with limited formal authority. He must use his knowledge, competence, relationships, force of personality, and skills in group management to get people to do what is necessary to the success of the project or business.

This role of the matrix organization (business) boss creates both real and imagined demands for new behaviors that can be particularly anxiety producing for individuals who face the job for the first time. The matrix (business) manager must rely more heavily on his personal qualities, on his ability to persuade through knowledge about a program, business, or function. He must use communication and relationships to influence and move things along. His skills in managing meetings, in bringing out divergent points of view and, it is to be hoped, working through to a consensus are taxed more than the skills of general managers in conventional organizations.

Thus, for individuals who face these demands for the first time, the world is quite different. They can easily experience frustration, doubt, and loss of confidence as they begin to rely on new behaviors to get their job done. They begin to question their competence as they experience what in their eyes is a discrepancy between final and complete responsibility for a program and less certain means of gaining compliance from others. Some individuals learn the required new behaviors; others never do.

Not only does the actual and required change in behavior create a problem for new matrix organization business managers, but so does their own attitude toward the change. In our experience, individuals assigned to this role must first break through their perception of the job as impossible. Individuals who have spent all their time in traditional organizations have firmly implanted in their minds the notion of hierarchy and formal authority as the source of influence and power. They are convinced that the job cannot be done because they have never had to think through how power and influence, in reality, are wielded in the traditional organization. They cling to the myth that the formal power a boss has is what gives him influence.

This myth remains even after they themselves have developed and used other means of gaining influence. The myth about power and influence is often the first barrier that must be broken before the individual can be motivated to address the real demands for new behavior.

In his relations with his peers in both arms of the matrix organization, a business manager needs to assume a posture that blends reason and advocacy, bluster and threats are out. It is through these relations that he obtains the human resources needed to accomplish his goals. He has to expect that a number of these resources will be in short supply and that competing claims will have to be resolved.

In these dialogues the business manager must stand up for his requirements without developing a fatal reputation for overstating them. He must search with his peers for imaginative ways to share scarce resources. He must reveal any developing problems quickly while there is still time for remedial action. These actions do not come easily to managers conditioned in more traditional structures.

Last, in his relations with the various functional specialists represented on his team, the matrix organization business manager must establish a balanced or intermediate orientation. He cannot be seen as biased toward one function. He cannot have an overly long or short time horizon. His capacity to obtain a high-quality decision is dependent on an approach that seeks to integrate the views and orientations of all the various functions. If he shows a bias, team members will begin to distrust his objectivity and his capacity to be a fair arbiter of differences. This distrust can be the seed of a team's destruction.

For many individuals, this is a difficult task. A career spent in one side of the matrix structure creates a bias imperceptible to the individual but quite obvious to others. The need to wear multiple hats believably and equally well creates heavy attitudinal and behavioral demands.

It requires of an individual the capacity to have empathy with people in a number of functional areas and to identify with them while at the same time maintaining a strong personal concept and orientation that guides his own behavior and role performance.

Since the heir to the chief executive office is likely to come from this rank, there is generally a great, though diplomatic, battle going on for supremacy among the shared-subordinate bosses. The statesman's posture is an ingredient essential to success. The appearance of being threatened by sharing subordinates is fatal: This brands the individual as not being top-management material.

Top leadership often uses the matrix structure to let the candidates for the top spar with each other in a constructive arena. The matrix structure is a better form than the pyramid for testing managers' ability to make things happen because of the strength of their personalities, their ability to lead, and the validity of their perceptions rather than because of their superior position in the hierarchy.

The perceptive matrix organization manager is aware that subordinates have other voices to attend to, other masters to please. Orders that seem irrational or unfair can more easily be circumvented under the protection of the other boss, than they can in a single chain of command. More care is therefore given to making clear the logic and importance of a directive.

For senior managers who must share their people with other senior managers, the matrix organization is both a training ground for how to assume the institutional reins and an incentive to go beyond having to share those reins equally with anyone else.

The rule for success in this role is to accept that while it can place contradictory demands on people, it is the best solution to accommodate simultaneous competing demands. Assume that there is no one best way to organize; each alternative has equally important claims, and the correct choice is both—in varying proportions.

2-BOSS MANAGERS

The most obvious challenge built into this matrix organization role is the sometimes conflicting demands of two bosses. For example, a representative from a manufacturing plant on a business team may know that his plant is having profitability problems and that the last thing the plant manager wants is to disrupt ongoing production activities with developmental work such as making samples or experimenting with a new process. Yet, as a business-team member, the plant's representative may see the importance of doing these things immediately to achieve project success.

In this situation the individual in a 2-boss position experiences a great deal of anxiety and stress. These come from the difficulties of weighing the conflicting interests of his function and his project team. Both have legitimate viewpoints. But which is the more important viewpoint from the perspective of the whole organization? This is not an easy question to answer or an easy conflict to resolve. But added to this are the questions of identification and loyalty to the individual's function or business team and the consequences of rejection or even punishment from the side of the matrix organization that perceives it has lost in a given conflict. To compound the problem, even if the plant representative on a project team decides that he needs to go against what he knows is in the interest of his plant, how does he communicate this back to his organization members and convince them of the merits of his views? The same problem would exist if he were to favor his functional orientation and have to persuade the team that sample runs will have to be delayed.

We can see from this description and the earlier discussion that there are problems of dual group membership—new demands for communication, uncertainty about the kinds of commitment that can be made, uncertainties about how to influence other people in the function or team, and uncertainties created by a more generalist orientation not demanded in a conventional functional organization. There are of course differences in the capacity of individuals to deal with ambiguity, but all individuals new to matrix management lack some of the knowledge and the skills needed to navigate through the ambiguities and conflicts generated by a matrix organization.

Remember that this manager is also at the apex of his or her own pyramid—subordinates to this role need not be shared. It is the multiple demands from above and beyond the immediate command that must be managed. But his approach, to be successful, must be no different from that of the top role: Both must pay heed to competing demands, make tradeoffs, and manage the conflicts that cannot be resolved. Any skillful politician knows that alternative sources of power increase one's flexibility. It is the unimaginative 2-boss manager who would trade extra degrees of freedom for finite and singular sources of action.

One operating manual for this role, developed after about a year's experience in a matrix organization, included the following points in a section titled "Practices for Managing Matrix Relationships":

- Lobby actively with relevant 2-boss counterparts and with your matrix bosses to win support before the event.

- Understand the other side's position in order to determine where tradeoffs can be negotiated; understand where your objectives overlap.

- Avoid absolutes.

- Negotiate to win support on key issues that are critical to accomplishing your goals; try to yield only to the less critical points.

- Maintain frequent contact with top leadership to avoid surprises.

- Assume an active leadership role in all committees and use this to educate other matrix players; share information/help interpret.

- Prepare more thoroughly before entering any key negotiation than you would in nonmatrix situations; and use third-party experts more than normally.

- Strike bilateral agreements prior to meetings to disarm potential opponents.

- Emphasize and play on the supportive role that each of your matrix bosses can provide for the other.

- If all else fails:
  a. You can consider escalation (going up another level to the boss-in-common).
  b. You can threaten escalation.
  c. You can escalate.

Before traveling this road, however, consider your timing. How much testing and negotiating should be done before calling for senior support? Does the top leadership want to be involved? When will they support and encourage your approach? Does escalation represent failure?

This kind of advice relies on managerial behavior, not on organization structure, for success. It sees personal style and influence as more important than power derived from either position or specialized knowledge. Success flows from facilitating decisions more than it does from making them. To remain flexible in this managerial role, it suggests, the manager must minimize the formal elements; move from fixture to actor, from bureaucracy to process.

The role problems of the 2-boss manager can of course become manageable in a mature matrix organization. This happens primarily because for the most part the functional and business managers learn to avoid making irreconcilable demands of their shared subordinates. This will still happen on occasion, however, even in a smoothly functioning matrix organization. In a familiar instance, the 2-boss manager may be directed to be in two places at the same time.

In addition to a balanced structure and shared roles, a matrix organization should have mechanisms for processing information along overlapping dimensions simultaneously. In a product-area matrix organization, a way of dealing with such situations is to establish the norm that the 2-boss individual is expected, and even directed, to convene a meeting between his two bosses to resolve any such conflict. The 2-boss manager is reprimanded only if he suffers such a conflict in silence.

Beyond handling such occasional problems, the 2-boss manager learns in a mature matrix organization that his role gives him a degree of influence not usually experienced at his level in a conventional organization. He not infrequently finds himself striking a balance in a discussion with his two bosses over some point of conflict. If he knows his facts and expresses his judgment on the merits of the particular issue, he often finds it is taken very seriously. This is the heart of training for general management.

This is exactly how the matrix organization is intended to work—with decisions being made at a level where the relevant information is concentrated and where time is available for a thorough airing of the options. In such a framework a higher percentage of decisions will, in fact, be given careful attention and decided on for their unique merits rather than in terms of a single orientation.

In reviewing the general characteristics of the mature matrix organization, we have emphasized the quality of flexibility. By looking in some detail at the four roles unique to the matrix we have discovered where that flexibility comes from— from the individuals in key roles who have been challenged by the matrix structure to respond to each new situation in a fresh and flexible fashion. This constant pressure for fresh thinking and for learning in the mature matrix organization has, in fact, seemed to greatly increase the organization's productivity, especially at middle-management levels. This may be fine for the organization, but how about the individuals as they initially face new and demanding role expectations? Is this a problem or an opportunity? In most cases it is probably both.

THE FUTURE OF THE MATURE MATRIX

A matrix organization includes matrix behavior, matrix systems, and a matrix culture, as well as a matrix structure. After years of working with a matrix, some organizations find that they no longer need the contradictory architecture of the matrix structure to accomplish their goals. Instead, they revert to the simpler pyramid for their structural form, while at the same time retaining the dual or multiple perspective in their managerial behavior, in their information processing, and in the culture of their firms.

This interpretation suggests that the matrix organization is not likely to become the dominant feature in the *structure* of American organizations. Its utility is more likely to be in helping organizations become more flexible in their responses to environmental pressures. Structures are intended to channel people's behavior in desired ways. Like laws, they are strongest when they are not invoked or tested. To the extent that managers behave effectively, they have little need to bump up against formal structures and reporting walls. In traditional pyramids, managers were always bumping against something—either the structure was centralized, and there wasn't enough freedom, or it was decentralized, and there wasn't enough control.

Organizations with mature matrix structures therefore appear to follow one of two paths, and the extent to which the structural framework survives depends on the path an organization takes. One is to maintain dual command, shared use of human resources, and an enriched information processing capacity. The other is to maintain matrix behavior, matrix systems, and a matrix style or culture, but without using the matrix's structural form. Some organizations tear down the matrix entirely and revert to the traditional forms, practices, and managerial behavior of the pyramid.

The distinction between a pathological breakdown and an evolutionary rotation, where the matrix is a transitional form, is a matter of interpretation. As we observe the change in these organizations we may ask, was the matrix thrown out or did the firm grow beyond it? The distinction is more than academic. As long as the environmental pressures that initially propelled an organization into a matrix structure remain, the original inadequacies of the pyramid form will reappear if the matrix structure is actually abandoned. Our observations suggest that this would be fairly evident in three to six months and painfully obvious within one to one and a half years.

Because the structural element of the matrix is so fiendishly difficult to many, we observe organizations trying to shed the form while maintaining the substance. Our diagnosis is that it can be done successfully only where appropriate matrix behavior is so internalized by all significant members that no one notices the structural shift. Even then, however, we anticipate that through the years the structural imbalances will increase.

Where We Stand on the Learning Curve

Not too many years ago few managers in our classrooms had heard of matrix organization, and to-day nearly half of them raise their hands when asked whether they work in a matrix organization. Objectively, this self-reporting is inaccurate. What is relevant, however, is the perception itself. Like Molière's gentleman who was surprised to learn that he had been speaking prose all his life, many managers find that they have been "matrixing" all along. The word is jargon, but the grammar connotes people's behavior more than the form of their organization. The unrealistically high self-reporting also demonstrates an increasing comfort and familiarity with the idea among a very large body of executives.

Our major purposes have been to broaden traditional treatments of the matrix structure by demonstrating its applicability in diverse settings and by suggesting ways to change a seemingly radical conception into a familiar and legitimate design. The matrix structure seems to have spread despite itself. It is complex and difficult; it requires human flexibility in order to provide organizational flexibility. But the reverse is also true. For these reasons, we believe, many managers shied away. The academic literature, until now, has limited the utility of the matrix structure to high-technology project organizations. We have shown how both in organization theory and in application, the matrix structure has a much broader applicability. Behavioral descriptions were replete with words like "tension," "conflict," and "confusion." For many it was not pleasant, but it seemed to improve performance. Success gave it legitimacy, and as the concept spread, familiarity seemed to reduce the resistance.

Matrix structure gained acceptance in the space age of the late 1960s. In fact, for a while in the early 1970s it almost seemed to be a fad. Organizations that should never have used it experimented with the form. It was in danger of becoming another hot item from the behavioral science grab bag for business. When this occurred, the results were usually disastrous, thus fueling the sense that if an organization played with the matrix structure it might easily get burned. Despite many misadventures, however, the matrix structure gained respectability. What was necessary was made desirable.

More organizations are feeling the pressure to respond to two or more critical aspects of their businesses simultaneously—that is, to consider and organize by function *and* by product, by service *and* by market area at the same time. There is also increasing pressure to improve information processing capacity, and recent technological advances make multiple matrix systems feasible. Last, it is clear that there is an increased sense of the scarcity of all resources and hence pressures for achieving economies of scale. As we described, these were the necessary and sufficient conditions for the emergence of matrix organizations in the first place. Because these conditions are increasingly prevalent, we feel that more organizations will be forced to consider the matrix organizational form.

Each organization that turns to the matrix structure has a larger and more varied number of predecessors that have charted the way. Despite our belief that matrix structures must be grown from within, the examples of wider applicability must nevertheless suggest that we are dealing less and less with an experiment and more and more with a mature formulation in organization design. Familiarity, here, reduces fear. As more organizations travel up the matrix structure learning curve, the curve itself becomes an easier one to climb. Similarly, as more managers gain experience operating in matrix organizations they are bound to spread this experience as some of them move into other organizations on their career journeys.

When pioneers experiment with new forms of organization, the costs are high and there are usually many casualties. In the case of the matrix structure, this has been true for both organizations and individuals. As the matrix has become a more familiar alternative, however, the costs and pressures have been reduced. Today, we believe that the concept is no longer a radical one, the understanding of the design is widespread, and the economic and social benefits have increased.

People in the Middle Ages had a very clear view of the world order. Galileo changed that. Newton changed the view of universal order once more, and Einstein did too in a later age. In each period there was certainty of the logic and correctness of the structure of the universe. And each period lasted until a new formulation posed a previously unthinkable question. After varying periods of resistance or adjustment, people become comfortable with the new formulation and in each instance assume it to be the final word.

The organization of large numbers of people to accomplish uncertain, complex, and interdependent tasks is currently nowhere as susceptible to the same exactness in calculation as the physical world. And there are those who would say that to compare the world of physics and the world of organizations is to compare the sacred with the profane. But the process of acceptability and then increased applicability of new formulations is similar, even if rather more humble. We believe, therefore, that in the future matrix organizations will become almost commonplace and that managers will speak less of the difficulties of the matrix structure and will take more of its advantages almost for granted.

SELECTED BIBLIOGRAPHY

Chris Argyris's "Today's Problems with Tomorrow's Organizations" (*The Journal of Management Studies*, February 1967, pp. 31–55) is an empirical study of nine British matrix organizations. The study is positive about the structure, but demonstrates how implementation has been unsuccessful because of traditional management behavioral styles. Arthur G. Butler's "Project Management: A Study in Organizational Conflict" (*Academy of Management Journal*, March 1973, pp. 84–101) contains an excellent review of the project management literature and deals extensively with the conflict faced by professionals involved in project work. David I. Cleland and William R. King's *Systems Analysis and Project Management* (McGraw-Hill, 1968) is one of the best and most thorough books available that explains project management and locates it in the larger setting of systems and organization theory. And Stanley M. Davis's "Two Models of Organization: Unity of Command versus Balance of Power" (*Sloan Management Review*, Fall 1974, pp. 29–40) spells out the basic theories and how they evolved in both domestic and international organizations.

Jay R. Galbraith's "Matrix Organization Design" (*Business Horizons*, February 1971, pp. 29–40) contains a fictitious case through which the author describes the decisions involved in adding a product orientation to a functional organization until an appropriate balance is reached. The article delimits the boundaries of matrix organization. William C. Goggin's "How the Multidimensional Structure Works at Dow-Corning" (*Harvard Business Review*, January-February 1974, pp. 54–65) is a case description of how Dow-Corning expanded a matrix form of organization into one that added an area dimension to the product and function areas plus a fourth dimension to consider organizational evolution. And Sherman K. Grinnell and Howard P. Apple's "When Two Bosses Are Better Than One" (*Ma-*

chine Design, January 9, 1975, pp. 84–87) includes brief but practical guidelines on when to use a matrix organization and how to make it work.

Leonard R. Sayles' recent article in *Organizational Dynamics*, "Matrix Management: The Structure with a Future" (Autumn 1976, pp. 2–18), expresses a viewpoint similar to our own and has developed a suggestive typology that encompasses five different types of matrix structures.

Managing Organizations over Time— Adapting and Implementing

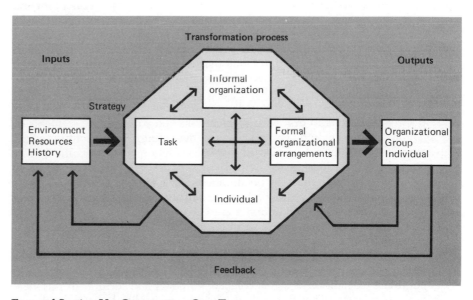

Focus of Section V—Organizations Over Time

INTRODUCTION AND OVERVIEW

The past four sections have focused on organizations as behavioral systems. We have argued that the basic components of these systems are individuals, the informal organization, organizational arrangements, and the inherent task requirements. We have stated that behavior in organizations is a result of the interactions between these interdependent components and that effective performance is a function of achieving balance or consistency between each of these components. This model is useful because it helps integrate and synthesize the literature on organizations and because it provides a systematic framework and set of concepts for diagnosing and evaluating organizations. Although this model does not capture the full complexity of organizations, it is useful for those interested in understanding and managing organizations.

The core operating hypothesis of the congruence model is based on functional logic. The individuals and the formal and informal organizations must be internally consistent; they must facilitate task accomplishment. Task requirements, in turn, must be based on the firm's strategy. Once strategy and tactics have been clarified, it is management's function to define the task requirements, then choose the appropriate individual and formal structure, and facilitate appropriate informal dynamics. Taken to an extreme, this functional analysis treats organizations as machines. From this perspective, managers can be seen as engineers guided by a clear set of objectives—engineers who steer the organization by clever and internally consistent choices of individuals, structures, and central systems.

We know, however, that the managerial role is not that unambiguous; that managers must accomplish their objectives with and through sometimes recalcitrant and contentious individuals and groups; and that managers must continually make choices between competing and conflicting objectives. We know that technical skills are necessary but not sufficient to carry out managerial responsibilities. Taken together the readings in this section argue that technical skills must be bolstered with political as well as artistic skills. Managers must develop a range of diverse skills; they must be engineers, politicians, and artists.

Organizations are messy, underdefined systems. As organizations grow they must develop specialized units to deal with specific tasks and with specific segments of the organization's task environment, for example, marketing or manufacturing areas. This specialization is, in turn, associated with the evolution of idiosyncratic norms, values, languages, and local goals. This division of labor is the basic source of conflict, complexity, and chaos in organizations. Organizations must be seen as conflictive or mixed-motive settings where participants have reasons to cooperate and to compete, to be open and honest and to be opportunistic.

If organizations are mixed-motive settings, we must extend our image of organizations as machines under managerial control to an image of organizations as political systems where managers take different, often competing, positions. From this political point of view, organizational goals and strategies are problematic and under continual redefinition as actors compete for power and control. In this view organizations are organized anarchy; they are driven by coalitions between cliques of unequal influence. Decisions are an outcome of compromise, accommodation, and bargaining between multiple actors, each with distinct bases of power. Objectives in organizations may be inconsistent because the organization copes with conflict through sequential attention to alternative objectives.

This political point of view forces managers to develop an alternative range of skills beyond those of an engineer. Managers must develop those conceptual skills that help them diagnose this complicated reality and those interpersonal/intergroup skills necessary to accomplish objectives with and through others who do not necessarily share values and objectives. Part V.A of this section presents readings that introduce several concepts and approaches for understanding and managing organizations as political systems.

Even with our consideration of political dynamics, our focus has been on achieving consistency at a point in time; we have taken a relatively static or "snapshot" approach to organizations. We have asked the analyst to choose or facilitate the appropriate individuals, structure, control system and informal dynamics to get the work done. Following the logic of the congruence model, however, we know that if any component of the organization changes (whether due to internal or external factors), then the other components of the organization must make appropriate shifts. If the strategy of the unit changes due to contextual conditions or if the nature of the unit's tasks change because of changes in demand or technology, then the nature of the organization must also evolve to reestablish congruence. Parts V.B and V.C discuss the notion of organizing over time and methods to effectively implement change.

Organizations have an inherent bias away from uncertainty and towards stability and bureaucratization. This evolutionary bias, due to contextual and inherent organizational processes, has profound benefits and costs. The entrepreneurial firm influenced by its customers and competition must eventually decide on a dominant design for its product line; instead of making many variations on a theme, these firms will decide on a relatively standard product or formulation (for instance, the Model T Ford). To take advantage of this dominant design, organizations will decrease their investment in product changes and increase their investment in process (production) changes. The previously entrepreneurial firm will learn better and more effective methods and procedures to produce a relatively standardized product; it becomes more and more like a bureaucracy.

These changes may occur gradually or rapidly depending on competitive conditions. Whatever the rate of change, the mature organization or productive unit at time 2 must be systematically different than the entrepreneurial firm at time 1 (see Galbraith and Nathanson, Reading 32). These changes or transitions do not just happen; most entrepreneurial firms or venture units fail to make these transitions. To be successful, management must actively manage these transitions; managers must shift the nature of the structure, controls, rewards, and informal organizations as the unit learns more about its task and its task environment.

This organizational learning and the shift towards more formalized systems and processes is a double-edged sword. While it is vital for short-run competitive reasons (that is, costs are reduced and benefits accrue due to division of labor and economies of scale), there are also profound dysfunctional consequences. As organizations evolve towards more formalized mature business units, there is increasing emphasis on narrow-focused problem solving and adaptation of rules and regulations, increased commitment to and inertia supporting the status quo, and a narrowing of environmental scanning. The organization's capacity to learn and adapt becomes increasingly stunted. If contextual conditions change, then today's success will sow the seeds of tomorrow's failure.

Managers must develop the conceptual skills to predict and deal with these inherent organizational dilemmas. Today's appropriate structure will be tomorrow's

Figure V-1.   Organizing: Balancing Stability and Change

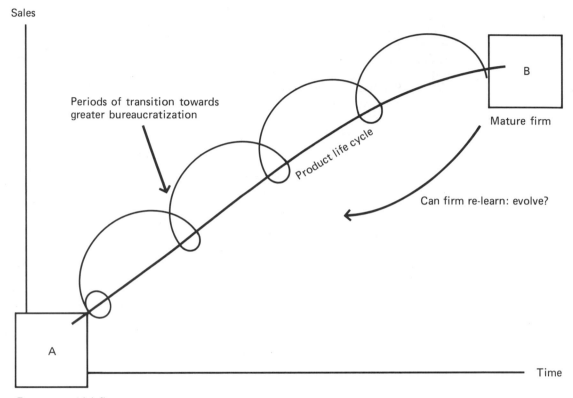

Sales

Periods of transition towards
greater bureaucratization

Product life cycle

Mature firm

B

Can firm re-learn: evolve?

A

Time

Entrepreneurial firm

dysfunctional structure; commitment will generate today's motivation but tomorrow's resistance to change. Managers must see to it that their organizations retain the ability to learn and unlearn; to generate commitment for yet be able to discard past decisions and processes; and to structure and unstructure, depending on contextual conditions. To be successful over time, organizations must balance stability with change, congruence with incongruence; they must be able to make transitions towards greater formalization as well as towards greater informality.

Managers must be able to deal with these inherent organizational paradoxes and dilemmas in a creative fashion. A vital managerial role is to take paradoxical situations and create and implement synergistic solutions over time. From this perspective, the general manager's role is not unlike that of an artist.

In summary, we argue that the manager's role is that of shaping, influencing, and motivating the behavior of relatively autonomous and recalcitrant individuals over time. Given the inherent complexity of organizations and their requirement to produce a competitive product, managers need a range of complementary skills. The engineer's skills are required to choose the right structure, reward systems, and so forth; the politician's skills are required to get things done in mixed-motive settings; and the artist's skills are required to handle the paradoxes and dilemmas faced by managers as their organizations face inconsistent objectives. Finally, we argue that managers must make systematic diagnoses of their organizations. Managers use the diagnoses to make a range of explicit decisions. They must make major, relatively infrequent decisions, such as what kind of organization (product, function, matrix) should be built; incremental decisions that fine-tune those major decisions (for instance, tailoring the reward systems to better meet task or individual requirements); and a range of mundane decisions (what meetings to attend, where to sit at meetings). We argue that these decisions must be congruent. When they make any of these decisions, managers must keep before them the image of the present and future organization.

THE READINGS IN SECTION V

The readings in this section are divided into three parts. Part V.A (Readings 28–30) presents several readings on power and politics and their implications in organizations. In Reading 28, Tushman and Nadler give a general approach to organizations as political systems. They argue that politics is a natural outcome in settings where there are different preference orderings and where there are scarce resources. In Reading 29, Salancik and Pfeffer discuss the questions of power, control, and legitimation in organizations and give insight on managing strategic contingencies as a basis for power. In Reading 30, Walton discusses the lack of diffusion of work redesign programs in several organizations. His discussion elaborates upon and enhances our understanding of the conditions under which political behavior is most likely to be observed.

Part V.B (Readings 31 and 32) focuses on organizing. Greiner's seminal article, Reading 31, discusses organizational revolutions and evolutions. He suggests that factors in today's success are the seeds of tomorrow's revolutions. In Reading 32, Galbraith and Nathanson describe their concept of consistency and then discuss the evolution of productive units over time and the different patterns of organization that are required at different points in time.

Part V.C (Readings 33–35) focuses on implementation. In Reading 33, Nadler suggests that successful change management must attend to several strategic issues: motivating change, controlling the change process, and shaping political behavior. Nadler points out several implications that flow from our congruence model. In Reading 34, Kotter and Schlesinger investigate different strategies for implementing change. They base their strategies on an analysis of the sources of resistance to change as well as key situational variables. Finally, Peters, in his innovative article (Reading 35), argues that perhaps too much attention has been paid to big decisions as a way of moving organizations and too little to the day-to-day behavior of managers. Peters suggests that managers should explicitly attempt to shape and motivate behavior by attending to symbols, patterns of concrete behavior, and managing settings.

V.A
The Informal Organization—
Political Concepts

28
Implications of political models of organizational behavior

Michael L. Tushman
and David A. Nadler

In the early 1970's, a leading food products manufacturer experimented by creating a new plant designed along lines of participative management. By mid 1977, reports indicated that the experiment was a success. Employee satisfaction was high, turnover was low, and the new system was credited with economic savings of approximately $1 million a year as compared to traditional factories. At the same time, however, reports filtering out from the company indicate that many of the key managers involved in the experiment have now left the company and that the experimental plant might be switched to a traditional system. As one ex-employee reported, "economically it was a success, but it became a power struggle. It was too threatening to too many people."
—From *Business Week*, March 28, 1977. Reprinted by permission of the publisher.

Source: From Michael L. Tushman and David A. Nadler, "Implications of political models of organizational behavior," in R. Miles, *Resource Book in Macro Organizational Behavior*, 1980, pp. 177–190. Reprinted by permission.

A large financial institution had experienced a long period of growth and prosperity under the leadership of a hard-driving CEO. After 13 years, the CEO retired. During the next 6 years, the firm went through 5 different CEO's. The senior staff, who advised the Board of Directors on executive selection, were reported to have chosen individuals of limited power and/or ability. Organizational performance deteriorated. Finally, a CEO was brought in who was so universally perceived as lacking competence that the senior staff asked the Board to remove him. Only then was a concerted search made for a competent and powerful new CEO. By then, however, the organization had lost much ground.

These two episodes of organizational life are not atypical. As one observes the various events that occur within organizations, the frequency of events that seem to defy rationality is overwhelming. More importantly, many of the existing models of organization and management seem unable to explain why these events occur.

Recent work by those who study organizational behavior indicates that much of the seemingly "irrational" behavior can in fact be understood by making use of political models to analyze organizations. This paper builds on the growing work in the area of political approaches to organizations and is an attempt to define the political perspective in terms that may provide managers with insights into the actual workings of organizations. This will be done by examining several issues. First, the political perspective will be defined in contrast to existing views of organizations. Second, some emerging models of political processes in organizations will be presented as a complement to existing models of organizational behavior (such as Nadler and Tushman, 1977). Third, political models will be used as a basis for identifying some of the dynamics of managerial power and behavior within a political context.

A COMPLEMENTARY ORGANIZING PERSPECTIVE: A POLITICAL PERSPECTIVE ON ORGANIZATIONS

Rational Actor Approach

Many of the existing approaches to understanding organizational behavior implicitly build on rational models of behavior. From this point of view, the organization is seen as a system within which individuals and groups will act in internally consistent ways to reach explicit objectives. Thus, organizational structures and processes are deliberately planned and coordinated for the most efficient realization of explicit objectives.

A rational actor model takes dysfunctional behavior into account yet tends to assign these departures to either ignorance, miscalculation, or managerial error. Thus, inconsistent behaviors can be diagnosed, alternative interventions can be considered, and the best intervention selected. Individual organizational elements are subject to planned intervention, while the development of the organization as a whole is also regarded as subject to planned direction. The rational actor model views change as the rational adaptation by the organization to feedback from its environ-

ment. The role defined for the manager implied from the rational actor model follows the prescriptions of classical management theory: plan, organize, coordinate, and control based on clearly articulated and systematically derived objectives.

Organizational Politics Approach

As the examples cited above suggest, the rational actor approach often fails to predict or explain important aspects of organizational life. Frequently, individuals, groups, and organizations do not act in internally consistent ways. Public or explicit goals often have little relation to what actually brings about behavior. The resulting patterns of behavior are therefore often completely different than that which utility maximizing models would predict.

An interesting and dramatic example of the failure of the rational model is presented in Allison's (1971) book in which he examines the various decisions and events that were involved in the 1962 Cuban Missile Crisis. Allison reconstructs the events that led up to the crisis, and attempts to explain these events using several different models. His analysis indicates that the rational actor model fails to explain many of the critical incidents, and leaves unexplained questions like "why did the Russians put in the missiles," "why did Kennedy choose the embargo as a response," and "why did the Russians remove the missiles."

It is only when Allison develops a model which he labels as the political model that he is able to explain much of what occurred. The political model views behavior as the *result* of conflicts between different interest groups as opposed to a calculated plan to secure the State's interests. For example, the decision of the Russians to put missiles in Cuba makes most sense in light of the internal conflicts between the Russians' land forces and the Russian missile command over scarce resources.

Some Basic Concepts

What then is the political perspective? It is basically an orientation towards organizations as systems characterized by conflict, value dissensus, and bargaining. Some definitions are needed. *Politics* as referred to here indicates the structure and process of the use of authority and power to effect definitions of goals, directions, and other major parameters of the organization (Wamsley and Zald, 1973). The political perspective, therefore, emphasizes the view that a range of decisions in organizations are not made in a rational or formal way, but rather through compromise, accommodation, and bargaining. This occurs because different groups within the organization (subunits) have different preferences for outcomes and behave in ways that will enable them to realize their desired outcomes. Implicit in this conception of politics is the issue of *conflict*. Conflict (where one group seeks to advance its own interests at the expense of another group) arises in organizations when interdependent subunits either have inconsistent goals, have differing perceptions on how to reach a commonly held goal, or when they must share scarce resources (March and Simon, 1958; Schmidt and Kochan, 1972; Pfeffer, 1977).

Obviously, if one talks of political behavior, the question of *power* must also be considered. While many definitions exist, several converge on the notion that power is the potential (or capacity) of an actor to influence the behavior of another actor in a particular issue area (Crozier, 1973; Katz and Kahn, 1966).

The political perspective therefore views organizations as sets of groups or subunits which exercise different amounts of power and who are potentially in conflict with each other to obtain scarce resources and realize locally valued outcomes. The behavior of organizations (e.g. decision making, profit, innovation) is the result of these political processes operating inside the organization.

POLITICAL MODELS OF ORGANIZATIONS

The Need for Models

Having been sensitized to the political nature of organizations, most would agree that political behavior occurs and that being aware of the political nature of organizations could be helpful in understanding organizational behavior. On the other hand, the mere awareness of the political nature of organizations may not, in itself, be enough. Political behavior, as other phenomena, abound in organizations and seem to occur in random or unpredictable ways. For the manager to begin to function effectively within a political environment, he or she must have tools with which to analyze that environment. What this implies is the need for models of organizations as political systems that can aid the manager in understanding the regularities of political behavior, to diagnose the nature of political systems, and to aid in the formulation of managerial action.

Two recent models seem to provide some useful guides for the manager. The first, a network approach, provides a framework for looking at entire organizations as politically functioning systems. The second, based on intergroup conflict concepts, gives some idea as to how different groups within networks relate to each other.

A Network Model

A number of political scientists and sociologists have argued for the value of looking at communities and organizations as networks of individuals and groups linked together in various ways. A recent statement of this model by Tichy, Tushman, and Fombrun (1979) provides some useful terms and applies this specifically to the understanding of formal organizations.

Organizations are viewed as networks of individuals who can be linked in three different ways. Individuals can be linked together by information; simple flows of information between two individuals establish a link between them. Second, individuals can be linked by influence; the ability of one individual to induce behavior in another is another form of linkage. Third, individuals can be linked together through affect—positive or negative feeling. For diagnostic purposes, linkages can be identified by asking individuals within an organization whom they normally interact with the most (informational linkages), who they feel influences them the most, or whom they look to for help and guidance (influence linkages), or who they ideally like to interact with (affect linkage). With these pieces of information, it is possible to graphically plot the various relationships among a set of individuals. Such a plot yields what is called a network (see Figure 1) which represents the sum total of relationships (lines) among individuals (represented by the points).

Networks in organizations tend to display certain characteristics or patterns. First, when the network is plotted, there usually emerges sets of points (individuals) that are highly interconnected. These dense areas represent individuals who are collectively related by linkages of information, influence, or affect (see, for instance Schwartz and Jacobson, 1977). They represent critical subunits of the political organization (analogous to the subunits of the formal organization) and are referred to as cliques (Tichy, 1973). Cliques are the basic building blocks of political organizations, much as the formal work group or subunit is seen as the major building block of formal organizations. Within these cliques one can also identify those individuals who have more frequent interactions with their peers (for example, person A in Figure 1). These sociometric stars tend to be more powerful than others in the clique and are a vital point in the organization's influence-information system. These key individuals may or may not have formal status or authority (Tushman, 1977; Pettigrew, 1972).

Over time, one can observe the functioning of cliques. One pattern that has been observed

frequently is the tendency of different cliques to develop cooperative (or collusive) strategies of action. They tend to act in concert around a certain set of issues, activities, or decisions. When a set of cliques group together to take cooperative action, they are called a *coalition*. Coalitions, being sets of cliques, tend to be less stable than cliques (although some may endure over relatively long periods of time). Coalitions tend to develop around specific issues, values, decisions, etc. Thus, the nature and composition of coalitions may change over time as different issues become salient (Baldridge, 1971). For example, a set of cliques that cooperate around an important aspect of strategy may dissolve and reform with different composition around a question of executive succession. Thus, the membership of cliques in coalitions may be multiple and/or overlapping. A simple diagramatic representation of a set of cliques in coalition within a network is presented as Figure 2.

The network model therefore provides the manager with a way of beginning to identify what Tichy et al. (1979) call the "emergent" system as opposed to the formal or "prescribed" structure of the organization. Social networks are, then, a basic tool for identifying the structure of political relationships.

The Political Conflict Model

The network model enables identification of the system and outlines some broad parameters for understanding how the system functions. Another model, however, when combined with the network model provides a clearer picture of how cliques and coalitions relate to each other over time. This model, described by Tushman (1977) will be called the political conflict model, since it focuses on the interactions (typically conflict) among the various subunits of the organization (in the political sense, the various cliques and coalitions).

Drawing on the existing literature on political behavior in organizations, Tushman puts forth a set of propositions which he hypothesizes describe the interaction of subunits (cliques and coalitions) within organizations. These propositions are as follows:

Figure 1. An Example of a Simple Network

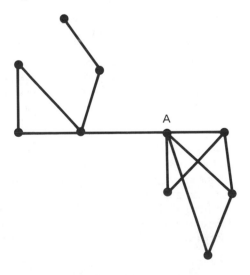

Figure 2.   A Simple Graph of Cliques and Coalitions

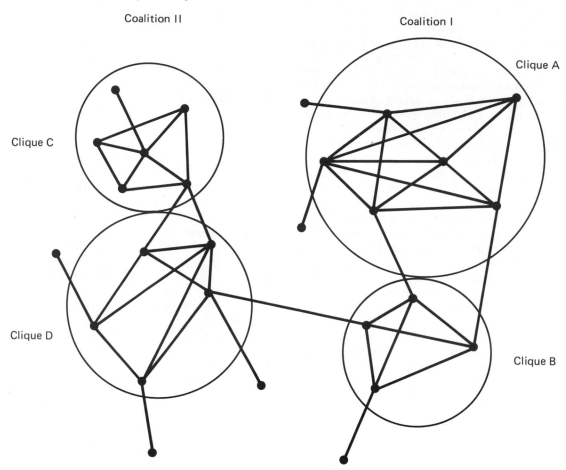

1. To understand the behavior of organizations, one must understand the dynamics and relationships among and between the subunits which make up the organization.
2. Subunits may not be equally powerful over different issues area; subunits which are better able to deal with critical sources of uncertainty in a particular decision making area will be more powerful than other subunits in that issue area.
   a. Since tasks and task environments are potentially unstable, the distribution of power and status within organizations will not be fixed or stable.
3. Subunits will act to decrease their internal dependence on others in order to limit the uncertainty which they must face and to increase their opportunities for growth and survival.
4. The greater the differentiation between subunits, the greater the difficulty of distortion-free communication and the greater the potential for organizational conflict.

These propositions thus present a picture of cliques involved in a constant interaction, with each clique attempting to maximize its own power (by minimizing its dependence on other groups), with shifting relationships, shifting coalitions, and differential power depending upon the realm of activity involved. Subunits that can deal with uncertainty tend to be more powerful and tend to engage in activity to maintain that power (Ritti and Gouldner, 1969).

This view supplements the network model and provides at least an initial picture of how the different components of the network interact with each other over time.

THE MANAGER WITHIN THE POLITICAL SYSTEM

The Managerial Role

Given a view of organizations as networks made up of interacting and conflicting groups, the role of the manager, sources of power for managers, and the kinds of tools that managers need must be re-examined. The first concern is to re-examine the aspects of the managerial role in light of political models.

Much of the leadership literature has focused on the relationship between the manager and his or her subordinates (see for example Stogdill, 1974). If, however, the political model has relevance, then one would expect that managers would spend a substantial amount of time outside their subunit developing or maintaining lateral relationships as well as working up the bureaucracy (e.g., persuading their superiors). Studies of what managers (and in particular top managers) actually do provide data in support of the political perspective. Research indicates that middle and upper level managers spend between 35 and 70 percent of their interaction time with subordinates (the higher the level, the less time with subordinates). Thus, a full 30 to 65 percent of their time was spent interacting with peers, professional colleagues, members of other departments, and outsiders (Sayles, 1979). Mintzberg's (1973) research suggests that this extra-unit managerial responsibility may be more important than is usually recognized. Of the ten basic roles Mintzberg argues typify most managerial jobs, only two deal with intra-unit activity.

Besides this dual focus of managerial activity, a number of studies indicate that managerial behavior is phrenetic; characterized by brevity, variety, and fragmentation. In Mintzberg's study, half of the executives' activities lasted nine minutes or less and only a tenth lasted more than an hour. Further, since managers have relatively little control of their pace of work, they are frequently forced to be "proficient at superficiality" (Mintzberg, 1973). To deal with this superficiality and yet attend to intra and extra unit decision making requirements, research emphasizes the importance of the manager's oral communication network. Managers simply do not utilize written or formal media. Oral communication is so heavily utilized in exchanging information, ideas, and live data since it is rapid, timely, and an efficient communication medium (Sayles, 1979; Keegan, 1974; Edstrom and Galbraith, 1977).

The growing mosaic of data on managerial behavior suggests that managers must be sensitive to both internal (supervisor-subordinate) as well as external (peer, cross departmental, extra-organizational) relations. Further, the available data indicates that in order to make sense out of their potentially overwhelming situation and to have the current data to make rapid yet informed decisions, managers must have extensive and well developed oral communication networks throughout the organization. More effective managers will have developed intra-unit *and* extra-unit oral communication networks. The higher up in the organization, the more critical external leadership roles become and the more the manager must be sensitive to his or her oral communication network.

Sources of Managerial Power

If the manager is to function within a network made up of cliques and coalitions, and if a large part of the interaction occurs with individuals other than subordinates, then the issue of managerial power (the capability of influencing the behavior of others) needs to be re-examined (Schein, 1977). French and Raven (1966) in their classic work provide a list of five "bases of power" which have often been applied to the managerial role. French and Raven see the bases of power as being:

1. Reward Power
2. Coercive Power

3. Legitimate Power
4. Referent Power
5. Expert Power

These bases of power continue to be operative within the political environments described above. However, there is a need to build on the French and Raven approach and identify other sources of power which are particularly salient within the context of political systems. Although some work on identifying sources of power has already been done, this list represents an early and probably incomplete conception of the additional bases of managerial power in organizations. Additional bases of power are as follows:

Control over critical resources.   At different points in time, different sets of resources may be critical to an organization's effectiveness. Similarly, different groups within organizations have control over alternative resources. Putting this together, it follows that those groups that control resources that are critical to the organization's functioning will be those that exercise greatest power. This position has been developed by Hickson et al. (1971) and Salancik and Pfeffer (1977) in what they call the strategic contingency model of power within organizations. Several studies have demonstrated the validity of this model. As an example, within a university which was highly dependent upon outside funding (research grants) for a large portion of its operating budget, Salancik and Pfeffer found that knowing which departments brought in what amounts of research funds enabled the prediction of how much power they had in critical decisions. Thus, the power stemming from the control over a resource (for instance, money or information) is contingent on whether that resource is perceived as being critical to the organization.

Avoid routinization.   An important source of power is the absence of routinization. To the extent that a manager's job (or the job of his or her unit) is routinizable or highly predictable, that manager has less power (Ritti and Gouldner, 1969). Sayles and Chandler's (1971) analysis of professionals working for NASA and Crozier's (1964) discussion of maintenance workers each demonstrate power accruing to individuals who work to make their tasks unpredictable yet important to the organization.

Access to powerful others.   In many organizations, one sees individuals and groups who are, on the face of it, not powerful, yet exercising great amounts of power. Newman and Warren (1977) have observed that a basis of power within political systems is access or proximity to others who have power. Individuals tend to perceive that proximity and access lead to transference of some power to the less powerful individual. Thus, those who have their office next to the chief executive, or those who have contact or connections with important others are perceived to have power, when in fact they may not. Obviously, access and proximity also tend to relate to issues of critical resource availability and control (Pettigrew, 1972).

Assessed stature and gaining visibility.   From a political perspective, managers persuade, negotiate, and exercise power they can mobilize. Assuming the manager is able to identify important others, an important constraint on his or her ability to negotiate will be the manager's assessed stature or visibility (i.e. the process of positive impression formation or of developing positive feelings in the perceptions of relevant others). Assessed stature derives from the manager being able to identify what is salient in the other party's perspective, and from demonstrating technical or managerial competence in areas salient to the other party. Sayles (1979) and Pettigrew (1972) emphasize the importance of assessed stature by suggesting that the manager's ability to negotiate and persuade depends directly on his or her assessed stature with significant others in the political network.

Exchange as a source of power.   Newman and Warren (1977) also point out that the ability to influence others often starts when one individual does a favor for another individual. This is consistent with concepts of exchange theory (Blau, 1962) and would indicate that when individuals provide resources, come to the assistance of others, do favors, etc., they set up a state of imbalance and obligation. This is what is frequently called the process of building up credits or points. The existence of such obligations, which can be called on in later time periods, is an additional source of power (Blau, 1963).

Group support.   To the extent that the manager has a cohesive work group, he or she will be better able to attend to inter-organizational issues. Conflict within a manager's work area will use up time, energy, and resources which could otherwise be used in developing inter-organizational linkages. In general, the more a manager has group support, the more he or she will be able to develop inter-organizational power.

The basic idea of this section is that if managerial behavior is embedded in a political network, and if power is an important resource in these systems, then managerial behavior can be facilitated by an awareness of different bases of power. Control of critical resources, avoiding routinization, control over information, access, exchange, assessed stature, visibility, and group support can each be seen as bases of power in organizations which go beyond formal bases of power which the organization gives the manager.

CONCLUSION— MANAGERIAL SKILLS

This paper has sought to emphasize the political nature of organizations and the idea that managerial behavior takes place in settings where struggles over power and control are pervasive and real. The organizational politics model was developed to serve as a counterpoint to the more traditional rational actor models of organizational behavior. It is the basic argument of this paper that the use of both models will provide managers with a perspective on organizations as mixed-motive situations.

The paper has focused on the organizational bases of political behavior and has suggested the following broad implications.

A. Importance of Diagnostic Models

Recent leadership research suggests that the demands on the managerial role are overwhelming. To deal with this complexity, managers need an organizing model to track the political topography, the dominant issues, key values and the flow of information in the system. A network based conceptual model was suggested. This approach focused on the dynamic of cliques, coalitions, and managers as they bargain and negotiate over scarce resources. It was suggested that the use of both the network model along with a general diagnostic model would provide an effective way of organizing organizational complexity.

B. The Importance of the Manager's External Role

If political behavior is an important aspect of organizational life, then managers must attend to organizational issues outside of their work area. To effectively deal with these external issues, managers must develop effective external communication networks. The importance of external information combined with the intensity of the managerial role suggests that managers must rely on well developed oral communication networks. Oral networks are best able to keep the manager current and permit rapid yet informed decision making, and are a source of potential allies throughout the organization. The challenge to the manager is to keep up with his or her oral network as well as to be able to use more formal and analytical informational inputs.

C. Bases of Power

Power is directly related to the manager's ability to produce outcomes consistent with his or her interests. Several bases of power have been discussed here; control of critical resources, control of information, avoiding routinization, access, exchange, assessed stature, visibility, and group support. These bases of power complement those suggested by French and Raven (1966) and indicate power resources beyond that defined by the formal organization.

These implications suggest that in order to be effective, managers must develop several distinct types of skills—analytic and interpersonal. *Analytic skills* are necessary so that the manager can develop models on how the organization and its components actually work (e.g., budget, financial, or inventory system). *Interpersonal skills* are critical if the manager is to be an effective actor within political systems. Decisions hinge on the ability to influence other actors. This influence will be contingent on the manager's power and on his or her ability to gain support, enthusiasm, and commitment from other, possibly indifferent, actors. Thus, more effective managers will have extensive contacts throughout the organization (possible allies and sources of information), and will be able to mobilize these actors for different issue areas. Vital interpersonal skills would include developing peer relations and information networks, carrying out negotiations, resolving conflicts, and developing cohesive teams (Sayles, 1979; Mintzberg, 1973).

In conclusion, the fact that political dynamics are ignored in much of the managerial literature does not detract from their importance. This paper has addressed itself to some aspects of the managerial role given a political perspective. The core idea of the paper is that in order to be successful, a manager must be aware of political constraints and opportunities. Managers can use diagnostic skills, network development, and developing power bases to take a proactive stance in implementing valued objectives. If this political involvement is not proactive, then it will be reactive, as the political behavior of others will act as a constraint on possible behavior and action.

REFERENCES

Allison, G. *Essence of Decision.* Boston: Little, Brown, 1971.

Baldridge, V. *Power and Conflict in the University.* New York: Wiley and Sons, 1971.

Blau, P. M. *Exchange and Power in Social Life.* New York: Wiley, 1967.

Blau, P. M. *The Dynamics of Bureaucracy.* Chicago: University of Chicago Press, 1963.

Crozier, M. "Problem of Power." *Social Research,* 1973, 40–43.

Crozier, M. *The Bureaucratic Phenomenon.* Chicago: University of Chicago Press, 1964.

Edstrom, A. and J. Galbraith. "Transfer of Managers as a Coordination and Control Strategy in Multi-national Organizations." *Administrative Science Quarterly,* 22 (1977), 248–263.

French, J. and B. Raven. "The Bases of Social Power." In Cartwright, D. (ed.) *Studies in Social Power.* Ann Arbor: Institute for Social Research, 1966.

Hickson, D., C. Hinnings, R. Lee, R. Schenck, and J. Pennings. "A Strategic Contingencies Theory of Intra-Organizational Power." *Administrative Science Quarterly,* 16, (1971), 216–229.

Katz, D. and R. Kahn. *The Social Psychology of Organizations.* New York: Wiley, 1966.

Keegan, W. "Multi-National Scanning: A Study of Information Sources Utilized by Executives in Multi-National Companies." *Administrative Science Quarterly,* 19 (1974), 411–421.

March, J. and H. Simon. *Organizations.* New York: Wiley, 1958.

Mintzberg, H. *The Nature of Managerial Work.* New York: Harper & Row, 1973.

Nadler, D. A. and M. L. Tushman. "Diagnostic Model for Organizational Behavior." In Hackman, J. R., E. E. Lawler, and L. W. Porter. *Perspectives on Behavior in Organizations.* New York: McGraw-Hill, 1977, 85–100.

Newman, W. H. and E. K. Warren. *The Process of Management* (Fourth Edition). Englewood Cliffs, N.J.: Prentice-Hall, 1977.

Pettigrew, A. "Information Control as a Power Resource." *Sociology,* 6 (1972), 187–204.

Pettigrew, A. "Towards a Political Theory of Organizational Intervention." *Human Relations,* 28 (1975), 191–208.

Pfeffer, J. "Power and Resource Allocation in Organizations." In Staw, M. B. and G. Salancik (eds.) *New Directions in Organizational Behavior.* Chicago: St. Clair Press, 1977.

Ritti, R. and F. Gouldner. "Professional Pluralism in an Industrial Organization." *Management Science,* 16 (1969), 233–246.

Salancik, G. R. and J. Pfeffer. "Who Gets Power and How They Hold on to it: A Strategic-Contingency Model of Power." *Organizational Dynamics,* 1977, 5 (3), 3–21.

Sayles, L. *Leadership.* New York: McGraw-Hill, 1979.

Sayles, L. and M. Chandler. *Managing Large Systems.* New York: Harper & Row, 1971.

Schein, V. "Individual Power and Political Behavior in Organizations." *Academy of Management Review,* 2 (1977), 64–72.

Schmidt, S. and T. Kochan. "Conflict: Toward Conceptual Clarity." *Administrative Science Quarterly,* 17 (1972), 359–370.

Schwartz, D. and E. Jacobson. "Organizational Communication Network Analysis." *Organizational Behavior and Human Performance,* 18 (1977), 158–174.

Stogdill, R. M. *The Handbook of Leadership*. New York: Free Press, 1974.

Tichy, N. M. "An Analysis of Clique Formation and Structure in Organizations." *Administrative Science Quarterly*, 18 (1973), 194–208.

Tichy, N. M., M. L. Tushman, and C. Fombrun, "Social Network Analysis for Organizations." *Academy of Management Review*, 4 (1979), 507–520.

Tushman, M. L. "A Political Approach to Organizations: A Review and Rationale." *Academy of Management Review*, 2 (1977), 206–216.

Tushman, M.L. "Special Boundary Roles in the Innovation Process." *Administrative Science Quarterly*, 22 (1977), 587–605.

Wamsley, G. and M. Zald. *The Political Economy of Public Organizations*. Lexington: Heath Co., 1973.

29

Who gets power— and how they hold on to it: A strategic-contingency model of power

Gerald R. Salancik
and Jeffrey Pfeffer

Power is held by many people to be a dirty word or, as Warren Bennis has said, "It is the organization's last dirty secret."

This article will argue that traditional "political" power, far from being a dirty business, is, in its most naked form, one of the few mechanisms available for aligning an organization with its own reality. However, institutionalized forms of power—what we prefer to call the cleaner forms of power: authority, legitimization, centralized control, regulations, and the more modern "management information systems"—tend to buffer the organization from reality and obscure the demands of its environment. Most great states and institutions declined, not because they played politics, but because they failed to accommodate to the political realities they faced. Political processes, rather than being mechanisms for unfair and unjust allocations and appointments, tend toward the realistic resolution of conflicts among interests. And power, while it eludes definition, is easy enough to recognize by its consequences—the ability of those who possess power to bring about the outcomes they desire.

The model of power we advance is an elaboration of what has been called strategic-contingency theory, a view that sees power as something that accrues to organizational subunits (individuals, departments) that cope with critical organizational problems. Power is used by subunits, indeed, used by all who have it, to enhance their own survival through control of scarce critical resources, through the placement of allies in key positions, and through the definition of organizational problems and policies. Because of the processes by which power develops and is used, organizations become both more aligned and more misaligned with their environments. This contradiction is the most interesting aspect of organizational power, and one that makes administration one of the most precarious of occupations.

WHAT IS ORGANIZATIONAL POWER?

You can walk into most organizations and ask without fear of being misunderstood, "Which are the powerful groups or people in this organization?" Although many organizational informants may be *unwilling* to tell you, it is unlikely they will be *unable* to tell you. Most people do not require explicit definitions to know what power is.

Power is simply the ability to get things done the way one wants them to be done. For a manager who wants an increased budget to launch a project that he thinks is important, his power is measured by his ability to get that budget. For an executive vice-president who wants to be chairman, his power is evidenced by his advancement toward his goal.

People in organizations not only know what you are talking about when you ask who is influential but they are likely to agree with one another to an amazing extent. Recently, we had a chance to observe this in a regional office of an insurance company. The office had 21 department managers; we asked ten of these managers to rank all 21 according to the influence each one had in the organization. Despite the fact that ranking 21 things is a difficult task, the managers sat down and began arranging the names of their colleagues and themselves in a column. Only one person bothered to ask, "What do you mean by influence?" When told "power," he responded, "Oh," and went on. We compared the rankings of all ten managers and found virtually no disagreement among them in the managers ranked among the top five or the bottom five. Differences in the rankings came from department heads claiming more influence for themselves than their colleagues attributed to them.

Such agreement on those who have influence, and those who do not, was not unique to this insurance company. So far we have studied over 20 very different organizations—universities, research firms, factories, banks, retailers, to name a few. In each one we found individuals able to rate themselves and their peers on a scale of influence or power. We have done this both for specific decisions and for general impact on organizational policies. Their agreement was unusually high, which suggests that distributions of influence exist well enough in everyone's mind to be referred to with ease—and we assume with accuracy.

WHERE DOES ORGANIZATIONAL POWER COME FROM?

Earlier we stated that power helps organizations become aligned with their realities. This hopeful prospect follows from what we have dubbed the strategic-contingencies theory of organizational power. Briefly, those subunits most able to cope with the organization's critical problems and uncertainties acquire power. In its simplest form, the strategic-contingencies theory implies that when an organization faces a number of lawsuits that threaten its existence, the legal department will gain power and influence over organizational decisions. Somehow other organizational interest groups will recognize its critical importance and confer upon it a status and power never before enjoyed. This influence may extend beyond handling legal matters and into decisions about product design, advertising production, and so on. Such extensions undoubtedly would be accompanied by appropriate, or acceptable, verbal justifications. In time, the head of the legal department may become the head of the corporation, just as in times past the vice-president for marketing had become the president when market shares were a worrisome problem and, before him, the chief engineer, who had made the production line run as smooth as silk.

Stated in this way, the strategic-contingencies theory of power paints an appealing picture of power. To the extent that power is determined by the critical uncertainties and problems facing the organization and, in turn, influences decisions in the organization, the organization is aligned with the realities it faces. In short, power facilitates the organization's adaptation to its environment—or its problems.

We can cite many illustrations of how influence derives from a subunit's ability to deal with critical contingencies. Michael Crozier described a French cigarette factory in which the maintenance engineers had a considerable say in the plantwide operation. After some probing he discovered that the group possessed the solution to one of the major problems faced by the company, that of troubleshooting the elaborate, expensive, and irrascible automated machines that kept breaking down and dumbfounding everyone else. It was the one problem that the plant manager could in no way control.

The production workers, while troublesome from time to time, created no insurmountable problems; the manager could reasonably predict their absenteeism or replace them when necessary. Production scheduling was something he could deal with since, by watching inventories and sales, the demand for cigarettes was known long in advance. Changes in demand could be accommodated by slowing down or speeding up the line. Supplies of tobacco and paper were also easily dealt with through stockpiles and advance orders.

The one thing that management could neither control nor accommodate to, however, was the seemingly happenstance breakdowns. And the foremen couldn't instruct the workers what to do when emergencies developed since the maintenance department kept its records of problems and solutions locked up in a cabinet or in its members' heads. The breakdowns were, in truth, a critical source of uncertainty for the organization, and the maintenance engineers were the only ones who could cope with the problem.

The engineers' strategic role in coping with breakdowns afforded them a considerable say on plant decisions. Schedules and production quotas were set in consultation with them. And the plant manager, while formally their boss, accepted their decisions about personnel in their operation. His submission was to his credit, for without their cooperation he would have had an even more difficult time in running the plant.

Ignoring Critical Consequences

In this cigarette factory, sharing influence with the maintenance workers reflected the plant manager's awareness of the critical contingencies. However, when organizational members are not aware of the critical contingencies they face, and

do not share influence accordingly, the failure to do so can create havoc. In one case, an insurance company's regional office was having problems with the performance of one of its departments, the coding department. From the outside, the department looked like a disaster area. The clerks who worked in it were somewhat dissatisfied; their supervisor paid little attention to them, and they resented the hard work. Several other departments were critical of this manager, claiming that she was inconsistent in meeting deadlines. The person most critical was the claims manager. He resented having to wait for work that was handled by her department, claiming that it held up his claims adjusters. Having heard the rumors about dissatisfaction among her subordinates, he attributed the situation to poor supervision. He was second in command in the office and therefore took up the issue with her immediate boss, the head of administrative services. They consulted with the personnel manager and the three of them concluded that the manager needed leadership training to improve her relations with her subordinates. The coding manager objected, saying it was a waste of time, but agreed to give more priority to the claims department's work. Within a week after the training, the results showed that her workers were happier but that the performance of her department had decreased, save for the people serving the claims department.

About this time, we began, quite independently, a study of influence in this organization. We asked the administrative services director to draw up flow charts of how the work of one department moved on to the next department. In the course of the interview, we noticed that the coding department began or interceded in the work flow of most of the other departments and casually mentioned to him, "The coding manager must be very influential." He said "No, not really. Why would you think so?" Before we could reply he recounted the story of her leadership training and the fact that things were worse. We then told him that it seemed obvious that the coding department would be influential from the fact that all the other departments depended on it. It was also clear why productivity had fallen. The coding manager took the training seriously and began spending more time raising her workers' spirits than she did worrying about the problems of all the departments that depended on her. Giving priority to the claims area only exaggerated the problem, for their work was getting done at the expense of the work of the other departments. Eventually the company hired a few more clerks to relieve the pressure in the coding department and performance returned to a more satisfactory level.

Originally we got involved with this insurance company to examine how the influence of each manager evolved from his or her department's handling of critical organizational contingencies. We reasoned that one of the most important contingencies faced by all profit-making organizations was that of generating income. Thus we expected managers would be influential to the extent to which they contributed to this function. Such was the case. The underwriting managers, who wrote the policies that committed the premiums, were the most influential; the claims managers, who kept a lid on the funds flowing out, were a close second. Least influential were the managers of functions unrelated to revenue, such as mailroom and payroll managers. And contrary to what the administrative services manager believed, the third most powerful department head (out of 21) was the woman in charge of the coding function, which consisted of rating, recording, and keeping track of the codes of all policy applications and contracts. Her peers attributed more influence to her than could have been inferred from her place on the organization chart. And it was not surprising, since they all depended on her department. The coding department's records, their accuracy and the speed with which they could be retrieved, affected virtually every other operating department in the insurance office. The underwriters depended on them in getting the contracts straight; the typing department depended on them in preparing the formal contract document; the claims department depended on them in adjusting claims; and accounting depended on them for billing. Unfortunately, the "bosses" were not aware of these dependences, for unlike the cigarette factory, there were no massive breakdowns that made them obvious, while the coding manager, who was a hard-working but quiet person, did little to announce her importance.

The cases of this plant and office illustrate nicely a basic point about the source of power in organizations. The basis for power in an organization derives from the ability of a person or subunit to take or not take actions that are desired by others. The coding manager was seen as influential by those who depended on her department, but not by the people at the top. The engineers were influential because of their role in keeping the plant operating. The two cases differ in these respects: The coding supervisor's source of power was not as widely recognized as that of the maintenance engineers, and she did not use her source of power to influence decisions; the maintenance engineers did. Whether power is used to influence anything is a separate issue. We should not confuse this issue with the fact that power derives from a social situation in which one person has a capacity to do something and another person does not, but wants it done.

POWER SHARING IN ORGANIZATIONS

Power is shared in organizations; and it is shared out of necessity more than out of concern for principles of organizational development or participatory democracy. Power is shared because no one person controls all the desired activities in the organization. While the factory owner may hire people to operate his noisy machines, once hired they have some control over the use of the machinery. And thus they have power over him in the same way he has power over them. Who has more power over whom is a mooter point than that of recognizing the inherent nature of organizing as a sharing of power.

Let's expand on the concept that power derives from the activities desired in an organization. A major way of managing influence in organizations is through the designation of activities. In a bank we studied, we saw this principle in action. This bank was planning to install a computer system for routine credit evaluation. The bank, rather progressive-minded, was concerned that the change would have adverse effects on employees and therefore surveyed their attitudes.

The principal opposition to the new system came, interestingly, not from the employees who performed the routine credit checks, some of whom would be relocated because of the change, but from the manager of the credit department. His reason was quite simple. The manager's primary function was to give official approval to the applications, catch any employee mistakes before giving approval, and arbitrate any difficulties the clerks had in deciding what to do. As a consequence of his role, others in the organization, including his superiors, subordinates, and colleagues, attributed considerable importance to him. He, in turn, for example, could point to the low proportion of credit approvals, compared with other financial institutions, that resulted in bad debts. Now, to his mind, a wretched machine threatened to transfer his role to a computer programmer, a man who knew nothing of finance and who, in addition, had ten years less seniority. The credit manager eventually quit for a position at a smaller firm with lower pay, but one in which he would have more influence than his redefined job would have left him with.

Because power derives from activities rather than individuals, an individual's or subgroup's power is never absolute and derives ultimately from the context of the situation. The amount of power an individual has at any one time depends, not only on the activities he or she controls, but also on the existence of other persons or means by which the activities can be achieved and on those who determine what ends are desired and, hence, on what activities are desired and critical for the organization. One's own power always depends on other people for these two reasons. Other people, or groups or organizations, can determine the definition of what is a critical contingency for the organization and can also undercut the uniqueness of the individual's personal contribution to the critical contingencies of the organization.

Perhaps one can best appreciate how situationally dependent power is by examining how it is distributed. In most societies, power organizes around scarce and critical resources. Rarely does power organize around abundant resources. In the United States, a person doesn't become powerful because he or she can drive a car. There are simply too many others who can drive with equal facility. In certain villages in Mexico, on the other hand, a person with a car is accredited with enormous social status and plays a key role in the community. In addition to scarcity, power is also limited by the need for one's capacities in a social system.

While a racer's ability to drive a car around a 90° turn at 80 mph may be sparsely distributed in a society, it is not likely to lend the driver much power in the society. The ability simply does not play a central role in the activities of the society.

The fact that power revolves around scarce and critical activities, of course, makes the control and organization of those activities a major battleground in struggles for power. Even relatively abundant or trivial resources can become the bases for power if one can organize and control their allocation and the definition of what is critical. Many occupational and professional groups attempt to do just this in modern economies. Lawyers organize themselves into associations, regulate the entrance requirements for novitiates, and then get laws passed specifying situations that require the services of an attorney. Workers had little power in the conduct of industrial affairs until they organized themselves into closed and controlled systems. In recent years, women and blacks have tried to define themselves as important and critical to the social system, using law to reify their status.

In organizations there are obviously opportunities for defining certain activities as more critical than others. Indeed, the growth of managerial thinking to include defining organizational objectives and goals has done much to foster these opportunities. One sure way to liquidate the power of groups in the organization is to define the need for their services out of existence. David Halberstam presents a description of how just such a thing happened to the group of correspondents that evolved around Edward R. Murrow, the brilliant journalist, interviewer, and war correspondent of CBS News. A close friend of CBS chairman and controlling stockholder William S. Paley, Murrow, and the news department he directed, were endowed with freedom to do what they felt was right. He used it to create some of the best documentaries and commentaries ever seen on television. Unfortunately, television became too large, too powerful, and too suspect in the eyes of the federal government that licensed it. It thus became, or at least the top executives believed it had become, too dangerous to have in-depth, probing commentary on the news. Crisp, dry, uneditorializing headliners were considered safer. Murrow was out and Walter Cronkite was in.

The power to define what is critical in an organization is no small power. Moreover, it is the key to understanding why organizations are either aligned with their environments or misaligned. If an organization defines certain activities as critical when in fact they are not critical, given the flow of resources coming into the organization, it is not likely to survive, at least in its present form.

Most organizations manage to evolve a distribution of power and influence that is aligned with the critical realities they face in the environment. The environment, in turn, includes both the internal environment, the shifting situational contexts in which particular decisions get made, and the external environment that it can hope to influence but is unlikely to control.

THE CRITICAL CONTINGENCIES

The critical contingencies facing most organizations derive from the environmental context within which they operate. This determines the available needed resources and thus determines the problems to be dealt with. That power organizes around handling these problems suggests an important mechanism by which organizations keep in tune with their external environments. The strategic-contingencies model implies that subunits that contribute to the critical resources of the organization will gain influence in the organization. Their influence presumably is then used to bend the organization's activities to the contingencies that determine its resources. This idea may strike one as obvious. But its obviousness in no way diminishes its importance. Indeed, despite its obviousness, it escapes the notice of many organizational analysts and managers, who all too frequently think of the organization in terms of a descending pyramid, in which all the departments in one tier hold equal power and status. This presumption denies the reality that departments differ in the contributions they are believed to make to the overall organization's resources, as well as to the fact that some are more equal than others.

Because of the importance of this idea to organizational effectiveness, we decided to examine it carefully in a large midwestern university. A university offers an excellent site for studying power. It is composed of departments with nominally equal power and is administered by a central executive structure much like other bureaucracies. However, at the same time it is a situation in which the departments have clearly defined identities and face diverse external environments. Each department has its own bodies of knowledge, its own institutions, its own sources of prestige and resources. Because the departments operate in different external environments, they are likely to contribute differentially to the resources of the overall organization. Thus a physics department with close ties to NASA may contribute substantially to the funds of the university; and a history department with a renowned historian in residence may contribute to the intellectual credibility or prestige of the whole university. Such variations permit one to examine how these various contributions lead to obtaining power within the university.

We analyzed the influence of 29 university departments throughout an 18-month period in their history. Our chief interest was to determine whether departments that brought more critical resources to the university would be more powerful than departments that contributed fewer or less critical resources.

To identify the critical resources each department contributed, the heads of all departments were interviewed about the importance of seven different resources to the university's success. The seven included undergraduate students (the factor determining size of the state allocations by the university), national prestige, administrative expertise, and so on. The most critical resource was found to be contract and grant monies received by a department's faculty for research or consulting services. At this university, contract and grants contributed somewhat less than 50 percent of the overall budget, with the remainder primarily coming from state appropriations. The importance attributed to contract and grant monies, and the rather minor importance of undergraduate students, was not surprising for this particular university. The university was a major center for graduate education; many of its departments ranked in the top ten of their respective fields. Grant and contract monies were the primary source of discretionary funding available for maintaining these programs of graduate education, and hence for maintaining the university's prestige. The prestige of the university itself was critical both in recruiting able students and attracting top-notch faculty.

From university records it was determined what relative contributions each of the 29 departments made to the various needs of the university (national prestige, outside grants, teaching). Thus, for instance, one department may have contributed to the university by teaching 7 percent of the instructional units, bringing in 2 percent of the outside contracts and grants, and having a national ranking of 20. Another department, on the other hand, may have taught one percent of the instructional units, contributed 12 percent to the grants, and be ranked the third best department in its field within the country.

The question was: Do these different contributions determine the relative power of the departments within the university? Power was measured in several ways; but regardless of how measured, the answer was "Yes." Those three resources together accounted for about 70 percent of the variance in subunit power in the university.

But the most important predictor of departmental power was the department's contribution to the contracts and grants of the university. Sixty percent of the variance in power was due to this one factor, suggesting that the power of departments derived primarily from the dollars they provided for graduate education, the activity believed to be the most important for the organization.

THE IMPACT OF ORGANIZATIONAL POWER ON DECISION MAKING

The measure of power we used in studying this university was an analysis of the responses of the department heads we interviewed. While such perceptions of power might be of interest in their own right, they contribute little to our understanding of how the distribution of power might serve to align an organization with its critical realities. For this we must look to how power actually influences the decisions and policies of organizations.

While it is perhaps not absolutely valid, we can generally gauge the relative importance of a department of an organization by the size of the budget allocated to it relative to other departments. Clearly it is of importance to the administrators of those departments whether they get squeezed in a budget crunch or are given more funds to strike out after new opportunities. And it should also be clear that when those decisions are made and one department can go ahead and try new approaches while another must cut back on the old, then the deployment of the resources of the organization in meeting its problems is most directly affected.

Thus our study of the university led us to ask the following questions: Does power lead to influence in the organization? To answer this question, we found it useful first to ask another one, namely: Why should department heads try to influence organizational decisions to favor their own departments to the exclusion of other departments? While this second question may seem a bit naive to anyone who has witnessed the political realities of organizations, we posed it in a context of research on organizations that sees power as an illegitimate threat to the neater rational authority of modern bureaucracies. In this context, decisions are not believed to be made because of the dirty business of politics but because of the overall goals and purposes of the organization. In a university, one reasonable basis for decision making is the teaching workload of departments and the demands that follow from that workload. We would expect, therefore, that departments with heavy student demands for courses would be able to obtain funds for teaching. Another reasonable basis for decision making is quality. We would expect, for that reason, that departments with esteemed reputations would be able to obtain funds both because their quality suggests they might use such funds effectively and because such funds would allow them to maintain their quality. A rational model of bureaucracy intimates, then, that the organizational decisions taken would favor those who perform the stated purposes of the organization—teaching undergraduates and training professional and scientific talent—well.

The problem with rational models of decision-making, however, is that what is rational to one person may strike another as irrational. For most departments, resources are a question of survival. While teaching undergraduates may seem to be a major goal for some members of the university, developing knowledge may seem so to others; and to still others, advising governments and other institutions about policies may seem to be the crucial business. Everyone has his own idea of the proper priorities in a just world. Thus goals rather than being clearly defined and universally agreed upon are blurred and contested throughout the organization. If such is the case, then the decisions taken on behalf of the organization as a whole are likely to reflect the goals of those who prevail in political contests, namely, those with power in the organization.

Will organizational decisions always reflect the distribution of power in the organization? Probably not. Using power for influence requires a certain expenditure of effort, time, and resources. Prudent and judicious persons are not likely to use their power needlessly or wastefully. And it is likely that power will be used to influence organizational decisions primarily under circumstances that both require and favor its use. We have examined three conditions that are likely to affect the use of power in organizations: scarcity, criticality, and uncertainty. The first suggests that subunits will try to exert influence when the resources of the organization are scarce. If there is an abundance of resources, then a particular department or a particular individual has little need to attempt influence. With little effort, he can get all he wants anyway.

The second condition, criticality, suggests that a subunit will attempt to influence decisions to obtain resources that are critical to its own survival and activities. Criticality implies that one would not waste effort, or risk being labeled obstinate, by fighting over trivial decisions affecting one's operations.

An office manager would probably balk less about a threatened cutback in copying machine usage than about a reduction in typing staff. An advertising department head would probably worry less about losing his lettering artist than his illustrator. Criticality is difficult to define because what is critical depends on people's beliefs about what is critical. Such beliefs may or may not be based on experience and knowledge and may or may not be agreed upon by all. Scarcity, for instance, may itself affect conceptions of criticality. When slack resources drop off, cutbacks have to be made—those "hard decisions," as congressmen and resplendent administrators like to call them. Managers then find themselves scrapping projects they once held dear.

The third condition that we believe affects the use of power is uncertainty: When individuals do not agree about what the organization should do or how to do it, power and other social processes will affect decisions. The reason for this is simply that, if there are no clear-cut criteria available for resolving conflicts of interest, then the only means for resolution is some form of social process, including power, status, social ties, or some arbitrary process like flipping a coin or drawing straws. Under conditions of uncertainty, the powerful manager can argue his case on any grounds and usually win it. Since there is no real consensus, other contestants are not likely to develop counter arguments or amass sufficient opposition. Moreover, because of his power and their need for access to the resources he controls, they are more likely to defer to his arguments.

Although the evidence is slight, we have found that power will influence the allocations of scarce and critical resources. In the analysis of power in the university, for instance, one of the most critical resources needed by departments is the general budget. First granted by the state legislature, the general budget is later allocated to individual departments by the university administration in response to requests from the department heads. Our analysis of the factors that contribute to a department getting more or less of this budget indicated that subunit power was the major predictor, overriding such factors as student demand for courses, national reputations of departments, or even the size of a department's faculty. Moreover, other research has shown that when the general budget has been cut back or held below previous uninflated levels, leading to monies becoming more scarce, budget allocations mirror departmental powers even more closely.

Student enrollment and faculty size, of course, do themselves relate to budget allocations, as we would expect since they determine a department's need for resources, or at least offer visible testimony of needs. But departments are not always able to get what they need by the mere fact of needing them. In one analysis it was found that high-power departments were able to obtain budget without regard to their teaching loads and, in some cases, actually in inverse relation to their teaching loads. In contrast, low-power departments could get increases in budget only when they could justify the increases by a recent growth in teaching load, and then only when it was far in excess of norms for other departments.

General budget is only one form of resource that is allocated to departments. There are others such as special grants for student fellowships or faculty research. These are critical to departments because they affect the ability to attract other resources, such as outstanding faculty or students. We examined how power influenced the allocations of four resources department heads had described as critical and scarce.

When the four resources were arrayed from the most to the least critical and scarce, we found that departmental power best predicted the allocations of the most critical and scarce resources. In other words, the analysis of how power influences organizational allocations leads to this conclusion: Those subunits most likely to survive in times of strife are those that are more critical to the organization. Their importance to the organization gives them power to influence resource allocations that enhance their own survival.

HOW EXTERNAL ENVIRONMENT IMPACTS EXECUTIVE SELECTION

Power not only influences the survival of key groups in an organization, it also influences the selection of individuals to key leadership positions, and by such a process further aligns the organization with its environmental context.

We can illustrate this with a recent study of the selection and tenure of chief administrators in 57 hospitals in Illinois. We assumed that since the critical problems facing the organization would enhance the power of certain groups at the expense of others, then the leaders to emerge should be those most relevant to the context of the hospitals. To assess this we asked each chief administrator about his professional background and how long he had been in office. The replies were then related to the hospitals' funding, ownership, and competitive conditions for patients and staff.

One aspect of a hospital's context is the source of its budget. Some hospitals, for instance, are run much like other businesses. They sell bed space, patient care, and treatment services. They charge fees sufficient both to cover their costs and to provide capital for expansion. The main source of both their operating and capital funds is patient billings. Increasingly, patient billings are paid for, not by patients, but by private insurance companies. Insurers like Blue Cross dominate and represent a potent interest group outside a hospital's control but critical to its income. The insurance companies, in order to limit their own costs, attempt to hold down the fees allowable to hospitals, which they do effectively from their positions on state rate boards. The squeeze on hospitals that results from fees increasing slowly while costs climb rapidly more and more demands the talents of cost accountants or people trained in the technical expertise of hospital administration.

By contrast, other hospitals operate more like social service institutions, either as government healthcare units (Bellevue Hospital in New York City and Cook County Hospital in Chicago, for example) or as charitable institutions. These hospitals obtain a large proportion of their operating and capital funds, not from privately insured patients, but from government subsidies or private donations. Such institutions rather than requiring the talents of a technically efficient administrator are likely to require the savvy of someone who is well integrated into the social and political power structure of the community.

Not surprisingly, the characteristics of administrators predictably reflect the funding context of the hospitals with which they are associated. Those hospitals with larger proportions of their budget obtained from private insurance companies were most likely to have administrators with backgrounds in accounting and least likely to have administrators whose professions were business or medicine. In contrast, those hospitals with larger proportions of their budget derived from private donations and local governments were most likely to have administrators with business or professional backgrounds and least likely to have accountants. The same held for formal training in hospital management. Professional hospital administrators could easily be found in hospitals drawing their incomes from private insurance and rarely in hospitals dependent on donations or legislative appropriations.

As with the selection of administrators, the context of organizations has also been found to affect the removal of executives. The environment, as a source of organizational problems, can make it more or less difficult for executives to demonstrate their value to the organization. In the hospitals we studied, long-term administrators came from hospitals with few problems. They enjoyed amicable and stable relations with their local business and social communities and suffered little competition for funding and staff. The small city hospital director who attended civic and Elks meetings while running the only hospital within a 100-mile radius, for example, had little difficulty holding on to his job. Turnover was highest in hospitals with the most problems, a phenomenon similar to that observed in a study of industrial organizations in which turnover was highest among executives in industries with competitive environments and unstable market conditions. The interesting thing is that instability characterized the industries rather than the individual firms in them. The troublesome conditions in the individual firms were attributed, or rather misattributed, to the executives themselves.

It takes more than problems, however, to terminate a manager's leadership. The problems themselves must be relevant and critical. This is clear from the way in which an administrator's tenure is affected by the status of the hospital's operating budget. Naively we might assume that all administrators would need to show a surplus. Not necessarily so. Again, we must distinguish between those hospitals that depend on private donations for funds and those that do not. Whether an endowed budget shows a surplus or deficit is less important than the hospital's relations with benefactors. On the other hand, with a budget dependent on patient billing, a surplus is almost essential; monies for new equipment or expansion must be drawn from it, and without

them quality care becomes more difficult and patients scarcer. An administrator's tenure reflected just these considerations. For those hospitals dependent upon private donations, the length of an administrator's term depended not at all on the status of the operating budget but was fairly predictable from the hospital's relations with the business community. On the other hand, in hospitals dependent on the operating budget for capital financing, the greater the deficit the shorter was the tenure of the hospital's principal administrators.

CHANGING CONTINGENCIES AND ERODING POWER BASES

The critical contingencies facing the organization may change. When they do, it is reasonable to expect that the power of individuals and subgroups will change in turn. At times the shift can be swift and shattering, as it was recently for powerholders in New York City. A few years ago it was believed that David Rockefeller was one of the ten most powerful people in the city, as tallied by *New York* magazine, which annually sniffs out power for the delectation of its readers. But that was before it was revealed that the city was in financial trouble, before Rockefeller's Chase Manhattan Bank lost some of its own financial luster, and before brother Nelson lost some of his political influence in Washington. Obviously David Rockefeller was no longer as well positioned to help bail the city out. Another loser was an attorney with considerable personal connections to the political and religious leaders of the city. His talents were no longer in much demand. The persons with more influence were the bankers and union pension fund executors who fed money to the city; community leaders who represent blacks and Spanish-Americans, in contrast, witnessed the erosion of their power bases.

One implication of the idea that power shifts with changes in organizational environments is that the dominant coalition will tend to be that group that is most appropriate for the organization's environment, as also will the leaders of an organization. One can observe this historically in the top executives of industrial firms in the

United States. Up until the early 1950s, many top corporations were headed by former production line managers or engineers who gained prominence because of their abilities to cope with the problems of production. Their success, however, only spelled their demise. As production became routinized and mechanized, the problem of most firms became one of selling all those goods they so efficiently produced. Marketing executives were more frequently found in corporate boardrooms. Success outdid itself again, for keeping markets and production steady and stable requires the kind of control that can only come from acquiring competitors and suppliers or the invention of more and more appealing products—ventures that typically require enormous amounts of capital. During the 1960s, financial executives assumed the seats of power. And they, too, will give way to others. Edging over the horizon are legal experts, as regulation and antitrust suits are becoming more and more frequent in the 1970s, suits that had their beginnings in the success of the expansion generated by prior executives. The more distant future, which is likely to be dominated by multinational corporations, may see former secretaries of state and their minions increasingly serving as corporate figureheads.

THE NONADAPTIVE CONSEQUENCES OF ADAPTATION

From what we have said thus far about power aligning the organization with its own realities, an intelligent person might react with a resounding ho-hum, for it all seems too obvious: Those with the ability to get the job done are given the job to do.

However, there are two aspects of power that make it more useful for understanding organizations and their effectiveness. First, the "job" to be done has a way of expanding itself until it becomes less and less clear what the job is. Napoleon began by doing a job for France in the war with Austria and ended up Emperor, convincing many that only he could keep the peace. Hitler began by promising an end to Germany's troubling postwar depression and ended up convinc-

ing more people than is comfortable to remember that he was destined to be the savior of the world. In short, power is a capacity for influence that extends far beyond the original bases that created it. Second, power tends to take on institutionalized forms that enable it to endure well beyond its usefulness to an organization.

There is an important contradiction in what we have observed about organizational power. On the one hand we have said that power derives from the contingencies facing an organization and that when those contingencies change so do the bases for power. On the other hand we have asserted that subunits will tend to use their power to influence organizational decisions in their own favor, particularly when their own survival is threatened by the scarcity of critical resources. The first statement implies that an organization will tend to be aligned with its environment since power will tend to bring to key positions those with capabilities relevant to the context. The second implies that those in power will not give up their positions so easily; they will pursue policies that guarantee their continued domination. In short, change and stability operate through the same mechanism, and, as a result, the organization will never ₋₋ completely in phase with its environment or its needs.

The study of hospital administrators illustrates how leadership can be out of phase with reality. We argued that privately funded hospitals needed trained technical administrators more so than did hospitals funded by donations. The need as we perceived it was matched in most hospitals, but by no means in all. Some organizations did not conform with our predictions. These deviations imply that some administrators were able to maintain their positions independent of their suitability for those positions. By dividing administrators into those with long and short terms of office, one finds that the characteristics of longer-termed administrators were virtually unrelated to the hospital's context. The shorter-termed chiefs on the other hand had characteristics more appropriate for the hospital's problems. For a hospital to have a recently appointed head implies that the previous administrator had been unable to endure by institutionalizing himself.

One obvious feature of hospitals that allowed some administrators to enjoy a long tenure was a hospital's ownership. Administrators were less entrenched when their hospitals were affiliated with and dependent upon larger organizations, such as governments or churches. Private hospitals offered more secure positions for administrators. Like private corporations, they tend to have more diffused ownership, leaving the administrator unopposed as he institutionalizes his reign. Thus he endures, sometimes at the expense of the performance of the organization. Other research has demonstrated that corporations with diffuse ownership have poorer earnings than those in which the control of the manager is checked by a dominant shareholder. Firms that overload their boardrooms with more insiders than are appropriate for their context have also been found to be less profitable.

A word of caution is required about our judgment of "appropriateness." When we argue some capabilities are more appropriate for one context than another, we do so from the perspective of an outsider and on the basis of reasonable assumptions as to the problems the organization will face and the capabilities they will need. The fact that we have been able to predict the distribution of influence and the characteristics of leaders suggests that our reasoning is not incorrect. However, we do not think that all organizations follow the same pattern. The fact that we have not been able to predict outcomes with 100 percent accuracy indicates they do not.

MISTAKING CRITICAL CONTINGENCIES

One thing that allows subunits to retain their power is their ability to name their functions as critical to the organization when they may not be. Consider again our discussion of power in the university. One might wonder why the most critical tasks were defined as graduate education and scholarly research, the effect of which was to lend power to those who brought in grants and contracts. Why not something else? The reason is that the more powerful departments argued for those criteria and won their case, partly because they were more powerful.

In another analysis of this university, we found that all departments advocate self-serving criteria for budget allocation. Thus a department with large undergraduate enrollments argued that enrollments should determine budget allocations, a department with a strong national reputation saw prestige as the most reasonable basis for distributing funds, and so on. We further found that advocating such self-serving criteria actually benefited a department's budget allotments but, also, it paid off more for departments that were already powerful.

Organizational needs are consistent with a current distribution of power also because of a human tendency to categorize problems in familiar ways. An accountant sees problems with organizational performance as cost accountancy problems or inventory flow problems. A sales manager sees them as problems with markets, promotional strategies, or just unaggressive sales people. But what is the truth? Since it does not automatically announce itself, it is likely that those with prior credibility, or those with power, will be favored as the enlightened. This bias, while not intentionally self-serving, further concentrates power among those who already possess it, independent of changes in the organization's context.

INSTITUTIONALIZING POWER

A third reason for expecting organizational contingencies to be defined in familiar ways is that the current holders of power can structure the organization in ways that institutionalize themselves. By institutionalization we mean the establishment of relatively permanent structures and policies that favor the influence of a particular subunit. While in power, a dominant coalition has the ability to institute constitutions, rules, procedures, and information systems that limit the potential power of others while continuing their own.

The key to institutionalizing power always is to create a device that legitimates one's own authority and diminishes the legitimacy of others. When the "Divine Right of Kings" was envisioned centuries ago it was to provide an unquestionable foundation for the supremacy of royal authority. There is generally a need to root the exercise of authority in some higher power. Modern leaders are no less affected by this need. Richard Nixon, with the aid of John Dean, reified the concept of executive privilege, which meant in effect that what the President wished not to be discussed need not be discussed.

In its simpler form, institutionalization is achieved by designating positions or roles for organizational activities. The creation of a new post legitimizes a function and forces organization members to orient to it. By designating how this new post relates to older, more established posts, moreover, one can structure an organization to enhance the importance of the function in the organization. Equally, one can diminish the importance of traditional functions. This is what happened in the end with the insurance company we mentioned that was having trouble with its coding department. As the situation unfolded, the claims director continued to feel dissatisfied about the dependency of his functions on the coding manager. Thus he instituted a reorganization that resulted in two coding departments. In so doing, of course, he placed activities that affected his department under his direct control, presumably to make the operation more effective. Similarly, consumer-product firms enhance the power of marketing by setting up a coordinating role to interface production and marketing functions and then appoint a marketing manager to fill the role.

The structures created by dominant powers sooner or later become fixed and unquestioned features of the organization. Eventually, this can be devastating. It is said that the battle of Jena in 1806 was lost by Frederick the Great, who died in 1786. Though the great Prussian leader had no direct hand in the disaster, his imprint on the army was so thorough, so embedded in its skeletal underpinnings, that the organization was inappropriate for others to lead in different times.

Another important source of institutionalized power lies in the ability to structure information systems. Setting up committees to investigate particular organizational issues and having them report only to particular individuals or groups, facilitates their awareness of problems by members of those groups while limiting the awareness of problems by the members of other groups. Obviously, those who have information are in a better position to interpret the problems of an organization, regardless of how realistically they may, in fact, do so.

Still another way to institutionalize power is to distribute rewards and resources. The dominant group may quiet competing interest groups with small favors and rewards. The credit for this artful form of cooptation belongs to Louis XIV. To avoid usurpation of his power by the nobles of France and the Fronde that had so troubled his father's reign, he built the palace at Versailles to occupy them with hunting and gossip. Awed, the courtiers basked in the reflected glories of the "Sun King" and the overwhelming setting he had created for his court.

At this point, we have not systematically studied the institutionalization of power. But we suspect it is an important condition that mediates between the environment of the organization and the capabilities of the organization for dealing with that environment. The more institutionalized power is within an organization, the more likely an organization will be out of phase with the realities it faces. President Richard Nixon's structuring of his White House is one of the better documented illustrations. If we go back to newspaper and magazine descriptions of how he organized his office from the beginning in 1968, most of what occurred subsequently follows almost as an afterthought. Decisions flowed through virtually only the small White House staff; rewards, small presidential favors of recognition, and perquisites were distributed by this staff to the loyal; and information from the outside world—the press, Congress, the people on the streets—was filtered by the staff and passed along only if initialed "bh." Thus it was not surprising that when Nixon met war protestors in the early dawn, the only thing he could think to talk about was the latest football game, so insulated had he become from their grief and anger.

One of the more interesting implications of institutionalized power is that executive turnover among the executives who have structured the organization is likely to be a rare event that occurs only under the most pressing crisis. If a dominant coalition is able to structure the organization and interpret the meaning of ambiguous events like declining sales and profits or lawsuits, then the "real" problems to emerge will easily be incorporated into traditional molds of thinking and acting. If opposition is designed out of the organization, the interpretations will go unquestioned. Conditions will remain stable until a crisis develops, so overwhelming and visible that even the most adroit rhetorician would be silenced.

IMPLICATIONS FOR THE MANAGEMENT OF POWER IN ORGANIZATIONS

While we could derive numerous implications from this discussion of power, our selection would have to depend largely on whether one wanted to increase one's power, decrease the power of others, or merely maintain one's position. More important, the real implications depend on the particulars of an organizational situation. To understand power in an organization one must begin by looking outside it—into the environment—for those groups that mediate the organization's outcomes but are not themselves within its control.

Instead of ending with homilies, we will end with a reversal of where we began. Power, rather than being the dirty business it is often made out to be, is probably one of the few mechanisms for reality testing in organizations. And the cleaner forms of power, the institutional forms, rather than having the virtues they are often credited with, can lead the organization to become out of touch. The real trick to managing power in organizations is to ensure somehow that leaders cannot be unaware of the realities of their environments and cannot avoid changing to deal with those realities. That, however, would be like designing the "self-liquidating organization," an unlikely event since anyone capable of designing such an instrument would be obviously in control of the liquidations.

Management would do well to devote more attention to determining the critical contingencies of their environments. For if you conclude, as we do, that the environment sets most of the structure influencing organizational outcomes

and problems, and that power derives from the organization's activities that deal with those contingencies, then it is the environment that needs managing, not power. The first step is to construct an accurate model of the environment, a process that is quite difficult for most organizations. We have recently started a project to aid administrators in systematically understanding their environments. From this experience, we have learned that the most critical blockage to perceiving an organization's reality accurately is a failure to incorporate those with the relevant expertise into the process. Most organizations have the requisite experts on hand but they are positioned so that they can be comfortably ignored.

One conclusion you can, and probably should, derive from our discussion is that power—because of the way it develops and the way it is used—will always result in the organization suboptimizing its performance. However, to this grim absolute, we add a comforting caveat: If any criteria other than power were the basis for determining an organization's decisions, the results would be even worse.

SELECTED BIBLIOGRAPHY

The literature on power is at once both voluminous and frequently empty of content. Some is philosophical musing about the concept of power, while other writing contains popularized palliatives for acquiring and exercising influence. Machiavelli's *The Prince,* if read carefully, remains the single best prescriptive treatment of power and its use. Most social scientists have approached power descriptively, attempting to understand how it is acquired, how it is used, and what its effects are. Mayer Zald's edited collection *Power in Organizations* (Vanderbilt University Press, 1970) is one of the more useful sets of thoughts about power from a sociological perspective, while James Tedeschi's edited book, *The Social Influence Processes* (Aldine-Atherton, 1972) represents the social psychological approach to understanding power and influence. The strategic contingencies' approach, with its emphasis on the importance of uncertainty for understanding power in organizations, is described by David

Hickson and his colleagues in "A Strategic Contingencies Theory of Intraorganizational Power" (*Administrative Science Quarterly*, December 1971, pp. 216–229).

Unfortunately, while many have written about power theoretically, there have been few empirical examinations of power and its use. Most of the work has taken the form of case studies. Michel Crozier's *The Bureaucratic Phenomenon* (University of Chicago Press, 1964) is important because it describes a group's source of power as control over critical activities and illustrates how power is not strictly derived from hierarchical position. J. Victor Baldridge's *Power and Conflict in the University* (John Wiley & Sons, 1971) and Andrew Pettigrew's study of computer purchase decisions in one English firm (*Politics of Organizational Decision-Making*, Tavistock, 1973) both present insights into the acquisition and use of power in specific instances. Our work has been more empirical and comparative, testing more explicitly the ideas presented in this article. The study of university decision making is reported in articles in the June 1974, pp. 135–151, and December 1974, pp. 453–473, issues of the *Administrative Science Quarterly*, the insurance firm study in J. G. Hunt and L. L. Larson's collection, *Leadership Frontiers* (Kent State University Press, 1975), and the study of hospital administrator succession will appear in 1977 in the *Academy of Management Journal*.

30
The diffusion of
new work structures:
Explaining why success didn't take

Richard E. Walton

When organizations engage in experimental projects in work restructuring, an underlying assumption is that if the innovation is effective, it will be adapted and used by other units in the organization. Most of us would expect that an orga-nizational pattern that is working better than the one it replaced will be recommended by superiors and emulated by peers. Experience, however, shows this to be not necessarily true: The assumed tendencies are sometimes nullified and offset by competing organizational dynamics.

I have studied a sample of organizations that made early efforts at the comprehensive redesign of work, asking: How much diffusion has occurred, particularly within the same firm? What are the vehicles for diffusion? What barriers are encountered? How does the character of the innovation affect the rate of its diffusion? Answers to questions such as these can help us formulate better diffusion strategies and tactics.

Source: Reprinted, by permission of the publisher, from *Organizational Dynamics*, 1975, © 1975 by AMACOM, a division of American Management Associations. All rights reserved.

Author's Note: I wish to acknowledge the helpful comments of Chris Argyris on an earlier draft of this paper and the support for this research provided by the Ford Foundation and the Division of Research, Harvard Graduate School of Business Administration.

EIGHT EXPERIMENTS

The eight firms included in the study had the following characteristics: All started their research on work redesign in the 1960s; their early experiments involved relatively comprehensive work restructuring; these experiments were all judged initially successful; the firms had a number of physically separate facilities, usually geographically dispersed; the change efforts of all the firms received substantial publicity.

Of the eight firms, two are in the U.S., two in Canada, one in Great Britain, two in Norway, and one in Sweden. The firms in the U.S. are Corning Glass, which initiated a study in its Medfield, Mass., assembly plant in 1965, and the General Foods Corporation, which initiated an experiment in its pet food plant in Topeka, Kansas, in January 1971, although it had begun planning for change in 1968. The Canadian organizations are the Sales and Fabrication Division of Alcan and the Advanced Devices Center, a division of Northern Electric Company, subsequently renamed Microsystems International, Ltd. In 1964, a group of Alcan managers launched a project in one plant in the works at Kingston, Ontario; over time the innovations developed in the first effort at Kingston were extended to other existing Sales and Fabrication Division plants and eventually to a new cold rolling mill. The Northern Electric unit designed a radically different organization for a new semi-conductor facility that was occupied in January 1966.

The European companies form the remainder of the sample. Shell U.K. introduced change in several locations in the mid-1960s, including a new refinery at Teesport, which came on stream in 1968. Several Norwegian projects were carried out in different industries under the Industrial Democracy Project, an action research program sponsored jointly by the Norwegian Federation of Employers and the Trades Union Council of Norway and guided by social scientists associated with the Work Research Institute in Oslo. The two projects included in this study were the fertilizer plants at Norsk Hydro in Porsgrunn and a department in the Hunsfos pulp and paper complex near Kristiansand. They were initiated in the mid-1960s.

A Swedish experiment in Volvo's truck assembly plant in Lundby, begun in 1969, has been followed by similar changes in a neighboring auto assembly plant, the design of a revolutionary car plant at Kalmar that went on stream in 1974, and a commitment to an advanced form of work structuring in a new Volvo plant in the U.S. planned for 1975.

An important similarity existed in the change strategies employed by seven of these eight firms. An early experiment in one unit of the firm was regarded as a pilot project from which the larger organization could learn. The positive results, if any, could demonstrate the value of work restructuring. Lessons gained from the experiment then could be made available to other units. The eighth, Shell U.K., by contrast followed a change strategy in which the demonstration projects were not the point of departure.

The extent of diffusion that has occurred within these eight firms has varied widely. In four companies (Corning, Northern Electric, Hunsfos, and Norsk Hydro) diffusion has been nonexistent or small. In three companies (General Foods, Shell U.K., and Alcan) somewhat more diffusion has occurred; however, the rate either has been slow or it has not been sustained. Only in one company in my sample, namely Volvo, was diffusion truly impressive. Managers involved in all the changes, including those at Volvo, clearly had expected more rapid and extensive change.

GENERAL MODEL

Before exploring the diffusion of "work restructuring," or the lack of diffusion, let us clarify what we mean by the term. The work restructuring approach pursued in the eight cases studied embraces many aspects of work, including the content of the job, compensation schemes, scope of worker responsibility for supervision and decision making, social structure, status hierarchy, and so on. The design of each element is intended to contribute to an internally consistent work culture—one that *appropriately* enlarges workers' scope for self-management, enhances their opportunity for learning new abilities, strengthens their sense of connectedness with co-workers, increases their identification with the product and manufacturing process, and promotes their sense of dignity and self-worth. The word "appropriately" is used in the preceding sentence to signify that the extent to which work structures can realistically depart from today's conventional work organization depends upon many situational factors, especially the type of technology involved, composition of the work force (Is it educated and skilled?), and economic forces (Do they favor the expenditures of time and money involved in a comprehensive attempt at job restructuring?).

Each diffusion effort had its own unique characteristics, but they all also shared many points. A generalized model of the change efforts, containing seven aspects or steps, will highlight both the similarities and the differences. Although I have viewed the early experiments as the first of a number of steps in transforming work throughout the larger corporation, they were not necessarily so conceived at the time they were initiated, either by direct participants or by corporate officials.

Step 1: Initiation of the pilot experiment. Although perhaps similarly inspired, pilot experiments took a variety of forms. Some were in new plants—GF's Topeka, Corning's Medfield, Alcan's Center Plant at the Kingston Works, and Northern Electric's plant at Montreal. Others were in established plants—Hunsfos' pulp and paper mill and Volvo's Lundby truck plant. At Norsk Hydro, experiments were initiated simultaneously in an existing and a new fertilizer facility. The Shell U.K. demonstration projects occurred as a later step in the process of restructuring work, but they too embraced both existing and new facilities.

Some experiments involved relatively radical and comprehensive work restructuring at the outset—especially GF's pet food plant, Norsk Hydro's fertilizer plants, Hunsfos' chemical pulp department, and Shell U.K.'s new Teesport refinery. Significantly, each of these four facilities is relatively small, employing fewer than 100 workers, and involves a continuous-processing technology. Also, the way work was restructured in these continuous-processing plants is remarkably

similar: Self-managing teams were formed to take responsibility for large segments of the process. Job rotation among team members was encouraged both to improve control of the technology and to provide intrinsically satisfying learning experiences for workers. Support activities, such as maintenance, quality control, and cleaning were incorporated into operating team responsibilities. Because of the diverse abilities required to manage, operate, and maintain these technologies, team members received heavy doses of skills training. Pay was based on the relevant skills and knowledge a worker had acquired rather than on the particular job he was performing. New information and measurement systems were developed to enable teams to keep on top of their enlarged responsibilities.

Northern Electric's Advanced Devices Center, because it focused mostly on professional and managerial personnel, differed from the four continuous-processing facilities. The Advanced Devices Center featured a matrix organization, functional and business teams, elaborate communication schemes, open office layouts, and nontraditional titles and reporting relationships.

Other experiments—in the new plants at Alcan and Corning and the existing facilities at Volvo and Shell U.K.—involved more moderate change. Significantly, two of these, Corning and Volvo, are assembly plants where the nature of the tasks and technology provided relatively little opportunity for upgrading the abilities of the work teams. Thus in these plants emphasis was placed on freeing workers from the tedium of short repetitive work cycles and on steps that would improve communication. Within those constraints, both were bold efforts at work restructuring. The changes that evolved over several years were rotation among and/or enlargement of assembly tasks, the formation of teams, and mechanisms for worker participation or consultation.

An incremental approach to work restructuring in the initial projects in both the Alcan plants and Shell's existing refineries was necessary in part because of constraints related to collective bargaining.

The initial experiment in a majority of cases occurred at the urging of a middle-level line manager, typically a plant manager, or with his active participation. Staff people and outside consultants or researchers also played an active role in designing and implementing most of the initial experiments. In the Norwegian projects, the researchers actually sought out the companies and persuaded them to collaborate in undertaking the projects. Similarly, in the Corning experiment, a corporate consultant began by stimulating interest among supervisors to try their own mini-experiments, which, if successful, could lead to plantwide work restructuring. Interestingly, although the management and worker members of the Norwegian and the Corning experiments subsequently came to "own" the projects, dependency upon outside experts long remained a factor in these cases, each of which resulted in little intracompany diffusion.

Step 2: Pilot experiment declared early success. The study included only those experiments that were judged successful after a year or two, when participants had had significant experience with the new work structures and when operating results could be assessed.

Spokesmen for these projects claimed that they had produced improved performance, increased worker knowledge and skills, and resulted in a generally more responsible and motivating work culture. In no case were there wholly independent performance audits or measurements that would persuade the most ardent skeptics of work restructuring. While my own field visits led me to conclude that in most cases some discounting of claims seemed to be required, I accept the original judgments of early success.

Results claimed on both the hard and soft sides of the benefits ledger varied: Only about 25 percent of the Northern Electric workers said they experienced a relatively large gain in the quality of their working life; among General Foods workers it was 80 percent. The balance, at least during the initial periods, would fall somewhere between. Six cases reported quality improvement and more efficient production due to decreased scrap, less down-time, or more efficient methods. Also, most companies reported reduced turnover and absentee rates. A case in point: The pet food plant after 18 months reported an overhead rate that was 33 percent lower than in the old plant. The absentee rate was 9 percent below the industry norm, and turnover was far below average.

Step 3: Recognition and resources provided for further work restructuring. After becoming acquainted with the results of the pilot experiment, top management typically gave its blessing to the approach. In several cases, notably GF, Alcan, and Norsk Hydro, it became company or division policy to diffuse work restructuring throughout the various facilities. In Hunsfos, it became company policy to spread work restructing to other departments in the mill complex. In the case of Volvo, the recognition of work restructuring became very strong. The new president took a special interest in the subject and had made a dramatic commitment to the program in existing plants in the early 1970s. He personally had pressed for and contributed to a revolutionary approach to the designing of a new auto assembly plant in Kalmar that involved a 10 percent higher capital investment to accommodate the desired work structure. This action gave work restructuring a high priority in other plants. Exceptions should be noted in the cases of Corning and Northern Electric, where apparently no strong encouragement of diffusion came from the corporate level other than from organizational development groups.

In Northern Electric, in fact, the reverse was true. A new manager who took over in the third year of the experiment terminated it before it could have reached the diffusion stage. The new organization was regarded as a success at its home base, but corporate management took a different view.

In a few cases, recognition eventually took the form of a management philosophy hammered out by a group of line managers with the assistance of staff consultants more familiar with work restructuring. A General Foods statement, for example, emerged shortly after other corporate measures had been taken to promote diffusion.

Another diffusion measure was the assignment of specific responsibility for promoting work restructuring. For example, in General Foods, the line manager responsible for pet food operations at the divisional level was transferred to the corporate level and made an internal consultant to several dozen plants.

Step 4: More general interest in work restructuring aroused. In every case, these experiments have been the subject of widely circulated written reports in the news media, oral presentations to other groups, and visits by interested parties to the experimental site. Dissemination activities often helped the project leaders secure top management recognition and approval, but they had other objectives as well. They were intended to interest and inform managers and union officials of sister units within the same firm and those outside the firm. The visibility and favorable acclaim, of course, were gratifying to the participants, who were proud of the work culture they had created and the performance results they had achieved.

Step 5: Change agents' interventions extend throughout the corporate system. We have already noted the tendency to designate some individuals or committees to help initiate projects and monitor their development. The change interventions led by the internal consultant at General Foods will help illustrate this aspect of a diffusion effort, although the activities are more elaborate than in other cases, except Shell U.K.

In late 1971, the newly appointed GF internal consultant, Lyman Ketchum, addressed a group of 150 top managers from operations, engineering, quality assurance, and personnel, together with several corporation group vice-presidents. Forms of work restructuring and their rationale were discussed. The chairman of GF and a key vice-president were present and sanctioned the role of the new change agent.

A steering committee comprised of the division operating managers was formed to guide the change activities. As a committee the managers assessed the progress of diffusion, and as individuals they were expected to collaborate with the change agent in his work in their divisions.

Change initiatives occurred at the plant level. Priority was given to new and recent plants over existing plants because more progress could be made with less effort. Further priority was given to larger plants because of their greater importance. Recognizing these priorities, the change agent began working with plant managers who manifested the most interest in change.

The change agent's initial work with plants involved a three-day meeting with the plant manager and his staff, who were encouraged to explore

their own values and the connections between values and work structures.

These initial three-day meetings by themselves seldom produced much action. After a month or so had elapsed, the change agent usually scheduled another meeting with a group drawn from the next level below the plant manager's staff.

As a parallel activity, the corporate change agent organized three-day seminars on the techniques of work analysis and design; these were attended largely by staff personnel such as engineers.

Where a commitment to work restructuring developed, the change agent helped form a plant steering committee comprised of key line and staff managers, and union officials where appropriate. Subordinate action committees were formed to explore and recommend specific projects within a limited area of the plant. The change agent himself and other consulting resources were made available to the plant committees to assist them in the action work restructuring.

Diffusion interventions at Norsk Hydro took a somewhat different form: The first major event was a policy clinic where managers and their union counterparts could discuss the ideas and techniques of achieving employee participation at the shop floor in the planning and introduction of change. These discussions were somewhat inhibited by managers who believed that the area manager was authoritarian and unsympathetic. The area manager discovered the content of these policy discussions and stopped them.

In 1971, a second effort was made with the responsibility for work restructuring initiatives assigned to the Joint Consultation Board. A supervisory training program was also introduced. Some new initiatives worked out; others did not.

By 1972 top management concluded that the diffusion policy still was not working. Middle managers were told to "get cracking," and a training program was devised to better equip them to play their role. In the meantime the area manager had been replaced, in part because he had not helped implement the work restructuring project. This development was offset by the departure of an influential union official who was interested in diffusing the work structures pioneered in the fertilizer plants.

A supplementary vehicle for diffusion was the conversion of the ten-man professional staff of the firm's industrial engineering methods group "from MTM engineers to socio-technical consultants." The head of this department understood the need for reshaping the role of the department and began in 1971 to reeducate the staff. Over time this development may greatly facilitate diffusion of the work restructuring ideas pioneered in the fertilizer plants.

Step 6: Facilitative networks develop.   This is a step taken in only a few of the change programs studied. An interunit network of personnel involved in work restructuring is created to exchange ideas, to provide a supportive reference group for its members, and to build a constituency for change in corporate policies and procedures more favorable to work restructuring. In GF, networks of plant managers and their personnel managers are evolving to a point where many of their members can serve others generally as outside consultants.

Step 7: Personnel movement occurs.   The transfer of experienced personnel from an innovative unit is a way of exporting the knowledge, values, and skills at the heart of work restructuring. The innovative unit then can educate the new managers who transfer into the unit.

A few favorable moves can be cited to illustrate the possibilities. In a strategic move at Norsk Hydro, the person who had been personnel manager in the Porsgrunn area was promoted to corporate headquarters. He was intimately familiar with the fertilizer project and an articulate proponent of the underlying philosophy. He moved to a better position to advise top management on the diffusion of work restructuring. Not surprisingly, the advantage of this move to headquarters was partly offset by the loss felt in the local area.

The manager at Alcan's Kingston Works was promoted to a division-level position after the program was well under way at Kingston. Later, however, he reportedly lost touch with the innovations and became less supportive.

In Shell U.K., the transfer of key personnel was disruptive of the program under way in the U.K., but some moves seeded other parts of the Shell International organization—for example, the Australian unit—with managers who were committed to finding better ways of organizing work.

THE SHELL U.K. APPROACH

A major variation on the procedure in the other seven firms—that of starting small with a single experiment—is provided by Shell U.K. From the outset, the approach was conceived as companywide, comprehensive in its effect on the work situation, and planned to last from five to ten years.

The first step was not a demonstration project. Work redesign was undertaken only after large amounts of organizational time had been spent in sessions developing and affirming a supportive managerial philosophy.

Attitudes, in short, were changed before structure. Tavistock social scientists worked closely with an internal staff resource group to design the activities in this and subsequent phases, beginning in 1965 with the development of a philosophy to which senior managers could commit themselves.

The second phase was intended to ensure that the operating philosophy was freely accepted by all 6,000 members of the organization from senior managers to hourly workers. To accomplish this dissemination—involving active testing and consensus building—required 18 months, from fall 1965 to spring 1967—and a cascade of conferences.

The implementation phase was launched in March 1966 by a third top-management conference. The first strategic approach to implementation was to set up pilot projects that "could act as centers of organizational learning." These projects, set up in one refinery, did not go well. Moreover, the concentration of attention on a few groups at one site created resentment among many others who had been through the philosophy discussions, and who were emotionally and intellectually primed to implement the philosophy.

Next, the implementation strategy was altered, and responsibility for change was placed on the department-manager level across the company—an approach made possible by the massive dissemination process. To enable department managers to initiate their own change projects, short training courses were provided to teach them techniques of work analysis and principles of work restructuring.

A network of committees representing both management and unions helped to change work rules that otherwise would prevent many types of restructuring, such as flexible manning patterns and paying workers for multiple job skills.

Although pilot projects as centers for organization learning no longer formed the primary foundation for implementation, it was decided to apply the concepts to a new refinery at Teesport, where construction began in 1965 and which came on stream in April 1968.

Evaluation conferences were held in March 1967 on the previous two major sites covered, Stanlow and Shell Haven. Shortly thereafter, a number of changes took place that served to arrest the diffusion process and tended to demoralize the innovative systems already introduced.

PROBLEM AREAS IN DIFFUSION

My investigation attempted to find out why diffusion was not more rapid and extensive. The reasons ranged from defects in the design of the original experiment to unanticipated consequences of the success of the initial pilot project.

Regression in the Pilot Project

Because diffusion typically occurs over a significant period of time, the sustained success of early experiments can help build momentum for companywide change; conversely, emergent weaknesses in the pilot projects can erode initial support for change.

A clear correlation between the continued success of initial projects and the rate of diffusion is found in several extreme cases. Volvo's truck plant experiment has continued to be effective and has been followed by relatively high diffusion. The Northern Electric experiment was discontinued, and also produced no significant diffusion within the company. A similar consistency is

found in the demoralization of Corning's Medfield experiment, after a period of effectiveness, and the lack of diffusion throughout the firm.

Both Shell U.K. and Alcan experienced moderate effectiveness in their early experiments and have shown moderate amounts of diffusion, although causal connections are not indicated. Shell U.K. achieved its diffusion soon after its change program was undertaken; the initial projects subsequently became somewhat demoralized and no further diffusion has occurred. Alcan has recently diffused the ideas of the earlier experiments into a new mill, although there has been a decline in management and worker involvement in the plants in which the earlier innovations were established.

There is not always a correlation between initial project success and diffusion. The strong success of the Topeka plant in GF is not matched so far by a high amount of diffusion, and in the cases of Norsk Hydro and Hunsfos, there is even less correlation. Continued success of initial change projects appears to be only one of many influences on diffusion.

What can cause a successful early experiment to deteriorate later on? I have noted several factors: (1) internal inconsistencies in the original design; (2) loss of support from levels of management above the experimental unit; (3) premature turnover of leaders, operators, of consultants directly associated with a project; (4) stress and crises that lead to more authoritarian management, which in turn demoralizes the innovative unit; (5) tension in the innovative unit's relations with other parties—peer units, staff groups, superiors, labor unions; (6) letdown in participants' involvement after initial success with its attendant publicity; (7) lack of diffusion to other parts of the organization, which isolates the original experiment and its leaders.

The seventh factor or principle, succinctly stated, is "diffuse or die"; it suggests that a circular relationship can *eventually* undermine the viability of the initial project, just as weaknesses that develop in the initial project can undermine the diffusion effort. The converse of this circular relationship is not strong; as I have noted above, continued success in the initial project does not necessarily lead to diffusion throughout the larger organization.

Poor Model for Change

Even if the pilot project remains viable over time, it may be an ineffective model for diffusion in the firm because it lacks either visibility or credibility. These deficiencies may reflect the behavior of leaders of the experiment, or they may relate to the way policy is formulated by higher officials. Also, many characteristics inherent in the site of the initial experiment affect its ability to stimulate further change. Consider the many conditions of the GF pet food plant that enhanced the success of that project: The Topeka plant was new, was located in a favorable labor market, required few workers, and was geographically separate from headquarters and other existing facilities of GF. Since it was a new plant with a new work force, no union agreement was required to establish the new work structure. Many of these conditions, of course, did not exist elsewhere in GF, and many managers asked, "Is work restructuring possible in other situations—for example, in a large, established, unionized plant?"

The credibility of the Corning and Northern Electric projects suffered not only for similar reasons but also from an additional site characteristic: The technology involved in the experimental plant was significantly different from that employed in other plants in the system.

In terms of site characteristics, Volvo, Alcan, and Shell U.K. appear to have presented relatively good prospects for further diffusion of a successful experiment. They were initiated in large, established, unionized facilities and involved technologies typical of the larger systems of which they were a part.

The prospects for diffusion of the work restructuring innovations at the Norsk Hydro fertilizer plants would have to be regarded as even more favorable. By 1973 a dozen different plants were adjacent to each other in the Porsgrunn area, each producing a different product—ammonia, nitric acid, urea, formic acid, magnesium, plastics, and so on. They were similar in ways that made the fertilizer work organization generally relevant: They employed continuous-process technologies, and large pieces of capital were manned by relatively small work forces. In addition, Norsk Hydro had operations in a number of other locations, and in fact was the largest industrial undertaking in Norway. Thus, one could project the spread of demonstrably successful ideas throughout the Porsgrunn works and other parts of the firm, and because of the firm's prominence in Norway, to other industrial firms in this small country. Obviously, for an explanation of why much diffusion did not occur, we will have to look elsewhere than to site characteristics.

The way the project leaders present the experiment to others in the firm will influence its visiblity and credibility. One basic choice is whether to maintain a low profile or to seek visibility in the corporate environment.

A low profile reduces the career risks associated with failure, and less publicity also minimizes the risk of creating a "showcase" complex with longer-run adverse effects on the work climate. However, in the cases studied, the incentive to publicize the experiments increased substantially once they appeared to be successfully established. Visibility, it was felt, was essential if diffusion were to occur, and the natural pride in the innovation was accompanied by a desire for wider recognition—inside the company and beyond. Some favorable publicity often created an appetite for more. The project leaders sometimes lost control of publicity to other corporate officials and the media.

Except possibly for Corning's Medfield and Northern Electric's Advanced Devices Center, the initial experiments in my sample achieved sufficient visibility throughout their corporate organizations.

Confusion over What Is to Be Diffused

Even if the initial site is favorable for eventual diffusion and the project leaders manage the publicity effectively, higher management can botch up the process in the way they formulate, and communicate the diffusion policy.

If the form of work structure indicated by company policy is stated too conceptually, the policy may be dismissed as abstract and platitudinous or action may be delayed because managers don't know how to translate the concepts.

On the other hand, if the ideas about the desired forms of work structure are stated too operationally, then they may be rejected as inappropriate by managers whose units have different types of work forces, different technologies, or different economic conditions.

Norsk Hydro presents an interesting case in point. Six years after the initiation of the fertilizer experiment and many years after it had become official company policy to diffuse this type of work innovation, managers still complained about the lack of clarity. Was the policy to diffuse "job enrichment," "autonomous groups," "organizational development," "socio-technical systems," or something more general that underlies all of these?

There was general agreement that diffusion would have proceeded more rapidly if it had been clear that the policy was for managers to pursue certain *aims* (such as making better use of the talents of employees and allowing for more day-to-day influence by employees over their work) rather than to employ particular *techniques*.

Inappropriateness of Concepts Employed

The long-run diffusion of work restructuring is affected by another issue: While the concepts should be inspiring, they must also be realistic.

"Autonomous groups" was the key concept employed in the Norwegian experiments to characterize the work restructuring innovations. The term, which many found inspiring, was later dropped because it was not feasible for many groups to become truly autonomous.

"Equal status" was a concept in the design of Shell U.K.'s Teesport work system. The term captured the imagination of the workers as well as the originators, but overstated what higher management was prepared to do. Differences persisted between blue- and white-collar workers, although all employees were placed on salary. The differences remaining were especially resented because of the expectations aroused by the "equal status" concept.

Deficient Implementation

The initial project may be viable in itself, but the follow-through may be inadequate, in terms of locating accountability for the change and providing "how-to" knowledge.

The first point has already been illustrated. Norsk Hydro unsuccessfully attempted to place the responsibility for diffusion with Joint Consultation Boards and then shifted it to middle management. Shell U.K. started implementation by selecting a few projects with heavy reliance upon a few staff people but then shifted to a policy in which all department heads become accountable for change in their units. Accountability for work restructuring in Volvo was clearest—it was an essential part of the plant managers' responsibility, period!

As is true with many types of change in organizations, "how-to" knowledge must be provided through training, consulting, or both. Resources for this seemed to have been a limiting factor at one time or another in GF, Corning, and Alcan.

Lack of Top Management Commitment

A period of sustained priority for work restructuring is important in achieving diffusion. The continuing interest and commitment of Volvo's president is a prime case in point. By contrast, the shifting priority given work restructuring in several other firms' studies hindered diffusion. An illustrative case is Norsk Hydro, where the work restructuring objective received lower priority during 1970–73 than it did in the period 1967–69.

Priority declined for several reasons. First, when the initial experiment was launched there was a high sense of urgency about improving industrial relations and productivity. But with a general improvement in industrial relations and the competitiveness of the business, the sense of urgency declined.

Second, according to the middle-level managers, they have come under increasing pressure to meet demanding volume and cost objectives, making it risky in the short run to start any major projects. One manager said, "I have the freedom to innovate but not the time."

Third, the company has been transformed by rapid expansion and revolutionary change in the raw materials and processes used in much of its business. The changes absorbed the attention of top management and the director-general became more formal and less accessible to members of the organization—at least to those who wanted to lobby for work restructuring.

The Shell U.K. managers perceived a similar set of changes as weakening their work restructuring program. In 1971, Hill reported that after mid-1967 there was a lack of continuing visible commitment at the top. In 1967, the U.K. company was reorganized to include North Sea exploration and production as well as U.K. refining activities, and a new chief executive was appointed. The refineries repeatedly requested assurances that the top management of the enlarged company endorsed and supported the philosophy behind the work restructuring program. When the new management team became absorbed in supply problems created by the 1967 Middle East War and failed to formally endorse an amended statement of philosophy tailored to the company's enlarged role, managers in the refineries became less willing to embark on change.

In many cases, including those just mentioned, inconsistencies in higher-management behavior weakened diffusion efforts. Even before they perceived that the program was downgraded, Shell U.K. managers were concerned that although they were asked to protect and develop their human resources, they were being assessed mainly on their handling of the technical system alone.

In the latter part of the 1960s, Alcan division management reportedly shifted toward a more directive, top-down type of leadership and away from a consultative, problem-oriented management pattern. This directly contradicted and undermined the innovative work structure that had been developed at the Kingston works and had an inhibiting effect on further diffusion of work restructuring in the division.

Union Opposition

Like sustained top management commitment, union support or acceptance is a necessary condition for any significant diffusion of work restructuring. In some cases, union support has been, on balance, a positive factor. In other cases, perceived opposition by the union has been a reason for not trying to diffuse work restructuring into unionized plants. Mostly, unions have had more complicated effects—on the process of introducing change, the nature of the work structures introduced, and the work climate.

The Scandinavian union movement has been more positive toward work restructuring than trade unions in the U.K. and North America. Clearly, joint union-management sponsorship of the Norwegian experiments served to legitimize the program for workers. However, the actual effects of the union officials on diffusion within Norsk Hydro and Hunsfos were mixed, just as the effects on the management side were mixed.

In Norsk Hydro a particularly key union official had moved from the area and the loss of his support hurt the diffusion effort. In Hunsfos, where the chief shop steward and the company president were strongly committed to the diffusion program, local effort received no backing from the trade union movement. Although the trade union movement as a whole was not averse to the changes pioneered at Hunsfos, the chief shop steward reported criticism from other quarters. He said he took risks with his own constituency every time he "stuck his neck out" (for example, on a change that resulted in a crew reduction). Also, radical sociologists accused him of selling out to management, increasing company efficiency at the expense of workers.

At Volvo, the unions have played an active and positive role in the work restructuring program. Management had initiated the job redesign aspects of the program and the union the consultative aspects. Both parties, moreover, claim joint ownership of the total program.

In the case of the Shell U.K. program, the union deliberately slowed down the rate of diffusion of work restructuring during 1965–68 until productivity bargaining had progressed to the point where they had been able to establish the economic quid pro quo for certain changes.

The union had played its role in the recent demoralization of the Shell U.K. change program. Management negotiated wage increases in 1971 and 1972 that were below the national pattern, and then in 1973 the government constraints prevented the parties from making up the difference. The union has reflected and perhaps amplified worker resentment.

Another factor at Shell is tension around manning. Top management continues to put pressure on refinery managers to reduce the work force.

When we recall that guarantees against dismissal and provisions for extra pay were a quid pro quo in the initial change program, we can see how reviving the same issue has led to poorer union-management relations and inhibited the further diffusion of work restructuring.

Three projects started in nonunion plants of firms whose other plants were mostly unionized. Unions representing these other plants were expected to oppose or otherwise complicate work restructuring in them. The three firms were General Foods, Corning, and Northern Electric. In the case of GF, where work restructuring efforts have actually been undertaken in unionized plants, the collective bargaining relationship complicated change in the early steps but has not prevented it. With Corning and Northern Electric little or no attempt was made to diffuse change to union plants.

To summarize, unions' effect has taken many forms:

First, unions have influenced the basic climate for change. Sometimes the effect was positive, helping to legitimize work restructuring or entering into an informal problem-solving pattern consistent with the work culture sought by the work restructuring experiment. Sometimes the effect of unions was negative, inhibiting management from trying to diffuse change or formalizing and politicizing relations contradictory to the spirit of the work culture being diffused.

Second, unions have complicated the change process by requiring additional consensus-seeking efforts.

Third, unions have affected the preconditions for change or limited the nature of the change itself. Sometimes they have obtained assurances on job security and earnings maintenance and have bargained for workers to obtain a share of the increased productivity that resulted from more flexibility and reduced work crews. Sometimes they have prevented certain changes, e.g., modifications in job content that affect union jurisdictional boundaries or historical patterns.

Bureaucratic Barriers

The importance of this issue belies the simplicity with which it can be stated. Diffusion efforts are frustrated by vested interests and existing organizational routines that limit local autonomy.

Innovative plant managements have often felt harassed by staff groups, who for their part have often become irritated and impatient with many of the plants' demands for self-sufficiency and exemption from uniform company policies. These tensions may be present during the establishment of the initial experiment, and they are escalated when serious diffusion begins. "Experiments," by definition, minimize the scope and duration of the effects of the change involved. However, when the changes are declared enduring or an attempt is made to spread them, the stakes are raised for groups affected.

Bureaucratic barriers can be illustrated from the experience of one company, where managers themselves introduced the term. One problem relates to the level at which decisions are made in the line organization. In 1973, workers were operating informally without supervisors on two of the four shifts, but formalization of this arrangement and extension to a third and fourth shift was not within the authority of the manager of the innovative plant.

Another example involved the method for judging operator qualification for increased pay in the innovative plant. Central personnel insisted that the "theoretical" tests of knowledge appropriate for each job had to be mastered before "practical" knowledge could be compensated. Previously, theoretical knowledge could be learned and compensated *after* a person had shown he could perform the day-to-day operations associated with a particular job and had received an adjustment for that practical mastery. These events not only demoralized the participants of the project, but also discouraged other managers from initiating projects.

The experience of General Foods, Shell U.K., and other firms in which an ambitious diffusion effort has been undertaken are rich with similar illustrations, involving such issues as whether quality assurance procedures at plant level must be uniform throughout the corporation, whether a common job evaluation scheme should be applied to plants with radically different work structures, what should be the respective roles of central engineering and local staff in plant expansion programs, how much local autonomy should exist in creating and filling plant manage-

ment positions, and whether reporting requirements must be applied uniformly throughout the
system.

Threatened Obsolescence

A restructured work situation requires new roles
and new skills and makes others obsolete. We
have already mentioned the resistance of staff
groups who may have to acquire new knowledge,
develop new consultative patterns for imparting
their expertise, and see some of their functions
being performed by nonspecialists.

However, the greatest threat was to first-line
supervision. The number of first-line supervisors
was often decreased. Sometimes the position was
even eliminated. Where the position was retained, the role was changed in the ways that
required new attitudes and greater interpersonal
and group skills.

Supervisors individually and as a group are
weak compared with other groups potentially affected by new work structures. They themselves
have not mounted much effective opposition to
the diffusion or tried to shape the form of work
restructuring, with one exception—Volvo, where
within the past year the supervisors' union has
taken an active role to protect its members' interests. In at least one case, Hunsfos, concern by
workers about the effect of work restructuring on
their supervisors created a major snag in the diffusion process. In many other cases, management's uncertainty about how to handle the
potential obsolescence of existing foremen has
been a factor inhibiting diffusion.

In some cases the resistance of supervisors and
other salaried personnel was not due to a direct
threat to their existing roles; rather, they felt neglected by comparison with blue-collar workers.
They resented the fact that the blue-collar worker's job was enriched and his status and influence
upgraded, while their lot had not improved.

Self-limiting Dynamics

In companies that employed the most comprehensive diffusion strategy, there was a tendency
for pilot projects to be self-limiting or "self-seal-

ing." The tendency was strongest in instances like
Norsk Hydro, Hunsfos, and General Foods,
where a single small unit was involved in the
original experiment and where serious efforts to
introduce work restructuring into other units
came only after widespread publicity on the success of the experimental unit.

One dynamic involved a "star-envy" phenomenon, which can be illustrated by Norsk Hydro.
The original experiment in the fertilizer plants
received an enormous amount of publicity within
Norway and outside. The fertilizer plants became
the object of innumerable visits by managers,
trade union officials, social scientists, and school-
children. Top management looked approvingly
on the project and made it company policy for
others to follow the lead of the fertilizer project.
Not surprisingly, the attention given the fertilizer
groups engendered resentment and envy among
the other persons who were asked to adopt the
innovation in their own operations. The resentment was accompanied by resistance to the work
restructuring program. The experience of the Topeka plant in General Foods was strikingly
similar.

A second dynamic involved a shift in the reward structure. Payoffs for pioneers and those who
followed them in the same organization differed
in important respects, providing a much less favorable benefit-risk picture for the subsequent
users of organizational innovations. Managers
who adapted the innovation and succeeded received less credit than the pioneer received, and
if they had failed, they probably would have lost
more standing in management than the pioneer
would have if he had failed. Managers who did
not utilize the innovation often figured that while
they might be prodded and goaded for not taking
any organizational initiatives, ultimately they
would be judged on the basis of production and
profit performance. In short, they felt that they
could afford to resist pressure.

A third dynamic involved the tendency for
participants to feel special and to regard their experimental work system as superior. On the one
hand, this feeling reinforced their commitment
to the group and was a positive factor in helping
establish a new form of social organization. On
the other hand, this tended to lead outsiders to
conclude that the culture created was unique and

to discount the general applicability of the experiment.

A fourth dynamic came into play at a later date. Rivalry sometimes developed among those engaged in work restructuring. They stressed minor differences in their approaches, while ignoring the similarity in underlying values and assumptions. One effect of this form of rivalry among change agents and among innovative units was to weaken their ability to form the collegial networks described as part of the general diffusion model.

A fifth dynamic also came into play at a later stage in those cases where diffusion did not occur fairly rapidly. It was a secondary consequence of two factors related above: the bureaucratic barriers and the special self-image developed by experimental units. The leaders of some innovative units had engaged in so many skirmishes with superiors and staff groups over corporate practices and were so aggressive in asserting the correctness of their positions that they hurt their careers. Observing this, some peers resolved not to get similarly burned.

Other Influential Factors

After having studied the diffusion process in eight companies and after having analyzed the situational factors that seemed to account for a generally slower-than-expected rate of diffusion, I became interested in assessing how inherently difficult or easy these new structures are to diffuse.

The early classic studies of diffusion traced the adoption of improved agricultural practices. More recent studies have covered other innovations, including farm practices, medical drugs, educational techniques, machinery, management control techniques, and so on. Should we expect diffusion of work restructuring to be relatively slower or faster than diffusion of innovations in these other fields?

Recent reviews of the literature on diffusion consistently concurred on a number of attributes of innovations that influenced their adoption rate. Most are plausible, at least on the surface.

1. Relative advantage. This is an obvious attribute that enhances the rate of diffusion. The cost-benefit analysis implied in this attribute includes not only financial but also perceived social costs and benefits. The problem with work restructuring is that there is a singular lack of agreement among its proponents over the benefits derived. Some stress tangible impacts on such factors as productivity and turnover; others choose to emphasize the psychic dividends paid to workers.

2. Communicability. Diffusion will be enhanced if the innovation can be explained easily and if its effects are easily separable from other influences in the environment. Work restructuring innovations rate low on this attribute compared with all other types of innovations cited. Volvo may be an exception. The changes were straightforward and readily grasped. Well-established production norms permitted an easy assessment of any loss of efficiency, and the desired decrease in turnover was quickly measured (although not always persuasively explained). Thus communicability may help explain why Volvo's relatively simple changes on the existing assembly lines were diffused relatively rapidly.

3. Compatability. Diffusion is aided if the innovation is perceived as being congruent with existing norms, values, and structures. Again, work restructuring innovations must be rated low because by definition they call for important structural and normative changes in the existing industrial organizations. (Work restructuring threatens what many managers in the United States continue to regard as their prerogatives.) However, the same innovations would rate higher in compatability in Scandinavia than in the U.S.

4. Pervasiveness. This term refers to the number of aspects of the system affected by the innovation. Less pervasiveness permits more rapid diffusion. By definition, what we refer to as "work restructuring" strives to be comprehensive, embracing divisions of labor, rewards, supervision, status systems, and power relations. This factor, too, makes diffusing work restructuring inherently difficult.

5. Reversibility. Can an innovation be adopted on an experimental basis and reversed without serious consequences? If the status quo ante cannot be readily restored, diffusion will be inhibited. Many managers believe that work restructuring creates expectations that will become a liability if the innovation must be abandoned. My limited observations support that belief. Thus work restructuring may rate moderate to low on the reversibility factor.

6. *Number of gatekeepers.* Numerous approval channels that must be satisfied before an innovation can be adopted will tend to inhibit the rate of diffusion. In work restructuring, top management, departmental or plant managers, staff groups, supervisors, unions, and workers themselves all have some gatekeeping role to perform. One could hardly imagine gatekeeping conditions less favorable for diffusion of new work structures.

Finally, a major difficulty in diffusing work restructuring is that frequently it's not literally a matter of "adoption." Because work forces, technologies, and economics affect the appropriate work structure, tailored application of the general principles of work restructuring is required rather than adoption of a predetermined model.

CONCLUSION

One important reason for the unimpressive rate of diffusion in the eight companies studied is that, especially in their more comprehensive form, these innovations have many attributes that make their diffusion inherently slow. Even if they offer relative advantages over existing work structures, their character and results are not highly communicable; they are not congruent with existing norms and values; their potential effect in a given work situation is pervasive rather than fractional; they are not readily reversed without incurring social costs; and too many affected parties serve as gatekeepers for the effective implementation of the innovations.

Another set of explanations for the actual diffusion observed in the eight companies relates to the barriers the diffusion efforts encountered and the efficacy of companies' strategies and tactics.

Many key areas are readily identifiable: Does the experiment continue to show good results? Is the experiment sufficiently visible and sufficiently convincing? Is organizational accountability for initiating change clear, and is know-how for implementation available? Is there sustained support for diffusion from powerful groups such as top management and union officials? Careful planning is required to ensure that the answers to these questions are positive.

Two problem areas deal with organizational dilemmas generated by the nature of the innovations. Work restructuring requires an increase in local autonomy, thereby threatening the power of central staff groups and some managers. It also threatens to make some roles obsolete or to eliminate the positions of some staff specialists and first-line supervisors. These problems are not easily resolved and require imaginative solutions—solutions not yet obvious to me.

Last, perhaps the most interesting type of barrier to diffusion is the self-limiting dynamics of pilot projects. Ironically, several of these are unexpected consequences of the success of the project: The greater the attention given pilot units, the more likely are managers of peer units to be "turned off" by the example. The more successful the pioneer, the less favorable are the payoffs and the greater the risks for those who follow. The more esprit de corps and sense of being special that develops in the unit, the less generalizable it appears to others.

Some of the implications of our analysis of these and other self-limiting tendencies are apparent once the dynamics are understood: There is an advantage in (1) introducing a number of projects at the same time in the same firm, (2) avoiding overexposure and glorification of particular change efforts, and (3) having the innovative program identified with top management as the initial project stage.

As the examples of work restructuring in the larger society become more numerous, however, the self-limiting tendencies should pose less of a problem.

In conclusion, I expect relatively little diffusion of potentially significant restructuring in the work place—over the short run. Hopefully the long run may tell a different story.

Increasingly, what many employees expect from their jobs is different from what organizations are prepared to offer them. Work restructuring is the preeminent answer to closing the gap. I would expect the latent dissatisfactions of workers to be activated and pressure for work restructuring to increase as the issues receive more public attention and as more successful examples of comprehensive work restructuring raise the general level of worker expectations. I would also be surprised if future experiments did not profit from the pioneering efforts. Together, these factors should generate an increase in the number of diffusions and a hastening of the pace of diffusion. But how many diffusions and how fast the pace, I can't even begin to guess.

SELECTED BIBLIOGRAPHY

A useful volume of papers on the problems associated with work is *The Worker and the Job: Coping with Change*, edited by Jerome M. Rosow (Prentice-Hall, Inc., 1974).

Included in that volume is a paper of mine, "Innovative Restructuring of Work," which reports on other aspects of the study on which the present article is based. It describes the rationale for, nature of, and results achieved by a dozen pilot projects in work restructuring. It also analyzes the viability of these projects over time.

Two recent reviews of the factors influencing diffusion of innovations in a wide range of fields are Gerald Zaltman, Robert Duncan, and Jonny Holbek's *Innovations and Organizations* (John Wiley & Sons, 1973) and John Kimberly's "Policies for Innovation in the Service Sector," prepared for the OECD Directorate for Scientific Affairs, October 1973.

The studies at the Work Research Institute in Oslo, Norway have also noted that Philip Herbst has called the "self-encapsulating" effects of experimental changes in work design. See Herbst's "Some Reflections on the Work Democratized Project—1974. I: The Process of Diffusion," Work Research Institutes, Oslo, Document 13, 1974.

V.B
Organizations over Time

31
Evolution
and revolution
as organizations grow

Larry E. Greiner

A small research company chooses too complicated and formalized an organization structure for its young age and limited size. It flounders in rigidity and bureaucracy for several years and is finally acquired by a larger company.

Key executives of a retail store chain hold on to an organization structure long after it has served its purpose, because their power is derived from this structure. The company eventually goes into bankruptcy.

A large bank disciplines a "rebellious" manager who is blamed for current control problems, when the underlying cause is centralized procedures that are holding back expansion into new markets. Many younger managers subsequently leave the bank, competition moves in, and profits are still declining.

The problems of these companies, like those of many others, are rooted more in past decisions than in present events or outside market dynamics. Historical forces do indeed shape the future growth of organizations. Yet management, in its haste to grow, often overlooks such critical developmental questions as: Where has our organization been? Where is it now? And what do the answers to these questions mean for where we are going? Instead, its gaze is fixed outward toward the environment and the future—as if more precise market projections will provide a new organizational identity.

Companies fail to see that many clues to their future success lie within their own organizations and their evolving states of development. Moreover, the inability of management to understand its organization development problems can result in a company becoming "frozen" in its present stage of evolution or, ultimately, in failure, regardless of market opportunities.

My position in this article is that the future of

Source: Reprinted by permission of the *Harvard Business Review.* "Evolution & Revolution as Organizations Grow" by Larry E. Greiner (July–August 1972). Copyright © 1972 by the President and Fellows of Harvard College; all rights reserved.

Author's note: This article is part of a continuing project on organization development with my colleague, Professor Louis B. Barnes, and sponsored by the Division of Research, Harvard Business School.

an organization may be less determined by outside forces than it is by the organization's history. In stressing the force of history on an organization, I have drawn from the legacies of European psychologists (their thesis being that individual behavior is determined primarily by previous events and experiences, not by what lies ahead). Extending this analogy of individual development to the problems of organization development, I shall discuss a series of developmental phases through which growing companies tend to pass. But, first, let me provide two definitions:

1. The term *evolution* is used to describe prolonged periods of growth where no major upheaval occurs in organization practices.

2. The term *revolution* is used to describe those periods of substantial turmoil in organization life.

As a company progresses through developmental phases, each evolutionary period creates its own revolution. For instance, centralized practices eventually lead to demands for decentralization. Moreover, the nature of management's solution to each revolutionary period determines whether a company will move forward into its next stage of evolutionary growth. As I shall show later, there are at least five phases of organization development, each characterized by both an evolution and a revolution.

KEY FORCES IN DEVELOPMENT

During the past few years a small amount of research knowledge about the phases of organization development has been building. Some of this research is very quantitative, such as time-series analyses that reveal patterns of economic performance over time.[1] The majority of studies, however, are case-oriented and use company records and interviews to reconstruct a rich picture of corporate development.[2] Yet both types of research tend to be heavily empirical without attempting more generalized statements about the overall process of development.

A notable exception is the historical work of Alfred D. Chandler, Jr., in his book *Strategy and Structure*.[3] This study depicts four very broad and general phases in the lives of four large U.S. companies. It proposes that outside market opportunities determine a company's strategy, which in turn determines the company's organization structure. This thesis has a valid ring for the four companies examined by Chandler, largely because they developed in a time of explosive markets and technological advances. But more recent evidence suggests that organization structure may be less malleable than Chandler assumed; in fact, structure can play a critical role in influencing corporate strategy. It is this reverse emphasis on how organization structure affects future growth which is highlighted in the model presented in this article.

From an analysis of recent studies,[4] five key dimensions emerge as essential for building a model of organization development:

1. Age of the organization.
2. Size of the organization.
3. Stages of evolution.
4. Stages of revolution.
5. Growth rate of the industry.

I shall describe each of these elements separately, but first note their combined effect as illustrated in *Exhibit 1*. Note especially how each dimension influences the other over time; when all five elements begin to interact, a more complete and dynamic picture of organizational growth emerges.

After describing these dimensions and their interconnections, I shall discuss each evolutionary/revolutionary phase of development and show (a) how each stage of evolution breeds its own revolution, and (b) how management solutions to each revolution determine the next stage of evolution.

Age of the Organization

The most obvious and essential dimension for any model of development is the life span of an organization (represented as the horizontal axis in *Exhibit 1*). All historical studies gather data from various points in time and then make comparisons. From these observations, it is evident that the same organization practices are not maintained throughout a long time span. This makes a most basic point: management problems and principles are rooted in time. The concept of de-

Exhibit 1.   Model of Organization Development

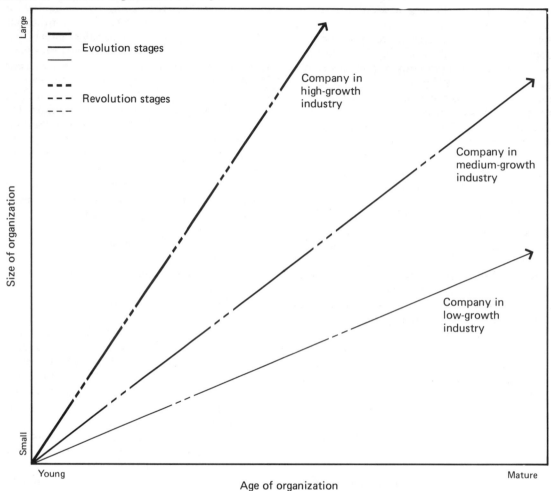

centralization, for example, can have meaning for describing corporate practices at one time period but loses its descriptive power at another.

The passage of time also contributes to the institutionalization of managerial attitudes. As a result, employee behavior becomes not only more predictable but also more difficult to change when attitudes are outdated.

Size of the Organization

This dimension is depicted as the vertical axis in *Exhibit 1*. A company's problems and solutions tend to change markedly as the number of employees and sales volume increase. Thus, time is

not the only determinant of structure; in fact, organizations that do not grow in size can retain many of the same management issues and practices over lengthy periods. In addition to increased size, however, problems of coordination and communication magnify, new functions emerge, levels in the management hierarchy multiply, and jobs become more interrelated.

Stages of Evolution

As both age and size increase, another phenomenon becomes evident: the prolonged growth that I have termed the evolutionary period. Most growing organizations do not expand for two years and then retreat for one year; rather, those that survive a crisis usually enjoy four to eight years of continuous growth without a major economic setback or severe internal disruption. The term evolution seems appropriate for describing these quieter periods because only modest adjustments appear necessary for maintaining growth under the same overall pattern of management.

Stages of Revolution

Smooth evolution is not inevitable; it cannot be assumed that organization growth is linear. *Fortune*'s "500" list, for example, has had significant turnover during the last 50 years. Thus we find evidence from numerous case histories which reveals periods of substantial turbulence spaced between smoother periods of evolution.

I have termed these turbulent times the periods of revolution because they typically exhibit a serious upheaval of management practices. Traditional management practices, which were appropriate for a smaller size and earlier time, are brought under scrutiny by frustrated top managers and disillusioned lower-level managers. During such periods of crisis, a number of companies fail—those unable to abandon past practices and effect major organization changes are likely either to fold or to level off in their growth rates.

The critical task for management in each revolutionary period is to find a new set of organization practices that will become the basis for managing the next period of evolutionary growth. Interestingly enough, these new practices eventually sow their own seeds of decay and lead to another period of revolution. Companies therefore experience the irony of seeing a major solution in one time period become a major problem at a latter date.

Growth Rate of the Industry

The speed at which an organization experiences phases of evolution and revolution is closely related to the market environment of its industry. For example, a company in a rapidly expanding market will have to add employees rapidly; hence, the need for new organization structures to accommodate large staff increases is accelerated.

While evolutionary periods tend to be relatively short in fast-growing industries, much longer evolutionary periods occur in mature or slowly growing industries.

Evolution can also be prolonged, and revolutions delayed, when profits come easily. For instance, companies that make grievous errors in a rewarding industry can still look good on their profit and loss statements; thus they can avoid a change in management practices for a longer period. The aerospace industry in its infancy is an example. Yet revolutionary periods still occur, as one did in aerospace when profit opportunities began to dry up. Revolutions seem to be much more severe and difficult to resolve when the market environment is poor.

PHASES OF GROWTH

With the foregoing framework in mind, let us now examine in depth the five specific phases of evolution and revolution. As shown in *Exhibit 2*, each evolutionary period is characterized by the dominant *management style* used to achieve growth, while each revolutionary period is characterized by the dominant *management problem* that must be solved before growth can continue. The patterns presented in *Exhibit 2* seem to be typical for companies in industries with moderate growth over a long time period; companies in faster growing industries tend to experience all five phases more rapidly, while those in slower growing industries encounter only two or three phases over many years.

It is important to note that *each phase is both an effect of the previous phase and a cause for the next phase.* For example, the evolutionary management style in Phase 3 of the exhibit is "delegation," which grows out of, and becomes the solution to, demands for greater "autonomy" in the preceding Phase 2 revolution. The style of delegation used in Phase 3, however, eventually provokes a major revolutionary crisis that is characterized by attempts to regain control over the diversity created through increased delegation.

The principal implication of each phase is that management actions are narrowly prescribed if growth is to occur. For example, a company experiencing an autonomy crisis in Phase 2 cannot

Exhibit 2.   The Five Phases of Growth

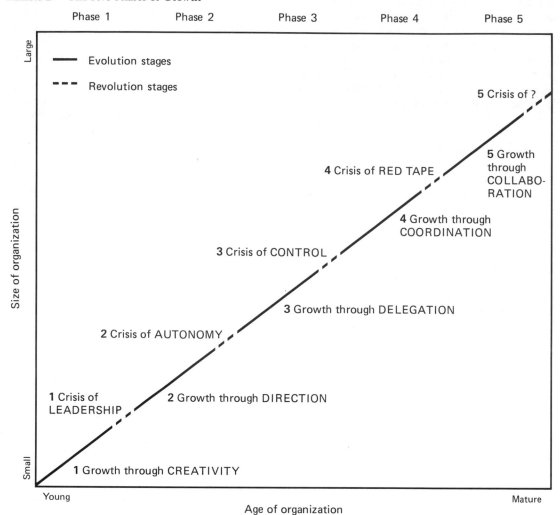

return to directive management for a solution—it must adopt a new style of delegation in order to move ahead.

Phase 1: Creativity . . .

In the birth stage of an organization, the emphasis is on creating both a product and a market. Here are the characteristics of the period of creative evolution:

• The company's founders are usually technically or entrepreneurially oriented, and they dis-

dain management activities; their physical and mental energies are absorbed entirely in making and selling a new product.

• Communication among employees is frequent and informal.

• Long hours of work are rewarded by modest salaries and the promise of ownership benefits.

• Control of activities comes from immediate marketplace feedback; the management acts as the customers react.

. . . *& the leadership crisis.*   All of the foregoing individualistic and creative activities are essential for the company to get off the ground. But therein lies the problem. As the company grows, larger production runs require knowledge about the efficiencies of manufacturing. Increased numbers of employees cannot be managed exclusively through informal communication; new employees are not motivated by an intense dedication to the product or organization. Additional capital must be secured, and new accounting procedures are needed for financial control.

Thus the founders find themselves burdened with unwanted management responsibilities. So they long for the "good old days," still trying to act as they did in the past. And conflicts between the harried leaders grow more intense.

At this point a crisis of leadership occurs, which is the onset of the first revolution. Who is to lead the company out of confusion and solve the managerial problems confronting it? Quite obviously, a strong manager is needed who has the necessary knowledge and skill to introduce new business techniques. But this is easier said than done. The founders often hate to step aside even though they are probably temperamentally unsuited to be managers. So here is the first critical developmental choice—to locate and install a strong business manager who is acceptable to the founders and who can pull the organization together.

Phase 2: Direction . . .

Those companies that survive the first phase by installing a capable business manager usually embark on a period of sustained growth under able and directive leadership. Here are the characteristics of this evolutionary period:

• A functional organization structure is introduced to separate manufacturing from marketing activities, and job assignments become more specialized.

• Accounting systems for inventory and purchasing are introduced.

• Incentives, budgets, and work standards are adopted.

• Communication becomes more formal and impersonal as a hierarchy of titles and positions builds.

• The new manager and his key supervisors

take most of the responsibility for instituting direction, while lower-level supervisors are treated more as functional specialists than as autonomous decision-making managers.

. . . & the autonomy crisis. Although the new directive techniques channel employee energy more efficiently into growth, they eventually become inappropriate for controlling a larger, more diverse and complex organization. Lower-level employees find themselves restricted by a cumbersome and centralized hierarchy. They have come to possess more direct knowledge about markets and machinery than do the leaders at the top; consequently, they feel torn between following procedures and taking initiative on their own.

Thus the second revolution is imminent as a crisis develops from demands for greater autonomy on the part of lower-level managers. The solution adopted by most companies is to move toward greater delegation. Yet it is difficult for top managers who were previously successful at being directive to give up responsibility. Moreover, lower-level managers are not accustomed to making decisions for themselves. As a result, numerous companies flounder during this revolutionary period, adhering to centralized methods while lower-level employees grow more disenchanted and leave the organization.

Phase 3: Delegation . . .

The next era of growth evolves from the successful application of a decentralized organization structure. It exhibits these characteristics:

• Much greater responsibility is given to the managers of plants and market territories.

• Profit centers and bonuses are used to stimulate motivation.

• The top executives at headquarters restrain themselves to managing by exception, based on periodic reports from the field.

• Management often concentrates on making new acquisitions which can be lined up beside other decentralized units.

• Communication from the top is infrequent, usually by correspondence, telephone, or brief visits to field locations.

The delegation stage proves useful for gaining expansion through heightened motivation at lower levels. Decentralized managers with greater authority and incentive are able to penetrate larger markets, respond faster to customers, and develop new products.

. . . & the control crisis.   A serious problem eventually evolves, however, as top executives sense that they are losing control over a highly diversified field operation. Autonomous field managers prefer to run their own shows without coordinating plans, money, technology, and manpower with the rest of the organization. Freedom breeds a parochial attitude.

Hence, the Phase 3 revolution is under way when top management seeks to regain control over the total company. Some top managements attempt a return to centralized management, which usually fails because of the vast scope of operations. Those companies that move ahead find a new solution in the use of special coordination techniques.

Phase 4: Coordination . . .

During this phase, the evolutionary period is characterized by the use of formal systems for achieving greater coordination and by top executives taking responsibility for the initiation and administration of these new systems. For example:

• Decentralized units are merged into product groups.

• Formal planning procedures are established and intensively reviewed.

• Numerous staff personnel are hired and located at headquarters to initiate companywide programs of control and review for line managers.

• Capital expenditures are carefully weighed and parceled out across the organization.

• Each product group is treated as an investment center where return on invested capital is an important criterion used in allocating funds.

• Certain technical functions, such as data processing, are centralized at headquarters, while daily operating decisions remain decentralized.

• Stock options and companywide profit shar-

ing are used to encourage identity with the firm as a whole.

All of these new coordination systems prove useful for achieving growth through more efficient allocation of a company's limited resources. They prompt field managers to look beyond the needs of their local units. While these managers still have much decision-making responsibility, they learn to justify their actions more carefully to a "watchdog" audience at headquarters.

. . . & the red-tape crisis.   But a lack of confidence gradually builds between line and staff, and between headquarters and the field. The proliferation of systems and programs begins to exceed its utility; a red-tape crisis is created. Line managers, for example, increasingly resent heavy staff direction from those who are not familiar with local conditions. Staff people, on the other hand, complain about uncooperative and uninformed line managers. Together both groups criticize the bureaucratic paper system that has evolved. Procedures take precedence over problem solving, and innovation is dampened. In short, the organization has become too large and complex to be managed through formal programs and rigid systems. The Phase 4 revolution is under way.

Phase 5: Collaboration . . .

The last observable phase in previous studies emphasizes strong interpersonal collaboration in an attempt to overcome the red-tape crisis. Where Phase 4 was managed more through formal systems and procedures, Phase 5 emphasizes greater spontaneity in management action through teams and the skillful confrontation of interpersonal differences. Social control and self-discipline take over from formal control. This transition is especially difficult for those experts who created the old systems as well as for those line managers who relied on formal methods for answers.

The Phase 5 evolution, then, builds around a more flexible and behavioral approach to management. Here are its characteristics:

• The focus is on solving problems quickly through team action.

• Teams are combined across functions for task-group activity.

• Headquarters staff experts are reduced in number, reassigned, and combined in interdisciplinary teams to consult with, not to direct, field units.

• A matrix-type structure is frequently used to assemble the right teams for the appropriate problems.

• Previous formal systems are simplified and combined into single multipurpose systems.

• Conferences of key managers are held frequently to focus on major problem issues.

• Educational programs are utilized to train managers in behavioral skills for achieving better teamwork and conflict resolution.

• Real-time information systems are integrated into daily decision making.

• Economic rewards are geared more to team performance than to individual achievement.

• Experiments in new practices are encouraged throughout the organization.

. . . & the ? crisis. What will be the revolution in response to this stage of evolution? Many large U.S. companies are now in the Phase 5 evolutionary stage, so the answers are critical. While there is little clear evidence, I imagine the revolution will center around the "psychological saturation" of employees who grow emotionally and physically exhausted by the intensity of teamwork and the heavy pressure for innovative solutions.

My hunch is that the Phase 5 revolution will be solved through new structures and programs that allow employees to periodically rest, reflect, and revitalize themselves. We may even see companies with dual organization structures: a "habit" structure for getting the daily work done, and a "reflective" structure for stimulating perspective and personal enrichment. Employees could then move back and forth between the two structures as their energies are dissipated and refueled.

One European organization has implemented just such a structure. Five reflective groups have been established outside the regular structure for the purpose of continuously evaluating five task activities basic to the organization. They report directly to the managing director, although their reports are made public throughout the organization. Membership in each group includes all levels and functions, and employees are rotated through these groups on a six-month basis.

Other concrete examples now in practice include providing sabbaticals for employees, moving managers in and out of "hot spot" jobs, establishing a four-day workweek, assuring job security, building physical facilities for relaxation *during* the working day, making jobs more interchangeable, creating an extra team on the assembly line so that one team is always off for reeducation, and switching to longer vacations and more flexible working hours.

The Chinese practice of requiring executives to spend time periodically on lower-level jobs may also be worth a nonideological evaluation. For too long U.S. management has assumed that career progress should be equated with an upward path toward title, salary, and power. Could it be that some vice presidents of marketing might just long for, and even benefit from, temporary duty in the field sales organization?

IMPLICATIONS OF HISTORY

Let me now summarize some important implications for practicing managers. First, the main features of this discussion are depicted in *Exhibit 3*, which shows the specific management actions that characterize each growth phase. These actions are also the solutions which ended each preceding revolutionary period.

In one sense, I hope that many readers will react to my model by calling it obvious and natural for depicting the growth of an organization. To me this type of reaction is a useful test of the model's validity.

But at a more reflective level I imagine some of these reactions are more hindsight than foresight. Those experienced managers who have been through a developmental sequence can empathize with it now, but how did they react when in the middle of a stage of evolution or revolution? They can probably recall the limits of their own developmental understanding at that time. Perhaps they resisted desirable changes or were

Exhibit 3.   Organization Practices During Evolution in the Five Phases of Growth

Category	Phase 1	Phase 2	Phase 3	Phase 4	Phase 5
Management focus	Make & sell	Efficiency of operations	Expansion of market	Consolidation of organization	Problem solving & innovation
Organization structure	Informal	Centralized & functional	Decentralized & geographical	Line-staff & product groups	Matrix of teams
Top management style	Individualistic & entrepreneurial	Directive	Delegative	Watchdog	Participative
Control system	Market results	Standards & cost centers	Reports & profit centers	Plans & investment centers	Mutual goal setting
Management reward emphasis	Ownership	Salary & merit increases	Individual bonus	Profit sharing & stock options	Team bonus

even swept emotionally into a revolution without being able to propose constructive solutions. So let me offer some explicit guidelines for managers of growing organizations to keep in mind.

Know Where You Are in the Developmental Sequence

Every organization and its component parts are at different stages of development. The task of top management is to be aware of these stages; otherwise, it may not recognize when the time for change has come, or it may act to impose the wrong solution.

Top leaders should be ready to work with the flow of the tide rather than against it; yet they should be cautious, since it is tempting to skip phases out of impatience. Each phase results in certain strengths and learning experiences in the organization that will be essential for success in subsequent phases. A child prodigy, for example, may be able to read like a teenager, but he cannot behave like one until he ages through a sequence of experiences.

I also doubt that managers can or should act to avoid revolutions. Rather, these periods of tension provide the pressure, ideas, and awareness that afford a platform for change and the introduction of new practices.

Recognize the Limited Range of Solutions

In each revolutionary stage it becomes evident that this stage can be ended only by certain specific solutions; moreover, these solutions are different from those which were applied to the problems of the preceding revolution. Too often it is tempting to choose solutions that were tried before, which makes it impossible for a new phase of growth to evolve.

Management must be prepared to dismantle current structures before the revolutionary stage becomes too turbulent. Top managers, realizing that their own managerial styles are no longer appropriate, may even have to take themselves out of leadership positions. A good Phase 2 manager facing Phase 3 might be wise to find another Phase 2 organization that better fits his talents, either outside the company or with one of its newer subsidiaries.

Finally, evolution is not an automatic affair; it is a contest for survival. To move ahead, companies must consciously introduce planned structures that not only are solutions to a current crisis but also are fitted to the *next* phase of growth. This requires considerable self-awareness on the part of top management, as well as great interpersonal skill in persuading other managers that change is needed.

Realize That Solutions Breed New Problems

Managers often fail to realize that organizational solutions create problems for the future (i.e., a decision to delegate eventually causes a problem of control). Historical actions are very much determinants of what happens to the company at a much later date.

An awareness of this effect should help managers to evaluate company problems with greater historical understanding instead of "pinning the blame" on a current development. Better yet, managers should be in a position to *predict* future problems, and thereby to prepare solutions and coping strategies before a revolution gets out of hand.

A management that is aware of the problems ahead could well decide *not* to grow. Top managers may, for instance, prefer to retain the informal practices of a small company, knowing that this way of life is inherent in the organization's limited size, not in their congenial personalities. If they choose to grow, they may do themselves out of a job and a way of life they enjoy.

And what about the managements of very large organizations? Can they find new solutions for continued phases of evolution? Or are they reaching a stage where the government will act to break them up because they are too large?

CONCLUDING NOTE

Clearly, there is still much to learn about processes of development in organizations. The phases outlined here are only five in number and are still only approximations. Researchers are just beginning to study the specific developmental problems of structure, control, rewards, and management style in different industries and in a variety of cultures.

One should not, however, wait for conclusive evidence before educating managers to think and act from a developmental perspective. The critical dimension of time has been missing for too long from our management theories and practices. The intriguing paradox is that by learning more about history we may do a better job in the future.

NOTES

1. See, for example, William H. Starbuck, "Organizational Metamorphosis," in *Promising Research Directions*, edited by R. W. Millman and M. P. Hottenstein (Tempe, Arizona, Academy of Management, 1968), p. 113.

2. See, for example, the *Grangesberg* case series, prepared by C. Roland Christensen and Bruce R. Scott, Case Clearing House, Harvard Business School.

3. *Strategy and Structure: Chapters in the History of the American Industrial Enterprise* (Cambridge, Massachusetts, The M.I.T. Press, 1962).

4. I have drawn on many sources for evidence: (a) numerous cases collected at the Harvard Business School; (b) *Organization Growth and Development*, edited by William H. Starbuck (Middlesex, England, Penguin Books, Ltd., 1971), where several studies are cited; and (c) articles published in journals, such as Lawrence E. Fouraker and John M. Stopford, "Organization Structure and the Multinational Strategy," *Administrative Science Quarterly*, Vol. 13, No. 1, 1968, p. 47; and Malcolm S. Salter, "Management Appraisal and Reward Systems," *Journal of Business Policy*, Vol. 1, No. 4, 1971.

32

Strategy implementation
and organizational growth

Jay R. Galbraith and Daniel A. Nathanson

. . .

THE CONCEPT OF FIT

The concept of fit or congruence among all the dimensions of the organization has emerged from several sources. Scott began talking of his stages as consisting "of a cluster of managerial characteristics" (Scott 1971, p. 6). In addition, he suggested that a cluster was not just an organizational form but a "way of managing," even a "way of life". He then identified the characteristics and specified them for each stage. These are shown in Table 1.

The same scheme has been elaborated by consulting firms in their own strategy and structure packages. They distinguished between products or businesses in a multi-divisional firm by the stage of the product life cycle. Then they assume that the "way of managing" will vary with the stages and go on to prescribe managerial characteristics that are appropriate for the various stages. The package currently being used by Hay Associates is shown in Table 2. The packages of other firms are similar, with due regard for variations in characteristics and descriptors. The main point is that business divisions need to adopt an internally consistent set of practices in order to implement the product strategy effectively.

Another source of development of the congruence or fit concept is organization theory. Leavitt was one of the first to discuss the degree to which task, structure, people, and processes form an integrated whole (Leavitt 1960, 1965). He suggests that organizational change strategies should take all dimensions into account. One cannot successfully change structure without making com-

pensating and reinforcing changes in information and budgeting systems, career systems, management development practices, and compensation policies. In organizations, everything is connected to everything else.

The major developer and empirical investigator of the fit concept has been Jay Lorsch (Lawrence and Lorsch 1967; Lorsch and Allen 1973; Lorsch and Morse 1974). Much of his work has already been discussed in the sections devoted to the individual dimensions. He is the primary investigator to examine structure, task, people and administrative practices; the congruence between these dimensions; and the degree to which congruence is related to organizational performance. The results of his research support the hypothesis that a fit between the dimensions leads to high organizational performance. Those organizations that were not high performers were experiencing a situation in which either structure or process did not fit with the degree of task uncertainty.

Two other studies also support the concept of fit or congruence. Using the same data base mentioned before, Khandwalla proposed that internal consistency of structural design was related to performance (Khandwalla 1973). He found that it was the more effective firms that adopted uncertainty reducers, internally differentiated their structures, formalized procedures, and decentralized decisions all in proportion to one another. There was far less congruence between these practices in less effective firms. These findings led him to suggest that it was the whole package or *gestalt* that was more important than any single factor acting alone.

Some preliminary results of a study by Child also reinforce this hypothesis. He is studying five international airlines, their structures and their performance. In examining the two most profitable airlines, he finds that they have contrasting administrative practices and structures even though they face similar problems, have similar route structures, and equivalent sizes. But the one fea-

Table 1. Three Stages of Organizational Development

Stage Co. Characteristics	I	II	III
1. Product line	1. Single product or single line	1. Single product line	1. Multiple product lines
2. Distribution	2. One channel or set of channels	2. One set of channels	2. Multiple channels
3. Organization structure	3. Little or no formal structure—"one man show"	3. Specialization based on function	3. Specialization based on product-market relationships
4. Product-service transactions	4. N/A	4. Integrated pattern of transactions	4. Not integrated
5. R&D	5. Not institutionalized-oriented by owner-mgr.	5. Increasingly institutionalized search for product or process improvements	5. Institutionalized search for *new* products as well as for improvements
6. Performance measurement	6. By personal contact & subjective criteria	6. Increasingly impersonal using technical and/or cost criteria	6. Increasingly impersonal using *market* criteria (return on investment and market share)
7. Rewards	7. Unsystematic and often paternalistic	7. Increasingly systematic with emphasis on stability and service	7. Increasingly systematic with variability related to performance
8. Control system	8. Personal control of both strategic and operating decisions	8. Personal control of strategic decisions, with increasing delegation of operating decisions based on control by decision rules (policies)	8. Delegation of product-market decisions within existing businesses, with indirect control based on analysis of "results"
9. Strategic choices	9. Needs of owner vs. needs of firm	9. —Degree of integration —Market share objective —Breadth of product line	9. —Entry and exit from industries —Allocation of resources by industry —Rate of growth

ture they have in common is congruence among their processes and structure. One is not divisionalized, has short time horizons, is centralized, and uses high and continuous involvement of the top management team which meets often. It operates a personal control process and has open communications among a management cadre which has long tenure. Conflicts are expressed and decisions are made and acted upon rapidly. The other airline has a multi-divisional, regional

Table 2. Hay Associates—Strategic Issues Matrix

		Phases of business development			
		1. Emergence	2. Developmental	3. Mature	4. Liquidation
Characteristics	A Style characteristics	• Limited delegation by strong leadership • Variety of schemes are possible	• Highest degree of delegation and freedom supported	• Delegative to controlled • Flexibility in meeting fixed goals	• Very limited delegation and freedom
	B Decision making characteristics	• Formalized goals virtually non-existent • Information limited	• General goals exist • More information for decisions	• High degree of clarity • Information based decisions	• Rigid goals • Information for control
	C Planning and control systems characteristics	• Informal, highly qualitative (milestone-oriented)	• Capable of setting broad goals and measuring results (program oriented)	• Supportive of careful goal setting and control (P & L oriented)	• Deemphasize long-term planning, quantitative controls (balance sheet oriented)
	D Responsiveness to external conditions characteristics	• Limited responsiveness at first, focus on establishing a position	• Highly responsive • Adapt to market opportunities	• Less responsiveness required due to decreasing rate of change in markets	• Responsive but under very limited conditions
	E Integration and differentiation characteristics	• High degree of differentiation among organization units • Integration at top	• Decreasing differentiation among units • Integrative function becoming more "local" to markets, products	• Continuing decrease in differentiation • Integration "local"	• Low differentiation • Integration at the top (corporate)
	F Leadership characteristics	• Entrepreneur, strong leader	• Entrepreneur/ business manager	• Sophisticated manager	• Administrator, S.O.B.
	G Motivations characteristics	• Venturesome • Accepts unaccustomed risks	• Venturesome to conservative • Accustomed and unaccustomed risks	• Conservative primarily • Generally risk adverse	• Conservative • Risk adverse
	H Reward management characteristics	• High base compensation to attract people • Discretionary bonus	• High levels related to job • Incentives for building results	• More average levels related to job • Incentives for results above high goal	• Average level • Incentives for cost control
	I Know-how and development characteristics	• Know-how depth important near top • Development needed to support expected expansion	• Ever broadening scope and increasing numbers of managers required	• Development needs and know-how becoming specialized, static	• Specialized depth and scope of know-how

Reprinted by permission of Hay Associates.

form with decentralized profit centers. It operates with impersonal controls and sophisticated planning processes. It has a large number of administrative staff personnel who operate the impersonal control system. These observations lead Child to suggest that it is the consistency among these practices, structure and people that makes them effective.

The poor performers also had multi-divisional structures for decentralization but placed restrictions on the amount of discretion that could be exercised. Although they had the structure and incurred the administrative cost of large staff overhead, they received none of the benefits of decentralization. Child's explanation of the effect of inconsistency upon performance is based on its impact on managerial behavior. The inconsistent practices give mixed signals that frustrate managers and weaken their motivation.

Thus, there are three researchers that have offered data to support the consistency or congruence hypothesis. These studies should be followed by others using different methodologies, however, because the above research is methodology bound. That is, each of the studies is a small sample, cross sectional, comparative study. This methodology could lead to rejection of the fit hypothesis and has not. But it has several flaws. The concept of fit involves consistency among multiple organizational dimensions, performance, and strategy. Consequently, a small sample size does not permit a fully orthogonal experimental design. Thus, there are still multiple interpretations that cannot be rejected either. Some of these interpretations concern causation. For example, does noninvolvement of corporate offices create the autonomy that divisions use to respond to the uniqueness of their market, thereby performing at a high level? Or, does high divisional performance create confidence in the minds of corporate management, who then give high performing divisions autonomy while concentrating on the low performing divisions? Here the cross-sectional nature of the research does not permit a rejection of the alternative explanations. Some large sample and longitudinal empirical studies are needed to complement and build upon the Lorsch, Khandwalla, and Child research.

Some further conceptual development has recently appeared (Galbraith 1977). Galbraith has built upon both the Lorsch scheme and the Lorsch research. He has attempted to identify the major design variables to be considered when matching organization form to strategy. These are shown schematically in Figure 1.

The product-market strategy chosen by the firm determines to a large extent the task diversity and uncertainty with which the organization must cope. The organization must then match the people with task through selection, recruitment, and training and development practices. The people must also match the structure. The structure, also chosen to fit the task, is specified by choices of the division of labor (amount of role differentiation), the departmental structure, the shape (number of levels, spans of control), and the distributions of power (both horizontal and vertical). Across the structure, processes are overlaid to allocate resources and coordinate activities not handled by the departmental structure. These information and decision processes are planning and control systems, budgeting processes, integration mechanisms, and performance measurements. And finally, the reward system must be matched with the task and structure through choices of compensation practices, career paths, leader behavior, and the design of work. In total, all these choices must create an internally consistent design. If one of the practices is changed, the other dimensions must be altered to maintain fit. Similarly, if the strategy is changed, then all the dimensions may need to be altered so that the form of organization remains consistent with the product-market strategy.

There is a great deal of research yet to be done in testing the concept of congruence, because it comprises many interacting variables. Although the concept of fit is a useful one, it lacks the precise definition needed to test it and to recognize whether an organization has it or not. There is also a trade-off between short-run fit and long-run fit. That is, the short-run congruence between all the organization design variables may be so good that they cannot be disentangled and rearranged into a new configuration in order to meet an environmental challenge or to implement a new strategy. For example, the Swiss watch makers achieved an excellent fit between strategy and structure for the making of mechan-

Figure 1. Major Illustration of Fit Among an Organization's Design Variables

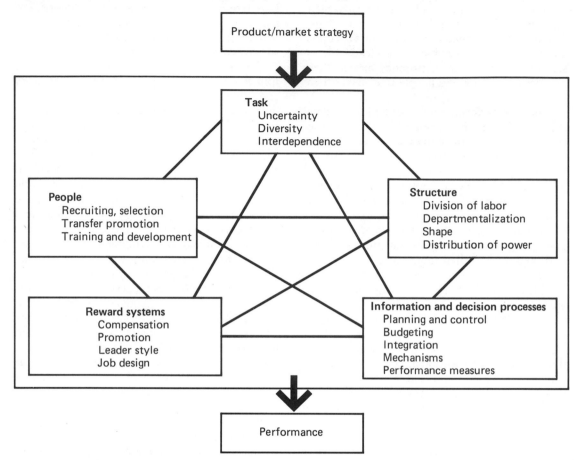

ical watches. The institutionalization of the mechanical technology has prevented these firms from adapting to the new technology. The fit is so strong that the Swiss became ready buyers from American watch makers who wanted to dump their subsidiaries. . . . Thus the corporate designer must choose a time over which to optimize the fit. . . .

. . .

. . . [Restructuring] is a major undertaking that moves an organization to a qualitatively different form. When a number of organizations repeat the same sequence of major structural changes, researchers propose that something systematic is at work and that there may be different stages of organizational growth involved, with

each stage having its own peculiar combination of structure, process, reward and people dimensions. In this section we will review the various models that have been proposed for different strategy-structure stages of growth and development.

Every area of inquiry has its own stages model. One can find proposed stages in individual cognitive development and socioemotional development, in group development, and in the economic development of countries. Organization and management theory is no exception. Several reviews of this literature already exist and will not be repeated here (Starbuck 1965, 1971; Child and Keiser 1978). Instead, we will select only those models that are relevant to choices of strategy and structure. These models are referred to as metamorphosis models, as opposed to continuous, smooth development models.

METAMORPHOSIS MODELS

Metamorphosis models of development are based on the premise that growth is not smooth and continuous, but is characterized instead by abrupt, discrete, and substantial changes in organizational strategy and structure. That is, organization structures are systems of limited adaptability. The structural parameters of the organization are capable of providing adjustments to routine disturbances such as daily operating problems and the turnover of non-central personnel. But long-run shifts such as technological change, change of government, and the like pose problems for which the existing set of structural parameters cannot adequately provide smooth adaptation. In order to return the organization to equilibrium with its environment, a metamorphosis is required. That is, a simple alteration in structure or rewards will be inadequate. The entire constellation of systems, rewards, processes, and structures must be disengaged, realigned, and then reconnected. For these reasons strategy and structure changes are major undertakings, and a complete transition often requires up to five years. It is usually hypothesized that a crisis is necessary to provoke the effort to change the status quo power structure (Greiner 1972).

A number of metamorphosis growth models have been offered. They vary in the number of stages that constitute the developmental sequence, in the number of organizational strategy and structure dimensions that are included, and in the particular determinant that drives the metamorphosis, for example, age, size or complexity. The latter distinction accounts for the greatest variance in the models. For example, James (1974) has proposed a growth model based on time phases or age of the organization, whereas Pugh and his colleagues (1969) propose that size is the primary driving force generating changes in organization form. The problem with all of these models is not that they are wrong, but that they are only partially correct. Clearly, young or-

ganizations are different from old ones. They have fewer institutionalized practices and are more entrepreneurial, creative, informal, and fragile. Similarly, a fifty person organization is very different from one that has fifty thousand, and there are major transitions along the way to the latter size. In reality age, size, and complexity are confounded, and it is virtually impossible to disentangle their separate effects. All contribute to development. Which model one uses will vary to some extent with the questions that one is asking. Because we are interested in choices of strategy and structure, the complexity models are most relevant for our purposes.

. . .

SMITH AND CHARMOZ MODEL

Smith and Charmoz report that predictable problems arise in the growth of the multi-national corporations, because the U.S. organizations must invent coordination and control devices in the international sphere, since the existing devices were designed for domestic operations. They invented control mechanisms for domestic operations before going international; therefore they must start again with Stages I, II, III on an international basis. The evolution is one of establishing control points that move from country to the corporate level, as the organization moves from the initial steps to a global enterprise. They propose a five phase model for this evolution which is illustrated in Figure 2.

Phase I represents the first move into a new area, an action that is guided by an attempt to minimize risk. The capital risk is minimized by using local distributors and participating in joint ventures. This allows the U.S. firm to "learn the ropes." Often, returns on the original investments are held as reserves against future losses. During this phase, there are no systems to process international information, no international staffs, and no plans or strategies. Decisions are made through direct personal contact as problems arise. Control is located at the corporate office, because new operations need cash.

An overload at the top provokes a move to Phase II. Either too many decisions must be

Figure 2. Evolution of Control, Coordination, and Organizational Crises in the Development of MNC

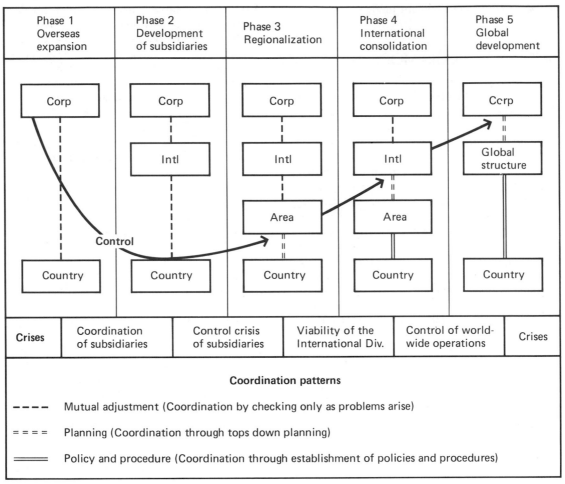

Source: Smith and Charmoz 1975.

made, or not enough decisions are made. Whatever the case may be, the result is that the subsidiaries go their own way. Also, because of lack of time and expertise at the top, poor decisions often are made. Whatever the case may be, the result is that the subsidiaries go their own way. Also, because of lack of time and expertise at the top, poor decisions often are made.

Phase II is marked by subsidiary development and the appointment of an international executive and staff. The executive acts to support the subsidiaries and allocates capital accordingly. Large subsidiaries therefore get the most atten-

tion, because they require most of the investment. Control now moves into the hands of the subsidiaries, who initiate, propose, and act. The domestic company is essentially left out of the process because of its lack of knowledge. Up to this point, there has been little movement of people to the international division, and U.S. centered thinking still predominates. Control remains on a basis of personal contact between the international executive and both corporate offices and the subsidiaries. By the end of Phase II, however, the international executive becomes overwhelmed. He is continuously traveling and has little, if any, time left to plan. Subsidiary managers begin to run their subsidiaries according to their own needs, not the corporate office's. Competition between subsidiaries develops over new areas and territories.

Phase III, then, can be called the phase of regionalization. A regional international executive is added, as well as staffs, and possible rationalizations are made for cross-border moves. These moves require a regional plan. Impersonal planning control replaces personal contact as control moves from subsidiary to region. By now the corporation recognizes the international group as a source of investment and is no longer satisfied with informal personal decision making. Use of return on investment criteria is instituted either across the board or is modified for the differential risk levels of countries. The international president is now a politician, a buffer. Since little data is available for making decisions, the domestic executives are ignorant of the international affairs. The international president must simultaneously get support from domestic product divisions and ward off ignorant staff groups who want information and may flood the fledgling subsidiaries with procedures.

The international president may be seen as a block by both international and domestic subsidiaries. At this point, the domestic subsidiaries and corporate offices realize how little they know about the international group and notice that the international group is a competitor for capital, research and development, people, and so forth. The problem at this point, however, is to prevent a move to a global structure that would be premature, because staffs are still ignorant about international affairs, and there are no planning and information systems to provide a link with the corporate office.

Phase IV is marked by international consolidation. In this stage, control moves to the international CEO to bring order and rationality to the dispersion characterizing the previous three periods of development. This period is one in which the corporate officers take a real and direct interest in the international divisions. The size of investments and interdependency of areas dictate a greater degree of centralization. However, there are no blanket solutions here, because of the differential rate of development of the geographic areas and the firm's own product lines. It is in the establishment of distinctive patterns of coordination that most firms differ. International consolidation is marked by executive international committees, planning and evaluation systems, more sophisticated financial measures, and task forces. By now the international division rivals the domestic divisions even more. There is an increasingly greater need for worldwide data and for a global mechanism to overcome parochial local interests. The corporate staff wants more control and information at this point; the area managers resent the planning and control. The international executive may again moderate a still ignorant staff, since the corporate officers might press prematurely for the kind of "planning control" that is better suited for the next phase of development.

Phase V, which can be termed "global development," is marked by corporate control. Through the increased contacts of the previous phase, corporate and domestic product groups have a more realistic awareness of foreign operations. The "planning" coordination provided by the international division is now superfluous. The particular organizational format that evolves is governed by product diversity and proportion of foreign sales as presented by Stopford. Phase V is also marked by significant improvements in global information and planning systems. Most companies maintain some form of international specialist coordination. This role is more integrative than controlling.

Our view is that transition to a global structure constitutes a metamorphosis. There are changes in the financial control system designed to handle such factors as national variations, profits by product and region, and transfer pricing. Different and multiple standards of evaluation appear; careers and compensation practices are changed; new committees and staffs evolve. Most important, an international mentality gets created to various degrees. All together, we feel these changes constitute a different "way of life" and therefore a different form.

The global form is not, however, a single distinct form like a functional or holding company form. There is no single global form. In its different manifestations it resembles the multidivisional forms which are all profit centers, but in which the profit center could be based on products, markets, or regions. Global structures can also assume any of those three multi-divisional forms, or they can take global functional or a holding company form. In fact Franko's description of European mother-daughter forms are descriptions of global holding companies. Thus we conceive of four different types of organization, each of which constitutes a distinct way of life— the simple, the functional, the holding company (or conglomerate), and the multi-divisional form. Each of these, but probably only the latter three, can exist in a domestic or in a global form. We prefer to talk about these eight possible organizations as forms rather than stages. All the forms are possible. Whether there are stages is in part an empirical question. Two studies have addressed themselves to this question.

STOPFORD AND FRANKO STUDIES

Two major empirical studies by Stopford and Wells (1972) and Franko (1974, 1977) have dealt with the stage of growth of American multi-nationals and European multi-nationals, respectively. These studies have both been discussed earlier in this paper. It is important at this point, however, to focus on their findings concerning the sequence of the stages. Figure 3 illustrates, comparatively, the sequence of both American and European multi-nationals (Franko 1977).

The American multi-national's first phase in international growth is characterized by an initial period of autonomy for the foreign subsidiary. The second phase is a period of organizational consolidation when an international division is developed. The international division is typically considered an independent enterprise and is not subject to the same strategic planning that guides domestic activities. In the third phase, strategic planning is carried out on a consistent and worldwide basis, and the structure of the foreign activities is altered to provide close links with the rest of the structure. As indicated by the chart, most American firms went through one of two major sequences of structural change. Either they moved from a functional Stage II structure to a divisional Stage III structure for their domestic

businesses before adding an international division, or they added an international division to a domestic Stage III structure. The figure also indicates that forty-nine of fifty-seven firms that replaced their international divisions did so after they had developed Stage III structures for their domestic activities. The few firms that moved directly from a Stage II structure with an international division to a global system are exceptions to the trend, and all of them adopted area divisions.

> Only twenty-four firms, or *14 percent of the 170 firms,* have moved directly from the phase of autonomous subsidiaries to a global structure without ever using an international division. In almost every instance, these firms have expanded abroad primarily by acquisitions or mergers with other firms that had international interests.
>
> Only six cases of firms reversing the directions of change were observed. These reversals are associated with failures in the decentralized systems and with decisions to recentralize authority and to establish tighter controls. (Stopford and Wells 1972, p. 48).

Unlike American multi nationals, the continental enterprises that adopted supranational organization structures typically did so after achieving a relatively large spread of multi-national operations. Moreover, when the continental multi-nationals changed their organization structures, they also did so in a sequence very different from that followed by their American counterparts.

One sees that most continental firms simply skipped the international division phase passed through by nearly 90 percent of the 170 American multi-nationals surveyed by the Comparative Multi-national Enterprise Project. One also observes that in all but three cases, Continental moves to the global forms of worldwide product divisions, area divisions, or mixed and matrix structures accompanied rather than followed divisionalization moves at home. In contrast, more than three-quarters of the American enterprises classified as multi-national saw fit to change their domestic organization structures from functional to divisional prior to adopting one of the so-called global structures.

In the competitive environment of their home market, American firms adapted their structures to their product diversification strategies. In prac-

Figure 3. International Organizational Evolution of Multinational Enterprise

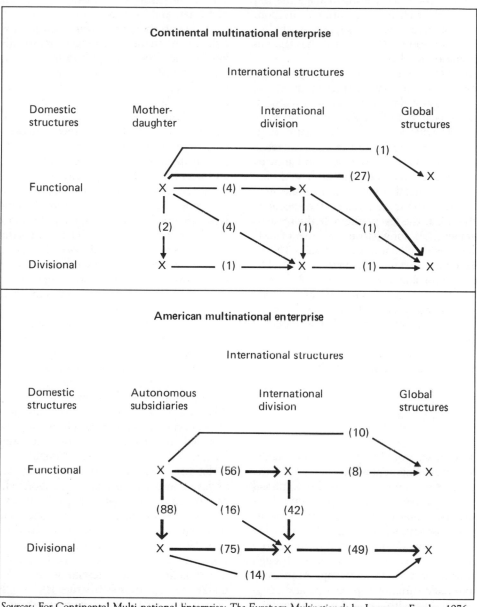

Sources: For Continental Multi-national Enterprise: *The European Multinationals* by Lawrence Franko, 1976, p. 203. Reprinted by permission of Greylock Press. For U.S. Enterprise: *Managing the Multinational Enterprise: Organization of the Firm and Ownership of the Subsidiaries* by John M. Stopford and Lewis T. Wells, Jr., p. 28. Copyright © 1972 by Basic Books, Inc. By permission of Basic Books, Inc., publisher, New York, and Longman Group Ltd.

tice, this meant that diversified American firms forsook functional for divisional organization structures well before they had had much of a chance to involve themselves in foreign operations.

Further examination of the data reveals some consistency between the European and American experiences. Those firms that did establish international divisions were French and German firms which came from large countries with large domestic markets. Also, if Europe is considered a single market, then many firms manage the rest of the world through an international division. Both these observations lend support to the international division stage, provided that there is a large domestic market.

In summary, these studies support the stagewise thesis of growth from a domestic functional organization to global multi-divisional structures. They also repeat Salter's assertion of alternate paths to worldwide structures. As organizations come from different sized countries, face domestic markets varying in competitiveness, and grow by acquisition rather than internally, they choose different but predictable paths to a similar final stage. However, the more detailed the specification of the stage, the less predictable the sequential movement. As long as we conceive of only three stages, with global forms considered to be a Stage III type, the stages of growth model holds. As soon as we consider other types of global structure or consider substages such as the international division phase, more alternate paths appear, more outcomes are possible, and more detailed specifications of strategy, such as Rumelt's nine categories, are required in order to match strategy with structure and process.

A REVISED MODEL

In this section we would like to offer our model of growth and development which summarizes the thinking of others and builds on the empirical evidence. The model is based upon several assumptions and empirical findings. First it is assumed that, starting with the simple form, any source of diversity could be added to move to a new form. There is no set sequence through which firms must move in lock step. An organization could add functions, products, and geography and wind up with a global multi-divisional structure passing through functional and domestic multi-divisional forms along the way. Or it could add functions, geography, and products and still wind up with a global multi-divisional form by passing instead through functional and global functional forms as intermediate transitions. As a result of this assumption, alternate paths

through the developmental sequence are possible. The comparison of American and European multi-nationals is a case in point.

Although there are possible alternative paths, a dominant sequence emerges empirically. Both Franko and Stopford report dominant sequences when multiple sequences are possible. This result is attributable in part to the effects of the environment. When faced with similar environments, firms choose to do similar things. The particular scenario that emerged consisted of specific patterns of population growth, economic growth, technological change, political changes, and world wars. Particular strategies resulting in particular structures proved to be profitable at various times. However, if a different scenario could have emerged, then a different dominant sequence would be observed. The point is that there is no set sequence; in all cases, however, development was dominated by the particular pattern of organization growth. Even though a pattern dominates, there are other routes taken by a minority of the firms.

Another feature of all developmental models is that an organization can stop anywhere along the way. Not every American organization is going to become a global, multi-divisional form. Various niches can be found, and any of the forms can be adopted which happen to fit that niche. Also, a firm can reverse direction and retrace its steps. Some firms are busy selling off their international subsidiaries and could very well move back to a domestic multi-divisional.

Finally, the resulting structure of any sequence of development is, as Chandler suggested, a concatenation of all previous steps. If one examined global structure based on areas, one would find that, within an area, structure is based on products. Within the product substructure, the organization could be market based by breaking out government and commercial sectors. Within a market sector, the substructure is probably functional. Thus each level of the hierarchy is a mechanism for coping with a source of diversity.

The resulting stages model is shown in Figure 4. The starting point is the simple structure with one function and product line. The first major structural change results from a growth in volume. The increased size brings about a division of labor and the simple functional organization

Figure 4. A Summary of Stages Model

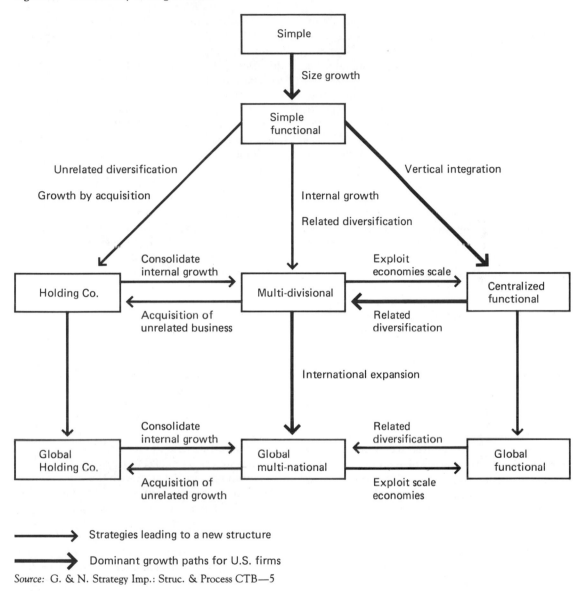

Source: G. & N. Strategy Imp.: Struc. & Process CTB—5

to coordinate the divided work. From this structure several paths are possible. Some firms with crucial supply or distribution problems will pursue strategies of vertical integration. These forms will continue to elaborate the functional organization into large, centralized firms. The mining companies are good examples. Other organizations will diversify product lines through internal growth and acquisition. The internal developer tending to pursue a related diversification strategy will adopt the multi-divisional structure. The third path an organization can follow is to diversify through acquisition and pursue an unrelated diversification strategy. These firms would adopt a holding company or conglomerate form. In each case the structure fits the strategy.

Although the next stages increase rapidly in number of possibilities, empirically there is a dominant movement. The majority of large enterprises have moved to the multi-divisional form either from a holding company type like General Motors, or from a functional form as did Du Pont. In the former case the move is an attempt to consolidate acquisitions, exploit a source of relatedness, and switch to internal growth. The latter case is the classic example of a functional organization unable to manage diversity.

Two other possible paths are not observed in the particular sample of firms that make up the empirical study. The multi-divisional could change to the centralized functional form or to the holding company model. A firm could introduce standardization across related product lines and attempt to exploit economies of scale by moving to the functional organization. General Motors may be an example. In its automobile business General Motors moved towards a functional organization by placing all manufacturing in a GM Assembly Division. Alternatively, the multi-divisional firm could pursue external growth and diversify into less related businesses. A transition to a holding company could occur if the new acquisitions are not integrated into the existing structure. The original core business will probably become an autonomous group managed from a small headquarters office that has been removed from its original location. There probably are examples of organizations not on the *Fortune 500* that have followed these paths.

The next different stage of development for those organizations that choose to pursue strategies of international expansion is the global form. Most organizations will adopt either the area or product global form as indicated in the Stopford research. Global holding companies and global functional forms are possible too, although less likely.

In summary, firms do follow developmental sequences characterized by a metamorphosis between the stages. There is also a dominant path that has been followed by large American enterprises. However, alternative paths are possible. We feel that it is preferable to refer to types of organization form rather than to stages. The multi-

divisional form need not be Stage III. It can be Stage II for some firms who adopt a holding company form for Stage III. Thus the model proposed here allows alternative paths, permitting organizations to stop at any type and even to reverse direction. The primary point of the discussion is to separate what has been observed in a biased sample from what is possible.

A second feature of the model is that it does identify some stages of development. Not all paths are possible. An organization cannot move to a global form without passing through a domestic type as well. A simple organization cannot become a global multi-divisional without passing through at least one transitional form. That is, an organization must learn to manage one and two sources of diversity before handling a third. In this sense we can speak of stages, but we cannot equate any of the types of structure, after the simple structure, with a particular stage.

TYPES OF ORGANIZATION

The previous section emphasized different types of organization, each of which constitute a different way of life. In this section we want to present our model of these different types. In so doing we will build upon the Scott model which was presented earlier. Our model is shown in Table 3. Its characteristics are similar both to those of the research we reviewed and to those used by Scott.

The characteristics start with the strategy classification that has been used throughout this [reading]. They represent the increasing diversity absorbed and managed by large enterprises. The second characteristic shows the degree of integration between divisions. This characteristic varies from the tight interdependence between divisions in the vertically integrated firm, through the loose coupling of the multi-divisional firm exploiting some type of relatedness, to the almost self-contained holding company divisions. The structures that administer these relations are the functional, the holding company, and the multi-divisional (domestic and global) forms. . . .

The research and development function is increasingly institutionalized as one moves from the simple form of organization to the multi-division-

Table 3. Model Illustrating Five Organizational Types

Type / Characteristic	Ⓢ Simple	Ⓕ Functional	Ⓗ Holding	Ⓜ Multi-divisional	Ⓖ Global— M
Strategy	Single Product	Single Product and Vertical Integration	Growth by Acquisition unrelated diversity	Related diversity of product lines—internal growth some acquisition	Multiple products in multiple countries
Inter-unit and Market Relations					
Organization Structure	Simple functional	Central functional	Decentralized Profit Centers around product divisions Small Headquarters	Decentralized Product or area division profit centers	Decentralized profit centers around World wide product or area divisions
Research and Development	Not institutionalized Random search	Increasingly institutionalized around product and process improvements	Institutionalized search for new products and improvements—Decentralized to divisions	Institutionalized search for new products and improvements—Centralized guidance	Institutionalized search for new products which is centralized and decentralized in centers of expertise
Performance Measurement	By personal contact subjective	Increasingly impersonal based on cost, productivity but still subjective	Impersonal based on return on investment and profitability	Impersonal, based on return on investment profitability with some subjective contribution to whole	Impersonal with multiple goals like ROI, profit tailored to product and country
Rewards	Unsystematic paternalistic based on loyalty	Increasingly related to performance around productivity and volume	Formula based bonus on ROI or profitability Equity rewards	Bonus based on profit performance but more subjective than holding—Cash rewards	Bonus based on multiple planned goals More discretion Cash rewards
Careers	Single function specialist	Functional specialists with some generalist interfunctional moves	Cross function but intra-divisional	Cross functional interdivisional and corporate-divisional moves	Interdivisional Intersubsidiary Subsidiary/Corporate moves
Leader Style and Control	Personal Control of strategic and operating decisions by top management	Top control of Strategic decisions Some delegation of operations [through] plans, procedures	Almost complete delegation of operations and strategy within existing businesses Indirect control [through] results and selection of management and capital funding	Delegation of operations with indirect control three results Some decentralization of strategy within existing business	Delegation of operations with indirect control [through] results according to plan Some delegation of strategy within countries and existing businesses Some political delegation
Strategic Choices	Need of owner vs. needs of firm	Degree of integration Market share Breadth of Product line	Degree of diversity Types of business Acquisition targets Entry and Exit from businesses	Allocation of resources by business Exit and Entry from businesses Rate of Growth	Allocation of resources across businesses and countries Exit and entry into businesses and countries Degree of ownership and type of country involvement

als. The functional organizations orient their research and development toward improvements of product and process. The holding company and multi-divisional types institutionalize the search for new products. In the holding company, the search is completely decentralized. In the multi-divisional, there is usually a centralized research and development function with product line extensions and process improvements decentralized to the divisions. The global multi-divisional is usually somewhere between the holding company (II) and the multi-divisional (M) form. Centers of expertise develop or are acquired in various countries. Thus, although some new product search is decentralized, it is coordinated centrally.

The measurement of performance becomes

more formal and explicit as a firm progresses from the S form to the F form and then to the H and M forms. The H, M and G forms all explicitly measure performance against plan, but [the] H form gives the clearest measures. The relatedness of the M form strategy and market, and political variations encountered by the G form all require multiple measures and some subjective assessments. Similarly, as a firm moves from the S form to others, the rewards are more systematically tied to performance. The H form again is the clearest, with formula based bonuses which most often take the form of equity compensation. The M and G forms also tie bonuses to performance, but use other indices and assessments for base salary.

Another major characteristic that changes is the career path followed by top management. In the S and F forms they are usually functional specialists, with a few generalists in the F form. The H form requires more general managers; therefore, one finds cross functional careers. However, they are predominantly intra-divisional careers. It is in the M form and particularly the G form that one finds the greatest need for general managers and general managers with international experience, respectively. Each type needs managers who have experienced multiple sources of diversity. This experience is the greatest difference between the G form and the others. It requires managers with interfunctional, interdivisional, and international experience: these renaissance people are part of the unifying substance that holds these far flung enterprises together.

The style of leadership and control changes significantly with the type of organization. In the S form, the leader is a decision maker very involved in strategy and operations. As a firm moves to F and M forms, the leader increasingly delegates operational decisions which are indirectly controlled through performance measures and procedures. In the M and G forms, some strategic decisions within the existing business are delegated to the divisions. The H form has the greatest amount of delegation and the greatest degree of indirect control through performance measures and rewards tied to performance.

The strategic choices are the same as the Scott model. The choices involved increasing choices about entry into and exit from various businesses, markets, and countries. For the G form, there is the choice of type of relation with a country. A firm can invest in its own facilities, use a joint venture, find a licensee, sign a management contract, and so on. Here the choice is the amount of risk to be managed.

The firm changes all these characteristics when moving from one form to another. Collectively the characteristics constitute the way of life of the organization. They form an integrated whole which fit together to permit effective implementation of the respective strategies. When the organization changes strategies, these characteristics must be disengaged, realigned, and reconnected. This change constitutes a metamorphosis.

SUMMARY

A number of the growth models have been reviewed in this [reading]. All present a sequence of stages through which all organizations must pass. The models differ in the number of stages, but are similar in all other respects. They see the change from one stage to another as a metamorphosis leading to a qualitatively different structure. The reason is that each stage consists of a package of structures, processes, systems, rewards, managerial styles, and so on. A movement to a new stage is a repackaging of all dimensions.

The three-stage model proposed by Scott has been the most popular and is most used in the empirical studies, which support the three-stage models. However, when we consider international expansions, variations on the Stage III multidivisional structure must be introduced. The variations in form also introduce variations in the paths, so that growth and development is not a lock step mechanical process. Organizations have a choice as to the path they want to take. The paths are not however, infinite; they vary according to chosen strategy. The chosen structure should fit the strategy, and vice versa.

A modified sequence of types and an elaboration of each type of structure was presented. An attempt was made to distinguish what is possible from what has been observed. When identifying types, one is led to ask whether or not we are experiencing a new type at present. Is the matrix a different type?

REFERENCES

Child, John, and Alfred Keiser. "The Development of Organizations over Time." in P. Nystrom and W. Starbuck, *The Handbook of Organizational Design*, Vol. I, Amsterdam: Elsevier/North Holland, 1978.

Franko, Lawrence. "The Move Toward a Multi-Divisional Structure in European Organizations." *Administrative Science Quarterly* 19 (1974): 493–506.

Franko, Lawrence. *The European Multinationals.* Greenwich, Connecticut: Greylock Press, 1977.

Galbraith, Jay R. *Organization Design.* Reading, Massachusetts: Addison-Wesley, 1977.

Greiner, Larry. "Patterns of Organizational Change." *Harvard Business Review,* May–June 1972: 121–138.

Khandwalla, Pradip. "Mass Output Orientation of Operations Technology and Organization Structure." *Administrative Science Quarterly* 19 (1973): 74–97.

Lawrence, Paul, and Jay Lorsch. *Organization and Environment.* Boston: Division of Research, Harvard Business School, 1967.

Leavitt, Harold. "Unhuman Organizations." *Harvard Business Review,* July–August 1960: 90–98.

Leavitt, Harold. "Applied Organizational Change in Industry," in James March (ed.) *The Handbook of Organizations.* Chicago: Rand McNally, 1965.

Lorsch, Jay, and Stephen Allen. *Managing Diversity and Interdependence.* Boston: Division of Research, Harvard Business School, 1973.

Lorsch, Jay, and John Morse. *Organizations and Their Members.* New York: Harper & Row Publishers, 1974.

Pugh, Derek, D. J. Hickson and C. R. Hinnings. "An Empirical Taxonomy of Structures of Work Organizations." *Administrative Science Quarterly* 14 (1969): 115–126.

Scott, Bruce R. "Stages of Corporate Development," 9-371-294, BP 998, Intercollegiate Case Clearinghouse, Harvard Business School, 1971.

Smith, William, and R. Charmoz. "Coordinate Line Management," Working Paper, Searle International, Chicago, Illinois, February, 1975.

Starbuck, William. "Organizational Growth and Development," in J. G. March (ed.) *Handbook of Organization.* Chicago: Rand McNally, 1965.

Starbuck, William. *Organizational Growth and Development.* London: Penguin Books, 1971.

Stopford, John, and Louis Wells. *Managing the Multinational Enterprise.* London: Longmans, 1972.

V.C
Implementing
Organizational Changes

33
Concepts for
the management of
organizational change

David A. Nadler

INTRODUCTION

Bringing about major change in a large and complex organization is a difficult task. Policies, procedures, and structures need to be altered. Individuals and groups have to be motivated to continue to perform in the face of major turbulence. People are presented with the fact that the old ways, which include familiar tasks, jobs, procedures, and structures, are no longer applicable. Political behavior frequently becomes more active and more intense. It is not surprising, therefore, that the process of effectively implementing organizational change has long been a topic that both managers and researchers have pondered. While there is still much that is not understood about change in complex organizations, the experiences and research of recent years provide some guidance to those concerned with implementing major changes in organizations.

Source: This article appears here for the first time. Copyright © 1982 by David A. Nadler. Printed by permission.

The [reading] is designed to provide some useful concepts to aid in understanding the dynamics of change and to help in the planning and managing of major organizational changes. We will start with a brief discussion of a model of organizational behavior. This discussion is necessary since it is difficult to think about changing organizations without some notion of why they work the way they do in the first place. Second, we will define organizational change and identify criteria for effective management of change. Third, we will discuss some of the basic problems of implementing change. In the last section, we will list some specific methods and tools for effective implementation of organizational change.

A VIEW OF ORGANIZATIONS

There are many different ways of thinking about organizations and the patterns of behavior that occur within them. During the past two decades, however, there has been an emerging view of organizations as complex open social systems (Katz and Kahn, 1966). Organizations are seen as mechanisms that take inputs from the larger environment and transform them into outputs.

As systems, organizations are seen as composed of interdependent parts. Change in one element of the system will result in changes in other parts of the system. Similarly, organizations have the property of equilibrium; the system will generate energy to move towards a state of balance. Finally, as open systems, organizations must maintain favorable transactions of input and output with the environment in order to survive over time.

While the systems perspective is useful, systems theory by itself may be too abstract a concept to be a usable tool for managers. A number of organizational theorists have attempted to develop more pragmatic theories or models based on the system paradigm. There are a number of such models currently in use. One of these will be employed here.

The particular approach, called a *congruence model of organizational behavior* (Nadler and Tushman, 1979; 1981), is based on the general systems model. The model uses [an] input, transformation process, and output perspective. In this framework, the major inputs to the system of organizational behavior are the *environment* which provides constraints, demands, and opportunities; the *resources* available to the organization; and the *history* of the organization. A fourth input, perhaps the most crucial, is the organization's *strategy*. Strategy is the set of key decisions about the match of the organization's resources to the opportunities, constraints, and demands in the environment within the context of history.

The output of the system is in general the effectiveness of the organization to perform in a manner consistent with the goals of strategy. Specifically, the output includes *organizational performance* as well as *group performance* and *individual behavior and affect*. The last two, of course, contribute to organizational performance.

The basic framework thus views the organization as being the mechanism that takes inputs (strategy and resources in the context of history and environment) and transforms them into outputs (patterns of individual, group, and organizational behavior). This view is portrayed in Figure 1.

The major focus of organizational analysis is this transformation process. The model conceives of the organization as having four major components. The first component is the *task* of the organization, or the work to be done and its critical characteristics. The second component is the *individuals* who are to perform organizational tasks. The third component includes all of the *formal organizational arrangements*, including various structures, processes, and systems designed to motivate and help individuals perform organizational tasks. Finally, there is a set of *informal organizational arrangements*, which are usually neither planned nor written, but which tend to emerge over time. These include patterns of communication, power, and influence; values and norms; and the like. These informal arrangements characterize how an organization actually functions.

How do these four components relate to one

Figure 1.   The Systems Model Applied to Organizational Behavior

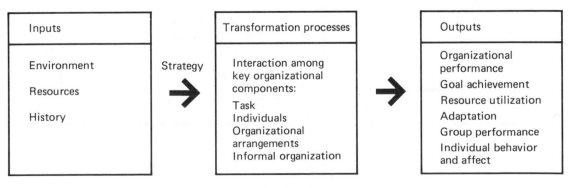

another? The relationship among components is the basic dynamic of the model. Each component exists in some relationship to each other component. Between each pair, then, we can think of a relative degree or consistency, congruence, or fit. If we look at the type of work to be done (task) and the nature of the people available to do the work (individuals), we could make a statement about the congruence between the two by seeing whether the demands of the work are consistent with the skills and abilities of the individuals. At the same time we would compare the rewards the work provides against the needs and desires of the individuals. By looking at these factors, we would be able to assess how congruent the nature of the task was with the nature of the individuals in the system.

We could look at the question of congruence between all the components, or in terms of all six of the possible relationships among them (see Figure 2). The basic hypothesis of the model is therefore that *organizations will be most effective when there is congruence among the major components.* To the extent that organizations face problems of effectiveness due to management and organizational factors, these problems will stem from poor fit, or lack of congruence, among organizational components.

This approach to organizations is thus a contingency approach. There is not one best organization design, or style of management or method of working. Rather, different patterns of organization and management will be most appropriate in different situations. The model recognizes the fact that individuals, tasks, strategies, and environments may differ greatly from organization to organization.

THE TASK OF IMPLEMENTING CHANGE

Having briefly presented some concepts that underlie our thinking about organizations, we can now address the question of change. Managers are frequently concerned about implementing organizational changes. Often changes in the environment necessitate organizational change. There are frequent shifts in factors related to competition, technology, or regulation; these shifts demand changes in organizational strategy.

Figure 2.   A Congruence Model of Organizational Behavior

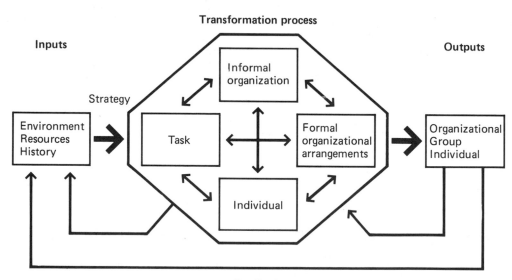

Source: Nadler and Tushman, 1979.

If a new strategy is to be executed, then the organization and its various subunits (departments, groups, and divisions) must perform tasks different from those previously performed. Building on the organizational model presented above, we can state that modification may be needed in organizational arrangements, individuals, and the informal organization.

Typically, implementing a change involves moving an organization to some desired future state. As illustrated in Figure 3, changes may be viewed in terms of transitions (Beckhard and Harris, 1977). At any point in time, the organization exists in a current state, A. The current state describes how the organization functions now. The future state, B, is how the organization should function in the future. B is the ideal future state after the change. The period between A and B can be thought of as the transition state, C. In its most general terms, then, the effective management of change involves developing an understanding of the current state A, developing an image of a desired future state B, and moving the organization from A through transition period C to state B (Beckhard and Harris, 1977).

Major transitions usually occur in response to changes in the nature of organizational inputs or outputs. Most significant changes are in response to or in anticipation of environmental or strategic shifts or problems of performance. In terms of the congruence model, a change occurs when managers determine that the configuration of the components in the current state is not effective and that the organization must be reshaped. Often this means a rethinking and redefining of the organization's task followed by changes in

other components to support that new task (see Figure 4).

What constitutes effective management of change? Several criteria emerge. Building on the transition framework presented above, we say that organizational change is effectively managed when the following occur:

1. The organization is moved from the current state to the future state.
2. The functioning of the organization in the future state meets expectations and works as planned.
3. The transition is accomplished without undue cost to the organization.
4. The organization is accomplished without undue cost to individual organizational members.

Of course, not every organizational change can be expected to meet these criteria, but such standards provide a target for planning change. The question is how to manage the way in which the change is implemented so as to maximize the chances that the change will be effective. Experience has shown that the process of implementing a change can influence the effectiveness of the transition as much as the content of the change.

PROBLEMS IN IMPLEMENTING CHANGE

Experience and research have shown that the process of creating change is more difficult than it might seem. It is reassuring to think of an organization as a large machine whose parts can be replaced at will. Managers know, however, that the task of changing the behavior of organizations, groups, and individuals is a difficult and often frustrating endeavor.

Using the organizational model presented above, we can envision how organizations, as systems, are resistant to change. The forces of equilibrium tend to work to cancel out many changes. Changing one component of an organization may reduce its congruence with other components.

Figure 3.   Organizational Change As a Transition State

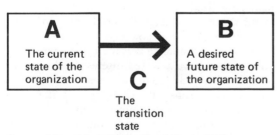

Source: Adapted from Beckhard and Harris, 1977.

Figure 4. Problems of Change in Relation to the Components of the Organizational Model

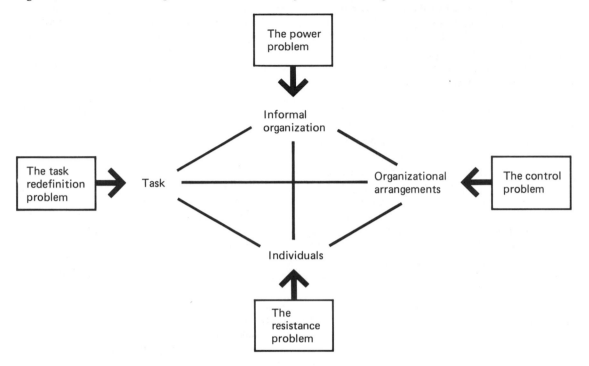

As this happens, energy develops in the organization to limit, encapsulate, or revise the change.

The first step in many changes is to diagnose the current system to identify the source of problems or opportunities for improvement. In a large organization, this step frequently leads to a rethinking of strategy and a redefinition of the organization's task or work. AT&T might examine the environment and determine, for example, that it needs to change the primary orientation of its strategy, and thus its task, from service to marketing.

Although the analysis of strategy and redefinition of task is an important step in changing an organization, many of the most troublesome problems of changing organizations occur not in the strategic/task shift but in the implementation of the organizational transition to support the change in the nature of the strategy and the work. More specifically, any major organizational change presents three major problems which must be dealt with.

First is the problem of *resistance* to change (Watson, 1969; Zaltman and Duncan, 1977). Any individual faced with a change in the organization in which he or she works may be resistant for several reasons. People have needs for a certain degree of stability or security. Change presents unknowns that cause anxiety; change imposed on an individual reduces his or her sense of autonomy or self-control. Furthermore, people typically develop patterns for coping with or managing the current structure and situation. Change means that they will have to find new ways of managing their own environments—ways that might not be as successful as old ways. In addition, those who have power in the current situation may resist change because it threatens that power. They have a vested interest in the status quo. Finally, individuals may resist change for ideological reasons; they believe that the proposed change is not an improvement. Whatever the source of resistance, individuals resistant to change block successful implementation.

Second is the problem of organizational *control*. Change disrupts the normal course of events within an organization. It thus disrupts and undermines existing systems of management control, particularly those developed as part of the formal organizational arrangements. Change may make those systems irrelevant or inappropriate. As a result, it may become easy to lose control of the organization during a change. As goals, structures, and people shift, it becomes difficult to monitor performance and make corrections as in normal control processes.

A related problem is that most formal organizational arrangements are designed for stable states, not transition states. Managers fix on the future state B and assume that all that is needed is to design the most effective organizational arrangements for the future. They think of change from A to B as simply a mechanical or procedural detail. The problems created by the lack of concern for the transition state are compounded by its inherent uniqueness. In most situations, the management systems and structures developed to manage A or B are simply not appropriate for C. They are steady statement management systems, designed to run organizations already in place rather than transitional management systems.

The third problem is *power*. Any organization is a political system made up of different individuals, groups, and coalitions competing for power (Tushman, 1977; Salancik and Pfeffer, 1977). Political behavior is thus a natural and expected feature of organizations and occurs in both states A and B. In transition state C, however, these dynamics become even more intense as the old order is dismantled and a new order emerges. Intensified political behavior happens because any significant change poses the possibility of upsetting or modifying the balance of power among groups. The uncertainty created by change creates ambiguity, which in turn tends to increase the probability of political activity (Thompson and Tuden, 1959). Individuals and groups may take action based on their perceptions of how the change will affect their relative power position in the organization. They will try to influence their positions in the organization that emerges from the transition and will be concerned about how the conflict of the transition period will affect the balance of power in the future state. Finally, individuals and groups may engage in political action because of their ideological position on the change—it may be inconsistent with their shared values or image of the organization (Pettigrew, 1972).

In some sense, each of these problems related primarily to one of the components of the organization (see Figure 4). Resistance relates to the individual component, getting people to change their behavior. Control concerns the design of appropriate organizational arrangements for the transition period. Power relates to the reactions of the informal organization to change. The implication is that if a change is to be effective, all three problems—resistance, control, and power—must be addressed.

GUIDELINES FOR IMPLEMENTING CHANGE

Each of the three basic problems inherent in change has a general implication for the management of change (see Figure 5).

Resistance implies the need to *motivate* changes in behavior by individuals. This involves overcoming the natural resistance to change and get-

Figure 5. Problems of Change and Implications for Change Management

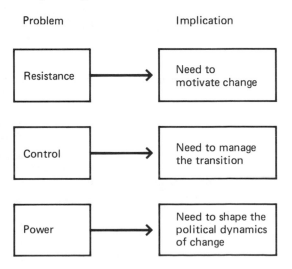

Problem	Implication
Resistance	Need to motivate change
Control	Need to manage the transition
Power	Need to shape the political dynamics of change

ting individuals to behave in ways consistent with both the short-run goals of change and long-run organizational strategy.

Lack of control implies the need to *manage the transition* period. Organizational arrangements need to be designed and used to ensure that control is maintained during and after the transition. These devices and approaches need to be ones appropriate specifically to the transition period rather than to the current or future state.

Intensified political activity implies the need to *shape the political dynamics of change* so as to develop power centers that support the change rather than block it (Pettigrew, 1978).

Each of these general implications suggests specific actions that can be taken to improve the probabilities of achieving an effective change. A number of those action steps can be identified for each of the three implications (see Table 1).

Action Steps to Motivate Change

The first action step is to *identify and bring to the surface dissatisfaction with the current state*. As long as people are satisfied with the current state, they will not be motivated to change; people need to be shaken from their inertia in order to be receptive to change (Lewin, 1947; Bennis, Berlew, Schein, and Steele, 1973). The greater the pain and dissatisfaction with the current state, the greater the motivation to change and the less the resistance to change. As a consequence, the management of change may require the creation of pain and dissatisfaction with the status quo. Dissatisfaction most commonly results from information concerning some aspect of organizational performance different from either desired or expected performance. Discrepancies therefore can be used to create dissatisfaction. As a result, data can be an important tool to initiate a process of change (Nadler, 1977).

The second action step is to build *participation* into the change. One of the most consistent findings in the research on change is that participation in the change tends to reduce resistance, build ownership of the change, and motivate people to make the change work (Coch and French, 1948; Vroom, 1964; Kotter and Schlesinger, 1979). Participation also facilitates the communication of information about what the change will be and why it has come about. Participation

Table 1. Implications for Change Management and Related Action Steps

Implication	Action Steps
Need to motivate change	1. Surface dissatisfaction with the present state
	2. Participation in change
	3. Rewards for behavior in support of change
	4. Time and opportunity to disengage from the present state
Need to manage the transition	5. Develop and communicate a clear image of the future
	6. Use multiple and consistent leverage points
	7. Develop organizational arrangements for the transition
	8. Build in feedback mechanisms
Need to shape the political dynamics of change	9. Assure the support of key power groups
	10. Use leader behavior to generate energy in support of change
	11. Use symbols and language
	12. Build in stability

also may shed light on new information held by participants, information that may enhance the effectiveness of the change or the future state.

However, participation has costs because it involves relinquishing control, takes time, and may create conflict. For each situation, different degrees of participation may be most effective (Vroom and Yetton, 1973). Participation may involve work on diagnosing the present situation, in planning change, in implementing change, or in combinations of the above. Participation may also vary in the devices that are used, ranging from large-scale data collection to sensing groups, to questionnaires, to cross unit committees, and the like.

A third action step is to build in *rewards* for the behavior that is desired both during the transition state and in the future state. Our understanding of motivation and behavior in organizations suggests that people will tend to be motivated to behave in ways that they perceive as leading to desired outcomes (Vroom, 1964; Lawler, 1973). The management implication of this tendency is that both formal and informal rewards need to be identified and tied to the behavior needed for the transition and for the future state. The most frequent problem is that organizations expect individuals to behave in certain ways (particularly in a transition) yet reward them for other conflicting behaviors (Kerr, 1975). In particular, rewards such as bonuses, pay systems, promotion, recognition, job assignment, and status symbols all need to be examined carefully during major organizational changes and restructured to support the direction of the transition.

Finally, people need to be provided with the *time and opportunity to disengage from the present state*. Change, like death, frequently creates feelings of loss. People need to mourn for the old system or familiar way of doing things. This need frequently manifests itself in stories or myths about the "good old days," even when those days were far from good. Dealing with loss and going through mourning takes time, and those managing change need to take this into account. This factor underscores the need to provide information about the problems of the status quo and also to plan for enough time in advance of a change to allow people to deal with the loss and prepare for it.

Action Steps to Manage the Transition

One of the first and most critical steps for managing the transition state is to *develop and communicate a clear image of the future* (Beckhard and Harris, 1977). Resistance and confusion frequently develop during an organizational change because people have no clear image of the future state. Thus the goals and purposes of the change become blurred, and individuals form expectancies from frequently erroneous information. With no clear image of the future, people listen to rumors, design their own fantasies, and then act on them. The implication is that as clear an image as possible of the future state needs to be developed. This image serves as a guideline, target, or goal. In particular, a written statement or description of the future state may be of value in clarifying the image. Similarly, it is important to communicate to those involved in the change information about what the future will hold, how the transition will come about, why the change is being implemented, and how individuals will be affected by the change. This communication can be accomplished in a variety of ways, ranging from written communications to small group meetings, large briefing session, video-taped presentations, and so on.

A second action step for managing the transition involves the use of *multiple and consistent leverage points*. If we accept the model presented above that an organization is made up of interdependent components, then we must use multiple leverage points to bring about the successful alteration of organizational behavior patterns. Structural change, task change, change in the social environment, as well as changes in individuals themselves are all needed to bring about significant and lasting changes in the patterns of organizational behavior. Changes targeted at individuals and social relations (such as training and group interventions) tend to fade out quickly with few lasting effects when done in isolation (Porter, Lawler, and Hackman, 1975). Task and structural changes alone, while powerful and enduring, frequently produce unintended and dysfunctional consequences (see, for example, literature on control systems, such as Lawler and Rhode, 1976). Lasting change in the intended direction requires the use of multiple leverage points, or modifications in the larger set of components that shape the behavior of the organization and the people in it. (Nadler and Tichy, 1980). The changes must be structured to be consistent; the training of individuals, for example, should dovetail with new job descriptions, rewards systems, or reporting relationships. Without consistency, changes may create new "poor fits" between organizational components. The result is either an abortive change or decreases in organizational performance.

The third action step involves a number of different activities. The implication is that *organizational arrangements for the transition* need to be explicitly considered, designed, and used. As mentioned earlier, the organizational arrangements that function in either the present or future state are typically steady-state designs rather than designs for managing the transition state. The whole issue of developing structures to manage the transition has been discussed in depth elsewhere (see Beckhard and Harris, 1977), but a number of the most important elements should be mentioned here. In particular, the following organizational arrangements are important for managing the change:

A transition manager.   Someone should be designated as the manager of the organization during the transition. This person may be a member of management, a chief executive, or someone else, but frequently it is difficult for one person to manage the current state, prepare to manage the future state, and simultaneously manage the transition. This person should have the power and authority needed to make the transition happen and should be appropriately linked to the steady-state managers, particularly the future-state manager.

Resources for the transition.   Major transitions involve potentially large risks for organizations. For this reason, transitions are worth doing well; they repay the investment of the resources needed to make them happen effectively. The transition manager needs personnel, dollars, training expertise, consultative expertise, and the like.

Transition plan.   A transition is a movement from one state to another. To have that occur

effectively, and to measure and control performance, a plan is needed with benchmarks, standards of performance, and similar features. Implicit in such a plan is a specification of the responsibilities of key individuals and groups.

Transition management structures.   Frequently it is difficult for a hierarchy to manage the process of changing itself. It may be necessary to develop other structures or use other devices outside of the regular organizational structure during the transition management period. Special task forces, pilot projects, and experimental units should be designed for and employed during this period (see Beckhard and Harris, 1977, for a discussion of these different devices).

The final action implication for transition management involves developing *feedback mechanisms* to provide transition managers information on the effectiveness of the transition and data on areas that require additional attention or action. A commonplace in anecdotal data are reports of senior managers ordering changes and assuming those changes were made only to find out to their horror that the change never was made. Such a situation develops because managers lack feedback devices to tell them whether actions have been effective. During stable periods, effective managers tend to develop various ways of eliciting feedback. During the transition state, however, these mechanisms often break down due to the turbulence of the change or to the natural inclination not to provide bad news. It is important for transition managers to develop multiple, redundant, and sensitive mechanisms for generating feedback about the transition. Devices such as surveys, sensing groups, consultant interviews, as well as informal communication channels need to be developed and used during this period.

Action Steps for Shaping the Political Dynamics of Change

If an organization is a political system composed of different groups, each competing for power, then the most obvious action step involves *assuring or developing the support of key power groups*. For a change to occur successfully, a critical mass of power groups must be assembled and mobilized in support of the change. Those groups that oppose the change must be compensated for or have their effects neutralized. Not all power groups have to be intimately involved in the change. Some may support the change on ideological grounds, while others may support the change because it enhances their own power position. Other groups must be included in the planning of the change so that their participation will motivate or coopt them (Selznick, 1949). Yet others may have to be dealt with by bargaining or negotiations. The key point is to identify the key groups who may be affected by the change and to develop and carry out strategies for building support among a necessary portion of those groups (Sayles, 1979).

A major factor affecting the political terrain of an organization is the behavior of key and powerful leaders. Thus a second major action step involves *using leader behavior to generate energy in support of the change.* Leaders can mobilize groups, generate energy, provide models, manipulate major rewards, and do many other things that affect the dynamics of the informal organization. Sets of leaders working in a coordinated manner can have a powerful effect on the informal organization. Leaders need to think about using their own behavior to generate energy (see House, 1976, on charismatic leadership) as well as building on the support and behavior of other leaders (both formal and informal) within the organization.

The third action step also is related to the question of leadership. The use of *symbols and language* can be a source of energy (Peters, 1978; Pfeffer, 1980). By providing a language to describe the change and symbols that have emotional impact, managers can create new power centers or bring together power centers under a common banner. Language is also important in defining an ambiguous reality. If, for example, a change is declared a success then, it may be perceived by others as a success.

Finally, there is the need to *build in stability.* Organizations and individuals can stand only so much uncertainty and turbulence. An overload of uncertainty may create dysfunctional effects; people may panic, engage in extreme defensive behavior, and become irrationally resistant to any new change proposed. The anxiety created by constant change has its costs. One way of dealing with this anxiety is to provide some sources of stability (structures, people, physical locations, and so on) that stay the same, serve as anchors for people to hold on to, and provide a means for definition of the self in the midst of turbulence. While too many anchors can encourage resistance, it is important to provide some stability. More importantly, it is necessary to communicate the stability. People may not take comfort from something that is stable if they are unsure of its stability. Those aspects of the organization that will not change during a transition period need to be identified and communicated to organization members.

SUMMARY

This paper has attempted to identify some of the problems and issues associated with bringing about changes in complex organizations. At the same time, a number of general and specific action steps have been suggested. To understand how to change organizational behavior, we need a tool to understand how it occurs in the first place. The model used here (Nadler and Tushman, 1979; 1981) suggests that people contemplating and implementing any change will encounter three general problems: resistance, control, and power. In general, these problems imply three areas of solutions: the need to motivate change, manage the transition, and shape the political dynamics of change. For each of these three general implications, a number of specific action steps have been identified (see Table 1).

Obviously, each of these action steps will be more or less critical (and more or less feasible) in different situations. Students of organization and managers alike need to be diagnostic in their approach to the problems of managing change. Each situation, while reflecting general patterns, is unique because of differences in individuals, history, and situation. Variants of the action steps need to be developed for specific situations. To find appropriate variants, managers need diagnostic models to understand problems as well as guidelines for implementing changes. Together, these two tools can be powerful aids in building and maintaining effective organizations.

REFERENCES

Beckhard, R., and Harris, R. *Organizational transitions.* Reading, Mass.: Addison-Wesley, 1977.

Bennis, W. G., Berlew, D. E., Schein, E. H., and Steele, F. I. *Interpersonal dynamics: Essays and readings on human interaction.* Homewood, Ill.: Dorsey Press, 1973.

Coch, L., and French, J. R. P., Jr. Overcoming resistance to change. *Human Relations,* 1948, *11,* 512–532.

House, Robert J. A 1976 theory of charismatic leadership (mimeo). Faculty of Management Studies, University of Toronto, 1976.

Katz, D., and Kahn, R. L. *The social psychology of organizations.* New York: Wiley, 1966.

Kerr, S. On the folly of rewarding A while hoping for B. *Academy of Management Journal,* December, 1975, *21,* 769–783.

Kotter, J. P., and Schlesinger, L. A. Choosing strategies for change. *Harvard Business Review,* 1979 (March–April), 106–114.

Lawler, E. E. *Motivation in work organizations.* Belmont, Calif.: Wadsworth, 1973.

Lawler, E. E., and Rhode, J. G. *Information and control in organizations.* Santa Monica, Calif.: Goodyear, 1976.

Lewin, K. Frontiers in group dynamics. *Human Relations,* 1947, *1,* 5–41.

Nadler, D. A. *Feedback and organization development: Using data based methods.* Reading, Mass.: Addison-Wesley, 1977.

Nadler, D. A., and Tichy, N. M. The limitations of traditional intervention technology in health care organizations. In N. Margulies and J. Adams (eds.). *Organization development in health care organizations.* Reading, Mass.: Addison-Wesley, 1980.

Nadler, D. A., and Tushman, M. L. A congruence model for diagnosing organizational behavior. In D. Kolb, I. Rubin, and J. McIntyre (eds.). *Organizational psychology: A book of readings* (3rd edition). Englewood Cliffs, N. J.: Prentice-Hall, 1979.

———. A congruence model for diagnosing organizational behavior. In D. A. Nadler, M. L. Tushman, and N. G. Hatvany (eds.). *Approaches to managing organizational behavior: Models, readings, and cases.* Boston: Little, Brown, 1981.

Peters, T. J. Symbols, patterns, and settings: An optimistic case for getting things done. *Organizational Dynamics,* 1978 (Autumn), 3–23.

Pettigrew, A. *The politics of organizational decision-making.* London: Tavistock Press, 1972.

———. Towards a political theory of organizational intervention. *Human Relations,* 1978, *28,* 191–208.

Pfeffer, J. Management as symbolic action: The creation and maintenance of organizational paradigms. In L. L. Cummings and B. M. Staw (eds.). *Research in organizational behavior,* vol 3. Greenwich, Conn.: JAI Press, 1980.

Porter, L. W., Lawler, E. E., and Hackman, J. R. *Behavior in organizations.* New York: McGraw-Hill, 1975.

Salancik, G. R., and Pfeffer, J. Who gets power and how they hold on to it: A strategic-contingency model of power. *Organizational Dynamics.* 1977 (Winter), 3–21.

Sayles, L. R. *Leadership: what effective managers really do and how they do it.* New York: McGraw-Hill, 1979.

Selznick, P. *TVA and the Grass Roots.* Berkeley: University of California Press, 1949.

Thompson, J. D., and Tuden, A. Strategies, structures and processes of organizational decision. In J. D. Thompson et al. (eds.). *Comparative studies in administration.* Pittsburgh: University of Pittsburgh Press, 1959.

Tushman, M. L. A political approach to organizations: a review and rationale. *Academy of Management Review,* 1977, *2,* 206–216.

Vroom, V. H. *Work and motivation.* New York: Wiley, 1964.

Vroom, V. H., and Yetton, P. W. *Leadership and decision making.* Pittsburgh: University of Pittsburgh Press, 1973.

Watson, G. Resistance to change. In W. G. Bennis, K. F. Benne, and R. Chin (eds.). *The planning of change.* New York: Holt, Rinehart and Winston, 1969.

Zaltman, G., and Duncan, R. *Strategies for planned change.* New York: Wiley, 1977.

"It must be considered that there is nothing more difficult to carry out, nor more doubtful of success, nor more dangerous to handle, than to initiate a new order of things."[1]

In 1973, The Conference Board asked 13 eminent authorities to speculate what significant management issues and problems would develop over the next 20 years. One of the strongest themes that runs through their subsequent reports is a concern for the ability of organizations to respond to environmental change. As one person wrote: "It follows that an acceleration in the rate of change will result in an increasing need for reorganization. Reorganization is usually feared, because it means disturbance of the status quo, a threat to people's vested interests in their jobs, and an upset to established ways of doing things. For these reasons, needed reorganization is often deferred, with a resulting loss in effectiveness and an increase in costs."[2]

Subsequent events have confirmed the importance of this concern about organizational change. Today, more and more managers must deal with new government regulations, new products, growth, increased competition, technological developments, and a changing work force. In response, most companies or divisions of major corporations find that they must undertake moderate organizational changes at least once a year and major changes every four or five.[3]

Few organizational change efforts tend to be complete failures, but few tend to be entirely successful either. Most efforts encounter problems; they often take longer than expected and desired, they sometimes kill morale, and they often cost a great deal in terms of managerial time or emotional upheaval. More than a few organizations have not even tried to initiate needed changes

because the managers involved were afraid that they were simply incapable of successfully implementing them.

In this article, we first describe various causes for resistance to change and then outline a systematic way to select a strategy and set of specific approaches for implementing an organizational change effort. The methods described are based on our analyses of dozens of successful and unsuccessful organizational changes.

DIAGNOSING RESISTANCE

Organizational change efforts often run into some form of human resistance. Although experienced managers are generally all too aware of this fact, surprisingly few take time before an organizational change to assess systematically who might resist the change initiative and for what reasons. Instead, using past experiences as guidelines, managers all too often apply a simple set of beliefs—such as "engineers will probably resist the change because they are independent and suspicious of top management." This limited approach can create serious problems. Because of the many different ways in which individuals and groups can react to change, correct assessments are often not intuitively obvious and require careful thought.

Of course, all people who are affected by change experience some emotional turmoil. Even changes that appear to be "positive" or "rational" involve loss and uncertainty.[4] Nevertheless, for a number of different reasons, individuals or groups can react very differently to change—from passively resisting it, to aggressively trying to undermine it, to sincerely embracing it.

To predict what form their resistance might take, managers need to be aware of the four most common reasons people resist change. These include: a desire not to lose something of value, a misunderstanding of the change and its implications, a belief that the change does not make sense for the organization, and a low tolerance for change.

Parochial Self-Interest

One major reason people resist organizational change is that they think they will lose something of value as a result. In these cases, because people focus on their own best interests and not on those of the total organization, resistance often results in "politics" or "political behavior."[5] Consider these two examples:

• After a number of years of rapid growth, the president of an organization decided that its size demanded the creation of a new staff function—New Product Planning and Development—to be headed by a vice president. Operationally, this change eliminated most of the decision-making power that the vice presidents of marketing, engineering, and production had over new products. Inasmuch as new products were very important in this organization, the change also reduced the vice presidents' status which, together with power, was very important to them.

During the two months after the president announced his idea for a new product vice president, the existing vice presidents each came up with six or seven reasons the new arrangement might not work. Their objections grew louder and louder until the president shelved the idea.

• A manufacturing company had traditionally employed a large group of personnel people as counselors and "father confessors" to its production employees. This group of counselors tended to exhibit high morale because of the professional satisfaction they received from the "helping relationships" they had with employees. When a new performance appraisal system was installed, every six months the counselors were required to provide each employee's supervisor with a written evaluation of the employee's "emotional maturity," "promotional potential," and so forth.

As some of the personnel people immediately recognized, the change would alter their relationships from a peer and helper to more of a boss and evaluator with most of the employees. Predictably, the personnel counselors resisted the change. While publicly arguing that the new system was not as good for the company as the old one, they privately put as much pressure as possible on the personnel vice president until he significantly altered the new system.

Political behavior sometimes emerges before and during organizational change efforts when what is in the best interests of one individual or group is not in the best interests of the total organization or of other individuals and groups.

While political behavior sometimes takes the form of two or more armed camps publicly fighting things out, it usually is much more subtle. In many cases, it occurs completely under the surface of public dialogue. Although scheming and ruthless individuals sometimes initiate power struggles, more often than not those who do are people who view their potential loss from change as an unfair violation of their implicit, or psychological, contract with the organization.[6]

Misunderstanding & Lack of Trust

People also resist change when they do not understand its implications and perceive that it might cost them much more than they will gain. Such situations often occur when trust is lacking between the person initiating the change and the employees.[7] Here is an example:

When the president of a small midwestern company announced to his managers that the company would implement a flexible working schedule for all employees, it never occurred to him that he might run into resistance. He had been introduced to the concept at a management seminar and decided to use it to make working conditions at his company more attractive, particularly to clerical and plant personnel.

Shortly after the announcement, numerous rumors began to circulate among plant employees—none of whom really knew what flexible working hours meant and many of whom were distrustful of the manufacturing vice president. One rumor, for instance, suggested that flexible hours meant that most people would have to work whenever their supervisors asked them to—including evenings and weekends. The employee association, a local union, held a quick meeting and then presented the management with a nonnegotiable demand that the flexible hours concept be dropped. The president, caught completely by surprise, complied.

Few organizations can be characterized as having a high level of trust between employees and managers; consequently, it is easy for misunderstandings to develop when change is introduced. Unless managers surface misunderstandings and clarify them rapidly, they can lead to resistance. And that resistance can easily catch change initiators by surprise, especially if they assume that people only resist change when it is not in their best interest.

Different Assessments

Another common reason people resist organizational change is that they assess the situation differently from their managers or those initiating the change and see more costs than benefits resulting from the change, not only for themselves but for their company as well. For example:

> The president of one moderate-size bank was shocked by his staff's analysis of the bank's real estate investment trust (REIT) loans. This complicated analysis suggested that the bank could easily lose up to $10 million, and that the possible losses were increasing each month by 20%. Within a week, the president drew up a plan to reorganize the part of the bank that managed REITs. Because of his concern for the bank's stock price, however, he chose not to release the staff report to anyone except the new REIT section manager.
>
> The reorganization immediately ran into massive resistance from the people involved. The group sentiment, as articulated by one person, was: "Has he gone mad? Why in God's name is he tearing apart this section of the bank? His actions have already cost us three very good people [who quit], and have crippled a new program we were implementing [which the president was unaware of] to reduce our loan losses."

Managers who initiate change often assume both that they have all the relevant information required to conduct an adequate organization analysis and that those who will be affected by the change have the same facts, when neither assumption is correct. In either case, the differ-

ence in information that groups work with often leads to differences in analyses, which in turn can lead to resistance. Moreover, if the analysis made by those not initiating the change is more accurate than that derived by the initiators, resistance is obviously "good" for the organization. But this likelihood is not obvious to some managers who assume that resistance is always bad and therefore always fight it.[8]

Low Tolerance for Change

People also resist change because they fear they will not be able to develop the new skills and behavior that will be required of them. All human beings are limited in their ability to change, with some people much more limited than others.[9] Organizational change can inadvertently require people to change too much, too quickly.

Peter F. Drucker has argued that the major obstacle to organizational growth is managers' inability to change their attitudes and behavior as rapidly as their organizations require.[10] Even when managers intellectually understand the need for changes in the way they operate, they sometimes are emotionally unable to make the transition.

It is because of people's limited tolerance for change that individuals will sometimes resist a change even when they realize it is a good one. For example, a person who receives a significantly more important job as a result of an organizational change will probably be very happy. But it is just as possible for such a person to also feel uneasy and to resist giving up certain aspects of the current situation. A new and very different job will require new and different behavior, new and different relationships, as well as the loss of some satisfactory current activities and relationships. If the changes are significant and the individual's tolerance for change is low, he might begin actively to resist the change for reasons even he does not consciously understand.

People also sometimes resist organizational change to save face; to go along with the change would be, they think, an admission that some of their previous decisions or beliefs were wrong. Or they might resist because of peer group pressure or because of a supervisor's attitude. Indeed, there are probably an endless number of reasons why people resist change.[11]

Assessing which of the many possibilities might apply to those who will be affected by a change is important because it can help a manager select an appropriate way to overcome resistance. Without an accurate diagnosis of possibilities of resistance, a manager can easily get bogged down during the change process with very costly problems.

DEALING WITH RESISTANCE

Many managers underestimate not only the variety of ways people can react to organizational change, but also the ways they can positively influence specific individuals and groups during a change. And, again because of past experiences, managers sometimes do not have an accurate understanding of the advantages and disadvantages of the methods with which they *are* familiar.

Education & Communication

One of the most common ways to overcome resistance to change is to educate people about it beforehand. Communication of ideas helps people see the need for and the logic of a change. The education process can involve one-on-one discussions, presentations to groups, or memos and reports. For example:

> As a part of an effort to make changes in a division's structure and in measurement and reward systems, a division manager put together a one-hour audiovisual presentation that explained the changes and the reasons for them. Over a four-month period, he made this presentation no less than a dozen times to groups of 20 or 30 corporate and division managers.

An education and communication program can be ideal when resistance is based on inadequate or inaccurate information and analysis, especially if the initiators need the resistors' help in implementing the change. But some managers overlook the fact that a program of this sort requires a good relationship between initiators and resistors or that the latter may not believe what they hear. It also requires time and effort, particularly if a lot of people are involved.

Participation & Involvement

If the initiators involve the potential resistors in some aspect of the design and implementation of the change, they can often forestall resistance. With a participative change effort, the initiators listen to the people the change involves and use their advice. To illustrate:

> The head of a small financial services company once created a task force to help design and implement changes in his company's reward system. The task force was composed of eight second- and third-level managers from different parts of the company. The president's specific charter to them was that they recommend changes in the company's benefit package. They were given six months and asked to file a brief progress report with the president once a month. After they had made their recommendations, which the president largely accepted, they were asked to help the company's personnel director implement them.

We have found that many managers have quite strong feelings about participation—sometimes positive and sometimes negative. That is, some managers feel that there should always be participation during change efforts, while others feel this is virtually always a mistake. Both attitudes can create problems for a manager, because neither is very realistic.

When change initiators believe they do not have all the information they need to design and implement a change, or when they need the wholehearted commitment of others to do so, involving others makes very good sense. Considerable research has demonstrated that, in general, participation leads to commitment, not merely compliance.[12] In some instances, commitment is needed for the change to be a success. Nevertheless, the participation process does have its drawbacks. Not only can it lead to a poor solution if the process is not carefully managed, but also it can be enormously time consuming. When the change must be made immediately, it can take simply too long to involve others.

Facilitation & Support

Another way that managers can deal with potential resistance to change is by being supportive. This process might include providing training in new skills, or giving employees time off after a demanding period, or simply listening and providing emotional support. For example:

> Management in one rapidly growing electronics company devised a way to help people adjust to frequent organizational changes. First, management staffed its human resource department with four counselors who spent most of their time talking to people who were feeling "burnt out" or who were having difficulty adjusting to new jobs. Second, on a selective basis, management offered people four-week minisabbaticals that involved some reflective or educational activity away from work. And, finally, it spent a great deal of money on in-house education and training programs.

Facilitation and support are most helpful when fear and anxiety lie at the heart of resistance. Seasoned, tough managers often overlook or ignore this kind of resistance, as well as the efficacy of facilitative ways of dealing with it. The basic drawback of this approach is that it can be time consuming and expensive and still fail.[13] If time, money, and patience just are not available, then using supportive methods is not very practical.

Negotiation & Agreement

Another way to deal with resistance is to offer incentives to active or potential resistors. For instance, management could give a union a higher wage rate in return for a work rule change; it could increase an individual's pension benefits in return for an early retirement. Here is an example of negotiated agreements:

> In a large manufacturing company, the divisions were very interdependent. One division manager wanted to make some major changes in his organization. Yet, because of the interdependence, he recognized that he would be forcing some inconvenience and change on other divisions as well. To prevent top managers in other divisions from undermining his efforts,

the division manager negotiated a written agreement with each. The agreement specified the outcomes the other division managers would receive and when, as well as the kinds of cooperation that he would receive from them in return during the change process. Later, whenever the division managers complained about his changes or the change process itself, he could point to the negotiated agreements.

Negotiation is particularly appropriate when it is clear that someone is going to lose out as a result of a change and yet his or her power to resist is significant. Negotiated agreements can be a relatively easy way to avoid major resistance, though, like some other processes, they may become expensive. And once a manager makes it clear that he will negotiate to avoid major resistance, he opens himself up to the possibility of blackmail.[14]

Manipulation & Co-optation

In some situations, managers also resort to covert attempts to influence others. Manipulation, in this context, normally involves the very selective use of information and the conscious structuring of events.

One common form of manipulation is cooptation. Co-opting an individual usually involves giving him or her a desirable role in the design or implementation of the change. Co-opting a group involves giving one of its leaders, or someone it respects, a key role in the design or implementation of a change. This is not a form of participation, however, because the initiators do not want the advice of the co-opted, merely his or her endorsement. For example:

> One division manager in a large multibusiness corporation invited the corporate human relations vice president, a close friend of the president, to help him and his key staff diagnose some problems the division was having. Because of his busy schedule, the corporate vice president was not able to do much of the actual information gathering or analysis himself, thus limiting his own influence on the diagnoses. But his presence at key meetings helped commit him to the diagnoses as well as the solutions the group designed. The commitment was subsequently very

important because the president, at least initially, did not like some of the proposed changes. Nevertheless, after discussion with his human relations vice president, he did not try to block them.

Under certain circumstances co-optation can be a relatively inexpensive and easy way to gain an individual's or a group's support (cheaper, for example, than negotiation and quicker than participation). Nevertheless, it has its drawbacks. If people feel they are being tricked into not resisting, are not being treated equally, or are being lied to, they may respond very negatively. More than one manager has found that, by his effort to give some subordinate a sense of participation through co-optation, he created more resistance than if he had done nothing. In addition, co-optation can create a different kind of problem if those co-opted use their ability to influence the design and implementation of changes in ways that are not in the best interests of the organization.

Other forms of manipulation have drawbacks also, sometimes to an even greater degree. Most people are likely to greet what they perceive as covert treatment and/or lies with a negative response. Furthermore, if a manager develops a reputation as a manipulator, it can undermine his ability to use needed approaches such as education/communication and participation/involvement. At the extreme, it can even ruin his career.

Nevertheless, people do manipulate others successfully—particularly when all other tactics are not feasible or have failed.[15] Having no other alternative, and not enough time to educate, involve, or support people, and without the power or other resources to negotiate, coerce, or co-opt them, managers have resorted to manipulating information channels in order to scare people into thinking there is a crisis coming which they can avoid only by changing.

Explicit & Implicit Coercion

Finally, managers often deal with resistance coercively. Here they essentially force people to accept a change by explicitly or implicitly threatening them (with the loss of jobs, promotion possibilities, and so forth) or by actually firing or

transferring them. As with manipulation, using coercion is a risky process because inevitably people strongly resent forced change. But in situations where speed is essential and where the changes will not be popular, regardless of how they are introduced, coercion may be the manager's only option.

Successful organizational change efforts are always characterized by the skillful application of a number of these approaches, often in very different combinations. However, successful efforts share two characteristics: managers employ the approaches with a sensitivity to their strengths and limitations (see *Exhibit 1 . . .*) and appraise the situation realistically.

The most common mistake managers make is to use only one approach or a limited set of them *regardless of the situation.* A surprisingly large number of managers have this problem. This would include the hard-boiled boss who often coerces people, the people-oriented manager who constantly tries to involve and support his people, the cynical boss who always manipulates and co-opts others, the intellectual manager who relies heavily on education and communication, and the lawyerlike manager who usually tries to negotiate.[16]

A second common mistake that managers make is to approach change in a disjointed and incremental way that is not a part of a clearly considered strategy.

CHOICE OF STRATEGY

In approaching an organizational change situation, managers explicitly or implicitly make strategic choices regarding the speed of the effort, the amount of preplanning, the involvement of others, and the relative emphasis they will give to different approaches. Successful change efforts seem to be those where these choices both are internally consistent and fit some key situational variables.

The strategic options available to managers can be usefully thought of as existing on a continuum (see *Exhibit 2*).[17] At one end of the continuum, the change strategy calls for a very rapid implementation, a clear plan of action, and little

Exhibit 1.   Methods for Dealing with Resistance to Change

Approach	Commonly used in situations	Advantages	Drawbacks
Education + communication	Where there is a lack of information or inaccurate information and analysis.	Once persuaded, people will often help with the implementation of the change.	Can be very time-consuming if lots of people are involved.
Participation + involvement	Where the initiators do not have all the information they need to design the change, and where others have considerable power to resist.	People who participate will be committed to implementing change, and any relevant information they have will be integrated into the change plan.	Can be very time-consuming if participators design an inappropriate change.
Facilitation + support	Where people are resisting because of adjustment problems.	No other approach works as well with adjustment problems.	Can be time-consuming, expensive, and still fail.
Negotiation + agreement	Where someone or some group will clearly lose out in a change, and where that group has considerable power to resist.	Sometimes it is a relatively easy way to avoid major resistance.	Can be too expensive in many cases if it alerts others to negotiate for compliance.
Manipulation + co-optation	Where other tactics will not work, or are too expensive.	It can be a relatively quick and inexpensive solution to resistance problems.	Can lead to future problems if people feel manipulated.
Explicit + implicit coercion	Where speed is essential, and the change initiators possess considerable power.	It is speedy, and can overcome any kind of resistance.	Can be risky if it leaves people mad at the initiators.

Exhibit 2.   Strategic Continuum

Fast	Slower
Clearly planned.	Not clearly planned at the beginning.
Little involvement of others.	Lots of involvement of others.
Attempt to overcome any resistance.	Attempt to minimize any resistance.

Key situational variables

The amount and type of resistance that is anticipated.

The position of the initiators vis-à-vis the resistors (in terms of power, trust, and so forth).

The locus of relevant data for designing the change, and of needed energy for implementing it.

The stakes involved (e.g., the presence or lack of presence of a crisis, the consequences of resistance and lack of change).

involvement of others. This type of strategy mows over any resistance and, at the extreme, would result in a fait accompli. At the other end of the continuum, the strategy would call for a much slower change process, a less clear plan, and involvement on the part of many people other than the change initiators. This type of strategy is designed to reduce resistance to a minimum.[18]

The further to the left one operates on the continuum in *Exhibit 2,* the more one tends to be coercive and the less one tends to use the other approaches—especially participation; the converse also holds.

Organizational change efforts that are based on inconsistent strategies tend to run into predictable problems. For example, efforts that are not clearly planned in advance and yet are implemented quickly tend to become bogged down owing to unanticipated problems. Efforts that involve a large number of people, but are implemented quickly, usually become either stalled or less participative.

Situational Factors

Exactly where a change effort should be strategically positioned on the continuum in *Exhibit 2* depends on four factors:

1. The amount and kind of resistance that is anticipated. All other factors being equal, the greater the anticipated resistance, the more difficult it will be simply to overwhelm it, and the more a manager will need to move toward the right on the continuum to find ways to reduce some of it.[19]

2. The position of the initiator vis-à-vis the resistors, especially with regard to power. The less power the initiator has with respect to others, the more the initiating manager *must* move to the left on the continuum.[20] Conversely, the stronger the initiator's position, the more he or she can move to the right.

3. The person who has the relevant data for designing the change and the energy for implementing it. The more the initiators anticipate that they will need information and commitment from others to help design and implement the change, the more they must move to the right.[21] Gaining useful information and commitment requires time and the involvement of others.

4. The stakes involved. The greater the short-run potential for risks to organizational performance and survival if the present situation is not changed, the more one must move to the left.

Organizational change efforts that ignore these factors inevitably run into problems. A common mistake some managers make, for example, is to move too quickly and involve too few people despite the fact that they do not have all the information they really need to design the change correctly.

Insofar as these factors still leave a manager with some choice of where to operate on the continuum, it is probably best to select a point as far to the right as possible for both economic and social reasons. Forcing change on people can have just too many negative side effects over both the short and the long term. Change efforts using the strategies on the right of the continuum can often help develop an organization and its people in useful ways.[22]

In some cases, however, knowing the four factors may not give a manager a comfortable and obvious choice. Consider a situation where a manager has a weak position vis-à-vis the people whom he thinks need a change and yet is faced with serious consequences if the change is not implemented immediately. Such a manager is clearly in a bind. If he somehow is not able to increase his power in the situation, he will be forced to choose some compromise strategy and to live through difficult times.

Implications for Managers

A manager can improve his chance of success in an organizational change effort by:

1. Conducting an organizational analysis that identifies the current situation, problems, and the forces that are possible causes of those problems. The analysis should specify the actual importance of the problems, the speed with which the problems must be addressed if additional problems are to be avoided, and the kinds of changes that are generally needed.

2. Conducting an analysis of factors relevant to producing the needed changes. This analysis should focus on questions of who might resist the change, why, and how much; who has information that is needed to design the change, and

whose cooperation is essential in implementing it; and what is the position of the initiator vis-à-vis other relevant parties in terms of power, trust, normal modes of interaction, and so forth.

3. Selecting a change strategy, based on the previous analysis, that specifies the speed of change, the amount of preplanning, and the degree of involvement of others; that selects specific tactics for use with various individuals and groups; and that is internally consistent.

4. Monitoring the implementation process. No matter how good a job one does of initially selecting a change strategy and tactics, something unexpected will eventually occur during implementation. Only by carefully monitoring the process can one identify the unexpected in a timely fashion and react to it intelligently.

Interpersonal skills, of course, are the key to using this analysis. But even the most outstanding interpersonal skills will not make up for a poor choice of strategy and tactics. And in a business world that continues to become more and more dynamic, the consequences of poor implementation choices will become increasingly severe.

REFERENCES

1. Niccolo Machiavelli, *The Prince.*

2. Marvin Bower and C. Lee Walton, Jr., "Gearing a Business to the Future," in *Challenge to Leadership* (New York: The Conference Board, 1973), p. 126.

3. For recent evidence on the frequency of changes, see Stephen A. Allen, "Organizational Choice and General Influence Networks for Diversified Companies," *Academy of Management Journal,* September 1978, p. 341.

4. For example, see Robert A. Luke, Jr., "A Structural Approach to Organizational Change," *Journal of Applied Behavioral Science,* September-October 1973, p. 611.

5. For a discussion of power and politics in corporations, see Abraham Zaleznik and Manfred F. R. Kets de Vries, *Power and the Corporate Mind* (Boston: Houghton Mifflin, 1975), Chapter 6; and Robert H. Miles, *Macro Organizational Behavior* (Pacific Palisades, Calif.: Goodyear, 1978), Chapter 4.

6. See Edgar H. Schein, *Organizational Psychology* (Englewood Cliffs, N.J.: Prentice-Hall, 1965), p. 44.

7. See Chris Argyris, *Intervention Theory and Method* (Reading, Mass.: Addison-Wesley, 1970), p. 70.

8. See Paul R. Lawrence, "How to Deal with Resistance to Change," HBR May–June 1954, p. 49; reprinted as [Harvard Business Review] Classic, January–February 1969, p. 4.

9. For a discussion of resistance that is personality based, see Goodwin Watson, "Resistance to Change," in *The Planning of Change,* eds. Warren G. Bennis, Kenneth F. Benne, and Robert Chin (New York: Holt, Rinehart, and Winston, 1969), p. 489.

10. Peter F. Drucker, *The Practice of Management* (New York: Harper and Row, 1954).

11. For a general discussion of resistance and reasons for it, see Chapter 3 in Gerald Zaltman and Robert Duncan, *Strategies for Planned Change* (New York: John Wiley, 1977).

12. See, for example, Alfred J. Marrow, David F. Bowers, and Stanley E. Seashore, *Management by Participation* (New York: Harper and Row, 1967).

13. Zaltman and Duncan, *Strategies for Planned Change,* Chapter 4.

14. For an excellent discussion of negotiation, see Gerald I. Nierenberg, *The Art of Negotiating* (Birmingham, Ala.: Cornerstone, 1968).

15. See John P. Kotter, "Power, Dependence, and Effective Management," [Harvard Business Review] July–August 1977, p. 125.

16. Ibid., p. 135.

17. See Larry E. Greiner, "Patterns of Organization Change," HBR May–June 1967, p. 119; and Larry E. Greiner and Louis B. Barnes, "Organization Change and Development," in *Organizational Change and Development,* eds. Gene W. Dalton and Paul R. Lawrence (Homewood, Ill.: Irwin, 1970), p. 3.

18. For a good discussion of an approach that attempts to minimize resistance, see Renato Tagiuri, "Notes on the Management of Change: Implication of Postulating a Need for Competence," in John P. Kotter, Vijay Sathe, and Leonard A. Schlesinger, *Organization* (Homewood, Ill.: Irwin, . . . 1979).

19. Jay W. Lorsch, "Managing Change," in *Organizational Behavior and Administration,* eds. Paul R. Lawrence, Louis B. Barnes, and Jay W. Lorsch (Homewood, Ill.: Irwin, 1976), p. 676.

20. Ibid.

21. Ibid.

22. Michael Beer, *Organization Change and Development: A Systems View* (Pacific Palisades, Calif.: Goodyear, 1979).

35
Symbols, patterns and settings: An optimistic case for getting things done

Thomas J. Peters

The most important decisions are often the least apparent.

Karl Weick

What tools come to mind when you think about changing an organization? If you came up through the ranks in the 1950s and 1960s, the answer is quite likely to be divisionalizing and developing a strategic planning system. Shifting the organizational structure and inventing new processes are still options for change. But increasingly thorny and overlapping international, competitive, and regulatory problems call for increasingly complex responses—and such responses are getting increasingly difficult to devise and problematical in their application.

It is reasonable to propose, however, that an effective set of change tools is actually embedded in senior management's daily message sending and receiving activities, and that these tools can be managed in such a way as to energize and redirect massive, lumbering business and government institutions. The tools will be characterized as symbols (the raw material), patterns (the systematic use of the raw material), and settings (the showcase for the systematic use).

It is not suggested that these tools merely be added to the traditional arsenal of formal change instruments—primarily structure and process. Rather, it will be argued that historically effective prescriptions are losing some of their impact, and their formal replacements—such as the matrix structure—have comparatively little leverage. Moreover, the typical top management is seldom

around for much more than five or six years—too little time in which to leave a distinctive and productive stamp on a large, history-bound institution solely by means of the available formal change alternatives. Hence effective change may increasingly depend on systematic use of the informal change mechanisms, derived from coherent daily actions.

PESSIMISM: FROM RATIONAL MEN TO GARBAGE CANS

Many leading organizational researchers seem to imply "You'll never get much done." James March describes organizations as "garbage cans," in which problems, participants, and choices circle aimlessly around, connecting—with resultant decisions—only occasionally. Other colorful metaphors or contrived terms have sought to convey similar images of confusion: for example, "organizational seesaws" (William Starbuck), "organized chaos" (Igor Ansoff), "loosely coupled systems" (Karl Weick). The theory of resource dependency developed by Jeffery Pfeffer and Gerald Salancik depicts the typical executive as having but a single course for inducing stable outcomes: Diversify to cope with uncertainty by reducing dependence on any one source of supply or market segment. The common message seems to be one of nearly unrelieved pessimism: It is a confusing, messy world.

It would be hard to quarrel with the researchers' descriptions of the complexity and ambiguity of real life in organizations. The trouble is that most of them fail to address in any but the most general terms the question of whether (and how) one can operate in such a world.

It may be well to begin by briefly examining the origin of the pessimistic views. Herbert Simon, the most noted analyst of organizational complexity, coined the term *satisficing* in 1957 to

Source: Reprinted, by permission of the publisher, from *Organizational Dynamics*, Autumn 1978, © by AMACOM, a division of American Management Associations. All rights reserved.

Author's note: The author wholeheartedly acknowledges the help of Anne Hartman Peters in the preparation of this article, along with the thoughtful comments of Anthony G. Athos, Harold J. Leavitt, and Eugene J. Webb.

suggest that organizations seek satisfactory rather than optimal solutions to problems.

Simon and his successors were reacting to decades of management and organization theorizing in search of reliable management prescriptions. The quest for certainties in management began at least as early as Frederick Taylor's time and motion studies and soon expanded to a search for highly rational principles of management—for example, optimal spans of control and rules of delegation. After the Hawthorne experiments, a competing form of prescriptive certainty, based on an opposite set of assumptions about human nature, emerged. Enhancing participation in decision making became a substitute panacea.

When Simon and his successors revolted against the quest for certainty, their line of attack (based on descriptions of ambiguity in managerial settings) was not surprisingly marked by a refusal to develop prescriptions for the management of change. Their complex models in general provide little comfort for the struggling executive. It is in fact commonplace in organizational behavior articles to dismiss most practical advice as "not contingent enough." The contingency theorists correctly assert that different organizational solutions work in different settings. In practice, this frequently seems to imply that every solution is unique, hence the search for generally useful principles is essentially futile.

Carefully reading the work of the leading architects of complexity, one can, however, unearth the rudiments of some practical prescriptions for beleaguered managers. Almost as an aside, for example, Michael Cohen and James March in *Leadership and Ambiguity*, a study of university presidents, offer "eight basic tactical rules for those who seek to influence the course of decisions." The sorts of rules that Cohen and March propose (see Figure 1) have a particularly startling

Figure 1. Rules for Managing Change

Rule	Interpretation
1. Spend time	Spending time exerts, in itself, a "claim" on the decision-making system.
2. Persist	Having more patience than other people often results in adoption of a chosen course of action.
3. Exchange status for substance	One of the most effective ways to gather support for programs is to reward allies with visible tokens of recognition.
4. Facilitate opposition participation	Often those outside the formal decision centers overestimate the feasibility of change; encouraged to participate, they will often become more realistic.
5. Overload the system	Bureaucracies chew up most projects, but on the other hand, some sneak through; merely launching more projects is likely to result in more successes.
6. Provide garbage cans	Organizations endlessly argue issues; to induce desired outcomes, put "throw-away" issues at the top of agendas (to absorb debate) saving substantive issues for later.
7. Manage unobtrusively	Certain actions can influence the organization pervasively but almost imperceptibly; moreover, the resulting changes will persist with little further attention.
8. Interpret history	By articulating a particular version of events, the leader can alter people's perception of what has been happening; whoever writes the minutes influences the outcome.

property: Although, as the authors demonstrate, some such tools as these may be the most effective change vehicles available in today's environment, they are too "trivial" to be at the forefront of most managers' minds—one reason, perhaps, why they have not been explored.

The author's research has focused on what many audiences have called the "theory of the small win." Patterns of consistent, moderate size, clear-cut outcomes—patterns of small wins—are a special subclass of managerial activity patterns influencing future change. The effectiveness of these patterns was first validated in laboratory experiments with M.B.A. graduates. In addition, patterns of small wins were repeatedly noted in the literature of business and politics. Successful executives in both the private and public sectors apparently often attend to manageable situations where the value of their own persistence and ability to control intermediate events maximizes their influence on subsequent outcomes. Strings of these controlled successes are used over time to shape and manage attention and perceptions, thereby affecting the course of interactions and outcomes.

During the past year, several colleagues and I have been testing similar change techniques in a handful of large American and European corporations. The results so far obtained by sensitive application of these "mundane tools"—as practical alternatives to ponderous weapons such as structural overhauls—have been impressive enough to give grounds for cautious optimism. Based on these experiences, I will propose in the following pages a simple set of change instruments whose practical value seems to warrant trial and application on a broader scale.

A FRAMEWORK FOR THINKING ABOUT CHANGE

In the minds of senior managers, what does it mean to induce effective change? Surely speed of effect and control over outcomes would be near the top of any list of criteria. Consider the typology derived from these two dimensions:

- Category 1: High control, low speed.

- Category 2: High control, high speed.
- Category 3: Low control, high speed.
- Category 4: Low control, low speed.

Our revised view of organizational change may be considered in the framework of this categorization. First, some historical change tools will be assigned to each category; next, the apparently decreasing effectiveness of several tools will be discussed; last, some alternative change levers will be suggested.

Historically, the most regularly considered tools for change have been formal processes, structure, and human resource development programs. The first two of these levers have been at the forefront of organization change in the past; the third has never attained its purported full potential.

The modern planning system is the most typical formal process. Its roots go back decades. Planning, as managers generally think of it today, received its major impetus during World War II. Strategic planning systems burgeoned in the 1960s; General Electric and Texas Instruments, among others, have attributed much of their continuing success to the planning revolution. Planning tends to affect organizational outcomes over a period of years, as experience and skill accumulate at many levels within the organization. Historically, then, planning systems are perhaps the most important and typical change tool in Category 1 (high control, low speed).

Structural solutions, especially decentralization and divisionalization, have commonly been employed for strategically realigning increasingly complex organizations into manageable, typically product-line–oriented chunks. Having reached its highwater mark in the United States in the years after World War II, decentralization spread to Europe in the 1960s in response to the U.S. multinational invasion. The vast majority of major business enterprises today are organized on the divisional principle—or some variation thereof, for example, GE's recent sectoral reorganization. Working out the problems of divisionalization took years in many cases, but noticeable change more often than not came quickly and was generally in the hoped-for direction. Thus it seems fair to consider this historical solution as the leading candidate for Category 2 (high control, high speed) change tools.

An obvious candidate for Category 4 (low control, low speed) change appears to be human resource development, particularly typified by bottom-up team building. Numerous organizations, under a wide range of circumstances, have noted the benefits of team building. By and large, however, organizational development, no matter what its form, seems not to have had the hoped-for impact. Chief executives are frequently unaware of ongoing experiments in their own organizations. Few corporations with stable, energetic cultures attribute much of their success to formal application of behavioral science techniques.

TRADITIONAL TOOLS: WHAT'S HAPPENED

Meanwhile, something rather disturbing has been happening to the traditional, controlled-change tools. In effect, they have largely been migrating to the low-speed, low-control category. Left with no obvious set of replacement tools, the senior manager may well adopt the pessimistic view noted earlier.

Over time, government and competitive pressures requiring recentralization along various dimensions have nibbled away at the decentralization principle until most organizations today are a hodgepodge of centralized and decentralized activities. The matrix structure, which has arisen in response to these conflicting demands, has as often as not multiplied rather than resolved coordination problems. Even the foremost advocates of the matrix, for example Paul Lawrence and Jay Galbraith, point to imposing lists of pathologies leading to failures—or at least significant delay in implementation.

Similarly, strategic planning systems are no longer viewed as a panacea by many executives. Their greatest value often came soon after they were put in place: They provided novel perspectives on the business. Now, in many large organizations, the strategic planning system has become a rather routine and highly politicized part of the bureaucracy. It is seldom the font

of new directions or the spearhead of rapid adaptation to changing economic or political conditions.

SOME SPECULATIONS

My thesis in this article is that there are a variety of practical controlled change tools appropriate to today's complex and ambiguous organization settings. Most have been around a long time and need only to be consciously packaged and managed. Some are rather new. Few have been thought of as major instruments for achieving organizational redirection. Almost all are associated with the informal organization.

Figure 2 arrays some of those change tools along the previously noted dimensions of controllability and speed of change, and Figure 3 presents some mundane change tools. By briefly assessing the reasons for the failure or obsolescence of the conventional tools and their successors (shown here as having drifted to the low-control, low-speed category), a very general rationale for the nature of the new change-tool candidates can be developed. Then each new category of tools can be assessed in turn.

There are at least two reasons why the conventional solutions have failed to achieve their full promise or have declined in effectiveness. One is that none of them takes time explicitly into account. In the case of structural solutions, management typically miscalculates in two different ways. On the one hand, it grossly underestimates the growing time lag between changed structure and changed behavior. On the other hand, it overestimates their durability under growing environmental pressures and consequently tends to leave them in place long after they have outlived their effectiveness.

The second reason for the weakness of conventional solutions is over- or underdetermination. Several solutions seem to rest on an overestimation of managers' ability to determine the best way to accomplish great purposes—overdetermination. For example, complex planning systems, multiple project teams, and the matrix structure proceed from the implicit assumption that effective organizing flows from fig-

Figure 2.   Speculation About Current Change Tools

	Speed of Short-Term Change	
	Low	High
High	Manipulation of symbols–*a* Patterns of activity–*b* Settings for interaction–*c* 1	Single element structural thrust focusers Total systems of top managers' interaction Dominating value 2
Low	4 Overdetermined approaches: • Complex planning systems • Multiple project teams • Matrix structures Underdetermined approaches: • Bottom-up team building	3 Change for change sake: • Structure • Senior managers

(vertical axis label: **Control Over Direction of Change**)

Figure 3.   Mundane Tools

a–Symbols:	b–Patterns:	c–Settings:
Calendars Reports Agenda Physical settings Public statements Staff organization	Positive reinforcement Frequency and consistency of behavior Implementation/solution bias Experimenting mode	Role of modeling Location Agenda control Presentation format Questioning approaches Deadline management Use of minutes

uring out the correct wiring diagram—an assumption increasingly at odds with today's organizational tasks. Koppers' chief executive officer, Fletcher Byrom, recently remarked, "Of all the things that I have observed about corporations, the most disturbing has been a tendency toward over-organization, producing a rigidity that is intolerable in an era of rapidly accelerating change."

At the other end of the spectrum—underdetermination—bottom-up team building has been based on the opposite presumption: Overall or-

ganizational purposes can be largely ignored; seeding effective new behavior patterns at the bottom of the organization or in the ranks of middle management will somehow eventuate in desirable organizational performance levels.

The proposed "new" change tools partially address both issues. First, they explicitly take time into account, recognizing both that change typically comes slowly as the result of the application of many tools and that the organizational focus of prime importance today is temporary and will almost certainly have changed substantially four or five years hence. Second, they are tools of the experimenter: That is, they neither assume an ability to fix organizational arrangements with much precision—the failing of overdetermination—nor do they ignore purposiveness—the failing of underdetermination.

OBSESSION WITH THE MUNDANE

Cell 1 of Figure 2 (high control, low speed change), the realm of what my colleagues and I have come to call "mundane tools," reflects the notion that the management of change—small or large—is inextricably bound up with the mundane occurrences that fill an executive's calendar.

By definition, managing the daily stream of activities might be said to consist of the manipulation of symbols, the creation of patterns of activity, and the staging of occasions for interaction. The mundane tools are proposed as direct alternatives to structural manipulation and other grand solutions to strategic organization needs. Conscious experimentation with these tools can provide a sound basis for controlled, purposive change.

Manipulation of Symbols

Because they have so often been applied by the media to the performances of politicians intent on reshaping or repairing an image, the terms *symbolic behavior* and *symbol manipulation* have lately acquired something of a perjorative connotation: symbol vs. substance. In a much more basic sense, however, symbols are the very stuff of management behavior. Executives, after all, do not synthesize chemicals or operate lift trucks; they deal in symbols. And their overt verbal communications are only part of the story. Consciously or unconsciously, the senior executive is constantly acting out the vision and goals he is trying to realize in an organization that is typically far too vast and complex for him to control directly.

What mundane tools might best aid the executive interested in effecting change through symbol manipulation? To signal watchers, which includes nearly everyone in his organization, there is no truer test of what he really thinks is important than the way he spends his time. As Eli Ginsberg and Ewing W. Reilley have noted:

> Those a few echelons from the top are always alert to the chief executive. Although they attach importance to what he says, they will be truly impressed only by what he does.

Is he serious about making a major acquisition? The gossip surrounding his calendar—Has he seen the investment banker?—provides clues for senior and junior management alike.

As reported in *Fortune*, Roy Ash's early activities after assuming the reins at Addressograph-Multigraph suggest mastery of the calendar and other mundane tools:

> Instead of immediately starting to revamp the company, Ash spent his first several months visiting its widely scattered operations and politely asking a lot of searching questions. . . . His predecessors had always summoned subordinates to the headquarters building, which had long lived up to its official name, the Tower. Rather than announcing his ideas, Ash demonstrated them. He left his office door open, placing his own intercom calls to arrange meetings, and always questioned people in person, not in writing. Then he removed some of the company's copying machines "to stop breeding paperwork." Spotting a well-written complaint from an important customer in Minneapolis, Ash quickly flew off to visit him. As he now explains, "I wanted the word to get around our organization that I'm aware of what's going on." Ash's next dramatic step to reshape company attitudes will be moving its headquarters to Los Angeles . . . he justifies the move primarily on psychological grounds. "We must place ourselves in a setting where—partly through osmosis—we get a different idea of our future." For much the same reason, he wants to change the corporation's name, too.

Calendar behavior includes review of reports and the use of agenda and minutes to shape expectations. What kinds of questions is the executive asking? Does he seem to focus on control of operating costs, quality, market share? How is his memory about what was "assumed" last month? Last quarter? What kinds of feedback is he giving? What sorts of issues get onto his agenda?

Other symbolic actions include the use of physical settings and public statements. By attending operating meetings in the field, the top man can provide vital evidence of his concerns and the directions he wants to pursue. By touching or ignoring a particular theme, a public statement—boilerplate to a skeptical outsider—can lead to a rash of activity. In a talk to investment bankers, a president devoted a paragraph to new departures in an R&D area that had previously been underfunded. Almost overnight, a wealth of new proposals began bubbling up from a previously disenchanted segment of the labs.

Last, his use of his personal staff—its size, their perquisites, how much probing he allows them to do—will indicate, not only the chief executive's style of doing business, but the direction of his substantive concerns as well.

The executive's ability to manage the use of symbols is at the heart of the case for optimism. Laterally at his fingertips, he has powerful tools—his day-timer and phone—for testing the possibilities of change and, over time, substantially shifting the focus of the organization.

Patterns of Activity

Success or failure in exploiting these simple tools is seen in the pattern of their use. Richard E. Neustadt in *Presidential Power* maintained:

> The professional reputation of a President in Washington is made or altered by the man himself. No one can guard it for him; no one saves him from himself. . . . His general reputation will be shaped by signs of pattern in the things he says and does. These are the words and actions he has chosen, day by day.

In short, the mundane tools that involve the creation and manipulation of symbols over time have impact to the extent that they reshape beliefs and expectations. Frequent, consistent, positive reinforcement is an unparalleled shaper of expectations—and, therefore, inducer of change.

Patterns of positive reinforcement can be applied in at least two ways: (1) use of praise and design of positive reinforcement schemes for individuals (or groups), and (2) allowing the bad to be displaced by the good, instead of trying to legislate it out of existence.

The White House, for example, has historically made meticulous use of the tools of praise. Selecting the attendees for major events and controlling the use of various classes of presidential letters of praise is a key activity controlled by very senior staff and the President himself.

Along the same lines, a research vice-president, responsible for about 2,000 scientists, has his executive assistant provide him with a sample of about 50 reports produced each month. He sends personal notes to the authors, often junior, of the best half-dozen or so.

Without touching on the complex ramifications of reinforcement theory, these instances merely support the point that senior managers are signal transmitters, and signals take on meaning as they are reiterated. Moreover, there is ample evidence that giving prominence to positive efforts and exposing them to the light of day induces constructive change far more effectively than trying to discourage undesired activities through negative reinforcement. As an associate of mine succinctly observed, "It's a hell of a lot easier to add a new solution than attack an old problem." An example illustrates the point in a broader context:

> The information system unit of a multibillion-dollar conglomerate had a disastrously bad reputation. Rather than "clean house" or develop better procedures, the vice-president/systems installed, with some fanfare, "Six Programs of Excellence." Six reasonably sizable projects—out of an agenda of over 100—were singled out for intensive management attention. The effort was designed to build, from the inside out, a reputation for excellence that would gradually increase user confidence and group motivation alike.

Frequency and consistency are two other primary attributes of effective pattern shaping. A pattern of frequent and consistent small successes is such a powerful shaper of expectations that its creation may be worth the deferral of ambitious short-term goals:

In one large company, the top team wished to establish a climate in which new product development would be viewed more favorably by all divisional managers. Rather than seeking an optimal product slate the first year—with the attendant likelihood of a high failure rate—the top team instead consistently supported small new product thrusts that gradually "made believers out of the operators."

Since consistency becomes a driving force in inducing major change over time, the executive committed to change ought to be constantly on the lookout for opportunities to reinforce activities, even trivial activities, that are congruent with his eventual purpose. He scours his in-basket for solutions—bits of completed action—to be singled out as exemplars of some larger theme. Support of completed actions typically generates further actions consistent with the rewarded behavior. The executive who keeps on testing tools to produce this result will find that by varying his patterns of reinforcement he can substantially influence people's behavior over time, often several levels down in the organization. (Figure 4 offers advice to pattern shapers based on my research.)

Settings for Interaction

The third class of mundane tools is settings. Senior management's development of a symbolic pattern of activities occurs somewhere. These are some of the setting variables that can directly reinforce or attenuate the impact of the symbolic message:

Presence or absence of top managers. Psychologists now agree on the high impact of modeling behavior—the most significant finding of the last decade, according to many. The senior execu-

Figure 4.   Guiding Assertions for the Pattern Shaper

—The world is a stream of problems that can be activated, bound in new ways, or bypassed.

—His associates are pattern watchers and are acutely aware of his and their impact, over time, on each other.

—Above all, timing is important.

—An early step in analyzing a situation is careful assessment of the levers he does or does not control.

—Most change occurs incrementally, and major change typically emerges over a long period of time.

—Much of the change induced in subordinates results from consciously acting as a model himself.

—Frequent rewards—directed at small, completed actions—effectively shape behavior over time.

—Good questioning, focusing on the short term, helps him and his subordinates learn about system responses to small nudges one way or another.

—Creating change in organizations is facilitated by unusual juxtaposition of traditional elements with small problem-making subunits that seed changes.

—Long-term goals are of secondary importance since control of change follows from learning about multiple, small, real-time adjustments.

—Consistency in delivering small, positive outcomes is an efficient and effective way to manipulate others' perceptions when attempting to induce change.

—Patience, persistence, self-control, and attention to the mundane are often keys to achieving small, consistent outcomes.

—Surprise should usually be avoided in an attempt to present stable expectations to peers, subordinates, and bosses.

—It is possible approximately to calculate the opportunity value of others' and one's own time, thus substantially increasing the ability to pick change opportunities.

—Adding new solutions is often better than tackling old problems; that is, as much or more change and learning can ensue from the effective implementation of new solutions as from time-consuming efforts to over-come typically deep-seated resistance to old problems.

---

tive's presence and his minor actions can bring to life and rather precisely shape an institutional point of view—about investment, competitive response, the importance of tight controls. The careers of top executives abundantly reflect their intuitive awareness of this point.

Location of groups and meetings. Moving a meeting or a staff unit or a new activity is often a dramatic signal that something new is afoot. At one company, the previously isolated top team began holding meetings in the field, thus signaling a sincere intent to make decentralization work after three previous failures.

Agenda control. Since agenda directly symbolize priorities, agenda management can be a potent change tool. A division's top team changed its basic approach to management by suddenly devoting more than half its meeting time to issues of project implementation, previously a relatively minor item on its agenda. To cope with the new questions they were getting from the top, managers throughout the organization were soon following suit.

Attendance. Who attends which meetings, and who presents material, can signal new approaches to management and new substantive directions. When one company president decided to force his vice-presidents, instead of junior staff, to present reviews and proposals, the atmosphere of his meetings perceptibly changed. All at once, heated battles between analytic guns-for-hire over numerical nuances were replaced by sober discussion of the issues.

Presentation/decision memorandum formats. Format control can shift managers' focus to new issues and fundamentally reshape the process of organizational learning. One management team vastly improved its approach to problem solving by meticulously starting every decision presentation with an historical review of "the five key assumptions." At a second major corporation, the chief executive brought to life his major theme—focus on the competition—by requiring all decision documents to include much greater depth of competitive analysis.

Questioning approaches. Among the clearest indicators of the direction or redirection of interest are the sorts of questions the top team consistently asks. Accounts of the working methods of Roy Ash, Harold Geneen, and others stress their unique questioning style and its pervasive effect on the issues the organization worries about. For instance, *Forbes* describes how A. W. Clausen of the Bank of America shifted concern from revenue to profit: "Ask an officer, 'How's business,' and you'd immediately hear how many loans he's made. I tried to leave my stamp by making everyone aware of profit."

Approaches to follow-up. Effective use of minutes, ticklers, and history can become the core of top management's real control system. Genuine accountability was introduced into a lax management organization by introducing a "blue blazer" system that made follow-up a way of life. In tracking issues, whenever operating executives' proposals had been modified by staff, the impact of the changes was explicitly noted. This put the staff and its contribution on stage. Accountability was further substantially sharpened by revamping a previous forecast-tracking procedure to highlight assumptions and outcomes.

Professor Serge Muscovici has asserted that:

> Social status, leadership, majority pressure . . . are not decisive factors to social influence. A minority can modify the opinions and norms of a majority, irrespective of their relative power or social status, as long as, all other things being equal, the organization of its actions and the expression of its opinions and objectives obey the conditions . . . of consistency, autonomy, investment, and fairness.

Fairness takes on added meaning in the context of mundane management tools, intended as they are to shape expectations, over time, through minor shifts of emphasis. To be effective, the management of expectations must be unfailingly honest, realistic, and consistent. Violation of this property, especially if perceived as intentional, automatically destroys the effectiveness of patterned symbolic manipulation.

Richard Neustadt captures the essence of the use of mundane tools:

[Franklin D. Roosevelt] had a strong feeling for a cardinal fact in government: That Presidents don't act on policies, program, or personnel in the abstract; they act in the concrete as they meet deadlines set by due dates, act on documents awaiting signatures, vacant posts awaiting appointees, officials seeking interviews, newsmen seeking answers, audiences waiting for a speech.

Note that the tools he mentions are all at hand. Though rarely disruptive or threatening, they have the potential to revolutionize an organization's ways of thinking and doing over time—particularly if, instead of being used intuitively and implicitly, they are consciously packaged and managed.

MAJOR CHANGE VIA TEMPORARY FOCUS

Big bureaucracies are run largely on inertia. Salesmen make their calls, products roll off the line, and checks get processed without any intervention by senior management. The task of today's slate of top managers, then, might well be viewed as time-bound: "How do we make a distinctive, productive difference over the next four years?" Or, "How do we leave our mark?"

It has been suggested above that certain prescriptions—undertaking structural shakeups or introducing new formal processes—are less effective than they once were in altering corporate perspectives. Constructing temporary systems to redirect the organization's attention and energies may be a better way to coax along institutional change. The high-impact devices proposed for this purpose are a natural extension of the mundane tools just discussed, in that in and of themselves they act as strong signals (or accumulations of symbols) of attention to new corporate directions.

Major—but limited—shifts in emphasis have been accomplished by public and private bureaucracies through three kinds of temporary focusing mechanisms: single-element focusers, systems of interaction, and dominating values. Each of these focusing mechanisms is discussed below.

Single-Element Focusers

To begin with, single-element focusers have been used time and again as a strategic signaling and implementing device. Consider how General Motors, a massive bureaucracy by any definition, recently adapted more swiftly than any other major automobile maker to the need to downsize its entire product line:

> The project center [says *Fortune*] was probably GM's single most important managerial tool in carrying out that bold decision. . . . It has eliminated a great deal of redundant effort, and has speeded numerous new technologies into production. Its success . . . rests on the same delicate balance between the powers of persuasion and coercion that underlines GM's basic system of coordinated decentralization.

Some other business examples of single-element focusers similarly wrested the attention of major organizations—temporarily—to something new:

—Harris Corporation created an interdivisional technology manager to oversee transfer of technology—Harris's "main strategic thrust"—between previously isolated groups.

Product family managers—three to five senior men with small staffs—were introduced as a means of wrenching the attention of two huge functional bureaucracies toward the marketplace; the creation of these high-visibility positions was thought to be a clearer, more efficient signal of strategic redirection than a major structural shift. Similarly, the establishment of just one job, executive vice-president for marketing, at White Consolidated is credited with sprucing up the long-stagnant sales of White's newly acquired Westinghouse appliance group.

—ITT's product group managers are a freewheeling band of central staff problem solvers and questioners who have brought a common market-based orientation to a highly diversified conglomerate.

—An oil company's central technology staff (a

roving group of top-ranking geologists and engineers) has markedly upgraded exploration and production quality.

In surveying these and other instances of success, some common threads can be identified (see Figure 5). Most important of these is singleness of focus. That is, the single-element focuser should not be confused with multiple-team project management. Its effectiveness rests on achieving a limited, temporary focus on one, or at most two, major new items. Note, also, that the structural manifestations tend to be about half staff, half line. On one hand, the focusing element often has the look of a traditional staff unit, but its manager, as the unmistakable agent of the top team's highest priority, visibly intrudes on operating managers' territory.

Kenneth Arrow, the Nobel laureate economist, describes an analogous approach to galvanizing massive government institutions into acting on new agenda: "Franklin D. Roosevelt . . . saw the need of assigning new tasks to new bureaus even though according to some logic [such a task] belonged in the sphere of an existing department." Congressional Budget Office Deputy Director Robert Levine summarizes the thesis this way:

Figure 5.   Attributes of Single-Element Focusing Devices

Success characteristic	Related failure mode
—Focus: limited number of "devices," no more than two and preferably one.	—Use usually—simultaneously—of many devices (e.g., teams, meetings) dilutes attention and can become just a bureaucratic encumbrance.
—Focus within focus: The limited device must, moreover, have a limited agenda and not take on everything at once.	—Limited devices charged with turning the world around in 12 months are likely to fail (i.e., a failure of expectation).
—Incumbent: Manned with a very senior contender(s) for the top.	—Selection of good men, but not those recognized as members of "the top ten" or sure-fire top ten contenders.
—Startup: Either a pilot element (e.g., one product family manager of an eventual set of five) or a "pilot decision," (e.g., a visible output— perhaps a decision—by the new event/ process) will affect acceptance.	—Groups/processes invented, but no clear sign of early progress or shift of emphasis.
—Need: A clear-cut, agreed-upon business need for the element exists.	—The new element's agenda is not clear and/or is not viewed as urgent.
—CEO role: CEO is reinforcer of project *and* lets it make its mark.	—CEO nonsupporter or a supporter but preempts the new role by continuing to play the game by the old rules.
—Conscience: Systems—formal or informal—to "watch" the top team and ensure that actions are being taken consistent with the purpose of the shift.	—Element "implemented," but top team regularly takes decisions inconsistent with purpose.
—Implementation duration: Even though single device, implementation should be expected to take a couple of years at least.	—Since it is only a simple new element, put it in place and let it go.

Since it seems impossible . . . to change overall public bureaucratic systems substantially either by changing their direction at the top by devices like program budgeting, or by changing their culture à la organization development, it may be useful to look for a third class of solutions . . . specifically, trying to treat bureaucratic units as if they were competing business units. . . . Even if it worked very well, this would be less well than program budgeting or organization development if they worked well. But the contention here is that in the real world this alternative concept is substantially more likely to work.

System of Interaction

Attention-directing organization elements are only the first of the three high-impact focusing mechanisms to be considered here. The second is the construction of a coherent system of senior management interaction, again with the purpose of shifting management attention either to some new direction or to some new method of reaching overall consensus. Under some circumstances, this second mechanism might even be preferred to the first. On the one hand, a system of forums has perhaps less symbolic impact than a single high-visibility element. On the other hand, however, such a system does directly manipulate the agenda of senior managers.

Systems of forums designed to turn top management's eyes to new horizons range from one company's five "management forums"—a formal system of interaction designed to force regular discussion of strategic issues—to a president's regular informal breakfast meetings where senior executives, free of their staffs and the attendant bureaucratic insulation, engage in untrammeled discussion of key issues.

One particularly striking class of forums is special operating or strategic review sessions. Texas Instruments, ITT, and Emerson Electric, among others, focus top-management direction setting in regular sessions where—as everyone in the organization knows—"things get done" or "the buck stops." Another notable example is cited by *Fortune:*

One of the enduring questions of management, a subject of constant concern and endless analy-

sis, is how a large corporation can best monitor and direct operations spread over many industries and throughout many parts of the world. A number of companies have sought the answer in ponderous and elaborate management mechanisms. . . . But there is at least one large company whose top management continues to rely on plain, old-fashioned, face-to-face contact. Richard B. Loynd, the president and chief operating officer of Eltra Corp. . . . visits each of Eltra's thirteen divisions as many as eight times a year, and puts managers through formal grillings that last several hours at a time. The people at Eltra call this the "hands-on" management technique. Loynd says: "I think I spend more time with our operating people than the president of any other major company."

Invariably, like the single-element focusers, these systems are temporary in nature. Since most of them tend to become rigid and lose their unique value in the course of time, they need to be modified at intervals. One executive reports:

The monthly breakfast meeting finally got the chairman and his operating presidents away from staff. For two years these sessions, preliminary to the regular monthly review, became the real decision-making/enervating forum. But then the staffs caught on. One by one, *they* began coming to breakfast.

Dominating Value

The discussion of change mechanisms has had a consistent undercurrent. The three classes of mundane tools have been presented as apparently trivial signaling devices for redirecting organizational attention and energy over time toward a theme, while the first two major change tools have been characterized as just larger-scale or agglomerated devices for the same purpose.

One final tool, which may be labeled the *dominating value*, addresses the role and utilization of the theme itself. It is, on the one hand, more delicate than the other tools, in that its use demands consummate political commitment-building skills and a shrewd sense of timing. In another sense it is more robust than the others, in that, if handled effectively, it can generate substantial, sustained energy in large institutions.

For the senior manager, therefore, thinking about and acting on the value management process is, although imprecise, extremely practical.

Business researchers have coined various terms for an effective, predominant institutional belief. Richard Normann calls it a business idea or growth idea. He devotes an entire book, *Management and Statesmanship,* to documenting a case for the power of an effective, simply articulated business idea and describing the unique role and leverage of top management in indirectly guiding the process of belief establishment and change. He argues that "the interpretation of ongoing and historical events and the associated adjustment and regulation of the dominating idea is probably the most crucial of the processes occurring in the company."

Some other recent scholarly work, well-grounded in the leading edge of social science findings, provides a corroborating point of view. Andrew Pettigrew's anthropological study of the creation of organization culture is representative:

> One way of approaching the study of the entrepreneur's relationship with his organization is to consider the entrepreneur as a symbol creator, an ideologue, a formulator of organizational vocabularies, and a maker of ritual and myth. Stylistic components of a vision, which may be crucial, might include the presence of a dramatically significant series of events, rooting the vision back into history, and thus indicating the vision was more than a fad. Visions with simple, yet ambiguous content expressed in symbolic language are not only likely to be potent consciousness raisers, but also flexible enough to sustain the ravages of time and therefore the certitude of events. Visions contain new and old terminology perhaps organized into metaphors with which it is hoped to create new meanings. Words can move people from a state of familiarity to a state of awareness. Some people have the capacity to make words walk. I suspect this is one of the unexplored characteristics of successful entrepreneurs.

Louis Pondy, in "Leadership is a Language Game," quite similarly equates leadership effectiveness with the capacity to achieve what he calls "language renewal."

Roy Ash puts the same notion in more concrete terms:

At a sufficiently high level of abstraction, he says, "all businesses are the same." Ash's plans for testing that theory are summed up in the notes that he continually pencils on yellow legal pads. One of the most revealing of these notes says: "Develop a much greater attachment of everybody to the bottom line—more agony and ecstasy." As he sees it, the really important change in a company is a process of psychological transformation.

If one combs the literature for the lessons extracted by business leaders, the crucial role of a central belief emerges. The biographies of Cordiner at GE, Vail at AT&T, Greenewalt at Du Pont, and Watson at IBM all stress the quest to give operational force and meaning to a dominant, though imprecise, idea. Such accounts may be dismissed as self-serving, but it would seem a bit more cynical than even these times call for to write off the extraordinary consistency of so many closing statements.

Among active business leaders, the pattern of evidence is repeated. Richard Pascale, for example, has described the management style of several particularly effective chief executive officers. He notes the recurrence of a simple, over-arching theme captured in a few words: for example, Harold Geneen's ceaseless "search for the unshakable facts," reflected in all kinds of organizational arrangements from structural contrivances—his controllers reporting to the chief executive and his intrusive product group managers—through interaction mechanisms—the famed ITT monthly review sessions. Further examples dot the business press:

• *A. W. Clausen at Bank of America:* "Stay around Tom Clausen for about 15 minutes and he'll talk about laying pipe," says *Forbes.* "That's his shorthand for anticipating events and readying a response. Subordinates lay pipe to Clausen when they tell him about potential problems; he lays the pipe the other way when he sketches his expectations. The expression isn't especially catchy, the process isn't particularly glamorous. But it does help to explain why Bank of America isn't facing huge loan losses—and this big, slow-moving tortoise seems perfectly able to keep up with the flashier, more dynamic hares."

• *John DeButts at AT&T* incessantly uses the term "the system is the solution." The concept, professed by DeButts in every setting from management meetings to television commercials, is aimed at starting the process of shifting the massive million-person Bell System's focus to the market place.

• *Tom Jones at Northrup, Fortune* notes, has been particularly successful at gaining more than a fair share of defense contracts—largely, he believes, by bringing to life the theme "Everybody at Northrup is in marketing."

• *Walter Spencer at Sherwin Williams*, according to *Forbes*, spent his five years as CEO working to introduce a "marketing orientation" into a previously manufacturing-dominated institution. Says Spencer: "When you take a 100-year old company and change the culture of the organization, and try to do that in Cleveland's traditional business setting—well, it takes time; you just have to keep hammering away at everybody. . . . The changeover to marketing is probably irreversible now. It's not complete, but we've brought along a lot of young managers with that philosophy, and once you've taken a company this far, you can't go back."

When the scholarly research and the anecdotal evidence are drawn together, some characteristic attributes of an effective dominating value can be discussed:

It is both loose and tight. That is, it connotes a clear directional emphasis—focus on the competition, stand for quality, become low-cost producer—but ample latitude for supporting initiatives.

It must, almost always, emerge rather than be imposed. Though it may be crystallized in a succinct phrase, it usually represents the end product of time-consuming consensus-building processes that may have gone on for a year or more.

Just as it cannot be imposed by fiat, it cannot be changed at will. Typically, a major shift in the dominant belief can be brought about only when an important change is perceived to be at hand. The process of gaining commitment requires so much emotional commitment and institutional energy that it can be repeated only infrequently.

It has a reasonably predictable life cycle. Beginning with a great deal of latitude, it be-

comes progressively less flexible over time—though never approaching the rigidity of a quantified goal.

It may be a definition or characterization of the past, meant primarily to mark the end of a period and provide the energy to start a search for new modes of organizational behavior. For example, one might choose to label the past five years as "the era of tight control" in order to suggest that something now coming to an end should be replaced with something new, as yet unspecified.

It imposes choices. Despite the general nature of most effective beliefs, they do require management to face up to the limits of the organization's capacities. Of course, any huge enterprise does a bit of everything, but, for example, a choice to stress controls, if effectively implemented, is likely also a choice not to push harder for new products.

It can be anything from a general management principle to a reasonably specific major business decision. At the management-principles end, it can become a commitment to something like "fact-based analysis." At the business-decision end, it can be a commitment to a revised position for a key product line. In the middle are hybrids such as "enhanced focus on competition."

It suggests movement (e.g., toward becoming the industry quality leader or dominating a particular market niche), thus implying some sort of tension or imbalance. Few leaders have been noted for achieving balance. Most have been known for going from somewhere to somewhere else.

Figure 6 gives a graphic portrayal of the essentials of the process I have been discussing. It depicts a five- to nine-year cycle of strategic transition marked by the tightening, executing, loosening, and redirecting search for an operational dominating value.

CHANGE FOR CHANGE'S SAKE

At least one significant tool remains to be considered: namely, change for its own sake.

Figure 6. Five- to Nine-Year Cycle of Strategic Transition

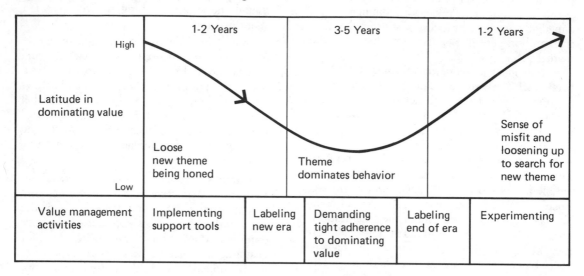

This is the device assigned, in Figure 2, to Cell 3 (low-control, high-speed change). Sometimes things are such a muddle that significant change for its own sake is a good bet to produce, on balance, a more desirable outcome than any directionally managed program.

In *The Economist,* Normal McRae recently observed:

> . . . the most successful companies have been those restless enough to be unsure what their management styles should be. Successful big American corporations today will often centralize their policy making, and get a significant initial gain in effectiveness; but then, as time passes, will find that this does not work because the central planners do not know what is really going on out in the field. So these corporations will then decentralize, and get a significant initial gain in effectiveness. This constant reorganization is in fact very sensible, and is a main reason why I judge that big American corporations are still the most efficient day-to-day business operators in the world.

A somewhat less radical dose of the same medicine is the rather arbitrary reshuffling of top team member responsibilities, even when it results in a seemingly less rational match of skills to tasks. A fresh juxtaposition of perspectives, per se, is often of value.

At least one word of warning about high-early impact, low-control prescriptions is in order. The secret of their success is novelty. Routine reorganizing or all-too-regular shakeups of top team assignments all too readily evoke the sense of déjà vu. "Nobody on the top team has been in the same job for more than 15 months," remarks an executive of a high-technology company. "Of course, all they do is trade bureaucratic barbs. That's all they've got. No one sees the results of his own initiatives."

Although it certainly merits much more discussion, the analysis of this last class of tools must necessarily be cut short at this point.

IN CONCLUSION: LIMITS AND OPTIMISM

The purpose of this essay has been twofold: first, to provide a simple classification of change tools and some speculative hypotheses in support of the case for pessimism about the old favorites among them; second, to suggest that for the alert senior manager, today's organizational garbage cans are still full of powerful change tools—tools that he uses intuitively, and therefore not systematically, but which nevertheless are numerous and potentially powerful enough to justify a measure of optimism.

A limited measure, to be sure. Even with a mastery of all the change tools reviewed here, today's senior manager is unlikely to be able to develop real consensus, commitment, and change in more than a single new direction. Richard Neustadt's metaphor captures the essence of his role:

> Presidential power is the power to persuade. Underneath our images of Presidents-in-boots, astride decisions, are the half-observed realities of President-in-sneakers, stirrups in hand, trying to induce particular department heads . . . to climb aboard.

As he tries to coax his senior colleagues aboard, the senior executive has at his command a variety of settings—settings in which he can experiment, implement, and build patterns to provide a general conception of what's possible. He can, with luck and to a limited extent, grasp control of the signaling system to point a general direction and mark out limited areas of expected new institutional excellence. By adroitly managing agenda, he can nudge the day-to-day decision-making system, thus simultaneously imparting new preferences and testing new initiatives.

And some day, in retrospect, he may be able to see himself as an experimenter who attempted to build consensus on a practical (and flexible) vision of what was possible over a five-year time horizon, and through incessant attention to the implementation of small, adaptive steps, eventually made that vision a reality.

If so, he should be well content.

SELECTED BIBLIOGRAPHY

Richard Pascale in "Three Chief Executives: The Effect of Style on Implementation" (Research Paper 357, Stanford Graduate School of Business) developed with the subjects' cooperation, detailed case studies of Harold Geneen, Roy Ash, and Ed Carlson. He meticulously describes the links between their everyday behavior patterns, supporting organizational systems, and effectiveness.

John Kotter and Paul Lawrence in *Mayors in Action* (Wiley, 1974) discuss in a series of case studies the relationship, for example, between mayoral agenda setting and implementation success.

Four studies of bureaucratic politics offer particularly detailed analyses of the mundane attributes of influence accumulation and exercise: Graham Allison's *Essence of Decision* (Little, Brown, 1971); Edward Banfield's *Political Influence* (Free Press, 1961); Robert Caro's *The Power Broker* (Knopf, 1974); and Richard Neustadt's *Presidential Power* (Wiley, 1960).

Henry Mintzberg's unique observational study of senior executives, *The Nature of Managerial Work* (Harper & Row, 1973), vividly portrays the fragmented nature of real senior-management activity. If one finds his analysis credible, then presumably the kinds of change levers discussed in this article are of particular importance.

H. Edward Wrapp's "Good Managers Don't Make Policy Decisions" (*Harvard Business Review*, September–October 1967) and James Quinn's "Strategic Goals: Process and Politics" (*Sloan Management Review*, Fall 1977) provide good examples of effective muddling-about processes that typically attend development of what is called a "dominating value" in this paper.

The notion of organizations as temporary systems discussed in the paper is treated at length by E. J. Miller and A. K. Rice in *Systems of Organization* (Tavistock, 1967).

Last, James March and Johan Olsen's *Ambiguity and Choice* (Universitelforlaget: Norway, 1976) proposes and supports a novel, complex model of organizational choice. The decision-making environment they describe clearly calls for radically different management prescriptions. The tools offered in this paper seem, to the author, to be reasonably consistent with their view of the world.

PNB University Branch

People's National Bank (PNB) is the lead bank of a moderate-sized bank holding company located in the capital of a large midwestern state. As the major bank in the company, PNB accounts for $600 million of the company's $2 billion in assets. At the core of PNB is its branch marketing system. Unlike many East Coast banks, branch banking accounts for a large percentage of PNB's income, and many of the top managers of the bank have come up through the branch system.

The senior vice-president for branch operations, John B. Green, directly supervises the operations of twenty-one branch banks. Approximately ten more branches are planned for the next three years. Each branch is headed by a branch manager, who runs the branch with a relatively high degree of freedom. A typical branch includes a group of tellers, directed by a teller supervisor, and a "desk" staff of financial consultants, loan officers, and some clerical personnel.

Some of the larger branches have assistant managers who may supervise either operations or the loan activity. Although the actual work is extremely standardized (procedures for opening accounts, processing loans, and so on), branch managers are free to manage the branch as they desire, and different branches have greatly varying structures, procedures, and atmospheres.

Each branch is a profit center within the larger bank. Branch revenue is figured by adding income from loan volume to a figure representing income derived from the funds the branch has brought in (based on deposit figures). From the revenue figure actual branch expenses, building expenses, and allocated overhead are subtracted to yield a monthly branch profit figure. Each year, the branch manager and John B. Green develop a profit plan for the coming year, and managers are paid a sizeable bonus depending upon the performance of their branch against the profit plan.

A CHANGE AT THE UNIVERSITY BRANCH

On the first Friday in April 1974, the manager of the University Branch of PNB informed John B. Green that he would be leaving the bank at the end of the following week to join the ministry of God. Faced with an unanticipated managerial vacancy in a large and critical branch, Green met with his staff and decided to appoint Gary Herline, an up-and-coming young man in the commercial lending department, as manager of the University Branch. Herline was notified on Wednesday and was told to report to the University Branch on the following Monday to take up his duties as branch manager.

HERLINE'S BACKGROUND

Herline had been with the bank for a few years when he received notice of his appointment as branch manager. After receiving his MBA from a well-known business school in 1970, he accepted an offer from PNB rather than those of the large New York banks because he felt that there would be greater opportunities to move up in the organization quickly at PNB. He started out his first year in the bank's training program and was rotated through a wide variety of assignments, including a brief assignment as a financial consultant at a branch. During this period, Gary learned that he had been identified by management as a "hot prospect" and that his performance

Exhibit 1.

Herline's Summary of Important Information About University Branch

---

—It's a large branch; eight desk people, eighteen tellers, fairly good physical plant, high volume.

—Loan volume has been very poor during the past three years, but there has been an increase over the past two or three months. Some people feel that this reflects an absence of any management and that the loans are not "good" ones (that delinquency will go up in the coming months).

—The staff is very young, particularly the tellers. All except two of the tellers are women and many have B.A. degrees; some have Master's degrees.

—Branch has the largest number of accounts and highest volume of transactions of any branch in the system; however, many accounts are very small, and many transactions are for small amounts of money (checks for 50¢ to $5.00).

—There is no official assistant manager, but one of the loan officers seems to function as an assistant manager. He is resented by the tellers, however, and seems to get into disagreements with the teller supervisor, who has been at the branch for seventeen years.

—The desk staff seems to be of uneven quality. Some are excellent, but there is some deadwood also.

—Turnover among tellers is very high. It has run at about 75 percent per year for the last five years. Recently the tellers submitted an informal group grievance to the manager complaining about working hours and low pay.

—Competition for the university area business is keen. The other two major commercial banks in town have branches on the same blocks as PNB. Both branches are newer and better laid out than the PNB branch. Also, several savings and loan offices are close by.

—Some of the key commercial accounts in the University Branch area have been taken away by aggressive loan officers and branch managers of other nearby PNB branches as well as by competing banks.

—For the last year, the branch has consistently failed to meet the profit plan and has even shown losses in several months.

---

was being watched closely. After training he spent two years in the trust department and had worked in the commercial lending department for a year when he heard about his move to the University Branch.

INFORMATION ABOUT UNIVERSITY

Having heard about his move late on Wednesday, Gary spent most of Thursday and Friday talking to some of his contacts within the bank about the University Branch. At the same time he tried to conclude his work in commercial lending. The University Branch, one of the largest in the system, had been a problem branch for some time.

There was quite a bit of turnover among the employees and the managerial staff. Located adjacent to the state university campus, it served a different market than almost any other branch in the system. By Friday afternoon, Gary had listed the important things he had learned about the branch (see Exhibit 1). As he prepared to start at University on Monday morning, he asked himself the following questions:

"From what I know about the branch, what are the critical issues I am going to have to deal with during the next six months at University Branch?

"When I get to the branch on Monday, what are the first things I should do—what should my first day be like?"

CASE **2**

The Medtek Corporation (A)

"We have a basic problem of performance here in the technical division." John Torrence, Senior Vice-President of the Medtek Corporation and Director of the company's technical division (R&D) was talking with several members of a consulting team he had brought in to help with problems in the division. "We have a bad case of technical constipation; this division has not brought out a successful new product in two years. If we don't do something about this problem soon, the whole company is going to be in big trouble."

COMPANY BACKGROUND

The Medtek corporation is an international company that designs, manufactures, and markets automated instruments for the analysis of blood and serum as well as for similar industrial applications. The company was founded in 1939 by Paul Torres; the father of the present chairman and chief executive officer, Arthur Torrence; and the grandfather of the present senior vice-president for research and development, John Torrence. Torres died in 1968.

Medtek was formed in 1939 as a small operation in a Bronx loft. They handcrafted a new device called the Automed, a product still manufactured by the company. This product automated the preparation of human tissue for microscopic examination by pathologists.

In the early 1950s the firm employed approximately twenty-five people. The R&D section was composed of two engineers and two draftsmen. The organization was very informal. New employees and consultants were brought in as needed to work on specific tasks.

During this period, Ben Kless, one of Medtek's salesmen, met an inventor named Dennis Rettew. Rettew was employed in a Cleveland hospital. After observing both the kidney dialysis and laboratory procedures in the hospital, he applied the mechanical techniques used in dialysis to the development of a rudimentary device that could automate one laboratory procedure.

Rettew and his invention were brought to Medtek. Technical development of this device resulted in the single channel Autoxam—an innovation which today is still one of the company's major products.

The single channel Autoxam works by plucking up a small blood sample and pumping it through a continuous system in which the sample is properly diluted; reagents added and mixed; the solution heated and/or cooled, filtered, pigmented, and spectrographically analyzed; and the results recorded and compared to a norm. Successive samples can be introduced continuously to the Autoxam. The innovation of separating the samples with a small air bubble both permitted the continuous flow of samples and scrubbed the pathway clean of the previous sample. Prior to the Autoxam, each sample was handled manually by a lab technician. Obviously the new device allowed a saving in lab technicians' time and in the amount of reagents used. Further savings were realized by the Autoxam's ability to examine a larger number of samples per day than a technician.

In 1957 the Autoxam was introduced to the market. It was a great success and ushered the firm into an era of rapid and continuous growth. By the early 1960s the firm had grown to about 125 employees. The bulk of the research and development work was centered around the blood analyzer. Development work during this period focused on a multichannel version of the Autoxam that could automate additional laboratory tests and could also automate some industrial tests such as the measurement of trace metals in water used in powering steam turbines for generating electricity. New applications and new clinical procedures compatible with Autoxam technology were developed both internally and by users and researchers external to and independent of the company. Much new information came to Medtek through professional journal reports of research inspired by the introduction of the Autoxam.

The years 1967 and 1968 brought a crisis to Medtek. This crisis was precipitated by the development of the 60/12, a second generation analyzer that produced a patient profile of 12 lab tests from one sample at the rate of 60 tests per hour. First, an internal fight arose over whether to finance an expansion of the company to tap the possible profits of the 60/12 or whether to restrain the firm's growth. Second, the rapid growth resulted in errors and slippage for which no one was accountable. A consulting firm proposed a vast change in the formal organization in order to better handle these accountability problems. Vice-presidents, senior vice-presidents and a divisional structure were introduced. Some believed that the switch to this formal structure was too quick and that the company did not have enough properly trained personnel to staff the new organization. Third, the company went public through a sale of common stock, the implications of which still seem to be sensitive.

The choice was made to expand, and the period of 1969 to 1972 was a time of extremely rapid growth. The technical division grew to 150 employees. Its 1971 budget was some five times greater than its 1967 budget. Lou Bidder, who was brought on in the early 1950s to work on the Autoxam hydraulics, became the first technical division vice-president.

The 60/12 was a huge success. The company moved to suburban Washington, D.C. Task groups were introduced in the technical division. This innovation changed the long-standing structure of the three functional departments: mechanical, electrical, and clinical chemistry. Development focused on HORSE (High Operation Repeated Sequential Examiner), a third generation computer-controlled blood analyzer with a capacity of 20 tests per profile and 150 tests per hour.

The years 1972 to the present have not been easy ones for the company. The National Institute of Health retrenched, and federal funds to buy Medtek's products were no longer as readily available to hospitals. HORSE developed numerous technical problems. Underwriters' requirements for insuring installed HORSEs varied from

city to city and in the international market necessitating modifications to fit local conditions. The company experienced problems with its formal organization structure.

In addition to the analyzers the firm also offers a white cell testing and diagnosis device, reagents for the analyzers, an infrared analyzer, and a hospital-oriented management information system. The analyzers, however, continue to account for the vast majority of hardware sales. Organization charts for the company as well as financial highlights are included as Exhibits 1, 2, and 3.

Exhibit 1.   Organization Chart of Medtek

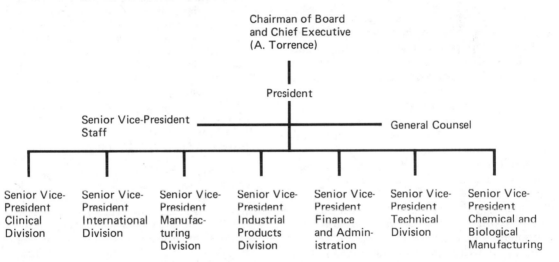

Exhibit 2.   Organization Chart of the Technical Division

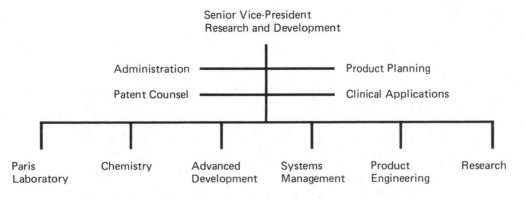

Exhibit 3.   Selected Financial Data (years 1965–1975)

	1965	1966	1967	1968	1969	1970	1971	1972	1973	1974	1975
Sales (millions)	23	32	44	54	79	102	100	109	131	166	202
R&D expenditures (millions)	.93	1.26	1.97	2.9	4.9	9.8	10.6	10.1	10	10.5	
R&D expenditures as % of sales	4	4	4.5	5.4	6.2	9.6	10.6	9.3	7.6	6.3	
Number of employees		50		150						250	
Introduction of major products			60/12					HORSE			

THE TECHNICAL DIVISION

As the R&D arm of Medtek, the technical division is responsible for basic research in areas relevant to the products of the firm. Its major goal, however, is the development of new product ideas that can be developed successfully into new commercial products for the firm. In addition, the division is responsible for development and refinement of existing products as well as investigating and responding to problems with products already in the field.

John Torrence, age 30, was given the assignment of heading up the technical division about a year ago after having rotated through a number of different positions within the company at large. He has been charged with revitalizing the division and increasing its performance.

In initial discussions with this new consulting team, Torrence provided some perspective on the problems the technical division faces:

> Our biggest problem, of course, is the failure to come up with new products. The future of the company depends upon us developing new technologies that will be commercially successful. Many of the problems, I think, stem from the way that we manage ourselves. With a few exceptions, we have high quality people here in the division. We do have the necessary scientific and technical talent. The problem is that they are not coming up with new ideas; and when they do come up with ideas, they don't seem to be able to get through the process of moving an idea to the product stage. Part of our problem, I think, is the way we are organized within the division. I have too many people reporting to me, and I am thinking about changing the structure. Beyond that, however, there are problems in the attitudes of people. When I talk to people in the division, they just don't seem to have much drive or ambition. They don't seem fired up. This attitude is reflected in the large number of projects that are either behind schedule, over budget, or both. Finally, we don't seem to have a good feel of where we are going as a division, where we ought to be putting our resources, and how we determine priorities.

Hausser Food Products Company

Brenda Cooper, the southeastern regional sales manager for the Hausser Food Products Company (HFP) expressed her concern to a researcher from a well-known eastern business school:

> I think during the past year I've begun to make some progress here, but the situation is a lot more difficult than I thought when I first arrived. Our currect methods of selling products just are not adequate, and the people in the field don't seem interested in coming up with new ideas or approaches to selling.

BACKGROUND

Hausser Food Products Company is a leading producer and marketer of baby foods in the United States. The company manufactures and markets a whole line of foods for the baby market including strained meats, vegetables, fruits, and combination dishes. The product line includes foods that are completely strained, for infants, as well as foods that are partially strained or chopped, for children six months and older. HFP has traditionally been the leader in this field. The company has no other major product lines. Its products are known for their high quality and the Hausser name is well known to most consumers.

HFP owns its production and warehousing facilities. Its well-developed distribution network provides direct delivery of products to the warehouses and stores of most major food chains. The smallest segment of its market is composed of a limited number of institutions for children, which purchase HFP products in bulk.

HFP has a long history in the baby food business. Traditionally the market leader, it has over the years maintained a market share of approximately 60 percent. During the 1960s the firm experienced rapid expansion and growth. The number of different types of baby food products increased tremendously to keep up with increasing demand for more foods and a greater variety of products. During the period from the middle 1960s through the mid 1970s, growth in sales approached 15 percent compounded yearly.

During the past few years, HFP has faced a greatly changing market for infant foods. The sudden decrease in the birth rate brought about major changes in the infant food business, and projections of sales had to be altered drastically. In addition, the new concern about food additives, including flavorings, dyes, and preservatives, also had its impact on the baby food market. Many consumer advocates argued that it would be safer for parents to make their own baby foods than to purchase the commercially prepared products such as those manufactured by HFP. Finally, competition in the baby food market also increased. Private names competed on the basis of price against the nationally advertised brand names.

These changing conditions have been viewed with great alarm by the top management of HFP. The drop in growth of sales (to 3 percent in the most recent year) was accompanied by an even greater drop in earnings as management found itself with unused plant and warehouse capacity. Management is currently concerned with looking for new ways of stimulating demand for HFP products as well as the longer-range problem of finding new complementary products to develop and market.

THE MARKETING ORGANIZATION

In 1975 a researcher from a major business school became involved in studying the marketing organization of HFP as part of a larger-scale research project. His inquiries led him to look closely at the sales department and to investigate some of the problems that were being experienced there.

The marketing function at HFP is directed by a vice-president for marketing who reports directly to the president of HFP (see a partial organizational chart in Exhibit 1). The vice-president for marketing has five functional directors reporting to him. Each of these directors is responsible for one of the major areas of marketing activity, including market research, market planning, sales promotion, advertising, and sales. The sales department, which has been the focus of much recent concern, is headed by the director of sales, who directs selling activities for the entire United States. The country is broken up into seven regions, each of which has a regional sales manager. Regions are further broken up into districts (each of which may include a range of area from several states to part of a city, depending upon the particular location). The district manager heads up the HFP "sales team" for each district. It is this sales team that has the ultimate job of selling HFP products to customers, offering promotions, maintaining contact with the customers, assuring adequate shelf space, and so on.

A key element in the marketing organization is the regional sales manager. This has been an entry position to HFP for many bright, aggressive, and well-trained young people who subsequently have risen to high-level jobs within the company.

Exhibit 1.   Partial Chart of Formal Organization Structure of Hausser Food Products

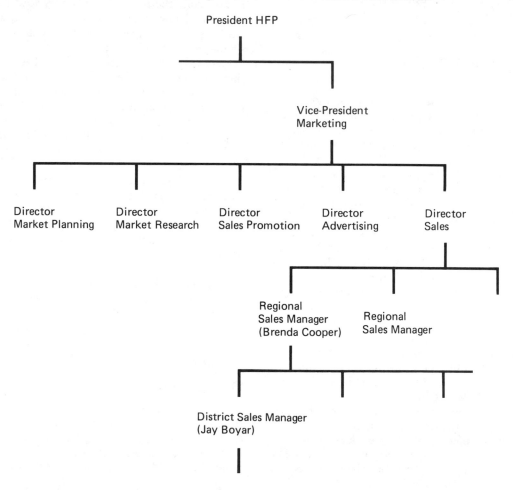

The current president of the company, the vice-president for marketing, and three of the five marketing directors all began their careers at HFP as regional sales managers.

Brenda Cooper, the southeast regional sales manager, is fairly typical of the kind of person who is placed in that position. Brenda entered an MBA program immediately following graduation from one of the best women's colleges in the country. Majoring in marketing, she did extremely well in business school and graduated near the top of her class. Upon graduation she received many job offers and took a position as an assistant product manager in a large nonfood consumer products company. During four years at that firm she performed extremely well both in the management of existing products and in the launching of new products. By the end of her fourth year, however, she was becoming restless, and seeing no opportunities for quick advancement, decided to accept an offer to become a regional sales manager at HFP. The salary was attractive, plus she would receive a potentially large bonus based on the profit performance of the entire company. Brenda was also attracted by the possibility of advancement within the company. She had heard that many of the senior staff had started as regional managers. At the end of her first year Brenda is still very concerned about doing well in her job; in particular she is adjusting to her role as manager with six district managers reporting to her.

THE SALES PLAN

Much of the activity of the regional managers centers around the yearly sales plan. The sales plan is essentially a budget that includes projections of sales, expenses, and profit. It serves as the basic yardstick against which the performance of regional managers is measured.

Each year the sales plan is developed through the following multistage process:

1. The director of market planning comes up with a projection of sales for the coming year. At the same time, the director of sales asks regional managers for their projections of sales for the next year. These projections are usually extrapolations of the previous year's figures with adjustments for major changes in the market year (if any).

2. The two directors (market planning and sales) and their staffs go through a negotiation process to resolve the difference that usually exists between their two projections (market planning always tending to be higher). Out of these negotiations emerges the sales plan for the coming year. This plan includes budgeted expenditures for promotions, advertising, expenses, and the like, as well as projected sales volume and profit.

3. The sales director allocates portions of the sales plan to regional managers, who are responsible for "meeting plan" within their own regions. Regional managers in turn allocate parts of the plan to each of their district sales managers and teams.

4. The district managers receive the plan in the form of sales targets and expense budgets for the coming year. The district manager typically receives a relatively low base salary combined with a relatively large yearly bonus, which is based entirely on the performance, as measured against the sales plan, of the sales team. At the end of the year, the district manager is also given a pool of bonus dollars, also based on team performance against plan, to be distributed to the individual salespeople. Salespeople also receive relatively low base salaries and look to their yearly bonuses as a major source of income.

THE PROBLEM OF THE REGIONAL SALES MANAGERS

As part of his investigation, the researcher visited Brenda Cooper in her Atlanta office. After describing the operations of her region, Brenda began to talk about some of the problems she was facing:

We in HFP are currently wrestling with the problem of a very mature product line. Top management has begun to see the critical need to diversify, in other words to hedge our bets with some other lines of products which are not dependent upon a steadily increasing birth rate. They have been talking about some interesting and exciting things, but any new product is still a few years away from being introduced. . . .In the meantime, it is the job of us out here in the field to come up with new ideas to help keep up sales of our existing product line. I think there must be better ways of selling our product, and I am sure that there are new things that we can do to get much more performance out of the line than we are seeing now. The problem is that the best ideas usually come in from the field, from the salesmen themselves, and we really have had very little from our sales teams. They seem content to continue to let the products sell themselves and just keep the shelves stocked, as they have for years. I just don't get any new ideas or approaches from my sales teams.

Brenda and the researcher then spent some time going over the figures for sales in her region, and in particular the sales performance of the different regions. As they were going over the figures, Brenda noted:

Look here at Jay Boyar and his group in Florida. This is a prime example of the kind of problem I am facing. While we have been facing decreasing growth in sales, and actual drop off of sales some places, Jay's group consistently comes in at 10 percent above the sales plan. I've been down there and met with them and I've talked with Jay numerous times, but I can't figure out how they do it. They must be doing something that could be used in other places; but every time I ask how they do it, I get very vague answers like, "Well, we work very hard down here," or "We work together as a group; that's how we are able to do well." I'm sure it must be more than that, but I can't seem to get them to open up.

A VISIT TO THE FLORIDA SALES TEAM

Intrigued with the Florida figures, the researcher arranged an extended visit (during January and February) with the Florida sales team. The researcher was given a letter of introduction from the vice-president for marketing. This letter explained that he was collecting background information for a major research project that would help the company, that any information collected would be confidential, and that the sales team should provide him with any assistance that he needed.

At first Jay Boyar and his group made no attempt to hide their suspicion of the researcher. Slowly, however, as the researcher spent numerous days in the field, riding around the Florida roads with each of the salespeople, they began to trust him and open up about how they felt about their jobs and the company. (See Exhibit 2 for a listing of the staff of the Florida sales team.)

David Berz, the unofficial assistant team manager, talked at length about why he liked his job:

What I really like is the freedom. I'm really my own boss most of the time. I don't have to be sitting in an office for the whole day, with some supervisor hanging over my shoulder and looking at all my work. I get to be outside, here in the car, doing what I like to be doing—being out in the world, talking to people, and making the sale.

Neil Portnow, who had been with the company longer than any of the other team members, commented on the group:

This is really a great bunch of guys to work with. I've been with a couple of different groups, but this is the best. I've been together with Dave and Jay for about fifteen years now, and I wouldn't trade it for anything. Jay is really one of us; he knows that we know how to do our jobs, and he doesn't try to put a lot of controls on us. We go about doing the job the way we know is best, and that is OK with Jay.

The guys are also good because they help you out. When I was sick last year, they all pitched in to cover my territory so that we could make our plan plus 10 percent without reporting my illness to the company. They can also be hard on someone who doesn't realize how things work here. A few years back, when one of the young guys, Fred, came with us, he was all fired up. He was gonna sell baby food to half the mothers in Florida, personally! He didn't realize that you have to take your time and not waste your effort for the company. The other guys gave him a little bit of a hard time at first—he found his orders getting lost and shipments being changed—but when he finally came to his senses, they treated him great and showed him the ropes.

Exhibit 2.   Listing of Staff of Florida Sales Team

Name	Position	Age	Years w/HFP	Education
Jay Boyar	District sales manager	52	30	high school
David Berz	Salesman (assistant manager)	50	30	high school
Neil Portnow	Salesman	56	36	high school
Alby Siegel	Salesman	49	18	1/2 year college
Mike Wolly	Salesman	35	12	2 years college
John Cassis	Salesman	28	4	B.A.
Fred Hopengarten	Salesman	30	3	B.A.

Following up on the references to the company, the researcher asked Neil to talk more about HFP as a place to work:

It's all pretty simple; the company is out to screw the salesperson. Up in Atlanta and New York, all they are concerned about is the numbers; meet the plan, no matter what. The worst thing is if you work hard, meet the plan, and then keep going so you can earn some decent money. Then they go and change the plan next year. They increase the sales quota so that you have to work harder just to earn the same money! It just doesn't pay to bust your ass. . . .

The people in Atlanta also want all kinds of paperwork; sales reports, call reports, all kinds of reports. If you filled out all of the things that they want you to fill out, you'd spend all your time doing paperwork and no time out selling, looking for new accounts, making cold calls, or any of the things that a salesman really is supposed to do if he's gonna keep on top of his area.

As he talked with the other salesmen, the researcher found general agreement with Neil's views on the company. Alby Siegel added:

The biggest joke they got going is the suggestion plan. They want us to come up with new ideas about how the company should make more money. The joke of it is, if you come up with an idea that, for instance, makes the company a couple of hundred thousand in profit across the country, they are generous enough to give you $500. That's the top figure; $500 for your idea. That amount of money is an insult. . . .

One thing you have to remember is that in one way or another, we're all in this for the money. Despite what they say, it's not the greatest life being out on the road all of the time, staying in motels, fighting the competition. But it's worth it because I can earn more money doing this job than anything else I could do. I can live better than most professional men with all their college degrees. . . . Jay is pretty good about the money thing, too. He makes sure that we get our bonus, year in and year out, and he keeps the people in Atlanta from taking our bonus checks away from us. He's not management—he's one of us. You can really tell it during the team meetings. Once every two months we all meet in Tampa and spend a day going over the accounts and talking about ideas for selling. We spend the whole day in this hotel room, working, and then we go out and spend the whole night on the town, usually drinking. Jay is one of us . . . many is the night that I've helped carry him back to the hotel.

After about four weeks with the team, the researcher got a chance to participate in one of the bimonthly team meetings. During lunch, Jay came over to him and began to talk:

Listen, I need to talk over something with you before we start the afternoon meeting. We trust you so we're going to let you in on our little discovery. You may have noticed that we aren't doing so badly, and you're right. The reason is a little finding made by Alby about three years ago. He was out in one of the stores and he noticed that a lot of people buying our products were not mothers of young children, but old people! We started looking around, and we began to notice that a lot of older people were buying HFP jars. We talked with some of them, and it turns out that they like our stuff, particularly those people who have all kinds of teeth problems.

Since then we've developed a very lucrative trade with a number of old folks' homes, and we've been able to sell to them through some of the supermarkets that are located in areas where there is a larger older population. It's a great new piece of the market; it takes the pressure off of us to make plan, and we don't even have to push it very hard to keep making plan and about 10 percent.

We've also been pretty successful in keeping Atlanta from finding out. If they knew, they'd up our plan, leaving us no time to sell, no time to develop new customers, no time to make cold calls, or anything. This way we use this new area as a little cushion, and it helps us to stay on top of our territory. I had to tell you because we'll be talking about the old people this afternoon. The boys seem to think you are OK, so I'm trusting you with it. I hope I'm not making a mistake telling you this.

BACK IN ATLANTA

Soon after the Tampa meeting, the researcher left the Florida sales team and headed back for New York. On the way back he stopped off for a final brief visit with Brenda Cooper. He found her even more concerned about her problems:

I'm getting all kinds of pressure from New York to jack up my sales in the region. They are pushing me to increase plan for the next year. I really am beginning to feel that my job is on the line on this one. If I can't come up with something that is good in the coming year, the future for me at HFP looks bleak.

At the same time I'm getting flak from my district managers. They all say that they're running flat out as is and they can't squeeze any more sales out of the district than they already are. Even Jay Boyar is complaining that he may not make plan if we have another increase next year. At the same time, he always seems to pull out his 10 percent extra by the end of the year. I wonder what they're really doing down there.

Michael Simpson

Michael Simpson is one of the most outstanding managers in the management consulting division of Avery McNeil and Co.[1] A highly qualified individual with a deep sense of responsibility, Simpson had obtained his MBA two years ago from one of the leading northeastern schools. Before graduating from business school, Simpson had interviewed a number of consulting firms and decided that the consulting division of Avery McNeil offered the greatest potential for rapid advancement.

Simpson had recently been promoted to manager, making him the youngest individual at this level in the consulting group. Two years with the firm was an exceptionally short period of time in which to achieve this promotion. Although the promotions had been announced, Simpson had not yet been informed of his new salary. Despite the fact that his career had progressed well, he was concerned that his salary would be somewhat lower than the current market value that a headhunter had recently quoted him.

Simpson's wife, Diane, soon would be receiving her MBA. One night over dinner, Simpson was amazed to hear the salaries being offered to new MBAs. Simpson commented to Diane,

I certainly hope I get a substantial raise this time. I mean, it just wouldn't be fair to be making the same amount as recent graduates when I've been at the company now for over two years! I'd like to buy a house soon but with housing costs rising and inflation following, that will depend on my pay raise.

Several days later, Simpson was working at his desk when Dave Barton, a friend and colleague, came across to Simpson's office. Barton had been hired at the same time as Simpson and had also been promoted recently. Barton told Simpson, "Hey Mike, look at this! I was walking past Jane's desk and saw this memo from the personnel manager lying there. She obviously forgot to put it away. Her boss would kill her if he found out!"

The memo showed the proposed salaries for all the individuals in the consulting group that year. Simpson looked at the list and was amazed by what he saw. He said, "I can't believe this, Dave! Walt and Rich will be getting $2,000 more than I am."

Walt Gresham and Rich Watson had been hired within the past year. Before coming to Avery McNeil they had both worked one year at another consulting firm. Barton spoke angrily:

Mike, I knew the firm had to pay them an awful lot to attract them, but to pay them more than people above them is ridiculous!

Simpson: You know if I hadn't seen Walt and Rich's salaries, I would think I was getting a reasonable raise. Hey listen Dave, let's get out of here. I've had enough of this place for one day.

Barton: Okay Mike, just let me return this memo. Look, it's not that bad; after all, you are getting the largest raise.

On his way home, Simpson tried to think about the situation more objectively. He knew that there were a number of pressures on the compensation structure in the consulting division.

If the division wished to continue attracting MBAs from top schools, it would have to offer competitive salaries. Starting salaries had increased about $3,500 during the last two years. As a result, some of the less experienced MBAs were earning nearly the same amounts as others who had been with the firm several years but had come in at lower starting salaries, even though their pay had been gradually increasing over time.

Furthermore, because of expanding business, the division had found it necessary to hire consultants from other firms. In order to do so effectively, Avery McNeil had found it necessary to upgrade the salaries they offered.

The firm as a whole was having problems meeting the federally regulated Equal Opportunity Employment goals and was trying especially hard to recruit women and minorities.

One of Simpson's colleagues, Martha Lohman, had been working in the consulting division of Avery McNeil and Company until three months ago when she was offered a job at another consulting firm. She had become disappointed with her new job and on returning to her previous position at Avery McNeil was rehired at a salary considerably higher than her former level. Simpson had noticed on the memo that she was earning more than he was, even though she was not given nearly the same level of responsibility as he was. Simpson also realized that the firm attempted to maintain some parity between salaries in the auditing and consulting divisions.

When Simpson arrived home, he discussed the situation with his wife:

Diane, I know I'm getting a good raise, but I am still earning below my market value—$3,000 less than that headhunter told me last week. And the fact that those two guys from the other consulting firm are getting more than I shows the firm is prepared to pay competitive rates.

Diane: I know it's unfair Mike, but what can you do? You know your boss won't negotiate salaries after they have been approved by the compensation committee, but it wouldn't hurt to at least talk to him about your dissatisfaction. I don't think you should let a few thousand dollars a year bother you. You will catch up eventually, and the main thing is that you really enjoy what you are doing.

Simpson: Yes I do enjoy what I'm doing, but that is not to say that I wouldn't enjoy it elsewhere. I really just have to sit down and think about all the pros and cons in my working for Avery McNeil. First of all, I took this job because I felt that I could work my way up quickly. I think that I have demonstrated this, and the firm has also shown that they are willing to help me achieve this goal. If I left this job for a better paying one, I might not get the opportunity to work on the exciting jobs that I am currently working on. Furthermore, this company has time and money invested in me. I'm the only one at Avery that can work on certain jobs, and the company has several lined up. If I left the company now, they would not only lose me, but they would probably lose some of their billings as well. I really don't know what to do at this point, Diane. I can either stay with Avery McNeil or look for a higher paying job elsewhere; however, there is no guarantee that my new job would be a "fast track" one like it is at Avery. One big plus at Avery is that the people there already know me and the kind of work I produce. If I went elsewhere, I'd essentially have to start all over again. What do you think I should do, Diane?

NOTE

1. Avery McNeil is primarily an accounting firm that has two divisions besides accounting—tax and management consulting.

CN Information Services

David Orlinoff, the new director of marketing for Columbia National (CN) Information Services, was sitting at his desk, trying to list the various major tasks that he had to tackle in his new job. On the piece of paper before him, he had listed a number of major headings, each representing a major piece of the job of getting his new unit up, running, and producing revenue within a short period of time. One of the headings was *staffing*. David decided that this evening he was going to try to attack that piece of the job, and that he would try to identify all of the various things that had to be done in order to build an effective staff.

BACKGROUND

Columbia National Bank (CN) is a major financial institution in a large city in the eastern United States. During the late 1970s, CN had been very concerned about the increasing costs of information processing, and in particular, the cost associated with the processing of information that had to do with retail banking, such as checks, credit card information, and so on. A major decision was made by the management of CN to invest resources in the development of the most advanced technology and systems for doing this work. From 1975 on, the bank made considerable investments in the development of new computer systems for the support of retail banking operations. These systems were, by and large, successful. They enabled the bank to maintain service quality while expanding volume dramatically and in the process reducing the expenses of this "back office" operation.

Having accomplished the job of developing the state-of-the-art information technology, top management of the bank began to discuss other ways of gaining a return on the investment that had been made to develop the information systems. The executive vice-president in charge of operations, whose responsibilities included the back office operations, developed a proposal that involved selling the bank's systems to other organizations facing similar information management problems. The executive vice-president reported that he had received numerous inquiries about the information systems from other businesses, and that many of these were willing and eager to purchase the expertise of the bank in this area. The executive committee of the bank reviewed the proposal and agreed to move ahead in this area.

The executive vice-president appointed a senior vice-president to head up the CN Information Services Group. This senior vice-president, Matthew Diaz, in turn set up two major departments, operations and marketing. Operations would develop and implement the systems. Marketing would have responsibility for identifying customers, generating sales, and working with customers to pinpoint needs and thus determine the type of product that operations would be required to develop and install.

THE MARKETING DEPARTMENT

Diaz had recruited an old friend of his, David Orlinoff, to be the director of marketing. Diaz and Orlinoff had been in the same MBA program several years earlier, and had kept in touch since then. Orlinoff had gone to a major computer firm in marketing after getting his MBA. After several years in a number of jobs in that firm, he had been recruited by a major consumer products organization. As a product manager, he had established a tremendous record of performance, but had been frustrated with the lack of opportunities for growth within that particular organization.

Thus, when approached by Diaz, Orlinoff decided to take the job at CN Information Services.

THE STAFFING PROBLEM

Orlinoff was given approximately six months to put together a marketing group. David knew that over the long run, his performance would be judged based on the performance of the entire Information Services Group (essentially Diaz, Orlinoff, and the operations director). More specifically, David knew that his responsibility would be to identify a marketing approach and generate sales volume. Obviously, he would have to work with the operations people closely.

It was now January, and Orlinoff had the goal of being "staffed up" and ready to start active marketing work by June at the latest. He knew that he had approximately $750,000 yearly in budget for direct expenses (salary) for staff for his department. As he began to plan for the next six months, a major concern was how he would go about assembling an effective staff for the department.

CASE **6**

Windelle Faculty Secretaries

At Uris Hall, two kinds of roles have been developed to provide direct clerical and secretarial support for faculty in the Graduate School of Business. Each floor has a number of faculty secretaries who are assigned to faculty members. These secretaries perform normal clerical support activities, including typing of correspondence, class materials, examinations, research proposals, manuscripts for articles, and so on. In addition these individuals perform other routine clerical duties as appropriate. Secretaries do not, however, have any responsibilities concerning phone communications (or related communication) with faculty. Each floor also has a receptionist whose job is answering telephones when faculty are absent and taking messages for faculty, either over the phone or from visitors. The receptionist also may have secretarial responsibilities for a number of faculty members.

PHYSICAL ARRANGEMENTS

Each of the major faculty floors (4–7) contains approximately twenty-six faculty offices all facing the outside of the building and situated around a core of cubicles. Each floor also has partitioned space allocated for clerical support and doctoral students (see Exhibit 1 for a typical floor diagram). There are at least four regular faculty secretaries per floor, usually at the ends of the floor, and one receptionist, in the small office directly opposite the elevator. Most of the remaining

Exhibit 1. Design of Faculty Floors

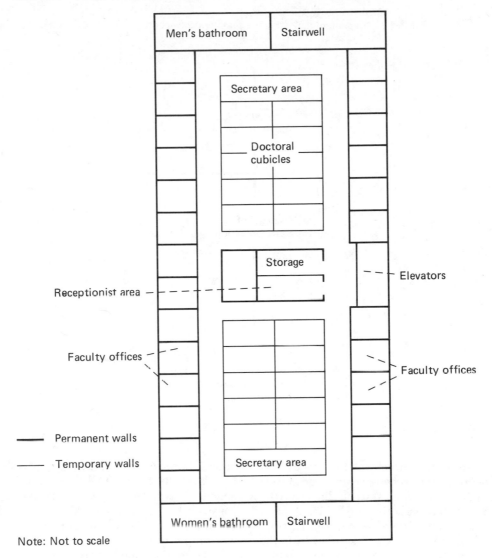

Note: Not to scale

space is allocated to doctoral students as study cubicles. On some floors, however, some of the cubicle space has been utilized differently; it is allocated to extra clerical personnel, research projects, "chair secretaries" (who report to chair professors), and so on. The cubicles are all locked regularly to prevent theft.

REPORTING RELATIONSHIPS

Each secretary may be assigned to a number of faculty members. Secretaries may work for as few as three and as many as five faculty members at any time. Allocation of secretaries to faculty members is made on the basis of expected work load determined by various factors (previous faculty productivity, existence of other support in the form of funded research clerical staff, leave status, and the like). No formal procedures exist for secretaries to make decisions among the potentially conflicting demands of different faculty members other than the rule that class-related work takes priority over other types of work.

Although secretaries are assigned to work with faculty members, they do not formally report to

Exhibit 2. Organizational Structure for Clerical Support

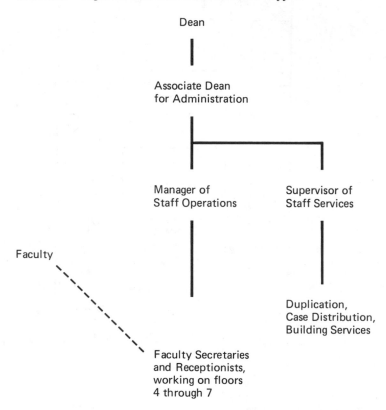

faculty within the hierarchy. All faculty clerical personnel (with the exception of those on outside funding or chair secretaries) report directly to the manager of staff operations. (See Exhibit 2 for an organizational chart.) The manager of staff operations has direct supervisory authority over the secretaries and receptionists and makes determinations in areas such as hiring and firing, disciplinary activities, job assignments, promotion, and pay. Faculty who want to affect any of these areas with regard to the clerical personnel reporting to them must work through the manager.

WORKING ARRANGEMENTS

Over the years, a number of working arrangements have developed. The rule exists that the receptionist's desk must be covered at all times because of the heavy volume of phone calls coming for faculty members who frequently may be absent. Thus whenever the receptionist needs to leave the desk (to take a break, to go to the bathroom, or to go to lunch) he or she must arrange with one of the other secretaries to cover the desk for that time. On most floors a rotation schedule has been developed so that secretaries share the coverage of the receptionist position on an equitable basis.

SYMPTOMS

The current system of job design and organization has been in place, with a few minor modifications, for a number of years. There are varying opinions on the effectiveness of the structure.

Some feel that it works effectively, given limited resources of space, budget, and personnel. Others feel that the system is cumbersome and overly rigid. Secretaries and receptionists themselves express varying degrees of satisfaction with the structure. It should be noted, however, that turnover in these positions has been relatively high, and that on some floors the receptionist job in particular may have turned over as many as four or five times within a year. Additional data on the perceptions of job holders is in Exhibit 3, which summarizes responses to the *Job Diagnostic Survey* (Hackman and Oldham, 1975) for a nonrandom sample of employees in these jobs. Typical responses are given in Exhibit 4.

CONSTRAINTS ON REDESIGN

Any structural or technological redesign must be done within some general constraints. First, no additional secretaries can be added. Assume approximately 3.5 faculty members to each secretary. Also assume that competing uses of space (research projects, doctoral cubicles) will continue unchanged; the proportion of space allocated to these activities should remain constant. However, changes can be made in any temporary partitions, including those in the doctoral cubicles. Changes can also be made in job assignments, reporting relationships, routines, responsibilities, and so on.

Exhibit 3.   Job Diagnostic Survey Data[*]

Survey scales	Secretaries	Receptionists
Job dimensions		
Skill variety	2.3	1.0
Task identity	5.3	5.0
Task significance	2.7	3.7
Autonomy	3.8	1.0
Feedback from the job	4.7	2.0
Feedback from agents	4.1	2.0
Dealing with others	3.8	5.7
Experienced psychological states		
Meaningfulness of work	2.6	2.3
Responsibility for work	5.1	4.5
Knowledge of results	4.0	4.0
Affective responses to job		
General satisfaction	3.5	1.0
Internal work motivation	5.1	2.3
Specific satisfactions		
Pay satisfaction	2.8	1.0
Security satisfaction	5.5	2.5
Social satisfaction	5.4	1.3
Supervisory satisfaction	5.2	1.3
Growth satisfaction	2.9	1.0
Individual growth need strength	6.4	7.0
Motivating Potential Score (MPS)	61.32	6.5

[*]Based on a nonrandom sample of staff from different floors. Numbers in each job are not included to protect confidentiality.
Source: J. Richard Hackman and Greg R. Oldham, "Development of the Job Diagnostic Survey," Journal of Applied Psychology 60: 159–170.

Exhibit 4. Means of Job Dimensions by Equal Employment Opportunity Commission (EEOC) Categories

Job dimension	Overall sample	Administrators	Professionals	Technicians	Protective services	Paraprofessionals	Office, Clerical	Skilled craft	Maintenance, service
					EEOC job categories				
Skill variety	5.18	5.98	5.84	5.33	5.83	5.05	4.47	5.06	4.23
Task identity	3.09	5.42	5.30	5.18	4.58	5.11	4.89	5.15	5.12
Task significance	6.06	6.26	6.22	5.94	6.43	6.20	5.90	5.78	5.87
Autonomy	5.04	5.60	5.50	5.20	4.97	4.89	4.75	4.85	4.59
Feedback from job	5.12	5.39	5.25	5.22	4.92	4.83	5.13	5.14	4.92
Feedback from agents	4.01	4.58	4.31	3.80	4.07	4.02	3.90	3.68	3.70
Dealing with others	5.68	6.29	6.05	5.70	6.13	5.95	5.36	5.09	5.14
Experienced meaningfulness of work	5.68	6.08	5.86	5.69	5.95	5.46	5.47	5.50	5.36
Experienced responsibility for work	5.67	6.10	5.89	5.63	5.52	5.52	5.73	5.42	5.34
Knowledge of results	5.40	5.52	5.32	5.46	5.21	5.06	5.53	5.48	5.40
Internal work motivation	5.64	5.96	5.86	5.66	5.68	5.48	5.62	5.42	5.33
Motivating Potential Score (MPS)	140	178	167	149	137	129	124	133	115
N	3059	368	477	380	352	159	582	287	427

Source: Work in the public sector. Washington, D.C. National Training and Development Service Technical Report, 1974.

Katz, Gefford & Associates

Katz, Gefford & Associates (KGA) is a well-known, medium-sized consulting firm that provides a variety of services to a range of corporate and public sector clients. The firm was founded in 1952 by a small group of academics from well-known universities who were interested in putting their talents to work in solving various kinds of business and organizational problems. Over the years, through a program of planned but conservative growth, the organization grew so that by the late 1970s it employed approximately 300 individuals and booked approximately $9 million a year in billings. Recently, top level staff in KGA became aware of problems of staff utilization in a number of the operating units of the firm and concerned about the potential impact of these problems on the firm's effectiveness.

BACKGROUND

Over the more than quarter century of its existence, KGA had grown primarily by attracting business that capitalized on the capabilities and reputation of the core group who had established the firm, known informally as "the founders." Each of the founders had assembled around him or her a group of talented individuals who worked on a variety of projects. The majority of current senior staff members started out as junior-level members of the organization, rose through the ranks, and gradually began to generate their own business and assemble a staff to work with them.

Although growth came largely through the gradual expansion of "home-grown" staff, over the years KGA also broadened its line of services and products offered. Throughout this period, KGA maintained its image as a "think tank," attracting highly competent individuals, providing high-quality service, and charging top fees. The found-

ers, who had expertise largely in the accounting field, developed clients based on the firm's expertise in the design of internal control systems for organizations. In the early 1960s a group of the senior staff began to specialize in the design of computer-based systems and finally was organized into a separate group to provide services related to computer applications. As the founders' interests began to broaden and as new senior staff developed, new divisions were set up in the areas of market research (1968) and personnel planning and selection (1972). By the late 1970s the structure of the organization stabilized into four major operating divisions, each headed by a senior vice-president, and one staff group directed by a chief of staff who reports directly to the president. (See Exhibit 1.)

THE ORGANIZATIONAL STRUCTURE IN OPERATION

Within each of the four operating divisions no formal organizational structure has developed. Each senior vice-president has a number of vice-presidents reporting to him or her, ranging from five in the personnel planning area to twenty in the management control area. The vice-presidents who work in related areas are talked about as "working groups," but in reality, each vice-president is an autonomous operator, with a set of clients, a yearly amount of billings, and so on. In many ways, the vice-presidents function as small profit centers. As a vice-president signs a project with a client, he or she assembles a group of junior level staff to work on the project. (For a brief listing and description of staff titles, see Exhibit 2.) While most junior staff work exclusively for one vice-president, they are in theory free to float and sell their services to any project or group

Exhibit 1.   KGA Organization Chart

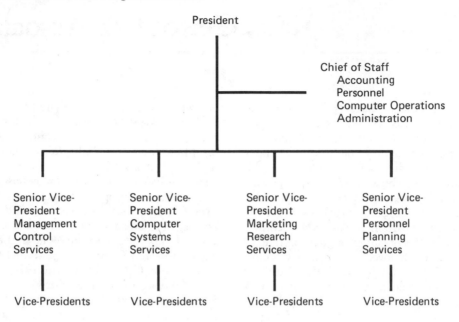

Exhibit 2.   Descriptions of KGA Job Titles

Senior Staff	Senior Vice-President	Responsible for management of operating division, total profit performance for the Vice-Presidents within the division, and planning for growth, new markets, services, staff, and so on
	Vice-President	Responsible for obtaining contracts and coordinating delivery of services. Profit-center responsibility for performance of staff assigned to him or her
Junior Staff	Group Manager	Responsible for day-to-day management of junior staff and work activities on different projects. Responsible for client relations as back-up to Vice-President
	Senior Associates	Primary professional staff for analysis, system design, and other professional work on projects
Non-professional Staff	Associates	Responsible for providing administrative support for professional staff with emphasis on computer operations and coordination of paperwork products
	Clerical Staff	Includes secretaries, clerks, administration aides, and the like

within the firm. About one-quarter of the professional junior staff work for more than one vice-president.

As project groups form and begin to work with clients, some of the divisions between staff roles become blurred, while others tend to stay very rigid. Senior staff, by and large, retain primary contact with top-level staff in the client organizations. However, the day-to-day activity and relations with members of the client organization are carried on by the junior professional staff. The distinction between senior associates and group managers tends to fade, with many senior associates taking day-to-day management responsibilities for projects and frequently coordinating the work of other senior associates or even group managers. The dividing line between the junior professional staff and the administrative staff is very distinct, with the administrative staff rarely getting into the field and having contact with clients.

The different roles reflect the nature of the career paths in KGA. Most professionals are hired at the senior associate level. These individuals at entry typically are bright and aggressive MBAs, usually with several years of experience. Occasionally Ph.D.s are also hired into the senior associate position. Senior associates typically move within five years to become group managers, and within ten to fifteen years into vice-president positions. At the same time, many senior associates have chosen not to move up the hierarchy, preferring to remain at the senior associate level, which provides them with considerable freedom and more than adequate compensation. The associates typically are college or technical school graduates with no advanced degrees. During the history of KGA, no associate has ever moved into a senior associate position or above.

The career path has created problems at varying times. A major point of friction in the organization is the relationship between the new senior associates and the relatively experienced associates. Frequently the new MBAs coming in at the senior associate level end up clashing with the associates who have been with the firm for some time over issues of status, authority, and interpersonal relations. The associates, many of whom have been with the firm for fifteen years or more, frequently resent what they see as the arrogant and insensitive attitude of these new employees, whom they perceive as relatively young and inexperienced. Similarly, the hiring of group managers from outside the firm has created problems; new group managers come into conflict with established senior associates who have had managerial responsibility over projects and may even have brought client projects into the firm.

INTERNAL CONTROL AND COMPENSATION

As a project is signed, the internal accounting office sets up a project account to which all expenses are assigned. Because of the nature of the consulting work, the largest single direct expense is salary, with computer costs, travel, and supplies as the other major expenses. Indirect expenses are allocated to projects as a percentage of the direct salary dollars charged to the account (at a rate of 67.5 percent).

At the end of each week, every employee of the organization fills out a time sheet. All of the forty working hours of the week have to be allocated to some account. All hours that are not charged to active projects or to accounts established or product/service development are allocated to an overhead account. Officially, junior staff may not charge time to overhead unless specifically authorized by senior staff. Senior staff are permitted to charge time to overhead but are discouraged from doing so. There is great informal pressure for all individuals to "cover their time," which means to avoid charging any hours to overhead and to bring in enough contracts to enable the time of senior and junior staff working on projects to be fully allocated.

KGA has had a policy of paying top dollar in its field. The company's official policy is to keep its middle range of salaries in the top quartile of the industry. Beginning salaries for senior associates are high, averaging about $26,000 in 1976. Each year salary recommendations for each junior staff member are made by the senior vice-presidents of the four divisions. In view of the length of service and high base salaries of employees, these yearly increases are relatively insignificant compared to the dollars earned through the company bonus plan. Under the bonus plan, a fixed percentage (15 percent) of pretax earnings is put into a pool and distributed to each employee as a standardized percentage of salary. In recent years employees have been averaging bonuses of approximately 12 percent of yearly salary. Thus, a major portion of the variable compensation of all employees (from senior staff through clerical) is tied to the performance of the company as a whole. In addition, senior staff receive an "executive bonus," which is determined by the president and which reflects the performance of the various profit centers.

THE FINANCIAL SERVICES GROUP

One of the groups that has recently been experiencing problems in performance and utilization of staff is the financial services group. This group, located in the management control services division, is organized around a vice-president, Emmett Lawson. Lawson joined KGA approximately four years ago, having left a high position in a competing consulting firm. One of the few vice-presidents hired from the outside, he came in with a good reputation; however, his experience was mainly working directly with clients, rather than managing a group of junior staff. Lawson brought with him John Courtland, a group manager who had worked closely with him in his old firm.

During the first year, Lawson began to cultivate new clients. He specialized in the area of long-range financial planning services for medium-sized corporations. After a year of hard work, contracts began to come in, and Lawson assembled a staff. He began by hiring two new senior associates, Guy Jones and Al Nader, and recruiting an associate, Marge Brown, internally. During the second year, he built his staff largely by attracting senior associates from other projects and groups within the firm, including Nancy Gradford, Ronnie Gerstein, and Jeff Waltz. At the end of the second year he hired a new group manager, Larry Gamble, and several new senior associates from the outside, including Howie Berg, Don Perkins, and Bill Murpis (recruited by Courtland

and Nader). In the third year he hired Ron Klash, Joe Caine, and Mark Richmond from outside the firm.

As the project work continued, Lawson recognized the need to devote time to developing specific packaged services (or "products," as they were called) that would give the firm a competitive advantage in this market. He was authorized by his senior vice-president to establish several product accounts.

At the end of four years, Lawson had established a major group with KGA accounting for a sizeable percentage of the division's billings. His staff was involved in eight major ongoing client projects and had three to four more under negotiation. In addition, work was proceeding on six different "products," several of which were being tested and developed as part of the current project activity (see Exhibits 3, 4, and 5 for data on the group).

Different staff members work on different project and product teams. While junior staff members officially are hired or placed into various teams by vice-presidents, job assignment actually

Exhibit 3.

Staff in the Financial Services Group	
Vice-president	Emmett Lawson
Group managers	John Courtland
	Larry Gamble
Senior associates	Howie Berg
	Guy Jones
	Bill Murpis
	Nancy Gradford
	Ronnie Gerstein
	Mark Richmond
	Jeff Waltz
	Don Perkins
	Al Nader
	Ron Klash
	Joe Caine
Associates	Marge Brown
	Gary Van
	Mary Compter
	Gus Campbell
Clerical	Susan Kahn
	Gayle Zander
	Lois Cartwright

Exhibit 4.   Current Work Assignments of Staff in the Financial Services Group

Assignment	Staff*
Major projects with clients	
Cutler project	Don Perkins, Ronnie Gerstein, Gary Van
PNB project	John Courtland, Al Nader, Bill Murpis
Rocky Ridge project	Emmett Lawson, Guy Jones
Colbork project	Guy Jones, Ron Klash
Microproducts project	Emmett Lawson, Joe Caine
Department of Transportation project	John Courtland, Nancy Gradford, Guy Jones, Jeff Waltz, Marge Brown, Gus Campbell
IBG project	Larry Gamble, Bill Murpis
Fenlon Crunch project	John Courtland, Howie Berg
Product/service development	
General coordination of product development	Emmett Lawson, John Courtland, Al Nader
Computer-based analysis	Guy Jones, Ron Klash, John Courtland, Mark Richmond
In-depth analysis procedures	Don Perkins, Al Nader, Ronnie Gerstein, Mark Richmond
Inventory control programs	Larry Gamble, Bill Murpis
Key indicators	Guy Jones, Al Nader
Data bank	Gary Van, Mary Compter

*First person listed usually has management responsibility for the project.

evolved into more of a bargaining process. Different people were assigned by Lawson to head up a project, and those individuals would then attempt to interest other people in "signing on" with the project by committing a certain fraction of their time (¼ time, ½ time, and so on) to it. Although in theory anyone could be removed from a project team at any time by the vice-president heading up the area, in practice such actions were never taken. The only time people had ever been reassigned was when funding had been exhausted for a particular project. It was strongly felt in the firm that junior staff could manage their own work assignments.

PROBLEMS IN THE FINANCIAL SERVICES GROUP

Although Lawson was pleased with his own performance and the work of his group, he was trou-

bled by a number of problems that he felt threatened the future of the unit. Talking with a close friend, he described some of the issues that were troubling him.

I'm pleased with where the group is these days in general. In many ways I've tried to shape the group, to provide as much individual freedom as possible. At first, this caused some of the other people in the firm to view us as somewhat strange. We were seen as the "wildmen" since we were more aggressive, less conservative, and different in our own style of relating. I'm close personally with many of the people in the group. We go out socially together and enjoy each other's company. But that's not the way things have been done traditionally around here. I guess many of the other vice-presidents sat back and waited for me to fail, but we succeeded. In this last year, I billed more business than any other vice-president in the firm, and I'm looking for a bigger year coming up.

Part of my problem is that I'm a consultant

Exhibit 5. Floor Plan of Financial Services Group

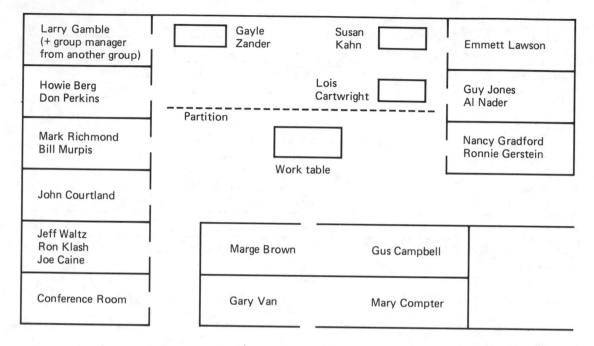

and a salesman, not a manager. I enjoy being out dealing with clients, and I've tried to recruit people who can take care of themselves. I've looked for people who are self-starters and don't need a lot of support or guidance from me, since I don't give it to them. Even if I did, managing is not the kind of thing that I'm comfortable with or good at. I really don't want to spend my time managing this group, and I don't believe that the firm would be getting full value out of me if I did.

During the first two years here I tried to get John [Courtland] to serve as a sort of chief of staff to actually manage the group. That has not worked out as well as I would like it to. John is also not a good manager—he gets involved with so many things that he loses sight of time deadlines and priorities. He's good on the administrative side, getting budgets together and proposals written, but he does not seem to be able to manage the actual project work and coordinate it as it needs to be done. In part, John may never be able to because most of the people here have come to the group to work with me. I was involved in recruiting many of them, and they tell me working with me is a big part of the attraction of the job. In fact, they talk about us as

Lawson's group, rather than the financial services group.

Some people, such as Don Perkins, Al Nader, or Bill Murpis, have taken some leadership, but this has mainly been in relation to specific projects. Since they are at the senior associate level and relatively new, the other senior associates see them as peers and are not ready to take direction from them. Given their newness, I would have trouble promoting them to group managers at this point also.

Recently, I've become aware of problems. We just are not getting the performance out of this group that we should be getting. Several of the projects are seriously over budget, such as the Department of Transportation Project and Colbork. We're also running behind schedule in some of the product development. Inventory control is doing well, but computer-based analysis is running about six months behind schedule. I've talked with the groups, but they complain about unrealistic deadlines and about my having underbid for contracts resulting in insufficient funds to do the work that we have contracted to do. Some of that may be true, but I think that it's being used as an excuse for less than top performance.

A symptom of the problems in the group is the informal groups—cliques you might call them—that have formed. In our first year when it was basically John [Courtland], Al [Nader], Guy [Jones] and myself, we were a tight-knit team, and we worked well together. During the past year, I've seen the development of some groups within the unit, and I'm not sure that it's for the good. (See Exhibit 6 for a rough charting of the groups as described by Lawson.)

One group in particular is troublesome. I call

this the "happy hour group" since they all seem to go out together at five in the afternoon to the happy hour at a local bar about three times a week. Two people seem to be at the core of the group, Guy and Nancy [Gradford]. The attitude they've developed is very negative, and it's beginning to tear the group apart. For example, about two years ago, I hired Larry Gamble as a group manager. Larry had been working in another consulting firm and seemed to show great promise. I brought him in to meet the staff, and

Exhibit 6. Informal Groups in the Financial Services Group

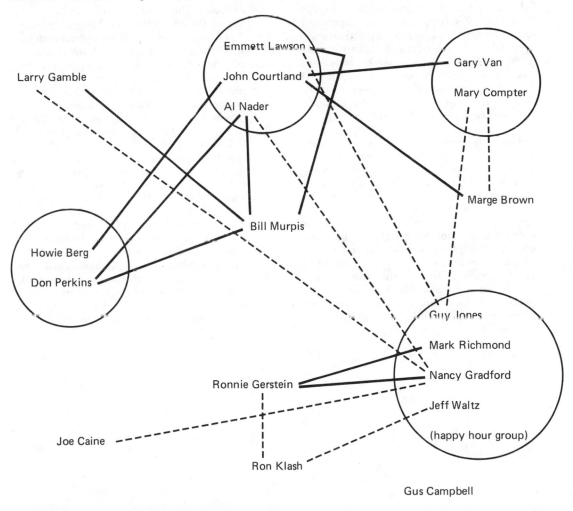

————— Signifies major positive relationships

– – – Signifies major negative relationships

Guy and Nancy in particular did not like him. They seemed to base their dislike on the fact that he was being recruited from a firm that was not "first rate" and that he did not have his MBA from one of the top ten schools, as they do. I hired him anyway, and since then, they have created problems all along. Anything Larry does, they criticize. When he gets up to present in staff meetings, they tend to not pay attention or give nonverbal signals indicating their dislike. They've refused to work with him on any of the projects.

Similarly, some of the new senior associates have also run into problems with this group. They have basically ostracized Joe Caine and Ron Klash, but at the same time, they immediately brought Mark Richmond into their group and helped to train him. Perhaps the most graphic example is the way that they have taken over the work table in our area (see Exhibit 5) and claimed it, informally, as their territory. They tend to eat lunch there, work at the table, and sit there for hours chit-chatting.

The problem is that the people in this group are basically competent, and given the current work load and new projects, I cannot afford to be without them. Guy, in particular, is extremely important. He is the most competent computer man we have, and we sorely need his skills in several of the projects. He is important to the group, since many people go to him for help on thorny computer problems. He's very good in helping them, although he tends to help people in a way that makes them continue to depend on him. That way they have to come back to him repeatedly. Therefore, he's a major power in the group and also a critical resource in the unit. It's not all bad—at times he's run informal seminars on new computer technology

for the rest of the group and has really helped us develop our capability in that area. We'd really be a lot worse off without him.

In some ways, I can understand how some of the members of that group feel. I've talked with them, and most of them are not particularly interested in promotion. They like the senior associate job, like the money and the freedom, and also like the people they work with. Much of their social life centers around the office—most of them are single—and they see a lot of each other on weekends. They have a pretty good existence and seem to be enjoying it.

What disturbs me is the generally negative outlook of this group and the fact that it is infecting the rest of the unit. Many of the other staff members have talked to me about their frustration when they have to work with these people. At different times, I've had complaints—well, not actually complaints but just comments—from Gary Van, John Courtland, Al Nader, and Larry Gamble. It's beginning to get people down. I've talked in staff meetings about the need to take a more positive attitude, both towards the work and towards each other, but that seems to have no effect. I'm out of town dealing with clients about 80 percent of the time, so it's hard for me to take much action on a day-to-day basis. The problem is that the negative and criticism-oriented attitude is beginning to spread. People in the group seem to feel that our whole set of projects and products is destined to ultimately fail; that we are understaffed, underfunded, and undermanaged. That may be true, but there's a lot of talent and time currently being wasted, and a lot of energy is being directed towards talking about how bad things are, rather than trying to make things better.

Office of State and Local Grants

The office of state and local grants is part of a large federal department, part of whose function is to provide grants-in-aid to local government units (including state governments, city and town governments, and other public or community units). These grants are given to support programs that are consistent with the federal department's mission. This granting function constitutes a major activity, as it does in many other federal departments.

The office of state and local grants (OSLG) is headed up by S. Campbell, a graduate of a well-known business school located in a large eastern city. Campbell has been with the department for seven years, working in a variety of different functional areas, and was only recently promoted to the directorship of OSLG. Although OSLG has a number of subunits, the major work of reviewing and deciding on grants is performed by three different groups. (See Exhibit 1 for a partial organizational chart of OSLG.) The three groups are organized functionally and include the grants application processing group (three professional staff members), the grants review and approval group (four professionals), and the grants administration and monitoring group (eight professionals). The grants administration and monitoring group has a supervisor, while the other two groups are directly responsible to Campbell.

A recent issue of concern has been the productivity of the grants application processing group. This group, made up of three fairly recent college graduates, M. Black, L. Shephard, and M. Compton, has the responsibility for processing the grants as they come in from the local agencies, reviewing them, and getting them ready for substantiation by the grants review and approval group. See the table below for the basic work flow.

The grant application packages that come in from the state and local government units are typically fairly involved and complicated. They include many pages of text, forms, technical information, budgets, and the like. The standard application runs from 200 to 300 pages.

Black, Compton, and Shephard all work in

Step	Person assigned to the step
1. *Forms review.* Review all standard grant application forms to make sure that all necessary documentation is included (such as EEOC compliance, accounting procedures, and assurance) and that forms have been filled out completely and correctly.	Black
2. *Program review.* Read the application for program relevance and determine which program area it falls into (of the forty or so program areas in which grants are given).	Compton
3. *Financial review.* Review the financial portion of the grant application to assure that all necessary information is present and that no obvious nonallowable expenditures are included in the budgets.	Shephard

Exhibit 1.　Partial Organizational Chart of OSLG

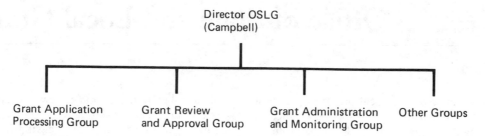

the same large office and have a secretary to help in clerical matters. Since they are in close proximity, they can help each other out if they wish. Since each of the jobs requires each individual to become very familiar with the grant application packages, each has been able to learn the other two jobs. Every few days the three trade positions in the application processing sequence. This idea of trading positions fairly regularly was developed by the three themselves. This does not seem to create problems for them in that it is hard to evaluate individual output anyway, and the thing that higher management has tended to look at for merit raises has been group output.

CASE 9
Trans-Europa Business Credit

Trans-Europa Business Credit (TEBC), a commercial finance company, was acquired as a wholly owned subsidiary by a large conglomerate holding company 10 years ago. It is headquartered in New York and has 30 branches, most of them located in North America and Europe, and a few in the Middle East. The branches have always operated separately and autonomously.

TEBC's primary business is accounts receivable financing, but it also books loans secured by inventory or other collateral when a borrower needs more money than can be secured by accounts receivable alone. The minimum loan is $100,000 and the average is $250,000. The District Manager, who usually has four or five Branch Managers reporting to him, has authority to approve all loans.

When TEBC was acquired, the management

of Trans-Europa Corporation decided it wanted more control over the subsidiary. There was an overall concentration of loans in a few business areas that could become dangerous should the world economy change and undermine one of those business areas. To reduce the risk, Paul Bergonzi, the President of the finance company, hired George Praeger, an experienced loan executive, as Vice President of Commercial Finance Lending. Praeger was to reorganize the branch system and diversify the loan portfolio. Bergonzi assigned Tom Baldwin as Praeger's assistant. Over the years, Baldwin had worked in several areas of TEBC and knew most of the Branch Managers personally.

One of Praeger's first decisions was to centralize the loan approval process by requiring that head office be notified of all loans over $250,000 and that head office make final approval of all loans over $350,000. This would include any increases in existing accommodations that would bring the loan line over $350,000.

Praeger discussed this idea with Bergonzi who presented it to the conglomerate management. They approved the plan.

Praeger then drafted the following letter to the Branch Managers:

Dear _____:

Paul Bergonzi and the directors of the Trans-Europa Corporation have authorized a change in our loan approval procedures. Hereafter, all Branch Managers will notify the Vice President of Commercial Finance Lending of any loans in excess of $250,000 before the preliminary approval and before TEBC's auditors conduct the survey. In addition, final approval of all loans for more than $350,000 will come from the New York office. This includes new accommodations and increases in the loan line which brings the limit up to $350,000 or more.

By centralizing loan approval, we can ensure that our monies are not concentrated in only a few areas and we can broaden our base of operation. I am sure you will understand that this step is necessary in such times of increasing economic uncertainty. By effecting this change, the interests of each branch and the company as a whole will best be served.

Yours very truly,

George Praeger

George Praeger
Vice President of
Commercial Finance Lending

Praeger showed the letter to Tom Baldwin and asked for his opinion. Baldwin said he liked the letter but suggested that since Praeger was new to TEBC, he might visit the branches and meet the managers to talk to them in person about the new procedure. Praeger decided that there was so much to do at the head office that he could not take the time to go to each branch. He sent the letter instead.

In the next 2 weeks, most of the branches responded. Although some managers wrote more, the following is a characteristic reply:

Dear Mr. Praeger:

We have received your recent letter about notifying the head office about negotiations of loans of $250,000 and the change in the approval process for loans in excess of $350,000. This suggestion seems a most practical one, and we want to assure you that you can depend on our cooperation.

Sincerely yours,

Jack Foster

Jack Foster
Branch Manager

For the next 10 weeks, the head office received no information about negotiations of loan agreements from any of the branch offices.

Executives who made frequent trips to the field reported that the offices were busy making somewhat more loans than usual.

CASE 10
Ross Martin & Associates

INTRODUCTION

T. Rendy is an MBA student who has completed two semesters at a well-known business school located in a large eastern city. Rendy is one of a group of summer interns at Ross Martin & Associates, an advertising agency formed in 1976. For the past month Rendy has been observing various projects and providing assistance to some of the account executives. Rendy likes this small dynamic company and hopes to work full time for them next year. Rendy is concerned, however, over the fact that the company has been doing badly recently and that a number of accounts have been taken elsewhere. The problem seems to lie with the creative people and their squabbles with the account executives.

This week, National Brand has approached Ross, Martin & Associates to handle a new account on a trial basis. The account is for a new product that National Brand is about to launch. The account executive in charge of the project is Glenn Pladde. Acting on the advice of the vice-president for accounts, Pladde has convened all the summer interns and is giving them a chance to exercise their creativity.

NATIONAL BRAND'S PRODUCT

The product about to be launched is a refined plastic-based spray for small houseplants and flowers of all kinds. It is transparent and thinly coats the plant or flower. The spray bonds to the plant to form an almost invisible seal so that no physical deterioration can take place. A preserved plant is thus formed that is as durable as a plastic plant but far superior to plastic plants because of the fine detail and natural color. Indeed, the light sheen that the spray gives the stems and leaves of plants makes sprayed plants appear healthier than their natural counterparts.

The product is packaged as an aerosol spray, although it is not fluorocarbon based. The spray is designed to be used at a distance of six inches from the plant and can be held at an angle.

It is expected that an 8 ounce can of the product will sell at a retail price of $4.99. This compares very favorably with the price of plastic flowers, which ranges from 89¢ a flower to $10 for an expensive and finely crafted flower. The price of a plant is naturally substantially higher than that for a single bloom.

The main retail outlet for the product is expected to be "home centers," stores where fertilizer, lawn-maintenance tools, and the like are sold. As well as being sold in these stores, the product will be sold in flower and plant stores, hardware stores, and various supermarket chains.

Market research indicates that this product will compete with the artificial flower market, which consists of homemakers as well as commercial establishments, including offices and restaurants.

National Brand envisions an advertising mix including perhaps short radio and television spots, as well as magazines and on-site promotion displays.

The Task

The summer interns are to come up with a name for the new product as well as a short slogan that includes the name. The issue here is not to come up with new uses or markets for the product. National Brand has their own employees for this. They expect, however, that a good name and a catchy slogan for an unusual product such as this will figure importantly in its success or failure.

Words of Wisdom, Inc. (A)

INTRODUCTION

Words of Wisdom, Inc. is a simulation exercise designed to model some aspects of organizational functioning, structure, and design. It provides an opportunity to experiment with organizational design variables and to see the impact they have on behavior. The case and simulation attempt to represent some valid real-life organizational design issues. At the same time some obviously unrealistic assumptions and constraints are provided in order to simulate certain real-life phenomena.

COMPANY BACKGROUND AND STRUCTURE

Words of Wisdom, Inc. designs, creates, manufactures, and markets a line of distinctive custom-made, one-of-a-kind decorative wall plaques engraved with "wise sayings." These plaques have sold very well in the recent past, and management anticipates continued growth in sales over the next few years. The plaques are sold through a direct mail operation. The company advertises in Sunday supplements and the like.

The company, located in Englewood, New Jersey, is divided into four major departments (see Exhibit 1). Marketing coordinates the advertising campaign, conducts market research, and handles the taking of orders. Product development is responsible for developing new wise sayings to be produced as plaques. Manufacturing works from the product development prototypes to produce and package finished plaques. Quality control inspects the final product for both creative content and production quality before final shipping. This case focuses on two of these departments, product development and manufacturing.

PRODUCT DEVELOPMENT DEPARTMENT

The product development department is responsible for creating new, distinctive, and meaningful wise sayings. Sayings are constructed from creative raw material, which the company purchases in the form of index cards with words on them. Each card has five words on it, from which wise sayings can be constructed. Several constraints exists on the use of these cards:

1. Each product developer can work with only one card at a time. Once a product developer is finished with a card he or she must discard it before going on to use a new card.

Exhibit 1. Organization of Words of Wisdom, Inc.

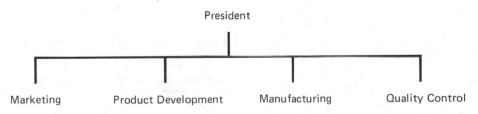

2. Product developers may, however, pool cards (up to a maximum of three cards) by working together and developing sayings from the larger set of words on the pooled cards. Once a set of cards has been pooled, no new cards may be purchased by any of the product developers until the entire pooled set has been discarded.
3. Cards are purchased by the company at a cost of $2.00 per card.

The work by the market research group indicates that while demand is strong for all plaques of three words or more, demand is much greater for longer plaques. Current estimates indicate that within any production period (five minutes in the simulation) the market can absorb the following number of plaques:

Number of words in the plaque	Maximum number of each length plaque to be sold
3 words	4 plaques
4 words	5 plaques
5 words	7 plaques
6 words	As many as can be produced

Exhibit 2.   Production Specifications

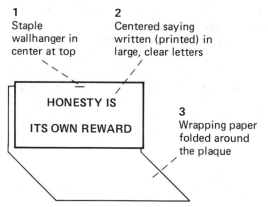

1
Staple wallhanger in center at top

2
Centered saying written (printed) in large, clear letters

3
Wrapping paper folded around the plaque

Wise sayings developed are to be written on the prototype forms (small white pads) and dropped into the manufacturing "in" box.

MANUFACTURING

The plaque (see Exhibit 2) is manufactured from plans provided on the prototype sheets developed by product development. The plaque is packaged by wrapping it in yellow shipping paper to prevent damage and then inserting it in a shipping envelope for mailing. Envelopes are sealed (using gummed flap, metal clasp, and scotch tape) and addressed for mailing directly to customers. Manufacturing works alphabetically down a mailing list provided by marketing. Each plaque should have the saying "engraved" neatly and clearly in the appropriate size and centered on the large index cards, which serves as the plaque. A wall hanger (staple) should be attached in the appropriate place.

Quality control examines products for both creative work (appropriate product mix, sayings that make sense, and so on) as well as proper

4
Plaque then put in envelope

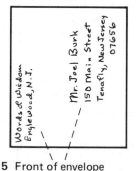

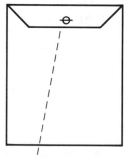

5 Front of envelope
Both name and address and return address printed clearly in appropriate places

6 Back of envelope
Envelope sealed by
(a) gummed flap,
(b) metal clasp, and
(c) scotch tape

production and packaging. Those finished plaques passed by quality control at the end of a production period will be sold for $2.00/each. Work in process inventory (that is, sayings created but not yet produced) will be valued at 25¢ per saying. Plaques completed and in an envelope but not completely sealed, taped, and addressed will be valued at $1.00.

Words of Wisdom, Inc. (B)

INTRODUCTION

Words of Wisdom, Inc. has enjoyed several years of growth in sales and earnings. Marketing indicates that there is growing interest in the product on the West Coast. Initial investigations, however, indicate a number of major problems including shipping costs, mailing delays, and local taste differences. (West Coast customers seem to want less formal, more frivolous, and less "work-oriented" plaques than those in the East. They also seem to prefer the plastic simulated redwood models as opposed to the hand-polished, natural wood oak and maple models sold in the East.)

As a result of these considerations, top management has decided to open a new product development and manufacturing facility in La Jolla, California. Marketing will continue to be coordinated from Englewood and quality control will be contracted out to a consulting firm. Thus, the West Coast operation will be a wholly autonomous subsidiary with two functions, product development and manufacturing.

THE FIRST YEAR

You have been recruited to be the vice-president for West Coast operations. You will have complete responsibility for the operations of this unit. You will receive a modest salary and a relatively large bonus based on the profitability of the operation on a quarterly basis. If you do well, you are in line for an equity share in the company.

A relatively large building, all on one floor, has been leased. Its interior design is up to you. Contracts have been signed for raw materials, equipment, machinery, and so forth, to be used by you as they are needed.

For the first year, you have been given a budget for wages and salaries of $850,000.

LABOR MARKET INFORMATION

Wage and salary surveys in the La Jolla area indicate the following midpoints of salary ranges for the type of personnel you will be hiring:

- Product developers—$18,000/yr

- Product development managers—$24,000; $28,000; or $30,000/yr, depending upon level
- Production workers—$8,000/yr
- Manufacturing managers — $12,000; $16,000; or $30,000/yr, depending upon level

Make reasonable estimates for salaries of other personnel.

CASE 13
Steinberg & Ross

Tom Boyd's footsteps rang loudly off the raw cement floor and echoed against the still unfinished walls of the office tower. He was inspecting the new office facility for Steinberg & Ross, an accounting firm. Steinberg & Ross was also new, having been created only recently by the merger of two established firms. As administrative partner, Tom oversaw all phases of the move to the new quarters. In conjunction with the move, all existing office practices and procedures were being evaluated, revised, or replaced. One area that had long been a source of friction and difficulty for both of the predecessor firms was the organization of the administrative staff and its relationship to the professional staff. Tom's regular responsibilities would include the management of this administrative staff once the move was completed. He was determined to prevent the troubles that had beset this area in the past and to organize

the administrative staff in a manner that would best serve the needs of the firm. Tom's concerns were shared by the other partners in the firm. As he gazed around the vast, empty space before him, Tom thought again of the clean-slate mandate he had requested and received at the last partners' meeting: he was to use any combination of functions, employees, and organizational arrangements he thought necessary, as long as it worked and he stayed within budget.

COMPANY BACKGROUND

Steinberg & Ross was created in the fall of 1978 by the merger of two established, mid-size accounting firms, Steinberg, Newman & Company and Ross, Easley & Grey. At the time, it also became affiliated with a large, national accounting firm, although not one of the "big eight." This affiliation provided Steinberg & Ross with a special ancillary services, a Washington, D.C. tax office, a New York City office that monitored the activities of the Securities and Exchange Commission, and a national management consulting practice, specializing in health care and electronic data processing (EDP) consulting. The merged firm represented the tenth largest firm in its market (and the largest local firm) and was positioned to offer its clients the full range of accounting and related services associated with a "big eight" firm, while still providing a local character, personalized service, and reasonable fees. The partners believed that this strategy would enable the firm to grow rapidly, primarily by attracting smaller clients from local firms with the promise of more professional service.

ORGANIZATION

The firm was formally organized as a partnership, an arrangement typical of accounting, consulting, legal, and other service firms. Exhibit 1 presents an organizational chart. The firm was run by the twenty-six partners, who also owned the business. They met at least monthly to set policy, discuss business developments, and monitor profits and profit-sharing. Sterling Grey, the partner-in-charge, played a coordinator's role and occasionally was called upon to represent the firm as a legal signatory or spokesman. He did not, however, have any direct, formal authority over the other partners. Indeed, the partners individually experienced very little control over their daily activities. Except for the monthly meetings and the fairly common practice of informally consulting with each other over practice development (attracting new business) or a particularly thorny accounting problem, the partners operated autonomously, building and maintaining their practices as they saw fit.

The differences in their management style were noteworthy. One partner, for example, was secretly referred to as "five-o'clock Phil" for his irritating habit of leaving everything until the last minute. By contrast, Don Landsdowne, the new-

est partner, who had joined the firm after reaching the level of manager in a "big eight" firm, was a model of organization and planning whose work always seemed on schedule and under control. The widespread differences in management style was exacerbated by Steinberg & Ross's history; different partners had developed different styles in the two predecessor firms. Although Tom Boyd was not pleased with this state of affairs, he seriously doubted that any improvement was likely in the near future. Eventually, he thought, the old or premerger partners would retire, to be replaced by new partners, trained in a consistent Steinberg & Ross management style. Until then, however, the partners' idiosyncracies were a fact of life with which he and the administrative staff would have to cope.

Beneath the partners was arrayed the *professional staff*. These 148 individuals were the accountants who produced the firm's services. They were grouped according to an explicit hierarchy reflecting seniority, authority, and pay. They ranged in age and responsibility from managers, in their late forties, who were candidates for partnership (hence ownership of the business), to staff accountants in their early twenties, who had yet to even complete the CPA licensing exam.

Their work environment was characterized by a pressured, grueling pace—especially during "the season," the January to April 15 period of year-end audits and tax return preparation when a six- or seven-day workweek was the norm. In addition, their career development was characterized by an "up or out" philosophy. The accountants were subject to a performance evaluation after each assignment. These evaluations were shared with the individuals involved and then maintained in personnel files by Tom Boyd. Shortly after the close of the season, the partners would meet to review these performance records and decide promotions and terminations, a process reputed to be highly subjective. Attrition was high; out of an entering "class" of a dozen staff accountants, only one would be likely to reach the level of manager. The combination of these factors tended to produce an atmosphere of stress and urgency in the office.

Before the merger, the *administrative staff* in both predecessor firms had been organized in a rather adhoc, patchwork manner. Some aspects of the organization arrangements followed conventional office practices, such as the assignment of one executive secretary to each partner. Other aspects, particularly in the area of annual report production, had developed erratically, reflecting the unsystematic adoption of new technologies in reproduction or word processing. Indeed, most of the problems between the administrative and professional staffs centered in the area of report production.

All administrative staff were hourly wage earners. Normally, they worked a 35 hour week. During the season, however, the normal week became $37\frac{1}{2}$ hours, with overtime pay (time and a half) paid after forty hours. Administrative staff were evaluated once a year by the immediate supervisor, or by Mildred Teicher, the office manager, when there was no direct supervisor. Evaluation was on the basis of overall performance. Bonuses and salary increases also reflected each employee's overall performance. These bonuses and salary increases were awarded by dividing up a fixed pool of dollars among the administrative staff, a task which was Tom Boyd's responsibility. The pool was determined each year by the partners, who generally set aside a fixed percentage of the firm's total profit. The exact profit figure was known only to the partners themselves, but in recent years the pool Tom was given to allocate had averaged about $60,000.00 (to be divided among approximately seventy administrative staff), an amount that Tom estimated to be about 2.5 percent of profits.

Profits were determined as follows: For each engagement, the client was charged a fee, based solely on the number of hours worked by each level of accountant (a staff accountant billed at about $40/hr, a partner might bill at $150/hr) plus out-of-pocket expenses such as travel or report production costs. When the fee was received, 10 percent was immediately deducted and paid to the partner in charge of the engagement as a new or continuing finder's fee. The remainder was pooled with like sums from other engagements, from which regular business expenses such as salaries, wages, and rent, were paid. Any remaining amount was profit. Some of this was retained as working capital, some distributed to the administrative staff bonus pool, and the rest was allocated among the partners on the basis of their proportional share of the business—that is, the dollar value of their individual clients as a percentage of the firm's total fees. It was thus in the individual partner's financial interest to maximize his or her own practice, developing it and serving it, even at the expense of a fellow partner's client service.

NATURE OF THE WORK— PROFESSIONAL STAFF

The professional accounting services offered by Steinberg & Ross fell roughly into two categories: audit work and tax work. The former constituted the bulk of the work and involved the auditing of a client's financial records and the certification of the financial statements in the client's annual report. Typically, the work was carried out in teams composed of a partner (who maintained client contact, reviewed final reports, and signed off on the report with a legally binding signature of the firm); a manager (who had overall responsibility for the scheduling of the audit work, especially the field work at the client's, the writing of the report in the office, and so on; the supervisor (who oversaw the on-site work on a daily basis and reviewed/authored the report in the office); and several senior and staff accountants (who verified records in the field, completed and checked calculations and figures, and composed initial report drafts). These teams varied in size and composition according to the size and needs of the client. Staff accountants were usually assigned sequentially, to one assignment (or engagement, in the accounting parlance) at a time. All others, however, commonly juggled multiple assignments. There was a formal system, administered by the scheduling department, for assigning available accountants to a team. (See Exhibit 1.) However most managers preferred to build a team by recruiting individuals with whom they had worked in the past and/or who offered a special expertise relevant to the engagement.

Despite an elaborate and rigorous planning system, engagements frequently fell behind schedule. In addition, last-minute negotiations with clients often resulted in changes in the figures or footnotes on the annual report. Thus ac-

Exhibit 1.   Organization Chart of Steinberg & Ross

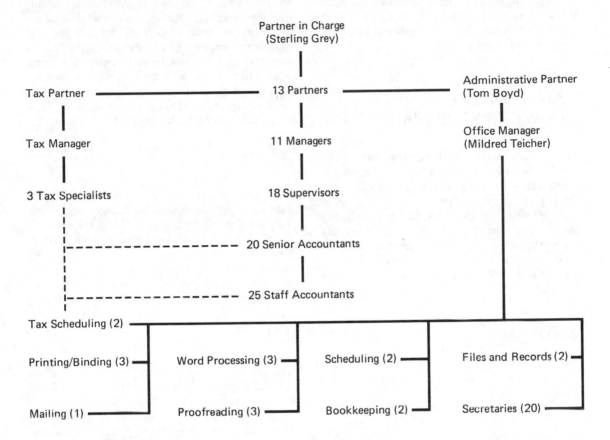

countants often found themselves pulled off one job to meet some crisis on another. Furthermore, partners, indeed all the accountants, were often absent from the office. Their absences were necessitated by their personal involvement in maintaining client contact or developing new business. As a result, the manager, and often the supervisor as well, needed to be kept fully informed of the status of an audit in order to respond to client questions and complaints and to effect necessary rescheduling or personnel redeployment. Although much of the field work could normally be done in the fall, the final audit could not conclude, and the audit report could not be written, until the client had actually closed the books for the year. Although frequent efforts had been made to convince clients to change their fiscal

year, most preferred to end it on the traditional December 31, a situation that exacerbated the pressures of the season in conjunction with tax return work.

Tax work, unlike audit work, tended to be more individualized. While corporate tax returns presented complex problems and were a lucrative practice area, individual tax returns were not. Many of the larger accounting firms had phased out this latter practice area, except for those returns prepared as a professional courtesy for officers of important corporate clients. Steinberg & Ross, however, still maintained a practice in this area, viewing it as a part of their personalized service much valued by many of their clients. Individual tax returns were not that complex or difficult to prepare; they were simply numerous and required a corresponding time commitment, usually from staff or senior accountants, before being passed to the firm's tax specialists. The demands of this work served chiefly to add to the pressure and office tensions.

NATURE OF THE WORK— ADMINISTRATIVE STAFF

The administrative staff support performed a number of functions necessary for the effective operation of the office. This support staff included secretaries (individual for the partners, shared for the managers), bookkeepers, file clerks (who kept track of the myriad records required for accounting work), and those employees involved in the production of audit reports. Tom had broken down the key functions of this latter group as follows.

Word Processing

Transfers the accountant's handwritten pencil copy into printed format suitable for mass reproduction.

Proofreading

In accounting work, accuracy was paramount. In-process reports needed to be checked for both computational and grammatical errors.

Report Review

This was a critical function, performed by Sidney Weiss. Although a manager-level accountant, Sidney had long ago realized that he would never make partner and had accepted this post as a kind of sinecure rather than face the likely termination. His task was to review and edit each report to ensure that it was in compliance with the latest edicts and standards set by the several regulatory groups that affected the accounting profession. Failure to conduct such reviews could leave the firm and the relevant partner dangerously liable to legal action. Sidney had developed a formidable expertise in this area; there had been no instances of successful legal actions brought against the firm or its partners since he had taken over this area. He was the one person in the firm who could overrule a partner on when to release a report. A thin and frail-looking chain-smoker, he was as overworked as he was accurate. At present, there was no back-up person for this work.

Corrections

Both proofreading and report review routinely discovered errors. In view of Sidney's work load, Tom felt that all computational and grammatical errors should be corrected before the report review stage. However, Sidney often inserted long, precisely worded paragraphs into the reports. Tom was unsure whether these inserts should be checked by proofreading or by Sidney himself.

Partner Sign-off

The partner in charge of each engagement was the only person who could legally sign the firm's name on the report. Ostensibly, partners thoroughly reviewed each report before signing, but except for Don Landsdowne, no partner had noticed a mistake within memory. The major difficulty here, Tom thought, was that partners were frequently out of the office. A report could sit unsigned for days while its delivery date drew closer and closer.

Printing

Steinberg & Ross had recently purchased a high speed offset press and photographic plate-maker. Unfortunately, the press required extensive set-up time, and the high speed could only be utilized through long production runs. Bob Berens, the current pressman, also looked after the ordering of paper stocks. The print shop also housed a high-speed [photocopying] machine, run by a technician, and a low-speed machine for "casual" operators.

Binding

Ideally, binding could take place twelve or more hours after a report was printed, to allow for drying of the ink. In practice, reports were often bound "hot off the press," a practice that inevitably lead to blurred or smeared reports and on occasion to complaints from clients, complaints that the partners never hesitated to pass on to Tom.

Mailing

When time permitted or distance demanded, reports were mailed to clients. Often partners would hand deliver the reports to the client, or express and courier services would be used.

The administrative staff employee complement for each of these key functions is shown in Exhibit 1. Tom felt that the current staffing levels were sufficient to handle the current and anticipated work load. He had reviewed the individual personnel and concluded that they were sufficiently hard-working and competent (several even had advanced degrees); they were capable of doing a number of different jobs and were also nonunion and thus not contractually restricted to one function. There were, however, some restrictions. In the short run, there was limited flexibility of staff across functions. Word processing required extensive training, effectively excluding the use of other administrative staff in this area. Similarly, printing required specialized skills and knowledge to run the press, although not to do the binding (a technology which could be taught in half a day). Proofreading's functions were equally divided between correcting for "grammar" —a catchword for a number of sophisticated editing skills—and correcting for calculations—a far more routine rechecking of the accountants' math. Up until now, there had been no way to determine the capacity of the whole staff working together because their income was largely dependent on overtime pay earned during the season, a situation which discouraged cooperation among them. Tom knew that, if he should decide additional staff were needed, he could spend approximately $100,000, if he could justify it. It was in the partners' (and thus his own) interest, however, to spend less, or none. The administrative staff employees fell into four rough "salary and fringe" categories, as follows:

Level	Position Type	Cost
I	Professional (for instance, Sidney in report review)	$60,000
II	Managerial (for instance, M. Teicher)	$20,000
III	Clerical (skilled/trained)	$12,000
IV	Clerical (unskilled)	$ 8,000

Nevertheless, Tom felt that he probably possessed sufficient employee strength in each function and that his major task was to organize them into an effective arrangement.

In order to facilitate this arrangement, Tom had devised a tentative work-flow chart (see Exhibits 2 and 3) that laid out the tasks to be performed in the report production process. He was not fully satisfied with his attempt; it seemed to raise more questions than it answered:

- Although he felt he had captured all of the required tasks, Tom was interested in additional, "optional" tasks. In particular, he wondered how the reports might best be transferred from one task to the next (the black arrows). Currently, it was done by the individual who had performed the preceding task, but was that the best way?

- Tom was also far from confident that his sequence of the tasks was optimal. Perhaps the task order could be more effectively arranged.

- Although the work-flow chart made the system look very rational and planned, Tom knew that the chart misrepresented the daily chaos. He knew that the generation of a client review copy of the report and the partner's ensuing discussions with the client initiated a continuing demand on the system (the "hollow" arrow) for corrections, revisions, schedule changes, and the like. How could the system be organized to respond effectively to this demand?

Exhibit 2. Tentative Work Flow

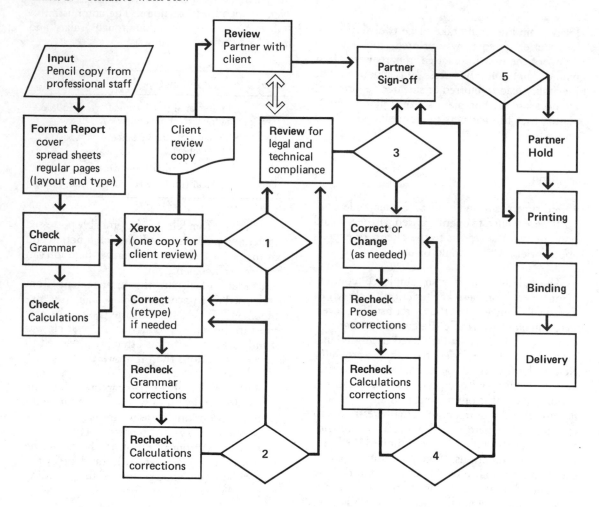

Exhibit 3.

Decision Points in Tentative Work Flow

1. If report is OK, send to REVIEW. If corrections are needed, send on to CORRECT.
2. If report is OK, send to REVIEW. If corrections still needed, send back to CORRECT.
3. If report passes REVIEW, send on to PARTNER for signature. If modifications/changes have been made, send on to CORRECT or CHANGE.
4. If review modifications have been correctly made, send on to PARTNER for signature. Otherwise, send back to CORRECT or CHANGE.
5. Sometimes, partners will hold a report until a client is ready to release it. (Sometimes, partners hold reports accidentally, for instance, five-o'clock Phil.) The choice here is to hold or send on to printing.

- There were five major decision points in the process. Were these opportunities for quality control activities and for recording report progress, or were they merely unnecessary roadblocks?
- Was there really only one system? Could there actually be a number of smaller, simpler, parallel systems?

CURRENT PROBLEMS

In considering his assignment, Tom had spoken at length with a number of the employees. Bob Berens, the pressman, seemed particularly irritated:

I guess I just don't know what they want. All the reports I get in here all say the same thing—date due: ASAP [as soon as possible]. They just don't understand how the press works. I run three stock sizes: covers, spread sheets, and regular pages. It takes me about twenty minutes to change from one format to another. If I can run all covers, then all spread sheets, then all regular pages I can get twelve reports out every day; but if I have to do each report separately—covers, spreads, regulars, covers, spreads, regulars—I'll be lucky to get four out. Even then, sometimes I can't tell which report to run first. I've had scenes where I had two partners right down in the shop, arguing with me and each other over which of their reports to run first. Two guys each making over a hundred grand a year, partners, ready to stick each other in the back over a lousy half an hour. They agree on one thing, though. If I tell 'em I'll run both reports at the same time—you know, take a little longer on both instead of one on time and one real late—they both say, "No, me first!"

Don Landsdowne saw things a little differently:

The situation here is absurd. All the way through an engagement, I bust my hump, and everybody else's for that matter, to make sure things are on time. Then the thing goes into report production, and it disappears! If I've got a worried client on the phone, can I put him on hold, make a quick call and find out when his report will be ready? No way! There's no use in even telling him I'll call him back with the an-

swer. When I go looking for it no one can tell me. No one knows where the report is. I have to chase it down step by step. Even when I find where it is, each person there can only tell me when they'll be through with it, not when it will be completely done. The way it stands now, my best bet is to tell the client a date I think we can live with and then go kick Sidney's, Bob's, and everybody else's butt to get the thing done by that date. It's a waste of my time, but so far it's the only way. Sometimes I even think they do five-o'clock Phil's stuff faster, just to get rid of him and his constant hassles.

Bernice Segal, who ran a word processing machine spoke of a different problem:

A big problem for word processing is how we divide up the work. People bring us reports all the time and say, "Here, do this." Lately, Mildred [Teicher] has tried to regulate what we get and divide it equally among us. But she's busy being the office manager, so it's kind of hit or miss. You can't really divide up a report to work on because you don't know the advance page numbers until the beginning pages have been typed. So it's one report for you, one report for me, except that some reports are thirty pages long and some are eight. The overtime is nice to get, but not when they're yelling at you all day for the report.

Carolyn Miller, the youngest and only female manager, had her own view of the situation:

When a partner is out of the office, it's up to me to make sure the report gets out. Half the time, I hear the same thing, "Sidney's got it and won't release it." It's really frustrating; there's nothing you can do but wait for the shit to hit the fan. Sidney wants to clear things with the partner, but the partner's not here, and Sidney won't clear it with me. The other managers have the same trouble. Once, on a report we were just dying for, I stole the thing out of Sidney's office during his lunch hour and had Bob start running it even though it hadn't been cleared. Later, when Sidney was finished with it, we did have to rerun a few pages, but overall we'd saved a bundle of time. Bob was real nice about it, but it was definitely a one-time thing. He has enough problems with clients making last-minute changes, never mind us.

As Tom paced about the new office, he reviewed the demands his new organization would have to meet:

Quality	Demand
Speed	Clients
Accuracy	Regulatory Agencies
Responsiveness	
Flexibility	Partners' styles
"Reportability"	Need to know report progress
Differentation	Workers' skills, identity, and rewards
Balanced work flow	Efficiency, employee morale

Tom laughed silently. All it has to be is all things to all people, he thought. He glanced around the office once more. Completion was expected in three weeks.

CASE 14
State Employment Agency

Frank Duncan, the commissioner of the State Employment Agency in a state along the Eastern Seaboard, was reviewing the agency's system for evaluating the results of its efforts. He gave the casewriter some background on state employment agencies in general and on the changes made in the review system in his agency over the past year.

State employment agencies were set up during the Depression years to administer unemployment benefits to workers unfortunate enough to lose their jobs. The agencies are largely federally funded but state-administered, and a large proportion of their federal funding is tied to the state unemployment level. Since their foundings and in particular in the Great Society years of Lyndon

Johnson, the role of these agencies expanded to cover helping people assess their own training needs and helping them to find jobs. The typical agency has several district offices within the state and is staffed by employment counselors. These counselors hold a series of interviews with clients in an attempt to assess their skills and the jobs for which they would be best suited. Suitable candidates are referred to local employers with vacancies. Those clients who remain unemployed because they are not offered jobs continue to receive unemployment benefits.

In general, the job of an employment counselor is a routine one, involving standardized interview formats and detailed bureaucratic routines for referrals and placements. The duties of counselors are as follows: They receive requests for workers over the phone. The order forms on which job openings are described are filed in a common pool in each office. Most of the officials' time is spent interviewing applicants for jobs. After ascertaining the client's qualifications, the interviewer searches the office files for suitable vacancies. If an acceptable job is found, he or she refers the client to it and later phones the employer to learn whether the client has been hired. The bulk of an employment counselor's time, aside from interviewing, is spent filling out the forms necessary for completion of each stage of the successful processing of a client.

A district office of the State Employment Agency was located in each of the sixteen counties of the state (see Exhibit 1). These offices varied greatly in terms of the population and degree of industrialization of the area in which they were located and hence in terms of the number of unemployed persons and the number of available jobs. However, the overall mission of the agency was clear: to serve workers seeking employment and employers seeking workers throughout the state. Operations within each of the district offices were also performed in a similar fashion. Most of the counselors employed by the agency viewed themselves as professionals, but this orientation was strongest in the Walden County office. While employees in the other districts had been assigned, and had received their training, at different times, the majority of those in Walden County received their training together after the Vietnam War at a time when intensive counseling had been stressed, since many returning veterans needed occupational advice. In this situation, the group developed a common professional code, which discouraged speedy placement as constituting defective employment service. Quality, rather than quantity, was stressed in this office. In addition, counselors in this office were not particularly concerned with performance because almost all of them were veterans, whose employment could not be terminated except for cause. At the same time, while a system of merit pay existed, it offered little motivation as bonuses were small in comparison to base pay, which depended solely on number of years in service. Overall, external motivation was small—

Exhibit 1. State Employment Agency: Organizational Chart*

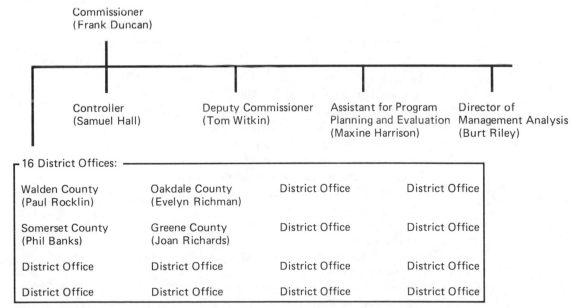

*Names of persons mentioned in the case are included.

salary increases were automatic and career paths were limited. There was nowhere to go from counselor as the opportunities for promotion were relatively scarce.

A year previously, on being appointed, Frank Duncan had reviewed the management control practices in the agency and had noted that the number of interviews held per month was the only operation that was statistically counted for each district office. Duncan recognized the obvious limitations of such an evaluation method. An individual district office could look good relative to other district offices if employment counselors concentrated on maximizing the number of interviews they conducted. There was no guarantee that this approach to performance of the agency's mission would result in effective matching of jobs and clients. Consequently, Duncan resolved to give high priority to the development of an alternative management control system.

Duncan stated:

I requested Burt Riley, director of management analysis, and Maxine Harrison, assistant to the commissioner for program planning and evaluation, to develop a system for measuring overall performance of each district office. It was my general plan that Riley and Harrison would draw up a list of objectives that they thought every district office should meet if performance is to be considered satisfactory. After checking these with me for approval, they would go out to the districts and get the approval of the district managers around the state. My thought here was that if the district managers would agree in advance to a set of objective criteria there would be no personal ugliness attached when, at the end of the year, one of the standards is not met. It would simply be a matter of saying, "Well, we agreed at the beginning that the annual ratio of placements to interviews should be 60 percent. If it turns out to be 50 percent, that's that." It is an objective fact to be dealt with, not a personal blame put on the districts by my staff.

After two months of project work, including discussions with several district office directors, Riley and Harrison recommended a system of fifteen controls (Exhibit 2) for all district offices. The controls were about equally divided between budgetary items relating to the outputs of the agency. As Burt Riley explained,

The advantage of such a system of controls is that the top management of the agency can very quickly look across one page of the computer output to detect there is trouble in a district. On that output, the sixteen districts are listed across

Exhibit 2.

Areas of Measurement
1. The number of interviews held
2. The number of clients referred to a job
3. The number of placements made (referred client was hired)
4. The proportion of interviews resulting in referrals
5. The proportion of referrals resulting in placements
6. The proportion of interviews resulting in placements
7. The number of notifications sent to the insurance office
8. The number of application forms made out
9. Employment interview expense
10. Unemployment claim expense
11. Overhead expense
12. Supervisory and management overhead expense
13. New program expense
14. Hours of unallocated personnel time
15. Total office expenditures

the top. Down the left is the quantitative level expected for that item. Under each district's column is listed the actual performance of that district. Performances rated satisfactory or above are listed in the ordinary way, and those below satisfactory are starred. Scanning down a column, one can get a complete and quick picture of what went wrong in that district. Or, if one scans across columns, he can see instantly which district is performing below satisfactory and which above. This kind of document enables us to manage by exception. We do not have to have our minds filled with thousands of details and figures. The factors for success are already there. The figures are all there. The exceptions are highlighted. We can evaluate the whole agency in a few hours and can have letters of inquiry going out within a day, asking why something went wrong. This is a real help to us and to the district offices.

During the process of setting standards, Maxine Harrison proposed one standard that dealt with the total district office expenditures (item 15 in Exhibit 2). Burt Riley suggested that this one expense standard was insufficient and added to various expense breakdowns shown as items 9 and 14 in Exhibit 2. Harrison objected to this level of detail, and so the two staff managers presented the issue to Duncan. Riley explained, "If we only get a lump sum expenditure figure, it will be practically useless to top management. All we could say is 'Your expenditures are exceeding budget.' We ought to include at least the additional six breakdowns."

After Harrison and Riley finished debating the issue, Duncan responded, "Well, it seems that you two cannot agree on this matter. My own inclination is that we in headquarters must be informed. I believe we should include these additional items." Maxine Harrison's comment on the discussion was, "That settled that."

Duncan had one additional suggestion to make at this meeting.

It appears that most of the standards you've set are technically correct. That is, they represent reasonable expectations regarding what the average district office should achieve. But there is another aspect of standards you have overlooked. I'm referring to the need to capture the attention and imagination of people who must carry out these standards. No person will exceed an easy goal. Have you set these standards in relation to an individual's extra effort—the kind one has to stretch to achieve?

Riley and Harrison agreed that they had set the standards as if personnel were working at a normal pace. "Just what 'normal' is," Riley said, "is not too clear. But I think it means a person working with average energy at a job the person hopes to accomplish. If you set individual standards too high, then competition among counselors will be encouraged. We don't want counselors hiding job openings from one another."

Duncan said that eventually he got Riley and Harrison to agree to raising the achievement levels on a number of items.

I told them that achievement didn't occur without challenge. I offered to take some time out to review all of the fifteen standards working out challenging levels item by item. We ended, for example, by raising the level of performance on the ratio of referrals to interviews from 75 percent to 80 percent. The acceptable unemployment claim expense figure was decreased by 5 percent. Similar changes were made on most standards.

Later, at a meeting of all district office directors, I explained that forces beyond our control are continuously setting demanding standards for the agency—the state of the overall economy, new unemployment legislation at the federal and state levels, geographical differences in employment demand, the changing mix of occupational skills, and other such factors make it essential that we properly control agency activities. There was a certain amount of reaction against both the standards we put into the list and the level we specified for each standard. However, in the end I told them that they could change the levels of the standards if they really wanted to. At that point, they all seemed to see both the necessity for checkpoints by headquarters and for challenging performance levels.

Mr. Duncan described the first year of operation under the new control system.

We've been operating under the new management control system for one year. Overall, I'm quite pleased with the system. I'm confident that it's been a major factor in our overall improvement over the previous fiscal year when the comparable figure was 55 percent. Of course, no system is perfect. I will give you some examples of the issues we're concerned about. We all are interested in learning from this first year of experience and implementing any necessary revisions.

At the end of the first year (we review the performance of each district office on an annual basis only), Samuel Hall, the agency controller, sent out a routine inquiry to Paul Rocklin, director of the district office in Walden County. Under the procedures, the whole results tabulation is sent in multiple copies to Hall, Riley, Harrison, myself, and Tom Witkin, my deputy commissioner. Each of us concentrates on particular items. Hall pays special attention to budgetary controls. As he scanned the control report, he noted that unemployment claim expense for the Walden County District Office was 6 percent above the standard. It was one of the few starred figures in the row for unemployment claim expense. Most districts were in the black. So Hall sent out the letter to Rocklin listing this exception. Riley also sent Rocklin a letter for an exception in the number of clients referred to jobs.

Rocklin exploded when he received the letters of inquiry. He called me on the telephone and said that the system was grossly unfair. Boy, was he steamed. Since his total district office expenditures were under the targeted figure, he wanted to know why my staff people were pestering him about details. He also said, "In the expense area, the real need is to have low total expenditures. I performed according to the spirit of that need by compensating for some unexpected turnover in the unemployment claims section. We were short-handed most of the year and had to spend some time training the new personnel we did hire. My supervisors and I worked overtime to help. In addition, we made concerted efforts to become more efficient in all other sections of the office."

I assured Rocklin that we appreciated his extra efforts and ingenuity in compensating for the turnover problem. That didn't seem to do a lot of good. He said that as the headquarters people like Riley and Hall scan the reports they form impressions without knowing the facts. That under the guise of "management by exception" or "management by objective" they look for the starred figures in a report, send out their letters of inquiry, and get a negative picture of his operating abilities. Of course, I assured him that the letter was one of inquiry.

Rocklin suggested that the way to correct this situation is simply to remove the detailed expenditure standards [items 9–14] and to leave only the total district office expenditure standard [item 15]. Actually, I will have to give this some more thought. That would defeat the original arguments we settled when we included them. This is one alternative for overcoming this, but I'm hoping I can achieve both Rocklin's and Riley's objectives.

Another problem is actually in Rocklin's favor. On that total expenditure measure, his district was one of only four districts that achieved the standard. All the others were in the red. We circulated the whole evaluation report to all district managers, and I got seven suggestions from different districts that this target was too demanding. I must admit that I don't like to see a horizontal row of figures all starred. It looks as if something is wrong with the agency. And the seven district managers complained that it looks as if there's something wrong with them. On the other hand, my "stretch" theory worked with Rocklin. His back was against the wall, and he devoted a lot of creativity and energy to obtaining efficiencies in other areas, so that he would make a good showing on his total cost. Maybe the other district managers ought to do that.

While Rocklin is certainly the most vocal critic of our new control system, I learned of some other problems during a meeting last week with district directors in the southern part of the state. The purpose of the meeting was to discuss some regional unemployment problems specific to that area. After we completed the major business discussion, the conversation turned to the new management control system. Phil Banks, director of the Somerset County district, began the conversation.

"Frank, I'm afraid there are some consequences of implementing this system that we didn't completely anticipate. In particular, I'm referring to the relationship between the quantitative figures reported in the control system and the annual performance review for an individual interviewer. Several of my interviewers are completely alienated by the new system. One interviewer came to see me complaining about the rating she received from her supervisor. Before the new system had been introduced, the supervisor gave her a low rating because her production wasn't high enough.

After the new system was introduced, the interviewer was high on the various performance indices. However, her rating was low again. As a result of this, the interviewer and her coworkers believe that some supervisors will use statistics to confirm their subjective judgments. As they see it, 'Figures can't lie, but liars can figure.' "

Joan Richards, director of the Greene County office, spoke next: "I'm also disturbed about the new system. Apparently, some of my interviewers have resorted to some ingenious means for outgaming the system by maximizing their performance indices.

"For example, occasionally a client who has been temporarily laid off expects to return to the former job within the next few days. After confirming this with the employer, the interviewer makes out a job order and 'refers' the client to his own job. In this way the interviewer improves his or her number of referrals and placements (and the corresponding proportional indices) without having accomplished the objective that these indices were designed to measure, that is, without having found a job for a client."

The next manager to speak was Evelyn Richman of the Oakdale County office: "The worst thing about these records is that they create unhealthy competition between interviewers. The records lead to competition and outright falsification. I don't say they all do that, but it happens. . . . You can't expect anything else. If you make production so important, some people will feel that they have to increase their figures by any means. The only way you can stop it is by discontinuing the control reports."

I [Frank Duncan] interrupted at this point and indicated my dismay at their reports. I indicated that it was essential to determine if these negative practices were widespread in the agency.

More significantly, these comments along with Rocklin's complaints have convinced me that we should review the control system to see if changes are needed.

CASE **15**
People's National Bank

John B. Green, vice-president for branch operations at People's National Bank (PNB) was concerned whether the current organizational structure for the branch system would be adequate to meet the demands of the near future. He had been giving some thought to modifying the organization of the branch system but was not clear about the direction those changes should take. A central issue, he felt, was how to coordinate the activities of twenty-two branch offices in a fast-changing and competitive environment.

BACKGROUND

PNB is a large consumer-oriented bank located in the capital city of a moderate-sized midwestern state. The bank was formed in the early part of the century through the merger of two other banks and is an old and established institution in the city. The bank remained relatively small until about 1960. At that time, the current management took over and started an expansion program. Throughout its history, the bank has been noted for a number of "firsts." It was one of the first banks in the country to affiliate with a major bank credit card system, had the first branch banking facilities in the state, installed the first drive-in banking windows, and was the first bank in the area to have twenty-four-hour automated banking machines in regular use. It also has experimented with other innovations including automated funds transfer systems, completely automated branches, and other new ideas in banking.

In recent years, the bank has attempted to create a specific image in the eyes of the public and create a niche for itself in the competitive environment. Although not the largest bank in the city in terms of assets, it has outperformed the others in earnings. Because it is not located in a major money center, the bank has chosen to be retail-oriented; 40–50 percent of the bank's income comes from retail rather than commercial loans. Because of this emphasis, the branch system is relatively important to the overall performance of the bank. Bank management thus invests much time, energy, and money in the maintenance of the branch system and the image of the bank presented to the public.

Another major development in recent years has been the formation of a bank holding company. State law prohibits the establishment of branch bank offices in more than one county of the state. This feature of the law encouraged the formation of a number of bank holding companies, which enable the operation of a group of banks over a multicounty area. In 1968, PNB formed the core of a newly organized bank holding company called the State Bank Group (SBG). In the following years, a number of other banks were acquired by SBG. By 1974, the group included close to twenty banks with total assets approaching $2 billion. Most of the banks, however, were somewhat smaller than PNB. Because of this, PNB, with assets of approximately $600 million, remained as the core of the SBG organization. The former chief executive of PNB now serves as chief executive of State Bank Group, and the PNB and SBG offices are in the same facility.

As development of industry, commerce, and housing in the capital city area has increased, competition among the banks in the metropolitan area has also become more intensive. PNB faces two other major commercial banks with headquarters and branch offices in the capital city area, as well as numerous smaller banks and savings and loan associations. Although in previous years each of the major banks tended to dominate certain areas (particularly in outlying suburban towns), competition has increased so that most sections of the city include at least one branch of each of the three major banks.

In early 1974 evidence of increased competition was seen in the sudden proliferation of "group accounts" in the capital city area. These accounts provided (for a low monthly fee) a variety of banking services. Typically, the account included such features as free checking accounts, reduced bank credit card rates, free traveler's checks, one statement for all accounts, overdraft coverage, and so on. For a variety of reasons, PNB was the third of the three major banks to offer this service, lagging behind the first by several months.

By late 1974, the economic crunch was being felt throughout the capital city area and was seen in PNB in the form of increasing delinquency rates on loans, decreasing loan volume, fewer new accounts, and more pessimistic forecasts of business growth.

THE BRANCH SYSTEM

At the heart of PNB's operations is the branch banking system. This system includes approximately 400 employees in twenty-two branch locations. The branches account for approximately a third of the total employees of the bank; the centralized computer center accounts for another third. The system is headed by the vice-president for branch operations, John B. Green, who serves as a member of the bank executive committee along with other senior level vice-presidents. (See Exhibit 1 for an organization chart.)

Exhibit 1. Organization of the Senior Staff

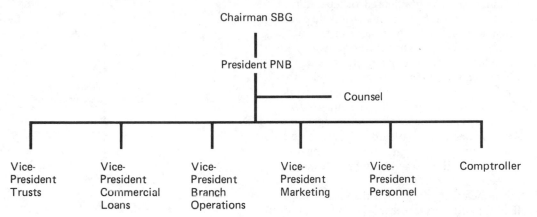

Each branch performs essentially the same functions. Branches are responsible for providing various banking services involved in the maintenance of customer accounts (checking, savings, certificates of deposit, and so on) as well as making loans of various types (commercial, installment, mortgage) to customers. There are two major groups of employees within a typical branch. The teller group is responsible for making and posting various transactions, while the "desk" group is responsible for providing information, opening new accounts, making loans, developing new business, and dealing with a range of customer problems. The desk group typically includes financial consultants, receptionists, loan interviewers, and other clerical personnel. There are three individuals with managerial responsibility in each branch. These three are the branch manager, the assistant branch manager (in most branches), and the teller supervisor.

The branch manager is responsible for all operations of the branch and is accountable for the profit performance of the branch. The teller supervisor has direct supervisory control over the operations of the teller line. The assistant manager may serve in different roles in different branches. In some branches, he or she may supervise the desk area in a role parallel to the teller-supervisor, while in others he or she may work in the operations area and direct the teller supervisor; the branch manager may have some mix of these two roles. A chart of the organizational structure of a typical branch is provided as Exhibit 2. This structure is descriptive of most of the branches, although size may vary from eleven to twenty-four employees.

The key person in the branch is the branch manager, who essentially runs his or her own small bank. While a large part of the branch's operations are standardized (including standardized forms, loan policies, interest rates and charges, general procedures for account and loan applications, salary rates, personnel practices, and so on), the branch manager does have a lot of leeway in determining how the branch will operate. Branch managers differ in the degree of responsibility they provide to subordinates; the

Exhibit 2. Structure of a Typical Branch

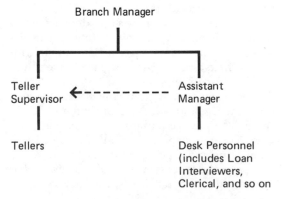

way the branch is structured; the hours worked by the staff; and the methods used for supervision, coordination, and information sharing. In addition, managers differ in their views of the manager's role. Some see themselves primarily as sellers of loans (the internal operations of the branch either run themselves or are under the responsibility of the assistant manager), while others see themselves primarily as managers and only secondarily as sellers of loans. Managers also differ on the degree of market development work they do; some go out aggressively seeking new customers, and others stay in the branch waiting for business to walk in the door.

At the heart of the branch manager's role is the lending authority the bank provides him or her. The manager is authorized to lend up to a certain amount of money (varying from manager to manager and depending on size of branch, track record, and so forth). Similarly, the branch manager can choose to delegate part or all of the lending authority to subordinates in his or her branch. Branch managers are paid a base salary plus a bonus, which is based on the branch's performance as a profit center. The branch profit figure, which is reported each month as part of a 17 page computer generated statement, includes a number of items. It is obtained by adding total loan income to an income credit figure based on the level of deposits maintained. From this figure, branch operating expenses (largely salary costs, but also including items such as sizeable discretionary expenses, advertising, and so on) are subtracted to yield a profit figure. Each year, profit figures are projected by the branch manager, meeting with John B. Green, and bonuses are based on the relationship between actual profit and budgeted profit.

The twenty-two branches are administered by John B. Green and his staff. Exhibit 3 provides a chart of the branch system. Green's staff includes three assistant vice-presidents. Fred Roberts has responsibility for control and is largely concerned with maintaining the reporting system on branch performance and analyzing trends in those data. George Jenkins has responsibility for branch operations and is basically concerned with monitoring and supervising the system-wide operation of the teller-groups. Fred Woodworth has responsibility for staff levels, staff development,

Exhibit 3.   Branch System Structure

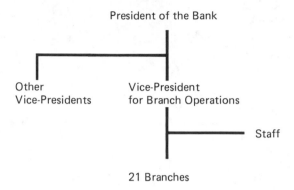

and special projects. He also is involved in planning for growth.

The branches themselves vary greatly in size, location, and type of market served. Exhibits 4 and 5 provide branch locations and basic information about the different branches.

THE FORMAL COMMUNICATION SYSTEM

As the branch system has grown, a major issue has been maintaining lines of communication among Green, his staff, and the twenty-two branches. To do this, Green set up a series of meetings to help communicate policy and deal with problems. Every Thursday he meets with the senior staff (the other vice-presidents of the bank). On Monday mornings he meets with his own personal staff. Around the first of each month, all of the branch managers meet together with Green as a group at the bank's computer center. Because of the size of the group, the meetings do not generally permit much discussion and usually consist of presentations by Green and his staff. Every ten weeks, Green also meets with the assistant managers, while Jenkins meets with the teller supervisors monthly.

In addition, another series of meetings is held by Green to facilitate two-way communication. Each month he meets with managers in smaller groups (about seven in each group) "over a meal."

Exhibit 4.   Key Branch Characteristics

Branch Number	Size of branch	Nature of market area	Profit performance	Comments
1	Large	Downtown	Good	Home office
2	Large	Downtown	Moderate	In a declining area
3	Large	Industrial/commuters	Good	
4	Large	Blue-collar ethnic	Good	
5	Small	Small town	Moderate	Recently acquired (acquisition of small town bank)
6	Medium	Suburban upper-middle class	Good	
7	Large	University area	Mixed	
8	Small	Wealthy residential	Good	
9	Large	New residential (apts.)	Good	
10	Small	Small town	Moderate	Recently acquired
11	Medium	Declining industrial	Poor	
12	Small	Small town	Good	Acquired
13	Large	Wealthy residential	Mixed	
14	Small	Small town	Good	Acquired
15	Medium	Industrial/poverty	Poor	
16	Medium	New middle class	Moderate	
17	Small	New residential	Poor	
18	Medium	Upper-middle class	Moderate	
19	Small	Lower-middle class	Good	
20	Small	Lower-middle class	Poor	
21	Medium	Upper-middle class	Good	
22	Small	New middle class	Automated branch, no branch manager or loan activity, attached to 17

This usually is done over three consecutive meals for a day or two.

In addition to holding meetings, Green receives summaries of the operating reports for each branch, including a loan activity report (new loans, outstanding balance, income, and delinquency rates); a work measurement report (number of accounts, balancing time for tellers, balancing accuracy, docked time, overtime worked, absenteeism, number of transactions, and so on); and a branch activity report (deposits, each new account, and summaries of key sections of the other reports). In addition, each month Fred Roberts visits the five best branches, while Green visits the ten worst-performing branches.

Green's responsibilities also include planning and direction for the whole branch system, including decisions about new branches, new product policy (that is, new services), technical innovations, system level budgeting, and advertising, as well as general responsibility for bank policy as a member of the senior staff.

The formal communication system is only part of the way in which information gets communicated throughout the branches. Many people find out what they need to know from the grapevine, a set of informal relationships among management in the branches. There are several different grapevines, including a teller supervisor grapevine and several manager/assistant manager net-

Exhibit 5. Location of Branches

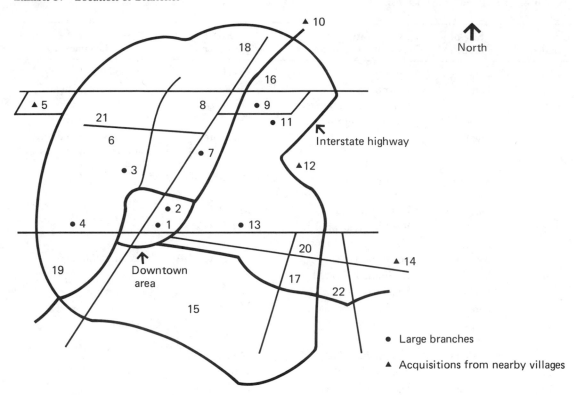

works. Among the managers and assistant managers there are subgroups who speak with each other on the phone or meet for lunch regularly. One group is composed of several branch managers who have been in the bank for twenty years or so, having started as tellers or clerks. Another is made up of the younger, "fast-track" managers who were recruited from graduate schools of business, have had special career tracks set up for them, and are rotating through the branch system, usually for two or three years. These people have contacts with other fast-track people in other parts of the bank.

RECENT PROBLEMS AND ISSUES

In recent staff meetings, Green and his staff have become aware of a number of problems and issues concerning the current organization of the branch

system. First, Green and his staff must consider a number of factors concerning the future; the bank has plans for the branch system to continue to grow, plans of perhaps adding eight new branches in the next two years. Because of this growth, there will be an increased need for good managers to staff these branches and also a need to prepare managers for positions in the other banks of the holding company. Second, the competitive pressures will continue to grow, necessitating more aggressive and better-coordinated marketing and service efforts by the branch system.

A third issue concerns problems in the branch system work force, particularly in the operational (teller) areas. The teller jobs tend to be highly structured and repetitive. The pay scale is relatively low, and pay tends to be based on seniority. In many branches, levels of absenteeism and turnover have been increasing, particularly in those branches where the work force is relatively young.

Given the costs of training tellers, this problem is potentially serious. In some branches, customer service has seemed to decline with the high turnover. Related to these problems are rumors of possible agitation for a tellers' union. As a result, Green feels that the branch managers might give more attention to the internal management of the branches.

There are also problems in Green's own organization. Because of the large number of branch managers reporting directly to him, he has had little opportunity to really provide in-depth support, direction, and help for his branch managers. He has also not been able to do any work in developing them as better managers. As a result, he has had to rely on a management by exception approach. Similarly, managers of branches have

expressed their discontent with the widening distance between themselves and the home office. Many of them express a desire to return to the "good old days" when the president of the bank knew everyone by his or her first name. Finally, Green realizes that he has not been able to do much work in coordinating efforts among the different branches so as to bring about a unified marketing and service approach in the branch system or even in selected geographical areas.

Given these issues, Green has felt the need to look at his organizational structure and to work out some better way of running the branch system. With ever-present time pressures and an approaching budget cycle, he feels there is a need for action soon.

CASE **16**

Kramer & Company, Inc.

Henry Williams, managing director of the Washington, D.C., office of Kramer & Company, Inc., a multinational management consulting firm, frowned intently as he skimmed a memo received from his secretary. Warren Daniels, an extremely talented consultant, had decided that the firm was no longer a viable career option and was in the process of forwarding his resignation. This was not the first such memo to cross Williams' marble-top desk; several people from various areas had left during the past eight months. As Williams finished the memo he began to count the number of recent departures. Since October, five consultants has resigned, including two senior

partners who had been offered positions in client organizations. In addition, two newly hired consultants had expressed significant discontent with their progress. The secretarial staff was nearly one-third brand new, including Williams' own; and office administration had lost three experienced people. This turnover problem greatly troubled Williams, as the success of the firm could be jeopardized if it continued.

Williams expressed his concern aloud:

This can't continue. We are entering into a heavy engagement cycle; and if I can't be certain about what resources we'll have, how can I artfully plan them? Continuity is essential to us. The SGM (senior group members) ranks are stretched far enough as it is, and we're going to need associates who'll be ready to manage engagements in the near term. Secretaries are easier to come by, but it costs so much to train them *if* you can find someone who can handle the pressure. The trouble with all of this is that I don't know where to begin. It's so difficult to get everyone together at the same time to talk about this.

He then picked up the phone and called Roland Davis, head of professional development, to get some input from him:

Williams: Roland, what's happening to us here? This turnover thing is going to hurt us down the road even more if we don't get to the source of it.

Davis: I know, I know. I've heard a lot of grumbling from the associates, but they're not all chomping at the bit. The SGMs don't really see it, but it's right under their noses. The support staff has totally dammed up, but I can feel the undercurrent. It could become an undertow if it doesn't get brought up to the surface.

Williams: My thoughts exactly. I want to get this out in the open, but it's hard to tell who's thinking what.

Several days later Williams contacted the case writer to have him get a feel for the attitudes within the office. Williams believed that an objective ear would receive more straightforward responses to sensitive questions.

COMPANY BACKGROUND

Kramer & Company, Inc., had achieved a prominent position within the industry since its founding in 1931 by John H. Kramer. Kramer stressed integrity and professionalism and exhorted his consultants to become "servant-leaders" for their clients. This attitude had been passed along intact, and the firm enjoyed a solid reputation. Prosperity had also been attributed to consistently excellent performance and demonstrated expertise in solving complicated management

problems. The firm's top-management approach provided tremendous visibility with both private sector leaders and high government officials. Each office had certain specialties, such as banking, insurance, industrial marketing, and strategic planning. The Washington office naturally formed the cutting edge of government client work, but its consultants were also involved with corporate clients along the East Coast and in the South. Although the firm continually explored new practice areas, it relied heavily upon groups of long-established clients who used Kramer's services extensively and productively. In most situations a team of consultants assigned to the project (known as an engagement) spent the better part of their time working in the client's own environment regardless of its distance from the home office. Good interpersonal skills were essential for interviewing key people, and many times the team members managed groups of client personnel to add continuity to the implementation of the results. Frequently consultants were needed at other offices as well, and it was common to be assigned to an entirely different office. Regardless of the location, hours were generally long and deadlines were closely spaced for informing the client of the progress to date and of the next stages of the investigation. The more effective a consultant became, the more often he or she found themself working on more than one engagement at a time.

ORGANIZATION

Exhibit 1 sets forth the formal organizational structure of the Washington office, which differed from the others in Kramer only in terms of the number of people needed. Of the thirteen offices within the firm, the Washington office was one of the smallest yet one of the most highly regarded.

PROFESSIONAL STAFF

The professional staff included only the consultants and a small number of research assistants.

Exhibit 1. Organization Chart of the Kramer Office in Washington

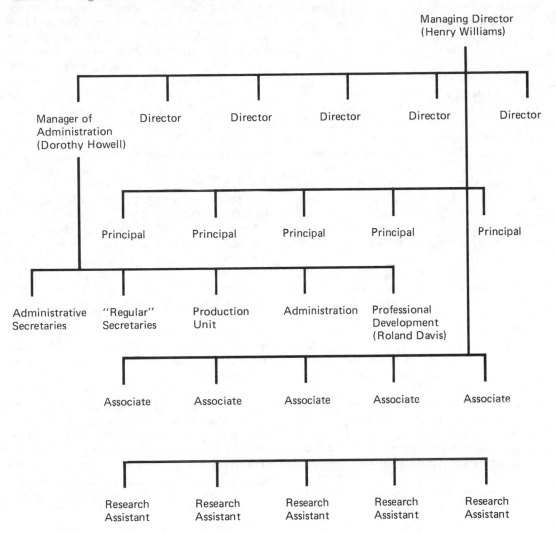

SGMs

There were two kinds of partners, or senior group members (SGM)—director and principal, the former being the more senior. Associates with five to seven years of experience in the firm could be elected to principal if they had a track record of successful client work. Following another four to six years of effective client development, one could be nominated for election as a director with responsibilities for opening up new practice areas or expanding existing ones. These elections were governed by the SGMs themselves and involved quite a substantial increase in salary and potential bonuses based upon the total firm's billings. It was obvious that SGMs had worked quite hard to arrive at their position and thrived upon the pressures involved in getting ahead. When asked how he felt about the reported discontent of several associates, one SGM replied: "During my eighteen years with the firm I never had any problems. You have to be aggressive around here. They just don't make associates like they used to. And where's the dedication? I surely don't see much of that these days."

Associates

The associate level also included different stages of experience and expertise. The newer associates were involved extensively in the nuts-and-bolts of client work, while the more senior managed the progress and direction of an engagement. As soon as an associate exhibited the ability to carry out an engagement, he or she was given the go-ahead regardless of tenure, although it usually took two years or so for a new associate to get into the swing of things. Within that two-year period there was little opportunity or real need to specialize in any of the practice areas since the main objective was to develop good consulting skills. However, to move forward one needed to gain expertise in at least one industry practice, field of discipline, or conceptual approach. At the end of the two-year period, associates were eligible for year-end bonuses and an informal stamp of approval from the other professionals. Performance was what really counted at Kramer, and thus there was significant pressure placed upon new associates to climb the learning curve. (This pressure was also felt at all levels of the Professional Staff as no "safe" position existed. The firm's "up or out" policy ensured that even the SGMs were motivated to perform continually.)

The case writer interviewed a number of associates, but there seemed to be no single reason for discontent. One particularly vocal associate, however, made the following comment: "I know my work is good or else I would have heard about it by now. But after 2½ years no one has ever said 'Good job, Randall.' A little encouragement could go a long way."

An Engagement

Although there was clear distinction between SGMs and associates on a formal basis, these distinctions became obscured during the course of an engagement. Typically, when a client requested Kramer's services in solving a management problem, a letter of proposal was put together by the SGM responsible for securing the opportunity. The document explicitly stated how the firm would approach the problem and what the specific outputs of their investigation would entail. Frequently, offers were simply turned down if the client's desires did not match the firm's own. Kramer's reputation hinged on the ability to be of value to the client; and if it was perceived that only limited results could be obtained, the firm would not hesitate to decline. Rather than cause any loss of potential clients, this policy engendered a strong measure of respect from top management everywhere and assured them that if the firm chose to undertake a project the fees were well worth it.

Once the proposal had been agreed upon, the SGM would select one of his peers, usually a principal, to monitor the overall progress. He was known as an engagement director (ED) and oversaw several engagements for different SGMs. From the ranks of the associates an engagement manager (EM) was selected to implement the work to be done. The remaining slots on the team were filled with associates and now and then an SGM. If necessary, a research assistant was added to assist in the collection of the massive amounts of data that would be required. In most instances, however, the engagement manager preferred to delegate these tasks among the team members to avoid having just "another warm body" around. Needless to say, research assistants resented this attitude. Typically, they had an advanced degree and had been involved in the research field for a number of years, although the firm from time to time would hire an especially gifted person with less experience. Research assistants seemed extremely efficient in data gathering, and the case-writer was impressed by their ability to locate information that was normally difficult to find. Their overall resentment reflected itself in the frustrations of one person in particular: "What am I doing here? I'm a damn good researcher but I spend most of my time watching my eyebrows grow. I feel like I'm waiting for someone to throw me a bone."

At the conclusion of the engagement, the EM would make an extensive final presentation to the client's top management, complete with audio-visual aides and a hard copy of the presentation's text. The results of the investigation were reviewed, and the recommended next steps were outlined. The EM was backed up by the team who assisted in responding to difficult client questions. In key client situations the managing director out of whose office the engagement sprang would be present. If the recommendations were accepted (which they usually were), an implementation team was formed. This implementation team could be totally different from the first team, although the EM was called upon for advice and insight. The implementation team relied on its ability to learn quickly in order to maintain the professional standards established by their predecessors. This produced obvious problems for new associates who found it challenging enough just to come up to speed on an engagement just beginning.

The Assignment Process

The forming of engagement teams was a rather informal process as consultants were chosen purely by request of the SGM handling the client. Associates, in particular, were selected on the basis of their perceived contributions to the problem-solving effort, in addition to their ability to work well with the other team members and client personnel. Although they frequently voiced their interests, associates were allocated as dictated by two needs; to meet the personnel demands posed by the great volume of work and to assure that each engagement had its fair share of talented consultants. The fact that the firm attempted to operate as a whole rather than merely as separate offices further complicated the assigning of associates; it was difficult to keep track of where they were located on a daily basis. On occasion newer associates were pulled out of engagements, if their expertise was no longer needed, and assigned elsewhere. As could be expected this practice created difficulties in achieving a large degree of continuity in the development of these individuals:

> I'm a new associate and I'm really tired of being batted around like a ping-pong ball. By the time I start production on an engagement, it's time to move on to another. And I also resent this

"new associate" albatross around my neck. I'm as good as anyone else, but I don't get the chance to prove it.

The case writer also discovered that even the more seasoned associates harbored ill feelings about their assignments although for the most part feelings stemmed from a different source. One highly regarded EM expressed his concern.

> I've managed three engagements back-to-back, and I don't think those SGMs know I'm alive. I've been running like a racehorse for a year and a half until my wife and kids think I'm a stranger. I love the work I do, but how about a break? I have vacation time I can't even get to.

The assignment task was slightly easier for the SGMs because they maintained more consistent contact with each other. It was usually a clear decision as to which SGMs should be assigned to particular types of engagements, but the extensive travel and time demands posed the same problems as with associates—both spent a good share of time out of the office and out of touch with assignment possibilities.

Performance Evaluations

The professional staff evaluated each other. By and large, SGMs obtained consensus on the progress and performance of directors and principals by getting input from those SGMs who had the most contact with the individual in question. Associates were assigned to one of the SGMs who was supposed to review their progress every six months and authorize salary increases and bonuses. The "group manager" system yielded results of little value because it was difficult to arrange an appropriate time for the two to meet. In addition the only real source of opinion was the EM, when a new associate was being evaluated, or the engagement director, when an EM was being evaluated. Soliciting detailed feedback from these sources was also a problem. Because of the intensity of the events during an engagement, no one really had time to keep in touch with an individual's progress: a successful overall effort was an accepted yardstick of individual performance.

SUPPORT STAFF

The support staff's chief responsibilities were providing all of the services needed by the professionals in their client work, handling the administrative details of the office, and maintaining contact with other Kramer offices. The manager of administration, Dorothy Howell, coordinated the efforts of the various subunits of the support staff interfacing with the key people in each subunit. Because of the diversity of support staff duties, subunits functioned more or less autonomously, taking their cues from the professionals on most issues. In this sense their environment could be characterized as informal and organic because they interacted closely and freely with the professionals. Howell did maintain control procedures to ensure a smooth work flow and to measure the productivity of individuals for promotional decisions. She also hired new support staff and helped plan resource needs and the allocation of people to special duties, such as overtime. This last duty was seldom executed since planning was a difficult task due to the variability of a consultant's day-to-day work.

Howell was evaluated solely on the basis of her ability to hold the fort together as judged by the managing director. In general, impressions of her competence were favorable although the recent departures had stirred some criticism: "Howell's got to keep a tighter rein on her support staff. You can't get anything done around here. It's bad enough that we have to be out of town so much; but when you discover your own secretary has flown the coop, you have to start at square one."

Secretarial

Both administrative secretaries for each SGM and "regular" secretaries, assigned to a group of four to six associates, were included in this unit. Their tasks fluctuated widely, ranging from structuring intricate travel arrangements and answering calls to the standard stenographic duties. It was not uncommon for a secretary simultaneously to perform duties for all of the associates to which he or she was assigned. In addition, secretaries were called upon to assist in the typing of drafts of client presentations, though personnel was specifically delegated for this. Several drafts and rewrites were usually done, which caused bottlenecks when much work was in progress. An even temperment was helpful because professionals facing deadlines blew off steam freely. In addition it seemed that the watchful eyes of Howell created friction from time to time:

> What good does it do a secretary to work hard for these consultants—you can't please them. After ten drafts from four different people I don't even get a thank-you. And when I do, along comes Howell breathing down my neck, bitching that I was fifteen minutes late for work and that the dress I picked out this morning looked a little too unprofessional. I did stay here until 12:00 last night, you know. And if support staff got bonuses like the professionals I could look like "Miss Businesswoman" every day.

When evaluating the units' performance overall, Howell relied upon the managing director's impression of how well the work flow was moving. For individual evaluations a consensus view was reached; Howell received written opinions of the secretary's performance from the professionals to which he or she was assigned. Punctuality and fast turn-around were important (and carefully monitored), but the ability to get along with the consultants could particularly influence the evaluation. Unfortunately, it appeared to the caseworker that this "ability-to-get-along" criterion stopped short of including the dedication he had seen exhibited by the secretarial staff.

Production

Kramer's production unit transformed the engagement teams' concept of how the presentation report should look into a bound and printed document complete with artistically displayed charts and exhibits. The high quality of this finished product was a constant source of pride. The production unit viewed themselves as craftsmen, and in effect they really were. Many had extensive experience in graphics, and one individual had been an instructor in a well-known technical school before joining the firm. As a whole they worked rather independently and set their own pace, at least until one of the professionals was caught in a bind:

> It takes time to do a good graphic. I don't mind being rushed. But when one of those damn consultants comes breezing through here at 10:00 in the morning and I've been at it since 7:00 A.M., it irks me to listen to them complain about their deadlines. We're *all* professionals as far as I'm concerned.

Much as the secretaries were required to rework by typing of excessive drafts, the production people did numerous reworks until the engagement team was satisfied. Every comma had to be in place, and no misspelled words could go unnoticed. Late hours were a normal occurrence, especially on the eve of presentations. Deadlines had to be met at all cost. Secretaries and other typists were borrowed, if necessary, to get a report completed.

Performance evaluations for the production unit were less formal. Rarely did they fail to meet a deadline, and the quality of their work was unquestioned. The only real source of control was punctual arrival to work and a minimum of days absent.

Administration

This unit handled the payroll and billing operations. Time and expense reports were received bimonthly from all firm members. The cost to the client was calculated from the hours worked on an engagement by various levels of personnel. Many professionals disliked the details of completing the time and expense forms but saw it as a potentially useful way of keeping track of each other. One interested associate mentioned this to the casewriter and expanded on his idea of incorporating it into the assignment and evaluation process:

> It's hard to believe that we're so good at organizing other people. Here we have a ready-made indicator of who's doing what, and we don't even use it. It takes a lot of time to fill those damn things out, and it irks me when SGMs ask me where I've been for the last month. If you want to know how productive I am, just take a look at the engagement list on my T&E.

Support staff rarely incurred personal expenses (charged to overhead) and needed prior authorization to do so. Because the consultants travelled constantly, they were given an open-ended expense account and were required to furnish receipts for charges in excess of $25. They viewed the account as sort of a "softener" to cushion the burden of the extensive demands of the job and used it liberally, but reasonably, with no supervision or double checking. This practice seemed to accentuate the resentment on the part of the support staff in general, who viewed the "free-and-easy" lifestyle of professionals as a sharp contrast to their far less exciting prospects of working in the office all the time.

Administrative personnel were evaluated on their punctuality and were monitored closely to ensure accurate information. They were seldom called upon to work overtime and were known as the "half-day" people ("half-day" referred to "only" the hours between 9:00 and 5:00).

Professional Development

Roland Davis was the sole member of this unit and represented the real interface with the professional staff. At 48 he was an "elder" in the firm and had amassed a great deal of autonomy among the support staff and respect from the professionals. A staff was formerly assigned to him, but he convinced the managing director that the job could be handled more efficiently by one man. The casewriter found him to be an extremely straightforward and objective person whose demeanor reflected a certain sageness and insight into people. He viewed himself as an administrator whose real strength was in orchestrating the resolution of conflicts. Although it was not his assigned task, he counseled (and consoled) associates on their career progress and was a sounding board for discontent. He would also, informally, keep track of pending engagements. Many associates would check with him, before trying to track down their group manager, to get filled in on the status of assignments and who was being considered. Davis' official duties included conducting initial screening interviews for new associate candidates and managing the recruiting process at the various graduate schools of business. As a conduit for information from other offices, he was in steady contact with most of the SGMs. No one really evaluated Davis, and his position was the closest to a "safe" one in the entire office.

THE REPORT

Following his discussions with members of the Washington office, the casewriter assembled his impressions and communicated them to Williams. The managing director reviewed the findings with a pained expression. He sighed heavily and placed the report on his desk. "This would be a lot easier if we didn't have to depend on each other like we do. This place should be a symphony and not a bunch of street-corner musicians playing different tunes."

CASE 17

Clearview Institute of Science

Jonathan Leigh, a case writer from the Columbia Business School, met Professor Sam Morris of the Clearview Institute of Science on a flight from New York to Geneva. Morris was on his way to report to a special United Nations committee on the development of alternative energy sources. In speaking to Leigh about Clearview, Morris seemed frustrated.

We always had such a great reputation—we did excellent research and published in the most prestigious scientific journals. We are always invited to major scientific conferences and always chair some of the sessions. Last year our department was awarded a United Nations grant for solar energy development. We are using solar energy to grow algae as a cheap source of protein and carbohydrates. We began working on this project several months ago, but somehow nothing has worked out. I'm on my way to Geneva now to report to the committee, but what can I tell them?

We have talented graduate students—we only accept the best. We also have an extremely skilled technical staff; and unlike other research institutes, each professor in our department has his own technician. Take my technician Saul Gardner. Even when I was working on the most complicated problems, I could count on him to carry out the daily experiments, and he learned to operate the equipment and report to me the next day. But now, everything is different. The technicians seem to have suddenly become incompetent, and the project is barely progressing.

The flight arrived before Leigh and Morris could discuss the problem; however, Leigh decided to spend some time at Clearview when he returned to New York.

BACKGROUND

Clearview is a world-famous institute of scientific research founded by James D. Clearview in 1948. He strongly believed in the promotion of scientific research for the benefit of mankind. It was his specific wish that each professor be granted the utmost academic freedom and that individual research be facilitated in every way.

A relatively small number of scientists and technicians were employed at Clearview in the early 1950s. The institute was organized as a single unit with a very informal structure.

Milt Irving was one of the first Ph.D. students to graduate from Clearview. Charming and brilliant, his advance was unprecedented. His frequent trips and personal contacts with outstanding members of the scientific community increased the institute's prestige. His name attracted many scientists, several of whom joined Clearview solely to collaborate with him. As time went by the institute expanded, ultimately requiring its division into departments. Irving was appointed head of biophysics.

Among those who joined Clearview because of Irving were Sam Morris and Jack Burton. Both proved to be excellent scientists and teachers who devoted most of their time to teaching in the graduate program. This activity did not interfere with their personal research because most of the laboratory work was performed by their technicians.

Impressed by Burton's and Morris's success, Irving decided to delegate to them full authority to manage and supervise their subordinates. Irving maintained his position as active head of the department but limited other responsibilities to his own graduate students and technicians.

In time, Clearview gained international fame. A national survey of scientific research topics revealed that Clearview's competitors had diversified by undertaking numerous applied research projects. A limited number of researchers at Clearview considered similarly diversifying their personal research interests but refrained from doing so mainly because it demanded a change in institutional policy and the restructuring of most existing departments.

The recent snowballing effect of the energy crisis made Irving reevaluate his approach. About one year ago, although initially hesitant, Irving decided to deviate from institutional policy; he applied for and was awarded the solar energy development grant.

The funds made available in the first year were impressive, although the terms of the grant were rigid. While the United Nations committee did not insist on controlling the spending and allocation of its grant, it did require payback of all funds not spent during the first year. Extension of the grant was subject to a review of the initial success of the project.

DEPARTMENT OF BIOPHYSICS

Walking into Irving's lab at 8:30 one morning, Jonathan Leigh was surprised to meet Ms. Smith, Irving's technician, preparing for an experiment.

Leigh: Are all of you such early birds?

Smith: No, only me! I come in around 7:00 and leave as soon as I finish. I've known Professor Irving since his first day as a graduate student here, twenty-five years ago! I work only for him. My hours are up to me, as long as I get the day's work done.

Ms. Smith's attitude reflects the strong position technicians enjoy at Clearview. Their union is very active, and firing a technician is unheard of. They receive tenure easily, and promotion is based on a seniority system. They are well paid, and many fringe benefits are provided by the local union. However, they do not receive rewards from their direct supervisors.

The scientific staff is comprised of graduate students, junior and senior scientists, and professors. Most graduate students leave the institute upon receiving their degrees.

The junior and senior scientists are promoted according to ability and performance. There are always a large number of applicants for junior staff positions even though their tenure rate is only 1 in 15. Because of this rate, the technicians are reluctant to work for the junior staff, since not only do they consider themselves superior but also they consider the juniors "temporary workers."

When Professor Irving arrived soon after 8:30, he told Leigh that he was very proud to have been awarded the grant. Despite his administrative load and his recent appointment as chairman of the board of directors, he was able to find sufficient time to spend in the laboratory. He loved the atmosphere and sometimes would work together with Ms. Smith. He relied fully upon Morris and Burton to carry out their share of the project. He did not believe in excessive interaction with those who were not his direct subordinates in the department; they were to report to Morris and Burton. The phone rang in Irving's office. When Irving hung up, he smiled and excused himself, explaining that an unexpected meeting of the board was to begin shortly.

Leigh's next stop was Morris's laboratory. Morris was still in Geneva, and Leigh found Gardner in Morris's recliner, reading the daily sports column. Leigh was not surprised by what he saw. He knew that the 10:00 A.M. coffee break was a well-established tradition at Clearview. The local union maintained a subsidized cafeteria that served mainly coffee and snacks. Each morning around 10:00 many of the technicians met in the relatively small lounge to exchange gossip and first-hand information on their research projects. A favorite topic for some time had been that some technicians had recently received a special bonus for their diligence during a recent project in the chemistry department.

The good news had raised the level of expectation among those employed in biophysics. They knew that working on the solar energy project would disrupt their established routine of the 10:00 o'clock break because they were expected to spend all day on the roof. However, they had confidence in their ability to perform well, and they had expected to receive a generous bonus in appreciation of their efforts. Their expectations had been disappointed, and technicians became discontented and hostile and lost all enthusiasm. Burton's and Morris's frequent absences from the laboratory only encouraged the technicians' indifference. Lacking supervision, they showed up and left whenever they pleased. Gardner spoke:

Ms. Smith told me you would be coming here. Let me show you our algae. We're growing them in containers on the roof. I find the whole thing rather stupid—last year our work was supposed to be free of traces of contamination, and now Morris is growing beasts on the roof! He must be out of his mind! I am really supposed to work all day on the roof, taking samples, etc., but it is actually Green who should be doing all this. He was appointed as my helper, but refuses to accept any orders from me. So for the time being he is doing nothing, and between you and me, neither am I. Morris never told us the real purpose of the whole project and never explained to us our specific tasks. A few days ago I found Ms. Smith taking samples from our containers. She seemed to be doing similar work to what we think we are supposed to be doing. If so, let her at least help us. She always refuses, and I know for a fact that she is hiding and locking all her equipment when she goes home. She belongs to Irving, so to whom can we complain?

Morris never even shows up during the day. He has ordered me to leave the experimental results in his office, and in the morning I always find messages from him on my desk. Actually, even when Morris is in the lab he is hardly to be seen. If he thinks that I will be bullied around by the "baby" graduate students, he is in for a surprise. So, I am enjoying life, not working too hard, I am receiving my salary anyhow—I have tenure—who can fire me?

Gardner's monologue was interrupted by the entrance of Ms. White, Burton's technician.

White: Saul, please help us with the vacuum pump. It's just come back from the workshop but something went wrong again!

Gardner: Tell Burton to help you, we don't work for Burton's group. If you think that you can get away with monopolizing the lab you're mistaken. We all know that you double order from the warehouse, and nothing is left in stock when we get there. If you guys are so smart, you can surely fix a simple pump!

White: So that's the way you see things. OK, there's nothing left for me to say!

Later in the cafeteria Leigh found himself seated next to Sue Cooper, one of Morris's graduate students. She told Leigh:

It's not my business to interfere, but I know something is very wrong. I'm not personally involved with this project and all I know is what I see and hear day in and day out. This department has not had a routine staff meeting for months, everyone seems to be busy with the solar energy project, the way Irving wants to carry it out. One or another of the professors seems always to be out of town or even out of the country. None of the technicians seems to be motivated, and I don't blame them. Working on the roof, they have turned into the laughing stock of the whole building! They demand incentives and rewards for "hard labor." I tried to talk to them and to explain the importance of this project to the department and to the institute, but they will not pay attention to a female graduate student. When I discussed the matter with Morris, he told me not to interfere and stick to my own work. Personally, I feel that it would benefit both the department and the project if the whole department became equally involved. We should exchange information and help one another. The truth is that Burton and Morris have independently decided that the project was their baby. As for the graduate students, our work seems good enough for the professors to put their names on the papers we write, but our advice is never taken seriously.

Some weeks later Jonathan Leigh was talking to Morris, who had returned from Geneva. Morris said, "I'm very worried about the fate of this whole project. If we don't start coming up with results soon, our grant will not be extended. Something drastic has to be done immediately."

CASE **18**

Friedrichs, Levine & Company

Carl Evans sat down with the management consultant he had recently engaged and asked, "Well, what do you think of this crazy place?" The consultant had been asked to study the entire firm and to formulate recommendations for dealing with the problems he perceived.

Evans had recently been hired as a first vice-president and de facto head of the corporate finance department of this prominant regional investment banking house. Evans had begun his career at Friedrichs, Levine & Company but had left seventeen years ago, after nine years at the firm. Since then, he had held a number of high-level jobs with New York investment banking firms, most recently as manager of the regional operations firm that had just merged.

He had been hired to take over from Jason Rosenthal, executive vice-president and head of the corporate finance department, an elderly man who had suffered from a long illness and was getting ready to retire. Rosenthal had run the corporate department since before the current president took over in 1954.

Evans had been attracted by more than the corporate department job, however. James Levine, the president of the firm, explained to him, "As you know, my family owns the majority of the firm. No one but myself has any interest in the business. I'd like to see the firm continue after I retire, and I'd like to see the employees running it." Levine had made it clear that Evans was expected to be the architect of this transition and to take the initiative in attacking the problems that had developed in the firm in recent years. After some study on his own, Evans decided to bring in a management consultant, who assembled the following information.

THE INDUSTRY

The securities industry raises capital primarily for industry and for municipal and state governments. The primary financing vehicles are corporate and municipal bonds, and stocks. Investment bankers perform many related services for companies and municipalities and for investors as well. Principal sources of revenue for an investment banking firm are commissions on brokerage transactions, underwriting spreads, placement fees, financial and other advisory fees, and profits on trading and investment in securities. Detailed information about the industry appears in Exhibit 1.

The 1960s witnessed a remarkable expansion of the securities industry, in tandem with a strong economy and rising stock prices. High stock prices and voracious demand tempted many small companies to sell shares to the public. In the general ebullience, investment banking and brokerage firms prospered, and a host of new firms came into being.

The bubble burst in the 1970s, with OPEC's ascendance, the severe recession of 1974–5, and the advent of an extended period of stagflation. Discouraged investors liquidated equities, and the market for new offerings of small company stocks all but evaporated. Capital markets in the 1970s exhibited significantly greater volatility than before.

Furthermore, the Securities and Exchange Commission ruled that the industry-wide commission rates on brokerage business amounted to price fixing and that commissions in the future would have to be negotiated. Institutional investors then used their market power to force commissions down, severely damaging the profitability of brokerage operations.

Although the industry had been highly regulated for many years, the regulatory environment continued to tighten. As a result of these occurrences, the industry began a period of drastic consolidation that continues to the present. Many firms merged or went out of business.

One result of the industry's consolidation has been an enormous increase in competition. Firms are scrabbling for underwriting business, which is still relatively profitable, as never before. Consequently, many regional firms feel a tighter squeeze than economic conditions alone indicate because the large New York firms are moving more aggressively into their territory.

THE FIRM

Friedrichs, Levine and Company was established in 1923. James Levine, the current president and nephew of the first president, took over in 1954, by which time Friedrichs, Levine was already the most prominent investment banking house in its region. Under James Levine's direction, the firm has grown rapidly, concentrating particularly on municipal bonds. In addition, the firm committed its own capital to several corporate ventures, under the direction of Jason Rosenthal. Some of these were spectacularly successful. As a result of its corporate finance deals and of the efforts of a highly professional sales force (directed primarily by Rosenthal), the firm developed an excellent reputation as a bold, competent regional investment banking house. The firm's emphasis has always been on traditional investment banking business, primarily underwriting, with minimal attention to brokerage and services.

Historically, Friedrichs, Levine has always been managed very informally. The firm employs no budgeting or planning procedures. Compensation practices are haphazard. Professionals in municipal and corporate finance are paid low salaries and rewarded for performance with bonuses based on the revenues they produce for the firm. Employees in nonproducing functions (for instance, traders and clerks), depend upon ad hoc negotiation with their superior or with Levine for compensation. Salespeople are paid a percentage of the commission or spread realized on a transaction. Although the commission system of pay-

Exhibit 1. The Investment Banking Business

Unit	Function	Tasks	Recipient of services
Corporate finance	Debt and equity underwriting Private placements Mergers and acquisitions Financial advice Valuations	Call on prospects and clients Monitor markets Monitor competition Learn about impending deals Develop proposals Execute transactions Develop new finance ideas	Corporations and partnerships
Municipal finance	Arrange underwritings of municipal bonds Financial advice	Call on state and local governments for business Monitor markets and competition Learn about impending deals Develop proposals Execute transactions Develop new finance ideas Develop political contacts	State and local governments and agencies thereof
Tax-exempt corporate finance: Pollution control and industrial revenue (IRB)	Arrange underwritings of tax-exempt bonds for corporations Private placements Provide information on relevant legislation	Keep abreast of legislative developments Inform corporate finance Monitor markets Monitor competition Call on companies, in conjunction with corporate finance Call on industrial development agencies Contact with realtors Execute transactions	Public utilities Other corporations Corporate finance department
Municipal underwriting	Make markets in municipals Inter-dealer trading Price issues firm underwrites Competitive bids on municipal issues Participation in other firms' underwritings Value customer's portfolios	Monitor and trade in municipal markets Maintain inter-dealer relations Bid on bonds and price firm's sales Monitor financial condition of municipalities Advise other departments on market conditions	Sales force Other dealers Finance personnel Municipalities
Sales	Sell securities Keep clients informed of developments in their holdings	Prospect for new accounts Constant contact with customers	Individuals Insurance companies Banks

(continued)

Exhibit 1.   *(continued)*

Unit	Function	Tasks	Recipient of services
Sales *(continued)*	Provide investment advice	Obtain investment information Execute trades for customers Sell merchandise finance departments generate	Mutual funds Pension funds Investment companies Finance departments Research
Research	Provide investment ideas and advice to salespeople Assist salespeople in sales to important customers Keep users of investment inform primarily through the sales force Assist corporate finance in valuations Advise syndicate personnel	Call on companies Develop investment ideas Monitor performance of companies in which clients may have positions Write research reports Develop economic scenario and investment policies Assist and act as liaison with salespeople, corporate finance, and syndicate	Corporate finance Investors Syndicate department
Equity trading	Make markets in stocks Execute orders on national and regional stock exchanges Trade stocks for profit	Keep informed on companies Maintain interdealer relations Perform transactions for salespeople Advise corporate finance, research, and syndicate departments on market conditions Monitor and trade in markets	Sales force Other dealers Corporate finance, research, and syndicate department
Syndicate	Participate in other dealers' underwritings	Inform salespeople of upcoming deals Maintain interdealer relations Determine participation in other firms' deals Keep corporate finance abreast of other dealers' activities	Other dealers Sales force Corporate finance
Cashier	Handle flow of funds and securities between firm and customers and firm and other dealers	Contact banks Maintain transaction records Bill customers	Investors Equity trading Municipal underwriting Syndicate department Sales force

ing salespeople and the salary/bonus arrangement for other employees are standard industry practices, Friedrichs, Levine is notable in its lack of established policies to set the amounts involved. Furthermore, although it is possible for a producer to earn a great deal in a good year, there is no mechanism to develop a personal stake in the firm. The profit sharing plan is based on base salary, which is low. Significantly, among the handful of employees, other than Levine, who own stock in the firm, the single largest position amounts to less than 2 percent. Such concentrated ownership is relatively rare in the industry.

Despite the formal organization chart depicted in Exhibit 2, the firm was basically split two ways: Levine ran the municipal department and Rosenthal ran the corporate and sales departments. The firm's salespeople sell both municipal and corporate securities. Until the past ten years, Rosenthal had run his show fairly tightly. However, as Levine grew ill and old, his concern with daily operations began to wane. Levine was not interested in detailed management (he preferred to stay in municipal underwriting and trade bonds), and nobody else stepped in to fill the vacuum left by Rosenthal's decline, though many high quality people had flowed through the firm in the past.

The corporate and sales departments deteriorated steadily over the past ten years. The firm's visibility among area companies had become very low; competitors had made enormous inroads; the firm was missing the chance to compete for deals because its personnel didn't know they were in the offing; and within Friedrichs, Levine, the corporate department was derisively referred to as the "Red Army," in reference to its lack of profitability. The sales force had recently lost a number of its successful senior brokers due to death or dissatisfaction. The remaining senior people were generally hard to control, and many were losing interest. The other salespeople were generally young and inexperienced. The firm had been unable to attract experienced securities salespeople, and turnover among trainees was very high. Consequently, the firm's reputation among investors had slipped, and a number of

Exhibit 2. Organization Chart of Friedrichs, Levine

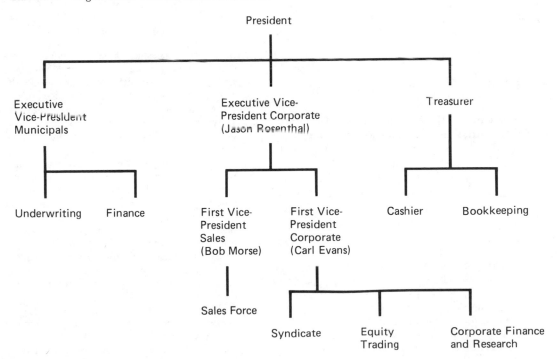

clients deserted the company. Naturally, the ability to distribute securities suffered. Many employees blamed the decline in the sales force on Bob Morse, first vice-president and sales manager for the past twelve years. It was felt that Morse often was unfair, indecisive, and disorganized. Nonetheless, he seemed to enjoy the confidence and support of the president, and, before Evans' arrival, appeared to be Levine's likely successor.

Municipal finance has been the single bright spot in the past few years (see Exhibit 3). Several new financing ideas had recently been developed in the industry, and some of the municipal finance people had exploited them very effectively. Because these deals were large and profitable, these employees had been very well rewarded: it was rumored within the firm that one of them had earned $500,000 in a recent year.

Nonetheless, there was some concern that routine, more reliable municipal business was being neglected to pursue these "trick" financings, which the IRS was steadily closing off as abuses of tax-exempt financing. And despite the municipal finance successes, overall profitability was disturbingly low: in a recent year, which had been good for the industry, the firm's net earnings from operations had amounted to only 10 percent of shareholders' equity.

CONVERSATIONS

After assembling the foregoing information from Evans and from general industry sources, the consultant decided to interview various members of the firm to observe different perspectives on its problems. For this purpose, he picked a young retail salesperson, an institutional salesperson, a corporate finance officer, one of the municipal finance people, and the senior research analyst. Their comments follow:

[Retail salesperson] The problem with this place is that no one tells you what to do. I'm supposed to go out and find new customers. I'm supposed to be giving investment advice to people. But we get no formal training in either salesmanship or investments! I've been a broker for eighteen months: how am I supposed to be competent to make investment judgments? It would help if we got more support from research, but we never hear from those guys. And when we do, it's the same stocks over and over: you can only sell so many people so many shares of the same company! Morse has got lots of advice, but I don't think it's very carefully considered. I've seen him stumble badly on stock recommendations and then deny he's made them.

[Institutional salesperson] One thing wrong is the way accounts are assigned. I work my ass off to develop a relationship with an institution we've never sold to before and end up accounting for half their business. Then a plum account comes up and Kahn [another institutional salesman] brown-noses it out of Morse. The research people can be helpful, but they always want me to sell stock. Sometimes, I don't happen to believe the market is attractive. I'm the one who loses a customer who gets burned.

[Corporate finance officer] I moved to Friedrichs, Levine five years ago from another regional firm, and it's been deteriorating steadily. Although things are generally tough in the industry, our department seems to do worse than most. A lot of that is our fault, but we're enormously handicapped by our sales force's inability to distribute. Also, we get no feedback from the market, and we don't know where to take private deals when we get them: our salesmen are simply not covering the institutions adequately. A few institutional salesmen have all the good accounts, so they make a lot of money with very little work. We recently went through all the possible buyers of industrial revenue bonds in the country, for a small private placement: our salesmen could tell us nothing about what sort of merchandise most of their accounts would buy. We have to call them ourselves!

In our own department, we're badly organized. I was calling on a company last week only to find when I got back that Ross had been there a month ago. It's pointless for him to try to get new business: he's smart enough, but to get business you've really got to be a salesman, and he's just not that type of guy. They barely remembered him! Meanwhile there are a lot of technical aspects of the business that we're not up on because we're all chasing after the same things.

We can be incredibly uncompetitive. We recently lost an industrial revenue deal for a major company because Carl wanted to charge a 2-point fee [2 percent of the principal amount].

Exhibit 3. Steps in a Financing

The hypothetical example below is of a company going public. Although every financing is different, this example encompasses many of the elements that typically are involved in a corporate financing.

1. A salesperson's customer mentions that the company (hereafter, "the company") he or she owns is growing rapidly and will need to raise new equity at some point. The salesperson suggests meeting with the investment firm's corporate finance people and promises to have them contact the customer.
2. Salesperson talks to corporate finance, which agrees to look into the matter.
3. Corporate finance obtains preliminary information on the company through Dun & Bradstreet credit reports, customers, competitors, and other sources. Quick check on viability of the industry is done.
4. Corporate finance decides that the company is worth examining. They hold meeting with the customer and obtain information about the company, its business, and its finances.
5. Research and corporate finance make preliminary study of company and industry.
6. Corporate finance recommends that the company go public and decides that the firm is willing to handle the deal. They give the company preliminary ideas about size, form, and pricing of the issue. Company engages the investment banker.
7. In depth study of industry, with research department, is performed.
8. In depth meetings with company officials to study the company are held, as are meetings with accountants, lawyers, and company officials to prepare registration statement.
9. Registration statement with S.E.C. is filed. Cooling-off period begins.
10. Red herring is circulated; syndicate and selling group are formed. Research and syndicate departments in each participating firm go over the issue with salespeople, who being preliminary work with customers.
11. Due diligence and information meetings held.
12. Cooling-off period ends. Issue becomes effective: issue period by syndicate department of managing firm. Manager signs underwriting agreement with company. Syndicate members sign agreement among underwriters.
13. Issue is offered. Salespeople call customers, who submit orders. Sales manager at each firm allocates stock among customers. Syndicate manager of the managing underwriter allocates stock among firms according to participation, demand, availability, and anticipated demand. Selling group members sign dealers agreement.
14. During offering period, trading department of managing firm places stabilizing bid with nonparticipating firm. Stock taken is returned to syndicate department control.
15. Offering ends and stabilizing bid is withdrawn. Manager pays company. Syndicate and selling group members pay manager. Syndicate members take delivery stock certificates. Customers pay investment banking firms. Syndicate members submit stock certificates to transfer agent, usually a commercial bank, to be transferred to ultimate buyers. All transactions are settled through cashier departments of firms involved.
16. Trading department makes a market in the stock.
17. Research department continues to monitor the company.
18. Stock may eventually be listed on one of the national exchanges.

We found out later that everyone else was talking 1 point. We've even stopped asking the municipal underwriters for price ideas: since they're afraid they'll get hung with a deal, they always price the bonds at least half a point above the market. Besides, they're out of touch with the IRB [industrial revenue bond] market since we've had so few deals. It's ridiculous, because IRBs are natural for us, but we're getting killed by other regional firms. And now the New York firms have been moving in. One problem is that it's never been made clear who is responsible for IRBs: us or the municipal finance boys.

Maybe the most serious problem is that you never know how well you're really doing. Corporate finance is a slow business: It takes time to build contacts and credibility. Companies don't finance as often as cities, and there are fewer companies for whom we would do deals. And we're not like salesmen, who do a number of transactions each day. I asked James to tell me how he thought I was doing, and he said he'd let me know if I screw up. Great, but between deals I starve. It's hardly reasonable when we have to support the research effort and when you consider that a healthy chunk of this firm's capital was generated by investment in corporate department ideas.

[Municipal finance officer] I'll grant you that you have to produce to do well here. But what the hell? You get well paid when you do. I admit it's disconcerting not knowing what will happen if James dies tomorrow. Still, I'm willing to take that chance: I'm 27 years old and I couldn't make nearly as much elsewhere. The one major complaint I do have is with the sales force: those guys can't sell worth beans, and I'm beginning to get embarrassed when I go back to a city whose finance officer sees a deal from a similar city sold by another house at a significantly lower interest rate. As for the municipal underwriters, they're disagreeable and closed-minded: I generally ignore them and wing it when it comes to price ideas.

[Senior research analyst] I've just about given up on the place. You come up with a good stock idea, and the salesmen can't even understand it, much less sell it. The latest crop is the least impressive I've seen in the past twenty years. Everyone wants to be an analyst, too: they don't seem to realize that they're securities salesmen: it's *our* responsibility to determine investment policy. I'm sick of talking to them. Frankly, I spend most of my time managing my own money.

It's hard to know what they want you to do around here. If I spend a lot of time on research, I can't be out trying to produce deals, so I don't get paid. Fortunately, Jason has always taken pretty good care of me, though. But when I'm doing deals, people bitch that they don't get research. There's another problem: as an analyst, my scope of interest in companies is much wider than for corporate finance, where for competitive reasons we're pretty much restricted to private companies and to smaller publicly held firms. So research contacts often are unlikely to result in finance business. In most firms, you know, corporate finance and research are entirely separate. Here, it's a matter of emphasis.

Following these discussions, the consultant returned to Evans, who offered the following comments:

The biggest single problem with Friedrichs, Levine is that everyone has his own special deal with James. The municipal finance people make out like nowhere else in the industry. People go off on their own trying to do deals who have no authority or expertise: one young salesman recently tried to generate an industrial revenue deal from a major company on the basis of an article in the newspaper. He made us look ridiculous! And this type of thing is not unique. Salesmen sometimes deal with company officers who could be useful to the corporate department, but they don't tell us. Municipal people sometimes will withhold information from one another and from us to pursue deals on their own. Our guys do it too. What the hell—you don't get paid for being a good team member here!

The firm is very loosely run, but all that means is that there's no management, no decision making. But you try to do something new and Levine'll scream bloody murder. Also, any time you step on somebody's toes for the good of the firm, he goes crying to James. The trouble is James often listens.

It's a real shame, because I think most of the people here are extremely competent. Admittedly, we've accumulated some dead weight over the years (I don't think Levine has ever fired anyone; he just starves them), but I think most people would really like to work hard. They just don't have any direction and they're skeptical about the likelihood of being rewarded for their efforts. Take our senior analyst. He makes much more than he's paid just from dividends on his stock holdings, and he started with nothing. That's a damned good investment story, but his talents don't go to anyone else's benefit. Also, we're very well capitalized, and it gives us a lot of flexibility that other firms just don't have. Besides, we're still a very strong force in the municipal bond market in this part of the country. If nothing else, we've got decades of history as managers of syndicates bidding on competitive sales, and those relationships are almost always honored. Of course, it's the manager who makes all the money on a public deal.

We've got to find some way to pull together: after all, we're all in the investment business and, with some variations, subject to the same basic economic, market, and industry conditions. This business is very fast paced, and new developments come up constantly. We're going to have to become more agile if we're going to survive.

GLOSSARY

Agreement among underwriters   Agreement whereby each firm in the syndicate agrees to purchase a fixed amount of securities from the issuer. Also names the manager as the representative of all members of the syndicate vis à vis the issuer.

Broker   Individual who arranges for purchase or sale of securities on behalf of investors. The broker is paid by commission based principally on the size of the transaction. See *salesperson*.

Brokerage firm   Firm comprising a number of individual brokers. An investment banking firm is a brokerage firm as well.

Commissions   Fee collected from investors by brokerage firm on a brokerage transaction. Also, the portion of the firm's fee paid to the individual broker who arranged the transaction.

Competitive sale   The issuer offers an issue in a public auction for bidding by a number of different syndicates of investment bankers. The syndicate with the highest bid underwrites the issue. This method is often used in municipal bond and public utility offerings.

Cooling-off period   Period between moment a deal is registered with the Securities Exchange Commission (S.E.C.) and moment it becomes effective. S.E.C. reviews the registration statement; suggests modifications in the prospectus; and permits proceeding with the issue or rejects it.

Dealer agreement   Agreement between selling group members and manager whereby firms agree to purchase a certain number of securities from the syndicate.

Diligence meeting   Meeting between syndicate members and issuer's officials. Syndicate members are expected to exercise due diligence in the investigation of the business and prospects of the issues.

Effective date   Date on which the S.E.C. grants permission to proceed with the offering.

Going public   The act of selling stock to the public at large, generally through an investment banker, by a company whose stock is held by a few entities.

Gross spread   Difference between prices at which securities are bought from the issuer and sold to the public in an underwriting.

Industrial revenue bonds (IRBs)   Bonds issued by a municipality on behalf of a corporation for the construction of facilities to be occupied by the company. Interest on the bonds is exempt from federal (and often state) income taxes. IRBs require close coordination between municipal and corporate departments within the investment banking firm arranging the issue. See *tax-exempt corporate finance*.

Information meeting   Meetings held by corporate finance and company officials with selling group members and other interested parties to answer questions about an issue. These are generally used when going public to generate interest in the issue.

Institution   Nonindividual purchasers of securities, generally insurance companies, pension funds, mutual funds, banks, investment advisers (sophisticated buyers).

Institutional salesperson   Salesperson dealing primarily with institutions. Assigned accounts and therefore represents investment banking firm vis à vis the institution, managing what is basically a firm-to-firm relationship. Assists finance departments in marketing private placements and syndicate and municipal underwriting departments in pricing public deals.

Manager   Generally the firm that originates an underwriting. The manager deals with the issuer, prepares the registration statement, forms the syndicate and selling group, and controls the offering. Collects a management fee in addition to the underwriting spread.

Market making   The attempt by an investment banking firm to sell securities from investors and other dealers. The market maker offers to buy the security by one price (bid) and to sell it at a higher price (asked).

Municipal bonds   Bonds issued by city or state governments to raise capital for various purposes. Interest on municipals is exempt from federal income taxes, so rates are significantly lower than they would be otherwise.

Participation   The portion an underwriting and investment banking firm agrees to purchase and attempts to sell to the public.

Private placement   An issue of securities that is not offered to the public but is sold privately to a few buyers, usually institutions.

Prospectus   Lengthy document circulated in an underwriting to prospective buyers. Provides financial and other information about the issuer and the issue.

Red herring   Preliminary prospectus filed as part of the registration statement and circulated to prospective buyers before the issue becomes effective.

Registration statement   Lengthy legal document filed with the S.E.C. to obtain permission for an underwriting.

Retail salesperson   Salesperson dealing primarily with individuals. Such a salesperson develops own clientele.

Salesperson   Industry parlance for a securities broker. See *Retail salesperson* and *Institutional salesperson*.

Securities and Exchange Commission (S.E.C.)   Regulatory body that oversees the securities industry.

Selling concession   Portion of gross spread allocated to selling group members.

Selling group   Firms that participate in an underwriting but have no legal obligation to buy securities from the issuer.

Stabilizing bid   A tactic in which the manager stands ready to purchase securities at a fixed price (generally slightly below the offering price) while an underwriting is in progress. Used to prevent the free market price from falling during the offering period if investors unload stock after buying from the syndicate or selling group.

Syndicate   Group of investment banking firms that commit themselves to purchase fixed portions of an underwriting. Also known collectively as the underwriters of an issue. Syndicate members can also act as selling group members.

Tax-exempt corporate finance   Highly specialized process of raising capital through industrial revenue and pollution control bonds. Such bonds require coordination between municipal officials, lawyers, municipal and corporate investment bankers, and company officials. Requires extensive expertise and detailed knowledge of governmental regulations.

Underwriting   Purchase and resale of an entire issue by a syndicate of investment bankers. The syndicate buys the issue from the issuer at one price and sells it at a higher price to other dealers (the syndicate collecting the underwriting spread), who in turn sell it at a higher price to investors (the dealer collecting the selling concession). The offering price to the public, the purchase price from the issuer, and the selling concession are set by the manager of the offering.

Underwriting agreement   Manager, on behalf of the syndicate, agrees to purchase an issue of securities from an issuer at a set price and terms.

Underwriting spread   Portion of the gross spread allocated to the underwriters: gross spread less management fee less selling concession.

The Medtek Corporation (B)

John Torrence, senior vice-president of the Medtek Corporation and director of the company's technical division (R&D) was talking with several members of a consulting team that he had brought in to help him with problems in the division.

> We have a basic problem of performance here in the technical division. Related to this problem is the low morale in my division and increased pressures from other parts of the company.
>
> We have had a bad case of technical constipation; this division has not brought out a successful new product in two years. Given our competition, if we don't do something about this problem soon, the whole company is going to be in big trouble.

COMPANY BACKGROUND

The Medtek Corporation is an international company that designs, manufactures, and markets automated diagnostic instruments for clerical and industrial users. The company was formed in 1939 as a small operation in a Bronx loft by the late Paul Torres; the father of the present chairman and CEO, Arthur Torrence; and the grandfather of the present senior vice-president for research and development, John Torrence.

Mr. Torres started Medtek by hand-crafting a new device called the Automed, a product still manufactured by the company, which automated the preparation of human tissue for microseopic examination by pathologists. The firm continued to grow until, in the early 1950s, it employed approximately 25 people. The R&D section was composed of two engineers and two draftsmen. At this stage, Medtek was organized very informally. New employees and consultants were brought in as needed to work on specific tasks.

During this period, an inventor named Dennis Rettew was brought in. Rettew had been employed in a Cleveland hospital. After observing both the kidney dialysis and laboratory procedures in the hospital, Rettew applied the mechanical techniques used in dialysis to the development of a rudimentary device that could automate one laboratory procedure. Technical development of this device resulted in the single channel Autoxam, an innovation that is still the basic technology for Medtek's major products.

The single channel Autoxam works by plucking up a small blood sample and pumping it through a continuous flow system where the sample is properly diluted; reagents added and mixed; the solution heated and/or cooled, filtered, pigmented, and spectrographically analyzed; and the results recorded and compared to a norm. Successive samples can be introduced continuously to the Autoxam. The innovation of separating the samples with a small air bubble both permitted the continuous flow of samples and scrubbed the pathway clean of the previous sample. Prior to the Autoxam, each sample was handled manually by a lab technician. Obviously, the new device allowed a saving in lab technicians' time and in the amount of reagents used. Further savings were realized by the Autoxam's ability to examine a larger number of samples per day than a technician.

In 1957 the Autoxam was introduced to the market. It was a great success and ushered the firm into an era of rapid and continuous growth. By the early 1960s the firm had grown to about 125 employees. The bulk of the research and development work was centered around the blood analyzer. Development work during this period focused on a multichannel version of the Autoxam that could automate additional laboratory tests and could also automate some industrial tests such as the measurement of trace metals in water. New applications and new clinical procedures compatible with Autoxam technology were developed both internally and by users and researchers external to and independent of the company. Much new information came to Medtek through professional journal reports of research inspired by the introduction of the Autoxam.

The years 1967 and 1968 brought a crisis to Medtek. This crisis was precipitated by the development of the 60/12, a second generation analyzer that produced a patient profile of 12 lab tests from one sample at the rate of 60 tests per hour. First, an internal fight arose over whether to finance an expansion of the company to tap the possible profits of the 60/12 or whether to restrain the firm's growth. Second, the rapid growth and the associated organizational consequences resulted in substantial engineering errors as well as cost and timing slippages. A consulting firm proposed a basic change in the formal organization in order to better handle accountability and coordination problems. Vice-presidents, senior vice-presidents, and a divisional structure were introduced. Some believed that the switch to this formal structure was too quick and that the company did not have enough properly trained personnel to staff the new organization.

The choice was to expand, and the period of 1969 to 1972 was a time of extremely rapid growth. The technical division grew to 150 employees. Its budget was some five times greater than its 1967 budget. Lou Bidder, who was brought in the early 1950s to work on the Autoxam hydraulics, became the first technical division vice-president. During this period, Medtek moved to suburban Washington, D.C. and greatly expanded its facilities.

The 60/12 was an instant success. None of Medtek's competitors could match or duplicate the 60/12's technology, speed, or versatility. Given the success of 60/12, development was initiated on HORSE (High Operation Repeated Sequential Examiner), a third generation computer-controlled blood analyzer with a capacity of 20 tests per profile and 150 tests per hour.

In the early 1970s work began on Scan-Lon—a complex high-speed diagnostic instrument oriented to the pharmaceutical industry. Scan-Lon was designed to take advantage of Medtek's core technology. Medtek also produces a white cell testing and diagnosis device; in addition, Medtek has developed and patented a range of reagents for its analyzers.

Medtek also produces an infrared analyzer and a hospital oriented management information system. These two products, however, constitute only a small, but growing, part of Medtek's sales of clerical systems and associated reagents.

The years 1972 to the present have not been easy ones for the company. Besides having to cope with the organizational consequences of growth, Medtek faces a range of environmental pressures. First, federal cutbacks to hospitals have decreased their ability to buy Medtek's products. This problem is acute because most of Medtek's new (and expensive) products are oriented to large clinical settings. Second, underwriters' requirements for insuring diagnostic equipment changed during the early 1970s in a number of cities and in the international market. These changes required making numerous modifications to fit local conditions. Similarly, the government, mostly through the Food and Drug Administration began to require extensive testing and product documentation before it would permit the diagnostic machines to be sold. Finally, during the 1970s a number of major companies began to directly compete with Medtek's diagnostic product line.

The organization chart for the company, financial highlights, and a description of the different divisions are included as Exhibits 1, 2, and 3.

THE TECHNICAL DIVISION

As the R&D arm of Medtek, the technical division is responsible for basic and applied research in areas relevant not only to present but also to future products of the firm.

John Torrence, age 30, was given the assignment of heading up the technical division about a year ago after having rotated through a number of different positions throughout the company. He expressed his views on the strategy of the technical division to the consultants:

> As my father has articulated it, we are in the business of benefiting mankind by serving the health care community. The best way to do this is for Medtek to develop innovative technology and be first to the market with new and patent-

Exhibit 1. Organization Chart of Medtek

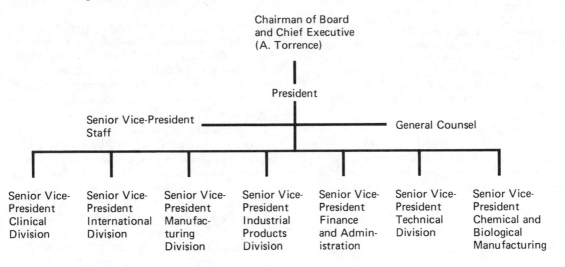

Exhibit 2. Organization Chart of the Technical Division

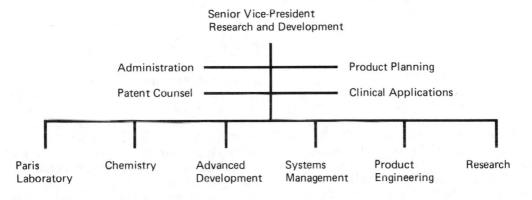

Exhibit 3. Selected Financial Data (years 1965–1975)

	1965	1966	1967	1968	1969	1970	1971	1972	1973	1974	1975
Sales (millions)	23	32	44	54	79	102	100	109	131	166	202
R&D expenditures (millions)	.93	1.26	1.97	2.9	4.9	9.8	10.6	10.1	10	10.5	
R&D expenditures as % of sales	4	4	4.5	5.4	6.2	9.6	10.6	9.3	7.6	6.3	
Number of employees		50		150						250	
Introduction of major products			60/12					HORSE			

able products. We are a "me first," not a "me too" firm.

The technical division is integral to this strategy and I believe that fully two-thirds of the division's time should be spent in generating new and creative ideas which can be developed into unique commercial products for the firm. The remainder of the division's time should be spent in developing and refining existing products.

The organization chart of the division can be found in Exhibit 2. Structurally, the division is organized into several departments. These departments are briefly described in the order of their involvement in the work flow of a typical project.

Research

Research concentrates on areas that relate to Medtek's basic technology and processes. There are small projects (4–6 members) investigating phenomena such as wave scattering properties and electrochemical principles.

Advanced Development

This department is chartered to do advanced development research (generating new knowledge or utilizing existing knowledge to solve a particular problem). The hydraulics, cell, and programming projects each conduct applied research on particular product problems in small teams. Each team's overall objective is to demonstrate the technical feasibility of a product idea.

Both these areas deal with state-of-the-art technology and are therefore particularly sensitive to new information from areas external to Medtek (universities, governmental agencies, professional societies). The technical personnel in these areas typically have advanced scientific or engineering degrees and are generally younger (with less organizational experience) than the rest of the staff in the division. Besides conducting research, these two departments are also responsible for assisting other divisional areas with technical problem solving.

Chemistry Methods

This department is in charge of developing the clinical test methods to be used in each system. As such, the department is divided into areas covering new system methods, existing system improvements, and reagent development. Different from the research and advanced development departments, this area not only develops the feasibility of a particular analysis but also develops the processes and reagents used in the analyses. This department is staffed with a range of professionals including biochemists, physicians, hematologists, organic chemists and hydraulic engineers. These professionals must also keep track of information from areas outside Medtek. Furthermore, since their products are at an intermediate stage of the work flow, the chemistry methods staff requires information not only from other departments in the technical division but also from areas in the larger corporation, such as manufacturing and marketing.

Engineering Services

This department provides support services to other departments in the division as well as to the larger corporation. The drafting design and model shop areas provide services to each product development program. The power supply area works on mechanical and electrical packaging questions as well as on power supply problems for each product line. A material assurance area monitors quality on all incoming technical components. The work in this department tends to be routine and requires less extradivisional communication than the other areas. The staff in this area tends to be older, more experienced within Medtek, and less educated than the rest of the division.

Systems Management

This department has overall responsibility for taking a "feasible project" and developing a manufacturing prototype (that is, a working model, with detailed designs, to be handed over to manufacturing). The department is organized into product-line program areas (HORSE, 60/12, Scan-Lon) as well as a systems support (computer) area. Each program has a product manager who has full responsibility for the project and a full-time technical project team. Since these teams do not have all the competence to carry a project to completion, the product manager must make arrangements with the different functional areas for assistance. Frequently a project will "buy" support teams from other areas for the full development phase of a project. Particularly important interfaces within the division are with chemistry methods and the service areas. Of vital importance to program development are effective links with manufacturing and marketing areas since the ultimate product must meet manufacturing constraints yet still meet market needs. The technical staff in this department are all engineers with varying amounts of experience at Medtek.

Product Planning

This is a two-person department whose responsibility is keeping track of and evaluating existing programs as well as investigating the possibilities of new products and new acquisitions. Product planning is a new department whose members are not yet sure of their roles. Indeed, there is a general confusion in the division as to the legitimate role of this department.

The product-line programs carried out in the division are each *unique systems* focusing on some aspect of clinical information and data analysis. Each system is made up of a range of components to handle the various stages in the work flow from material preparation, material transfer, and multiple diagnostic tests to automatic analysis and interpretation. The various system components have to be integrated to produce an automated, high-speed, and precise system. In order to be commercially successful, each system has to be tailored to fit the particular market as well as the legal requirements in the different locations.

The Scan-Lon system provides an example of the complexity of a particular program. To meet a need in the pharmaceutical industry, Medtek initiated a program to develop a system that would allow high-speed assays of the most critical parameters facing the pharmaceutical producer. The system required the development of a new form of photometric analysis to be integrated with continuous flow core technology. Once the measurement concept was found feasible, the program team had to come up with specially designed test procedures, mechanics, power systems, and computer program. Each of the component systems had to be compatible with the overall design and within cost specifications. The system is now in production but not without some accuracy and maintenance problems.

SOME CURRENT ISSUES IN THE TECHNICAL DIVISION

In order to probe the reasons for the problems with both technical innovation and with morale, the consulting team conducted a number of interviews in all parts of the laboratory.

The most frequently discussed problem was one termed "fragmentation." As one researcher suggested:

> The structure of the laboratory only encourages separate disciplines, each with a desire to do it their own way and with their own set of objectives. An example of this fragmentation problem was the initial photometric development by the advanced development department. Even though the research department had done substantial groundwork in the area, the advanced development group essentially started without the benefit of this in-house expertise.

Another researcher suggested:

> I think part of the fragmentation problem is that people in the various departments are so different. The guys in engineering services feel inadequate around us because, after all, their work really is not as important in the overall scheme

of things as ours is. However, when we *do* need them, they aren't very helpful.

A result of the fragmentation problem seemed to be inefficient transfer of work between departments. There was a tendency for each area to overlook or fail to take into account other related areas. "Communication and coordination among areas can best be characterized as hit or miss," said one division member.

The fragmentation problem was not unique to the technical division. Important marketing or manufacturing information was often not available in the formative and problem-solving stages of a project. As one researcher put it, "I am sick of receiving memos from marketing that give me out-of-date information. What's the point of my doing feasibility studies for a product without knowing about the regulation out there which directly affects the product?"

Another major problem was the role of the product managers. Product managers were assigned between one and three projects; their role was to marshal the needed resources and shepherd the project to completion. The power of these product managers varied greatly. As one manager described it:

> We have full responsibility for projects, but we don't have the influence—over budgets and staffing and so on—that we need to get the job done. The department heads have the authority here; except for one of us. We call him the Czar—he's a buddy of the chairman of the board. He gets all the resources and support he needs.

Day-to-day decision making seemed to present a basic problem for the product managers. In short, their real influence over divisional staff and other corporate personnel was minimal—coordination and joint problem solving suffered.

Another major problem faced by the division (and particularly by the product managers) was the absence of laboratory plans and project priorities and the attendant lack of systems to track and evaluate project progress. Ongoing projects were not subject to formal review procedures; there were no formalized cost, schedule, or timing systems. A product manager commented:

Not only are reviews done on a "catch-as-catch can" basis, but it's also unclear whether I am supposed to be doing the evaluating or not. Sometimes, Torrence Senior suddenly takes over and sometimes it all gets so confusing that a department head does it. To make it all worse, Arthur Torrence has actually been known to walk into the lab and unilaterally start or stop a project. We don't have formal controls, so it leaves us open to unpredictable tampering by top management. One project was started and stopped three times over a two-year period. We call it the "yo-yo effect."

Contributing to the confusion of the staff was the problem of project definition and interproject coordination. Since projects changed direction so frequently and since the product managers did not always have current information, project members often did not know either what their own objectives were or how they should fit into the overall project objectives. This lack of general project direction reinforced the fragmentation problem and the feelings of "isolation in the midst of chaos" and further undermined the influence of the product managers. The lack of control and the general planning problem also adversely affected the coordination among projects: "Decision making about resource allocation—space, time, budgets, staff—among projects is often made arbitrarily and by the seat of management's pants; the point is that there are just no priorities to systematically guide project decision making."

A final problem that was frequently mentioned was the role of the research and advanced development departments. One researcher complained:

> We're supposed to be doing real applied research, but we hardly ever get a chance to actually do any. We spend all our time fire fighting on existing products. What research work we do is all but ignored by top management. I helped develop a process a few months ago, and then we heard that top management had gone outside to get exactly the same process. I still feel terrible about it.

Another example often given of management's lack of support for in-house expertise was the fact that the basic technology of Scan-Lon was not developed in-house, but was bought from an outside laboratory. The results of these management actions were very low morale in these departments and a lack of real research activity in a firm dependent on new technology and new clinical processes. As one interviewee put it, "The researchers have just stopped thinking; their creativity has been burned out by management's neglect."

While particularly an issue in the research areas, the problem of employee motivation and morale existed throughout the division. Many employees felt either that their work was not recognized by management or that they were simply not being used to their full potential. A survey indicated that a full 70 percent of the division's staff did not believe that they were effectively utilized. Further, more than two-third of the staff felt that the pay and career systems did not recognize or reward creative work.

These problem areas seemed to feed on each other. The lack of planning and control procedures and the resultant start-stop of the projects only accentuated the fragmentation problem as each functional area focused on its narrow task. Further, the lack of clear project objectives also contributed to the narrow focus of the departments. Defects in the planning and control system and weakness of the product managers worked to drive the departments away from each other. The lack of project stability, the poor structure of reward systems, and the nature of the stop-and-start work each reduced commitment and involvement of the staff. Similarly, the "yo-yo effect" undermined the role of the product managers and further reduced their ability to develop motivation within their project and to influence others in the larger organization.

These interrelated problems along with the lack of any real research activity contributed to low morale and low motivation in the division. Between departments, communication decreased as did the amount of effective collaboration and cooperation. The HORSE project developed a number of clinical and engineering problems, while the 60/12 system and the Scan-Lon system could not shake off persistent technical problems. The reputation of the division had fallen sharply in the eyes of the rest of the corporation, and the R&D personnel were openly complaining of the lack of leadership and direction in the division.

JOHN TORRENCE'S PERSPECTIVE

John Torrence was clearly frustrated. In discussions with the consulting team, Torrence provided some perspective on the problems faced by the technical division.

> Something is rotten here. Given our corporate objectives and our commitment to R&D, the laboratory should have the highest status individuals in the company. Instead, our morale is low, and our reputation could not be lower within the firm as a whole. Our biggest problem, of course, is the failure to come up with new products. The future of the company depends upon our developing new technologies that will be commercially successful. Many of the problems, I think, stem from the way that we manage ourselves. With a few exceptions, we have high quality people here in the division. We do have the necessary scientific and technical talent. The problem is that they are not coming up with new ideas; also, they don't seem to be able to get through the process of moving an idea to the product stage. Part of our problem, I think, is the way we are organized within the division. I have too many people reporting to me, and I am thinking about changing the structure. Beyond that, however, there are problems in the attitudes of people. When I talk to people in the division, they just don't seem to have much drive or ambition. They don't seem fired up. This attitude is reflected in the large number of projects that are either behind schedule, over budget, or both. Finally, we don't seem to have a good feel of where we are going as a Division, where we ought to be putting our resources, and how we determine priorities.

Given their initial diagnosis, Mr. Torrence asked the consulting team for any intepretations as to what was going on. He also asked if they had any suggestions for new directions in the technical division.